STUDIES IN THE BUDDHIST TRADITIONS

WISDOM, COMPASSION, AND THE SEARCH FOR UNDERSTANDING

The Buddhist Studies Legacy of Gadjin M. Nagao

Edited by
Jonathan A. Silk

UNIVERSITY OF HAWAI'I PRESS, HONOLULU

01 02 03 04 5 4 3 2

The Institute for the Study of Buddhist Traditions is part of the Department of Asian Languages and Cultures at the University of Michigan, Ann Arbor, Michigan. It was founded in 1988 to foster research and publication in the study of Buddhism and of the cultures and literatures that represent it. In association with the University of Hawai'i Press, the Institute publishes Studies in the Buddhist Traditions, a series devoted to the publication of materials, translations, and monographs relevant to the study of Buddhist traditions, in particular as they radiate from the South Asian homeland. The series also publishes studies and conference volumes resulting from work carried out in affiliation with the Institute in Ann Arbor.

Library of Congress Cataloging-in-Publication Data

Wisdom, compassion, and the search for understanding : the Buddhist studies legacy of Gadjin M. Nagao / edited by Jonathan A. Silk

p. cm. — (Studies in the Buddhist traditions)

Includes bibliographical references and index.

ISBN 0–8248–2086–X (cloth : alk. paper)

1. Buddhism. I. Nagao, Gajin, 1907– II. Silk, Jonathan A. III. Series.

BQ120 . W56 2000
294.3—dc21

00–033780

University of Hawai'i Press books are printed on acid-free paper and meet the guidelines for permanence and durability of the Council on Library Resources.

This book is set in the Appeal font, designed by Urs App.

Cover Design by Yoko Silk

Contents

Preface

It is with great pleasure that I write these words of introduction to this volume, offered in honor of the tradition of great scholarship and great humanity that is the legacy of Professor Gadjin Masato Nagao. I hope he will be pleased with this tribute, which I believe contains insights and suggestions of interest to him and all others who study Buddhist traditions. The essays assembled here were contributed by students, colleagues, and friends of Prof. Nagao (designations which are far from mutually exclusive) from Japan, North America, and Europe. Although the result is a rather large volume, I have no doubt that had their publication been a possibility it would have been easy to gather twice as many papers only from those directly influenced by Prof. Nagao's teaching, not to mention those influenced by his published work. Given the influence he has had on the contributors, it is perhaps no coincidence that the breadth of material covered in this volume closely reflects the research interests of Prof. Nagao himself (although it was not planned that way), ranging over Madhyamaka and Yogācāra philosophical and doctrinal traditions, early Buddhism, Mahāyāna sūtras, Tibetan studies, Pure Land studies, the history of East Asian Sanskrit studies, and so on.

My original idea was that this volume be produced in honor of Prof. Nagao's eighty-eighth birthday. Accordingly, I proposed to call the volume *Beiju*, in the attempt to make a clever multivalent pun. *Beiju* 米寿 indicates the celebration of the eighty-eighth birthday in Japanese, and is a visual pun on the Chinese characters, since the first character is made up of the elements 八十八, namely the number eighty-eight. In addition, the character *bei* 米 is also used to indicate America. Since the volume was to appear in America, and be written in English, I was very proud of my suggestion. Alas, due to my own lack of energy and direction, and other adventitious factors, Prof. Nagao's eighty-eighth birthday is long past, and only now is the volume to see print. Almost the only good result of this long delay is the jettisoning of the original title. The present title much more straightforwardly states what it is that is remarkable about Prof. Nagao, which is most certainly not the mere fact that he has lived a long life.

The Buddhist traditions are often said to embody at their core the virtues of wisdom (*prajñā*), compassion (*karuṇā*), and the search for understanding the two (*mārga*—the path). Prof. Nagao himself tirelessly embodies these very same qualities in his life and work. His scholarly career and his personal life have been dedicated to a search for understanding and an effort to act on that understanding. Another way of putting this would be to say that for him the search for wisdom and compassion in its theoretical and practical aspects appears in the study of Buddhist philosophy and the living of a Buddhist life—which for Prof. Nagao, as a devout Buddhist and a devout scholar, are after all mutually dependent and coextensive.

Perhaps nothing could illustrate this better than the paper that Prof. Nagao has contributed to the present volume, and the very fact that he has contributed one. While it is no doubt somewhat unusual to include a paper by an honoree in a volume dedicated to his honor, here it serves to illustrate, I think, better than any editor's mere words could, Prof. Nagao's continued vitality and his continued commitment to encounter and struggle with the text, which is to say, his search for understanding. The *Mahāyānasūtrālaṁkāra* is a text Prof. Nagao has been studying carefully for more than sixty years. Yet, over the course of the editing of this volume, he took the opportunity several times over to reconsider, rethink, and revise his translations of certain passages, his understanding of Vasubandhu's intent, and so on. (This is one additional benefit of the delayed appearance of the volume.) The text is clearly very much alive for him, in a way that perhaps only more than half a century's intimacy with it can bring. And the topic that he has addressed, compassion, could not, of course, be more central to the Buddhist vision. If we can learn an overall lesson from all of this, and from Prof. Nagao's scholarly work and human character, perhaps it is that wisdom and compassion come about together with the process of the search for understanding, and not as an end result of that search.

From the beginning, the production of this volume has had the full cooperation of Prof. Nagao. Or, I should say, his full, but initially reluctant, cooperation. When I first proposed to him the idea for this volume, he refused to have anything to do with it, and more or less summarily ordered me to put the idea out of my head. But I persisted, and after a number of refusals—more than the customary Asian three—eventually he agreed. He later told me that the only reason he finally gave in was that he believed that nothing would come of it, and agreeing would get me off his back. If this is so, then Prof. Nagao failed to fully appreciate the love, respect, and admiration in which he is held by his students, friends, and colleagues. (Or perhaps he merely doubted my organizational and editorial capabilities, which is a different matter entirely.) In any case, although Prof.

Nagao has never sought recognition for himself, he has been extremely helpful to me in the task of putting together this volume. Without his cooperation I would have been unable to write an accurate brief biography; moreover, the bibliography presented here is based almost entirely on Prof. Nagao's own handwritten list of his publications. I regret that in a few cases I have been unable to verify the listings, especially of various ephemera, and several obscurities remain; it will be possible to clarify these points only with access to several large Japanese libraries.

Many have made the appearance of this volume possible. I am very grateful for the kindness shown me by Prof. Luis O. Gómez, whose enthusiasm for the publication of this volume in the series of which he is general editor has been a great encouragement for me. I have likewise received a great deal of support, material and otherwise, from Prof. Shōryū Katsura. Among other things, he arranged for the complete bibliography of Prof. Nagao's publications to be input onto disk, a project which was supported financially through the generosity of Prof. Masamichi Ichigō. The publication itself was supported by a generous subvention from the Bukkyō Dendō Kyōkai, for which I am most grateful.

Last, but far from least, my wife Yōko has helped in numerous ways, ranging from the creation of Chinese characters to the preparation of plates and the cover design. More than that, she has sustained me in everything I do; my gratitude to her is beyond verbal expression.

New Haven

Just as this volume was about to be sent to the printer, the sad news reached us of the death of our contributor Prof. J. W. de Jong. His excellent scholarship will be much missed.

A Short Biographical Sketch of Professor Gadjin Masato Nagao

Professor Gadjin Masato Nagao 長尾雅人 was born August 22, 1907 (the fortieth year of the Meiji 明治 period), in Sendai, Japan, the second son of Unryū 雲龍 and Shie 志ゑ.[1] In his younger days he was known as Masato Nagao, but later he preferred to adopt another reading of the same Chinese characters, Gadjin, taking Masato as a "middle" name.[2] On April 8, 1938, Nagao married Toshiko Gotō 後藤敏子, and the marriage produced two children, a son Shirō 史郎 and a daughter Mayako まや子. The couple now have five grandchildren. Professor and Mrs. Nagao continue to live in their lovely home in the foothills east of Kyoto, just outside the precincts of the Shingon temple Sennyūji 泉涌寺, a home which they have inhabited now for almost seventy years.

It is not possible or appropriate to offer a full biography here; I will concentrate on Prof. Nagao's contribution to scholarship, and leave to others a more detailed recounting of his life and character. But something of his background and his personality needs to be mentioned here. For indeed, in addition to being a fine scholar with a razor-sharp mind, and a perhaps equally razor-sharp wit which occasionally shows itself in a most delicate and precise use of irony, among other *rasa*s, Prof. Nagao has also been a witness to world events, having lived through two world wars and Japan's rebuilding after the second. He was the first Japanese to provide reliable reports on the uprising in Lhasa, which later led to the Dalai Lama's 1959 flight to India, since Nagao happened to be visiting the Sikkhimese royal family at the time (see G–19 in the Bibliography below). He has travelled extensively, and chatted with emperors, kings, and prime

---

1. The erroneous date August 24 is sometimes found, but this is an old uncorrected mistake.

In preparing the following, I have derived great assistance from the published conversation with Prof. Nagao (H–64), and have also consulted a sketch of his scholarly achievements prepared by Professors Aramaki and Kajiyama in support of Prof. Nagao's nomination to the Japan Academy in 1980. In addition to my memories of my own conversations with him, I have also had access to Prof. Nagao's Curriculum Vitae, for which I thank him. For additional information I am grateful to those students and friends of his who have spoken with me about him.

2. The spelling Gadjin reflects an older romanization convention. The same can be, and sometimes is, written Gajin.

ministers. Despite its brevity, it may be hoped that something of Nagao as a person will come through in the following outline of his academic career and scholarly achievements.

Although born in northeastern Japan, in Sendai, where his father had been assigned as a Chief Minister of the Nishi Honganji sect of Jōdo Shinshū Pure Land Buddhism, and spending his first years in Sapporo, the young Nagao attended school from the mid-primary level in Kyoto, the city that would become his home for the rest of his life. In 1925 he entered the Daisan Kōtō Gakkō 第三高等學校 (Third High School), part of the Imperial University system, and something like a junior college in the contemporary American system.[3] Graduates of these schools were guaranteed admission to one of the imperial universities, and so in 1928 Nagao entered Kyoto Imperial University (Kyōto Teikoku Daigaku 京都帝國大學, later renamed Kyoto University), from which he graduated with the degree of Bungakushi 文學士 (roughly equivalent to Master of Arts) in Buddhist Studies in March 1931. He subsequently entered the Graduate School of the same university. From 1935 until his retirement in 1971 he held a series of positions in Kyoto University, ranging from Research Assistant (*fukushu* 副手) through Dean of the Faculty of Letters (Bungakubuchō 文學部長), and finally Professor Emeritus (Meiyo kyōju 名誉教授). He also concurrently held a professorship at Kyūshū University from 1956–1958. In 1950 he was awarded the degree of Bungaku Hakase 文學博士 (D. Litt.) for his publication "Chūkan tetsugaku no konponteki tachiba" (The Fundamental Standpoint of Mādhyamika Philosophy) (D–17).

In addition to his various positions in the Faculty of Letters of Kyoto University, Nagao also held several research positions in the Research Institute of Oriental Culture (Tōhō Bunka Kenkyūjo 東方文化研究所) and its successor, now known as the Research Institute for Humanistic Studies of Kyoto University (Kyōto Daigaku Jinbun Kagaku Kenkyūsho 京都大學人文科學研究所).[4] Other teaching appointments included stints at Kyūshū, Dōshisha, Ryūkoku, and Kōyasan Universities and Tekkō Junior College (Amagasaki). He has been

3. The Third High School was later to become the General Education section (Kyōyōbu 教養部) of Kyoto University, in which students were required to study the first two years of general courses.

4. For an account of the early history of the Tōhō Bunka Kenkyūjo and the Jinbun Kagaku Kenkyūsho, see "A Short History of the Institute (1929–1954)," in *Silver Jubilee Volume of the Zinbun-Kagaku-Kenkyusho*, Kyoto University (Kyoto: Kyōto Daigaku Jinbun Kagaku Kenkyūsho, 1954): v–xii.

a Visiting Professor at Nagoya University and, in the United States and Canada, at the Universities of Wisconsin, British Columbia, Calgary, and Michigan. He has also travelled extensively throughout Asia, Europe, and North America, and has lectured at hundreds of universities, conferences, and other venues both in Japan and abroad.

Professor Nagao's excellence in numerous fields has not gone unrecognized. In 1959 he was awarded the Japan Academy Prize (Nihon Gakushiin-shō 日本學士院賞) for his participation in the publication *Chü-yung-kuan* (D–36). In 1978 he was conferred the Imperial decoration Second Class Order of the Sacred Treasure (Kun nitō zuihō-shō 勲二等瑞寶章), and in 1979 he was awarded the Culture Prize (Bukkyō dendō bunka-shō 佛教傳道文化賞) of the Society for the Promotion of Buddhism (Bukkyō Dendō Kyōkai 佛教傳道協會). In 1980 Nagao was selected as a Member of the Japan Academy (Nihon Gakushiin), and in 1993 he was awarded by the Patriarch (Monshu) of the Nishi-Honganji Temple the Honorary President Prize (Meiyo sōsai-shō 名誉総裁賞) of the Foundation for the Promotion of Buddhist Scholarship of the Nishi-Honganji, Kyoto (Honpa Honganji kyōgaku josei zaidan 本派本願寺教学助成財団).

Nagao's service to scholarship has also been notable. In addition to many behind-the-scenes activities, he has also engaged in more public work, including the execution of the duties of the large number of offices he has held in professional organizations. It is only possible to mention a few here. From 1949 until 1971 he was a member of the board of directors (*riji* 理事) of the Nippon Buddhist Research Association (Nippon Bukkyō Gakkai). Since 1950 he has been a member of the board of directors of the Japanese Association for Religious Studies (Nihon Shūkyō Gakkai), from 1951 through 1971, and again from 1983 to the present, of the Japanese Association for Indian and Buddhist Studies (Nihon Indogaku Bukkyō Gakkai), and from 1961 through 1991 of the Tōhō Gakkai (Institute of Eastern Culture). He was a Committee Member of the Suzuki Research Foundation from 1962 until 1978, the President of the Japanese Association for Tibetan Studies (Nihon Chibetto Gakkai) from 1968 through 1989, a founding member of the International Association of Buddhist Studies in 1976, and Chair of its Board of Directors from 1976 through 1978. In 1987 he was appointed to the chair of the Board of Directors of the Ueno Memorial Foundation for the Study of Buddhist Art, Kyoto, and from 1989 through 1995 to the same post in the Society for the Promotion of Buddhism, Tokyo. In 1988 he was a member of the selection committee for the Kyoto

Prize, awarded by the Inamori Foundation. He has been an editor of the English language journal *The Eastern Buddhist* since 1973.

There can be little doubt that Prof. Nagao is one of the most exacting and thoughtful Buddhist scholars of the modern age. And in fact, in many senses, he is one of the great innovative pioneers of the modern study of Buddhism, although his impressive *guruparamparā* links him to a glorious past as well. As a student at Kyoto University Nagao began his studies on Indian philosophy under the guidance of Matsumoto Bunzaburō 松本文三郎. A graduate of Tokyo Imperial University, Matsumoto came to Kyoto around 1906, after several years' study in Paris, as one of six professors appointed as founding members of the Faculty of Letters of the newly established Kyoto Imperial University. When Nagao approached him it was only two years before his retirement, but Nagao visited him rather often. As Matsumoto used to spend the summer season on the cooler Kōyasan to escape the heat of Kyoto, the young Nagao would stay in Matsumoto's Kyoto home to look after it in his absence.

As for Buddhism in general, Nagao studied under the guidance of Hatani Ryōtai 羽渓了諦, a specialist in Central Asian Buddhism and one of Matsumoto's first disciples. Although Hatani also had studied in Europe and had a knowledge of Sanskrit, almost all Buddhist studies in Japan were still carried out on Chinese sources. Hatani thus, like almost all Japanese scholars trained in the pre-war period, taught the *Vajracchedikā*, for instance, in Chinese. Nagao's first encounter with Yogācāra Buddhism, a subject that was to receive most of his scholarly attention later, came at around the same time, when the Hossō (法相, traditional East Asian Yogācāra) scholar Saeki Jōin 佐伯定胤 came to Kyoto from the Hōryūji 法隆寺 temple in Nara to lecture. Such traditional Yogācāra study was also, of course, based solely on sources written in classical Chinese. It was only later, and then more as a junior colleague than as a student, that Nagao would become close to Yamaguchi Susumu 山口益, the great specialist in the Yogācāra-Vijñānavāda and himself a student of Sylvain Lévi, the first scholar to make the Sanskrit literature of the Yogācāra school available.

Although the traditional scholastics of East Asian Buddhism contain a tremendous amount of great learning, a learning which he has certainly not ignored, Nagao also felt the need to turn to the Indic sources in their original Sanskrit. At that time the professor of Sanskrit philology and literature at Kyoto University was Sakaki Ryōsaburō 榊亮三郎. Although well known both in Japan and abroad as the editor of the Buddhist lexicon, the *Mahāvyutpatti*, Sakaki restricted attendance at his Sanskrit lectures to students with a background in Greek or Latin, or exceptionally in Pāli, which had the result, if not the intention, of excluding from his classes students of Buddhism. Thus Nagao's teacher of Sanskrit, and later Tibetan, became Hara Shinjō 原眞乘, the Associate Professor of Sanskrit at the university. Nagao has recalled the pain of working through Bühler's *Grammatik*, struggling not only with Sanskrit and the German but also with the boredom of sitting in class while the professor actually *read* the textbook aloud hour after hour. (On the other hand, Nagao has also spoken of the intensive German training required of high school students at that time—around fifteen hours of German per week. He and his friends, Nagao remembers, regularly used to speak German outside of class on a casual basis, so we must presume that studying a grammar book in German was in itself not such a chore.) The first Sanskrit Buddhist work Nagao read was, perhaps significantly, Vasubandhu's *Triṁśikā*. Helped along by the recently published Japanese translation of Wogihara Unrai 荻原雲来, Nagao worked through Vasubadhu's text, and the commentary of Sthiramati, more or less on his own.

In the old imperial system, the university was a three-year course. Therefore, already in his second year Nagao had to think about his graduation thesis. He initially was interested in working on the famous "Awakening of Faith in the Mahāyāna" 大乘起信論. But he realized that it would be impossible to understand this text without a firm grounding in its Yogācāra background, and the Yogācāra itself would elude his grasp without an understanding of the Madhyamaka. This conviction was to focus the main stream of his subsequent scholarship. In the end Nagao gave up his idea of studying the "Awakening of Faith" as too difficult, and wrote his graduation thesis on Sthiramati's idea of *vijñānapariṇāma* as it is found in the *Triṁśikāṭīkā*, a paper which became his first publication (D–1).

Nagao encountered the philological method which would shape all of his later work thanks to Yamaguchi Susumu, whom he, along with Nozawa Jōshō 野澤靜證, assisted in the study of the *Madhyānta-vibhāgaṭīkā*, another work of Sthiramati. The approach of comparatively studying the Sanskrit, Tibetan, and Chinese versions of texts, now quite ordinary and accepted, was at the time still rather rare. It might not be unreasonable to suggest that this method travelled from Sylvain Lévi through Yamaguchi to Nagao. Nagao also began to study the *Mahāyānasūtrālaṁkāra* at this time as well, a text which has continued to occupy him to this day, as his own contribution to the present volume illustrates. His studies of the *Mahāyānasūtrālaṁ-*

kāra eventually resulted, among numerous other publications, in a trilingual glossary of the text (see below), carried out on the plan that he had learned from working on the *Madhyāntavibhāgaṭīkā* with Yamaguchi. But at the same time that he was learning these philological skills, Nagao was also developing another aspect of his interests, one which would, as much as or even more than his philology, come to shape his later scholarly approach.

While in the last year of high school, Nagao was able to attend the final lectures delivered at Kyoto Imperial University by the famous philosopher Nishida Kitarō 西田幾太郎. Although he professes to have understood not a word, the following year, having entered the university proper, he attended the lectures of Nishida's successor, Tanabe Hajime 田邊元. He had, in addition, frequent friendly conversations with many of the philosophy students at the university. This seems to have deeply influenced his interest in philosophical problems such as "subjectivity" and "ascent and descent," themes to which he has continually returned over the years. Nagao's philosophizing is, however, based not on the German Kantian, Hegelian, or Heideggerian thought that characterized the thinking of Nishida and his successors, but rather upon Indian Yogācāra philosophy. For Nagao, profound insights into the human condition, and more especially into the human psyche, the workings of the human mind, were obtained by the great Yogācāra theoreticians, most especially by Asaṅga and Vasubandhu. The ability to understand the discoveries of such ancient thinkers in their own context, while simultaneously translating those discoveries into modern terms in a creative and yet faithful way, makes Nagao's scholarship much more than simple philology or creative philosophy. As examples of this approach one might look at any of a number of recent papers, for example that in English confronting the Yogācāra cognition theory with Jungian Depth Psychology (D–94). It is probably fair to say that it is both by nature and by training that Nagao has been able to develop his happy marriage of philological rigor, philosophical curiosity, and creative imagination, the result of which is not merely a combination but a synergy, a whole greater than the sum of its parts.

Nagao's first official position was in the Research Institute of Oriental Culture, in which he became a researcher after completing his graduate school courses. In some of the papers dating from this period, as later, Nagao employed Chinese sources extensively, partly because of his intention to reexamine aspects of Chinese Buddhism from an Indian perspective. With the above-mentioned Matsumoto Bunzaburō as his advisor, and assigned to assist Tsukamoto Zenryū

塚本善隆, the great historian of Chinese Buddhism and one of the researchers at the Institute,[5] Nagao worked on an important compendium of inscriptions, the *Chin-shih ts'ui-pien* 金石萃編, extracting references to Buddhism for Tsukamoto. Although he has never published on Chinese Buddhism per se, this early experience introduced Nagao to yet another method and approach to the study of Buddhism in historical perspective. At the same time that he received the assignment to assist Tsukamoto, Nagao was also permitted to choose his own research project, and what he selected was the *Mahāyānasaṁgraha*, a text he has continued to study to the present day, and to which we shall return below.

It is interesting how circumstances can shape a life or a career. Being barred by financial and political considerations from visiting Europe, America, or even India, and learning from a comment in a publication of Guissepe Tucci that the Tibetans had preserved traditional studies of the Madhyamaka and Yogācāra (although, as he has commented, with regard to the Yogācāra this is not strictly true), Nagao resolved to encounter Tibetan Buddhism (or "Lamaism," as it was then called) in the only area available to him, the Chinese mainland then under Japanese military occupation. Thus, in 1939 Nagao made the first of two visits to Northern China and Inner Mongolia. His "field work" in Tibetology consisted of these two visits (August–October 1939 and May–October 1943) to Mongolian "Lamaist" monasteries. It was not possible for Nagao to engage in the type of prolonged study with a *dge bshes* that is feasible today, but the travel and research that was within reach led to two very valuable works on Mongolian monasteries and their academic system, works which have lost little of their value over the years (A–1, 2). But Nagao's fundamental interest has always lain not in ethnography but in the study of philosophy and doctrine. Having been informed by Mihara Yoshinobu 三原芳信,[6] his former classmate at the Third High School, and at that time an official in the Japanese occupation government of Manchuria, that it was a great work, worthy of being translated into Japanese, Nagao was inspired to undertake a study of Tsong

---

5. Other researchers included the superb Sinologist Yoshikawa Kōjirō 吉川幸次郎 and the archaeologist Mizuno Seiichi 水野清一, with the eminent Sinologist Kanō Naoki 狩野直喜, and the specialist in Central Asian studies Haneda Tōru 羽田亨, as their advisors.

6. Mihara was himself a graduate of the famous program in Buddhist Studies at Tōhoku Imperial University, where he probably learned of the *Lam rim chen mo* from Tada Tōkan.

kha pa's *Lam rim chen mo*.[7] Although there were great Japanese pioneer Tibetologists in the generation before Nagao, figures such as Kawaguchi Ekai 河口慧海, Aoki Bunkyō 青木文教, Tada Tōkan 多田等観, and Teramoto Enga 寺本婉雅, Nagao was among the first to give a philosophically sophisticated reading of Tibetan materials concerning what is today called Indo-Tibetan Buddhism. While he gives full credit to the assistance he received from the excellent complete Chinese translation of Fa-tsun 法尊,[8] there is no question that Nagao's translation of the *vipaśyanā* chapter of the *Lam rim chen mo* is a tour de force (A–3). In addition to a philologically and philosophically sensitive reading of the text, which is deeply imbued with Candrakīrti's Prāsaṅgika Mādhyamika, Nagao also identified the numerous quotations in the text in their Sanskrit or Tibetan sources.[9]

Although he does not consider himself a Tibetologist per se, over the years Nagao continued to occasionally publish on Tibetan Buddhist topics. Among these publications one of the most important is his study of the Tibetan inscription on the Chü-yung-kuan 居庸關, the famous "Buddhist Arch" outside Peking which is adorned with images and multilingual inscriptions (D–36, 79). While future scholars may be able to improve on selected aspects,[10] only a scholar with Nagao's knowledge of the language, literature, and epigraphy of Tibetan, Chinese, and Sanskrit, not to mention Buddhist doctrine, would have been able to treat the inscription in such a satisfactory way.

---

7. The original plan called for a complete Japanese translation. The text was divided up among three scholars, Nagao, Yoshimura Shūki 芳村修基, and Funahashi Issai 舟橋一哉. The other two parts have never been published.

8. Published in installments in the journal *Hai-ch'ao-yin* 海潮音, and later published in book form as *Pu-t'i-tao tz'u-ti kuang-lun* 菩提道次第廣論 (Han-tsang chiao-li-yuan 漢藏教理院, 1936).

9. Nagao has stated that without the groundwork of Fa-tsun, who identified many of the quotations in Hsüan-tsang's Chinese versions, his own work would not have been possible. While this may be true, the labor of locating a large number of quotations in difficult-to-find Sanskrit books and unedited Tibetan collections should not be underestimated, and will be well understood by those who have tried it themselves!

10. See the study of Yael Bentor, "In Praise of *Stūpas*: The Tibetan Eulogy at Chü-Yung-Kuan Reconsidered," *Indo-Iranian Journal* 38 (1995): 31–54, in which, using recently published Tibetan sources entirely unavailable to Nagao, she has been able to improve on some of Nagao's interpretations of a small number of verses of the inscription. Clearly, however, without Nagao's groundbreaking work, Bentor's would have been impossible.

Despite his wide interests and equally wide expertise, the heart of Nagao's work, and of his personal commitment to scholarship and the intellectual investigation of Buddhism, lies in his studies of the two main philosophical traditions of mature Indian Mahāyāna Buddhism, the Madhyamaka and the Yogācāra. Although initially fascinated by the Madhyamaka, especially as developed by Candrakīrti, Nagao later came to feel that the rigorous critique of the Madhyamaka dialectic, the *prasaṅga* method, was necessarily complemented by the constructive and positive outlook of the Yogācāra, which he sees therefore as representing the culmination of the philosophical presentation of the Buddhist path to human perfection and self-knowledge (see D–72).

In terms of his more strictly philological contributions, Prof. Nagao has concentrated on some core works of the Yogācāra tradition of Maitreya, Asaṅga, and Vasubandhu, as well as the commentarial tradition of Sthiramati, giving us a superb edition of the Sanskrit text of the *Madhyāntavibhāga*, accompanied by an excellent trilingual index (A–5). He subsequently translated the entire text (C–15), and has published on it and its commentary, Sthiramati's *Ṭīkā*, which he had studied already with Yamaguchi Susumu (for example, D–68). His trilingual index to the *Mahāyānasūtrālaṁkāra*, a work published by his teacher's teacher, Sylvain Lévi, is justly famous, and an essential tool for anyone studying this literature (A–4). His continued commitment to this text is evident from his present engagement in the preparation of a complete Japanese translation, and the fact that he continues to teach weekly seminars on the work. Nevertheless, Nagao's painstakingly precise work on these classic texts was not an end in itself; these studies also served a greater purpose. For he has seen them all, in some sense, as precursors to, or tools to assist in, his study of the text which represents for him the culmination of the early Yogācāra, the *Mahāyānasaṁgraha*. The indices and detailed studies of vocabulary and thought have all been brought into focus on this great "Compendium of the Mahāyāna." Nagao's virtually lifelong effort bore its ultimate fruit in the two-volume edition with richly annotated translation published in the mid-1980s (A–9, 12). His interest in the text and his study of it did not stop with those volumes, of course, and the mid-1990s saw the appearance of two trilingual indices of the same text (A–15), with a final third volume still forthcoming.

In this regard it is interesting to note that Prof. Nagao has commented that it is easy to produce a mechanical index, but very hard to make a "clever" index. By this I think he means that to produce an index which lists every word is a trivial process (and nowadays it can be done by computer automatically), but to produce an index which lists the terms most likely to be of interest to a philosophically inclined investigator's understanding of the text and its thought can be a very difficult task indeed. It goes without saying that a trilingual glossary, Sanskrit-Tibetan-Chinese, compounds these problems almost to the breaking point. The reputation among scholars of Prof. Nagao's indices of the *Mahāyānasūtrālaṁkāra* and *Madhyāntavibhāga* is very high, but he himself has expressed his dissatisfaction with them. They are, he claims, full of oversights and faulty presentations. I very much doubt, however, that many who have used the indices feel the same way. Prof. Nagao's attitude reflects, I think, not on the quality of the indices but rather on the extremely high standards of their author, who it should be confessed is something of a perfectionist. It is another remarkable aspect of his personal qualities and intense dedication and energies that this perfectionism has not paralyzed him as it has some others, nor has it resulted in a small scholarly output, but on the contrary it has merely led him to examine, reexamine, and then reexamine again, with seemingly endless energy, everything he writes, constantly asking himself if he is right, and if this is the best way to express his understanding. His attitude toward precise use of language, as well as his constant reappraisal of his own ideas and conclusions, requires of the reader much attention to detail, and is part of the reason that Prof. Nagao has almost always insisted on personally revising English translations of his work. His command of English and its nuances is exceptional, and in those cases when he has not been able to monitor the English renderings of his work, the reader should understand that the English version is unlikely to express what Prof. Nagao himself would have wanted to say.

In addition to his more strictly philological projects, Prof. Nagao has published voluminously on the doctrine and philosophy of Buddhism, especially of the Madhyamaka and Yogācāra schools. His first major work of this type was "The Fundamental Standpoint of Mādhyamika Philosophy" (D–17). Here Nagao investigates many aspects of thought, concentrating on the Madhyamaka definition of emptiness as dependent origination, and the theory of the Two Truths. Already in this work Nagao's profoundly creative approach to philosophical problems, joined with a strict philological respect for his sources, is clearly evident. The former, of course, is difficult to imitate, but the latter is a trait which has been widely influential in modern Japanese Buddhist Studies, not only in the impact Nagao has had upon his many students at Kyoto University, but upon those who read his works as well, whether in Japan, Europe, or North America.

As important as Nagao's Madhyamaka studies are, it is his work on the Yogācāra school that will no doubt be his most lasting legacy. Many of these studies are already known to a non-Japanese audience, since they were originally published in English, or translated early on. More recently, a volume of his selected papers in English was published, including works previously available in English and others newly translated (A–14). Almost all of these papers deal with Yogācāra thought. Among the most important philosophical ideas investigated by Nagao are the theory of the so-called three natures (*trisvabhāva*), and the idea he calls "ascent and descent." Just as emptiness is the key to Madhyamaka thought, Nagao finds that emptiness to be the key to Yogācāra thought as well. But this continuity also provides the medium for change, since the interpretation of this idea, central to both systems, nevertheless differs. According to Nagao (see D-85), the dependent nature (*paratantra-svabhāva*) of the Three Nature theory, synonymous with dependent arisal (*pratītya-samutpāda*), is apt to fall into the imagined nature (*parikalpita*) on the one hand, and on the other becomes the consummated nature (*pariniṣpanna*) when awakened to it. The dependent nature, thus, is the pivot between the imagined nature, which is characterized as non-being (*asat*), and the consummated, which is none other than emptiness (*śūnyatā*). It is to this that Nagao attaches the notion—which is not a classical Buddhist one, but his own creative contribution—of "convertibility." It is this very convertibility which makes the path, attainment of spiritual progress, and ultimately awakening, possible.

While Nagao is certainly an expert in Buddhist philosophy, his interests go far beyond the abstract world of thought into many other fields. And the standard he set in the study of philosophy he upholds in his other researches as well. In 1967 Nagao took part in a venture that was to lead to an important change in the Japanese intellectual sphere. Together with Satō Masaru 佐藤優 and his successor Onoji Hidetada 小野地英忠 of Chūō Kōron Publishing, Nagao edited and presented what was essentially the first volume of translations of Buddhist scriptures into modern, colloquial Japanese to be published by a major publishing house (B–3). Encouraged by the success of this volume and a subsequent volume of works on early Buddhism (B–4), Onoji approached Nagao concerning the possibility of a series of publications to present texts of Mahāyāna Buddhism in their entirety in modern Japanese. Thus was born the *Daijō Butten* series (B–5). While including such well-known works as the *Sad-*

dharmapuṇḍarīka, the *Vajracchedikā*, and the *Sukhāvatīvyūha*, it also includes many works which, even today, more than twenty years later, have no other complete rendering in any modern language. The quality of these translations, which were made from Sanskrit or, when this was not available, Tibetan, is without exception of the highest level. The selection of texts itself, which was the responsibility of Nagao, tells us much about his catholic vision of Indian Mahāyāna Buddhism.[11] Since these translations were intended for an educated lay audience, the type of sometimes mind-numbing critical apparatus with which scholars fill their books is entirely absent. Whatever slight inconvenience this approach might cause the scholar is more than balanced by the fact that the natural translation into vernacular Japanese forced the translators to express in ordinary language what they actually felt the texts to mean. Western scholars who translate into English, German, or French have always been compelled to select words entirely different from those of their source language, and thus to actually interpret their texts. But for years the standard practice in Japanese Buddhist Studies had been to adopt the Sino-Japanese translation equivalents of Hsüan-tsang, almost mechanically inserting them into a text where corresponding Sanskrit forms were found. This naturally made such "translations" accessible only to the initiated. On the other side were entirely interpretive and non-critical devotional translations of a few select texts prepared for devotees. Nagao's project opened the door to a new generation of Buddhist publishing in Japan, in which reliable and yet accessible renderings of works were made widely available.

Nagao's own deep and broad interest in Mahāyāna sūtras is evidenced not only by his selection of the texts to be translated in the series, but by the fact that several of the volumes include his own renderings. Among these it is probably fair to say that the *Vimalakīrtinirdeśa* is the closest to his heart. He clearly considers this text to be one of the finest works of Buddhist literature, and he has returned to it time and again. His complete Japanese translation is probably the best in any language of the many available versions, both in terms of its philological accuracy and understanding of the point of the text and its accessible and clear language (A–7, C–2, 11). His lectures on the text present in simple terms his understanding of how we moderns might bridge the gap between the present day and

---

11. A discussion of the logic of selection and other matters concerned with the series is to be found in H–38.

the living world of the text (A–11). Prof. Nagao has also written other popular works which, while accessible to the non-specialist, also convey the fruits of his scholarship (for example, A–10). He has a rare ability to make carefully crafted academically sound points clear to a lay audience. Indeed, such works illustrate that the message of Buddhism, the heart of Śākyamuni's discovery, is something very real for Prof. Nagao.

In addition to the *Vimalakīrtinirdeśa*, Nagao has also published translations of the *Vajracchedikā*, *Kāśyapaparivarta*, and *Saddharmapuṇḍarīka*. An English translation of the *Kāśyapaparivarta* prepared by myself with Prof. Nagao's assistance should also be published before too long. In working with him on this translation over the period of a number of years I grew to learn something of the remarkable rigor with which he approaches a text, taking into careful account the original text, its translations, its commentary, and the location of the text within the great ocean of Buddhist thought. It is an approach one can aspire to emulate, without any reasonable expectation of ever being able to achieve it.

Nagao has also contributed many studies in the area of Buddhist art. His contributions to epigraphy include not only his work on the Siddham script (D–53) and Tibetan inscriptions (D–15), including the above-mentioned Chü-yung-kuan inscription, but more playfully an inscription in the 'Phags-pa script published in facsimile for the first time in the present volume. He is also an accomplished calligrapher in the Siddham script (H–67) and of course in Chinese (H–44). Nagao's wider interest in the arts and archaeology of Asia, and related subjects, is illustrated in his publications on Mongolian fearsome deities (D–21), Tibetan painting and other religious objects (E–3, G–40, H–42), religious art in India (D–43, G–28, 29, 31, 32, 33, 39, H–19, 28), Japanese art (G–15, 23, 25, 34, 41, H–16), and his general articles on a number of art-historical topics (F–3, 4). In 1958–59 Nagao organized an expedition from Kyoto University to tour Buddhist sites in South Asia, and the team was able during that time to engage in a short archaeological dig at Bodh Gaya. This experience in part contributed to a number of published studies on excavations in India, and monastic architecture and its relation to monastic life (A–6, D–38, 39, 46, 66, 75, E–7, G–17, 20, 21, 22, 26, 27, 30).

It is certainly far too early to begin talking of Prof. Nagao's legacy. Even at the age of ninety he is healthy, vital, and hard at work at numerous projects, including his above-mentioned Japanese translation of the *Mahāyānasūtrālaṁkāra*. But it is not too early to call for more attention to be paid to certain aspects of his work.

Outside of Japan Nagao's Tibetological studies remain poorly known, almost certainly due to the fact that although many of his studies on philosophy and Sanskrit philology have been published in English, either originally or later in translation, the Tibetological works are still largely available only in Japanese. This is unfortunate because even today, when Tibetan Buddhist studies is a growing field and sources and opportunities denied Nagao are available, at least one aspect of Nagao's work, his studies on the living "Lamaism" of the Inner Mongolia of fifty years ago, cannot be duplicated and retains virtually all of its original value. It is to be hoped that the recent reprinting of the two accounts of Nagao's journeys (A–1′, 2′) may stimulate renewed interest in his valuable discoveries. Likewise, his studies on the *Lam rim chen mo* of Tsong kha pa set a high standard. It is also no doubt due to a lack of knowledge of the Japanese language that Nagao's excellent works on a number of texts, perhaps most importantly the *Mahāyānasaṁgraha*, remain almost unknown to all but a handful of non-Japanese scholars.

As such works are translated, and as more Western Buddhist scholars realize the necessity of a knowledge of Japanese, it is beyond doubt that the influence of Prof. Nagao's work will only continue to grow.

Seal in 'Phags pa script, reading
dga' 'dzin (Gadjin), 21 × 9 mm.

Gadjin M. Nagao

Spring 1933.
Standing, right to left: Honda Giei, Yamaguchi Susumu, Matsumoto Bunzaburō.
Seated, right to left: Hatani Ryōtai, Nagao Gadjin; *second from left,* Tsukamoto Zenryū.

A Bibliography of the Publications of Gadjin M. Nagao (Through 1996)

Abbreviations:

AS	*Asahi Shinbun* 朝日新聞
CN	*Chūgai Nippō* 中外日報
EB	*The Eastern Buddhist*, New Series
IBK	*Indogaku Bukkyōgaku Kenkyū* 印度学仏教学研究
JIABS	*The Journal of the International Association of Buddhist Studies*
KS	*Kyōto Shinbun* 京都新聞
MS	*Mainichi Shinbun* 毎日新聞
NKS	*Nihon Keizai Shinbun* 日本経済新聞
SGZKN	*Suzuki Gakujutsu Zaidan Kenkyū Nenpō* 鈴木学術財団年報
SK	*Shūkyō Kenkyū* 宗教研究
TG	*Tōhō Gakuhō*, Kyoto, 東方學報 (京都)
TK	*Tetsugaku Kenkyū* 哲學研究

Additional printings of books are not mentioned if no changes were made to the contents or title.

A: Books and Monographs

1. *Mōko Ramabyōki* 蒙古喇嘛廟記 (ཧོར་ཡུལ་ལ་འགྲོ་སྐབས་ཀྱི་ལམ་ཡིག་བཞུགས) [A Record of Lamaistic Temples in Mongolia] (Kyoto: Kōtō Shoin 高桐書院, 1947).

1′. Reprinted as *Mōko Ramabyōki* 蒙古ラマ廟記. Chūkō bunko中公文庫 M344 (Tokyo: Chūō Kōronsha 中央公論社, 1987). The new edition is presented in revised orthography, with a new Afterword and Appendix (pp. 251–258), and reprints **D–14, G–4, 5**.

2. *Mōko Gakumonji* 蒙古學問寺 (ཧོར་ཡུལ་གྱི་གྲྭ་ས་ཆོས་སྡེ་ཆེན་པོ་རྣམས་ཀྱི་གདམ་བཤད) [Lamaistic College-monasteries in Inner Mongolia] (Kyoto: Zenkoku Shobō 全國書房, 1947).

2′. Reprinted in Chūkō bunko 中公文庫 640 (Tokyo: Chūō Kōronsha 中央公論社, 1992). The new edition is presented in revised orthography, and with a new Afterword (pp. 340–346).

3. *Chibetto Bukkyō Kenkyū* 西蔵佛教研究 [A Study of Tibetan Buddhism: Being a Translation into Japanese of the Exposition of Vipaśyanā in

Tsong kha pa's *Lam-rim Chen-mo*, with annotations and prefatory remarks] (Tokyo: Iwanami Shoten 岩波書店, 1954. Reprinted 1974).

English summary in *Bibliographie Bouddhique XXVIII-XXXI (Mai 1954–Mai 1958)* (Paris: Adrien Maisonneuve): #2039.

4. *Index to the Mahāyāna-sūtrālaṁkāra (Sylvain Lévi Edition)*. Part One: Sanskrit-Tibetan-Chinese (Tokyo: Nippon Gakujutsu Shinkōkai [Japan Society for the Promotion of Science], 1958). Part Two: Tibetan-Sanskrit & Chinese-Sanskrit (Tokyo: Nippon Gakujutsu Shinkōkai [Japan Society for the Promotion of Science], 1961).

5. *Madhyāntavibhāga-bhāṣya, A Buddhist Philosophical Treatise edited for the first time from a Sanskrit manuscript* (Tōkyō: Suzuki Research Foundation, 1964).

6. *The Ancient Buddhist Community in India and its Cultural Activities.* With appendices containing his personal history and a list of his publications (in Japanese). Edited by the Commemoration Committee on the Occasion of Professor Nagao's Retirement from Kyoto University, March 1971 (Kyoto: The Society for Indic and Buddhist Studies, Kyoto University, 1971).

An expanded English version of **D–46**.

7. *Yuimakyō* 維摩経 [The *Vimalakīrtinirdeśa*]. Chūkō bunko 中公文庫 D6 (Tokyo: Chūō Kōronsha 中央公論社, 1973).

7′. Revised reprint: *Kaihan Yuimakyō* 改版維摩経. Chūkō bunko 中公文庫 D6–2 (Tokyo: Chūō Kōronsha 中央公論社, 1983).
See **A–11, C–2, 11, D–50, 52, 84, 96**.

8. *Chūkan to Yuishiki* 中観と唯識 [Madhyamaka and Yogācāra: A Collection of Papers on Mahāyāna Philosophy] (Tokyo: Iwanami Shoten 岩波書店, 1978).

Contains **D–1, 2, 3, 5, 7, 8, 16, 17, 23, 24, 25, 26, 28, 31, 32, 44, 49, 54, 55, 69, 70, 71, F–1**.

9. *Shōdaijōron Wayaku to chūkai (Jō)* 摂大乗論・和訳と注解 (上) [An annotated Japanese translation of the *Mahāyānasaṁgraha*, Part I, chapters 1–2]. Indo Koten Sōsho インド古典叢書 (Tokyo: Kōdansha 講談社, 1982).

See **A–12, B–9, D–10**.

10. *Bukkyō no genryū: Indo* 仏教の源流—インド [The origins of Buddhism: India]. Asahi Karucyā Bukkusu 朝日カルチャーブックス 39

(Osaka: Ōsaka Shoseki Kabushiki Gaisha 大阪書籍株式会社, 1984. Reprinted 1987).

Partial English translation in **D–81, 91,** and see **D–90**.

11. *"Yuimakyō" o yomu* 「維摩経」を読む [Reading the *Vimalakīrtinirdeśa*]. Iwanami Seminā Bukkusu 岩波セミナーブックス 19 (Tokyo: Iwanami Shoten 岩波書店, 1986).

See **A–7, C–2, 11, D–50, 52, 84, 96**.

12. *Shōdaijōron Wayaku to chūkai* (*Ge*) 摂大乗論・和訳と注解 (下) [An annotated Japanese translation of the *Mahāyānasaṁgraha*, Part II, chapters 3–10]. Indo Koten Sōsho インド古典叢書 (Tokyo: Kōdansha 講談社, 1987).

See **A–9, B–9**.

12′. Chap.VIII, *Nirvikalpa-jñāna*, translated into English by Leslie Kawamura in *From Benares to Beijing: Essays on Buddhism and Chinese Religion*, ed. Koichi Shinohara and Gregory Schopen (Oakville, Ontario: Mosaic Press, 1991): 41–68.

13. *The Foundational Standpoint of Mādhyamika Philosophy*. Translated by John P. Keenan. SUNY Series in Buddhist Studies (Albany: State University of New York Press, 1989).

See the Japanese original **D–17**.

14. *Mādhyamika and Yogācāra: A Study of Mahāyāna Philosophies*. Collected Papers of G. M. Nagao. Edited, collected, and translated by L. S. Kawamura in collaboration with G. M. Nagao (Albany: State University of New York Press, 1991).

Contains **D–27, 29, 35, 37, 59, 67, 72, 74, 76, 77, 78, 85, 86, 87, 88, 89**.

15. *An Index to Asaṅga's Mahāyānasaṁgraha*. Part One: Tibetan-Sanskrit-Chinese. Part Two: Sanskrit-Tibetan-Chinese. Studia Philologica Buddhica, Monograph Series 9 (Tokyo: The International Institute of Buddhist Studies, 1994). 2 volumes.

B: Edited Works, Series, Volumes, and Collections

1. *Indo no Bunka* 印度の文化 [The Culture of India] (Tokyo: Seikatsusha 生活社 [Daitōa Gakujutsu Kyōkai 大東亞學術協会] 1943).

See **D–11**.

2. *Yamaguchi Hakase Kanreki Kinen: Indogaku Bukkyōgaku Ronsō* 山口博士還暦記念・印度學佛教學論叢 / *Studies in Indology and Buddhology:*

Presented in Honour of Professor Susumu Yamaguchi on the Occasion of his Sixtieth Birthday (Kyoto: Hōzōkan 法蔵館, 1955).

Edited with Nozawa Jōshō 野澤靜證; the introduction is by Nagao. See **D–29**.

3. *Sekai no Meicho* 世界の名著 2: *Daijō Butten* 大乗仏典 (Tokyo: Chūō Kōronsha 中央公論社, 1967).

See **C–1, 2, 3, 4, 5, H–21**.

4. *Sekai no Meicho* 世界の名著 1: *Baramon Kyōten / Genshi Butten* バラモン教典・原始仏典 (Tokyo: Chūō Kōronsha 中央公論社, 1969).

See **C–7, 8, 9, D–62, H–25**.

5. *Daijō Butten* 大乗仏典. 15 volumes (Tokyo: Chūō Kōronsha 中央公論社, 1973–1976).

Co-edited with Kajiyama Yūichi 梶山雄一.

Contents: 1: Shorter Prajñāparamitā texts; 2, 3: *Aṣṭasahāsrikā Prajñāparamitā*; 4, 5: *Saddharmapuṇḍarīka*; 6: Pure Land Sūtras; 7: *Vimalakīrtinirdeśa* and *Śūraṁgamasamādhi*; 8: *Daśabhūmika*; 9: *Mahāratnakūṭa* Sūtras; 10, 11: *Samādhirāja*; 12: *Tathāgatagarbha* Sūtras; 13: *Buddhacarita*; 14: Writings of Nāgārjuna; 15: Writings of Vasubandhu.

See **C–10, 11, 12, 13, 14, 15, H–38**.

6. *Kōza Bukkyō Shisō* 講座仏教思想 (Tokyo: Risōsha 理想社, 1974–1975).

General editor with Nakamura Hajima 中村元; edited by Saigusa Mitsuyoshi 三枝充悳.

7 volumes: 1: *Sonzairon / Jikanron* 存在論・時間論 [Ontology / Time]; 2: *Ninshikiron / Ronrigaku* 認識論・論理学 [Epistemology / Logic]; 3: *Rinrigaku / Kyōikugaku* 倫理学・教育学 [Ethics / Education]; 4: *Ningenron / Shinrigaku* 人間論・心理学 [Humanity / Psychology]; 5: *Shūkyōron / Shinri / Kachiron* 宗教論・真理・価値論 [Religion / Truth / Values]; 6: *Jinseikan* 人生観 [Human Life]; 7: *Bungakuron / Geijutsuron* 文学論・芸術論 [Literature / Art].

See **D–61**.

7. *Acta Asiatica* 29 [Special Issue: Tibetan Studies in Japan] (1975).

See **D–64**.

8. Volumes of the *Kokuyaku-Issaikyō* 国訳一切経 *Indosenjutsubu* 印度撰述部 128–135, *Shakkyōronbu* 釈経論部 1–8 (Tokyo: Daitō Shuppansha 大東出版社, 1977).

Indosenjutsubu 128–32–(2), *Shakkyōronbu* 1–5B (*ge* 下) is *Daichidoron* 大智度論 1–5A, 5B, translated by Mano Shōjun 眞野正順. Volumes 1, 3, 5A are edited with Tanigawa Risen 谷川理宣; 2, 4, 5B with Kan Eishō 菅英尚. Vol. 5B also includes *Ninnō-Hannyakyō* 仁王般若經, *Hannyashingyō* 般若心經, and *Butsumo-Hōtokuzō-Hannnyakyō* 仏母宝徳蔵般若經, translated by Shiio Benkyō 椎尾辨

匡. *Indosenjutsubu* 133, *Shakkyōronbu* 6 is *Jūjikyōron* 十地經論, translated by Ishii Kyōdō 石井教道, edited with Hayashima Osamu 早島理. *Indosenjutsubu* 134, *Shakkyōronbu* 7, is *Jūju-bibasharon*十住毘婆沙論, translated by Yabuki Keiki 矢吹慶輝, edited with Sasaki Eshō 佐々木惠精. *Indosenjutsubu* 135, *Shakkyōronbu* 8 is *Mirokubosatsu-shomon-kyōron* 弥勒菩薩所問經論, *Nehanron* 涅槃論, and *Nehangyō-hon-u-konmugeron* 涅槃經本有今無偈論, translated by Fuse Kōgaku 布施洪岳, with *Funbetsu-kudokuron* 分別功徳論, *Kuju-seigiron* 九頌精義論, *Enjūyōgiron* 円集要義論, *Enjūyōgishakuron* 円集要義釈論, *Hōmangyō-shihō-upadaisha* 宝鬘經四法憂波提舎, *Tenpōrinkyōron* 転法輪經論, and *Sangusokukyōron* 三具足經論, translated by Izumi Hōkei 泉芳憬, edited with Hayashima Osamu 早島理.

See **D–65**.

9. *Indo Koten Sōsho* インド古典叢書 (Tokyo: Kōdansha 講談社, 1980–).

Co-editor with Tsuji Naoshirō 辻直四郎, Kanakura Enshō 金倉圓照, Hikata Ryūshō 干潟龍祥, Kajiyama Yūichi 梶山雄一, and Takasaki Jikidō 高崎直道.

See **A–8, 12**.

10. *Iwanami Kōza: Tōyō Shisō* 岩波講座・東洋思想 (Tokyo: Iwanami Shoten 岩波書店, 1988–1990). 16 volumes.

Co-edited with Izutsu Toshihiko 井筒俊彦, Fukunaga Mitsuji 福永光司, Ueyama Shunpei 上山春平, Hattori Masaaki 服部正明, Kajiyama Yūichi 梶山雄一, and Takasaki Jikidō 高崎直道.
Vols. 1–2: Judaic thought; 3–4: Islamic thought; 5–7: Indian philosophy; 8–10: Indian Buddhism; 11: Tibetan Buddhism; 12: East Asian Buddhism; 13–14: Chinese religious thought; 15–16: Japanese thought.

11. *Daijō Butten: Chūgoku / Nihon-hen* 大乗仏典: 中国・日本篇. 30 volumes (Tokyo: Chūō Kōronsha 中央公論社, 1987–1996).

Co-editor with Yanagida Seizan 柳田聖山 and Kajiyama Yūichi 梶山雄一.

12. *Jōdo Bukkyō no Shisō* 浄土佛教の思想. 15 volumes (Tokyo: Kōdansha 講談社, 1991–).

Co-editor with Kajiyama Yūichi 梶山雄一, Bandō Shōjun 坂東性純, Fujita Kōtatsu 藤田宏達, and Fujiyoshi Jikai 藤吉慈海.

C: Translations of Buddhist Texts

1. "Kongō-Hannyakyō" 金剛般若経 [The *Vajracchedikā*]. **B–3**: 67–82.

Abbreviated translation from Sanskrit. See **C–10**.

2. "Yuimakyō" 維摩経 [The *Vimalakīrtinirdeśa*]. **B–3**: 83–194.

Translated from Tibetan. See **A–7, 11, C–11, D–52, 84**.

3. "Hōshakukyō" 宝積経 [The *Kāśyapaparivarta*]. **B–3**: 195–230.

Abbreviated co-translation from Sanskrit with Aramaki Noritoshi 荒牧典俊. See **C–12**, **D–63**.

4. "Akiraka na kotoba" (Chūron Gesshō-shaku, dai 15 shō, Bonbun wayaku) 明らかなことば (中論月称釈, 第15章, 梵文和訳) [The *Prasannapadā*, Chapter 15, from Sanskrit]. **B–3**: 269–286.

5. "Chūsei to ryōkyokutan to no benbetsu" (Chūhenfunbetsuron, dai 1, 3 shō, Bonbun wayaku) 中正と両極端との弁別 (中辺分別論, 第 1, 3 章, 梵文和訳) [The *Madhyāntavibhāga*, Chapters 1 and 3, from Sanskrit]. **B–3**: 397–426.

6. "*Jūnimonronso*: Kichizō-sen" 十二門論疏・吉蔵撰 [Chi-tsang's Commentary to Nāgārjuna's "Twelve Gate Treatise"]. *Kokuyaku-Issaikyō* 国訳一切経, *Wakan senjutsu* 和漢撰述 27, *Ronshobu* 論疏部 7 (Tokyo: Daitō Shuppansha 大東出版社, 1968): 323–355.

Co-translated with Tanji Teruyoshi 丹治昭義. Includes a commentary on pp. 325-339.

7. "Tanpen no kyōten: Hasshu" 短編の経典—八種 [*Saṁyutta Nikāya* 1.2.10; 3.3.1; 7.2.1; 8.5; 22.87; 32.200]. **B–4**: 440–459.

Six Pāli *sutta*s co-translated with Kudō Shigeki 工藤成樹.

8. "Chūhen no kyōten: Goshu" 中編の経典—五種 [*Majjhima Nikāya* 115]. **B–4**: 487–493.

Co-translated from Pāli with Kudō Shigeki 工藤成樹.

9. "Shukke no kudoku" 出家の功徳 [The *Sāmaññaphala-sutta*]. **B–4**: 503–538.

10. "Kongō-Hannyakyō" 金剛般若経 [The *Vajracchedikā*]. In *Daijō Butten* 大乗仏典 1: *Hannyabu-Kyōten* 般若部経典 [Prajñāpāramitā texts] (Tokyo: Chūō Kōronsha 中央公論社, 1973): 5–71. With notes pp. 297–303, and a commentary on pp. 317–324.

Translated from Sanskrit. See **B–5**, **C–1**. A translation of the sūtra text, along with Asaṅga's commentary *Triśatikāyāḥ Prajñāpāramitāyāḥ Kārikāsaptatiḥ* (published by G. Tucci in *Minor Buddhist Texts I* [Rome: IsMEO, 1956]). See below, **D–55**.

11. "Yuimakyō" 維摩経 [The *Vimalakīrtinirdeśa*]. In *Daijō Butten* 大乗仏典 7. *Yuimakyō / Shuryōgonkyō* 維摩経・首楞厳経 (Tokyo: Chūō Kōronsha 中央公論社, 1974): 6–180. Notes 372–392, commentary 416–430.

Translated from Tibetan. See **A–7**, **11**, **B–5**, **C–2**, **D–52**, **84**.

12. "Kashōbon" 迦葉品 [The *Kāśyapaparivarta*]. *Daijō Butten* 大乗仏典 9, Hōshakubu-kyōten 宝積部経典 (Tokyo: Chūō Kōronsha 中央公論社, 1974): 5–124, with notes: 314–323.

Co-translated from Sanskrit and annotated with Sakurabe Hajime 桜部建. Commentary by Nagao: 336–341. See **B–5**, **C–3**, **D–63**.

13. "Hokekyō" 法華経 [The *Saddharmapuṇḍarīka*]. *Daijō Butten* 大乗仏典 4, Hokekyō 法華経 I (Tokyo: Chūō Kōronsha 中央公論社, 1975).

Co-translated with Matsunami Seiren 松濤誠廉 and Tanji Teruyoshi 丹治昭義, through KN 223. Commentary by Nagao: 297–305. See **B–5**.

14. "Sanshōron" 三性論 [The *Trisvabhāvanirdeśa*]. *Daijō Butten* 大乗仏典 15, *Seshin Ronshū* 世親論集 (Tokyo: Chūō Kōronsha 中央公論社, 1976): 191–213.

See **B–5**.

15. "Chūhenfunbetsuron" 中辺分別論 [The *Madhyāntavibhāga*]. *Daijō Butten* 大乗仏典 15, *Seshin Ronshū* 世親論集 (Tokyo: Chūō Kōronsha 中央公論社, 1976): 215–358, notes 380–409.

See **B–5**.

D: Articles

1. "Anne no shikitenpensetsu ni tsuite" 安慧の識轉變説について [Sthiramati on *vijñānapariṇāma*]. *SK* 9/5 (1932): 107–122 (865–880), 10/2 (1933): 102–116 (470–484).

Reprinted in **A–8**: 341–372.

2. "Shoen-gyōsōmon no ichimondai" 所縁行相門の一問題 [Sthiramati on *ālambana* and *ākāra*]. *SK* 12/2 (1935): 33–49 (207–223).

Reprinted in **A–8**: 373–388.

3. "Kūgi yori sanshōsetsu e" 空義より三性説へ [From emptiness to the three natures theory]. *TK* 22/1 (250) (1937): 61–96.

Reprinted in **A–8**: 180–206.

4. "On the Publication of *Madhyāntavibhāgaṭīkā*." *The Young East* 7/3 (1937): 27–32.

An introduction to Yamaguchi Susumu's edition.

5. "*Jōyuishikiron* ni okeru zōron-ishu ni tsuite" 『成唯識論』における造論意趣について [The writer's motive in Hsüan-tsang's *Vijñaptimātratāsiddhi*]. *TG* 9 (1938): 197–217.

Reprinted in **A–8**: 389–405.

6. "Ramabyō to sono bunken" 喇嘛廟とその文獻 [Lamaist temples and their literature]. *TG* 11/2 (1940): 84–96 (232–244).

7. "Imon (*paryāya*) toiu kotoba" 異門 (*paryāya*) といふことば [On the term *paryāya*]. *SK* 2/4 (1940): 324–331 (978–985).

Reprinted in **A–8**: 406–412.

8. "Sanshōsetsu to sono hiyu" 三性説とその譬喩 [The theory of the three aspects (*trisvabhāva*) and its allegories (*upamā*)]. *TG* 11/4 (1941): 47–84 (489–526).

Reprinted in **A–8**: 207–236. English version **D–77**.

9. "Chibetto bunka no kenkyū to sono igi" 西藏文化の研究とその意義 [The study of Tibetan culture and its significance]. *Bukkyō Kenkyū* 佛教研究 5/5–6 (1941) [Bukkyōgaku no Genjō to Shōrai 佛教學の現状と將來, The present state and the future of Buddhist Studies]: 235–253.

10. "Shōdaijōron Seshin-shaku no kanzōbon taishō" 摂大乗論世親釋の漢藏本對照 [A comparison of the Chinese and Tibetan texts of Vasubandhu's commentary to the *Mahāyānasaṁgraha*]. *TG* 13/2 (1943): 119–175 (281–337).

The Tibetan translation and three Chinese translations, of Hsüan-tsang, Gupta, and Paramārtha, compared, and technical terms restored into Sanskrit, for the introductory section (*prastāvanā*) only. See **A–9**.

11. "Bukkyō no indoteki seikaku" 佛教の印度的性格 [The Indian character of Buddhism]. In **B–1**: 59–119.

12. "Ramakyō kyōri no gaiyō: Mui-kokū no shosetsu ni yorite" 喇嘛教教理の概要・無畏虚空の所説に依りて [An outline of Lamaist doctrine, according to 'Jigs med nam mkha']. *TG* 14/4 (1944): 1–47 (467–513).

13. "Mōko ramabyō chōsaki" 蒙古喇嘛廟調查記 [An investigation of Lamaist monasteries in Mongolia]. *TG* 14/4 (1944): 118–144 (584–611), 15/2 (1946): 101–128 (233–260).

14. "Kioku to gakumon" 記憶と學問 [Memory and scholasticism]. *Gakkai* 學海 3/2 (1946): 21–34.

Reprinted in **A–1′**: 229–249.

15. "Chibetto inshō moji" 西藏印章文字 [Tibetan seal script, the 'Phags-pa script]. *Gakkai* 學海 3/5 (1946): 39–48.

A discussion of the 'Phags-pa script, with illustrations of various seals.

16. "Shōgi to sezoku to no sekai" 勝義と世俗との世界 [The worlds of absolute and conventional truth]. *Gakkai* 學海 4/5 (1947): 1–6, *Gakugei* 學藝 4/7: 9–14.

Reprinted in **A–8**: 145–157.

17. "Chūkan tetsugaku no konponteki tachiba" 中觀哲學の根本的立場 [The fundamental standpoint of Mādhyamika philosophy]. *TK* 31/9 (366): 1–27 (505–531), 31/11 (368): 16–49 (646–679), 32/1 (370): 1–41 (1–41), 32/2 (371): 19–38 (87–106) (1947–1948).

Reprinted in **A–8**: 3–144. Compare the English translation **A–13**.

18. "Kyōhan no seishin" 教判の精神 [The idea of systematic rankings of Buddhist teachings]. *Mikkyō Bunka* 密教文化 5/6 (1949): 12–37.

19. "Gakusō Tson ka pa: sono den to chosaku mokuroku" 學僧宗喀巴—その傳と著作目録 [Tsong kha pa, the greatest pandit in Tibetan Buddhism, with a list of his Complete Works]. *TG* 17 (1949): 35–82.

20. "Kokusai tōyōgaku kaigi no koto nado" 國際東洋學會議のことなど [An international conference on Asian Studies]. *TK* 34/2 (395) (1950): 51–58.

21. "Mōko no fuizo" 蒙古の怖畏像 [Lamaist terrible deities]. *Bukkyō Geijutsu* 佛教藝術 [*Ars Buddhica*] 12 (1951): 64–77.

22. "Tson ka pa no kyōgaku ni tsuite" 宗喀巴の教學について [On Buddhist studies as authorized by Tsong kha pa]. *Nippon Bukkyō Gakkai Nenpō* 日本佛教學會年報 16 (1951): 1–27.

23. "Tenkan no ronri" 轉換の論理 [The logic of 'convertibility' in Buddhism]. *TK* 35/7 (405) (1952): 1–28.

Reprinted in **A–8**: 237–265. English version **D–85**.

24."Bukkyōteki shutaisei ni tsuite" 佛教的主体性について [Buddhist subjectivity]. *IBK* 1/1 (1952): 49–54.

Reprinted in **A–8**: 333–340. English version **D–37**.

25. "Chibetto ni nokoreru yuishikigaku" 西蔵に残れる唯識学 [The idealistic school of Buddhism (Vijñānavāda) preserved in Tibet]. *IBK* 2/1 (1953): 75–84.

Reprinted in **A–8**: 413–425.

26. "Chūron no kōzō: Tson ka pa *Chūron-shaku* o chūshin toshite" 中論の構造—宗喀巴『中論釈』を中心として [A Synopsis of Nāgārjuna's *Mūlamadhyamaka-śāstra*, according to the commentary by Tsong kha pa]. *Bukkyōgaku Kenkyū* 佛教學研究 8–9 (Akashi Kyōju Kanreki Kinen Ronbunshū 明石教授還暦記念論文集) (1953): 121–132.

Reprinted in **A–8**: 321–332.

27. "An interpretation of the term 'saṁvṛti' (convention) in Buddhism." *Silver Jubilee Volume of the Zinbun-Kagaku-Kenkyusho, Kyōto University* (Kyoto: Kyōto Daigaku Jinbun Kagaku Kenkyūsho, 1954): 550–561.

Reprinted in **A–14:** 13–22, 230–232. Japanese translation **D–69**.

28. "Butsuda no chinmoku to sono chūkanteki igi" 佛陀の沈黙とその中観的意義 [The silence of the Buddha and its Madhyamic interpretation]. *TK* 37/8 (430) (1955): 1–21 (435–455).

Reprinted in **A–8**: 158–179. English version **D–29**.

29. "The silence of the Buddha and its Madhyamic interpretation." In **B–2**: 137–151.

A translation by Yoshiaki Fujitani of **D–28**. Reprinted in **A–14**: 35–49, 236–238.

30. "Chibetto" チベット [Tibet]. In Uehara Senroku 上原専祿, Kamei Katsuichirō 亀井勝一郎, Furuta Shōkin 古田紹欽, and Nakamura Hajime 中村元, eds., *Gendai Bukkyō Kōza* 現代仏教講座, Vol. 3, *Rekishihen* 歴史篇 (Tokyo: Kadokawa Shoten 角川書店, 1955): 85–100.

31. "*Daijō-shōgon-kyōron* no yōgorei: tokuni chūron to no hikaku ni oite" 『大乗荘厳経論』の用語例—特に中論との比較に於いて [Terminologies employed in the *Mahāyānasūtrālaṁkāra*, a study with specific comparison with those in the *Mūlamadhyamakakārikā*]. *IBK* 4/2 (1956): 123–126 (430–433).

Reprinted in **A–8**: 426–431.

32. "Chibetto bukkyō ni okeru shinrikan" チベット佛教における眞理観 [The concept of truth in Tibetan Buddhism]. *Bukkyō no konpon genri* 佛教の根本原理, ed. by Miyamoto Shōson 宮本正尊 (Tokyo: Sanseido 三省堂, 1956): 651–673.

Reprinted in **A–8**: 584–606.

33. "Hōzō no sanshōsetsu ni taisuru jakkan no gimon" 法蔵の三性説に対する若干の疑問 [Fa-tsang's viewpoint in regard to the theory of three-fold nature (*Trisvabhāva*)]. In *Kyōto Daigaku Bungakubu Gojusshūnen Kinen Ronshū* 京都大学文学部五十周年記念論集 [Miscellanea

Kiotiensia, Essays in Celebration of the Semicentennial of the Faculty of Letters of Kyoto University]. Kyōto Daigaku Bungakubu Kenkyū Kiyō 京都大学文学部研究紀要 4 (Kyoto: Kyōto Daigaku Bungakubu 京都大学文学部, 1956): 183–205.

Reprinted in **A–8**: 502–525.

34. "Gotokuchi to Kenju Daishi" 後得智と賢首大師 [*Pṛṣṭhalabdhajñāna* and Fa-tsang]. *SK* 150 (1956): 46–47 (213–214).

35. "Connotations of the Word *āśraya* (basis) in the *Mahāyāna-sūtrālaṁkāra*." *Liebenthal Festschift / Sino-Indian Studies* V/3–4 (Santiniketan, Visvabharati, 1957): 147–155.

Reprinted in **A–14:** 75–81, 245–246. Japanese translation **D–70**.

36. Contributions to Murata Jirō 村田治郎, ed., *Chü-yung-kuan, the Buddhist Arch of the Fourteenth Century A.D. at the Pass of the Great Wall Northwest of Peking / Kyoyōkan* 居庸關. Text volume (Kyoto: Faculty of Engineering, Kyoto University, 1957).

Pages 121–127 (the inscription in six scripts; the *Uṣṇīṣavijayadhāraṇī*; the *Tathāgatahṛdayadhāraṇī*); 135–136 (Introduction to the large character inscriptions, with Ashikaga Atsuuji 足利惇氏); 137–142 (the large Lhantsa character inscription); 143–147 (the large Tibetan character inscription); 204–205 (remarks on the corrections to the inscriptions; corrections to the *Uṣṇīṣavijayadhāraṇī* inscription, with Ashikaga); 210 (corrections to the *Tathāgatahṛdayadhāraṇī* inscription); 221–222 (restored Sanskrit texts and Japanese translation of the additional *dhāraṇīs*, with Ashikaga); 225–242 (the small character inscriptions; the Tibetan inscription).

See **D–79**.

37. "Buddhist Subjectivity." In Japanese Association for Religious Studies and Japan Organizing Committee of the Ninth International Congress for the History of Religion, ed., *Religious Studies in Japan* (Tokyo: Maruzen Company Ltd., 1959): 257–262.

A translation by Dairokurō Kanzaki 神崎大六郎 and Masaaki Hattori of **D–24**. Reprinted in **A–14**: 7–12, 229–230.

38. "Indo busseki tōsaki: Karukatta kara Benaresu made" インド佛蹟踏査記—カルカッタからベナレスまで [A survey of Buddhist ruins in India: from Calcutta to Benares]. *Bukkyō Geijutsu* 佛教藝術 [*Ars Buddhica*] 41 (1959): 56–76.

39. "Zoku Indo busseki tōsaki: Kajurāho yori Bonbei e" インド佛蹟踏査記—カジュラーホよりボンベイへ [A survey of Buddhist ruins in India continued: from Khajurāho to Bombay]. *Bukkyō Geijutsu* 佛教藝術 [*Ars Buddhica*] 43 (1960): 67–88.

This and the preceding item are reports of the Japanese Expedition to Buddhist Sites in India (JEBI) which was organized, with Nagao as its leader, under the sponsorship of the Mainichi Shinbun and the Tōhō Gakkai (Tokyo), with assistance from the Indian Embassy (Tokyo), and carried out from December 1958 to March 1959. See **G–20**, **21**, **22**, **H–14**.

40. "Ichijō / Sanjō no rongi o megutte" 一乗・三乗の論議をめぐって [Aspects of the *ekayāna* and *triyāna* argument with particular reference to India]. In Tsukamoto Hakase Shōju Kinenkai 塚本博士頌寿記念会, ed., *Tsukamoto Hakase Shōju Kinen Bukkyōshigaku Ronshū* 塚本博士頌寿記念 佛教史学論集 (Kyoto: Tsukamoto Hakase Shōju Kinenkai 塚本博士頌寿記念会, 1961): 534–545.

Reprinted in **A–8**: 526–541.

41. "*Chūbenfunbetsuron* no bonbun shahon" 中邊分別論の梵文寫本 [A Sanskrit manuscript of the *Madhyāntavibhāga*]. *Tōhōgakkai sōritsu jūgoshūnen kinen Tōhōgaku ronshū* 東方學會創立十五周年記念東方學論集 (Tokyo: Tōhō Gakkai 東方學會, 1962): 182–193.

42. "Katomandu no bukkyō shahon tenseki" カトマンドゥの佛教寫本典籍 [Buddhist manuscripts in Sanskrit from Kathmandu]. *Iwai Hakase Koki Kinen Tenseki Ronshū* 岩井博士古稀記念典籍論集 (Tokyo: Iwai Hakase Koki Kinen Jigyōkai 岩井博士古稀記念事業会, 1963): 8–25.

43. "Indo no Shūkyō to sono Bijutsu" インドの宗教とその美術 [Religions and Religious Arts of India]. *Museum / Tōkyō Kokuritsu Hakubutsukan Bijutsushi* 東京国立博物館美術誌 (1963): 2–5.

44. "*Chūbenfunbetsuron* no daimei" 『中邊分別論』の題名 [On the title *Madhyāntavibhāga*]. *Yūki Kyōju shōju kinen: Bukkyō Shisōshi Ronshū* 結城教授頌寿記念・佛教思想史論集 (Tokyo: Daizō Shuppan 大藏出版, 1964): 197–209.

Reprinted in **A–8**: 443–454.

45. "Bukkyō: Muga shisō o chūshin ni" 佛教—無我思想を中心に [The Buddhist non-self]. *Shūkyō to Rinri* 宗教と倫理. Kōza Tetsugaku Taikei 講座哲学体系 7 (Jinbun Shoin 人文書院, 1964): 160–182.

46. "Bukkyō kyōdan to bunka katsudō" 仏教教団と文化活動 [The ancient Buddhist community in India and its cultural activity]. In Ueno Teruo 上野照夫, ed., *Sekai no Bunka* 世界の文化 3: *Indo* インド (Kawade Shobō Shinsha 河出書房新社, 1965): 80–93.

See **A–6** for an expanded version in English.

47. "Bukkyō no shisō to rekishi" 佛教の思想と歴史 [Buddhist thought and history]. In **B–3**: 5–66.

48. "Amarerumono" 餘れるもの [The term *avaśiṣṭa* in the Yogācāra philosophy]. *IBK* 16/2 (1968): 23–27 (497–501).

A revised version is **D–71**, itself a translation of the expanded English version, **D–67**.

49. "Yuishikigi no kiban toshite no sanshōsetsu" 唯識義の基盤としての三性説 [The *trisvabhāva* theory as the foundation of the *vijñāna* theory]. *SGZKN* 4 (1968): 1–22.

Reprinted in **A–8**: 455–501.

50. "Yuimakyō" 維摩経 [The *Vimalakīrtinirdeśa*]. In Takeuchi Yoshinori 武内義範 and Umehara Takeshi 梅原猛, eds., *Nippon no butten* 日本の佛典. Chūkō Shinsho 中公新書179. (Tokyo: Chūō Kōronsha 中央公論社, 1969): 45–54.

51. "Indo shisō no chōryū" インド思想の潮流 [Tides of Indian thought]. In **B–4**: 5–56.

Co-authored with Hattori Masaaki 服部正明.

52. "Chibetto-yaku Yuimakyō o meguru ni-san no mondai" 西蔵訳維摩経をめぐる二三の問題 [Some problems in the Tibetan translation of the *Vimalakīrtinirdeśa*]. In Shōtoku Taishi Kenkyūkai 聖徳太子研究会, ed., *Shōtoku Taishi Ronshū* 聖徳太子論集 (Kyoto: Heirakuji Shoten 平楽寺書店, 1971): 251–267.

See **A–7**, **11**, **C–2**, **11**, **D–84**.

53. "Siddham and Its Study in Japan." *Acta Asiatica* 21 (1971): 1–12.

54. "Busshinron o megurite" 佛身論をめぐりて [On the theory of Buddha-body (*buddha-kāya*)]. *TK* 45/3 (521) (1971): 1–26 (179–204).

Reprinted in **A–8**: 266–92. English version **D–59**.

55. "Kongō-hannyakyō ni taisuru Muchaku no shakuge" 金剛般若経に対する無着の釈偈 [Asaṅga's commentary in verse form on the *Vajracchedikā*]. *Tōhōgakkai sōritsu nijūgoshūnen kinen Tōhōgakuronshū* 東方学会創立二十五周年記念東方学論集 [Eastern Studies Twenty-fifth Anniversary Volume] (Tokyo: Tōhō Gakkai, 1972): 551–572.

Reprinted in **A–8**: 561–583. See **C–10** for a translation of this commentary.

56. Introductory Remarks to "*Daijōtaikushashō*" 14 kan, Genshin sen 大乗対倶舎抄 十四巻 源信撰. *Dainippon Bukkyō Zensho* 大日本佛教全書

97, kaidai 解題 1 (Tokyo: Zaidan Hōjin Suzuki Gakujutsu Zaidan 財団法人鈴木学術財団, 1973): 144–147.

57. Introductory Remarks to "*Kusharonju soshōmon*" 1 kan 倶舍論頌疏正文 一巻. *Dainippon Bukkyō Zensho* 大日本佛教全書 97, Kaidai 解題 1 (Tokyo: Zaidan Hōjin Suzuki Gakujutsu Zaidan 財団法人鈴木学術財団, 1973): 147–148.

58. Introductory Remarks to "*Kusha-gimon*" 1 kan 倶舍疑問 一巻. *Dainippon Bukkyō Zensho* 大日本佛教全書 97, Kaidai 解題 1 (Tokyo: Zaidan Hōjin Suzuki Gakujutsu Zaidan 財団法人鈴木学術財団, 1973): 148–149

59. "On the Theory of Buddha-Body (*Buddha-kāya*)." *EB* 6/1 (1973): 25–53.

Reprinted in **A–14**: 103–122, 249–255. English translation by Hirano Umeyo of **D–54**.

60. "Yuimakitsu to tomo ni" 維摩詰とともに [With Vimalakīrti]. *Shitennōji* 四天王寺 402 (Apr. 1974): 2–18.

61. "Daijō bukkyō ni okeru sonzairon" 大乗仏教における存在論 [Ontology in Mahāyāna Buddhism]. In **B–6**, volume 1: 55–94.

English version **D–87**.

62. "Bukkyō kyōdan no genshi keitai" 佛教教団の原始形態 [Early developments in the Buddhist community in India]. *Nippon Bukkyō Gakkai Nenpō* 日本仏教学会年報 39—Bukkyō kyōdan no shomondai (showa 48 nendo) 仏教教団の諸問題 (昭和48年度) (1974): 1–19.

This same volume was also printed as *Bukkyō kyōdan no shomondai* 仏教教団の諸問題 (Kyoto: Heirakuji shoten 平楽寺書店, 1974): 1–19.

63. "'*Kashōbon*' no shohon to '*Daihōshakukyō*' Seiritsu no Mondai" 『迦葉品』の諸本と『大宝積経』成立の問題 [Some problems of several versions of the *Kāśyapa-parivarta* and the formation of the *Ta pao-chi ching*]. *SGZKN* 10 (1973): 13–25.

See **C–3, 12**.

64. "Reflections on Tibetan Studies in Japan." *Acta Asiatica* 29 (1975): 107–128.

See **B–7**.

65. "Kokuyaku-Issaikyō Shakkyōronbu kaisetsu" 国訳一切経釈経論部解説 [Introduction to the Kokuyaku-Issaikyō section on sūtra commentaries]. *Kokuyaku-Issaikyō* 国訳一切経 *Indo senjutsu-bu* 印度撰述部

135, *Shakkyōronbu* 釈経論部 8 (Tokyo: Daitō Shuppansha 大東出版社, 1977): 1–10 (= 359–368).

See **B–8**.

66. "Gion shōja no mon o megurite" 祇園精舎の門をめぐりて [Koṭṭhaka, a gate of the Jetavana-vihāra]. In Nippon Oriento Gakkai 日本オリエント学会, ed., *Ashikaga Atsuuji Hakase Kiju Kinen: Orientogaku Indogaku Ronshū* 足利惇氏博士喜寿記念・オリエント学インド学論集 [Studies dedicated to Professor Atsuuji Ashikaga, On the Occasion of His Seventy-seventh Birthday] (Tokyo: Kokusho Kankōkai 国書刊行会, 1978): 499–511.

67. "'What Remains' in Śūnyatā: A Yogācāra Interpretation of Emptiness." In Minoru Kiyota, ed., *Mahāyāna Buddhist Meditation: Theory and Practice* (Honolulu: The University Press of Hawaii, 1978): 66–82.

Reprinted in **A–14**: 51–60, 239–242. Japanese version **D–71**, and see **D–48**.

68. "*Chūhenfunbetsuron Anne-shaku* no bonshahon to no shōgō: sono daiisshō sōhon nitsuite" 『中辺分別論安慧釈』の梵寫本との照合—その第一章相品について [Collation of the *Madhyāntavibhāgaṭīkā* with its manuscript, Chapter I, *Lakṣaṇa-pariccheda*]. *SGZKN* 15 (1978): 16–22.

69. "Bukkyō ni okeru 'sezoku' (saṁvṛti) toiu go no ichikaishaku" 仏教に於ける「世俗」(saṁvṛti) という語の一解釈 [An interpretation of the term 'saṁvṛti' (convention) in Buddhism]. In **A–8**: 305–320.

Japanese translation by Katsura Shōryū 桂紹隆 of **D–27**.

70. "*Daijō Shōgon Kyōron* ni okeru 'shoe (āśraya)' no goi." 『大乘荘厳経論』に於ける「所依 (āśraya)」の語意 [Connotations of the word *āśraya* (basis) in the *Mahāyāna-sūtrālaṁkāra*]. In **A–8**: 432–442.

Japanese translation by Katsura Shōryū of **D–35**.

71. "Kūshō ni okeru 'amarerumono'" 空性に於ける「余れるもの」['What Remains' in Śūnyatā]. In **A–8**: 542–560.

Japanese translation by Katsura Shōryū of **D–67**. A revision of **D–48**.

72. "From Mādhyamika to Yogācāra: An Analysis of MMK, XXIV.18 and MV, I.1–2." *JIABS* 2/1 (1979): 29–43.

Reprinted in **A–14**: 189–199, 260–261.

73. "Presidential Address by Professor Gadjin M. Nagao." *JIABS* 1/2 (1979): 79–85.

74. "Tranquil Flow of Mind: An Interpretation of *Upekṣā*." *Indianisme et bouddhisme: Mélanges offerts à Mgr Étienne Lamotte.* Publications de L'Institut Orientaliste de Louvain 23 (Louvain-la-Neuve: Institut Orientalisite, Université Catholique de Louvain, 1980): 245–258.

Reprinted in **A–14**: 91–102, 247–249.

75. "The Architectural Tradition in Buddhist Monasticism." In A. K. Narain, ed., *Studies in History of Buddhism* (Delhi: B. R. Publishing Corporation, 1980): 189–208.

76. "The Bodhisattva Returns to This World." In Leslie S. Kawamura, ed., *The Bodhisattva Doctrine in Buddhism*. SR Supplements 10 (Waterloo, Ontario: Wilfrid Laurier University Press / Canadian Corporation for Studies in Religion, 1981): 61–79.

Reprinted in **A–14**: 23–34, 232–236.

77. "The Buddhist World-View as Elucidated in the Three-Nature Theory and Its Similes." *EB* 16/1 (1983): 1–18.

Reprinted in **A–14**: 61–74, 242–245. English version of **D–8**.

78. "Ascent and Descent: Two-directional Activity in Buddhist Thought." [Presidential Address for The Sixth Conference of The IABS, Tōkyō, Japan, September 1983.] *JIABS* 7/1 (1984): 176–183.

Reprinted in **A–14**: 201–207, 261.

79. "The Tibetan Eulogy at Chü-yung-kuan: Text and Translation." In Michel Strickmann, ed., *Tantric and Taoist Studies in Honour of R. A. Stein.* Volume 3. Mélanges Chinois et Bouddhiques 22 (Brussels: Institut Belge des Hautes Études Chinoises, 1985): 835–861.

Revised English version of the Japanese translation of the small character Tibetan inscription, with notes, in **D–36**.

80. "Kanyaku butten to sono bongaku" 漢訳仏典とその梵学 [Merit and demerit of the Chinese translations of Buddhist texts]. *Tōhō gakkai sōritsu yonjusshūnen kinen Tōhōgaku Ronshū* 東方学会創立四十周年記念東方学論集 (Tokyo: Tōhō Gakkai 東方学会, 1987): 605–620.

81. "The Life of the Buddha: An Interpretation." *EB* 20/2 (1987): 1–31.

Translated by Mark Blum from chapter 2 of **A–10.** See **D–90**, **91**.

82. "Sekaikan toshite no sanshōsetsu" 世界観としての三性説 [The three-nature theory as a Buddhist world-view]. *Nippon Gakushiin Kiyō*

日本学士院紀要 [Transactions of the Japan Academy] 43/1 (1988): 1–19.

83. "Chibetto Bukkyō gaikan" チベット仏教概観 [An outline of Tibetan Buddhism]. *Iwanami Kōza Tōyō-shisō* 岩波講座東洋思想 11, *Chibetto Bukkyō* チベット仏教 (Tokyo: Iwanami Shoten 岩波書店 1989): 3–20.

84. "*Yuimakyō* o kien toshite: Hitei to kōtei no nihōkō ni tsuite" 『維摩経』を機縁として—否定と肯定の二方向について [The *Vimalakīrti-sūtra* in retrospect: two directions of negation and affirmation]. *Bukkyōgaku Seminā* 仏教学セミナー 50 (1989): 53–70.

See **A–7**, **11**, **C–2**, **11**, **D–52**.

85. "Logic of Convertibility." In **A–14**: 123–153, 255–259.

A translation of **D–23** by Leslie Kawamura.

86. "Emptiness." In **A–14**: 209–218, 262.

A translation of **F–1** by John Keenan.

87. "Ontology in Mahāyāna Buddhism ." In **A–14**: 155–187, 159–160.

A translation of **D–61** by Leslie Kawamura.

88. "Usages and Meanings of Pariṇāmanā." In **A–14**: 83–90, 247.

Read at the First Conference of the International Association of Shin Buddhist Studies, Kyoto, 1983, translated by Leslie Kawamura.

89. "Yogācāra—A Reappraisal." In **A–14**: 219–225, 262.

Read at the Annual Meeting of the American Academy of Relgion, Atlanta, Georgia, 1986.

90. "La vida de Buda, Una interpretación." *Revista de Estudios Budistas*, Año 1– No.2 (October 1991– March 1992): 9–49.

Re-translation by Marfa Urquidi of **D–81**.

91. "The Buddha's Life as Parable for Later Buddhist Thought." *EB* 24/2 (1991): 1–32.

Translated by Mark Blum from chapters 3 and 4 of **A–10**. See **D–81**.

92. "Bukkyō no kihonteki na kangaekata ni tsuite" 仏教の基本的な考え方について [The fundamental way of thinking of Buddhism]. *Shinshū kyōgakkai kaihō* 真宗教学会会報 (Yamaguchi Shinshūkyōgakkai 山口真宗教学会刊) 4 (1992): 3–20.

93. "Bukkyōteki shisaku no hōkōsei ni tsuite" 仏教的思索の方向性について [The bi-directional orientation of Buddhistic thinking]. *Buzan Kyōgaku Taikai Kiyō* 豊山教学大会紀要 20 (1992): 1–21.

94. "The Yogācāra Cognition Theory and Depth Psychology." *Asiatische Studien/Études Asiatiques* 46/1 (1992): 307–322.

95. "Chūkan kara Yuishiki e: Chūron to Chūhenfunbetsuron no hikaku o tsūjite" 中観から唯識へ—『中論』と『中辺分別論』の比較を通じて [An aspect of the development from Mādhyamika to Yogācāra]. *Bukkyō Bunka Kenkyūsho Kiyō* 仏教文化研究所紀要 31 (1992): 207–222.

96. "The *Vimalakīrti Sūtra*." In Takeuchi Yoshinori, ed., *Buddhist Spirituality: Indian, Southeast Asian, Tibetan, and Early Chinese*. World Spirituality: An Encyclopedic History of the Religious Quest 8 (New York: Crossroad, 1995): 155–159.

E: Book Reviews

1. "*Mu to U to no tairon* o yomite" 『無と有との對論』を讀みて [On reading Yamaguchi Susumu's *Mu to U to no tairon*]. *TK* 26/11 (308) (1941): 70–96 (1016–1042).

See **E–2** (XXI-XXIII): 1077. Yamaguchi's book, *Buddhist Controversies concerning Existence and Non-existence* (Kyoto: Kōbundō, 1941), concerns arguments between the Madhyamaka and the Yogācāra, especially as found in chapter 5 of Bhāvaviveka's *Tarkajvālā*.

2. Short reviews and notices in *Bibliographie Bouddhique* (Paris: Adrien Maisonneuve).

Between 1947 and 1958, Nagao and Yamaguchi Susumu together authored a number of entries in volumes XXI–XXIII (1947–1950), XXIV–XXVII (1950–1954), and XXVIII–XXXI (1954–1958). I list by serial number only those entries which contain some list of contents or summary (all are in English). Those which refer to other listed items are so noted:

XXI–XXIII: 156, 157, 814, 817, 946, 950, 960, 963, 964, 973, 988, 1002, 1004, 1028, 1067 [**D–22**], 1068, 1077 [cf. **E–1**], 1079, 1085, 1088, 1099, 1107, 1113, 1118, 1138, 1146, 1161 [**D–8**], 1177, 1192, 1253, 1428, 1437, 1523, 1750, 1761, 2166, 2203 [by SY alone, **A–2**].

XXIV–XXVII: 279, 280, 281, 282, 283, 297, 298, 340, 404, 405, 406, 416, 471, 527, 556, 583, 592, 711, 869, 871, 874, 875, 877, 878, 884, 885, 886, 889, 932, 933, 946, 947, 952, 1070, 1080, 1111, 1112, 1238, 1259, 1282, 1283, 1301, 1303, 1321, 1418, 1419, 1447, 1448, 1454, 1455, 1465, 1466, 1468, 1496, 1497, 2009, 2041, 2043, 2161, 2200, 2364, 2501.

XXVIII–XXXI: 24, 45, 85, 326, 483, 720, 743, 798, 1310, 1413, 1506, 1597, 1729, 1808, 1828, 1845, 1849, 1969, 1970, 2039 [**A–5**], 2181, 2412, 2590, 3215, 3404.

3. "Chibetto kaigashi ni okeru kingyō" 西蔵絵画史における近業 [A recent work on Tibetan painting]. *Bukkyō Geijutsu* 佛教藝術 22 (1954): 49–53.

A review of G. Tucci, *Tibetan Painted Scrolls* (Rome: Libreria dello Stato, 1949).

4. Kenneth W. Morgan, ed., *The Path of the Buddha: Buddhism interpreted by Buddhists* (New York: Ronald Press Co., 1956). *Philosophy East and West* 6/2 (1956): 175–176.

5. "Murti Kyōju no kingyō" ムルティ教授の近業 [A recent work of Prof. Murti]. *TK* 39/6 (452) (1958): 75–84 (469–478).

A review of T. R. V. Murti, *The Central Philosophy of Buddhism* (London: G. Allen and Unwin, 1955).

6. Inaba Shōju 稲葉正就 and Satō Hisashi 佐藤長, translators, *Fū ran teputeru* [*Hu lan deb ther*]*: Chibetto nendaiki* フゥラン・テプテル—チベット年代記 (Kyoto: Hōzōkan 法蔵館, 1964). *SGZKN* 1 (1965): 98–100.

7. Takata Osamu 高田修, *Butsuzō no kigen* 佛像の起源 (Tokyo: Iwanami Shoten 岩波書店, 1967). *Bijutsushi* 美術史 18/1 (69) (1968): 27–30.

8. Inaba Shōju 稲葉正就, "Enjiki: *Gejinmikkyōso* san'itsu bubun no kenkyū: Kanbunyaku-hen" 円測・解深密経疏散逸部分の研究・漢文訳篇 *Ōtani Daigaku Kenkyū Nenpō* 大谷大学研究年報 24 (Kyoto: Ōtani Gakkai 大谷学会, 1972; Kyoto: Heirakuji Shoten 平楽寺書店, 1973). *SGZKN* 9 (1973): 95–99.

9. Charles Luk, ed. and trans., *The Vimalakīrti Nirdeśa Sūtra* (Berkeley and London: Shambala Books, 1972). *EB* 6/2 (1973): 157–161.

10. Susumu Yamaguchi, *Index to the Prasannapadā Madhyamakavṛtti*. Part One: Sanskrit-Tibetan, Part Two: Tibetan-Sanskrit (Kyōto: Heirakuji-Shoten, 1974). *SGZKN* 12/13 (1975/1976): 121–125.

11. Tateshiro Ennō 健代渕応, *Abhisamayālaṃkāraśāstraṭīkā no Kenkyū* Abhisamayālaṃkāraśāstraṭīkāの研究 (Ōsaka: Shitennōji shiin Seikōin Kiyomizudera 四天王寺支院清光院清水寺, 1973). *SGZKN* 12/13 (1975/1976): 116–118.

12. Robert A. F. Thurman, trans., *The Holy Teaching of Vimalakīrti: A Mahāyāna Scripture* (The Pennsylvania State Univ. Press, 1976), and Étienne Lamotte, *The Teaching of Vimalakīrti* (*Vimalakīrtinirdeśa*),

rendered into English by Sara Boin from the French Translation with Introduction and Notes, *L'Enseignement de Vimalakīrti* (London: The Pali Text Society, 1976). *EB* 11/1 (1978): 109–112.

13. Akira Yuyama, *Prajñā-pāramitā-ratna-guṇa-saṃcaya-gāthā (Sanskrit Recension A)*. Edited, with an Introduction, Bibliographical Notes and a Tibetan version from Tun-huang (Cambridge Univ. Press, 1976). *SGZKN* 15 (1978): 64–66.

14. Edward Conze, *The Prajñāpāramitā Literature*. Second Edition, Revised and Enlarged. Bibliographia Philologica Buddhica, Series Maior 1 (Tokyo: The Reiyūkai, 1978). *EB* 13/2 (1980): 131–134.

F: Encyclopedia Articles

1. "Kū" 空 [Emptiness]. In TBS Buritanika TBSブリタニカ / *Buritanika Kokusai Daihyakkajiten* ブリタニカ国際大百科辞典 [Britannica International Encyclopaedia] 6 (1973): 1–3.

Reprinted in **A–8**: 293–302. English version **D–86**.

2. "Vasubandhu." In Mircea Eliade et al., eds., *The Encyclopedia of Religion* (New York: Macmillan Publishing Company, 1987): vol. 15: 191–193.

3. A series of contributions to the column "Sekai Bijutsu Shōjiten: Tōyō-hen: Indo / Tōnan Ajia 1–5" 世界美術小辞典・東洋編・インド・東南アジア [A small dictionary of art: Asia: India and Southeast Asia]. In the journal *Geijutsu Shinchō* 芸術新潮.

Anika 阿尼哥, あにか [Aniko, Anigo] (I—May 1975); Indo no Shinwa インドの神話 [Indian mythology] (II—June 1975); Shōjiron 生死論 [saṁsāra], Tantora タントラ [tantra], Chibetto no kenchiku チベットの建築 [Tibetan architecture], Chibetto no bijutsu チベットの美術 [Tibetan art], Nepal no bijutsu ネパールの美術 [Nepalese art] (III—June 1975); Purāna プラーナ [Purāṇa], Mahābārata マハーバーラタ [Mahābhārata], Manikoru マニコル [Maṇi 'khor], Ramakyō shinwa ラマ教神話 [Lamaist mythology] (IV—June1975); Ramakyō bijutsu ラマ教美術 [Lamaist art], Rāmāyana ラーマーヤナ [Rāmāyaṇa] (V—June 1975).

4. **F–3**, included in *Shinchō Sekai Bijutsu Jiten* 新潮 世界美術辞典 (Tokyo: Shinchōsha 新潮社, 1985).

G: Newspaper and Periodical Articles

1. “Mōko no Ramakyō” 蒙古のラマ教 [Mongolian lamaism]. *Hinomoto* ひのもと 5/11 (1942): 12–18.

2. “Hakka o sakanoboru” 白河を遡る [Sailing up the Po river]. *Hinomoto* ひのもと 6/1, Jan. 1943.

   Published under the Chinese pen name Chang Yajên 章雅仁 (章雅仁 is homophonous with 長雅人. The name was never again used). Due to flooding on the rail line, Nagao travelled from T’ang-ku 塘沽 to T’ien-tsin 天津 by river.

3. “Rama o tazunete (Jō, Chū, Ge)” 喇嘛を訪ねて (上・中・下) [My visit to Lamas]. *CN* Sept. 30, Oct.1, Oct. 2, 1943.

4. “Mōko no tabi” 蒙古の旅 [A journey in Mongolia]. *Gakugei* 學藝 1/4 (1943): 13–19.

   Reprinted in **A–1′**: 213–220.

5. “Mōko ni manabu” 蒙古に學ぶ [Study in Mongolia]. *Gakugei* 學藝 1/7 (1943): 12–18.

   Reprinted in **A–1′**: 221–228.

6. “Gaō o shinobite” ガ翁を偲びて [In memory of M. K. Gandhi]. *Kokusai Shinbun* 国際新聞, Feb. 18, 1948.

7. “Seimei ni tsuite”生命について [On life]. *Ningen Bigaku* 人間美学 (Usui Shobō 臼井書房) 1 (1948): 39–41.

8. “Rekishi—shizen, gō, kakumei, shinkō” 歴史—自然・業・革命・信仰 [History: nature, action, revolution, and faith]. *Chi to gyō* 知と行 (Daitō Shuppansha 大東出版社) 3–12 (1948): 36–44.

9. “Bukkyō no gakuteki hōkō” 佛教の學的方向 [The scholarly direction of Buddhism]. *Miyako Shinbun* 都新聞, Feb. 23, 1949.

10. “Hoko to josei” ほこと女性 [Festival floats and women]. *Yūkan Mainichi Shinbun* 夕刊毎日新聞, Jul. 23, 1951.

    The *hoko* is a festival float mounted with a halberd (鉾) used in the famous Gion Matsuri in Kyoto on July 17. In 1950 an old rule prohibiting women from entering the floats was overturned, but in 1951 a float toppled over, and there was a renewed call for the prohibition of women. Nagao discusses this issue.

11. "Kōkinaru chinmoku" 高貴なる沈黙 [The thundering silence]. *Eikō Shinbun* 叡光新聞 (published by Hieizan Kōkō 比叡山高校), Jun. 26, 1953,

12. "Monpō Seppō" 聞法説法 [Hearing the dharma—preaching the dharma]. *Kenshin* 見真 (Hiroshima Honganji Betsuin 広島本願寺別院発行), Oct. 10, 1954.

13. "Takutseru-shi to Chibettogo" タクツェル師とチベット語 [Rev. Stag-tsher and the Tibetan language]. *Tsukiji Honganji Shinpō* 築地本願寺新報, Dec. 1, 1954.

Rev. Stag-tsher, now known as Prof. Thubten Jigmed Norbu of Indiana University, is the eldest brother of the 14th Dalai Lama.

14. "Seiron to 'Wesaka': Buddha nisengohyakunensai ni yosete" セイロンと'ウェサカ'—仏陀二千五百年祭によせて [Ceylon and Vesak: on visiting the 2500 year anniversary celebrations of the Buddha]. *Yomiuri Shinbun* 読売新聞, Apr. 6, 1956.

15. "Shikaru kōkōya: Daikokuten" 叱る好々爺—大黒天 [A scolding kind old man: Daikokuten]. *KS* (Date unknown, but 1956).

15′. Later published in *Kyōto no butsuzō* 京都の仏像 (Kawade Shinsho 河出新書, Apr. 1956): 88–89.

16. "Seiron no bukki nisengohyakunensai" セイロンの仏紀二千五百年祭 [The Ceylonese festival celebrating 2500 years of Buddhism]. *AS*, Jun. 6, 1956.

17. "Patona no kōkogaku, nisengohyakunenkan no chiri o harau" パトナの考古学,二千五百年間のチリを払う [Patna archaeology: brushing aside the dust of 2500 years]. *MS*, Aug. 4, 1956.

18. "Indo no inshō: amari ni mo shūkyōteki" インドの印象—余りにも宗教的 [Impressions of India: too religious]. *AS*, Jan. 14, 1957.

19. "Rasa dōran no hi: Shikkimu ōke no kyaku to natte" ラサ動乱の日—シッキム王家の客となって [The days of disturbances in Lhasa: becoming a guest of the Sikkhimese Royal Family]. *MS*, Apr. 2, 1959.

20. "Indo: hito to tsuchi 1–13" インド・人と土 1–13 [The people and soil of India, in thirteen parts]. *MS* (Ōsaka), Jun. 22–Jul. 8, 1959.

A serial report of the events of the JEBI; see **D–38**, **39**.

21. “Indo no busseki 1–7” インドの仏跡 1–7 [Buddhist sites of India, in seven parts]. *MS* (Tōkyō), Jun. 29–Jul. 7, 1959.

These 7 correspond with items 2, 6, 8, 9, 10, 12, 11 in **G–20**.

22. “Indo busseki kenkyū chōsa no tabi o oete” インド仏蹟研究調査の旅を終えて [After a research trip to investigate Indian Buddhist sites]. *Nichi-In Bunka* 日印文化, Aug. 5, 1959.

23. “Kokedera” 苔寺 [The Moss Temple]. *KS* (Date unknown, but 1960)

23′. Later published in *Koto saiken* 古都再見. Kyōto Shinbunsha 京都新聞社 ed. (Kawade Shobō Shinsha 河出書房新社, 1961): 126–127.

24. “Hōnen Shinran no onki ni saishite” 法然・親鸞の遠忌にさいして [On the memorial days of Hōnen and Shinran]. *Nishinihon Shinbun* 西日本新聞, Mar. 3, 1961.

24′. Printed also under the main title “Wareware no hokoru ni-daisosei” われわれの誇る二大祖聖 [Two great saints we may be proud of (Hōnen and Shinran)] in *Kōbe Shinbun* 神戸新聞, Mar. 2, 1961, and under the title “Rekishi ni okeru isei” 歴史における偉聖 [Great saints (Hōnen and Shinran) in history] in *KS* (exact date unknown, but March 1961).

25. “Kiyomizu no sekibutsu: Jakunen toshita jōdo” 清水の石佛—寂然とした浄土 [The stone Buddhas of Kiyomizu temple: the silent Pure Land]. *KS*, May 26, 1961.

25′. Later published in *Zoku Koto saiken* 續古都再見 (Kawade Shobō Shinsha 河出書房新社, Nov. 1961): 150–151.

26. “Indo seifu no nesshinsa: Ajia kōkogakkai no inshō ” インド政府の熱心さ—アジア考古学会の印象 [The zeal of the Indian government: Impressions from attending the International Conference on Asian Archaeology]. *AS*, Jan. 10, 1962.

The International Conference on Asian Archaeology was sponsored by the Archaeological Survey of India on the occasion of its 100th anniversary.

27. “Gendai bunmei to isekihozon no akushu: Indo no Nāgārjyunakonda no iseki o tazunete” 現代文明と遺跡保存の握手—インドのナーガールジュナコンダの遺跡をたずねて [Contemporary culture and the preservation of ancient ruins: a visit to the Buddhist ruins at Nāgārjunakoṇḍa]. *AS*, May 15, 1962.

28. “Sanbō o sasagemotsu chi no megami” (Afuganisutan kodai bijutsuten kara 7) 三宝をささげ持つ地の女神 (アフガニスタン古代美術展から7) [The earth goddess reverently holding the Three Jewels: ancient Afghani art]. *NKS*, Sept. 4, 1963.

29. "Indo chōkoku no ayumi" インド彫刻のあゆみ [The development of Indian sculpture]. *NKS*, Oct. 16, 1963.

30. "Nāgārjyuna-konda" (Bi no gensen o tazunete: omoide no Indo kiko) ナーガールジュナコンダ (美の源泉をたずねて—思い出のインド紀行) [Nāgārjunakoṇḍa: a visit to the wellspring of art: memories of a visit to India]. *NKS*, Oct. 22, 1963.

31. "Pitarukōra no zaishinzō" (Indo kodai bijutsuten kara) ピタルコーラの財神像 (インド古代美術展から) [An image of the god of wealth from the Pitalkhora cave:]. *NKS*, Oct. 29, 1963.

32. "Matura no buttō" (Indo kodai bijutsuten kara) マトゥラの佛頭 (インド古代美術展から) [A Mathurā Buddha head]. *NKS*, Nov. 7, 1963.

33. "Butsuden no furīzu"(Indo kodai bijutsuten kara) 仏伝のフリーズ (インド古代美術展から) [A frieze depicting the life story of the Buddha]. *NKS*, Feb. 11, 1964.

34. "Banjaku ni zasu: Fudōmyōōzō" (Kyōōgokokuji) 磐石に坐す—不動明王像 (教王護国寺) [Sitting firmly like a rock: the Kyōōgokokuji image of Fudōmyōō]. *Sandē Mainichi* サンデー毎日, May 10, 1964.

35. "Nēru shushō no seikyo o itamu" ネール首相の逝去をいたむ [Grief over the death of Prime Minister Nehru]. *Nichi-In Bunka* 日印文化 Tokushūgō 特集号 III, Sept. 1964.

36. "Hai, Iie" ハイ、イイエ [Yes, no (Ja, aber nein)]. *MS*, Oct. 24, 1964.

Appeared in the column "Cha no ma" 茶の間 (The Family Room).

37. "Beikoku bukkyō no shōrai" 米国仏教の将来 [The future of American Buddhism]. *CN*(?) (No date given, but around 1966).

38. "Tenkai suru Amerika Bukkyōgaku" 展開するアメリカ仏教学 [Evolving American Buddhist Studies]. *AS*, Jun. 6, 1966.

39. "Nepāru no bijutsu: Hindoizumu to Bukkyō to no ittaika" ネパールの美術—ヒンドィズムと佛教との一体化 [Nepalese art: a fusion of Hinduism and Buddhism]. *MS*, Jul. 18, 1968.

40. "Pekin-ban Chibetto daizōkyō: Butsuzō to dōretsu, tera no hokori," 北京版西蔵大蔵経—佛像と同列、寺の誇り [The Peking edition of the Tibetan Buddhist canon: the temple's pride, revered equally with the Buddha images]. *KS*, Jun. 20, 1970, evening edition.

Appeared in the serial column "Mongai fushutsu" 門外不出 [Treasures forbidden to be removed] (18).

41. "Dōkyōzutsu: Bukkyō no negai matsudai ni" 「銅経筒」—佛教の願い末代に [A cylindrical copper case from Kyoto's Kuramadera, within which were placed sūtras with the wish to transmit the teaching to future generations]. *KS*, Dec. 7, 1970, evening edition.

Appeared in the serial column "Mongai fushutsu" 門外不出 [Treasures forbidden to be removed] (143).

41′. Later included in *Kyōto no Hihō* 京都の秘宝, edited by Kyōto Shinbunsha 京都新聞社 (Kyoto: Kyōto Shinbunsha 京都新聞社, 1971): 124–25.

42. "Hadami ni kanjita Chūgoku" 肌身に感じた中国 [An experience of China (interview)]. *Kyōdai Gakusei Shinbun* 京大学生新聞 26, May 1, 1975 .

43. "Chūgoku o hōmon shite" 中国を訪問して [A visit to China]. *Bukkyō Taimuzu* 仏教タイムス, May 5, 1975.

44. "Yamaguchi Susumu Hakase to Kindai Bukkyōgaku" 山口益博士と近代佛教学 [Yamaguchi Susumu and modern Buddhist Studies]. *KS*, Oct. 28, 1976, evening edition.

45. "Karada de Bukkyō o manabu kokoromi: Chibetto Seminā no kaigai kenshū" からだで仏教を学ぶ試み—チベット・セミナーの海外研修 [Learning Buddhism through experience: the Tibet Seminar's study abroad]. *CN*, Sept. 6, 1977.

46. "Gakumon no konteiteki na sagyō (Risshō Daigaku Hokekyō Bunka Kenkyūsho ni tsuite)" 学問の根底的な作業 (立正大学法華経文化研究所について) [A fundamental work of scholarship: on the Institute for the Comprehensive Study of the Lotus Sūtra, Risshō University]. *CN*, Jun. 27, 1982, p. 9.

Written in reference to the publication by the Institute for the Comprehensive Study of the Lotus Sūtra, Risshō University, of the volumes of photographs of *Sanskrit Manuscripts of the Saddharmapuṇḍarīka* (*Bonbun Hokekyō Shahon shūsei* 梵文法華經写本集成).

47. "Ārayashiki e no tankyū" アーラヤ識への探求 [In search of the *Ālayavijñāna*]. *CN*, May 10, 13, 14, 1991.

48. "Weisheit und Licht, Der Name Buddha Amidas." [Wisdom and Light: the Name of the Buddha Amida]. *Ekō-Blätter* [Düsseldorf: Ekō-Haus der Japanischen Kultur], Vol. 3 (Fall 1995): 3–5.

Translated by Tadashi Ōtsuru.

H: Miscellaneous Items

1. "Bukkyōgaku oyobi Indo tetsugaku" 佛教學及び印度哲學 [Buddhist studies and Indian philosophy]. *Tetsugaku Nenkan* 哲学年鑑 1, Showa 17 nenban 昭和十七年版 (Osaka: Seibunsha 靖文社, 1943): 97–103.

2. "Bukkyōgaku oyobi Indo tetsugaku" 佛教學及び印度哲學 [Buddhist studies and Indian philosophy]. *Tetsugaku Nenkan* 哲學年鑑 2, Showa 18 nenban 昭和十八年版 (Seibunsha 靖文社, 1944): 102–113.

3. "Showa 17–18 nendo no Tōyōshi Gakkai" dai-nana setsu "Shūkyō-shi" o tanto. 「昭和十七・八年度の東洋史学界」第七節「宗教史」を担当 [Directing section seven, History of Religions, at the 1942–43 Congress on Oriental History]. *Showa 17・8 nendo Tōyōshi Kenkyū Bunken Mokuroku* 昭和十七・八年度東洋史研究文献目録 (Kyoto: Kyōto Daigaku Jinbunkagaku Kenkyūsho 京都大学人文科学研究所, 1949): 20–23.

4. "Chibettogaku, toku ni Chibetto Bukkyō (Rama-kyō) no kenkyū" 西蔵学、特に西蔵佛教(ラマ教)の研究 [Tibetan studies: especially studies of Tibetan Buddhism (lamaism)]. In Monbushō-shokan Kenkyū-jochō Kaigi, Chōsa-iinkai 文部省所管研究所長会議, 調査委員会, ed., *Monbushō Chokkatsu oyobi Kokuritsu Daigaku Kenkyūjo Kenkyū Gyōseki Yōran* 文部省直轄及び国立大学研究所研究業績要覧 1950 (Tokyo: Monbushō-shokan Kenkyūjochō Kaigi, Chōsa-iinkai 文部省所管研究所長会議, 調査委員会, 1951): 191.

5. English co-translation, with William Fernström-Flygare, of the descriptions of the plates in Mizuno Seiichi 水野清一 and Nagahiro Toshio 長広敏雄, *Yun-kang: The Buddhist Cave-Temples of the Fifth Century A. D. in North China / Unkō Sekkutsu* 雲岡石窟, vol. 4, cave 7 (Kyoto: Kyōto Daigaku Jinbun Kagaku Kenkyūjo 京都大学人文科学研究所, 1952): 99–125.

6. "The fundamental standpoint of the Mādhyamika philosophy. (Chūkan-tetsugaku no konpon-teki tachiba)." *Bungaku, Tetsugaku, Shigaku Gakkai Rengō henshū: Kenkyū Ronbunshū* 文學・哲學・史學學會連合編集・研究論文集 *4 Kenkyū ronbun shōrokushi* 研究論文抄録誌 / *The Japan Science Review: Literature, Philosophy and History*, Vol. 4, Abstracts of Doctoral Dissertations (3). (Tokyo: Union of Japanese Societies of Literature, Philosophy and History, 1953): 177–179.

7. "Chūkan-tetsugaku no konpon-teki tachiba" 中觀哲学の根本的立場 [The fundamental standpoint of the Mādhyamika philosophy] *Bungaku, Tetsugaku, Shigaku Gakkai Rengō henshū: Kenkyū Ronbunshū* 文學・哲學・史學學會連合編集・研究論文集 *4 Kenkyū ronbun shōroku-shi* 研究論文抄録誌 Vol. 4 (Tokyo: Union of Japanese Societies of Literature, Philosophy and History, 1953): pages unknown.

8. "*Shōdaijōron* Seshin-shaku no kenkyū" 摂大乗論世親釈の研究 [Vasubandhu's commentary on the *Mahāyānasaṁgraha*]. *Kakko Josei Kenkyū Hōkoku shūroku* 各個助成研究報告集録 (Showa 27 nendo 昭和27年度) (1953): pages unknown.

9. "Jiun Sonja Selected Works, Introductory Remarks, by Juntaro Ishihama." English translation of the introduction by Ishihama Juntaro 石浜純太郎 to *Jiun Sonja bonpon chūso eika kaidai* 慈雲尊者梵本註疏英華解題 (Osaka: Jiun Sonja hyakugojūnen onki hōsankai 慈雲尊者百五十年遠忌奉讃会 / The Jiun Sonja One Hundred Fiftieth Death Anniversary Commemoration Society, 1953): 1–11.

10. Giuseppe Tucci ヂゥゼッペ・トゥチ, "Chibetto no rekishi bunken" 西蔵の歴史文献 [Tibetan historical literature]. *Tōhōgaku* 東方学 12 (1956): 100–114.

Japanese translation of a lecture delivered by Tucci at Kyoto University, October 14, 1955.

11. Preface to *Peoples of Nepal Himalaya, Scientific Results of the Japanese Expeditions to Nepal Himalaya*, 1952–53, Vol. III. Ed. by Hitoshi Kihara (Kyoto: Fauna and Flora Research Society, Kyoto University, 1957): i-iv.

12. "Kenkyū chōsa ryokō / Kyōto chiku [Dai 9 kai kokusai shūkyōshi kaigi] 研究調査旅行・京都地区 [第9回国際宗教史会議] [Research Trip, Kyoto District: the 9th International History of Religions Conference]. *Gakujutsu Geppo* 学術月報 (Nippon gakujutsu shinkōkai 日本学術振興会) 11/7 (1958): 29–31.

13. "Bādopūru no omoide: Indo busseki tōsa no nikki kara" バードプールの思い出—インド仏蹟踏査の日記から [Memories of Birdpūr: from the diary of a journey to Indian Buddhist sites]. *Tōhōgaku Kaihō* 東方学会報 2 (1959): 5–6.

14. "Ajyanta Nikki" アジャンタ日記 [A journey to Ajanta]. *Nichi-In Bunka* 日印文化, Tokushū-gō 特集号 (1960): 41–48.

The journey referred to in this and the preceding item is that of the JEBI; see **D–38, 39**.

15. “Rekishi ni kagayaku Ōtani Tankentai: Atama sagaru sono yūto” 歴史にかがやく大谷探険隊—頭下るその雄図 [The Ōtani expeditions shining in history: An appreciation of their grand enterprise]. *Daijō* 大乗 11/3 (Mar. 1960): 16–19.

16. “Sara no hana o tsumu otome” 沙羅の花を摘む乙女 [A girl picking śāla flowers]. *Kadokawaban Sekai Bijutsu Zenshū Geppō* 角川版世界美術全集月報 2 Indo インド. (Tokyo: Kadokawa Shoten 角川書店, Dec. 20, 1960): pages unknown.

17. “Inoru kokoro” 祈るこころ [The supplicating heart; an essay on dependent arisal]. *Zaike Bukkyō* 在家佛教 85 (1961): 8–10.

18. “*Hokekyō* no kankō o yorokobu” 『法華経』の刊行をよろこぶ [Joy at the publication of the *Saddharmapuṇḍarīka*]. *Tosho* 図書 157 (Tokyo: Iwanami Shoten 岩波刊, Sept. 1962): 46–47.

19. “Indo bijutsu zakkan” インド美術雑感 [Impressions of Indian art]. *Ōtani Gakuhō* 大谷学報 42–3 (1963): 46–48.

20. “Ashikaga / Zenba ryōhakase o okuru” 足利・善波両博士を送る [Dedication: on the retirement of Professors Ashikaga and Zenba from Kyoto University]. *Indogaku Shironshū* インド學試論集 [*Miscellania Indologica Kiotiensia*] 6–7 (Ashikaga Atsuuji Hakase, Zenba Makoto Hakase shōju kinen 足利惇氏博士, 善波周博士頌寿記念 [Dr. Atsuuji Ashikaga and Dr. Makoto Zenba Commemoration Volume]) (1965): 1–4.

21. “Gendaijin ni totte Bukkyō to wa nani ka” 現代人にとって仏教とはなにか [What is Buddhism to modern people?]. Supplement (*geppō* 月報) 22 to **B–3**. 12 pages.

A conversation with Umehara Takeshi 梅原猛.

22. “Butten annai 仏典案内 (1): Bukkyō no tenseki: sono rekishi” 佛教の典籍—その歴史 [An introduction to Buddhist texts: their history]. *Bukkyō no shisō Geppō* 「佛教の思想」月報 1 (Kadokawa Shoten 角川書店, Oct. 1968): 6–8.

23. “Butten annai 仏典案内 (2): Genshi Bukkyō” 原始佛教 [An introduction to Buddhist texts: early Buddhism]. *Bukkyō no shisō Geppō* 「佛教の思想」月報 2 (Kadokawa Shoten 角川書店, Nov. 1968): 6–8.

24. "Bukkyō no kotoba" 佛教のことば [The languages of Buddhism]. *Shindō* (Nagoya) 信道 25/3: 2–11, 30, and 4 (1969): 30–32.

25. "Kodai Indo Shisō no Tenkai" 古代インド思想の展開 [The Development of ancient Indian thought]. Supplement (*geppō* 月報) 36 to **B–4**. 12 pages.

A conversation with Ueyama Shunpei 上山春平 and Hattori Masaaki 服部正明.

26. "Ueno-san no hige:" 上野さんのひげ [Mr. Ueno's beard: on the retirement of Ueno Teruo]. In Ueno Teruo taikan shuppan kinen kankōkai 上野照夫退官出版記念刊行会, ed., *Aru teinen kyōju no ningenzō: Ueno Teruo kō* ある停年教授の人間像—上野照夫考 (Kyoto: Nagata Shobō 永田書房 1971): 128–130.

27. "Amerika no Chibetto kyōkai to Mōko kyōkai" アメリカの西蔵協会と蒙古協会 [The Tibet Society and Mongolia Society in the United States of America]. *Nippon Chibetto Gakkai Kaihō* 日本西蔵学会会報 17 (1971): 4.

28. "Shōka shuen no zu" 娼家酒宴の図 [A scene of a banquet at a brothel]. *Ibun* 以文 14 (1971): 9–12, with 3 plates.

Published by Kyōto Daigaku Bungakubu Ibunkai 京都大学文学部以文会, the Kyoto University Alumni Association. The article concerns a Mathurā sculpture depicting a drunken prostitute trying to escape an admirer. Contradicting several recent Japanese mistaken interpretations of the scene, Nagao introduces the theory of Calambur Sivaramamurti, published in 1956, with which he agrees.

29. "Gendai Bukkyōgaku no kadai" 現代佛教学の課題 1, 2, 3 [Topics in contemporary Buddhist Studies]. *Monshin* 聞眞 Vol. 11, Mar. 1972; Vol. 12, Jul. 1972; Vol. 13, Oct. 1972.

30. "Chibetto bunken ryakumokuroku" (Aoki Bunkyō 1886–1956 shōraibon) チベット文献略目録 (青木文教 1886–1956 将来本) [A short catalogue of Tibetan literature, from the collection brought back by Aoki Bunkyō]. In *Dai gojūhakkai Daizōe tenkan mokuroku* 第五十八回大蔵会展観目録 (A catalogue of the exhibition held in the Library of Ryūkoku University, Ōmiya campus, Nov. 17–18, 1972) (Kyoto: Ryūkoku Daigaku, 1972): 3–14.

31. "Various Views on the Buddha-Body." *Transactions of the International Conference of Orientalists in Japan* 18 (1973): 25–26.

32. "Unkō de no ikku: Mizuno-san no omoide" 雲岡での一齣—水野さんの思い出 [A snapshot from Yun-kang: remembering Mizuno Seiichi]. In Kaizuka Shigeki 貝塚茂樹 and Hibino Takeo 日比野丈夫, eds., *Mizuno Seiichi Hakase Tsuiokushū* 水野清一博士追憶集 (Kyoto: Kyōto Daigaku Jinbun Kagaku Kenkyūjo, 1973): 71–76.

33. "Arayashiki to Sanshō: Yuishiki shisō no kihonteki kōzō" アラヤ識と三性—唯識思想の基本構造 [*Ālayavijñāna* and *trisvabhāva*: the fundamental structure of Yogācāra thought]. *Chūō Kōron* 中央公論 (May 1974): 320–333.

A conversation with Ueyama Shunpei 上山春平.

33′. Later published in Ueyama Shunpei and Kajiyama Yūichi, eds., *Bukkyō no shisō: Sono genkei o saguru* 仏教の思想・その原形をさぐる. Chūkō Shinsho 中公新書 364 (Tokyo: Chūō Kōronsha 中央公論社, 1974): 82–111.

34. "Bukkyō ni dokujina tetsugakuteki shii: toku ni sanshōsetsu ni tsuite" 仏教に独自な哲学的思惟—特に三性説について [Philosophical thought unique to Buddhism: the three natures theory]. *Shuppan Daijesuto* 出版ダイジェスト 772 (Apr. 21, 1974): pages unknown.

35. "Hōchū nikki no ichibu kara: Yoshikawa-san no otomo o shite" 訪中日記の一部から—吉川さんのお伴をして [From a diary of a visit to China: as the companion of Yoshikawa Kōjirō]. *Yoshikawa Kōjirō zenshū* 吉川幸次郎全集 22 *Geppō* 月報 (Sept. 1975): 1–3.

36. "Hōchū inshōki" 訪中印象記 [My impressions from a visit to China]. *Gakujutsu bunka hōchū shisetsudan hōkokusho* 学術文化訪中使節團報告書 *Gaimushō Ajiakyoku Chūgokuka* 外務省アジア局中国課 (Oct. 1975): 89–93.

37. "Minami Ajia bukai o chūshin ni (Kokusai Ajia / Kita Afurika Jinbun kenkyū, Mekishiko kaigi no hōkoku 2)" 南アジア部会を中心に(国際アジア・北アフリカ人文研究、メキシコ会議の報告・2) [The (30-th) Mexico meeting of International Congress of Human Sciences in Asia and North Africa (ICANAS): especially the South Asia Presentations]. *Tōhōgakkai Kaihō* 東方学学会報 31 (1976): 3–5.

38. "*Daijō Butten* zen-jūgokan no kankō o oete" 「大乗仏典」全十五巻の刊行を終えて [On the completion of the publication of the 15 volumes of the *Daijō Butten*]. A note in **B–5**, vol. 15: 429–434.

39. "Yamaguchi Susumu, 1895–1976." *EB* 10/1 (1977): 163–166.

40. "Yamaguchi Susumu Hakase 1895–1976" 山口益博士—1895–1976 [Yamaguchi Susumu, 1895–1976]. *SGZKN* 14 (1977): 123–125.

41. "Yamaguchi Susumu Kyōju no goseikyo (1895–1976)" 山口益教授の御逝去 (一八九五-一九七六) [Yamaguchi Susumu, 1895–1976]. *Tōhōgaku* 東方学 54 (1977): 181–182.

42. Introduction to Inoue Takao 井上隆雄, *Chibetto mikkyō hekiga* チベット密教壁画 [Tibetan Esoteric Buddhist Wall Paintings] (Kyoto: Shinshindō 駸々堂, 1977): 9 –13.

43. "Bosatsu no kokoro" 菩薩のこころ [The bodhisattva's heart]. *Sanjūsangendō Kannon bosatsu kōza dayori* 三十三間堂観音菩薩講座だより (Published by the Myōhōin Monzeki kyōgakubu 妙法院門跡教学部): 12, Feb. 1977.

A lecture given to the monthly "Avalokiteśvara lecture series" (*Kannon bosatsu kōza*) held at the Myōhōin Monzeki temple in Kyoto, and published in the "report" (*tayori*) of that series. The famous Sanjūsangendō temple is a part of the Myōhōin Monzeki temple.

44. "Hana o motte Tayori to nasu" 華を以って信となす [Calligraphy of the phrase 以華為信 (Sending flowers as a greeting), with a short essay]. *Daihōrin* 大法輪 44/4, Apr. 1977: 21.

45. "Jinsei no mokuteki ni tsuite" 人生の目的について [The goal of life]. *Tekkō Tanki Daigaku dōsōkai kaihō* 鉄鋼短期大学同窓会会報 7 (1978): 9–10.

46. "Yamaguchi-sensei no Chibettogaku" 山口先生のチベット学 [The Tibetan studies of Yamaguchi Susumu]. *Nippon Chibetto Gakkai Kaihō* 日本西蔵学会会報 24 (1978): 1–4.

47. "The Śrāvaka Teaches." *Zero* 1 (1978): 13–14.

Published by the Rinzai-ji, Los Angeles, California.

48. "Butten honyaku" 仏典翻訳 [The translation of Buddhist scriptures]. *Chūō Kōron* 中央公論 (Jun. 1979): 48–49.

49. Introduction to Yoritomi Motohiro 頼富本宏, *Chūgoku mikkyō no kenkyū* 中国密教の研究 (Tokyo: Daitō Shuppansha 大東出版社, 1979): i-ii.

50. "Hisamatsu-sensei no omoide" 久松先生の思い出 [Remembering Prof. Hisamatsu Shin'ichi]. *Risō* 理想 563 (Apr. 1980): 155–159.

51. "Tsukamoto Zenryū 1898–1980." *EB* 13/2 (1980): 148–149.

52. "Bukkyō ni okeru kotoba no mondai" 仏教における言葉の問題 [The problem of language in Buddhism]. *Shūkyō Shinpojiumu* 宗教シ

ンポジウム (Kyoto: Ōtani Daigaku Gakuseika 大谷大学学生課 [1982]): 14–26.

52′. Reprinted in *Shūkyō to Bunka* 宗教と文化, Dai-i-shū 第一輯 (Kyoto: Ōtani Daigaku, 1987): 20–39.

53. "Dai-Chibetto-ten ni yosete" 大チベット展に寄せて [On the Tibet Exhibition in Japan, 1983]. *Dai Chibettoten* 大チベット展 / The Tibet Exhibition in Japan, 1983.

A message sent upon the opening of the exhibition.

54. "Omoidasu koto nado" 思い出すことなど [Memories of the early days of *Nichi-In Bunka*]. *Nichi-In Bunka* 日印文化 Sōritsu 25 shūnen kinen tokushūgo 創立25周年記念特集号 (1984): 8–9.

55. "*Tetsugaku Kenkyū* to watakushi" 『哲学研究』と私 [*Tetsugaku Kenkyū* and I]. *TK* 47/8 (550) (1984): 600–601.

56. "Introduction" to *Jūseige* (Vista, California: Private publication of the Takemoto Family, 1987). Unpaginated.

Co-written with Nagao's son-in-law, Ron Takemoto, for publication in a pamphlet commemorating the completion of the Takemoto family's temple in Vista, California.

57. "Kusagusa no omoide" くさぐさの思い出 [Some memories of Kyoto University]. In Kyōto Daigaku sōritsu kyūjusshūnen kinen iinkai 京都大学創立九十周年記念委員会, ed., *Kyōdai Shiki* 京大史記 (Kyoto: Kyōto Daigaku sōritsu kyūjusshūnen kinen kyōryoku shuppan 京都大学創立九十周年記念協力出版, 1988): 306.

58. Introduction to Ueno Teruo 上野照夫, *Indo Kikō* インド紀行 (Tokyo: Chūō Kōronsha 中央公論社, 1988): 1–4.

59. "Sengaku o kataru: Tsukamoto Zenryū Hakase" 先学を語る—塚本善隆博士 [Discussing Prof. Tsukamoto Zenryū]. *Tōhōgaku* 東方学 77 (1989): 190–212.

A roundtable discussion, the participants in which were: Nagao, Makita Tairyō 牧田諦亮, Fukui Kōjun 福井康順, Nogami Shunjō 野上俊静, Ōchō Enichi 横超慧日, Hibino Takeo 日比野丈夫, Fujiyoshi Masumi 藤善眞澄, Tsukamoto Kazuko 塚本和子, and Mano Takako 間野隆子.

60. A memorial note in *Zanshō: Hagami Ajari Tsuitōshū* 『残照』葉上阿闍梨追悼集. Ed. Hagami Ajari Tsuitōshū Kankōiinkai 葉上阿闍梨追悼集 刊行委員会 (Tokyo: Zenponsha 善本社, 1990): 205–207.

61. "Chūkan / Yugaha no keisei" 中観・瑜伽派の形成 [The formation of the Madhyamaka and Yogācāra schools]. *Bukkyō denpashi ni okeru*

Shoha no keisei to sono kiban 仏教伝播史における諸派の形成とその基盤 [The development of schools in light of the history of the development of Buddhism]. Heisei gannendo-ninendo kagaku kenkyū hihojo kenkyūseika hōkokusho 平成元年度〜二年度科学研究費補助研究成果報告書 (1991): 46–48.

A private publication resulting from a Ministry of Education Grant, representative Tsukamoto Keishō 塚本啓祥.

62. "Bukkyōgaku no hanashi" 仏教学の話 [On Buddhist Studies]. *Shinryō bunko* 神陵文庫 10, Sanko Jishōkai 三高自昭会 (1991): 1–35.

63. "Gakumon no omoide: Nagao Gadjin Hakase o kakonde" 学問の思い出—長尾雅人博士を囲んで [A conversation with Prof. Nagao]. *Tōhōgaku* 東方学 86 (1992): 179–212.

A roundtable discussion, the participants in which were: Nagao, Hattori Masaaki 服部正明, Kajiyama Yūichi 梶山雄一, Takasaki Jikido 高崎直道, Aramaki Noritoshi 荒牧典俊, and Mimaki Katsumi 御牧克巳.

64. "What we can do in the Cause of World Peace." *Journal of the Institute of Asian Studies* 9/2 (1992): 1–8.

65. "Izutsu-san no *Kishinron* Tetsugaku" 井筒さんの『起信論』哲学 [Izutsu Toshihiko and the philosophy of the *Awakening of Faith*]. In *Izutsu Toshihiko Chosakushū* 井筒俊彦著作集 (Tokyo: Chūō Kōronsha 中央公論社, 1993), Appendix volume (vol. 12): Supplement 12: 1–5.

66. "Marijuku no ongaku kyōshitsu" 真理塾の音楽教室 [Mari's music classroom]. In Ihashi Hatsuko 井橋初子, ed., *Hana o motte Tayori to nasu* 以華為信 (Kyoto: Privately published by Ihashi Hatsuko, 1994): 18–27.

67. *Namo 'mitābhāya*. A handout explaining the meaning of the Siddham calligraphy of *Namo 'mitābhāya* written by Nagao on a fan distributed to the audience at the Ekō-ji (Ekō-Haus), Düsseldorf, Germany, May 1995.

Text in Japanese, English, and German. A draft of what was later printed as **G–48** was included.

68. "Omoiokosu Toyohara-ke no hitobito" 憶い起す豊原家の人びと [In rememberance of the members of the Toyohara family who perished in the Kōbe earthquake]. *Onenbutsu to tomo ni: Toyohara Taijun-shi tsuitōshi* お念仏とともに—豊原大潤師追悼誌. Toyohara Taijun-shi tsuitōshi kankōkai 豊原大潤師追悼誌刊行会. (Kyoto: Dōbōsha 同朋舎, 1996): 58–60.

69. "Omoide no Tson ka pa" 思い出のツォンカパ (宗喀巴) [Remembering Tsong kha pa]. Supplement (geppō 月報) 30 to *Daijō Butten: Chūgoku, Nihon-hen 15: Tson ka pa* 大乗仏典・中国・日本篇 15 ツォンカパ (Tokyo: Chūō Kōronsha 中央公論社, 1996).

WISDOM, COMPASSION, AND THE SEARCH FOR UNDERSTANDING

The Bodhisattva's Compassion Described in the *Mahāyāna-sūtrālaṁkāra*[*]

Gadjin M. Nagao

Recently I was fortunate enough to have the opportunity to reread Chapter XVII of the *Mahāyāna-sūtrālaṁkāra*,[1] almost sixty years after I studied it for the first time. I was once again greatly impressed with its deep thought and beautiful expressions. The *Mahāyāna-sūtrālaṁkāra* (hereafter MSA) is constituted of verses more than 800 in number, and prose commentary on them and interspersed between them. The author is not known with certainty; its verse portion is ascribed either to Maitreyanātha or Asaṅga, and the commentary portion (hereafter Comm.) either to Asaṅga or his younger brother Vasubandhu. I realized once again that these people are highly distinguished, wise persons, especially so Asaṅga, in both philosophical and religious thinking and practice.

Chapter XVII of the MSA deals with the practical, not the theoretical, aspect of the Yogācāra school of the fourth to fifth century, C.E. The chapter explains first *pūjā*, worship of Buddhas and masters, then *sevā*, service to teachers and reverent friends, and lastly the four *apramāṇa* or immeasurables, which are *maitrī* (benevolence), *karuṇā* (compassion), *muditā*, (sympathetic joy), and *upekṣā* (equanimity). All of these items are expounded in the first twenty-eight verses. They

---

* I would like to express my hearty thanks to the editor, Jonathan Silk, for his assistance in the revision of this paper.

1. *Asaṅga, Mahāyāna-sūtrālamkāra: Exposé de la Doctrine du Grand Véhicule selon le Systéme Yogācāra.* Édité et traduit par Sylvain Lévi. Tome I, Texte (Paris: 1907); Tome II, Traduction, Introduction, Index (Paris: 1911). This includes all verses and the Commentary attributed to Vasubandhu inserted between verses. The same text was republished by S. Bagchi (*Mahāyānasūtrālaṁkāra of Asaṅga.* Buddhist Sanskrit Texts 13 [Darbhanga, 1970]) without much improvement. In the Tibetan Tanjur, we find its Tibetan versions (Tōhoku 4020 and 4026, Ōtani 5521 and 5527), together with several sub-commentaries produced in India. Among these sub-commentaries, the following two are very important: *Mahāyānasūtrālaṁkāra-ṭīkā* (hereafter Ṭīkā) by Asvabhāva (Tōhoku 4029, Ōtani 5530), and *Sūtrālaṁkāra-vṛttibhāṣya* (hereafter Vṛtti) by Sthiramati (Tōhoku 4034, Ōtani 5531). The Chinese translation of MSA was created by Prabhākaramitra (T. 1604) just before the time of Hsüan-tsang, but it seems not to have been much studied in the history of Buddhism in the East.

are then followed by thirty-six verses, XVII.29–64, which are solely devoted to the exposition of *karuṇā*, the second of the four immeasurables. At the beginning of this portion, the Comm. states that *karuṇā* is specifically selected and reexplained in detail because it is the most important and central among the four immeasurables. In fact, this portion is the most interesting in Chap. XVII. Finally, the chapter ends with two verses (XVII.65–66) that extol the greatness and merit of these virtues—worship, service, and the four immeasurables.

In the present paper, I will present the *karuṇā* portion, the thirty-six verses and the Comm. on them (Lévi's ed., 124–131), in an English translation, occasionally together with my own understandings or interpretations.

As stated above, the consideration of *karuṇā* belongs to the practical side of the Yogācāra school. Needless to say, however, theory and practice are always exercising influences on each other. Thus, the discussion of practice by the ācāryas is always based upon and supported by various Buddhist theories in general, especially theories unique to this school. And conversely, the theories are newly grown, nourished, and developed by age-old experiences of practice—the practices of generosity, compassion, and other virtues. An example of such a relationship between theory and practice may be seen in k.32.[2] As will be explained below, the theory of the so-called "not abiding in nirvāṇa" (*apratiṣṭhita-nirvāṇa*), a theory unique to this school, is suddenly introduced in connection with compassion, and through this introduction the practical aspect of compassion is clarified in relation to wisdom, the theoretical aspect.

The central theoretical aspect is represented by *prajñā*, wisdom, while the practical aspect is represented by *karuṇā*, compassion. It is often said that *prajñā* and *karuṇā* are the two main pillars of Buddhism; they are like two wings of a bird or two wheels of a cart, and the absence of either of them invites the corruption of Buddhist spirituality. Although both *prajñā* and *karuṇā* are the acme of Buddhist thought, they are apparently different in character and directly opposite in direction. It is one of the ultimate problems of Buddhist thought how to understand the relationship between the two.

Through wisdom, *prajñā*, wise men became enlightened and finally realized nirvāṇa; this can be characterized as ascending in direction

2. In the following, "k." [*kārikā*] means "verse," "k. 32," for instance, is equal to XVII.32, or the 32nd verse in Chapter XVII.

and negative in quality. This is because *prajñā* aims at a higher ideal status departing from this world of defilement and sufferings, and it is a wisdom that looks at this world as *śūnyatā* (emptiness), "zero-ness" or "negated-ness"; it is ascending in character through negating everything. However, the Buddha's compassion, his great love toward all sentient beings, is affirmative of this world and descending in direction. It is coming down from the ultimate *śūnyatā*, that is nirvāṇa itself, rather miraculously the negative turning around to the affirmative.[3]

However, I do not intend to discuss the relationship of *prajñā* and *karuṇā* in this paper, but simply to show how the latter, compassion, is described in the above-mentioned *karuṇā* portion of the MSA. It is always described in terms of "bodhisattva's compassion," which involves the Buddha's compassion also at the same time.[4]

In this text, the Sanskrit term *karuṇā* appears as the standard word corresponding to English "compassion"; the term *kṛpā* also is used frequently in the same meaning. Although I am unable to explain linguistically their original meanings, both of them seem to mean first "to mourn, to pity," corresponding to Chinese 悲, and then "to be compassionate." *Kṛpālu* means "one who is compassionate," and is used often as an epithet of bodhisattvas. Also *anukampā*, *anukampana*, and so on (the root of which, √*kamp*, means "to tremble") are used less frequently in a similar meaning. In contrast and in relation to these words, the term *sneha* is likely to be used to denote love or affection in general, including both the blamable and the blameless; similarly used are *priya*, *preman*, and so on. Apart from these, love and strong desire are expressed by *kāma*, *rāga*, and so on, which also denote sexual desire. The same may be thought with regard to the Buddhistic term *tṛṣṇā* (thirst-like craving).

Now, the *karuṇā* portion begins with an explanation of the object of *karuṇā*, that is, those on whom bodhisattvas are compassionate (k. 29–30). Specifically noticeable is the fact that a theoretical doctrine unique to this school is also introduced in relation to *karuṇā* (k. 32).

---

3. See my paper, "Ascent and Descent: Two-Directional Activity in Buddhist Thought," in *Mādhyamika and Yogācāra*. L. S. Kawamura, ed. (Albany: State University of New York Press, 1991).

4. Throughout the MSA, the term "bodhisattva" is used to denote a superior distinguished personality who seeks to obtain Buddhahood but has not yet reached it. Or rather in the opposite direction, it is a human being who has descended from out of Buddhahood, taking birth in this world in the form of human existence for the benefit of other beings. In any case, a bodhisattva is an ideal form of human being; hence it involves the Buddha's characteristics also.

That is, the idea of "not abiding in saṁsāra or in nirvāṇa" (*aprati-ṣṭhitasaṁsāranirvāṇatva*) is explained. The phrase has two aspects: "not abiding in nirvāṇa" means that on account of deep compassion the bodhisattvas do not dwell in and attached to nirvāṇa, the highest goal for all followers of the Buddha, but "not abiding in saṁsāra" means that on account of superior wisdom they are not tormented by the sufferings and wickedness of this world. The problem of the relationship between "wisdom and compassion" referred to above appears here to have been answered in this way. This idea is usually named simply "Not abiding in nirvāṇa" (*apratiṣṭhita-nirvāṇa*), which is one of the four exegeses of nirvāṇa in this school (see *Mahāyāna-saṁgraha*, IX.1ff.). After this statement, various aspects of *karuṇā* such as its real cause, classification, characteristics, and so on, are revealed.

Very interesting is a metaphor described with five verses, k. 36–40. In this metaphor, a tree of compassion is mentioned and the compassion itself is likened to the root of the tree. That which sprinkles water upon it is *maitrī* (benevolence). Thus its trunk, branches, and so on grow luxuriantly and vigorously and the tree of compassion flourishes and ripens good fruits.

Dāna, generosity, is often discussed among thirteen verses, k. 48–60, in relation to compassion. *Dāna* means simply giving freely, especially giving to others everything one possesses; this is a good and virtuous act everyone can perform. However, *dāna* given with compassion is much superior and is praised in k. 48 and k. 59–60. In the series *karuṇā* → *dāna* → *bhoga* (property, wealth), in which the former produces the latter in due order, each increases more and more, and brings forth happiness for the compassionate one (k. 50); and those who are languid in doing *dāna* are encouraged to practice *dāna* that finally produces great wealth (k. 51).

In connection with these instances, we have another very interesting topic in which compassion gives *dāna* some education and advice. From the above instances, it is apparent that *dāna* is, as it were, a disciple or a follower of *karuṇā*, the teacher. Thus *karuṇā* teaches *dāna* with six verses, k. 53–58. It is true that *dāna* is not always necessarily a virtue in its own right; instead, it is easy to see that there are many examples of *dāna* wrong in act or in spirit, such as the giving of a bribe to an official, and so on. Therefore *dāna* needs to be educated in order that right generosity should be carried out. Severe criticism against *dāna* is included here in k. 58, and compassion scolds *dāna*, saying, more or less: "Since without being worked on you, *dāna*, you do not offer anything to others, you are essentially the one who expects some kind of reward; and in this sense you are utterly different from me. I, compassion, do not at all expect any reward, and all of what I have acquired in turn will be given to others" (k. 58 paraphrased). While *dāna* is material,[5] compassion is spiritual.

Love (*sneha*) is joy—at least a fountainhead of joy; it is admirable in its beauty, tenderness, and so forth. This is the common idea we hold of love. Compassion is of course a kind of love, but it is quite contrary to such an ordinary kind of love, because it is first emphasized that it is painful and it is suffering (*duḥkha*) (k. 46, 49, etc.). In comparison with this compassion, ordinary love such as that of a father and mother and the like is referred to in the Comm. to k. 43 and is there condemned as constituted by "(thirst-like) craving" (*tṛṣṇā*) which is liable to invite things blamable (*avadya*). In fact, it is very often utterly selfish and blindly acting, finally turning into its opposite, hatred. In comparison to it, the superiority of compassion is clarified by three verses, k. 43–45. The term love or *sneha* itself, however, is not abolished but used in contexts both good and bad (k. 42, 45, etc.); we also find the expression "love born of compassion" *karuṇā-sneha, kṛpā-sneha*, which is called the supreme love (k. 43).

Compassion means "to share others' sufferings," and naturally it is itself characterized by pain and suffering. Observing the sufferings of all sentient beings, when a bodhisattva becomes compassionate toward them he shares the same suffering and himself comes to suffer greatly (k. 33, 49). Due to this suffering, a bodhisattva, while still in his beginning stages, feels fear terribly. This fear, however, is soon relinquished and the suffering turns out to be a great joy for him (k. 46–47). The reason for this transformation of suffering into joy is basically due to the bodhisattva's awakening to the reality (*dharmatā* or *śūnyatā*) of things, but actually through his producing happiness in others he makes himself happy. His happiness never occurs so long as other people are unhappy; his happiness is only constituted of other's happiness, apart from which there is no happiness independent and special to him (k. 52, 54).

That to be compassionate means to suffer greatly and that this suffering miraculously proves to be the supreme bliss, happiness, or joy for a bodhisattva (k. 46–47) is one of the characteristics of com-

---

5. The word "material" in this context means that *dāna* is not a mental factor (*caitta*), simply being a bodily (and verbal) act; compassion, on the other hand, is purely spiritual since it is equated with *ahiṁsā*, non-violence, one of the morally good mental factors.

passion. That in the bodhisattva's generosity he does not expect any reward, as stated in k. 56, is another remarkable characteristic. Further, he is equally compassionate toward all sentient beings, without discriminating between the suffering and the happy; and this equality (*samatā*) is also to be seen between self and others (*ātma-para*) (k. 35, 64). These mental characteristics of the compassionate one are the "basis" for all of the bodhisattva's activities. That *karuṇā* is the "basis" for the whole of a bodhisattva's career is apparent when it is likened to the "*mūla*" (root) in k. 36. The *Akṣayamatinirdeśa-sūtra* quoted in the note to the Comm. to this verse clarifies this fact eloquently.

It is beyond my capacity to compare these ideas of compassion developed in Indian Mahāyāna with that developed in Western or Christian theology together with such notions as Mitleid, sympathy, pity, and so on. But it seems to me that *agapē*, God's love specifically distinguished from the usual type of love or *eros*, is very near to the idea of Buddhistic *karuṇā*. As stated in the New Testament (Phil. ii,7), Jesus Christ "emptied himself (*kenosis*), taking the form of a servant," and took birth in this world. This is the incarnation of Christ for the purpose of absolving humans from their sins. It occurs through his "self-emptying love." The Greek term *kenosis*, emptying, reminds me of the Buddhist notion of *śūnyatā*, emptiness. Actually, Buddha's compassion arises in and from *śūnyatā*, which is reached through his *prajñā* and based on which he acts in this world, as is shown by the phrase *apratiṣṭhita-nirvāṇa* mentioned above. Further, God's love is freely bestowed on all mankind, unjust or just alike, without being asked for by man and without any expectation of recompense for his *agapē*. These points seem to me to be commonly emphasized in Christian and Buddhist traditions. Of course, on account of differences between the theistic and atheistic attitudes, or self-realizing and non-self realizing attitudes, of the two traditions, I believe the contextual formation of these ideas to differ greatly in the respective traditions.

In the following translation, although the rendering of the technical terms is my own, I benefited enormously from the translation of the text that was prepared by Prof. Robert A. F. Thurman more than ten years ago. My deep gratitude goes to Professor Thurman.

The following translation is based upon Lévi's edition and several revisions made to it. The revisions were made by consulting the Tibetan versions and several manuscripts: A, B (both kept in Ryūkoku University, Kyoto), and Ns, Nc (both kept in the National Archives, Kathmandu). See the list of revisions appended at the end of this paper. The Sanskrit text presented with this paper incorporates my suggested emendations. Words and phrases in double quotation marks (" ") in the Comm. and footnotes mean quotations mainly from the verse. The section titles inserted in brackets are added from the Comm. Other abbreviations are:

Ṭīkā:	Asvabhāva's subcommentary
Vṛtti:	Sthiramati's subcommentary
T1:	Tibetan translations of the MSA and its Ṭīkā
T2:	Tibetan translation of the Vṛtti

A Translation of *Mahāyāna-sūtrālaṁkāra* XVII, k. 29–64

[*Various Object of Compassion*]

Within the analysis of compassion, there are two verses concerning its various objects:[6]

> Inflamed (with lust), conquered by enemies (of Māra), oppressed by suffering, enveloped in darkness, fallen on the evil way (consisting of five kinds of decay), bound with great chains, (29)
> Fond of banquets mixed with poison, strayed from the (right) path, practicing on the wrong path, of little strength—(the bodhisattva) takes compassion on such living beings. (30)

Here (in the verse),[7] 1) "inflamed" refers to (living beings who are) inflamed by lustful greed and attached to lustful pleasure. 2) "Conquered by enemies" refers to those who, being impeded by Māra's deeds, stopped engaging in virtue. 3) "Oppressed by suffering" refers to those who are overcome by pain in the hells, and so on. 4) "Enveloped in darkness" refers to those who are, like butchers and the like, wholly given over to evil conduct, because they are ignorant of the fruits of their actions (in the next life). 5) "Fallen on the evil

6. This is the introductory passage for the section "Analysis of compassion," which comprises thirty-six verses, k. 29 through k. 64. The Ṭīkā comments: "Since, among the four immeasurables (*apramāṇa*), *karuṇā* is the highest (*mchog*) one, it is investigated in detail under the divisions of its objects, and so on."

7. The ten types of living beings are enumerated here as the objects of compassion. Here as well as in the following sections, their numberings are given by the present translator.

way"[8] refers to those whose nature it is to never attain the perfect nirvāṇa, because the course of saṁsāra is not radically severed (by them). 6) "Bound with great chains" refers to the heterodox people set out on (the path of) liberation, because they are bound with the tight chains of various wrong views. 7) "Fond of banquets mixed with poison" refers to those who are stuck to the pleasure of meditative absorption. For them, indeed, that pleasure of meditative absorption causes affliction, because it, like delicious food mixed with poison, causes them to divert from that (meditation).[9] 8) "Strayed from the (right) path" refers to arrogant persons, because they have wandered from the path to liberation.[10] 9) "Practicing on the wrong path" refers to those (bodhisattvas) (whose heritage is) not yet fixed (*aniyata-[gotra]*) and who are practising the way of the small vehicle.[11] 10) "Of little strength" refers to those bodhisattvas whose provisions are still incomplete.[12] These ten types of living beings are the objects of the bodhisattva's compassion.

[*Five Results of Compassion*]

There is one verse showing the five results of compassion:[13]

8. "Evil way" is *durga* in Sanskrit, lit. "hard to walk" and means saṁsāra (transmigration) according to the Ṭīkā, but the five *kaṣāya* (impurities, degradations) according to Edgerton (*Buddhist Hybrid Sanskrit Dictionary* [New Haven: Yale University Press, 1953]—hereafter BHSD).

9. If one is attached to the comfort of meditation, he becomes corrupted and diverts (*pracyāvana*) from the meditation.

10. The Vṛtti comments on the "arrogant persons" as the heterodox people who are arrogant with their practice of austerities. But the heterodox people have been referred to above as those "bound with great chains." The Ṭīkā, on the other hand, comments that those people become arrogant due to the belief that they are of the character of obtaining the perfect nirvāṇa and arrogantly believe that they have realized the truth (*tattva*) although they have not yet realized it, and consequently they are deprived of the path. The Ṭīkā's understanding may be better.

11. *Aniyatāḥ*, here in the text, may refer to *bodhisattvagotrā aniyatāḥ*, not *aniyata-śrāvakagotrāḥ*. Such a bodhisattva, although originally belonging to the bodhisattva family, often practises the Hīnayānic way, due to depression and exhaustion. The Vṛtti, however, includes both śrāvaka and bodhisattva in the term *aniyatāḥ*.

12. According to the Vṛtti, a bodhisattva who is "of little strength," due to his provisions being still incomplete, means a bodhisattva on the *adhimukticaryā-bhūmi*, the "stage of practicing through faith," which indicates that this bodhisattva is a beginner.

1) (Compassion) relinquishes injuring (others), 2) becomes the seed for superior enlightenment, 3) brings about happiness (to others) and makes (oneself) miserable, 4) is the cause for the desirable,[14] and 5) gives its own nature.[15] Enlightenment is not far from the son of the Victor[16] who resorts to these qualities (*dharma*) (of compassion). (31)

Here 1) by "relinquishes injuring," the binding-severance fruition (*visaṁyoga-phala*) is referred to, because its adversary, that is violence, is destroyed. 2) By "becomes the seed for superior enlightenment," the dominant fruition (*adhipati-phala*) is referred to. 3) It "brings about happiness" and "makes oneself miserable," to others and oneself, respectively; by this, the fruition of manly performance (*puruṣakāra-*

---

13. The result of compassion is described here in terms of the traditional Abhidharmic system of "five results" (*pañca-phala*) as numbered 1) to 5) in the translation. In his BHSD (p. 396, s.v. phala), Edgerton notices that the present MSA xvii.31 explains all five results which, however, are different from the usual five. It is true that the explanatory comments here are largely different from those found in, for instance, the *Bodhisattvabhūmi* (Wogihara, p. 102.24) or *Abhidharmakośa* (Pradhan, p. 96.1–2). I believe, however, that while those other texts give "definitions" of each category of the five results system, our text has employed the notion of that system to apply it to the description of the results. Hence, the difference.

In the five results system, it is generally understood that, while four results other than the binding-severance result (*visaṁyoga-phala*) are results of some causes, the binding-severance is not to be called a result and does not belong to the ordinary series of cause-and-effect, because the binding-severance means *nirodha*, cessation, severing and transcending all *saṁskṛta-dharmas*. In our text's explanation of the binding-severance result, the term "relinquishing" (*apaha* or *prahāṇa*) (of injuring) is used, which is parallel to this "cessation."

In k. 63 below, the cause for compassion is described in terms of the "four conditions" (*pratyaya*), also an Abhidharmic system. Thus, it seems to have been usual to employ these systems to explain some important characteristic notions.

14. "The desirable" seems to mean a desirable life that a bodhisattva wishes to assume. As the Comm. says, it is the "maturation fruition" and the maturation fruition refers to a new life assumed. The Vṛtti interprets that wherever a compassionate one wishes to take birth, he is able to be born there, and this is the maturation fruition of compassion. It is stated in k. 36 with the metaphor of the leaf and flower of a tree that a bodhisattva "vows for brilliant lives" and being born "in that brilliant life," he is able to benefit others. This brilliant life is meant here by the term "the desirable" life.

15. "Gives its own nature" (*svabhāvada*) simply means that the same distinctive compassion will be established in the future.

16. "Son of the Victor" (*jinātmaja*), in the meaning of "a Buddha's son," is an epithet for a bodhisattva.

phala) is referred to. 4) "Is the cause for the desirable" refers to the maturation fruition (*vipāka-phala*). 5) "Gives its own nature" refers to the issuance fruition (*niṣyanda-phala*), because it gives distinctive compassion as its fruit in the future. Know that Buddhahood is not far off when (the bodhisattva) resorts to the compassion that possesses this fivefold (fruition).

[*Abiding Neither in Saṁsāra nor in Nirvāṇa*]

There is one verse on abiding neither in saṁsāra nor in nirvāṇa:

> Having understood that all existence belonging to saṁsāra is both of the nature of suffering and also of the nature of non-self, the one who possesses compassion and the highest intelligence neither falls into disgust nor becomes tormented by faults. (32)

Having thoroughly comprehended all samsaric existence as it truly is, the bodhisattva does not fall into disgust (at saṁsāra), because he possesses compassion. Nor does he become tormented by the faults (of this world), because he possesses the highest intelligence. Thus he neither abides in[17] nirvāṇa nor in saṁsāra.[18]

[*Thorough Comprehension of Saṁsāra*]

There is one verse on the thorough comprehension of saṁsāra:

---

17. *Pratiṣṭha*, abide in, may have both meanings: to dwell in something and to attach to it.

18. In my introduction above, I have explained this verse which is introduced by the phrase *apratiṣṭhitasaṁsāranirvāṇatva*. Dividing the phrase into its component parts, *apratiṣṭhitasaṁsāra* and *apratiṣṭhitanirvāṇa*, the commentary here paraphrases it in reverse order. The former part means: due to *prajñā*, high intelligence, the bodhisattva does not abide in saṁsāra; but also: due to *karuṇā*, compassion, he does not abide even in nirvāṇa, the highest goal of Buddhism. In the verse a phrase states: "one who possesses compassion and the highest intelligence" (*kāruṇiko 'grabuddhiḥ*) and this phrase combines *prajñā* and *karuṇā* to constitute the uppermost status of a bodhisattva. He dare abide in saṁsāra due to compassion but is not tormented thereby due to his intelligence.

In this verse, the nature of saṁsāra is described with two terms, suffering and non-self. In this connection, the Vṛtti mentions the so-called four characteristics (*ākāra*) of the truth of suffering: impermanence, suffering, emptiness, and non-self. Of these four characteristics, the first two are represented here by "suffering," and the latter two by "non-self."

> Observing that the world is of the nature of suffering, the compassionate one (*kṛpālu*) suffers (by this fact), and he truly knows it, as well as the means to get rid of it. Or, further, he does not become exhausted (in his practice of those means). (33)

"Suffers (by this fact)" means that he is compassionate. "He truly knows it" means that (he knows) suffering just as it is. "As well as the means to get rid of it" means that he knows (the means) through which the suffering is to be removed. By this (statement), it is clarified that, even though acquainted with the suffering of saṁsāra, just as it is, as well as the means of expelling it, the bodhisattva does not become exhausted (in his practice of that means) because of his distinctive compassion.[19]

[*The Classification of Compassion*]

There are two verses on the classification of compassion (*karuṇā*):

> The compassionate ones (bodhisattvas) have four types of pity (*kṛpā*): 1) that from its nature (*prakṛti*),[20] 2) from its careful analysis (*pratisaṁkhyā*), 3) from methods of cultivation (*abhyāsa-vidhāna*) acquired in a former life, and 4) from gain of purity (*viśuddhi*) by destroying its adversary (*vipakṣa*). (34)

It (the pity) should be understood as proceeding respectively from: 1) the excellence of (the bodhisattva's) heritage (*gotra*), 2) an examination (*parīkṣaṇa*) of virtues and faults, 3) its cultivation (*paribhāvana*) in another (former) life, and 4) the gain of being free from greed (*vairāgya*). When its adversary, namely violence (*vihiṁsā*), is destroyed, purity is gained, hence, (it proceeds) from the gain of being free from greed.

---

19. In his Vṛtti, Sthiramati understands this verse as a realization of the four-fold noble truth, identifying the first half of the verse as the truth of suffering (*duḥkha*) and origin (*samudaya*), and the latter half as that of cessation (*nirodha*) and path (*mārga*). Interpretation referring to the fourfold *ārya-satya* is often encountered in Sthiramati's commentary, as seen with regard to the previous verse and elsewhere.

20. The Comm. here comments on the terms in the verse, replacing them with other terms not found in the verse; for instance, "nature" (*prakṛti*) is replaced by "heritage" (*gotra*). To make this fact clearer, Sanskrit terms are specifically inserted both in the verse and Comm.

> That is not pity which is: 1) not equal or 2) constant, 3) not from high resolve, 4) not from practice, 5) not from being free from greed, 6) nor from non-perception. One who is without pity (*akṛpa*) in that way is not a bodhisattva.[21] (35)

Here (a bodhisattva's compassion is): 1) "equal" (*sama*)[22] towards all sentient beings who are happy and so on, (because a bodhisattva is compassionate) having understood that whatever is experienced in this life is suffering.[23] It is 2) "constant" (*sadā*), because it is not exhausted in the nirvāṇa without remainder (*nirupadhiśeṣa-nirvāṇa*). It is 3) "from high resolve" (*adhyāśaya*), for those who enter the (first) stage attain the intention of the equality of self and others.[24] It is 4) "from practice" (*pratipatti*), for (the bodhisattva) acts to rescue beings from sufferings. It is 5) "from being free from greed" (*vairāgya*), when its adversary (*vipakṣa*), violence (*vihiṁsā*), is destroyed. It is 6) "from non-perception" (*anupalambha*) when the insight into the non-origination of all existences (*anutpattikadharmakṣānti*)[25] is attained.

---

21. While the previous k. 34 classifies compassion in accord with its causes for arising, the present k. 35 does the same by characterizing compassion with six kinds of negative expressions. When the negative utterance in them is reversed, they manifest the important characteristics of compassion, as is stated in the Comm. Most of them appear again in k. 64 (excepting item no. 2, *sadā*) to reveal the greatness of compassion, with slightly different wording.

22. The term "equal" or "equality" (*samatā*) conveys an idea very important in Buddhism. In the *Daśabhūmika-sūtra* it is stated that a bodhisattva enters the sixth stage through realization of the ten kinds of "equality of existence" (*dharma-samatā*). Below in the Comm. here "equality of self and others" (*ātma-para-samatā*) also is mentioned, which means that, in sharing others' sufferings, self and others are equal for a compassionate bodhisattva. The present "equal" is not equality of this kind, but means that the compassion is directed equally towards all beings without discriminating whether they are happy or unhappy. The same equality appears again in k. 64.

23. All sensations experienced in this life are none other than suffering. For this, see k. 63, its Comm., and note 65.

24. On entering the first stage (*bhūmi*), a bodhisattva attains the "intent of the equality of self and others," and this intent is called his "high resolve" which is a nickname for the first stage.

25. The "insight into (or receptivity to) the non-origination of all existence" (*anutpattikadharmakṣānti*), 無生法忍 in Chinese, is a higher awareness to be obtained on the eighth stage of bodhisattva path. As for the time of its obtainment, there are various views, but our Comm. almost always ascribes it to the eighth stage. The *kṣānti-pāramitā* (the perfection of patience) is divided into three kinds, the third of which is named *dharmanidhyānakṣānti*, "receptivity to the insight of existences."

[*Comparison to a Tree*]

There are five verses on the comparison of compassion to a tree:

> There are compassion, tolerance, thinking, vow, birth, and full maturation of living beings; this means the great tree of compassion beginning with the root and ending with the superior fruit.[26] (36)

The tree of compassion should be known as having stages of root, trunk, branches, leaves, flowers, and fruits. The root of this (tree) is compassion,[27] its trunk tolerance, the branches thinking for the benefit of living beings, the leaves vows for brilliant lives, the flower the birth in that brilliant life, and the fruit is full maturation of living beings.

> If compassion were not the root, there would be no tolerance (for a bodhisattva) to perform difficult tasks.[28] If the intelligent one (bodhisattva) could not tolerate suffering, he would never think for the benefit of living beings. (37)

This *kṣānti* is explicated to be *jñāna* (knowledge, insight) by MSA XVI.21. Thus *kṣānti*, patience or receptivity, 忍, is equal to *jñāna*, knowledge or insight, 認. The Chinese characters 忍 and 認 are also cognate. These ideas should be applied in understanding the term *anutpattikadharmakṣānti*.

26. In this verse, the bodhisattva's career and activities, i.e., compassion, tolerance, and so on, are compared to the growth of a tree, from root, trunk and so on, as explained in the Comm. In the following discussions, the stages of a growing tree and those of a bodhisattva's activities are often combined and mingled together.

27. In his Vṛtti, Sthiramati states: "The great compassion is the root for all virtues of bodhisattvas." And for this, he quotes the *Ārya-Akṣayamatinirdeśa-sūtra* which speaks roughly as follows: Great compassion never perishes, because it is the prerequisite (*pūrvaṁgamatva*). For instance, life force (*jīvitendriya*) is preceded by inhaling and exhaling. Similarly (all virtues are) preceded by great compassion.

This sūtra passage corresponds to the *Akṣayamatinirdeśasūtra* edited by Jens Braarvig (Oslo, 1993, Vol. I, p. 87f. = T. 397 [XII] 200a). It is quoted in Sanskrit in the (First) *Bhāvanākrama* (ed. Tucci, 187.2–6): *punar aparaṁ bhadanta śāradvatīputra bodhisatvānāṁ mahākaruṇāpy akṣayā | tat kasya hetoḥ | pūrvaṅgamatvāt | tad yathāpi nāma bhadanta śāradvatīputra āśvāsāḥ puruṣasya jīvitendriyasya pūrvaṅgamāḥ | evam eva mahāyānasaṁbhārasamudāgamāya bodhisatvasya mahākaruṇā pūrvaṅgamāḥ |*. A Sanskrit version almost the same as this is cited by Braarvig in Vol. II, p. 353.

28. *Duṣkaracaryā-sahiṣṇutā*.

> An intellect devoid of that thinking would not make the vow to be born in that spotless life. Without obtaining the glorious life, he would not be able to mature living beings. (38)

These two verses prove that compassion and the rest are of the nature of a root, and the rest through the analogy that the latter one is produced by the former one after another.[29]

> 1) The water for compassion (the root) is benevolence (*maitrī*), 2) (the trunk) grows broadly, since happiness (is born) out of that suffering, 3) and the vast spread of branches should be known as (coming) from right mental reflection (for the benefit of sentient beings). (39)
> 4) The abandoning of (old) leaves and presenting (new ones) is from the unbroken continuation of vows. 5), 6) On account of the fulfillment of two kinds of conditions the flower is not barren and, consequently, neither is the fruit. (40)

These two verses compare the tree of compassion to the root of a tree which is watered, and so on. 1) Compassion has been called the root. Benevolence is the water sprinkled upon it because it causes it

29. Beginning with the first verse, k. 36, compassion, tolerance, and other practices or activities of the bodhisattva are mentioned and compared to the root, trunk, and other stages of a tree. Their analogy is explained by these five verses as follows:

1.	*mūla*, root	*karuṇā*, compassion
2.	*skandha*, trunk	*kṣānti*, tolerance
3.	*śākhā*, branches	*cintā*, thinking
		yoniśomanaskāra, right mental reflection
4.	*patra*, leaves	*praṇidhāna*, vow
5.	*puṣpa*, flowers	*janman*, birth
6.	*phala*, fruits	*paripāka*, maturation

Among these, "tolerance" means that a bodhisattva endures the suffering produced by compassion, but when this suffering turns out to be his joy, the tree of compassion grows broadly. Hence it is likened to the trunk of a tree. "Thinking" or "right mental reflection" means to develop doctrinal theories of Mahāyāna thought. Buddhist philosophy, so to speak, is likened here to the leaves of a tree. "Vow" means, on the other hand, that a bodhisattva pledges to take birth in this world for the purpose of benefiting others; it is like old leaves which are continuously replaced by new ones, because a bodhisattva repeatedly makes his vow anew. Thus when "birth" is taken by him it is like a flower blossoming on a tree. The analogies of this kind are explained in detail by the following two verses and the Comm. on them.

to grow. 2) In fact, one who has the thought of benevolence suffers on account of the sufferings of others. And because for the bodhisattva who is engaged in benefiting living beings happiness is born within the suffering which is produced out of that compassion, "grows broadly" (in the verse) means tolerance grows (broadly). And since that (tolerance) has been called the trunk, the trunk becomes broad. 3) From right mental reflection there comes an abundant spread of branches (of doctrinal thinking) in the Great Vehicle (*mahāyāna*), for thinking has been called the branches. 4) Since the (bodhisattva's) vows are in an unbroken series in a manner that when the prior one ceases another (later one) begins, the (various) vows should be known as analogous to the abandoning and presenting of leaves.[30] 5) One's own continuum reaches maturity on account of the fulfillment of inner conditions (*pratyaya*); therefore know that his birth is not barren, like a flower is not barren.[31] 6) The continua of others reach maturity on account of the fulfillment of external conditions; therefore know that to cause living beings to mature is, like a fruit (of a tree), not barren.

---

30. The Vṛtti says: A bodhisattva abandons older, smaller vows and births, and undertakes newer, greater vows and births.

31. "Two kinds of conditions" stated in verse k. 40c means inner and outer conditions (*pratyaya*). According to the Vṛtti, the inner condition for a tree means: in the series of root, trunk, branch, etc., the former one is the cause for the later one. The outer conditions are water, warmth, winds, etc., for the growth of a tree. The inner condition for a tree of compassion is similar to that of a tree: here in this instance of 5) and 6), it means that on account of the fulfillment of vows, the glorious birth is obtained, and likewise on account of birth, the final fruit of maturation is accomplished. The outer condition, however, is so poorly explained by the Vṛtti that it is very hard to grasp its meaning correctly; but it seems to refer to the fact that, in whatever life a bodhisattva is born, he works always for the benefit of living beings and, specifically in this instance of 5) and 6), his birth and his act of maturation are the outer conditions for the maturation of his own continuum and of the continua of other beings, respectively. Although the above understanding of the Vṛtti seems to contradict 5) of the Comm., which interprets flower as inner condition, actually it does not, because all six items, compassion, tolerance, and so on, are working as inner conditions on the one hand and as outer conditions on the other.

This all may be illustrated in a chart:

leaves	vow		
↓	↓		
flowers	birth	→	outer condition for one's own maturation
↓	↓		
fruits	maturation	→	outer condition for maturation of living beings

(The marks ↓ and → indicate the inner and outer conditions, respectively.)

[*The Benefit of Compassion*]

There is one verse on the benefit (*anuśaṁsa*) of compassion:

Who would not be compassionate toward living beings who work to have those (bodhisattvas) attain the virtue of great compassion?[32] Even in (severe) suffering, for those (bodhisattvas) there is unequalled happiness which has arisen from compassion.[33] (41)

The second half of the verse shows the virtue of great compassion. The rest is self-evident.

[*The Non-attachment of Compassion*]

There is one verse on the non-attachment of compassion:

The mind of compassionate ones filled with compassion does not dwell[34] (even) in quietude. How indeed then could they be attached[35] to mundane happiness or their own lives? (42)

All the people of this world are attached to (five kinds of sensual) mundane happiness and to their own lives. And although disciples (*śrāvaka*) and self-enlightened sages (*pratyekabuddha*) are not attached

---

32. The Skt. for "who work to have those (bodhisattvas) attain the virtue of great compassion" is *mahākṛpāguṇakareṣu*. It is rendered by T2 correctly with *snying rje chen po'i yon tan byed pa yi*, but by T1 erroneously with *snying rje chen po yon tan 'byuṅ gnas kyi*, as if the Skt. were °*guṇākara*° (mine of virtue), which reading is, moreover, against the metre of this verse. The verse means that living beings are the source of a bodhisattva's virtue through the former's being the object of the latter's compassion.

33. The latter half of the verse, "Even in (severe) suffering ...," is worthy of being called "the benefit (*anuśaṁsa*) of compassion," as stated in the introductory phrase.

34. "Dwell" stands for Skt. *tiṣṭhati* and "abide" in the Comm. for Skt. *pratiṣṭhita.* Both of them mean "to stand" and at the same time "to attach to." "Not dwell in" and "not abide in" refer to *apratiṣṭhita-nirvāṇa* which has been explicated by k. 32 above.

35. The Skt. for this is *sneha* both in the verse and the Comm. *Sneha* originally means oiliness, and then love, attachment to, etc. I would prefer to translate *sneha* as "love" (see note 37), but since both T1 and T2 render it as *chags pa* here, and the introductory sentence of this verse also has "non-attachment" (*niḥsaṅgatā*), I feel compelled to follow them and render it "attached to" and "attachment."

to either (mundane happiness or their own lives), their mind abides[36] in nirvāṇa in which all suffering is quieted. But because they are filled with compassion the minds of bodhisattvas do not abide even in nirvāṇa. How much less, then, will there be attachment to both (mundane happiness and their own lives).

[*The Distinctiveness of Compassionate Love*]

There are three verses on the distinctiveness of compassionate love:[37]

> There exists no love which is (perfectly) blameless, and (no love) which is not mundane. But the compassionate love of intelligent ones is blameless and world-surpassing. (43) [38]

The love of father and mother, and so forth, is constituted by (thirst-like) craving (*tṛṣṇā*) and is blamable. For those who dwell in mundane compassion,[39] though (love) is blameless it is still mundane. On the other hand, the bodhisattva's love is constituted by compassion and is (both) blameless and transmundane.

Why is it said to be blameless?

> The world rests upon the great flood of suffering and ignorance, and upon the great darkness. How could (the bodhisattva's love working as) the means to lift up (the world from the flood and the darkness) not be blameless? (44)

---

36. See note 34.

37. Skt. *karuṇā-sneha*. Apart from k. 42, the term *sneha* appears in k. 43 and 45, where T1 renders it with *byams pa* (usually equivalent for *maitrī*) and T2 with *sdug pa*; in k. 50 both T1 and T2 have *byams pa*. I translated it as "love." But "compassionate love" or love through compassion is far superior to ordinary love, of course.

38. In this verse, three stages are divided concerning love in general: 1. mundane love that is blameworthy; 2. compassionate but still worldly love; and 3. the compassionate love of bodhisattvas. The term *sneha* at the top of this verse means the first stage, worldly love, and is compared to the third stage, the compassionate love of bodhisattvas.

39. It is a compassionate but still worldly love. This means compassionate love of those bodhisattvas who are still staying on the stage of practicing through faith (*adhimukticaryā-bhūmi*), hence worldly.

(In analyzing the wording in the verse) one should associate the great flood with suffering and the great darkness with ignorance. The rest is self-evident.

Why is it said to be transmundane?

> Those who have "destroyed enemies"[40] and those who are "enlightened in personal wisdom"[41] (both of whom are sages) in this world[42] do not have (such) love (for the world)—not to speak of other[43] (worldly beings). How could it not be supramundane? (45)

Those who have been awakened to wisdom individually are those who are "enlightened in personal wisdom." The rest is self-evident.

[*The Efficient Cause for Terror and Delight*]

There is one verse with regard to the efficient cause for (the bodhisattva's) terror and delight:

> In the nonexistence of suffering,[44] whatever suffering comes to the bodhisattvas due to compassion terrifies them at first, but when it is deeply penetrated it causes them delight. (46)

---

40. *arihat* = *arhat*. The *arhat*, one respectable or deserving (to be worshipped), an epithet for the highest stage of religious practitioner in Buddhism, is interpreted as *ari-han*, killing or having conquered the enemies. In Tibetan, *dgra bcom pa*, overcoming the enemy, is used as the equivalent for *arhat*. In Chinese, beside 阿羅漢, a transliteration of some form like *arhan* or *arahan*, the translation 殺賊, meaning killing the enemy, is also used widely to denote *arhat*.

41. Sanskrit *pratyekabodhibuddhāḥ*, which is paraphrased in the Comm. as *pratyekāṁ bodhiṁ buddhāḥ*. It is the so-called *pratyekabuddha*, the self-enlightened one, or a Buddha for himself alone.

42. The Vṛtti comments: both śrāvakas and pratyekabuddhas are regarded as the most excellent persons "in this world." The word *loke* here is translated in accordance with this idea of the Vṛtti. At the same time this idea of "most excellent in this world" seems to suggest implicitly or ironically that both of them remain worldly mundane beings.

43. The term *sneha*, love, in this verse is understood to mean the bodhisattva's compassionate love, since all these three verses are concerned with the compassionate love (*karuṇā-sneha*) of bodhisattvas. Therefore, "others" here means other worldly beings. That is, the verse says: not only the worldly beings, but also śrāvakas and pratyekabuddhas who are (the sages) of this world, "do not have such love." The term "it" in the last sentence refers to this love.

(The phrase) "in the nonexistence of suffering" (in the locative case) means the efficient cause (*nimitta*) "for the nonexistence of suffering among sentient beings." The suffering which comes about for bodhisattvas on account of their compassion terrifies them at first, on the stage of practicing through faith; this is because they have not yet penetrated into (*spṛṣṭa*) the true nature of suffering through (the realization of) the equality of self and others. But when it is penetrated on the stage of pure high resolve, (the same suffering) causes only delight. This is the meaning.

[*Suffering Surpasses Happiness*]

There is one verse concerning the fact that the suffering (born) of compassion surpasses (all mundane) happiness:

> That suffering surpasses all happiness—what could be more marvelous than this? That is, (that suffering) born from compassion (surpasses all) mundane (happiness). Even those who have accomplished their own aims are deprived of that (suffering which becomes happiness).[45] (47)

There is nothing more marvelous than this—that just that suffering of bodhisattvas born out of compassion becomes such a happiness that surpasses all mundane happiness; and even the arhats who have accomplished their aims are deprived of that happiness, not to speak of others.

---

44. The Sanskrit of the phrase "In the nonexistence of suffering" is *duḥkhābhāve* in the locative case. According to both the Vṛtti and Ṭīkā, this locative should be understood as a dative in the meaning of "in order to have sufferings eliminated." This is the efficient cause (*nimitta*) for a bodhisattva to work for the benefit of other beings, as well as for his terror to become delight, and may refer to the so-called *nimitta-saptamī*. Thus, the phrase means "In order to eliminate sufferings (of living beings, as well as of the bodhisattva himself)."

45. The Ṭīkā comments here roughly as follows: While the verse says that "that suffering surpasses all happiness," the Comm. says: "the suffering ... becomes such a happiness that surpasses all mundane happiness." The latter is more rational than the former. Otherwise, how can one say that those "who have accomplished their aims" do not possess such a happiness? Śrāvakas "who have accomplished their aims (= arhats)," however, do not possess such a happiness (= the happiness born out of severe suffering), but possess sufferings (i.e., worldly sufferings).

[*The Benefit of Compassionate Generosity*]

There is one verse on the benefit of compassionate generosity:[46]

Generosity accompanied by compassion provides the firm-hearted ones (bodhisattvas) with the happiness of generosity. Happiness that arises from enjoyments belonging to the three realms does not equal even a minute portion of it. (48)

That happiness which was produced by enjoyments in the three realms does not equal a minute portion of the happiness (born from giving). This is the meaning of the second half (of the verse). The rest is self-evident.

[*Accepting Suffering*]

There is one verse on accepting suffering out of compassion:

Out of compassion for the sake of living beings they do not forsake the suffering by which the transmigrational life is constituted. What suffering for the benefit of others will the compassionate ones not embrace? (49)

All suffering, in fact, is included in the suffering of the transmigrational life (*saṁsāra*). Because (they) accept that, (the compassionate ones) accept all suffering.

[*Three Things and their Fruits Increase*]

There is one verse on the growth of three things and their fruits:

Compassion, generosity, and wealth always increase for the compassionate one. From this comes happiness (of three kinds), born of love and assistance, and produced (due to) the capacity (to act). (50)

Because they possess compassion, three things increase for bodhisattvas in whatsoever rebirths they are born: compassion (increases) through its repeated practice, generosity through compassion, and

---

46. The benefit (*anuśaṁsa*) of compassion was explained in k. 41. Here that of generosity is referred to.

wealth through generosity. And from these three, three kinds of happiness come forth as their result: (happiness) born of love, due to compassion, (happiness) born of assistance to beings, due to generosity, and (happiness) produced from having the capacity to act in assisting those (beings), due to wealth.[47]

[*Encouraging Generosity*]

There is one verse on encouraging (the practice of) generosity:

> "I increase (through generosity), I cause (generosity) to increase, (by generosity) I mature, gladden, attract, and lead (living beings)"—it is as if compassion speaks to those who are languid in generosity.[48] (51)

---

47. The three things which increase for the bodhisattvas are compassion (*karuṇā*), generosity (*dāna*), and wealth (*bhoga*). One produces the next in due order. This is a natural sequence and it is a generally accepted idea that not only does compassion of course motivate generosity, but that as a result of generosity, one becomes wealthy. Further, from these three, three happinesses are born: happiness (*sukha*) born of love (*snehajanita*), born of assistance (*anugraha-janita*), and produced from the (material) capacity to assist (*anugrahaśaktikṛta*), respectively. These can be shown in a chart:

compassion	→	happiness of love
↓		
generosity	→	happiness from offering assistance
↓		
wealth	→	happiness from having the capacity to assist

48. At the beginning of the Comm., it is remarked that the phrase "those who are languid" (*sannān*) is to be connected with the word "(in/by) generosity" (*dāne*). It is necessary to note this because the two words appear distantly separated from each other in the verse: *sannān* is in pada d, while *dāne* is in pada b. I base my rendering "those who are languid in generosity" on the Comm.

Related to this, however, there are other problems. The word *dāne* in the verse is rendered by both T1 and T2 as *sbyin pas*, as if it were **dānena*. Moreover, adding a note to item 3) of the Comm., the Ṭīkā states that, with regard to the same *dāne*, "the locative case is used in the meaning of instrumental case" (*gsum paḥi don du bdun pa yin*); actually item 3) of the Comm. reads *dānena sattvaparipācanayā*, which is a paraphrase of the words *dāne paripācayāmi* in the verse. Hence my translation "(by generosity)" in the verse.

Thus, one and the same word *dāne* seems to have been understood in two ways: in the former case as purely a locative, and in the latter case as an instrumental, hence "(in/by) generosity."

The words "those who are languid" (in the verse) are to be connected with "in generosity." It is as if compassion, by enumerating six virtues (of generosity), encourages bodhisattvas who are languid in generosity.[49] (The six virtues are): 1) (Compassion) increases in itself (through generosity). 2) It (generosity) is increased by wealth (which is the fruit of generosity). 3) Generosity brings living beings to maturity. 4) (Generosity) produces happiness (not only in the receiver, but also) in the giver. 5) (Generosity) attracts the provisions for great enlightenment[50] and other (virtues).[51] And 6) it leads (beings) toward great enlightenment.

---

49. The phrase in the verse, "it is as if compassion speaks to those who are languid in generosity," reminds me of k. 54–58 below, in which compassion (personified as a teacher) teaches generosity (personified as a disciple). Similarly, in the present verse, compassion speaks to or encourages bodhisattvas who are languid in generosity; it is not generosity that compassion speaks to, but in Sthiramati's explication it is often presented as if compassion encourages generosity. The term "languid" does not appear in the Chinese version, which has only "bodhisattva".

Apart from this, the Chinese version has 大悲義言 (T. 1604 [XXXI] 638c11). Some scholars consider 大悲義 to be the name of a bodhisattva or the name of a treatise called "The Meaning of Great Compassion." However, it seems to me to mean "(Personified) compassion talks properly (義)," because in the following the six virtues enumerated above are explained one by one in the form of a conversation between two persons, replacing the prose explanation stated in the Sanskrit Comm. For instance, the first virtue is explained thus: "You, bodhisattva, practice me (compassion) and make me increase!"

50. "Provisions" (*saṁbhāra*) means materials gathered for the purpose of obtaining the highest Enlightenment in the future. Provision is of two kinds: provision of meritorious deeds and provision of wisdom (and see the next note).

51. The term "others" (*anyasya*) is omitted by Lévi from the original Sanskrit *mahābodhisaṁbhārasyānyasyākarṣaṇāt*, probably because both T1 and T2 do not have it. But I have emended the text to *°saṁbhārasyānyasya cākarṣaṇāt* because *anyasya* should be retained here, and accordingly *ca* is added. My reasons are as follows:

The Chinese version appears here in a conversation form (see n. 49 above), and corresponding to phrase 5) Prabhākaramitra, the Chinese translator, has: 汝若施者、招引大菩提二聚及餘、令向已來. "If you perform generosity, you may attract the two kinds of provisions for great enlightenment and others, and let them approach." The two characters 及餘 appear also in the next phrase 6): 汝若施者、将導二聚及餘、令向大菩提去. "If you perform generosity, you may lead the two kinds of provisions and others, and let them proceed toward great enlightenment." Thus the presence of the term "others" here is certain.

However, what is meant by "others," virtues other than the two provisions? Neither of the two commentaries remark on this point. The provisions are sometimes associated with the six perfections, as in MSA XVIII.38–41: *dāna* and *śīla* are the provision of meritorious deeds, *prajñā* is that of wisdom, while the other perfections, *kṣānti*, *vīrya*, and *dhyāna*, are regarded as both provisions, in that they provide for

[*Happiness through Others' Happiness*]

There is one verse on the experience of happiness through the happiness of others:

> How could one who, out of compassion, suffers by (others') suffering be happy without bestowing happiness on them? Therefore, by bestowing (happiness) on others, the compassionate one makes himself happy. (52)

Due to compassion the bodhisattva suffers through the sufferings of others.[52] How could he be happy if he does not bestow happiness upon living beings? Therefore it should be understood that when he bestows happiness upon others the bodhisattva is in fact making himself happy.

[*Compassion Instructs Generosity*]

There are six verses with regard to compassion instructing generosity:

> The compassionate one who never ever desires his own happiness instructs, as it were, generosity, his own (pupil), (saying): "Make happy through wealth others, or me as well, (I) who am without my own distinct happiness!"[53] (53)

---

them necessary assistance. Thus, as the six perfections cover almost all virtues, any other virtues are hardly conceivable. However, apart from the six perfections and two provisions, there are many other virtues cultivated by monks since early times. For example, there is a vast system of the thirty-seven *bodhipakṣa* that includes four *smṛtyupasthāna*, four *samyakprahāṇa*, four *ṛddhipāda*, and so on. This system of the *bodhipakṣa* is explicated, just following the explanation of the provision referred to above, with twenty-four kārikās, XVIII.42–65. The author of the Comm. here, I believe, added the term *anyasya* with a vague idea of these other virtues in mind.

52. *Paraduḥkhaiḥ*. In this connection Sthiramati quotes a very famous passage from the *Vimalakīrti-nirdeśa-sūtra*, IV, §6: "As all sentient beings are ill, therefore I am ill" (according to Kumārajīva's version), or "As long as beings are sick, I myself will also be sick" (Étienne Lamotte, *The Teaching of Vimalakīrti*, rendered into English by Sara Boin, p. 118).

53. The term *a-yutasaukhya* in pada-d is rendered by T1: *tha dad min bde … min*, and by T2: *bde ba tha dad ma yin pas*. They are precisely opposite in context, one being a double-negative and the other a simple negative. But this probably occurred due to a difference in understanding the root √*yu* of *yuta* as cl. 2 or cl. 3. T1 understands *yuta* as cl. 2, meaning "attached, fastened," while T2 understands it

The compassionate one, in fact, is not happy without the happiness of others, because he has no distinct happiness of his own. Without that (happiness of others), the bodhisattva does not desire (his own) happiness which is the fruit of (his) generosity.

> "(You) generosity are given to living beings together with your fruits because, in my (compassion's) case, their happiness (is my) happiness. If you (generosity) think that you have some duty towards me, you should bear fruit plentifully only for those (beings, not for me)." (54)

"Giving generosity, I give generosity and the fruit of generosity to living beings, since their happiness *is* my happiness. Thus you (generosity) should bear fruit only for those (beings) as long as any fruit remains to be borne." (Grammatically, in the verse the verb form "you should bear fruit") *phala* is an imperative. (In this way,) the bodhisattva instructs generosity out of compassion.

> "To the giver who hates wealth approaches more abundant wealth of a better quality. Happiness of this kind, however, is not what I intend to have, because I only desire to dwell in one act of generosity after another." (55)

"To the giver who turns his back on wealth approaches wealth more abundant and of a better quality. This is the natural way things are (*dharmatā*) (with giving) because the mind (of the giver) is highly exalted. The happiness (that comes) from wealth which approaches in this way, however, is not what I intend to have, since as I love continuous series of generosity, I desire to dwell in it in succession, not in happiness."

> "You observe me uninterruptedly giving up all of my property out of compassion. Should not you know, through this, that I have no interest in the fruit of that (generosity)?" (56)

---

as cl. 3, meaning "separate." Both are, however, intending to signify one and the same thing, which I finally rendered as "without one's own distinct happiness."

Lévi has pointed out that the verse, its metre being *āryā*, is defective in pada d, lacking four mora, but he did not propose any emendation. Other manuscripts I have consulted also are not helpful in this regard. Is it possible to read **māṁ vāpi tāvad ayutasaukhyaṁ*, or **mām api na tāvad ayutasaukhyaṁ*?

"I absolutely always give up all the fruits of generosity out of compassion. So, should not you thus understand that I have no interest in the fruits of my generosity?" Thus saying, the bodhisattva instructs generosity.

> "If I would not let go of its fruit that I obtained[54] I shall not be one who delights in generosity." (57ab)

> Because,

> (To remain) without generosity even for a moment is to be one who does not delight in generosity. (57cd)

> The meaning of the verse is self-evident.

> "Since you do not bear fruit when nothing is done, in expecting some requital (for your generosity) you are not equal to me, (58ab)

"You bear fruit (only) to someone who has acted for your benefit. Therefore in expecting some requital you are not equal to me. This is because, I am

> "One who does not expect any requital from you (generosity) and gives the fruits produced by you (generosity) to others quite freely."[55] (58cd)

> This is self-evident.

[*Pitying Generosity*]

There are two verses on generosity offered through pity:

---

54. "Its fruit that I obtained" may mean "wealth of a more abundant quantity and of a better quality," as explained in the Comm. to k. 55 above.

55. In 58cd, *pratikāranirvyapekṣaḥ paratra phalado 'sya kāmaṁ te*, it is difficult for me to understand *(a)sya* and *te*. T1 renders this half-verse: *khyod kyi lan la lta dang bral bas na | 'bras bu shing tu gzhan la gtong ba yin*, and T2 has a confusion here and simply gives almost the same idea as that of k. 58ab. Does Skt. *te* refer to Tib. *khyod kyi*? My translation, "requital from you," follows this understanding and means "requital for (the generosity) you have done." As for *asya*, I can say nothing with any certainty.

> Generosity (offered) through pity by the sons of the Victor is blameless, a pure footstep, conducive to benefit, equipped with protection, unsought, and without stain. (59)

Here it is 1) "blameless" because it is generosity without harm to others. It is 2) a "pure footstep"[56] because it gives appropriate objects (which is to say) excluding (such inappropriate objects as) poison, weapons, intoxicants, and so on. It is 3) "conducive to benefit" because it attracts (others) through generosity and fixes them in the virtuous life. It is 4) "equipped with protection" because it presents a retinue to others only after making them safe from hardship.[57] It is 5) "unsought" because when one perceives people in need or in hardship, even though they do not request it he performs generosity spontaneously. And also because (the giver gives) without seeking out one who is worthy of being given to.[58] It is 6) "without stain" because it is without desire for requital (with regard to one's generosity) and for the fruits (of that generosity).

There is another classification (of pitying generosity):

> It is exhaustive, vast, excellent, continual, joyous, free from sensual desires, and pure, tending toward enlightenment, and tending toward virtue. This is the generosity of the sons of the Victor (born) from pity. (60)

---

56. The Skt. for "pure footstep" is *śuddhapada* and its Tib. equivalent is T1: *dag pa'i gzhi* and T2: *dag pa'i gnas*. The term *pada* means first "a step, pace," and then is used in various meanings "sentence, clause; characteristic, token; abode, site; footing, standpoint," and so on. In this text, the usage in the meaning "locus, standpoint" is often met with, and the Tib. renderings mentioned above, which mean "basis, foundation," will be understood in this way. The Comm. here, however, says "it gives appropriate objects." This shows that it is not speaking of any theoretical or logical "basis" or "foundation" or "standpoint," but simply means an act of giving. Hence, my tentative and literal rendition is "pure footstep," implying the meaning "(first) footstep toward purity."

57. The Vṛtti comments: when asked, the bodhisattva gives his retinue, including his family members, to the beggar, but only after preparations are made for them to avoid various dangers and distress. Or, the bodhisattva gives even his wife and children, but not to yakṣas and māras who cause harm to them. Hence, "equipped with protection."

58. "Unsought" (*nirmṛgya*) is understood in two ways: the giver is unsought and the recipient is unsought. "Worthy of being given to" (*dakṣiṇīya*) is equivalent to the "field of merit" (*puṇyakṣetra*), the place where meritorious virtues can be cultivated.

It is 1) "exhaustive," because it gives (all) internal and external things. It is 2) "vast," because it gives things in abundance. It is 3) "excellent," because it gives the best things. It is 4) "continual," because it gives perpetually. It is 5) "joyous," because it delightedly gives without deliberation.[59] It is 6) "free from sensual desires," in the same way as "without stain" (was explained in the previous verse). It is 7) "pure," in the same way as "a pure footstep" (was explained in the previous verse). It is 8) "tending toward enlightenment," because it is dedicated towards great enlightenment. It is 9) "tending toward virtue," in the same way as "conducive to benefit" (was explained in the previous verse).[60]

[*Excellent Enjoyment*]

There is one verse on excellent enjoyment (of compassion):

> A voluptuary may obtain satisfaction from his wealth. But this cannot bear comparison with the satisfaction obtained by the pitying one (bodhisattva) whose mind is satiated with the three happinesses through renunciation. (61)

The three happinesses are the joy of giving, the joy of helping others, and the joy of gathering the provisions for enlightenment.[61] The rest is self-evident.

[*Compassion Accomplishes the Perfections*]

A verse on the compassion which accomplishes the perfections (*pāramitā*):

> (The compassionate one) 1) pities the pitiable, 2) pities the violent, 3) pities those disturbed (by anger), 4) pities the reckless,

---

59. "Deliberation" (*pratisaṁkhyā*) may mean to be hesitant, deliberating this or that.

60. Two kinds of classification of pitying generosity are explained with the two verses k. 59 and 60, but the difference between the classifying standards is not clear. The Vṛtti says that k. 60 classifies compassionate generosity from the viewpoint of the benefit to be obtained in both the present and future lives. However, the same meaning can be seen in k. 59 also; at the end of its Comm., "without desire for requital" is said to refer to the present life while "without desire for fruit" refers to the future life.

61. As for "provisions," see note 50.

5) pities those dependent on sense-objects, and 6) pities those attached to falsehood.[62] (62)

The 1) "pitiable" are the niggardly. The 2) "violent" are those who do harm to others by misbehavior (of ten kinds, killing, stealing, and so on).[63] Those 3) "disturbed (by anger)" are the wrathful. The 4) "reckless" are the lazy. Those 5) "dependent on sense-objects" are those whose thoughts are distracted toward objects of lust. Those who are 6) "attached to falsehood" are stupid heretics and others.[64] Compassion for "the pitiable" and the rest is compassion directed at those who are practising adversaries to the perfections. Since that (compassion) censures these adversaries (and thereby leads beings to the perfections), it causes the accomplishment of the perfections. Thus it is called the compassion which accomplishes the perfections.

[*Four Conditions for Compassion*]

A verse to show the conditions (*pratyaya*) for compassion:

The compassion of the bodhisattvas comes from happiness, from suffering, and from their conjunction (*anvaya*). The compassion of bodhisattvas comes from a cause, from a friend, and from (the immediately preceding moment of compassion) itself. (63)

The first half (of the verse) shows the objective condition (*ālambana-pratyaya*) of compassion, because (a bodhisattva), taking the three types of sensation (pleasurable, painful, and neutral) as objects, is compassionate through three kinds of suffering.[65] The sensation of

---

62. Here compassion is observed in relation to the practices of the six perfections (*pāramitā*) with the view that they act as a remedy (*pratipakṣa*) for adversaries (*vipakṣa*) of the pāramitās.

63. This interpretation follows Sthiramati, who seems to suggest the *daśa-akuśalāni.*

64. The six items correlate, of course, directly to the perfections: 1) *dāna*—generosity: the niggardly; 2) *śīla*—restraint: those who misbehave (*duḥśīla*); 3) *kṣānti*—patience: the wrathful; 4) *vīrya*—energy: the lazy; 5) *dhyāna*—concentration: those of distracted thoughts; 6) *prajñā*—wisdom: the stupid (*duḥprajña*).

65. The three kinds of sensation (*vedanā*) are permeated by the three kinds of suffering (*duḥkhatā*) and are destined to turn into them:

sukha-vedanā → *vipariṇāma-duḥkhatā*

(pleasure → the suffering due to change)

neither pain nor pleasure is a conjunction of pleasure and pain, because it leads to them once again.[66] The second half shows the causal (*hetu-*), dominant (*adhipati-*), and contiguous (*samanantara-*) conditions (*pratyaya*) of compassion which are respectively the cause, the spiritual friend, and (the immediately preceding moment of compassion) itself.[67]

[*The Greatness of Compassion*]

A verse on the greatness of compassion:

Know that the compassion of the bodhisattvas is equal (toward all sentient beings) because of its intention, right practice, being free from greed, non-perception, and purification. (64)

(Compassion) is "equal" (toward all beings).[68] (This is because the

---

duḥkha-vedanā → *duḥkha-duḥkhatā*
(pain → the suffering of suffering itself)
aduḥkhāsukha-vedanā → *saṁskāra-duḥkhatā*
(neutral → the suffering inherent in all conditioned things)

Although it is stated in the verse that compassion comes from three things, pleasure and so on, the actual cause which brings about compassion is the three kinds of suffering.

66. The sensation of neither pain nor pleasure does not mean that it has transcended and abandoned those two sensations; instead, it is still a sensation and possesses latent impressions (Vṛtti: *anuśaya, vāsanā*; Ṭīkā: *dauṣṭhulya*) both of which are, in turn, the cause for the same two sensations to arise anew.

67. The present verse explains the cause for compassion, in terms of the four conditions (*pratyaya*), an Abhidharmic system. It was developed side by side with two other categorical systems: one is that of five results which appeared in k. 31 above; the other is a system of six causes, including the executing cause (*kāraṇa-hetu*) and five other causes. The area of cause covered by the aforementioned system of four conditions, however, seems to be wider than that of the system of six causes; the categories of objective condition and contiguous condition are not found in the latter system. In our text, this latter system does not appear explained as a system. When the classification of compassion was discussed in k. 34, it was explained actually from the viewpoint of various causes for compassion to arise. Therefore the present verse can be considered as an additional Abhidharmic discussion, so to speak, of the cause for compassion.

68. As the introduction to this verse states, it explains the "greatness" of compassion. The "greatness," however, is actually expressed by being "equal" toward all sentient beings, happy or unhappy, alike. As for "equality," see k. 35, note 22. In the following, I understand that "because of its intention" (*āśayāt, āśayatas*) and the four other phrases in the ablative case modify this equality, the "greatness."

bodhisattva) knows that, whichever of the three kinds of sensation he experiences, that (sensation) is (nothing but) suffering.[69] Further, that (compassion) is (equal) also "because of its intention," since it is compassionate mentally; because of its "right practice," since it protects (other beings); because of its "being free from greed," since it relinquishes the violence which is its adversary; because of its "non-perception," since it does not perceive (three things, namely) self, other, and compassion (itself);[70] and because of its "purification," since on the eighth stage (of the bodhisattva's ten stages), (it becomes purified) by virtue of attaining the insight into the non-origination of all existences (*anutpattikadharmakṣānti*).

* * *

Corrections to Lévi's Edition

In his French translation of the MSA, Sylvain Lévi had already made various revisions to his edition. We are also fortunately favored with several manuscripts not available to Lévi with which we may

---

The contents of this verse are quite similar to those of k. 35 as stated before (k. 35, n. 21). However, the fifth phrase here, "purification," is absent in k. 35. The interpretation of each phrase by the Comm. also slightly differs between the two verses.

69. For "sensation is nothing but suffering," see k. 63, Comm., n. 65. With regard to the greatness of the compassion of Buddhas and bodhisattvas, the Vṛtti comments in the following way: "In the mundane world, too, there is compassion such as love of parents for children, friends, and so on, but there is no love for an enemy. Śrāvakas and pratyekabuddhas also have compassion for suffered beings, but not for beings who are happy and comforted. A bodhisattva, on the other hand, realizes that any sensation whatsoever is none other than suffering, and, looking at these sufferings, he pities not only beings of the Avīci-hell, the world of uppermost pain, but also equally beings of the Bhavāgra-heaven, the world of uppermost pleasure." This is the reason for the greatness.

70. While "non-perception" (*anupalambha*) was explicated by the Comm. to mean the "insight into the non-origination ..." in k. 35, it is elucidated here in terms of non-discriminative wisdom (*nirvikalpa-jñāna*) which does not discriminate between three things (*trimaṇḍala*). Often with regard to generosity the *tri-maṇḍala* is mentioned as giver, recipient, and the gift itself or act of giving, which three correspond in the present case to "self," "other," and "compassion," respectively. These three are the object of non-discriminative wisdom, which, however, is essentially equal to the "insight into the non-origination...." The latter phrase, on the other hand, is used here to explain the next item, "because of its purification," which did not appear in k. 35.

now collate the text. Based on the materials listed below, and for the reasons given, a number of corrections may be suggested. The following abbreviations are used:

L	Lévi's revision
A	Manuscript kept in Ryūkoku University, Kyoto
B	Another manuscript kept in Ryūkoku University, Kyoto
Ns	NGMPP* manuscript No. 3–291
Nc	NGMPP manuscript No. 4–6
T1	Tibetan translations of the MSA and Ṭīkā
T2	Tibetan translation of the Vṛtti
Tib	Tibetan version

* NGMPP: Nepal-German Manuscript Preservation Project

*

XVII.30	Comm[1]	kāmasukhabhaktāḥ	*read*	kāmasukhasaktāḥ (T1, B, Ns)
"	Comm[2]	duḥkhākrāntāḥ	"	duḥkhākrāntā (A)
"	Comm[2]	duḥkhābhūtā	"	duḥkhābhibhūtāḥ (L, T1)
"	Comm[4–5]	anyatīrthyāḥ | mo°	"	anyatīrthyamo° (L)
"	Comm[9]	°saṁbhārā bodhisatvāḥ	*emended by* (L) *to*	bodhisaṁbhārāḥ satvāḥ, *but the original reading is correct*
XVII.31	b	tāyaka°	*read*	tāpaka° (L, B)
"	Comm[1]	tataḥ	"	tatra (T1)
"	Comm[2]	tāyaka°	"	tāpaka° (L, B)
"	Comm[3]	niṣpandaphala°	"	niṣyandaphala°
XVII.32	Comm[2]	evaṁ nirvāṇe	"	evaṁ na nirvāṇe (B, Ns)
XVII.34	c	vipakṣahīnā	"	vipakṣahānau (A, B, Ns)
"		viśuddhilābhāt	"	viśuddhilābhāc (A, B, Ns)
XVII.35	Comm[1]	sukhitādiṣu yat°	"	sukhitādiṣu satveṣu yat° (T1, A, B, Ns)
XVII.36	d	puṣpapatraphalaḥ	"	paścimāntaphalaḥ (L), *but* paścimāgraphalaḥ (T1, Ns)
XVII.37	b	°caryā sahiṣṇu°	"	°caryāsahiṣṇu° (L)
XVII.40	Comm[2]	mūlavṛkṣā	"	mūlam ity uktā (L), mūlam uktā (Ns)
"	Comm[3]	karuṇodbhavaduḥkham	"	karuṇāto yad duḥkham (L, T1, B, Ns, Nc)

" Comm^{3}	svārtha°	"	sattvārtha° (L, T1)
" Comm^{9}	'bandhyo	*inserted before*	veditavyaḥ (T1)
XVII.43 b	'niravadyo	*read*	niravadyo (T1)
XVII.45 Comm^{1}	pratyekabodhibuddhāḥ	*inserted after*	pratyekāṁ bodhiṁ buddhāḥ (A, B, Ns)
XVII.46 Comm^{1}	duḥkhābhāvo nimittaṁ I satveṣu	*read*	duḥkhābhāvanimittaṁ satveṣu I (A, B, Ns, T1, T2)
XVII.46 Comm^{2}	saṁtrāsayati	*read*	saṁtrāsayaty (A, B, Ns)
XVII.47 d	vimukto api kṛtārthaḥ	"	vimuktā api kṛtārthāḥ (B *and* Ns *read* kṛtārthāḥ *instead of* kṛtārthaḥ. *Consequently* vimukto api *should be* vimuktā api, *although this is not supported by any manuscript.*)
XVII.49 b	tyajati	"	tyajanti (Ns)
" Comm^{2}	tatra tat°	"	trayatat° (A, B), traye tat° (Ns)
XVII.51 Comm^{3}	°saṁbhārasyānyasyākar°	"	°saṁbhārasyānyasya cākar° (L *omitted* anyasya, *but emended for various reasons, on which see n. 51 in the translation.*)
" Comm^{4}	sukhābhave	"	sukhānubhave (L, A, B, Ns, Nc)
XVII.52 a	duḥkhe	"	duḥkhair (Ns), °khai (A, B, Nc)
XVII.53 c	paraṁ	"	parāṁ (T1)
" Comm^{2}	vinā no	"	vinātmano (L, A, B, Ns)
XVII.59 Comm^{1}	anupahṛtya	"	anupakṛtya (L), *but* anupahatya (A, B, Ns, Nc)
" Comm^{1}	kalpikavasudānāt	"	kalpikavastudānāt (L)

* * *

The Sanskrit Text of *Mahāyāna-sūtrālaṁkāra* XVII.29–64

karuṇāvibhāge tadālambanaprabhedam ārabhya dvau ślokau |

pradīptān śatruvaśagān duḥkhākrāntāṁs tamovṛtān |
durgamārgasamārūḍhān mahābandhanasaṁyutān || 29 ||
mahāśanaviṣākrāntalolān mārgapranaṣṭakān |
utpathaprasthitān sattvān durbalān karuṇāyate || 30 ||

tatra 1) pradīptāḥ kāmarāgeṇa kāmasukhasaktāḥ | 2) śatruvaśagā mārakṛtāntarāyāḥ kuśale 'prayuktāḥ 3) duḥkhākrāntā duḥkhābhibhūtāḥ narakādiṣu | 4) tamovṛtā aurabhrikādayo duścaritaikāntikāḥ | karmavipākasaṁmūḍhatvāt | 5) durgamārgasamārūḍhā aparinirvāṇadharmāṇaḥ saṁsāravartmātyantānupacchedāt | 6) mahābandhanasaṁyutā anyatīrthyamokṣasaṁprasthitā nānākudṛṣṭigāḍhabandhanabaddhatvāt | 7) mahāśanaviṣākrāntalolāḥ samāpattisukhasaktāḥ | teṣāṁ hi tat kliṣṭaṁ samāpattisukhaṁ | yathā mṛṣṭam aśanaṁ viṣākrāntaṁ | tataḥ pracyāvanāt | 8) mārgapraṇaṣṭakā abhimānikā mokṣamārgabhrāntatvāt | 9) utpathaprasthitā hīnayānaprayuktā aniyatāḥ | 10) durbalā aparipūrṇasaṁbhārā bodhisattvāḥ | ity ete daśavidhāḥ sattvā bodhisattvakaruṇāyā ālambanaṁ |

pañcaphalasaṁdarśane karuṇāyāḥ ślokaḥ |

heṭhāpaham hy uttamabodhibījaṁ sukhāvahaṁ tāpakam iṣṭahetuṁ |
svabhāvadaṁ dharmam upāśritasya bodhir na dūre jinātmajasya || 31 ||

tatra 1) heṭhāpahatvena tadvipakṣavihiṁsāprahāṇād visaṁyogaphalaṁ darśayati | 2) uttamabodhibījatvenādhipatiphalaṁ | 3) parātmanor yathākramaṁ sukhāvahatāpakatvena puruṣakāraphalaṁ | 4) iṣṭahetutvena vipākaphalaṁ | 5) svabhāvadatvena niṣyandaphalam āyatyāṁ viśiṣṭakaruṇāphaladānāt | evaṁ pañcavidhāṁ karuṇām āśritya buddhatvam adūre veditavyaṁ |

apratiṣṭhitasaṁsāranirvāṇatve ślokaḥ |

vijñāya saṁsāragataṁ samagraṁ duḥkhātmakaṁ caiva nirātmakaṁ ca |
nodvegam āyāti na cāpi doṣaiḥ prabādhyate kāruṇiko 'grabuddhiḥ || 32 ||

sarvaṁ saṁsāraṁ yathābhūtaṁ parijñāya bodhisattvo nodvegam āyāti kāruṇikatvāt | na doṣair bādhyate 'grabuddhitvāt | evaṁ na nirvāṇe pratiṣṭhito bhavati na saṁsāre yathākramaṁ |

saṁsāraparijñāne ślokaḥ |

duḥkhātmakaṁ lokam avekṣamāṇo duḥkhāyate vetti ca tad yathāvat |
tasyābhyupāyaṁ parivarjane ca na khedam āyāty api vā kṛpāluḥ || 33 ||

duḥkhāyata iti karuṇāyate | vetti ca tad yathāvad iti duḥkhaṁ yathābhūtaṁ tasya ca duḥkhasya parivarjane 'bhyupāyaṁ | vetti yenāsya duḥkhaṁ nirudhyate | etena jānann api saṁsāraduḥkhaṁ yathābhūtaṁ tatparityāgopāyaṁ ca na khedam āpadyate bodhisattvaḥ karuṇāviśeṣād iti pradarśayati |

karuṇāprabhede dvau ślokau |

kṛpā prakṛtyā pratisaṁkhyayā ca pūrvaṁ tadabhyāsavidhānayogāt |
vipakṣahānau ca viśuddhilābhāc caturvidheyaṁ karuṇātmakānāṁ ||
34 ||

seyaṁ yathākramaṁ 1) gotraviśeṣataḥ | 2) guṇadoṣaparīkṣaṇataḥ | 3) janmāntaraparibhāvanataḥ | 4) vairāgyalābhataś ca veditavyā | tadvipakṣavihiṁsāprahāṇe sati viśuddhilābhata iti vairāgyalābhataḥ |

na sā kṛpā yā na samā sadā vā nādhyāśayād vā pratipattito vā |
vairāgyato nānupalambhato vā na bodhisattvo hy akṛpas tathā yaḥ ||
35 ||

tatra 1) samā sukhitādiṣu sattveṣu yatkiṁcid veditam idam atra duḥkhasyeti viditvā | 2) sadā nirupadhiśeṣanirvāṇe tadakṣayāt | 3) adhyāśayād bhūmipraviṣṭānām ātmaparasamatāśayalābhāt | 4) pratipattito duḥkhaparitrāṇakriyayā | 5) vairāgyatas tadvipakṣavihiṁsāprahāṇāt | 6) anupalambhato 'nutpattikadharmakṣāntilābhāt |

karuṇāvṛkṣapratibimbake pañca ślokāḥ |

karuṇā kṣāntiś cintā praṇidhānaṁ janma sattvaparipākaḥ |
karuṇātarur eṣa mahān mūlādiḥ paścimāgraphalaḥ || 36 ||

ity eṣa mūlaskandhaśākhāpatrapuṣpaphalāvasthaḥ karuṇāvṛkṣo veditavyaḥ | etasya karuṇā mūlaṁ | kṣāntiḥ skandhaḥ | sattvārthacintā śākhā | praṇidhānaṁ śobhaneṣu janmasu patrāṇi | śobhanaṁ janma puṣpaṁ | sattvaparipākaḥ phalaṁ |

mūlaṁ karuṇā na bhaved duṣkaracaryāsahiṣṇutā na bhavet |
duḥkhākṣamaś ca dhīmān sattvārthaṁ cintayen naiva || 37 ||
cintāvihīnabuddhiḥ praṇidhānaṁ śuklajanmasu na kuryāt |
śubhajanmān anugacchan sattvān paripācayen naiva || 38 ||

ābhyāṁ ślokābhyāṁ pūrvottaraprasavasādharmyāt karuṇādīnāṁ mūlādibhāvaṁ sādhayati |

karuṇāseko maitrī tadduḥkhe saukhyato vipulapuṣṭiḥ |
śākhāvṛddhir viśadā yonimanaskārato jñeyā || 39 ||
parṇatyāgādānaṁ praṇidhīnāṁ saṁtater anucchedāt |
dvividhapratyayasiddheḥ puṣpam abandhyaṁ phalaṁ cāsmāt || 40
||

etābhyāṁ ślokābhyāṁ vṛkṣamūlasekādisādharmyaṁ karuṇāvṛkṣasya darśayati | 1) karuṇā hi mūlam uktā | tasyāḥ seko maitrī tayā tadāpyāyanāt | 2) maitracitto hi paraduḥkhena duḥkhāyate | tataś ca karuṇāto yad duḥkham utpadyate bodhisattvasya sattvārthaprayuktasya tatra saukhyotpādād vipulapuṣṭiḥ kṣāntipuṣṭir ity arthaḥ | sā hi skandha ity uktā | skandhaś ca vipulaḥ |

3) yoniśomanaskārād bahuvidhā mahāyāne śākhāvṛddhiḥ। cintā hi śākhety uktā। 4) pūrvāparanirodhotpādakrameṇa praṇidhānasaṁtānasyānucchedāt। parṇatyāgādānasādharmyaṁ praṇidhānānāṁ veditavyaṁ। 5) ādhyātmikapratyayasiddhitaḥ svasaṁtānaparipākāt puṣpam iva janmābandhyaṁ veditavyaṁ। 6) bāhyapratyayasiddhitaḥ parasaṁtānaparipākāt phalabhūtaḥ sattvaparipāko 'bandhyo veditavyaḥ।

karuṇānuśaṁse ślokaḥ।

kaḥ kurvīta na karuṇāṁ sattveṣu mahākṛpāguṇakareṣu।
duḥkhe 'pi saukhyam atulaṁ bhavati yad eṣāṁ kṛpājanitaṁ।। 41 ।।

atra mahākaruṇāguṇa uttarārdhena saṁdarśitaḥ। śeṣo gatārthaḥ।

karuṇāniḥsaṅgatāyāṁ ślokaḥ।

āviṣṭānāṁ kṛpayā na tiṣṭhati manaḥ śame kṛpālūnāṁ।
kuta eva lokasaukhye svajīvite vā bhavet snehaḥ।। 42 ।।

sarvasya hi lokasya laukike saukhye svajīvite ca snehaḥ। tatrāpi ca niḥsnehānāṁ śrāvakapratyekabuddhānāṁ sarvaduḥkhopaśame nirvāṇe pratiṣṭhitaṁ manaḥ। bodhisattvānāṁ tu karuṇāviṣṭatvān nirvāṇe 'pi mano na pratiṣṭhitaṁ। kuta eva tayoḥ sneho bhaviṣyati।

karuṇāsnehavaiśeṣye trayaḥ ślokāḥ।

sneho na vidyate 'sau yo niravadyo na laukiko yaś ca।
dhīmatsu kṛpāsneho niravadyo lokasamatītaḥ।। 43 ।।

mātāpitṛprabhṛtīnāṁ hi tṛṣṇāmayaḥ snehaḥ sāvadyaḥ। laukikakaruṇāvihāriṇāṁ niravadyo 'pi laukikaḥ। bodhisattvānāṁ tu karuṇāmayaḥ sneho niravadyaś ca laukikātikrāntaś ca। kathaṁ ca punar niravadya ity āha।

duḥkhājñānamahaughe mahāndhakāre ca niśritaṁ lokaṁ।
uddhartuṁ ya upāyaḥ katham iva na syāt sa niravadyaḥ।। 44 ।।

duḥkhamahaugha ajñānamahāndhakāre ceti yojyaṁ। śeṣaṁ gatārthaṁ। kathaṁ lokātikrānta ity āha।

sneho na so 'sty arihatāṁ loke pratyekabodhibuddhānāṁ।
prāg eva tadanyeṣāṁ katham iva lokottaro na syāt।। 45 ।।

pratyekāṁ bodhiṁ buddhāḥ pratyekabodhibuddhāḥ। śeṣaṁ gatārthaṁ।

trāsābhinandananimittatve ślokaḥ।

duḥkhābhāve duḥkhaṁ yat kṛpayā bhavati bodhisattvānāṁ।
saṁtrāsayati tad ādau spṛṣṭaṁ tv abhinandayati gāḍhaṁ।।46 ।।

duḥkhābhāve iti duḥkhābhāvanimittaṁ sattveṣu। karuṇayā bodhisattvānāṁ yad duḥkham utpadyate tad ādau saṁtrāsayaty adhimukticaryābhūmau। ātmaparasamatayā duḥkhasya yathābhūtam aspṛṣṭatvāt। spṛṣṭaṁ tu śuddhādhyāśayabhūmāv abhinandayaty evety arthaḥ।

karuṇāduḥkhena sukhābhibhave ślokaḥ।

kim ataḥ paramāścaryaṁ yad duḥkhaṁ saukhyam abhibhavati sarvaṁ।
kṛpayā janitaṁ laukyaṁ yena vimuktā api kṛtārthāḥ।। 47 ।।

nāsty ata āścaryataraṁ yad duḥkham eva karuṇājanitaṁ bodhisattvānāṁ tathā sukhaṁ bhavati | yat sarvaṁ laukikaṁ sukham abhibhavati | yena sukhena vimuktā arhanto 'pi kṛtārthāḥ prāg evānye |

kṛpākṛtadānānuśaṁse ślokaḥ |

kṛpayā sahitaṁ dānaṁ yad dānasukhaṁ karoti dhīrāṇāṁ |
traidhātukam upabhogair na tat sukhaṁ tatkalāṁ spṛśati || 48 ||

yac ca traidhātukaṁ sukham upabhogaiḥ kṛtaṁ na tat sukhaṁ tasya sukhasya kalāṁ spṛśatīty ayam uttarārdhasyārthaḥ | śeṣaṁ gatārthaṁ |

kṛpayā duḥkhābhyupagame ślokaḥ |

duḥkhamayaṁ saṁsāraṁ yat kṛpayā na tyajanti sattvārthaṁ |
parahitahetor duḥkhaṁ kiṁ kāruṇikair na samupetaṁ || 49 ||

sarvaṁ hi dukhaṁ saṁsāraduḥkhe 'ntarbhūtaṁ | tasyābhyupagamāt sarvaṁ duḥkham abhyupagataṁ bhavati |

trayatatphalavṛddhau ślokaḥ |

karuṇā dānaṁ bhogāḥ sadā kṛpālor vivṛddhim upayānti |
snehānugrahajanitaṁ tacchaktikṛtaṁ sukhaṁ cāsmāt || 50 ||

trayaṁ bodhisattvānāṁ sarvajanmasu vardhate karuṇāyogāt | karuṇā tadabhyāsāt | dānaṁ karuṇāvaśāt | bhogāś ca dānavaśāt | tasmāc ca trayāt phalaṁ trividhaṁ sukhaṁ bhavati | snehajanitaṁ karuṇātaḥ | sattvānugrahajanitaṁ dānāt | tadanugrahakriyāśaktikṛtaṁ bhogebhyaḥ |

dānaprotsāhanāyāṁ ślokaḥ |

vardhe ca vardhayāmi ca dāne paripācayāmi sukhayāmi |
ākarṣāmi nayāmi ca karuṇā sannān pravadatīva || 51 ||

dāne sannān iti saṁbandhanīyaṁ | ṣaḍbhir guṇair dāne 'vasannān bodhisattvān karuṇā protsahayatīva | 1) svabhāvavṛddhyā | 2) bhogais tadvardhanayā | 3) dānena sattvaparipācanayā | 4) dātuś ca sukhotpādanāt | 5) mahābodhisaṁbhārasyānyasya cākarṣaṇāt | 6) mahābodhisamīpanayanāc ca |

parasaukhyena sukhānubhave ślokaḥ |

duḥkhair duḥkhī kṛpayā sukhāny anādhāya kena sukhitaḥ syāt |
sukhayaty ātmanam ataḥ kṛpālur ādhāya parasaukhyaṁ || 52 ||

karuṇayā bodhisattvaḥ paraduḥkhair duḥkhitaḥ sattveṣv anādhāya sukhaṁ kathaṁ sukhitaḥ syāt | tasmāt pareṣu sukham ādhāya bodhisattva ātmānam eva sukhayatīti veditavyaṁ |

kṛpayā dānasamanuśāstau ṣaṭ ślokāḥ |

svaṁ dānaṁ kāruṇikaḥ śāstīva sadaiva niḥsvasukhakāmaḥ |
bhogaiḥ sukhaya parāṁ vā mām apy ayutasaukhyaṁ || 53 ||

na hi kāruṇikasya vinā parasukhenāsti sukhaṁ | tasyāyutasaukhyatvād bodhisattvas tena vinātmano dānasya phalaṁ sukhaṁ necchati |

saphalaṁ dānaṁ dattaṁ tan me sattveṣu tatsukhasukhena |
phala teṣv eva nikāmaṁ yadi me kartavyatā te 'sti || 54 ||

dānaṁ dadatā dānaṁ ca dānaphalaṁ ca tan mayā sattveṣu dattaṁ। tat-sukham eva me sukhaṁ yasmāt। atas teṣv eva yāvat phalitavyaṁ tāvat phaleti loṭ। bodhisattvaḥ karuṇayā dānam anuśāsti।

bhogadveṣṭur dātur bhogā bahuśubhataropasarpanti।
na hi tat sukhaṁ mataṁ me dāne pāraṁparo 'smi yataḥ।। 55 ।।

bhogavimukhasya dātur bhogā bahutarāś copatiṣṭhante। śobhanatarāś ca। dharmataiveyaṁ cittasyodāratarātvāt। na hi tat sukhaṁ mataṁ me yad bhogās tathopatiṣṭhante। yasmād ahaṁ dāne pāraṁparas tatprabandhakāmatvān na sukhe।

sarvāstiparityāge yat kṛpayā māṁ nirīkṣase satataṁ।
nanu te tena jñeyaṁ na matphalenārthitā 'syeti।। 56 ।।

yo 'haṁ dānaphalaṁ sarvam eva karuṇayā nityaṁ parityajāmi nanv ata eva veditavyaṁ nāsti me dānaphalenārthitvam iti bodhisattvo dānaṁ samanu-śāsti।

dānābhirato na syāṁ prāptaṁ cet tatphalaṁ na visṛjeyaṁ।

tathā hi।

kṣanam api dānena vinā dānābhirato bhavati naiva।। 57 ।।

iti gatārthaḥ ślokaḥ।

akṛtaṁ na phalasi yasmāt pratikārāpekṣayā na me tulyaṁ।

yas tvā karoti tasya tvaṁ phalasi। tasmāt tvaṁ pratikārāpekṣayā na mat tulyaṁ। tathā hy ahaṁ।

pratikāranirvyapekṣaḥ paratra phalado 'sya kāmaṁ te।। 58 ।।

gatārtham etat।

kṛpādāne dvau ślokau।

niravadyaṁ śuddhapadaṁ hitāvahaṁ caiva sānurakṣaṁ ca।
nirmṛgyaṁ nirlepaṁ jinātmajānāṁ kṛpādānaṁ।। 59 ।।

tatra 1) niravadyaṁ param anupahatya dānāt। 2) śuddhapadaṁ kalpikava-studānāt। viṣaśastramadyādivivarjanataḥ। 3) hitāvahaṁ dānena saṁgṛhya kuśale niyojanāt। 4) sānurakṣaṁ parijanasyāvighātaṁ kṛtvā anyasmai dānāt। 5) nirmṛgyam ayācamāne 'py arthitvaṁ vighātaṁ vāvagamya svayam eva dānāt dakṣiṇīyāparimārgaṇāc ca। 6) nirlepaṁ pratikāravipākaniḥspṛhatvāt।

aparaḥ prakāraḥ।

sakalaṁ vipulaṁ śreṣṭhaṁ satataṁ muditaṁ nirāmiṣaṁ śuddhaṁ।
bodhinataṁ kuśalanataṁ jinātmajānāṁ kṛpādānaṁ।। 60 ।।

tatra 1) sakalam ādhyātmikabāhyavastudānāt। 2) vipulaṁ prabhūtavastu-dānāt। 3) śreṣṭhaṁ praṇītavastudānāt। 4) satatam abhīkṣṇadānāt। 5) muditam apratisaṁkhyāya prahṛṣṭadānāt। 6) nirāmiṣaṁ yathā nirlepaṁ। 7) śuddhaṁ yathā śuddhapadaṁ। 8) bodhinataṁ mahābodhipariṇāmanāt। 9) kuśalanataṁ yathā hitāvahaṁ।

upabhogaviśeṣe ślokaḥ।

na tathopabhogatuṣṭiṁ labhate bhogī yathā parityāgāt ǀ
tuṣṭim upaiti kṛpāluḥ sukhatrayāpyāyitamanaskaḥ ǀǀ 61 ǀǀ

tatra sukhatrayaṁ dānaprītiḥ parānugrahaprītiḥ bodhisaṁbhārasaṁbharaṇaprītiś ca ǀ śeṣaṁ gatārthaṁ ǀ

pāramitābhinirhārakaruṇāyāṁ ślokaḥ ǀ

kṛpaṇakṛpā raudrakṛpā saṁkṣubdhakṛpā kṛpā pramatteṣu ǀ
viṣayaparatantrakaruṇā mithyābhiniviṣṭakaruṇā ca ǀǀ 62 ǀǀ

tatra 1) kṛpaṇā matsariṇaḥ ǀ 2) raudrā duḥśīlāḥ paropatāpinaḥ ǀ 3) saṁkṣubdhāḥ krodhanāḥ ǀ 4) pramattāḥ kuśīdāḥ ǀ 5) viṣayaparatantrāḥ kāmeṣu vikṣiptacittāḥ ǀ 6) mithyābhiniviṣṭāḥ duḥprajñāḥ tīrthikādayaḥ ǀ eṣu pāramitāvipakṣadharmāvasthiteṣu yā karuṇā sā kṛpaṇādikaruṇā ǀ sā ca tadvipakṣavidūṣaṇāt pāramitābhinirhārāya saṁpadyate ǀ tasmāt pāramitābhinirhārakaruṇety ucyate ǀ

karuṇāpratyayasaṁdarśane ślokaḥ ǀ

karuṇā bodhisattvānāṁ sukhād duḥkhāt tadanvayāt ǀ
karuṇā bodhisattvānāṁ hetor mitrāt svabhāvataḥ ǀǀ 63 ǀǀ

tatra pūrvārdhenālambanapratyayaṁ karuṇāyāḥ saṁdarśayati ǀ trividhāṁ vedanām ālambya tisṛbhir duḥkhatābhiḥ karuṇāyanāt ǀ aduḥkhāsukhā hi vedanā sukhaduḥkhayor anvayaḥ punas tadāvāhanāt ǀ uttarārdhena yathākramaṁ hetumitrasvabhāvaiḥ karuṇāyā hetvadhipatisamanantarapratyayān saṁdarśayati ǀ

mahākaruṇatve ślokaḥ ǀ

karuṇā bodhisattvānāṁ samā jñeyā tadāśayāt ǀ
pratipatter virāgāc ca nopalambhād viśuddhitaḥ ǀǀ 64 ǀǀ

tatra samā trividhavedanāvastheṣu yat kiṁcid veditam idam atra duḥkhasyeti viditvā ǀ sā punar āśayato 'pi cittena karuṇāyanāt ǀ pratipattito 'pi tatparitrāṇāt ǀ virāgato 'pi tadvipakṣavihiṁsāprahāṇāt ǀ anupalambhato 'py ātmaparakaruṇānupalambhāt ǀ viśuddhito 'py aṣṭamyāṁ bhūmāv anutpattikadharmakṣāntilābhāt ǀ

Toward an Understanding of the *Vijñaptimātratā*

Noritoshi Aramaki

In my joint-seminars with Professor Lambert Schmithausen at the Universität Hamburg, 1979–1980,[1] I emphasized the necessity of undertaking two enterprises: 1) the stratification of the *Yogācārabhūmi* text-complex (YBh) and the other relevant philosophical texts in accordance with their textual development,[2] and 2) the tracing of the historical development of some fundamental concepts of their philosophy through those strata. In a preliminary attempt at these enterprises I have noticed that it is fundamentally important to understand how the older Hīnayānistic tradition of the yogācāras' *mārga* (path)-system, starting with Saṁgharakṣa's *Yogācārabhūmi*,[3] is "mahāyānized" into the newer Mahāyānistic version of the bodhisattvas' *mārga*-system from around the fourth century onward. Here in this short paper I do not intend to expound the mahāyānization process through the strata of the yogācāras' textual development as such, but confine myself to establishing one fundamental structure of their mahāyānized *mārga*-system so far, it seems, left unnoticed—namely, the *avavāda* (instruction receiving and delivering) structure of their mahāyānistic philosophy, that is to say, the fact that their mahāyānistic philosophical concepts, e.g., the *vijñaptimātratā* (truth of appearing-consciousness-

1. It is my happiest duty to record my indebtedness to Professor Schmithausen who gave me this rare opportunity, and has ever since been ready to give me corrections, advice, and encouragement not only in the joint seminars, but also later on; needless to say, all the errors and shortcomings of the paper are mine.

2. My very provisional working-hypotheses on the strata of those texts are as follows: 1) Saṁgharakṣa's *Yogācārabhūmi*; 2) the three strata of the *Śrāvakabhūmi*; 3) the *Vastusaṁgrahaṇī*; 4) the two strata of the *Bodhisattvabhūmi*; 5) the *Ratnagotravibhāga*; 6) the Maitreya, the Viśālamati, the Paramārthasaṁbhava, and the Guṇākara chapters of the *Sandhinirmocanasūtra* (SandhN), in that order; 7) the *Dharmadharmatāvibhāga*; 8) the *Madhyāntavibhāga*; 9) the *Mahāyānasūtrālaṁkāra*; 10) the so-called Proof, the Pravṛtti, and the Nivṛtti portions of the *ālayavijñāna* treatise of the *Viniścayasaṁgrahaṇī*; 11) the Sacittikabhūmi of the *Viniścayasaṁgrahaṇī*; 12) the Maulībhūmi; 13) the works of Asaṅga; 14) the works of Vasubandhu. The list is given here merely to explain the background against which the present paper is being written.

3. In one of those joint-seminars I tried to establish the development from this text to the oldest stratum of the *Śrāvakabhūmi*. Also see P. Demieville, "La Yogācārabhūmi de Saṅgharakṣa," *BEFEO* 44–2, 1954.

only), the *abhūtaparikalpa* (unreal conceptual imagination), the *mano-jalpa* (thinking in words), the *ālayavijñāna* (subconsciousness of being-in-the-world), the *trisvabhāva* (three essences of being), and so on all share in the fundamental structure of *avavāda* of the Buddhas and bodhisattvas toward all saṁsāric existences. By paying due attention to this *avavāda* structure underlying those mahāyānistic philosophical concepts I think I can find some clues which will help us trace back their "whences," which have so far remained mysteriously elusive in spite of the scholarly zeal exerted to search for their historical origins. Thus the present paper is designed, by way of illustration, to explain the most fundamental of those "whences": whence the *vijñaptimātratā*? (§2). But prior to trying to explain the "whence" of the *vijñaptimātratā* it may be advisable to define briefly what I mean by the term "the *avavāda* structure underlying" those mahāyānistic philosophical concepts (§1).

§1 The *Avavāda* Structure

In one of the joint seminars mentioned above, I tried to analyze the textual composition of the *Bodhisattvabhūmi* (BBh)—the very starting-point of the Yogācāra's mahāyānization process—into two strata, the old and the new,[4] and I found that the new stratum is so composed as to initiate the mahāyānization process with an *avavāda* interpolated into the context of the systematic exposition of the supernatural acts (*karmans*) of the ten *jñānabalas* (supernatural powers of knowledge) of the Tathāgatas. The fifth (but here in the exposition of their *karmans* the sixth) *tathāgatajñānabala*, *nānādhātujñānabala* (supernatural powers of knowledge on the variety of innate natures of all saṁsāric existences), is defined as follows, BBh 272.9 (394.15):[5]

> *nānādhātujñānabalena tathāgato hīnamadhyapraṇītadhātukatāś ca vibhajya yathābhūtaṁ prajānāti | yathendriyān yathāśayān yathānuśayāṁś ca sattvāṁs teṣu teṣv avatāramukheṣv avavādakriyayā samyag yathāyogaṁ saṁniyojayati |*
>
> With His [fifth] supernatural power of knowledge on the variety of innate natures [of all saṁsāric existences] the Tathāgata distinguishes [if they are of] the inferior, the middle, or the superior innate natures and knows

---

4. It is impossible to explain the old and the new strata of BBh within the compass of this paper. It would require a book-size study. Merely to give a general idea, I will append to this paper a table of the chapter titles of the respective strata, together with those of the *Mahāyānasūtrālaṁkāra*.

5. The page and the line numbers at the head of the quotations from the BBh are those of Dutt's edition; those of Wogihara's edition are given in parentheses.

truly which capacities, which aspirations, and which inclinations they have so that they may be instructed by His supernatural act of *avavāda* (instruction-delivering) on their respective initiatory *mārgas* in order for them to practise yogic practices rightly in accordance [with their capacities, aspirations, and inclinations].

Then begins a lengthy *avavāda* interpolation introduced by a question as follows, BBh 272.12 (394.20):

tatra yathā tathāgatāḥ śrāvakānāṁ teṣu teṣv avatāramukheṣu avavādam anuprayacchanti tathā śrāvakabhūmau sarveṇa sarvaṁ niraṁtaram ākhyātam uttānaṁ vivṛtaṁ prajñaptaṁ prakāśitam | *kathañ ca punas tathāgatā bodhisattvam ādikarmikaṁ tatprathamakarmikaṁ samādhisaṁbhāraparigrahe 'vasthitañ cittasthitikāmaṁ cittasthitaye 'vavadanti* |

Hereon it has been expounded completely in the *Śrāvakabhūmi* (ŚBh) how the Tathāgatas instruct *avavāda* to the śrāvakas on their respective initiatory *mārgas* (the Paths). How, then, do the Tathāgatas deliver *avavāda* to the initiatory bodhisattvas well prepared to practise *samādhi* (ecstatic concentration) and wishing to concentrate their mind in order for them to concentrate their mind?[6]

From this introduction it is clear that the new stratum of BBh is motivated to start the mahāyānization process in continuation to the completion of the old *mārga*-system of śrāvakas in the *Śrāvakabhūmi* and to formulate the new *mārga*-system of bodhisattvas, especially its initiatory *prayogamārga* (path of preliminary endeavor),[7] in accordance with the Tathāgatas' *avavāda*. The Tathāgatas' *avavāda* here must be understood as Their teachings, not only externally taught in any forms of language, but more fundamentally, internally inspired deep within the initiatory bodhisattvas.[8] The *avavāda* in the following

---

6. The repetitions are simplified in the translation.

7. The first and original occurrence of the technical term *prayogamārga* is, as far as I can see now, BBh 274.13 (396.10) in the context of the Tathāgatas' *avavāda* here. Thus the *prayogamārga* leading to the *āśrayaparivṛtti* on the *darśanamārga* is first formulated in the new stratum of BBh, under discussion, and will develop in the Maitreya chapter of the *Sandhinirmocanasūtra* (where the term does not occur) and further in the *Dharmadharmatāvibhāga*, etc.

8. It is Professor Nagao himself who has, on reading the first draft of this paper, pointed out that what I mean by the *avavāda* structure is nothing but the act of the *pṛṣṭhalabdhajñāna* (the knowledge with compassion to teach, which is realized in continuation to awakening by the true knowledge free from any conceptual imagination) of Buddhas and bodhisattvas. I now realize that the Tathāgatas' *avavāda* of BBh and the *dharma-* and *arthapratisaṁvedin* and the *prabhāva* of the Maitreya chapter of SandhN to be discussed later, are, indeed, the precursors of one of the fundamental concepts of Yogācāravijñānavāda philosophy: the *pṛṣṭhalabdhajñāna* to be accomplished in the *Dharmadharmatāvibhāga* and the *Mahāyānasūtrālaṅkāra*.

introduces a new Prajñāpāramitā-wise contemplation and instructs the initiatory bodhisattvas to contemplate (*manasikṛ-*) their own existence here and now as name (*nāma*)-only, concept (*saṁjñā*)-only, and appearance (*prajñapti*)-only so as to be concentrated in *samādhi* to penetrate into the reality (*vastu*) transcending all those verbal existences. Thus I may specify that the new *mārga*-system of bodhisattvas has the *avavāda* structure of contemplating one's own existence here and now as appearance (*prajñapti*)-only through being inspired by the supernatural act of the Tathāgatas' *jñānabala*s.

Now, the new stratum of BBh has been motivated to rework the old *mārga*-system of bodhisattvas into the new in accordance with this *avavāda*-interpolation in the last chapter of BBh, and therefore the element of this *avavāda* is recognizable throughout the new stratum of BBh. Here I will try to identify the element of this *avavāda* in two further chapters of BBh, "Balagotrapaṭala" and "Tattvārthapaṭala," so as to further define the *avavāda* structure of the new *mārga*-system of bodhisattvas.

Firstly this *avavāda* (instruction), being the supernatural act (*karman*) of the Tathāgatas' *jñānabala*s (powers of knowledge), must have given rise to a new system of the *prayogamārga*[9] to purify the *balagotra* (innate nature to attain the supernatural powers of knowledge) in the chapter of the Balagotra.[10] This new system of the *prayogamārga* for the initiatory bodhisattvas to purify their *balagotra* consists of the six bodhisattva practices as follows (BBh 67.1–79.27 [95.1–113.12]):

1. *adhimukti* (faith without any scepticism)
2. *dharmaparyeṣṭi* (search for teachings and truths)
3. *dharmadeśanā* (learning and teaching teachings and truths)
4. *dharmānudharmapratipatti* (practice on the truths in accordance with the stage of practice in order to realize the ultimate truth)
5. *samyagavavādānuśāsana* (reception and delivery of the right instructions and admonitions)
6. *upāyasahitakāyavāṅmanaḥkarman* (physical, verbal, and mental acts performed with expediency)

9. The term *prayogamārga* does not occur in this section of the Balagotra, BBh 67.1–79.27 (95.1–113.12), but I interpret on the basis of the following development of the *prayogamārga* that the six bodhisattva practices here are meant to be the *prayogamārga*.

10. The element of this *avavāda* may be recognized, in addition to the peculiar term *balagotra* discussed below, in the explanation of the *dharmānudharmapratipatti* where *śamatha* is defined as concentrated on the *nirabhilāpyavastumātra*, BBh 77.6 (109.12).

It is certain that the traditional system of the four *srotāpattyaṅgas* (constituent practices leading to conversion) for the śrāvakas to attain the *srotāpattiphala* (attainment of conversion to the new being of the holy disciples) on the *darśanamārga* (path of awakening insight) (*catvāri srotāpattyaṅgāni*: 1 *satpuruṣasaṁsevaḥ* [homage to and attendance upon Buddhist teachers and friends]; 2 *saddharmaśravaṇaṁ* [learning the Buddhist teachings and truths]; 3 *yoniśomanaskāro* [right contemplation in accord with the stages of practice]; 4 *dharmānudharmapratipattiḥ* [practice on the truths in accordance with the stage of practice in order to realize the ultimate truth])[11] is here "mahāyānized" into this system of the six bodhisattva practices, as the common term *dharmānudharmapratipatti* may suggest. But why is this new system of the six bodhisattva practices labeled with the peculiar term *balagotra*? What does *balagotra* mean exactly? The meaning of the term *balagotra* is to be inferred from such passages as the following, BBh 78.22 (111.18):

> *evam evāvavādaṁ parato vā labhamāno bodhisattvaḥ pareṣāṁ vānuyacchann aṣṭāṇāṁ balāṇāṁ gotraṁ krameṇa viśodhayati* |
>
> Just in this way the bodhisattva purifies [his] *gotra* (innate nature) of the eight [*jñāna-*] *balas* [of the Tathāgatas], one by one, while receiving *avavāda* from others and delivering *avavāda* to others.

Thus the *balagotra* is a bodhisattva's *gotra* (innate nature) of the ten *jñānabalas* (powers of knowledge) of the Tathāgatas. Then what is the exact meaning of this "of," and how is a bodhisattva's *gotra* related to the Tathāgatas' *jñānabalas*? The text says that the former *gotra* receives *avavāda* from the supernatural act of the latter *jñānabalas* and is thereby purified so as to be converted for himself to attain the latter *jñānabalas* delivering *avavāda*. Thus *avavāda*-receiving is converted to attain *avavāda*-delivering and *avavāda*-delivering is converted supernaturally to act onto *avavāda*-receiving. Here is, I think, recognizable "the logic of convertibility" which Professor Nagao has once coined to define the essence of this philosophy.[12] The term *balagotra* (innate nature of the supernatural powers of knowledge) is to be understood as an immature attempt to define the essential structure

---

11. Cf. V. Stache-Rosen, *Das Saṅgītisūtra und sein Kommentar Saṅgītiparyāya* (Sanskrittexte aus den Turfanfunden IX) 1968, S. 58, §4, 11.

12. Cf. G. M. Nagao (tr. L. Kawamura), *Mādhyamika and Yogācāra*, 1991, pp. 123–153. Prof. Nagao expounds convertibility with reference to three concepts: the *vijñānapariṇāma*, the *paryāyas* of the *trisvabhāvas*, and the *pariṇāmanā* of the bodhisattva practice. I interpret that at least the last two, if not the first, have the essential structure of this *avavāda* structure as defined here.

of the new *mārga*-system of bodhisattvas which consists of the convertibility of *avavāda* between the former *gotra* and the latter *jñānabalas*. The "of" between the two means this convertibility of *avavāda*. Thus I may specify that the new *mārga* system of bodhisattvas has the *avavāda* structure to be convertible from *avavāda*-receiving to *avavāda*-delivering and vice versa.

Secondly, the philosophically most important chapter of BBh, "Tattvārthapaṭala," is in its old stratum designed to expound four truths: 1) the truth commonly recognized in this world (*lokaprasiddhatattva*), 2) the truth proven by philosophical investigations (*yuktiprasiddhatattva*), 3) the truth being actually known by the knowledge which purifies [the bodhisattva practices] from the obscuration of mental defilements (*kleśāvaraṇaviśuddhijñānagocaratattva*), and 4) the truth being actually known by the knowledge which purifies [the bodhisattva practices] from the obscuration over the truths to be known (*jñeyāvaraṇaviśuddhijñānagocaratattva*), the last of which must have originally been defined as follows, BBh 26.11 (38.22):

> *bodhisattvāṇāṁ buddhānāṁ ca bhagavatāṁ dharmanairātmyapraveśāya praviṣṭena suviśuddhena ca ... jñeyasamena jñānena yo gocaraviṣayaḥ sā 'sau paramā tathatā niruttarā jñeyaparyantagatā yasyāḥ samyaksarvadharmapravicayā nirvartante nābhivartante* |

> The [fourth *jñeyāvaraṇaviśuddhijñānagocaratattva*] is the supreme and unsurpassed *tathatā* (one and the same essential reality) which is being actually and really known by the true knowledge of the bodhisattvas and the Bhagavat Buddhas, this true knowledge now being the same as the truth to be known. [The former bodhisattvas aim] with this knowledge to realize the selflessness [not only of personal beings (*pudgalanairātmya*), but also] of all beings (*dharmanairātmya*) and [the latter, the Bhagavat Buddhas] have, with this knoweldge, realized and purified their [selflessness] perfectly. [This supreme and unsurpassed *tathatā*] is the most fundamental of all the truths to be known and [therefore] no sooner is it [realized] than all philosophical investigations of truths, [even] the right ones, are calmed and do not work any more.

To this definition of the most fundamental truth in the old stratum of BBh, its new stratum adds an additional definition in the portion skipped by ... above as follows:

> *sarvadharmāṇāṁ nirabhilāpyasvabhāvatām ārabhya prajñaptivādasvabhāvanirvikalpena*

> [This true knowledge of the bodhisattvas and of the Bhagavat Buddhas] is free from any conceptual imagination of [individual] substances appearing in accordance with ordinary language, inasmuch as [it realizes] the essential [being] of all the beings which transcends any [individual] substances conceptually imagined [in accordance with] ordinary language.

This additional definition is clearly meant to make the most fundamental truth *tathatā* (one-and-the-same-being) realizable through the new bodhisattva practices taught in the Tathāgatas' *avavāda* above and therefore is essentially related with a large enlargement in the latter half of this chapter, BBh 30.1ff. (43.24ff.), which, after an exposition of *nirabhilāpyasvabhāvatā* (truth of the essential being which transcends any individual substances conceptually imagined in accordance with ordinary language) or *śūnyatā* (truth of void- or zero-being) as the middle path and of the eight kinds of *vikalpa*s (conceptual imaginations), proposes to systematize the new bodhisattva practices into the system of the four *paryeṣaṇā*s (investigations) and the four *yathābhūtaparijñāna*s (complete knowledge of reality as such)[13] as follows:

1. *nāmaparyeṣaṇā* (investigation of the name)	1. *nāmaparyeṣaṇāgataṁ yathābhūtaparijñānaṁ* (complete knowledge of being as the real, resulting from the investigation of the name)
2. *vastuparyeṣaṇā* (investigation of the real being)	2. *vastupryeṣaṇāgataṁ* ... (the same, resulting from the investigation) on the real being)
3. *svabhāvaprajñaptiparyeṣaṇā* (investigation of the appearance of individual substances in accordance with language)	3. *svabhāvaprajñaptiparyeṣaṇā gataṁ* ... (the same, resulting from the investigation of the appearance of individual substances in accordance with language)
4. *veśeṣaprajñaptiparyeṣaṇā* (investigation of the appearance of their attributes in accordance with language)	4. *veśeṣaprajñaptiparyeṣaṇāgataṁ* ... (the same resulting from the investigation of the appearance of their attributes in accordance with language)

Therefore I may specify that the new *mārga*-system of bodhisattvas has the *avavāda* structure to realize the most fundamental truth *tathatā*

13. There is no doubt that this system of the four *paryeṣaṇā*s and the four *yathābhūtaparijñāna*s has developed out of the Prajñāpāramitā-wise contemplation as taught in the *avavāda*-interpolation in the exposition of the Tathāgatas' ten *jñānabala*s above. But it may also be noteworthy that this system of the four *paryeṣaṇā*s and the four *yathābhūtaparijñāna*s will develop into the *vijñaptimātratā* contemplation in the Maitreya chapter of the SandhN as will be discussed later. This is the reason why this system of the four *paryeṣaṇā*s and the four *yathābhūtaparijñāna*s is expounded within the *vijñaptimātratā* exposition in §3.7 of the *Mahāyānasaṁgraha*.

or *śūnyatā* through the new Prajñāpāramitā-wise contemplation of the four *paryeṣaṇā*s and the four *yathābhūtaparijñāna*s.[14]

In concluding this section I may observe that in the new stratum of BBh the new *mārga*-system of bodhisattvas is developing in the direction of having the *avavāda* structure: 1) to contemplate one's own existence as *prajñapti* (appearance)-only through being inspired by the supernatural acts of Tathāgatas, 2) to be convertible from *avavāda*-receiving to *avavāda*-delivering and vice versa, and 3) to realize the most fundamental truth *tathatā* or *śūnyatā* through the four *paryeṣaṇā*s and the four *yathābhūtaparijñāna*s. In the next section I will discuss how and why this new *mārga*-system of bodhisattvas with its *avavāda* structure develops into the *vijñaptimātratā* in the Maitreya chapter of the *Sandhinirmocanasūtra* (SandhN).

§2 Whence the *Vijñaptimātratā*?

Any scholar working on any text of Yogācāra-Vijñānavāda philosophy must have time and again asked the question "whence the *vijñaptimātratā*?", because any philosophical concepts of this school must after all be traced back to this fundamental truth of *vijñaptimātratā* for their penetrating understanding. And it is perfectly natural and reasonable that all scholars must have come to the conclusion that the *vijñaptimātratā* originates in the Maitreya chapter of SandhN.[15] I do agree with this conclusion. Why not? And yet I say that the most fundamental question, "whence the *vijñaptimātratā*?", is still mysteriously elusive, inasmuch as it has not yet been understood from what historical and philosophical background the *vijñptimātratā* originates in the Maitreya chapter of SandhN. In the present section I will try to answer this most fundamental question by analyzing the philosophical structure of the Maitreya chapter itself, so identifying the *avavāda* structure therein, and then by postulating a historical back-

---

14. In the chapter Caryā one of the four *caryā*s, the *bodhipakṣyacaryā*, consists of 1) the thirty-seven *bodhipakṣyadharma*s and 2) the four *paryeṣaṇā*s and the four *yathābhūtaparijñāna*s. I think it is important that these two types of *bodhipakṣyacaryā* have the purpose (*kṛtya*) of *tattvārthaprativedha*, BBh 256.12f. and 258.9 (371.18f. and 373.27).

15. The most recent fundamental attempt to elucidate the origin of the *vijñaptimātratā* is perhaps L. Schmithausen, "Spirituelle Praxis und Philosophischen Theorie im Buddhismus," *Zeitschrift für Missionswissenschaft und Religionswissenschaft*, Heft 3, 1973, where he already discusses the crucial sentence of §8.7 of SandhN and says, "Mit dem Terminus *vijñaptimātra* ... hat das SandhN den zentrallen und charakteristischen Terminus des Yogācāra-Idealismus geschaffen."

ground for this specific *avavāda* structure to define the fundamental movement starting with this *avavāda* structure and leading to the following developments of Yogācāra-Vijñānavāda philosophy.

The philosophical structure of the Maitreya chapter of SandhN (§§8.1–41) may be analyzed as follows:[16]

8.1 The foundations of the bodhisattva's practice of *śamatha* (concentration) and *vipaśyanā* (contemplation) are the *dharmaprajña-ptivyavasthāna* (philosophical theories teaching Buddhist truth) and the *anuttarasamyaksaṁbodhipraṇidhānāparityajana* (never-abandoning of his vows to attain the supreme and perfect awakening).

8.2 The four kinds of *ālambana* (objects concentrated upon and contemplated) of the bodhisattva's practice of *śamatha* and *vipaśya-nā* are 1) the *savikalpaṁ pratibimbaṁ* (reflected images conceptually imagined), 2) the *nirvikalpaṁ pratibimbaṁ* (reflected images free from any conceptual imagination), 3) the *vastuparyantatā* (ultimate reality being realized *in toto*), and 4) the *kāryaparinișpatti* (perfection of supernatural acts of bodhisattvas and Buddhas).

8.3 The bodhisattva who is *śamathaparyeṣṭin* (pursuing concentration) attains the *kāya*- and the *cittapraśrabdhi*s (freedom from subconscious conditions, physical as well as mental).

8.4 The bodhisattva who is *vipaśyanākuśala* (expert of contemplation) attains the *vicaya* (examination), the *pravicaya* (deeper examination), the *parivitarka* (logical examination), the *parimīmāṁsām āpat-tiḥ* (attainment of conclusive examination), the *kṣānti* (realization of truth), etc. with reference to the *samādhigocarapratibimbajñeyārtha* (truth to be known, appearing as the reflected image of concentration).

8.5 The bodhisattva's practice of *śamatha* and *vipaśyanā* must be called the *śamatha*- and the *vipaśyanānulomikādhimuktisaṁprayukta* (practising with the trust guiding one to concentration and contemplation), in so far as it has not attained the stage defined above (8.3 and 8.4).

8.6 The *śamatha*- and the *vipaśyanāmārga*s (paths of concentration and contemplation) are neither different nor non-different from each other, because [not only the former, but also] the latter contem-

---

16. Here I provisionally follow Lamotte's sections in his editions of the Tibetan text and his French translation with annotation: Étienne Lamotte, *Saṁdhinirmoca-nasūtra* (L'explication des mystéres), texte tibétain édit et traduit (Louvain-Paris, 1935).

plates the mind, while the former does not contemplate the *savikalpa-pratibimba* (objective image conceptually imagined).

8.7–8 Henceforth the *vijñaptimātra* contemplation begins as follows: the *pratibimba* (reflected image) being contemplated in *samādhi* is *vijñaptimātra* and is not outside the mind, as an image of a mirror is not outside the mirror, while appearing as if outside. Here the revolutionary concept *vijñapti* implies that the *vijñāna* of this *pṛthagjana* (ordinary man) stage of the bodhisattva appears as the *ālambana* without any external *ālambana*, as supernaturally taught by the *prabhāva* (supernatural power of the omniscience of Buddhas and bodhisattvas). The crucial sentence here must be back-translated into the Sanskrit as follows:

> *ālambanavijñaptimātraprabhāvitaṁ vijñānaṁ.*
>
> It is instructed by the supernatural power of the omniscience of Buddhas and bodhisattvas that consciousness is consciousness-only appearing as objects.

I will discuss this sentence later.

8.9 *Śamatha* and *vipaśyanā* culminate in the *cittaikāgratā* (mind unified into oneness) which penetrates into the *vijñaptimātratā* (truth of appearing-consciousness-only) and begins to contemplate the *tathatā*.

8.10–12 The three kinds of *vipaśyanā* and various kinds of *śamatha* are enumerated.

8.13–15 *Śamatha* and *vipaśyanā* which contemplate the *saṁbhinnālambana* (one universal truth unifying entire objects) are directed to, tend to, and are destined to [attain] *tathatā*, *bodhi*, *nirvāṇa*, and the *āśrayaparivṛtti* (conversion of the old basis into the new).

8.16 *Śamatha* and *vipaśyanā* which contemplate the *saṁbhinnālambana* are realized on the first *bhūmi* and are accomplished on the third *bhūmi*.

8.17–18 *Śamatha* and *vipaśyanā* experience the three kinds of *samādhi* (ecstatic contemplation): 1) *savitarkasavicāra* (with logical examination), 2) *avitarkavicāramātra* (with trans-logical examination), and 3) *avitarkāvicāra* (free from trans-logical examination), and must be *upekṣā* (equanimous), being free from the two *upakleśa*s (contingent defilements), *laya* (inertia), and *auddhatya* (agitation).

8.19–23 The bodhisattva who has accomplished *śamatha* and *vipaśyanā* must now practise bodhisattva practices to be a *dharma-pratisaṁvedin* (one who has supernatural eloquence in teaching teachings) and an *arthapratisaṁvedin* (one who has supernatural eloquence in teaching truths), in order to realize the supernatural power to deliver *avavāda* omnisciently and omnipresently.[17] The *dharmapratisaṁvedin* here means one who is conversant in employing language, and the *arthapratisaṁvedin* one who is conversant in teaching philosophical truths. The latter *arthapratisaṁvedin* is expounded in detail in four alternative ways, perhaps because it is here for the first time that the yogācāras have begun to reflect on the philosophical foundations on which they will construct their mahāyānistic philosophy, later to develop into *ālayavijñāna* (subconsciousness of being-in-the-world), *trisvabhāva* (three essences of being-as-such), *vijñaptimātratā*, etc.

8.24 It is neither by his *śrutamayī prajñā* (wisdom attained through learning), nor by his *cintāmayī prajñā* (wisdom attained through understanding), but only by his *śamathavipaśyanābhāvanāmayī prajñā* (wisdom attained through repeated practice of concentration and contemplation) that the bodhisattva becomes the *arthapratisaṁvedī* for the purpose of liberating all saṁsāric existences.

8.25 The bodhisattva who has accomplished *śamatha* and *vipaśyanā* and is now practising to be the *dharma-* and the *arthapratisaṁvedin* has the *jñāna* contemplating the *saṁbhinnālambana* as well as the *darśana* (insight) contemplating the *asaṁbhinnālambana* (specific distinctions of the categories of objects).

8.26–28 The bodhisattva who has accomplished *śamatha* and *vipaśyanā* and is now practising to be the *dharma-* and the *arthapratisaṁvedin* must overcome (*vibhāvay-*) any and every *nimitta* (individual substance conceptually imagined) of *dharma*s (teachings) and *artha*s (truths) and even that of *tathatā* through the *śrutamaya-*, the *cintāmaya-*, and the *bhāvanāmayapratisaṁkhyā* contemplating the *vijñaptitathatā*.

---

17. The important terms *dharma-* and *arthapratisaṁvedin* must be traced back, on the one hand, to the *Śrāvakabhūmi* (Shukla ed.), 462, and, on the other, to the ninth bhūmi of the *Daśabhūmikasūtra* (Kondō ed.), 161–162 (Rahder ed. §N). In the former a śrāvaka accomplishes his *dhyāna* practices by acquiring the five *abhijñā*s through being *dharmapratisaṁvedin* and *arthapratisaṁvedin*. And in the latter a bodhisattva attains on the ninth *bhūmi* the four *pratisaṁvid*s: 1) *dharmapratisaṁvid*, 2) *arthapratisaṁvid*, 3) *niruktipratisaṁvid*, and 4) *pratibhānapratisaṁvid*. I think that here in SandhN the former is "mahāyānized" in relation to the latter, so that the Hīnayānistic supernatural power may now be reinterpreted as the bodhisattva's power to deliver *avavāda*. Cf. also BBh (Wogihara ed.), 258, where the four *bodhisatvapratisaṁvid*s are reinterpreted in accordance with the philosophy of BBh.

8.29–30 The bodhisattva who is now practising to be the *dharma-* and the *arthapratisaṁvedin* overcomes the ten most difficult to overcome *nimitta*s by means of the seventeen kinds of *śūnyatā*:

1. the *padavyañjananimtta* (individual substance of sentence and character) by means of the *sarvadharmaśūnyatā* (void- or zero-being of all teachings),
2. the *jātivināśasthityanyathātvasaṁtānānuvartananimitta* (individual substances of successive arising in continuity of being born, perishing, standing still and changing) by means of the *lakṣaṇaśūnyatā* (void- or zero-being of the [four] characteristics [of saṁsāric existence]) and the *anavarāgraśūnyatā* (void- or zero-being of beginningless and endless *saṁsāra*),
3. the *satkāyadṛṣṭi-* and the *asmimānanimitta*s (individual substances of conceiving the bodily subconsciousness as real and thinking "I am") by means of the *adhyātmaśūnyatā* (void- or zero-being of internal beings) and the *anupalambhaśūnyatā* (void- or zero-being of non-recognition),
4. the *bhogadṛṣṭinimitta* (individual substance of conceiving experienced objects) by means of the *bahirdhāśūnyatā* (void- or zero-being of external beings),
5. the *adhyātmasukha-* and the *bāhyapriyanimitta*s (individual substances of internal happiness and external pleasure) by means of the *bahirdhādhyātmaśūnyatā* (void- or zero-being of internal or external beings) and the *prakṛtiśūnyatā* (void- or zero-being of innate nature),
6. the *apramāṇanimitta* (individual substance of infinite beings) by means of the *mahāśūnyatā* (void- or zero-being of extensive beings),
7. the *adhyātmaśāntivimokṣanimitta* (individual substances of internal quietude and liberation) by means of the *saṁskṛtaśūnyatā* (void- or zero-being of the saṁsāric),
8. the *pudgalanairātmya-*, the *dharmanairātmya-*, the *vijñaptimātra-*, and the *paramārthanimitta*s (individual substances of the non-selfness of any persons, of the non-selfness of any beings, and that of the truth of appearing-consciousness-only) by means of the *atyantaśūnyatā* (void- or zero-being of ultimate beings), the *abhāvaśūnyatā* (void- or zero-being of non-being), the *abhāvasvabhāvaśūnyatā* (void- or zero-being of the essential being of non-being), and the *paramārthaśūnyatā* (void- or zero-being of the supreme truth),
9. the *asaṁskṛta-* and the *avikāranimitta*s (individual substances of the non-saṁsāric and of the non-evolving) by means of the *asaṁskṛtaśūnyatā* (void- or zero-being of non-saṁsāric beings) and the *anavakāraśūnyatā* (void- or zero-being of unlimited beings), and
10. the *śūnyatānimitta* (individual substance of void- or zero-being) by means of the *śūnyatāśūnyatā* (void- or zero-being of void- or zero-being).

8.31 The *śūnyatāsaṁgrahalakṣaṇa* (essential defining characteristics of void- or zero-being) is defined as the universal voidness (*virahitatā*) and non-existence in the sense that the *paratantra-* and the *pariniṣpannalakṣaṇa*s (defining characteristics of the dependently originated being and of the completely purified being) are void of any and every *parikalpitalakṣaṇa* (defining characteristic of conceptual imagined beings) of all the *saṁkleśa-* and the *vyavadānadharma*s (saṁsāric beings and purifying beings) and that the latter *parikalpitalakṣaṇa*s do not exist in the former *pariniṣpannalakṣaṇa*s.

8.32 *Śamatha* and *vipaśyanā* which comprise all kinds of *samādhi*s of śrāvakas, bodhisattvas, and tathāgatas have their cause in pure *śīla* (observing morality) and *śrutacintāmayadarśana*, have their result in pure *citta* (mind) and *prajñā* (wisdom), and have their function in liberating the bodhisattva from the bondage of *nimitta*s (individual substances conceptually imagined) and *dauṣṭhulya*s (subconscious conditions).

8.33 *Śamatha* and *vipaśyanā* have their respective *vibandha*s (obstructions) and *nīvaraṇa*s (obscurations) (each five in the total).

8.34 The bodhisattva practising *śamatha* and *vipaśyanā* experiences the five kinds of *cittavikṣepa* (dispersions of mind): 1) *manaskāra-vikṣepa* (dispersion caused by willing to contemplate), 2) *bāhyacitta-vikṣepa* (dispersion caused by externally oriented mind), 3) *adhyātma-cittavikṣepa* (dispersion caused by internally oriented mind), 4) *nimitta-vikṣepa* (dispersion caused by individual substances conceptually imagined), and 5) *dauṣṭhulyavikṣepa* (dispersion caused by subconscious conditions).

8.35 *Śamatha* and *vipaśyanā* are the *pratipakṣa*s (antidotes) of the respective *vipakṣa*s (opposites to be remedied) on the eleven *bhūmi*s from the first up to the *tāthāgatabhūmi*:

1. the *pratipakṣa* against the *āpāyikakleśakarmajanmasaṁkleśa*s (causality of defilements, acts, and rebirths to be reborn in unhappy being-in-the-world) on the first *bhūmi*,
2. " against the *sūkṣmāpattiskhalitasamudācāra*s (subtle offences being actually offended) on the second,
3. " against the *kāmarāga* (desire for the objects of desire) on the third,
4. " against the *samāpattisneha* and the *dharmasneha* (attachments to the higher levels of meditative concentration and to the truths) on the fourth,
5. " against the *ekāntavaimukhyābhimukhya* (extreme disgust) against *saṁsāra* and *ābhimukya* (extreme aspiration) to *nirvāṇa* on the fifth,
6. " against the *bahunimittasamudācāra*s (number of individual substances conceptually imagined being actualized) on the sixth,
7. " against the *sūkṣmanimittasamudācāra*s (subtle individual substances conceptually imagined being actualized) on the seventh,

8. the *pratipakṣa* against the *samārambha* (effort) toward the *ānimitta* (freedom from any individual substance conceptually imagined) state and of the *avaśitā* (imperfect mastery) in the *nimitta* state on the eighth,
9. " against the *avaśitā* in the *sarvākāradharmadeśanā* (teaching all varieties of teachings) on the ninth,
10. " against the non-attainment of the *dharmakāyaparipūraṇa-pratisaṁvids* (supernatural eloquences in teaching truths in order to complete the Truth-Body of Buddhas) on the tenth, and
11. " against the *sūkṣma paramasūkṣmakleśajñeyāvaraṇas* (subtlest of the subtle obscurations of defilements and of the truths to be known) on the *tathāgatabhūmi*.

8.36 The bodhisattva who has been practising *śamatha* and *vipaśyanā* accomplishes *anuttarasamyaksaṁbodhi* (supreme and complete awakening) through the *darśanamārga* and the *bhāvanāmārga*, respectively defined as follows:

1. the *darśanamārga* accomplishes the *vastuparyantatālmbana* (ultimate reality being realized *in toto* as the contemplated object) by realizing the seven kinds of *tathatā* and thus concentrating his mind so as to be equanimous and free from any *samudācāras* (actualizations) even of the *sūkṣmanimittas* (subtle individual substances conceptually imagined) such as *cittādānanimitta* (individual substance of attaching to one's own mind), *anubhavanimitta* (individual existence of direct experience), *vijñaptinimitta* (individual substance of appearing-consciousness), etc., and
2. the *bhāvanāmārga* accomplishes the *kāryapariniṣpattyālambana* (perfection of supernatural acts of bodhisattvas and Buddhas as the contemplated object) by contemplating the same *vastuparyantatālambana* higher and higher on the higher and higher *bhūmis*, so as to extirpate all the *nimittas* and *dauṣṭhulyas* in the way as hammering one peg in order to pull out another.

8.37 The bodhisattva who has been practising *śamatha* and *vipaśyanā* as taught so far accomplishes the infinite supernatural power (*mahāprabhāva*) through being conversant with the six conditions of all saṁsāric existences to deliver *avavāda* to them:

1. through being conversant with how their *citta* arises (*cittasyotpattikuśala*),
2. " with how their *citta* is concentrated (*sthitikuśala*),
3. " with how their *citta* is averted from the *nimitta*- and *dauṣṭhulya*-bondages (*vyutthānakuśala*),
4. " with how their *citta* increases to counteract the two bondages (*vṛddhikuśala*),
5. " with how their *citta* decreases so as to annihilate the two bondages (*hānikuśala*), and

6. " with how their *citta* attains the supernatural meditations (*upāyakuśala*).

The first condition how their *citta* arises is further expounded in detail as how the *citta* arises as the sixteen kinds of *citta*, as follows:

1. their *citta* arises as the *asaṁviditakadhruvabhājanavijñapti* (subconscious appearing as various kind of objects),
2. " as the *vividhākārālambanavijñapti* (consciousness appearing as various kinds of objects),
3. " as the *parīttanimittālambanavijñapti* (consciousness appearing as the object which is the narrow individual substance),
4. " as the *mahadgatanimittālambanavijñapti* (consciousness appearing as the object which is the extensive individual substance),
5. " as the *apramāṇanimittālambanavijñapti* (consciousness appearing as the object which is the infinite individual substance),
6. " as the *sūkṣmanimittālambanavijñapti* (consciousness appearing as the object which is the subtle individual substance),
7. " as the *niṣṭhāgatanimittālambanavijñapti* (consciousness appearing as the object which is the ultimate individual substance),
8. " as the *animittavijñapti* (consciousness appearing as the freedom from any individual substance),
9. " as the *duḥkhasaṁprayukta* (being united with suffering feelings),
10. " as the *miśravedanāsaṁprayukta* (being united with mixed feelings),
11. " as the *prītisaṁprayukta* (being united with pleasant feelings),
12. " as the *sukhasaṁprayukta* (being united with happy feelings),
13. " as the *aduḥkhāsukhasaṁprayukta* (being united with neither suffering nor happy feelings),
14. " as the *saṁkleśasaṁprayukta* (being united with the causality of suffering),
15. " as the *kuśalasaṁprayukta* (being united with good acts), and
16. " as the *avyākṛtasaṁprayukta* (being united with neither good acts nor bad acts).

Here the first *citta* is identified as the *ādānavijñāna* (subconsciousness of being-possessed-of-body), the second as the *sakṛdrūpādiviṣayodgraha* (simultaneous cognitions of color-and-form and other objects, i.e., *pañca cakṣurādivijñānāni*, or the five perceptive consciousnesses such as the eye-consciousness and others), *vikalpamanovijñāna* (consciousness of conceptual imagination and thinking), etc., and all the other *citta*s are enumerated merely to exhaust all the specific modes of the *citta* on the saṁsāric and meditative levels of existences.

8.38 In the *nirupadhiśeṣanirvāṇadhātu* (the being of *nirvāṇa* or Extinction without any residue of being-possessed-of-body) all the *vedanā*s (feelings) consisting of the *āśrayadauṣṭhulyavedanā*s (feelings of the subconscious conditions of one's basis) and the *tatphalaviṣaya-vedanā*s (feelings of the experienced objects effected by the former) are annihilated without any residue.

The remaining sections, §§8.39–41, are the praising and recapitulating conclusion, and so I will stop my analysis of the philosophical structure of the Maitreya chapter of SandhN at this point.

Having thus analyzed the philosophical structure of the Maitreya chapter, I may now recognize the *avavāda* structure of the *vijñaptimātra* contemplation of this chapter in the following facts: 1) One of the two foundations of the bodhisattva's practice, the *dharmaprajñaptivya-vasthāna* (philosophical theories teaching Buddhist truths) taught in §8.1, must be instructed either with or without language to the heart of the initiatory bodhisattva in the *avavāda* of Buddhas and bodhisattvas. 2) The *ālambanavijñaptimātra* (consciousness-only appearing as objects) in §8.7 must be understood as instructed and inspired in the *avavāda* by the *mahāprabhāva* (infinite supernatural power) of §8.37 which is conversant with the *citta* arising as the *asaṁviditaka-dhruvabhājanavijñapti* (subconsciousness appearing as the receptacle world being constantly there and invisible), the *vividhākārālambana-vijñapti* (consciousness appearing as various forms of objects), the *parīttanimittālambanavijñapti* (consciousness appearing as the object which is the narrow individual substance), etc. This *avavāda* structure of the *vijñaptimātra* contemplation, consisting in the identification of the *vijñaptimātra* of the first contemplation with that of the last *mahāprabhāva*, is the most fundamental. I will discuss this point further. 3) The *vijñaptimātratā* contemplation in §§8.9–15 leads to *tathatā* or *śūnyatā*, because the former is instructed and inspired by the *avavāda* which is nothing but the supernatural act realized freely and without *nimitta* on the basis of *tathatā* or *śūnyatā*. 4) The bodhisattva practices to become the *dharma-* and the *arthapratisaṁvedin* in §§8.19–28 must be understood as those to attain the bodhisattva's supernatural power to deliver *avavāda* freely and without *nimitta*. 5) The seventeen kinds of *śūnyatā* introduced from the *Pañcaviṁśatikā Prajñāpāramitā* in §§8.29–30 may be the starting-point to define what is to be known by the *arthapratisaṁvedin* and so what is to be instructed and inspired in the *avavāda*.[18] 6) The bodhisattva practices on the eleven *bhūmis* in §8.35 culminate in the supernatural act of *avavāda* here termed the *sarvākāradharmadeśanā* (teaching all varieties of teachings) and the *dharmakāyaparipūraṇa-pratisaṁvids* (supernatural eloquences in teachings truths in order to complete the Truth-Body of Buddhas). 7) The infinite supernatural power (*mahāprabhāva*) in §8.37 is nothing but the perfection of the *dharma-* and the *arthapratisaṁvids* to deliver *avavāda* freely and without *nimitta*. Thus in continuation to the new stratum of BBh discussed in §1, the Maitreya chapter of SandhN is trying to establish the new *mārga*-system of the bodhisattva centering around the *vijñaptimātratā* with the *avavāda*-structure as its formative principle. Then what is fundamentally revolutionary here? I think that the concepts *vijñapti* and *vijñāna* are revolutionary. How? Let me try to explain briefly.

In one of the joint-seminars referred to above, Professor Schmithausen and I had a lengthy and heated discussion over how to back-translate into Sanskrit the crucial sentence of §8.7—"the oldest extant passage enouncing the doctrine of *vijñaptimātra*" as Professor Schmithausen puts it—on the basis of all the available Chinese and Tibetan translations and commentaries. I proposed to solve the minute discrepancies among those sources by back-translating the sentence into the Sanskrit as follows:

**ālambanaṁ vijñaptimātraprabhāvitaṁ vijñānaṁ*

The objects are (nothing but) consciousness which has been instructed by the supernatural power to be consciousness-only appearing as objects.

Professor Schmithausen criticized this and argued for his previously attempted back-translation, namely:

**ālambanavijñaptimātraprabhāvitaṁ vijñānaṁ*

It has been instructed by the supernatural power that consciousness is consciousness-only appearing as objects.

Later he published a very exhaustive philological examination of the sentence in support of his own back-translation.[19] Here I need not add any philological examination of the sentence, for I now

18. I have come to this conclusion by noticing a remarkable parallelism between the list of the *arthas* in §8.20 and the list of the *arthapratisaṁvedins* corresponding to some of the seventeen *śūnyatās* in §8.29. A further study is needed to account for the lists of the *arthas* in §§8.20–8.23.

19. Cf. Lambert Schmithausen, "On the Vijñaptimātra Passage in SandhN VIII.7," *Studies of Mysticism in Honor of the 1150th Anniversry of Kobo-daishi's Nirvāṇam, Acta Indologica*, vol. VI, 1984.

accept Professor Schmithausen's back-translation not only on the basis of the philological examination of the sentence so superbly carried out by him, but more fundamentally on the basis of my own philosophical understanding of the *avavāda* structure of the *vijñapti-mātra-* contemplation as pointed out above. If I may recognize the *avavāda* structure of the *vijñāna* being defined in the sentence, then this *vijñāna* of the initiatory bodhisattva beginning to contemplate the *vijñaptimātra* at this *pṛthagjana* level must be identified, or rather must originally have been identical, with the three-layered *vijñāna*: the *ādānavijñāna* (subconsciousness of being-possessed-of-body), the *manovijñāna* (consciousness of conceptual imagination and thinking), and the *pañcavijñānas* (five perceptive consciousnesses), as instructed and inspired in the *avavāda* by the *prabhāva* of §8.37. I think that this is fundamentally revolutionary, because the fundamental concept of Early Buddhism, *vijñāna*, which has been developing into the three layered *vijñāna*: the *ādāna-*, the *mano-*, and the *pañcavijñānas* in the Vastusaṁgrahaṇī Portion of YBh,[20] has now in this chapter begun to be identified with that *vijñāna* to be instructed in the *avavāda* by the supernatural act of the *mahāprabhāva*, and therefore with the *vijñāna* appearing as the *asaṁviditakadhuruvabhājana* (the receptacle world being constantly there and invisible), the *vividhākārālaṁbanas* (various kinds of objects), the *parīttanimittālaṁbanas* (the object which is the narrow individual substance), and so on, without any such external *ālaṁbanas*. It must here be remembered that the *ādikarmika* (beginning to practice) bodhisattvas receive *avavāda* from Tathāgatas and the latter deliver *avavāda* to the former only on the foundation of the Mahāyānistic fundamental truth *tathatā* or *śūnyatā*. Therefore the Early Buddhist *vijñāna* is here for the first time brought into relation with the Mahāyānistic *tathatā* or *śūnyatā* so that the former may be re-interpreted as receiving *avavāda* and the latter as delivering *avavāda*. To the question "whence the *vijñaptimātratā*?" I must answer that the *vijñaptimātratā* is an outcome of the new movement among the Yogācāras to synthesize the Early Buddhist *vijñāna* and the Mahāyānistic *tathatā* or *śūnyatā* into one coherent philosophy through recognizing their interacting *avavāda* structure: *avavāda*-receiving and *avavāda*-delivering, respectively.[21] The crucial passage of the original

20. Professor Schmithausen is fully aware of this precursory development of the *ādāna-* and the *ālayavijñāna* in the Vastusaṁgrahaṇī portion in his fundamental study on the *ālayavijñāna*: L. Schmithausen, *Ālayavijñāna, On the Origin and the Early Development of a Central Concept of Yogācāra Philosophy*, Tokyo, 1987, §1.3.5 on the *sopādānaṁ vijñānaṁ* and n. 81.

enunciation of the *vijñaptimātra* must be interpreted in relation to §8.37 as follows:

The fundamental concept of Early Buddhism, *vijñāna*, which has been developing into the three layered *ādāna-*, *mano-*, and *pañcavijñānas*, is now supernaturally taught (*prabhāvita*) to be appearing as the *asaṁviditakadhruvabhājana*, the *vividhākārālambana*, the *parītta-nimittālambana*, etc., without any such external *ālambanas* (namely *ālambanavijñaptimātra*), and therefore is leading to the mahāyānistic fundamental truth *tathatā* or *śūnyatā*.

I think that if interpreted in this way this definition of *vijñāna* is fundamentally revolutionary, because it is here for the first time in the history of Buddhism[22] that the fundamental truth of Early Buddhism, *vijñāna*, is brought into relation with that of Mahāyāna Buddhism, *tathatā* or *śūnyatā*, so that 1) the former *vijñāna* develops into the multi-layered *ādāna-*, *mano-*, and *pañcavijñānas* appearing as the *ālambanas* without any external *ālambanas*, 2) the latter *tathatā* or *śūnyatā* also develops to be analyzed into the *trisvabhāvas* as already evident in §8.31, and finally 3) these two, the *vijñāna* and *tathatā* or *śūnyatā*, are practically mediated by this very *bodhisattvamārga* contemplating the *vijñaptimātratā*. Henceforth a new era is opened to create and develop Yogācāra-Vijñānavāda philosophy as *the* philosophy of Buddhism—a synthesis of Early and Mahāyāna Buddhisms: 1) the *ādāna-* or the *ālayavijñāna* (subconsciousness of being-in-the-world) will further be elaborated to be the fundamental truth of the *saṁkleśa* (causality of suffering) inherited from Early Buddhism, 2) the *trisvabhāvas* to be that of the *vyavadāna* (purifying being) inherited from Mahāyāna Buddhism, and 3) the *vijñaptimātratā* to be that of the *bodhisattvamārga* converting from the former to the latter. Once this new philosophical movement started among Yogācāras, they seem to have been bifurcated into the two schools: the conservative Yogācāras and the progressive Maitreya devotees, the former being

---

21. So far I have tried to propose the *avavāda* structure of the Maitreya chapter of SandhN as the very clue to explain the "whence" of the *vijñaptimātratā*. In this connection I would like to note that one of the motives of the present paper has been to understand the reason why the *Mahāyānasūtrālaṁkāra* expounds the full course of the *vijñaptimātratā* contemplation of the *bodhisattvamārga* in its Avavādānu-śāsanā section. I believe that the reason is now evident.

22. I do admit that Nāgārjuna's fundamental truth *śūnyatā* is open and related to that of Early Buddhism, *pratītyasamutpāda*, whose fundamental truth is *vijñāna*, but Nāgārjuna was concerned to establish *śūnyatā* as the fundamental truth and did not create a new philosophy to synthesize the two traditions of Buddhism.

more concerned to develop their older Yogācāra tradition into the more Abhidharmic direction (the Maulī Portion of YBh, the *Abhidharmasamuccaya*, etc.) and the latter to synthesize the three fundamental truths, the *ālayavijñāna*, the *trisvabhāva*, and the *vijñaptimātratā* further into the two fundamental truths, *abhūtaparikalpa* (unreal conceptual imagination) and *śūnyatā* or *dharmadhātu* (being-as-creativity) (the *Dharmadharmatāvibhāga*, the *Madhyāntavibhāga*, the *Mahāyānasūtrālaṁkāra*, etc.). With this historical background accepted, I may say that the definition of *vijñāna* in §8.7 of SandhN with its *avavāda* structure is indeed the starting-point for the following development of Yogācāra-Vijñānavāda philosophy and therefore is the origin of the *vijñaptimātratā*.

Epilogue

The present paper might look as if very much dependent upon Professor Schmithausen, my indebtedness to whom is so evident, but what I have endeavored to demonstrate here is not my dependence upon this now leading great scholar of Western Buddhist studies, but rather my independence from him, by which alone I have been able to have discussions with him, I hope, on the same ground—just because I have been educated here in Japan by another great scholar, Professor G. M. Nagao, to whose longevity this paper is cordially dedicated. Have I been able to show that the convertibility which Professor Nagao in his younger days has proposed as the fundamental structure of Yogācāra-Vijñānavāda philosophy does indeed prove to have played the fundamental role in the formation of this philosophy, if it is interpreted as the *avavāda* structure discussed in the paper?

Appendix

[the old stratum of BBh]	[the new stratum of BBh]	[the *Mahāyānasūtrālaṅkāra*]
		1 mahāyānasiddhi
		2 śaraṇagamana
1 ādhāra		
1.1 gotra		3 gotra
1.2 cittotpāda		4 cittotpāda
	(*yatra śikṣante*)	
	1.3 svaparārtha	5 pratipatti
	1.4 tattvārtha	6 tattva
	1.5 prabhāva	7 prabhāva
	1.6 paripāka	8 paripāka
	1.7 bodhi	9 bodhi
	(*yathā śikṣante*)	
	1.8 balagotra	
	1.8.1 adhimukti	10 adhimukti
	1.8.2 dharmaparyeṣaka	11 dharmaparyeṣṭii
	1.8.3 dharmadeśaka	12 deśanā
	1.8.4 dharmānudharmapratipanna	13 pratipatti
	1.8.5 samyagavavādānuśāsaka	14 avavādānuśāsanā
	1.8.6 upāyaprigṛhītakāyavāṅmanaḥkarma	15 upāyasahitakarma
(1.3 =) 1.9 dāna		16 pāramitā

(1.4 =) 1.10 śīla (including the bodhisattvaśīla of the new stratum)		
(1.5 =) 1.11 kṣānti		
(1.6 =) 1.12 vīrya		
(1.7 =) 1.13 dhyāna		
(1.8 =) 1.14 prajñā		
(1.9 =) 1.15 saṁgrahavastu		[17] saṁgrahavastu
	1.16 pūjāsevāpramāṇa	[18] pūjāsevāpramāṇa
	1.17 bodhipakṣya	[19] bodhipakṣa
	(*ye śikṣante*)	
	1.18 bodhisattvaguṇa	[20] guṇa
		21 caryāpratiṣṭhā
2 liṅga		21.1 liṅga
3 pakṣya		21.2 gṛhipravrajita-pakṣa
4 adhyāśaya		21.3 adhyāśaya
	5′ vihāra	
5 upapatti		21.4 parigraha
6 parigraha		21.5 upapatti
7 bhūmi		21.6 vihārabhūmi
8 caryā		21.7 caryā
9 lakṣanānuvyañjana		21.8 buddhaguṇa
10 pratiṣṭhā		

Samādhi in Hōnen's Hermeneutic of Practice and Faith

Assessing the *Sammai hottokki*

Mark L. Blum

I. Samādhi in Kamakura Pure Land Buddhism

The tremendous historical impact in Japan of the life and teachings of Hōnen is evidenced by the hagiography surrounding him that began not long after his death in 1212. Excluding the biographical material on Hōnen found within medieval nonsectarian works, such as *Gyokuyō* (玉葉, 1200), *Meigetsu-ki* (明月記, 1235), and *Azuma-kagami* (吾妻鏡, 1288–1306), at least fifteen biographies of Hōnen were written prior to the Muromachi period. This is testimony not only to the widespread influence of the charismatic living Hōnen, but also to the appeal of his image as sincere and insightful teacher to subsequent generations.

Among this material can be found a fairly consistent story which groups together Hōnen's religious experiences during states of *samādhi*, or meditative trance. These accounts relate extraordinary sensory events such as hearing the voices of heavenly birds, seeing Amitābha Buddha in different forms, or viewing some of the special attributes of that Buddha's realm known as Sukhāvatī. In the creed of twentieth-century sectarian Pure Land Buddhism in Japan, both in the Jōdo-shū and Jōdo Shinshū schools within which Hōnen is revered either as sectarian founder (Jōdo-shū) or inspirational mentor to the sectarian founder (Jōdo Shinshū), Hōnen's core message is encapsulated in his *Senchaku hongan nembutsu-shū* (hereafter *Senchakushū*) in which a pivotal, possibly even exclusive, focus on recitation *nembutsu* is presented as the raison d'être of Pure Land Buddhism precisely because it does not demand a highly focused state of mind. The role of samādhi practice in Pure Land Buddhism is a crucial and complex one, and in this paper I will limit my focus to the role of samādhi in the thought of Hōnen and its implications for our understanding of his notion of praxis. In all standard collections of Hōnen's writings there is nevertheless a group of materials which reference his trance experiences in samādhi states, among them an autobiographical account of his samādhi visions known as the *Sammai hottokki* (三昧發得記) or "Record of Samādhi Attainments."[1] This document is in the form of a personal testimony of Hōnen's samādhi visions experienced between 1198 and 1206, the period of his greatest influence, and has been enigmatic for the tradition because samādhi attainment requires an extreme degree of meditative concentration. To wit, if Hōnen had worked so hard to establish a new form of Buddhism in which difficult meditations are rejected for the more universal, easier approach of *nembutsu*, why would he himself be earnestly engaged in samādhi practice and so committed to it that he felt the need to leave behind a record of his experiences/attainments for his students to emulate?

I would like to suggest that the difficulty scholars have had with this material stems more from a faulty model of interpretation than from the content of the material itself. Although admittedly not a paradigm found in the original literature, I believe much confusion has resulted from an unwitting confusion between what are the two axial themes of so-called Pure Land Buddhism: soteriology and praxis. Careful reading of the *Senchakushū* reveals Hōnen's strong concern with delineating his position in both areas. In fact it has been the disagreement about the precise relationship between these two issues that has led to repeated schisms throughout the history of Japanese Pure Land Buddhism. In the twentieth century as well, what can only be described as apologist attempts to maintain the historical integrity of the Hōnen biographical material have resulted in struggles to justify the legitimacy of this record of Hōnen's samādhi attainments on a soteriological level at the expense of considering the significance of the text in terms of religious practice. But this attitude is not surprising if one recalls that it is in this very same *Senchakushū* that Hōnen raises questions of practice to a soteriological level in a way most unusual in the Buddhist tradition by arguing that recitation *nembutsu* has been designated by Amida Buddha himself as the optimal practice for anyone aiming at the goal of rebirth in his realm. What marks Hōnen's stance as new is his affirming that our *choice* of practice may have more of a direct consequence upon our salvation than our *ability* to do it. Here we move from traditional monastic Buddhism's unipolar valuing of *attainment* to a new scheme in which *commitment* to a certain set of religious values becomes equally esteemed alongside the attainments of practice or, viewed in another way, the measure of one's ability to adopt these religious values is itself a kind of attainment.[2] The very existence of a text like the *Sammai hottokki*

---

1. Cf. the authoritative collections of Hōnen's works for the Jōdo-shū, such as Ishii Kyōdō, ed., *Shōwa shinshū Hōnen Shōnin zenshū* (Kyoto: Heirakuji, 1955), 863–867, and Jōdo-shū Kaishū Happyaku-nen Kinen Kyōsan Junbi-kyoku, ed., *Jōdo-shū zensho* (third ed., Tokyo: Sankibō Bussho-rin, 1990): 9.454–455, 16.179–181, and the summary in 17.425.

tells us that recitation *nembutsu* practice as conceived of by Hōnen, despite his justification of its unique status in the *Senchakushū* and elsewhere in terms of its ease of performance, was never meant to be a formulaic ritual. My conclusion, rather, is that Hōnen located its value precisely in its efficacy as a means to the attainment of samādhi.

One of Hōnen's important statements on praxis lies in chapters 2 and 3 of the *Senchakushū*[3] in which he presents an outline of one of his hierarchies of practice, this one clearly based on the writings of the T'ang dynasty monk Shan-tao (善導, 613–681), in particular his *Kuan wu-liang shou ching shu.*[4] It discriminates first between practices which contribute to the religious goal of Birth in the Pure Land (called proper or critical practices, 正行) and those practices not specific to the Pure Land tradition (labeled as miscellaneous, 雑行), which include other religious goals. This phrasing is found in Shan-tao's treatise in which he begins this section with the poignant phrase, "one approaches practice in order to establish his belief/faith."[5] Chapter 2 lists five critical Pure Land practices which are also gleaned from Shan-tao: sūtra-chanting, contemplation, reverence, recitation of the Buddha's name, and giving praise and offerings.[6] Among these, Hōnen then selects recitation of the Buddha's name as the practice "chosen" by Amida Buddha based upon Hōnen's own reading of the Eighteenth Vow of the *Sukhāvatīvyūha sūtra.* The other four so-called Pure Land practices are thus relegated to a secondary category as "ancillary" (助業). In chapter 3, on the other hand, there is quite a different sort of discussion wherein different practices are recognized as leading to Birth in different Buddha lands, all of which can be considered "purified lands" because a Buddha is present.[7] Included

---

2. Ryūkan, for example, spoke in terms of different vows among the forty-eight enumerated in the *Sukhāvatīvyūha-sūtra* as being appropriate for different people, depending on their nature.

3. T. 83.2c14–6c9.

4. 觀無量壽經疏 *Kanmuryōju-kyō sho.* T. 37.245ff.

5. T. 37.272a28: *chiu-hsing li-hsin* (就行立信). This sentiment is echoed in the popular title of Shinran's magnum opus, the *Kyōgyōshinshō*, in which the order of the chapters—teaching (*kyō*), practice (*gyō*), faith (*shin*), realization (*shō*)—expresses the ideal sequence of an adept's spiritual progress.

6. T. 83.2c18ff. This list should not be confused with a similar list of five practices found in the *Ch'ing-tu lun* of Vasubandhu and generally referred to as the *wu-nien men/gonen mon* (五念門): worship of the Buddha image (禮拝門), invoking the name of Amitābha (讃嘆門), vowing to be born in the Pure Land (作願門), meditation on the splendor of the Pure Land (觀察門), and transferring merit to other sentient beings (廻向門).

among this latter group are both *bodhicitta* and the six perfections, that is, the *pāramitās* which normally form the backbone of any Mahāyāna *mārga* system. Hōnen's hermeneutic is such that these other forms of praxis were accepted but categorized as less efficacious, requiring a transfer of merit (*pariṇāma*, *ekō* 廻向) in order to bring an individual to the stated goal of birth in the Pure Land.

This scheme speaks of the often overlooked point that Hōnen clearly recognized the soteriological efficacy of practices which stemmed from mainstream Mahāyāna doctrines, even specifically for his stated goal of Birth in a Buddhaland. This suggests that the proper hermeneutic for reading Hōnen on practice, even one based solely on the *Senchakushū*, affirms a priority for recitation *nembutsu* which, while relegating other practices to a status of secondary efficacy, does not entirely reject them as counterproductive to the necessarily intermediate but nonetheless salvific goal of Birth in the Pure Land. It is thus a mistake to read too much exclusive implication in these terms, "ancillary" (*jo* 助) and "miscellaneous" (*zō* 雑), as Hōnen does not deny the soteriological value of these doctrines. Admittedly, in his discussion of the term *ikkō* 一向 within chapter 4 of the *Senchakushū*,[8] Hōnen implies a level of exclusivity regarding *nembutsu* practice that is not found in the *Wu-liang shou ching*, wherein those devoted to this practice are clearly urged to put forth the *bodhicitta*. But the form of this argument is such that *nembutsu* is the consequence or conclusion of all other forms of practice; as such *nembutsu* supersedes other forms of praxis without necessarily disparaging them.[9] In this approach the values associated with other practices traditional to the Mahāyāna path are also embraced; it is no coincidence, therefore, that this section of the sūtra also promises a samādhi vision of the Buddha on one's deathbed for those who take joy in hearing the Dharma, and manages to put forth even one *nembutsu*:

> If someone hears (this) profound Teaching and is overcome with a joy of faith that does not give rise to troublesome doubt, if he can then concentrate on that buddha (i.e., *nembutsu*) for just a single thought-moment (*nen*) and sincerely yearn for birth in that realm, when this person is facing death he will have a vision of that Buddha, obtaining Birth in the Pure Land (*ōjō*).[10]

---

7. T. 83.5b6ff.

8. T. 83.7a27.

9. At least this is the interpretation in the standard modern reference work on the *Senchakushū*, Ishii Kyōdō, *Senchakushū zenkō* (Kyoto: Heirakuji Shoten, 1974) 234, which skillfully pulls together an assortment of interpretations found in premodern canonical commentaries.

The encounter with a buddha in this important passage refers to what the East Asian tradition calls *chien-fo* (見佛 Jpn: *kenbutsu*) and is not limited to deathbed experiences, even in this same sūtra. The soteriological implications of having a "vision of the Buddha" are based in the orthodox tradition of *buddhānusmṛti-samādhi* introduced to East Asia with translations of such texts as the *Pan-chou san-mei ching* (般舟三昧經, *Pratyutpanna buddhasammukhāvasthita-samādhi sūtra*) from as early as the second century,[11] and elucidated in Chih-i's *Mo-ho chih-kuan* and Shan-tao's *Kuan-nien fa-men*, traditions that undergird Hōnen's hermeneutic. The importance for our discussion here is the clear link between *kenbutsu* and *ōjō* or Birth in the Pure Land. In reading Kamakura texts, it becomes clear to one that the experience of *ōjō* was understood by Hōnen and his contemporaries as essentially a samādhi experience. The argument put forth compellingly by Hōnen, and largely accepted by the populace judging by the enormity of his popularity, was that the one practice most likely to result in attaining the spiritual goal of reaching a pure Buddha Land is decidedly recitation *nembutsu*, regardless of whether one understands the soteriological implications of attaining a vision of Amida Buddha during the experience of what is essentially a *buddhānusmṛti-samādhi.*[12]

What is the nature of this valuing of *nembutsu*? Does this critical position necessarily imply an exclusivity toward other practices, or rather is it a statement intended to determine what is first among equals? Hōnen's focus on the soteriological dimension of praxis itself resulted in this critical problematic remaining for subsequent generations to debate, and the competing schools of the Hōnen legacy all define themselves to some degree on this point. There is no small amount of literature on this subject in Japanese, but the scholar must be wary of certain a priori assumptions which inevitably mask sectarian

---

10. T. 12.272c7–10.

11 See Lokakṣema's translations at T. 13.897 and 13.902.

12. Of course, the Chinese word *nien-fo* 念佛 was originally selected as a translation for *buddhānusmṛti* because of the previous use of the word *nien* 念 to translate *smṛti* which contained the primary meanings of "recall from memory" and "concentration." The practice of meditating or concentrating on a Buddha in such texts as the *Pratyutpanna-samādhi sūtra* (般舟三昧經) thus created the word *nien-fo* 念佛 to refer to recalling the image of a Buddha and holding it in mind. Even in this early sūtra, however, recitation of the name of the Buddha was one method of practicing such concentration. In this context Hōnen, as well as all subsequent Japanese Pure Land schools, based his creed upon the concept of *nembutsu* interpreted such that it specifically denoted recitation practice.

interests regarding Hōnen as the person who opened up Buddhism for the populace as a whole.

There was certainly nothing new in promoting the recitation of the Buddha's name as a central practice in Pure Land Buddhism, as Shan-tao is Hōnen's authority for this position. The key to the way in which Hōnen changed the paradigm lies in how he imbued the *nembutsu* with a religious significance beyond praxis. Although Shan-tao promises to those who engage in the proper practices that ten out of ten will reach the Pure Land and only one in a thousand who pursue the mixed practice path will achieve that goal, in my view Hōnen went one step further and raised the *nembutsu* from practice to the status of salvific symbol. After Hōnen, the *nembutsu* symbolized the meeting point between Buddha and "ordinary people" (*pṛthagjana*, 凡夫 Jpn: *bonbu*), much as the Christ symbol came to be seen as the best articulated if not the only link between God and mankind. Against the background of the Kamakura period, with its series of natural and human disasters, Hōnen's message of soteriological hope in a seemingly godless age proved famously popular. But it was a message doubly coded with respect to practice.

If grasping the symbolic meaning of *nembutsu* as an act of faith has now become the defining religious act for the individual, what is the purpose of practice? Is it indeed proper to speak of "an act of faith" in this context? Do we find such language in this period? One is tempted to see something akin to the Western notion of faith in the term *anjin* (安心) which is used extensively at this time to express an attainment of a state of spiritual grace in Pure Land Buddhism. *Shinjin* is a synonym favored by the Jōdo Shinshū school, although Rennyo used *anjin* more frequently. But *anjin* and *shinjin* are terms with a long history in East Asian Buddhism.[13] *Anjin* does indeed express the dimension of salvific assurance, though not necessarily in a passive or *tariki* sense. It is often glossed as *pu-tong* (不動 immovable or unshakable), expressing a strength of confidence in one's own understanding. And in the Ch'an/Zen tradition, *anjin* is used to denote the state of having realized the Buddha nature within oneself. Thus

13. *Shinjin* is generally considered the more narrow of the two, yet it appears in Kumārajīva's translation of the *Diamond Sūtra* and also appears in the commentary on that text by the Hua-yen patriarch Chih-yen (T. 33.241c28). In the same context, we can also find the use of *anjin* by Chih-i in his *Diamond Sūtra* commentary (T. 33.77c4). Do these examples refer to the same meaning as found in Kamakura Pure Land Buddhist usage? While the doctrinal contexts may differ, the core meaning of reaching a religious or spiritual plateau marked by a sense of assurance is most likely common to usage in both medieval China and Japan.

if Hōnen's notion of faith is best expressed by the word *anjin*, then precedent in Buddhist commentarial usage outside of Pure Land thought should also be considered in unpacking the full implication of Hōnen's language. I would argue that the encapsulation of Hōnen's message in terms like *anjin* and *shinjin* had resonance precisely because these words embodied a sense of salvific attainment in East Asian Buddhism that is not specific to a Pure Land context. Seen from this perspective, our understanding of these terms in the writings of Hōnen, Shinran, and others of this period should properly reflect the religious aspirations of East Asian Buddhism as a whole.

Hōnen nevertheless did take a position which consciously implied for the first time in Japanese history that both laymen and less than ideal monastics had an avenue of religious liberation open to them within a Buddhist context that did not demand either mastery of elaborate Buddhist philosophy or success at the rigorous psychological demands of advanced meditative practice. It is a mistake, however, to assume that in taking such a position Hōnen thereby rejected the value of spiritual attainments normally associated with difficult, focused practices, as implied in the general use of the term *anjin* in Chinese Buddhist thought. In other words, it is important to recognize that the religious potential of *nembutsu* practice was never diminished by the emphasis placed on its accessibility. While Hōnen may have imbued *nembutsu* with new salvific significance, this only served to intensify the meaning understood in all soteriological schema associated with the term, among them the attainment of *buddhānusmṛti-samādhi*. A good example of this can be found in the same chapter in the *Senchakushū* in which, after his hierarchy of path, practice, and so on, Hōnen quotes Shan-tao to illustrate the value of pursuing the proper practice of *nembutsu*: "If sentient beings desire to have a vision of the Buddha (見佛), the Buddha will thereby respond to this *nen(butsu)* and appear before their eyes."[14]

After Hōnen's death, this religious message centered on the power of the *nembutsu* continued to evolve, arguably most creatively expressed in the teachings of Shinran, Kōsai, and Shōkū. Its religious significance expanded with Shinran, whereby its performative aspect became nearly

---

14. T. 37.268a10. Although basing his statement on the passage mentioned above from the *Wu-liang shou ching*, Shan-tao abbreviates *nembutsu* with simply *nen/nien* (念), and it is certainly possible to read this as indicating *citta* (state of mind) rather than calling out the Buddha's name. But within the context of Shan-tao's discussion here in the "concentrated good practice" section where *nembutsu-samādhi* is frequently mentioned, it is most plausible to read this as signifying *buddhānusmṛti*, whether verbally expressed or not.

totally absent in the traditional sense of training or cultivation. For Shinran, understanding the *meaning* of *nembutsu* thus implied the end of the *practice* of *nembutsu* in the sense of personal accomplishment. Aside from bending an ear toward the Dharma itself, the notion of an individual, independent contribution toward one's own birth in the Pure Land is thoroughly deconstructed by Shinran, and even listening to the Dharma reflects the will of all buddhas. As one is drawn deeper and deeper into the words of the Buddha, the working of the Buddha in the individual reveals a realm of pure wisdom and bliss; thus Shinran upwardly displaces the *nembutsu* even further. In Shinshū, therefore, the issue of the purpose of practice after attainment is resolved by the affirmation of *nembutsu* practice as an expression of gratitude to the Buddha.

Although there are many today who look to Shinran as the one Japanese religious thinker whose ideas seem closest to Western notions of faith, much of what many find sympathetic in Shinran can in fact be found in his teacher Hōnen. Nonetheless there are major differences between the two, one of which is the role of samādhi. Although there is no space here to address fully the role of samādhi in Jōdo Shinshū, it is worth noting that Shinran frequently affirms the soteriological significance of *nembutsu-samādhi* in both the chapter on practice and the chapter on faith in his *Kyōgyōshinshō* by using the voices of Tao-ch'o (who quotes the *Kuan-fo san-mei [hai] ching* 觀佛三昧[海]經), Fa-chao, Tz'u-min (quoting the *Pan-chou san-mei ching*), Shan-tao, and others.[15] Unlike Hōnen, however, there is no record of Shinran's own attainment of such, either within his own writings or in the hagiographic biographies of him. This is despite the fact that the attainment of *nembutsu-samādhi* continues to be an important religious theme in canonical Jōdo Shinshū writings even after Shinran,

15. See *Shinshū shōgyō zensho II*: 16–18, 29–31, 76–78, etc. The many quotes selected by Shinran for inclusion in his *Kyōgyōshinshō* reveal a strong reverence for the authority of the *nembutsu-samādhi* attainment. For example, Fa-chao (法照, 766–822) is quoted as declaring, "How could Ch'an or the Vinaya be the right dharma (*shōbō* 正法)? *Nembutsu-samādhi* is the true doctrine (*shinshū* 眞宗). One who sees his own-nature and apprehends his mind is thus a buddha. How could [this practice] not be in accord with the truth?" (24.4–5). Here Shinran appears to accept *nembutsu-samādhi* as representing the apogee of Pure Land practice. He avoids the "self-power" (*jiriki*) hermeneutic trap by quoting Yuan-chao (元照, 1048–1116), who distinguishes between self-power samādhi practice and the *nembutsu-samādhi* which occurs precisely because it relies on the Buddha's power (佛力) (28.11–29.1). Far from proscribing samādhi practice as one might expect, Shinran instead quotes the T'ien-t'ai figure Fei-hsi (飛錫, eighth century) whom he identifies as of the "Ch'an school," as stating that *nembutsu-samādhi* is the king of all samādhis (三昧王) (31.12).

as evidenced, for example, in its favorable treatment in Zonkaku's *Rokuyōshō* (六要鈔) and Rennyo's embrace of the *Anjin ketsujōshō*, a Kamakura *nembutsu-samādhi* text of obscure origins.

Insofar as Hōnen was explicit regarding the paramount esteem he afforded to the writings of Shan-tao, particularly Shan-tao's commentary on the *Kuan wu-liang-shou ching*—a Pure Land sūtra extolling various means to attain visionary experience of the Buddha and his realm—one should not be surprised to find that many of Hōnen's samādhi experiences mirror the thirteen visualization practices outlined in that sūtra, particularly visualizations one through six.[16] While these extraordinary experiences are depicted in the early biographical materials on Hōnen, none of these texts assign it a title as such. In the account in Shinran's *Saihō shinanshō* (西方指南鈔, 1258), for example, this is mentioned in the form of an entry merely under the title of the date when the visions begin: the first day of the first month, 1198.[17] But by 1275, some fifty years after Hōnen's death, the biographies have begun referring to these accounts by the title *Sammai hottokki*."[18]

Below I will present an overview of the historical problems associated with the origins of the text, some doctrinal problems raised by the existence of the text which have led to its authenticity having been questioned on doctrinal grounds, and finally, what the existence of texts like the *Sammai hottokki* tells us about Hōnen's view of praxis as well as the meaning and function of praxis in post-Hōnen Kamakura Pure Land Buddhism. Given the lack of an extant holograph, it is far from certain that the *Sammai hottokki* was actually authored by Hōnen. It is nonetheless significant that by the end of the thirteenth century the story of Hōnen's achievements in samādhi had become an integral part of his historical identity, suggesting that the contents of the *Sammai hottokki* had achieved widespread acceptance. In fact, fragments of the *Sammai hottokki* can be found in at least thirteen of the earliest Hōnen biographies,[19] and mention of Hōnen's samādhi attain-

---

16. T. 12.342a4–c11.

17. T. 83.866b5ff.

18. See below.

19. For example, *Hōnen Shōnin denki* (Daigo-ji ed.), *Hōnen Shōnin denki* (9-fascicle ed.), *Chion kōshiki, Shūigo tōroku, Saihō shinanshō, Genkū Shōnin shinikki, Honchō soshi denki eshi, Hōnen Shōnin denbō-e, Chion-den, Hōnen Shōnin e, Hōnen Shōnin den* (10-fascicle ed.), *Hōnen Shōnin den* (Zōjōji ed.), *Hōnen Shōnin gyōjō ezu*. Cf. Tomatsu Keishin 戸松啓真, "Hōnen Shōnin no *Sammai Hottokki* ni tsuite," *Chizan Gakuho* 智山学報 1/19 (1971).

ments deriving from the *Sammai hottokki* is also included in many premodern texts not specifically of Pure Land origin, such as the *setsuwa* texts *Kokonchomon-jū* (古今著聞集, 1254) by Tachibana no Narisue,[20] *Shijuhyaku innen-shū* (私聚百因縁集, 1257) by Jūshin,[21] as well as the *Genkōshakusho* (元亨釋書, 1322) by the Rinzai monk Kokan Shiren.[22]

II. The *Sammai hottokki*

Regarding the textual issues surrounding the *Sammai hottokki*, all canonical editions appear to derive from one of three or four early recensions of the text, and it is still unclear which should be taken as the earliest.[23] The colophon to the Daigoji text explains that Hōnen wrote down this information by himself and passed it to his disciple Genchi. This story, if authentic, not only means that Hōnen wanted this record to be part of his legacy but also reveals the importance he attached to this wish, as Genchi is thought to have been central to administration of his organization.

It is odd that no one has as yet considered the fact that the year in which Hōnen's samādhi record supposedly began, 1198, is the same year in which he wrote the *Senchakushū*. More specifically, the *Senchakushū* is said to have been written in the third month of that year and according to the *Sammai hottokki* text found in the earliest sources—the *Hōnen Shōnin denki* (法然上人傳記) and the *Saihō shinanshō*—Hōnen's samādhi record begins in the first day of the first month in the same year.[24] Without any evidence to the contrary, therefore, these dates show the *Sammai hottokki* record commencing at least two months prior to the completion of the *Senchakushū*, a work judging by its length and extensive quotations that must have taken him quite some time to put together. In other words, the story of the creation of these two works as recorded in the earliest sources attests to the fact that Hōnen was writing both at the same time.

20. *Kōchū Nihon bungaku taikei*, vol. 10; *Shintei zōho Kokushi taikei*; etc.

21. *Dainihon bukkyō zensho* (Suzuki ed.), vol. 92.

22. *Dainihon bukkyō zensho* (Suzuki ed.), vol. 62; *Shintei zōho Kokushi taikei* (Yoshikawa Kōbunkan ed.), vol. 31.

23. A number of studies have been done comparing the material in the various recensions of the *Sammai Hottokki*. The most helpful are those by Tomatsu; *ibid.*, Arashi Zuichō 嵐瑞徴, "Hōnen Shōnin no *Sammai Hottokki* no kenkyū," *Bukkyō Ronsō* 仏教論叢 17 (1973); and Tamura Enchō 田村圓澄, *Hōnen Shōnin-den* 法然上人伝 (Kyoto: Hōzōkan, 1983): 240ff.

24. See n. 15 on *Hōnen Shōnin denki*. The *Saihō-shinan-shō* is in T. 83.847ff.

This fact tells us that the tradition considered both the *Senchakushū* and the *Sammai hottokki* to represent his thinking at this critical time in the formation of his doctrinal conclusions.

Then why does the *Senchakushū* appear to have had so much more impact? One important consideration here is the contrast between the manners in which the texts were transmitted. As explained below, the *Sammai hottokki* was initially shown to only one student and after Hōnen's death passed on to only one other. It was never printed and only moves into the general literature associated with Hōnen through the evolution of his biographical literature. By contrast, the *Senchakushū* was supposedly written at the behest of the highest minister in the land (Kwampaku Kanezane), and was said to have been copied by a limited number of Hōnen's disciples only with the master's permission. But it was printed thirteen years after Hōnen's death, a highly unusual event for a treatise at this time, obviously with the purpose of achieving wide distribution. Although it is exceedingly difficult to evaluate the extent to which manuscripts and xylographs were available in thirteenth-century Japan, the *Senchakushū* becomes a public document from its first printing in 1239, and we know blocks were carved for its printing again in 1251 and twice more in the early fourteenth century. The *Sammai hottokki* by contrast is a short record rather than a philosophical or doctrinal treatise and therefore probably of little interest to those other than Jōdo scholars. To my knowledge it was never printed until modern times. Thus, while the origins of each as incorporated into the lore of Jōdo-shū were private, the *Senchakushū* quickly entered the "public" domain, while the *Sammai hottokki* came to be defined as a chapter, albeit with its own title, within the Hōnen biographies.[25]

Although their purposes may have been different, there remain important historical implications to be drawn from the simultaneous composition of both works, compelling us to review our assumptions about Hōnen's hermeneutic of practice and attainment as something

25. Today there is considerable doubt about this story of the origins of the *Senchakushū*. Moreover, the oldest text, a manuscript from Rōsanji, is not only significantly different from the extant early printed editions, it is also written in three different hands. This suggests either that Hōnen wrote one version for Kanezane and another for the public, or that the Kanezane story was invented to give authority to the work's origins after Hōnen's movement faced political suppression. The notion that Hōnen restricted the number of people for whom he would allow a copy to be made also has clear political implications with regard to the post-Hōnen religious community's efforts to determine which of Hōnen's many students should be considered proper "disciples."

different from that which was developed for the Jōdo-shū during the assiduous scholarship of the Tokugawa period. Although beyond the scope of this paper, modern views of Hōnen are deeply informed by the work of eighteenth- and nineteenth-century scholars who generally devalued samādhi attainment in their formulations of a credo centered on *nembutsu*.[26] But the discovery by Mochizuki Shinkō of the *Hōnen Shōnin denki* at Daigo-ji (this text is thus known as the *Daigo-bon* 醍醐本) has given new credibility to the *Sammai hottokki* for modern scholarship. Some postwar scholars have reacted to this need to re-evaluate the *Sammai hottokki* by dismissing it as apocryphal. In the famous words of Tamura Enchō, who made a thorough study of the early Hōnen biographies, the *Sammai hottokki* must be a forgery because it is "anti-Hōnen" in spirit.[27] Of course this "spirit" refers to the sectarian interpretation of the *Senchakushū*, in which religious attainment is postponed until one reaches the postmortem state or at the earliest one's deathbed. Is Tamura necessarily correct? If so, then who wrote the text, when, and why?

Because of the controversy over its content, consideration of the historical value of the *Sammai hottokki* has led modern scholarship to focus on which of the earliest biographies of Hōnen contain it, and in what form it appears. In this regard it is important to note that the samādhi record of Hōnen appearing in the *Saihō shinanshō* is extant in an autograph of Shinran, although many believe this material to be something Shinran copied rather than composed. This edition contains a colophon stating that the material was compiled by Shinran over a two-year period beginning in 1256, and whether or not Shinran actually wrote it based on his own notes, his choice to include this samādhi material indicates its significance to him.

Tamura uses the *Sammai hottokki* as one means to establish temporal links among many of the earliest Hōnen biographies. In this regard,

---

26. A good example of the now established decoupling of samādhi from *nembutsu* practice can be seen in the essay on *nembutsu* found in the *Jōdoshū daijiten* 3.156–157, which echoes contemporary scholarship based on the foundation created in the Tokugawa period within the Chinzei school. Only in referencing classical Chinese T'ien-t'ai *nembutsu* practice are *nembutsu* and samādhi linked, in this case in the *Wu-fang-men nien-fo men* attributed to Chih-i (538–597). But no such link is mentioned for Hōnen or the Jōdo-shū. On the Chinzei faction's writing on samādhi and *nembutsu* during the Kamakura period, see below.

27. The phrase in Tamura (1983) is *hi-hōnen teki* 非法然的 (p. 245). It is also worth mentioning that Tamura points out (43–49) that the so-called 48-fascicle biography of Hōnen, *Hōnen Shōnin gyōjō-ezu* 法然上人行状絵図, reverses this trend, implying a definite step towards consolidation of power by the Chinzei faction and therefore a changing political climate.

the *Daigo-bon* is of pivotal importance because it contains a number of individual items that appear for the first time and are frequently found in other versions of the *Sammai hottokki* that are included in later biographies, suggesting a kind of archetypal influence. The *Daigo-bon* itself is thought to be the product of someone in the faction led by Hōnen's disciple Genchi. In addition to the *Daigo-bon*, discussion of Hōnen's samādhi attainment also appears in the *Shi-nikki* (私日記) and *Denbō-e* (傳法繪, also referred to as the *Shikan-den* 四卷傳), two biographies of Hōnen considered to be products of a rival faction led by Shinkū, another influential disciple.[28] Although there is some controversy over the relationship between the *Shi-nikki* and the *Denbō-e* because they share much material, Tamura feels that whichever is the older of the two predates the *Daigo-bon* by a few years. All three probably date to the early 1240s, some thirty years after Hōnen's death.

Although both the *Shi-nikki* and *Denbō-e* present descriptions of the extra-sensory perceptions experienced by Hōnen during samādhi in a way similar to the discussion in the *Daigo-bon* of Genchi's lineage, it is important to note that none of these three sources formally segregate this material into an independent work. Even its entry in Shinran's *Saihō shinanshō* is marked only by a date. In comparing the accounts given in the *Shi-nikki* and the *Daigo-bon*, for example, the description in the *Shi-nikki* is relatively vague, short, and appears in a rather anecdotal manner. The *Daigo-bon* presentation contains more detail as well as the addition of a colophon explaining a secret transmission of this samādhi material from Hōnen to Genchi.[29] If we take this addition in the *Daigo-bon* to represent a significant reorganization of the material motivated by sectarian concerns, it would support Tamura's view that the texts of Shinkū's group predate the *Daigo-bon*. In any case, Hōnen's samādhi record appears as the prototype of a literary work for the first time in the *Daigo-bon*, perhaps as part of an effort to legitimate Genchi's faction among competing disciples in the post-Hōnen era. Although the appellation *Sammai hottokki* 三昧發得記 as such does not occur in the *Daigo-bon*, the germ of the title does appear in the colophon with the phrase "this record of samādhi attainment" 此三昧發得之記. This point is emphasized here because, contrary to the *Daigo-bon* manuscript where this material is not marked

---

28. Ikawa Jōkyō 井川定慶, ed., *Hōnen Shōnin den zenshū* 法然上人傳全集 (revised edition, Osaka: Hōnen Shōnin-den zenshū kankōkai, 1967), 769ff. for the *Shi-nikki*, and 512ff. for the *Denbō-e*.

29. Ikawa 1967, 789b.14 and 790b12.

by any title, the heading *Sammai hottokki* does appear in the standard printed editions of the *Daigo-bon* contained in both the *Hōnen Shōnin-den zenshū* as well as in the modern printed canon of the Jōdo sect, the *Jōdo-shū zensho*.[30] The earliest instance I have been able to trace of the appearance of the title *Sammai hottokki* is in the *Shūi-gotōroku* (拾遺語燈録) by Ryōe (了慧, d. 1330–1331),[31] composed between 1264 and 1275, that is, at least twenty years after the compilation of the *Daigo-bon*.[32]

We can thus discern three stages in the evolution of this samādhi material within sixty years of Hōnen's death: 1) an anecdotal record appearing in the *Shi-nikki*, *Denbō-e*, and *Saihō shinanshō*; 2) an organized and expanded presentation replete with transmission colophon in the *Daigo-bon*; and 3) a conscious recognition of this body of information as an independent text in Ryōe's *Shūi-gotōroku*.

The colophon to the *Sammai hottokki* as it appears in the *Daigo-bon*, although missing from the *Shūi-gotōroku*, was frequently copied in later biographies and thus came to be accepted de facto as the standard origin of the text. There it is explained that upon receiving the samādhi record from the master himself, Genchi kept the text hidden from all except Myōhen (明遍, 1142–1224),[33] a Shingon monk from Mt. Kōya who studied with Hōnen between 1171 and 1175.[34] This resulted in the work being unknown to the world until it was discovered or, as the colophon reads, "unintentionally transmitted," sometime after Genchi himself died in 1238. No reasons are given why Genchi

---

30. Ikawa 1967, 789b; see also *Jōdo-shū zensho* 17.43. This fact only came to light with the publication of a photographic reprint of the original text of the *Hōnen Shōnin denki* in *Tōdo Kyōshun hakase koki-kinen: Jōdoshū tenseki kenkyū—shiryō hen* 東堂恭俊博士古希古稀記念 浄土宗典籍研究一資料編, 230–237.

31. Full title: *Shūi Kurodani Shōnin gotōroku* 拾遺黒谷語燈録, in *Jōdo-shū zensho* (Tokyo: Sankibō, 1973), 9.454–455.

32. Another early work in which the title appears is the *Kangyōsho denzuki kenmon* 観經疏傳通記見聞 written by Shinran's disciple Kenchi (顕智, 1226–1310). Although this work cannot be dated precisely, it probably appeared slightly after the *Shūi-gotōroku*.

33. Ikawa 1967, 789b14–15.

34. Although a Shingon monk of Mādhyamika training, Myōhen is considered one of the typical *nembutsu-hijiri* of Kōya-san. Only ten years younger than Hōnen, Myōhen was seen as a younger contemporary of the master, as evidenced by his appearance in fascicle 16 of the *Hōnen Shōnin gyōjō e-zu*. In the next generation, his student Jōhen (静遍, 1166–1224) became one of Hōnen's most influential disciples. Both left a number of works on Pure Land thought from a Tantric perspective. Myōhen's biography can be found in the *Honchō kōsō-den*, fascicle 13: *Dainippon bukkyō zensho* 102.212 (1979 ed.). He is also mentioned in the *Myōgi shingyō-shū* by Shinzui 信瑞 (see below, n. 44).

felt the need to hide the work, nor why Myōhen enjoyed the unique privilege of being able to borrow it for his own edification. Moreover, the biographical information extant on Myōhen contains no mention of his having seen this text. A clue as to when the material was first edited lies in a comment in the *Daigo-bon* located at the end of the discussion of Hōnen's death and just prior to the beginning of what is demarcated as the *Sammai hottokki* in modern editions, which begins: "In the thirty years that have passed since Hōnen passed away...."[35] Since Hōnen died in 1212, we can thus conclude that either the *Sammai hottokki* or the section that preceded it, later titled *Gorinjū nikki* (御臨終日記), has a *terminus a quo* of 1241. Indeed, this reference to a post-mortem editing of thirty years may reflect the date of the editing of the entire *Daigo-bon*. The date of 1241 also corresponds to the colophon statement regarding the public disclosure of the *Sammai hottokki* sometime after Genchi's death in 1238.

When one compares the description of Hōnen's death in the *Saihō shinanshō* with that found in the *Daigo-bon*, one finds that the latter is more detailed. Coupled with the absence of the transmission story in the *Saihō shinanshō*, this suggests Shinran's ignorance of the *Daigo-bon* biography and thus a separate transmission of the *Sammai hottokki* to Shinran either from Hōnen directly or from another of Hōnen's disciples to whom Shinran was close, such as Ryūkan or Seikaku. Since the two extent biographies of Hōnen attributed to Ryūkan both extol his samādhi attainments, Ryūkan is certainly a highly possible source.[36]

If the *Sammai hottokki* was apocryphally attributed to Hōnen, then the Genchi transmission story certainly points to someone in Genchi's line as author. As there are no known ties between Shinran and Genchi, however, the different version of the story in Shinran's record, written sometime after the *Daigo-bon*, indicates just how much broad acceptance this samādhi record achieved within the Pure Land Buddhist community within a single generation after Hōnen, whatever its origins.

---

35. Ikawa 1967, 789b8–9.

36. There are two works attributed to Ryūkan on the life of Hōnen that have been discovered in the last thirty years. Their content is somewhat different,but they agree on the importance of his samādhi achievement. The *Chion kōshiki* 知恩講私記 was first published by Kushida Ryōkō under the title "Shin-hakken no Hōnen denki—Chion kōshiki," *Nihon Rekishiki* 200, p. 217 (Jan. 1965). The *Hōnen Shōnin-den* 法然上人傳 was published by Udaka Ryōsetsu in *Taishō Daigaku kenkyū-kiyō*, 69, p.89 (Feb. 1984).

While one would hope for something that could corroborate this transmission story before pointing the finger at Genchi as author, in the absence of such, one wonders about the stated need for secrecy. Was this meant to restrict this material to the eyes of Genchi and his students? Or is the transmission story itself apocryphal but the text genuine? That is, was the story generated out of the same factional self-interest that Tamura and others see as the motivation for the creation of the text itself? In sharp contrast to its later canonization, the *Sammai hottokki* seems to have been unknown during Hōnen's lifetime—the only contemporary reference we have is the mention of Myōhen within the text itself—or at least it is never mentioned in any extant work from this period. But if the secret transmission story were genuine, it would satisfactorily explain this lack of corroboration, as well as its sudden appearance after the death of Genchi.

III. Samādhi Attainment and the Politics of Lineage

In addition to the micro-political dimension in which philosophical struggles were played out between rival disciples of Hōnen, it is also pertinent to consider the impact of the broader political realm in which the suppression of the entire Pure Land movement continued after Hōnen's death. In this regard, the period from 1219 to 1235, during which Hōnen's grave was supposedly desecrated and Kōsai, Ryūkan, Shinran, Kū'a, and others were exiled, is particularly important. Jōdo Shinshū scholars have long argued that in the wake of such social difficulties, the leading disciples of Hōnen, with the exception of Shinran, of course, sought to de-radicalize the movement by interpreting Hōnen's thought in ways more traditional than Hōnen himself had intended. Here the phrase "more traditional" means more in keeping with preexisting conceptions of Pure Land doctrine normative to the Tendai school. Although reductionist, there is some truth to this argument, and given the socio-political context of potential violence, it is certainly plausible that the *Sammai hottokki* might be a statement by one or more of his disciples expressing Hōnen's proximity to traditional Tendai beliefs and practices. Tamura makes a case for seeing the entire *Daigo-bon* as an expression of this stand, as evidenced in the editorial decision of its compilers to include not only the *Sammai hottokki*, but also a short biographical sketch called the *Ichigo monogatari* (一期物語), which traces Hōnen's Vinaya lineage specifically to Hui-ssu (Eshi 慧思 [Nangaku Daishi 南岳大師], 515–577), the second patriarch of Tendai.[37]

As mentioned above, among those claiming the mantle of succession of the Pure Land movement, possession of a posthumous record of Hōnen's miraculous samādhi attainments afforded legitimacy within what was still a fledgling sectarian movement held in suspicion. The efficacy of this move stems from the Sino-Japanese tradition of a genre of texts devoted to hagiographic stories about remarkable events in the lives of individual Buddhists. In the case of the Pure Land Path, these works are usually referred to as the *wang-sheng chuan*, or *ōjō-den* (往生傳),[38] and in the specific case of Hōnen such hagiographic tendencies extend well into *setsuwa* and even secular literature. Reading through the plethora of biographical material written on Hōnen in the thirteenth and fourteenth centuries one finds many fantastic descriptions. Indeed, none of the extant biographies are without some hagiographic content, even such early texts as the *Daigo-bon* and the *Shi-nikki*. Seen in this context, the paranormal events mentioned in such texts as the *Sammai hottokki* and the *Gorinjū-nikki* do not seem out of place. For example, the very early *Shi-nikki* expresses its own fascination at the transhistorical possibilities by using the now famous phrase in which a fellow monk remarked to Hōnen, "you are not merely a man, but a *nirmāṇa-kāya* incarnation (汝非直人、權者化身)."[39] This theme of apotheosis can be seen in some form in all these early biographies of Hōnen, usually in the form of the master identified as either a *nirmāṇa-kāya* of Mahāstāmaprāpta (*Seishi bosatsu*) or even Amida Buddha himself. It is probably not an exaggeration, therefore, to conclude that the easing of the political persecution at the end of the 1230s rather quickly yielded an intense effort at biographical composition in which individual lineages spawned by Hōnen succeeded by the middle of the thirteenth century in elevating Hōnen from seeker to savior.

Space does not permit concrete discussion of the *Gorinjū-nikki* section of the *Daigo-bon*, but in parallel with the *Sammai hottokki* it records the miraculous events that occurred during the last moments of Hōnen's life. Here he talks about his visions of the Buddha, the

---

37. Tamura 1983, 245.

38. The earliest work in this genre is probably the *Hsi-fang ch'ing-t'u jui-ying chuan* 西方淨土瑞應傳, compiled by Hsiao-k'ang and Wen-shen at the end of the eighth century. The three best known Chinese *wang-sheng chuan* are contained in T. 104–153. There were many in Japan, beginning with the *Nihon ōjō gokuraku-ki* 日本往生極楽記 compiled in 984 by Yoshishige no Yasutane. For the Japanese works, see *Dainippon bukkyō zensho*, vol. 107, and *Jōdo-shū zensho zoku-hen*, vol. 16.

39. Ikawa 1967, 769b.

Pure Land, and how his body was "originally from the Pure Land." Recalling the fact that in the oldest recension of the *Daigo-bon* the *Gorinjū-nikki* and the *Sammai hottokki* are not segregated chapters but appear as one continuous passage, we can infer an original editorial decision to present a consistent theme of supernatural perception as the result of samādhi attainment. Since attaining a vision of the Buddha and his Pure Land signified non-backsliding bodhisattva status, for some specifically equivalent to eighth *bhūmi* status, in contemporary writings these two sections should properly be understood to be one statement both visionary in personal experience and sanctifying in historical significance. These are clear expressions of presenting the case for Hōnen's doctrinal authority by means of his samādhi attainment. What is not clear is whether the apotheosizing of Hōnen as *nirmāṇa-kāya* is necessarily a part of the same interpretive framework, or if it represents a later level of hagiographic escalation.

In Ryōe's *Shūi-gotōroku*, there are two texts in addition to the *Sammai hottokki* that also relate accounts of a supernatural nature: the *Mukanshōsōki* (夢感聖相記) and *Jōdo zuimonki* (淨土随聞記).[40] The *Mukanshōsōki* material dates back to the *Saihō shinanshō* of Shinran,[41] appears in no less than seventeen biographies,[42] and is particularly important because it details Hōnen's dreaming of a face-to-face meeting with Shan-tao. This was an event of immense importance for all Pure Land schools which derived from Hōnen, because it encapsulated the Japanese conception of the transmission of the mantle of authority of the Pure Land teaching from Shan-tao to Hōnen despite the lack of any direct connection through teacher-student lineage between the two. We should not forget here that the core of Dōgen's claim to exclusive authority for his conception of Zen in the early thirteenth century lay in his having received transmission from a teacher in a recognized Ch'an lineage in China which traced itself back to the Sixth Patriarch, Hui-neng, and the fact that in contrast Hōnen never visited China. The *Jōdo zuimonki* was compiled by Genchi,and contains a version of the *Gorinjū nikki* under the title *Rinjū shōzuiki* (臨終祥瑞記). According to Ryōe's comment in the *Kurodani Shōnin go-tōroku*,

---

40. The *Mukanshōsōki* can be found in Ikawa, 860–861 (Japanese) and 862 (*kanbun*). The *Jōdo zuimonki* is in Ikawa, 435ff.

41. Cf. "Hōnen Shōnin gomusōki" 法然上人御夢相記 within the *Saihō shinanshō*, Ishii Kyōdō 1955, 860–863.

42. See Sanda Zenshin, *Seiritsushi-teki Hōnen Shōnin shoden no kenkyū* (Kyoto: Kōnenji, 1966), 40.

this was not a composition of Hōnen's but was written down by a witness during his final days.[43]

Taken together with the *Sammai hottokki*, such writings legitimate Hōnen's teaching by locating him within the orthodox Sino-Japanese hagiography of eminent monks. This is just one reason for us to resist the temptation to see Hōnen as an isolated religious figure intent on establishing an entirely new mode of salvation. Hōnen's new Buddhism of faith owes its social, organizational, cultural, and ultimately its political success on the one hand to existential issues that were inevitably grounded in preexisting forms of Buddhism, and on the other to political factors that framed the interpretations of his historical role in terms of Buddhist values no less traditional.

The encounter between Hōnen and Shan-tao in the *Mukanshōsōki* is but another expression of the paradoxical way in which Hōnen tied himself to the Chinese prelate and his views. Hōnen used rational argument to illustrate his doctrinal standpoint on recitation *nembutsu*, but his biographers also saw the importance of establishing a trans-historical, karmic link to the person of Shan-tao, which is accomplished through the imagery of samādhi. The former position is argued by means of intellectual debate, the latter is affirmed by the authority of charisma, and samādhi attainment in Buddhism always confers charismatic authority.

We can draw an analogy here between the transmission of teachings from Shan-tao to Hōnen and the story of Asaṅga receiving the Yogācāra teachings from Maitreya in the Tuṣita heaven, a story which promoted the legitimacy of Asaṅga's new school in India.[44] In both cases the new teachings met with resistance, and only through the continual efforts of the recipients Asaṅga and Hōnen in explaining them to others did they finally achieve general acceptance. While the importance of such ahistorical myths to the establishment of new

43. Ryōe's comment occurs at the end of the *kanbun* text as it appears in Ishii, 870.9. The *Jōdo-shū daijiten*, 3.478c, notes the accepted opinion that its author was probably Genchi.

44. This story appears in both the Chinese and Tibetan traditions, although the list of texts which Asaṅga received from Maitreya differs somewhat. Perhaps the most important differences are that the *Yogācārabhūmi* is recorded as being composed by Maitreya in China but attributed to Asaṅga in Tibet, and the *Dharmadharmatā-vibhaṅga* which is attributed to Maitreya and widely read in Tibet somehow never made it to China. The Chinese version of the myth can be seen in the *Yu-ch'ieh lun chi* by Tun-lun (遁倫): T. 42.311b. Bu-ston records the Tibetan story in his *Chos ḥbyuṅ*, in the translation by Obermiller, *The History of Buddhism in India and Tibet* (Heidelberg, 1932), I.53.

Buddhist schools cannot be overstated, we should also consider the elevated status such stories bring to the person who plays the dual role of sacred recipient and lineage founder. All Buddhist schools exhibit an imperative to extend their lineage back to earlier figures of authority, such as the Ch'an founding story of Mahākāśyapa receiving in silence the flower from Śākyamuni. In the case of the hagiographies surrounding Asaṅga and Hōnen, the special, charismatic status of the individual as founder/seer is implicit in the historically unique event of being "chosen" to receive the authoritative transmission. Thus, while subsequent lineages of the Yogācāra/Vijñāptimātra/Vijñānavāda traditions must all return to Asaṅga, he himself is not the "creator" of this new line of thinking, but merely one who was able to attain the samādhi state whereby he was afforded the interaction with Maitreya who, in turn, was one of Śākyamuni's disciples. In a similar manner, Hōnen is the one patriarch who stands at the top of all historical lineages connected with Japanese Pure Land Buddhism from the Kamakura period onward, and through his link to Shan-tao the lineage can then be traced back through Tao-ch'o, T'an-luan, and ultimately through Bodhiruci to India. This scheme is laid out in Gyōnen's history of the Pure Land school entitled *Jōdo hōmon genrushō*, completed in 1310.[45]

One important difference in the stories of Asaṅga and Hōnen is the fact that while the mythic figure of Maitreya had immediate authority by virtue of being designated as the future Buddha in the sūtras, Shan-tao was a relatively minor figure in Japan before Hōnen. Indeed, unlike Asaṅga, Hōnen had the added burden of somehow creating patriarchal status for his mythic figure of authority. While Shan-tao is mentioned in Genshin's *Ōjōyōshū*, he appears in that work as only one of many Chinese commentators and is not afforded a prominent role.[46] Moreover Genshin is more interested in Shan-tao's work on samādhi practice (*Kuan-hsin fa-men*) than his doctrinal analysis of the *Kuan ching* that so inspired Hōnen. But it is a measure of Hōnen's success at establishing the patriarchal status of Shan-tao that he appears among the list of Pure Land patriarchs not only in

---

45. T. 84.196a24–b9. To his credit, in this section Gyōnen notes that the Pure Land lineage was not one of direct transmission from teacher to disciple, yet he accepts its authoritative nature nonetheless.

46. For example, Shan-tao's interpretation of the three states of mind requisite for attaining Birth in the Pure Land is one of his most important contributions. Genshin notes his position at T. 84.58a22ff., but no comment is made.

the writings of Hōnen's disciples such as Benchō, Shinran, and Shōkū, but also in the nonsectarian writings of Gyōnen mentioned above.

It has been determined that Hōnen based his understanding of Shan-tao primarily upon the biographical material contained in the *Hsü kao-seng chuan*, the various *Wang-sheng chuan*, and in the record left by Shan-tao in the colophon to his *San-shan-i* (散善義) section of his *Kuan ching* commentary, in which his own visionary attainments during *nembutsu-samādhi* are mentioned. For Shan-tao himself, the one source in addition to the *Kuan ching* of demonstrable influence on his samādhi experience is the *Pan-chou san-mei ching*, one of the texts which form the basis of samādhi practice in Chinese T'ien-t'ai. In chapter 16 of the *Senchakushū*, Hōnen stages a dialogue about why he has chosen Shan-tao as his authority on the Pure Land teaching. Four reasons are given, which can be summarized as follows:[47]

1. Among the earlier commentators on the Pure Land teaching, Shan-tao is different in that he is based in the Pure Land Path rather than in the Path for Saints.
2. Among the other teachers who are similarly based in the Pure Land Path, many did not yet attain samādhi, but Shan-tao did.
3. Hui-k'an (Ekan, late eighth century, 懐感) also attained samādhi, but Shan-tao was his teacher.
4. Tao-ch'o (Dōshaku, 562–645, 道綽) was Shan-tao's teacher and devoted to the Pure Land Path, but he did not attain samādhi, so it cannot be known for certain that he in fact attained Birth in the Pure Land.

Thus, within the *Senchakushū* itself Hōnen plainly states that his assessment of Shan-tao as the preeminent, authoritative spokesman for the message of the Pure Land sūtras is based upon his attainment of samādhi because only in this way can it be known for certain that he in fact attained Birth in the Pure Land. In other words, the attainment of samādhi confirms the realization of *ōjō*, which itself confirms his legitimacy as a teacher. Elsewhere in the same work Hōnen wrote, "The Reverend Shan-tao is someone who attained samādhi, this is confirmation that he attained the Path" (善導和尚是三昧發得之人也、於道既有其證).[48] This is perhaps the clearest statement by Hōnen that, notwithstanding the philosophical attraction he felt to Shan-tao's conclusion that recitation *nembutsu* is the practice designated by the Buddha, his justification for accepting Shan-tao's

47. T. 83.19a5–24.

48. T. 83.19a15.

interpretation as authoritative is based on the traditional Tendai hermeneutic of highly focused samādhi attainment.

What I would like to suggest here is that posterity applied the same argument to Hōnen as he himself did to Shan-tao. In other words, the introduction of the *Sammai hottokki* into the Buddhist world simultaneous with the composition of Hōnen biographies reflects a natural effort to legitimate his teaching by means of authenticating his samādhi attainment, and in this the biographers used the same model as Hōnen employed in his *Senchakushū* for choosing Shan-tao as mythic founder of the true Pure Land Path. Evidence of a conscious linking of these two models can be found in Ryūkan's *Chion kō-shiki*, one of the early biographies. As one of Hōnen's closest disciples, Ryūkan explicitly states that Hōnen's samādhi attainment is of a piece with Shan-tao's experience.[49] This suggests that the issue of whether the *Sammai hottokki* was a genuine product of Hōnen's brush is of secondary importance to its historical significance for the Pure Land tradition in Japan. That is, whatever its veracity, the notion that Hōnen had achieved *buddhānusmṛti samādhi* was asserted as a plausible explanation for his charisma and authority because of a contemporary hermeneutic in which samādhi attainment resulting in entranced visions of religious themes functioned as a legitimating motif, a hermeneutic that was no less effective in Amidist piety than it was in all forms of Buddhism. The volumes of doctrinal explication of Hōnen's *nembutsu* thesis argued by subsequent generations of Pure Land followers are no less significant for this story of his transic attainments. But the presence of this samādhi material throughout the biographical literature, from Genchi to Shinkū to Shinran to Benchō to Shōkū to Ryūkan, tells us that the *Sammai hottokki* was as acceptable across the broad range of post-Hōnen thinkers as was the *Senchakushū* itself. And as subsequent generations of leaders in the Pure Land movement sought to rationalize the problems inherent in Hōnen's thesis that an ordinary person could be reborn in a *saṁbhoga-kāya* realm,[50] the widespread reference to his samādhi achievements in their writings implies that his particular historical experience of

49. The section of this work which contains the biographical material on Hōnen can be found in Ikawa, 1967, 1035–1038, and in *Shinshū shōkyō zenshso*, 5: 715–719.

50. One of the doctrinal difficulties of Hōnen's system of thought is that it is based upon the notion that through the special grace of the Buddha Amida, the *buddhakṣetra* of this Buddha in his *saṁbhoga-kāya* state is accessible to *pṛthagjana*, or ordinary people. Traditionally, a *saṁbhoga-kāya* realm of a Buddha is only visible to beings who are advanced-stage bodhisattvas. Ordinary beings by definition are only capable of experiencing a *nirmāṇa-kāya* Buddha.

just such an attainment not only helped establish Hōnen's authority but also provided an example of the truth of his doctrine.

Recognizing the universal acceptance of the *Sammai hottokki* by the Pure Land movement after Hōnen's demise also suggests that the question of its dubious origins is far more troublesome to modern scholarship than it was to Hōnen's contemporaries. I suggest above that arguing Hōnen's doctrinal positions seems to be distinct from arguing the authority of Hōnen as teacher, but can these two really be separated? Is it not more likely that we have an oversimplified understanding of Hōnen's message precisely because we have not sufficiently taken this samādhi material into consideration in our understanding of this new religious school which appears to denigrate the value of attainment through practice? In this light, is it still possible to place Hōnen as the conscious founder of a new sect of Buddhism which defined itself by a creed in which faith is sufficient (*tariki*) for the attainment of *bodhi* because the model of attainment through practice (*jiriki*) is no longer viable? Or should we instead consider a Pauline model whereby it is in the next generation or generations after Hōnen that the so-called Pure Land school was actually conceived and organized?

To better evaluate the possibility of Hōnen affirming the value of his own samādhi attainment, there are two more passages from the *Senchakushū* I would like to note. The first occurs within the so-called "five-fold relativity" (五番相對) scheme used in chapter 2 in which Hōnen sets up five dichotomies as a way to argue for the soteriological implications of his hermeneutic of segregating practices into critical and secondary (正助).[51] The second of the five is called the relativity of distance (近遠對), wherein he posits a "proximate link" (近緣) between the Buddha and the practitioner. How is this soteriological intimacy between self and Buddha to be understood? Here Hōnen dips into the *nembutsu-samādhi* rhetoric, explaining how the Buddha has promised to reveal himself before the eyes of the practitioner when the latter is striving for just such a vision—in other words, to appear when *anusmṛti samādhi* is attained.

The second passage is from chapter 12 of the *Senchakushū* in which Hōnen borrows a line from Shan-tao to state his own position affirming the unique value of *nembutsu-samādhi* within the purview of Pure Land Buddhism. The topic is the relative significance of *kanbutsu-samādhi* (觀佛三昧 *kanbutsu zammai*, *kuan-fo san-mei*) and *nembutsu-*

51. T. 83.3b24ff.

samādhi (念佛三昧 *nembutsu zammai, nien-fo san-mei*). Shan-tao's position can be seen in both the *hsüan-i* (玄義分) section of his *Kuan-ching shu* and in his *P'an-chou tsan* in which the sixteenth meditation of the *Kuan ching* is taken to suggest that the critical way of reaching *nembutsu-samādhi* as outlined in the *Pan chou san-mei ching* is to practice recitation *nembutsu*.[52] The purpose of his interpretation is to affirm the attainment of samādhi as available even to people of ordinary abilities, and in doing so he uniquely affirms the authority of both the *nembutsu-samādhi* of the *Pan chou san-mei ching* and the *kanbutsu-samādhi* of the *Kuan ching*.

Here is Hōnen's comment:

> Next is [the topic of] *nembutsu* as devotion to reciting the name of Amida Buddha. The meaning of *nembutsu* is always like this. And if one also speaks properly of the entrusting of the holy name of Amida for dissemination in later generations then, although the [*Contemplation*] *sūtra* has broadly extolled a variety of practices for both focused and unfocused minds, it was not these [practices] for focused and unfocused minds that were entrusted to Ānanda for dissemination to later generations. It was *only the one practice of nembutsu-samādhi* that was entrusted to Ānanda for dissemination to later generations. (emphasis mine)
>
> One might ask, why was it that the various practices for focused and unfocused minds were not entrusted to Ānanda for dissemination to later generations? ... Among the thirteen contemplations, the ninth is the contemplation of Amida Buddha; this refers to the *kanbutsu-samādhi*. [The intention] surely was to abandon the other twelve contemplations and entrust [only] the *kanbutsu-samādhi*. On this, the *hsüan-i* section of the same commentary [by Shan-tao] states, "this sūtra takes the *kanbutsu-samādhi* as its central theme and also the *nembutsu-samādhi* as its central theme." Thus this one sūtra has two practices for its central theme. How can you abandon the *kanbutsu-samādhi* and [only affirm] the entrusting of the *nembutsu-samādhi* [for future generations]?
>
> To this, [Shan-tao] has answered, "What we infer from the Original Vow of the Buddha [Śākyamuni] is his intention to have sentient beings single-mindedly recite the name of the Amida Buddha."[53] The various focused and unfocused practices are not in the Original Vow, and therefore they are not what has been entrusted [to Ānanda]. Moreover, on this

---

52. In other words, Shan-tao is designating a specific way to read the character *nien* 念 in the phrase *nien-fo san-mei*. Since *nien* can be read both as an exercise of mental concentration and as the practice of saying aloud sanctified words or phrases, Shan-tao exploits this ambiguity to assert his critical position affirming recitation as the correct reading.

53. This is a quote from the *sanshan-i* section of Shan-tao's *Kuan ching shu*, T. 37.278a25. The inference is drawn from Shan-tao's reading of the *Wu-liang shou ching* and reflects his interpretation that in the eighteenth vow Amida is only carrying out Śākyamuni's request to direct people to recite Amida Buddha's name as the best means to attain Birth in the Pure Land.

point, although the *kanbutsu-samādhi* is a most excellent practice, it is not the Original Vow [of the Buddha]. Therefore, it is not what has been entrusted [by the Buddha]. The *nembutsu-samādhi* is the Original Vow and therefore it is what has been entrusted. "What we infer from the Original Vow of the Buddha" is what is indicated in the eighteenth vow of the forty-eight vows found in the double fascicle [i.e., *Sukhāvatīvyūha*] sūtra.[54]

This passage stems from a line at the end of the *Kuan ching* in which the sūtra expresses Śākyamuni's admonition to Ānanda to hold on to what he has taught in the sūtra just as he holds on to the name of the Immeasurable Buddha (Amida).

The focus here on the implications of what has been entrusted to Ānanda represents a common hermeneutic move in East Asia wherein commentators insert their interpretations of what part of the sūtra message should be valued most highly, inferring that the Buddha also implied that some sections of the sūtra are relatively more significant. Hōnen is borrowing Shan-tao's view of the *Kuan ching* as promoting both forms of *buddhānusmṛti-samādhi* and his link of recitation *nembutsu* practice with the eighteenth vow in the *Sukhāvatīvyūha*. But Hōnen also somehow reads into this latter statement not only an affirmation of *nembutsu* as the practice chosen by the Buddha but also an affirmation of *nembutsu-samādhi* in this role. Shan-tao's *Kuan-ching shu*, however, does not make this connection; in fact there is no mention of samādhi in the original passage quoted by Hōnen.[55] By contrast, one can find statements in Shan-tao's writings which confirm his esteem for both methods of practice aimed at achieving *anusmṛti samādhi*, such as in his *Kuan-nien fa-men*, in which he quotes the *Kuan-fo san-mei hai ching* (T. 643) to illustrate that *mi-t'o-san-mei* (彌陀三昧 = *kuan-fo san-mei*) and *nien-fo san-mei* represent the same experience.[56] Regarding what the *Kuan ching* itself says regarding transmission and samādhi, there is nothing to support Hōnen's conclusion that the Buddha intended to entrust only the *nembutsu-samādhi*

54. T. 83.16a16–b11.

55. T. 83.16b2–10.

56. T. 47.22–30. Cf. H. Inagaki, "Amida Samādhi and Nembutsu Samādhi," *The Pure Land* 2 (new series), Dec. 1985, 85–86. While some scholars have argued that Shan-tao's commentary on the *Kuan ching* is a later and more mature work than his *Kuan-nien fa-men* and therefore supersedes it, the dating of these texts remains a mystery, and with our current knowledge such arguments seem too close to Japanese sectarian concerns to be convincing.

to Ānanda. The text reads only "those who practice *this* samādhi" (行此三昧者).[57]

In going beyond Shan-tao, this statement should be understood to be the locus classicus of Hōnen's core hermeneutic scheme to link the two sūtras. That is, the concept of Original Vow, or *hongan*, is defined as the eighteenth vow in the *Sukhāvatīvyūha sūtra* and understood on the ground of human praxis as the experience of *nembutsu-samādhi* as outlined in the *Kuan ching*. This therefore is the basis of *anjin*, the attainment of the path in Pure Land Buddhism. The fifteenth-century Shinshū patriarch Rennyo expresses this as *kihō-ittai*, the mystical formula in the *Anjin ketsujōshō*, which expresses the spiritual union of Buddha and sentient being.[58] Although this particular position of Rennyo is controversial within Shinshū today, it should be clear from this discussion that he is only reflecting the tradition set in place by Hōnen that views *buddhānusmṛti-samādhi* as the defining soteriological moment of the Pure Land Path. The views of Shōkū (證空, 1177–1247) followed this line of thought and can be seen today in the Seizan branch of Jōdo-shū. When Kōsai described this samādhi experience as the momentary meeting of the Buddha mind and the mind of an ordinary person, he was expressing the same standpoint. Seen against this background, the presence of a text like the *Sammai hottokki* is not at all surprising. We would even expect to find some testimony of the experiential basis of Hōnen's doctrinal conclusions. For those who view Hōnen as someone who advocated a new concept of faith, the *Sammai hottokki* is a statement to his followers expressing that faith as grounded in the experience of *nembutsu-samādhi*.

IV. *Nembutsu-Samādhi* as the Critical Practice of Pure Land Buddhism

Prior to the new Buddhist forms expressed in the Kamakura period, focus on the *goals* of practice in Buddhism was so pervasive that one does not find much critical discussion regarding the relative value of various *means* of practice, and Shan-tao's statements reflect this norm. Does Hōnen's unique interpretation of the Pure Land tradition imply a different outcome? That is, in following the axiom that the particular form of one's practice determines the nature of one's attainment, are we to infer that the attainment of *nembutsu-samādhi* is somehow

57. T. 12.346b9.

58. T. 83.921b21, 923c19, etc.

different from that of *kanbutsu-samādhi* because *nembutsu* is a different spiritual experience from visualization/contemplation? Nothing in Shan-tao's writings supports this position. Even in Hōnen's comment cited above, which asserts the Original Vow to be the source of only the *nembutsu-samādhi*, there is no implication that this is so because it designates a qualitatively different samādhi experience.

I believe a more persuasive interpretation is one which instead sees the *nembutsu-samādhi* as the "practice of the Original Vow" not because it yields a different sort of visionary samādhi but because it symbolically includes all *nembutsu* practice directed toward this aim, whether or not the practitioner actually achieves samādhi. Hōnen and his followers want to argue that the meditation practices which rely on the thirteen concentrated visualizations (*kanbutsu*) of the *Kuan ching* may be out of reach for the ordinary person, but that fact does not preclude their attainment of the liberating experience of *anusmṛti-samādhi*. The *Sukhāvatīvyūha sūtra* itself likens the Pure Land to an ultimate samādhi experience,[59] and promises the attainment of samādhi for bodhisattvas who only have to hear the Buddha's name (vows forty-two and forty-five).[60] When Shan-tao esteems the passage in the famous eighteenth vow that urges believers to practice *nembutsu* to obtain birth in the Pure Land and Hōnen links this *nembutsu* practice to samādhi attainment, it is thus not without doctrinal grounding in the same sūtra. While both the *Sukhāvatīvyūha-sūtra* and *Kuan ching* expound a wide range of praxis, the focus on the phrase *jū-nen/shi-nien* (十念) in the eighteen vow of the *Sukhāvatīvyūha sūtra* and its glossing as *recitation nembutsu* (稱名念佛) leading to samādhi by Shan-tao and Hōnen bestows a religious justification upon the practice of recitation *nembutsu* that is unprecedented and perhaps even undeserved, considering its Sanskrit equivalent *daśabhiś cittotpāda parivartaiḥ*.[61]

Hōnen's hermeneutic elevating *nembutsu-samādhi* above *kanbutsu-samādhi* in the *Senchakushū* is actually the development of a hermeneutic process begun much earlier by T'an-luan, Tao-ch'o and of course Shan-tao aimed at conflating the distance between the potential of the traditional path and the Pure Land Path. Hōnen accomplishes this by drawing out the symbolic, some might say Tantric, implications of the term *nen* 念, whereby its utterance in the proper ritual and

59. T. 12.272a18.

60. T. 12.269a15–18 and 269a25–28.

61. A. Ashikaga, ed., *Sukhāvatīvyūha* (Kyoto: Hōzōkan, 1965), 14.

psychological environment has the power to bring the devotee to a higher state of trance, much like the *bīja* syllable *A* does in Vajrayāna practice.

This attitude is strikingly common throughout Pure Land Buddhist writings of the thirteenth and fourteenth centuries, and makes for a sharp contrast with the reductionist creed of Japanese Pure Land sects in the twentieth century, which all but ignore samādhi attainment. Three contemporary examples from the works of Hōnen's closest disciples corroborate this interpretation of the importance of *nembutsu-samādhi* for his era. The first two are attributed to Ryūkan and represent the earliest strata of the Hōnen biographical literature: *Hōnen Shōnin-den*[62] and *Chion kōshiki*,[63] mentioned above. In the former, the disciple Shinkū queries Hōnen about whether or not he would like them to build a structure to commemorate his *iseki* (遺跡), remains or relics. Hōnen answers:

> My *iseki* will be the spread [of this teaching] to all groups, for that reason I have promoted the *nembutsu-samādhi* throughout the whole of this old man's life.[64]

Written as a liturgical eulogy on the anniversary of his teacher's death, *Chion kōshiki* extols five of Hōnen's most outstanding virtues. In the third section on the merits of his *nembutsu* practice, Hōnen's ability to perceive various aspects of the Pure Land, including the form of the Buddha and bodhisattvas located there, is described in detail, and finally Hōnen is described as having obtained "realization commensurate with that of Shan-tao and Hui-k'an," all clear references to his attainment of *nembutsu-samādhi*.[65] Elsewhere Ryūkan wrote, "The Venerable (Shan-tao) was someone who attained the samādhi

62. Cf. note 36 above. Nakai Shinkō has challenged Udaka's assertion of the early origins of this work in *Hōnen-den to jōdoshū-shi no kenkyū* (Kyoto: Shibunkan, 1994), 100–117.

63. This text can be found printed in Ikawa Jōkyō, 1035. A manuscript copy of this text made in 1228 by another disciple of Hōnen, Shin-amida butsu (心阿彌陀佛), was discovered in Tōji in 1964 and a photo reproduction published in the journal *Nihon rekishi*, no. 300 (1965). Shin-amida butsu is otherwise known as one of the monks who assisted the seven-day *nembutsu* vigil performed by Emperor Shirakawa when he took the tonsure in 1192 (cf. *Jōdo-shū zensho* 17.64a12, 17.121b5, 16.203a15, etc.).

64. Udaka, 99. This exchange is echoed in later biographies but not without important variation. The *Kukan-den* (九巻傳), thought to have been written about one century after Hōnen's death, maintains this reference to samādhi intact, but the *Hōnen Shōnin gyōjō ezu*, from the same period, has altered the phrase *nembutsu-samādhi* to read merely *nembutsu*, reflecting the political ambiguity of samādhi attainment for the Pure Land movement after Hōnen.

of [seeing] the *nirmāṇa-kāya* of Amida. His reasoning cannot possibly be incorrect":[66] Ryūkan has clearly stated the paradigm for us.

The final example is from Shōkō (聖光, 1162–1238), another disciple of Hōnen and the founder of the Chinzei branch of the Jōdo-shū. Shōkō wrote in his comprehensive outline, the *Jōdo-shū yōshū* (浄土宗要集):

> The matter of attaining *nembutsu-samādhi* is of great importance to the *nembutsu* practitioner and should be studied well. Just as all practices are focused on their expected outcome, it is not good to practice *nembutsu* with no thought of its [objective]. The attainment of *nembutsu-samādhi* is precisely what you should expect.[67]

In light of Hōnen's identification of *nembutsu-samādhi* with the Original Vow in chapter 12 of the *Senchakushū* and his professed esteem of Shan-tao described in chapter 16 as based in his samādhi attainment, Shōkō's statement positing *nembutsu-samādhi* as the normative goal of *nembutsu* practice similarly reflects the fact that the critical efficacy of *nembutsu* practice, notwithstanding its appeal as a simple practice accessible to every man, has always been linked with *nembutsu-samādhi* in a fundamental way. This is exactly the position taken by Shōkō who, along with Ryōchū (良忠, 1199–1287), created the line which has dominated the Jōdo-shū since the end of the thirteenth century. Returning to the fact that Hōnen's *Senchakushū* was written simultaneously with his *Sammai hottokki*, I believe this samādhi material suggests that the *Senchakushū* itself should be seen as an expression of religious confidence resulting from Hōnen's *samādhi* attainments.

Tōdō Kyōshun has gone so far as to suggest that whenever Hōnen spoke of recitation *nembutsu* as the practice chosen by the Buddha's vows, he was referring to *nembutsu* praxis directed at the attainment of samādhi.[68] Tōdō makes a useful distinction between what I would call the sacred or religious meaning of *nembutsu* for Hōnen and the practical sense of the term. The former refers to the principle that all those who devote themselves to *nembutsu* practice will fall within the purview of the Buddha's promise to bring them to his Pure

---

65. See above for Hōnen's specific mention of these two figures as authoritative because of their samādhi attainments.

66. *Gokuraku jōdo-shūgi*, contained in *Dainihon bukkyō zensho*, 102.199b.

67. *Jōdo-shū zensho* 10.219a12.

68. Tōdō Kyōshun, *Hōnen Shōnin kenkyū* (Tokyo: Sankibō, 1983), 148. Tōdō takes a similar position that we should regard the *Sammai hottokki* as a kind of confirmation of Hōnen's doctrines as expressed in the *Senchakushū*.

Land, regardless of their spiritual attainments or lack thereof. The latter addresses the concerns of serious or professional practitioners, people like Hōnen and Ryūkan who recite the *nembutsu* upwards of seventy thousand times every day and who do expect to reach states of samādhi.[69]

The genius of Hōnen is that he was able to speak to both audiences, and any understanding of Hōnen's religious contribution is insufficient if it does not consider his concern for samādhi attainment alongside his message of soteriology without samādhi. What many misunderstand is that such a position affirming both the attainment as well as the non-attainment of *samādhi* by means of recitation *nembutsu* does not violate the basic assumptions of Pure Land Buddhist doctrine. That is, the premise in Pure Land thought that it is not possible to properly maintain the traditional Buddhist goals of a life governed by morality (*śīla*), meditation (*samādhi*), and wisdom (*prajñā*) remains intact in Hōnen's thought. Indeed, what is astonishing about the so-called sūtras of Amida Buddha is that they expound a way of attaining liberation without such achievements. The existential acceptance of the poverty of the individual's ability to live by ideal religious standards is thus a given for Hōnen, but this conviction did not lead him to denigrate the value of attaining these states of morality, meditation, and wisdom. Rather, the position of Pure Land Buddhism in East Asia is that it is precisely because one understands the implications of the impossibility of an ideal spiritual life that one can attain these things. The doctrinal roots of this religious approach can be found in the Chinese notion of an "easy path" located in the partial Chinese translation of a commentary on the *Daśabhūmika* attributed to Nāgārjuna,[70] and elaborated on by T'an-luan and Tao-ch'o.

What we may call Hōnen's *p'an-chiao* 判教 of practice is thus based on both *faith*—the acceptance of soteriological significance attributed to a given practice—as well as what we might call *transic efficacy*—how well the pursuit of particular practices is acknowledged to lead to higher states of trance such as *buddhānusmṛti-samādhi*. It goes without saying that for Hōnen the practice of *nembutsu* uniquely fulfills both roles. Here one is reminded of the symbolic significance of *zazen* in Dōgen's assertion that this practice is ideal because it is what the

69. Tōdō, 151–155.

70. This text exists only in Chinese translation as the *Shih-chu p'i-p'o-sha lun* (十住毘婆沙論) / **Daśabhūmivibhāṣā*, T. 26.20.

Buddha himself practiced and yet, at the same time, Dōgen does not dispense with the significance of *kenshō*. In this way, *nembutsu* for Hōnen and *zazen* for Dōgen both embody two somewhat different dimensions: a religious imperative noumenal in nature and a pragmatic imperative based on empirical knowledge.

This piety of practice expresses one of the critical religious attitudes of Kamakura Buddhism and, having been made explicit by Hōnen perhaps for the first time (it is not seen in Eisai, for example), continues to evolve in subsequent generations. Dōgen is just one example. Among Hōnen's own disciples, Kōsai, Shōkū, and Shinran are best known for viewing the *nembutsu* with increasing religious significance in the course of their own development after Hōnen's death. Ryōchū, writing fifty years after Hōnen's death, focused, or one might say advanced, Hōnen's argument when he furthered the hermeneutic apparatus by affirming that *nembutsu-samādhi* should be regarded as the critical or proper practice (正業), while *kanbutsu-samādhi* should be seen only as secondary or provisional (助業).[71] One could argue that Ryōchū's interpretation is based on a synthesis of the *Senchakushū* and the *Sammai hottokki*.

V. Conclusion

It is worth remembering that in early Buddhism, samādhi experiences represented stages on the way to enlightenment rather than enlightenment itself. In this regard, we should recall that Śākyamuni at one point renounced samādhi practice when he abandoned his yoga teachers. This was precisely because they made the error of taking samādhi attainment itself as their final goal. Within the early tradition, samādhi was merely one aspect of the eightfold noble path, seen specifically as a means to the attainment of *dhyāna*.

But the Mahāyāna tradition seems to have been taken with the fact that Śākyamuni experienced *bodhi* while in samādhi, and apparently set the stage for many sūtras beginning with the scene of the Buddha emerging from samādhi to preach. When the tradition considered Śākyamuni's abandonment of his teachers together with his samādhi experience of *bodhi*, the lesson emerged that success in practice, i.e., samādhi or *dhyāna* attainment, does not in itself guarantee a successful grasp of religious truth. No matter how efficient, a raft is only a raft.

---

71. *Jōdo-shū zensho*, 2.155, as cited in Kobayashi Shōei 小林尚英, "Zendō no Kanbutsu-zammai to Nembutsu-zammai ni tsuite," *Indogaku-bukkyōgaku kenkyū* 50 (1977), 264.

When considered against this background, Hōnen's view of samādhi practice is interestingly parallel to the story of Śākyamuni. In his early years, Hōnen engaged in samādhi practices as part of his Tendai training. Yet, the result was something less than achieving the genuine religious experience that he sought so intently. When we compare his comments in the *Senchakushū* on the importance of samādhi attainment to his own simultaneously written samādhi record in the *Sammai hottokki*, however, it inevitably leads to the conclusion reached above that Hōnen's personal confirmation of the Pure Land Teaching came during his own achievement of samādhi states.

In contrast to the use of the term *samādhi* in early Buddhism, however, our discussion also tells us that for Hōnen the psychological state of *nembutsu-samādhi* should not be taken as praxis but rather as an attainment, that is, an experience in trance of communion with either the Buddha or an aspect of Sukhāvatī which symbolizes that Buddha. The practice of samādhi for Śākyamuni was in itself not necessarily of soteriological significance, as he had achieved the equivalent of the fourth *dhyāna* under his teacher Udraka Rāmaputra but remained dissatisfied until he realized the samādhi state based in *bodhi*. Similarly, it was not merely the attainment of samādhi or even *buddhānusmṛti-samādhi* that Hōnen valued but specifically *nembutsu-samādhi*, which signified confirmation of Birth in the Pure Land (*ōjō*). Shinran conflates the notions of *nembutsu*-with-*samādhi* and *nembutsu*-without-*samādhi* by stating that there can be no *nembutsu* without *samādhi*. In other words, the *nembutsu* is not something to practice but something to be realized. But Hōnen is not too far from Shinran's position when he concludes: "practices of both the concentrated and scattered minds are to be abandoned and the *nembutsu-samādhi* is to be established,"[72] for in this context "practices of the concentrated and scattered minds" is an inclusive phrase denoting *all* practices. In other words, this is an admonition to abandon practice in the usual sense of the term and only rely upon the experience of *nembutsu-samādhi*.

It has been my intention here to raise questions about the implications which the *Sammai hottokki* holds for Hōnen studies, rather than hazard a judgment about the authenticity of the work itself. By way of closing, however, there are a few points that are worth restating.

---

72. *Senchakushū*, T. 83.16b19. Hōnen displayed the attitude that attaining *nembutsu-samādhi* will eliminate the karma of past sins as early as his lectures at Tōdaiji. See Kikuchi Yūjiro 菊地勇次郎, *Genkū to sono monka* 源空とその門下 (Kyoto: Hōzōkan, 1975), 38.

If the text is genuine, then I think it safe to deduce that Hōnen never ceased his samādhi practice, even after the redirection of his faith toward the Pure Land Path. This we know from the simultaneity of the composition of the *Sammai hottokki* and the *Senchakushū* and the mimicking of Hōnen's massive sixty to seventy thousand *nembutsu* chanted per day by such late disciples as Ryūkan. On the other hand, if a genuine ascription to Hōnen seems improbable, then the political circumstances of the immediate post-Hōnen period also provide sufficient background to support an argument of forgery.

There is, however, a third possibility. While the lack of a holograph is indeed problematic, it is not at all difficult to conceive of Hōnen orally communicating some of his unusual samādhi experiences to close disciples like Genchi, Shinran, Shōkū, Ryūkan, and Shinkū. After his death, when so many of his students took it upon themselves to write down what they knew about the master, soteriologically significant experiences such as his epiphany when reading Shan-tao or his perception of the Pure Land in a samādhi-induced dream were naturally included. In this scenario, a formal presentation of Hōnen's samādhi experiences as a titled literary work probably did not emerge until after public discussion of this material was stimulated by its appearance in the earliest biographies. Seeing the positive reaction in the community upon learning of Hōnen's samādhi achievements, and seeing that this in fact did not detract from the strength of either the image of Hōnen or the Pure Land movement as a whole, an independent work evolved into what was labelled in due time as the *Sammai hottokki*, or *Record of (My) Samādhi Attainments*.

It is also important to note that nowhere in Kamakura and Muromachi literature do we see any doubt about the authenticity of this work. Indeed, the hagiographic material such as the *Sammai hottokki*, *Gorinjū-nikki*, and *Mukanshōsōki*, included in the biographies of Hōnen seem to have had the effect of increasing his fame and prestige. This historical fact of posthumous acceptance contains a very important message for us today seeking to understand the events of so many centuries ago. Despite the use of distinctions like *jiriki/tariki*, *shōdō-mon/jōdo-mon* in his own writings, Hōnen's point of view did not entail abandoning the traditional Mahāyāna *mārga*. Because Hōnen's conception of *nembutsu* is religious rather than practical, important markers of spiritual progress vis-a-vis the *mārga* such as samādhi attainment are very much relevant to his system of thought. It is worth noting in this context that all the sectarian biographies of Hōnen record the fact that as he faced death he put on the surplice (*kesa*) of Ennin. Scholars have noted this fact as indicative of his conscious Tendai affiliation but I think it means much more. Ennin was known for introducing the constant walking samādhi practice (*jōgyō-zanmai* 常行三昧) based on the *Pan-chou san-mei ching*, in which the practictioner for ninety days circumambulates a statue of Amida Buddha chanting his name, hoping to achieve the goal of a samādhi vision of buddhas from the ten directions, as promised by the sūtra. Within the Tendai Pure Land tradition Ennin was thus considered the patriarch who transmitted the specific praxis of *nembutsu-samādhi* from China, and from this ninety-day praxis various shorter forms of "continuous *nembutsu*" (*fudan nenbutsu* 不斷念佛) developed within Tendai and, later, within Hōnen's own Jōdo-shū. We can infer then that this death gesture of Hōnen to wear Ennin's robe and thereby identify with the sacred transmission of *nembutsu-samādhi* to Japan expresses the location of his own religious identity squarely on the ground of *nembutsu-samādhi*.[73]

73. Note how Ninchō 忍澂, in petitioning the *bakufu* for the building of a new Jōdo-shū temple in the Genroku period, described it as a *nembutsu-samādhi dōjō*.

Two Jars on Two Tables

Reflections on the "Two Truths"

Luis O. Gómez

> Monks, I do not quarrel with the world. The world quarrels with me.
>
> For there are not many and diverse truths, other than the notions [people] of the world have about permanent things. They construct arguments for these views and speak of two separate things: the true and the false.
>
> The [true] Brahmin does not construct and adopt conceptualizations, or hold as essential any view, nor is he a follower of [any special] knowledge. Understanding commonplace conventions and opinions, he is indifferent to them, while others latch on to them.[1]

Gadjin M. Nagao, the scholar and the gentleman, has been a source of inspiration in the life of many Buddhist scholars of my generation and of the upcoming younger generations. For many of us he has left an indelible mark both as an intellectual model and as a memorable human presence. However, what has always impressed me the most about Prof. Nagao's scholarly and human style (apart from his vitality, even keel, and sense of humor) is his capacity to live simultaneously commitments that others are unable to combine: a devotion to the highest ideals of scientific scholarship, a dedication to the analytic dimensions of Buddhist philosophy and doctrine, and a calm acceptance (*prasāda*) of Buddhism as a tradition, a faith, and a practice—a commitment that pervades his work, even at its technical best. In my mind there is no question that in Gadjin Nagao these three human experiences meet behind the reticence of the scholar and the restraint of the Japanese gentleman. I therefore wrote this essay with pleasure, pride, gratitude, and trepidation.

One of the topics Prof. Nagao addressed with special clarity was that of the so-called "two truths."[2] This is a topic of special relevance

---

1. These three passages are from the following sources: the first paragraph is translated from the Chinese text of the *Samyuktāgama*, Taishō 99 (II) 8b16–17. The second is from *Suttanipāta* 886, translated from the edition of Andersen and Smith 1965, and the third from *Suttanipāta* 911. All three passages are discussed in the body of the essay.

2. Worthy of special mention are his landmark essays of 1954 and 1955, referenced in the bibliography.

when one is speaking of the integration or coexistence of many commitments in a human being (presumed, rightly or wrongly, to be a single entity!). In this paper I wish to direct my reader's attention to the important question of the religious meanings of a doctrine such as this one, especially the significance of the claims expressed in the passage of the epigraph: that holding no doctrine is the highest aspiration in a life committed to a religious path.

Naturally, my understanding of the notions "religious meanings" and "religious commitment" is not limited by the parameters set by Buddhist scholastic reflection and systematization. In fact, it is not clear to me that the Buddhist scholastics used concepts corresponding exactly to what I may think are religious meaning and commitment (however vague my own conceptions may turn out to be). I do trust, however, that whatever is lost in scholastic faithfulness will be more than offset by the promise of a useful perspective on the topic.

Furthermore, "religious" is used here to characterize a constellation of practices and discourse genres that encompass the social, as well as the psychological, and, as we shall see presently, also involve formal issues of doctrinal reasoning. The puzzle is precisely in this multiplicity of meanings.

A Fascination with Truth

A fascination with truth and puzzlement in the face of problems that arise when we make claims about truth ties this paper, its reader, author, and editor, and the person honored with the book, to Nāgārjuna and those that have studied him for centuries. This fascination also is one of the reasons that for a brief, but prolific, period contemporary scholars showed an unusual enthusiasm for the doctrine of "the two truths," a "doctrine" that earlier generations of scholars (e.g., Louis de la Vallée Poussin) dismissed as nonsense. Especially since the decade of the 1960s we have heard many praises for this doctrine. Still, this enthusiasm seems to respond to our puzzlement: it is not clear what the doctrine means beyond the sophisticated rhetoric that some have in fact considered sophistry.

But alas, there are so many different ways to respond to this fascination and puzzlement! The question of the validity, truth, or rationality of the doctrine is not the only question. I am also puzzled by its meaning, especially in the context of a history of Madhyamaka *as a form of religious thought.* I understand "meaning" in this context to be in part social function and in part psychological function and process. My interest in this paper is, then, the two truths as categories of religious thought or rhetoric that may shed some light on the way in which certain Buddhists tried to make sense of their beliefs (which often also entails trying to make sense of their world).

Unfortunately, we are severely limited in our capacity to pursue this question successfully. The study of Indian Buddhism in the West is beset with a number of special limitations. Some of these are the result of the nature of the evidential material itself. Others are the result of the location of Buddhism in Western culture. In the first group, that of problems arising from the data itself, one must count the absence of sociographic and biographic data. Specifically in the study of Nāgārjuna, reliable data on his life, to say nothing of valid data, are virtually nonexistent. One cannot even come close to the type of information we have on figures like Plato and his times, much less to the historically nuanced portraits we can form of more recent figures in Western, and for that matter Indian, history. Admittedly, what one can say even of more recent Western figures (e.g., of the political ambiguities of Carl Jung, of the religious inclinations of Ludwig Wittgenstein, or of the personal struggles of Teresa of Ávila as a woman) is tentative. Judgements regarding cause and attributions of influences and motivations are at best probabilistic.

I mean this in the strictest sense of the word "probability," and apply it to most aspects of our investigation. For instance, the materials we have at out disposal are samples, and, in the case of ancient Indian Buddhism, they are restricted and inadequate samples. Or, consider the fact that often the probabilistic choice is hidden—as is the case when we use a particular human scenario to interpret a text, that is, whenever we read a text in light of human needs and aspirations that may not be universal.[3] When reconstructing those historical scenarios we do have a limited number of possibilities, but the data we possess often is not enough, or too idealized and normative, to allow us to set the scenario with any degree of confidence. Thus, the probability that we will accurately imagine, let alone reconstruct, the social and individual circumstances for human events, ideas, and ideologies when we know what we know of Jung or Teresa is certainly much higher than the probability of understanding Plato, and much

3. The nature of our evidence and the limits of our knowledge are sometimes obscured because we cultivate the illusion that our conclusions are reached by formal deductive processes, or we affect a certainty and overconfidence that is at best hyperbolic, and which is often not falsifiable. The problem is endemic to the Humanities, but much more serious in the study of ancient Indian thought.

more than the probability of understanding what Nāgārjuna sought, did, thought, or could have meant.

Problems that are due to the location of Buddhism in Western culture are only partly related to problems of the first type (paucity of historical data). These are problems of the-square-peg-in-the-round-hole type: a cultural phenomenon we barely understand (Nāgārjuna's Buddhism and Nāgārjuna the human being, and the man) has to fit into a foreign cultural mode (the forum of the Western academy). Thus, Nāgārjuna becomes a philosopher and yet finds no place in philosophy curricula. He becomes a mystic, yet no one understands the religious setting for his works (that is, not just the doctrine, but the type of religious life he led, or the community of belief and ritual universes in which he lived). Again, one only has to compare this situation (the social situation of this knowledge) with the situation of Spinoza the philosopher or Teresa the mystic to understand the magnitude of the problem.[4]

Problems of the first type (e.g., where did he live, what did he do on a normal day, what was his early childhood background and his social status as an adult) cannot be answered with much certainty for lack of reliable data. Yet some such questions must be asked. They have often been ignored because Nāgārjuna has been studied mostly from the perspective of a "philology of doctrine" or a history of philosophy content with a gloss of arguments, postulations, and propositions. This is an approach that forgives our inability to locate the work in any kind of social setting, perhaps forbids us to investigate this location, perhaps forbids us from discovering the impossibility of locating this setting.

Such problems lead to a number of desperate solutions. Some will want us to believe that Nāgārjuna's biography is irrelevant: either "it" is only a myth to be valued as myth, or "it" would tell us nothing of significance for understanding his thought. Others would want us to believe that, well, he really was not that important after all—which is another way of translating the absence of evidence into the evidence of absence. Still others seem to suggest that Nāgārjuna being beyond reproof, there is no point in investigating his social contexts. If he has no biography, he has no history, and he stands outside history and beyond criticism (that is, beyond critical investigation).

4. This is not to say that the study and presentation of these two figures are not without problems of their own, or free of the mystification and unwarranted attribution of ideas and beliefs that plagues much of what we say about Nāgārjuna.

Furthermore, there is a certain unavoidable ambivalence toward anything we conclude about Nāgārjuna. On the one hand, we are not in a Buddhist society, and we are in a so-called post-modern society to boot. It is not clear how questions of judgement and value should be treated in these confusing and confused times. And it is not clear what the significance of the study of Nāgārjuna could be in a non-Buddhist society. I have yet to meet the colleague whose work on Nāgārjuna is valued beyond the very limited confines of Buddhist studies, and then again sometimes even simply beyond the confines of Mādhyamika studies. This is frustrating, and confusing, but perhaps it is also liberating.

On the other hand we could hardly justify our interest in Nāgārjuna if we did not in some way value his work—or at least value the high regard in which he was held in Asia. And we would not be interested in his work if we did not feel that it may hold interesting clues about human beings and religion beyond Nāgārjuna himself. We may despair for fear that we will never find anything more than a very speculative recasting of Nāgārjuna that is meaningful only in a scholarly metalanguage foreign to Nāgārjuna. But despair is not the only option. One can proceed with full awareness of the fragility and tentativeness of our conclusions, and with a healthy skepticism regarding their usefulness.

To proceed in spite of the serious limitations that are inherent to the subject seems to me the only alternative acceptable to those of us for whom one or all of the following propositions are true: either Nāgārjuna was historically important, or his work is of some inherent value, or his work can teach us something about the cultural phenomena we call Buddhism, and the phenomena of philosophy and religion generally. It is primarily to the third of these assumptions that I now direct my reflections. And I do so accepting the limitations of our evidence, but suggesting that the bits and pieces of traces we possess can still teach us something about Nāgārjuna's religion (broadly understood), or at least about the religious contexts of statements attributed to this legendary figure.

In the next few pages, then, I will engage in reflections that, given the paucity of historical and social data, are mostly speculative, but which may prove of some heuristic value. These are preliminary reflections that may be described as social and critical, but which are intended as exegetical, and as "psychological" in the broadest meaning of this term. In other words, although the initial theoretical assumptions are assumptions as to the probable social context for the production of Nāgārjuna's work, they are intended as an aid towards a different way of reading his "work" as part of the "work" of religion and the work of religious philosophies.[5] This is a reading that starts out with much of the skepticism and the social eye that characterizes Western scholarship at the end of the twentieth century. It is nevertheless a reading that takes seriously the work of religion as something more than (not necessarily something totally other than and autonomous from) social function and social meanings. I believe that a reading of suspicion can still enrich our contemporary rereadings of the work. Although the perspective adopted is one of social criticism or suspicion, the goal is to enrich the work of the Humanities, which in this case involves, among other things, an inevitable rewriting of Nāgārjuna's words as religious thought.

The Two and the Many

The Nāgārjuna that I envision must have had more than one aim in the formulation of his philosophy, and of the two truths as a central component of this philosophy. I suggest that the two truths is a classical strategy for presenting in metaphysical terms what is in fact something more than just an ontology. In the following pages I analyze various applications of this strategy that may be conveniently classified in three broad classes. First, the two truths serve to sanctify orders of human relationships. Second, the doctrine of the two truths allows for the symbolic intensification of a given: the rupture between, on the one hand, the social and psychological realities of the profane and, on the other, the reality of spiritual liberation. And, third, the doctrine of the two truths bridges this same discontinuity even as it intensifies it.

Multiple Meanings

The constraints that the data impose on our capacity to historicize force us to concentrate mostly on the contradictions or tensions in the system that may reveal something about the social and psychological functions of the doctrine. Granted, some of these tensions may be projections of our own concerns, but not all of them are.

---

5. The term "work of religion" is borrowed from Bourdieu (1971, 1975). However, it is used here not only as a designation for the social functions of religion, but also as a term for all the cultural activities and psychological effects of religious practices, especially as they are considered to be valuable products or goals of human endeavor, hence, as potentially valuable in themselves.

I assume that our ambiguity about Nāgārjuna is not completely unrelated to the realities of the production of his work. In other words, our hesitation and stumbling may reflect in part the hesitation and stumbling of the ancient Indian Buddhists. Nāgārjuna's work is certainly the product of a small intellectual elite, most likely a privileged class, and the product of an author who by the very nature of his work placed himself apart from what we call mundane life.[6] This was, furthermore, an elite that was both similar to ours (that of the Western academy), and dissimilar to ours (that of the non-Buddhist, secular scholar).[7]

Or, to restate the same notion in much more radical terms: it is of the nature of academic reflection generally, including religious-theological speculation (and Nāgārjuna is no exception to this), to distance discourse from the groundings of its object in the life of its authors.[8] That is to say, academic reflection by necessity transforms the immediate and concrete into the discursive and abstract, and therefore risks becoming a type of disembodied rationalization (and in religious thinkers a disembodied religiosity). Religious discourse of the type we find in the *śāstra*s attempts to lead others into the isolated sphere of the mind. Yet the discourse is at the same time contained within

6. This is, of course, a placing or location defined by social role, not in fact an existence outside the mundane. Fortunately, in the case of Nāgārjuna, his two epistles, *Ratnāvalī* and *Suhṛllekha*, attest to his actual location in the socio-political arena. I assume that the royal recipients of these letters were in fact accessible to Nāgārjuna and amenable to his preaching. Conversely, this implies that Nāgārjuna was willing to serve as legitimator of their status—a conclusion that is in fact supported by the content of both of these works.

7. I distinguish privilege from power, social rank, and wealth (although all four are often found together). I also assume that privilege is attained and preserved by control over commodities, which, in the case of the Buddhist monk, include, but are not limited to, spiritual and intellectual commodities. Claims of special access to a transcendent truth, for instance, can also be interpreted as claims of privileged access to a valuable commodity: unquestioned and unquestionable truth. Special access to commodities is translated as power, rank, and privilege, or as all three—but the commodities may be valued in themselves. For a more detailed discussion of these notions, see Bourdieu, 1977a, 1977b, 1980.

8. I use the terms "theological" and "theology" in this article to refer to the *rationalizing task* of religious thinkers. Theology is thus the general drive to make religious belief and practice rational (coherent, convincing, ordered, and consistent with other sources of knowledge). This is only one aspect of the work of śāstric authors, but an important one, and also an important part of the work of religion. This usage does not imply, of course, that the discourse of Buddhist philosophers was about a "theos," or that their work was exclusively theological. On academic reflection and distancing, see Bourdieu, Passeron, and de Saint Martin 1994.

the cultural context that produces it. Unavoidably, it is part of a broader rhetoric of constructive theology and apologetics.[9]

I do not use these terms, "constructive theology" and "apologetics," disparagingly. Rather I am trying to call attention to several important aspects of theological discourse and, therefore, of Nāgārjuna's discourse as religious discourse. Religious speculation *is* religion, including religion in the sense of a clear separation of the sacred from the profane.[10] It is religion by serving at least three functions. First, theology is a form of celebratory ritual that can serve self-confirming purposes. Second, the self-confirmatory effects are generated by both behavioral and discursive processes. Theology also affects religious life generally by ordering or rationalizing the forms of language that a religious community will recognize as religious, authorized or authoritative. And, last, intellectualized discourse about religion can lead, perhaps paradoxically, to a return to the profane, or, better, a sacralization of the profane.

We may be reluctant to use the terms sacred and profane to talk about Mādhyamika, but the dichotomy is implicit in the separation between the privileged position of *paramārtha* and its association with the Buddha on the one hand, and the association of *saṁvṛti* with error, desire, and the state of unenlightenment, on the other.

Of course, the rhetoric of Nāgārjuna is a rhetoric of "return" (to adopt and adapt one of Prof. Nagao's conceptions). It belongs to a family of religious discourse in which two realms—worldly and supramundane, or profane and sacred—are separated and distinguished only to allow for an eventual reintegration. A division of reality into two realms is accepted provisionally, only to bring them back together by various rhetorical, philosophical, ethical, or ritual moves. Still, in Nāgārjuna's system, as in many other religious systems, two forces pull simultaneously in opposite directions. A centrifugal force pulls in the direction of a hierarchy (lower and higher "reality")—even as the doctrine, as dialectic, recognizes the centripetal force of an implicit identity of the two truths. Conversely, even as the dialectic recognizes

9. The term rhetoric is used in the contemporary sense extensively explored by Burke (1950, 1961, 1973). I consider "rhetoric" to be one of the most important aspects of the work of religion in institutionalized, literate traditions—it is one of several strategies for the construction of universes of meaning. Religious rhetoric, apologetic and non-apologetic, also serves to protect and isolate from other forms of human knowledge those experiences that might be termed "religious."

10. The words "sacred" and "profane" are used here as analytic terms in ways similar to Boyer's (1994) cognitive explanation of the concept of the "supernatural."

that there can be no hierarchy, the rhetoric reverts again and again to a hierarchical conception of the two truths.

Nāgārjuna's rhetoric embodies or demonstrates a tension between the withdrawal of the absolute truth of religious intuitions and the confused world of multiple voices (the world of *prapañca*). This tension is a good indicator of an underlying social and psychological tension, that we may attribute to Nāgārjuna the person with much hesitation, but that we can attribute to his social and religious context with a certain degree of confidence. The putatively univocal and monolithic discourse of Nāgārjuna the philosopher shows gaps and breaks suggestive of the social and psychological settings of his philosophical quest.

This can be further expanded as follows: (1) Privilege is based on a social disambiguity, which I presume to reflect an underlying ambiguity. By disambiguity I mean the process by which ideologies erase tensions and create closure where social and psychological contexts are in tension or where the potential for change is viewed as threatening. Ambiguity, on the other hand, is the term that designates the uncertain and contradictory ground upon which religious ideologies seek to create order. In terms of the focus of this paper, the leveling of difference and the closing down of uncertainty is brought about by rhetorical means. Not all religious strategies rely on rhetoric and not all religious rhetorics erase ambiguity, but the literature under consideration here does both.

The ambiguity reflects the inherent vulnerability of this discourse of certainty, the emptiness of hierarchies, the fact that hierarchies of truth paint over undeniable contradictions and differences, and the psychological insecurity of those who struggle to maintain the hierarchy. Thus, the successful maintenance of rigid hierarchies disambiguates social and psychological uncertainty.

(2) Religious life occurs on a number of planes that I assume reflect the very different interests of groups and individuals. Hence, the social function of a doctrine does not exhaust its meanings. These multiple meanings and interests may coincide in one person (in fact they often do), yet they may also generate conflict or ambivalence. Attempts to resolve this ambivalence involve processes of (a) isolation and selective attention/inattention; that is, the physical or mental reinforcement ("recollection") of particular orders of meaning.[11]

11. The term "selective inattention" is from Sullivan (1953), but variants of the same concept occur in other psychological theories, in W. James and Piaget, for instance. In Sullivan, it is the most important dimension of what he calls the "control

Especially successful in a religious context is the development of "techniques of the self," like asceticism, monasticism, and meditation practice.[12] One also struggles against ambivalence by means of (b) withdrawal or inattention other than separation or isolation, e.g., ritual delimitations of identity by excluding other, possible definitions of self (aspects of pseudospeciation or negative identity),[13] (c) doctrinal discourse ("theology") as abstract withdrawal (substitution of facticity with ideality), as ritualization, and as attempts to regulate experience, and, as a final corollary to all of the above, (d) moral discourse.

Some or all of these socio-psychological strategies are at play in the work of Nāgārjuna—or, at least, the assumption of such strategies helps us make sense of the complex interplay of discourses that one finds in his work.[14] On the basis of the extant works, and on the basis

---

of focal awareness," and is both a normal dimension of cognitive development and a defense mechanism. He describes it as "the relatively trifling and almost ubiquitous disturbance of awareness to which I give the term *selective inattention*, in which one simply doesn't happen to notice almost an infinite series of more-or-less meaningful details of one's living" (p. 319). I share with Sullivan his view of personality as an interpersonal reality, but I extend the model of inattention to think of theology and ideology as *cultural constructs* amenable to an explanation through cognitive models of the *individual personality*. More specifically, I see the work of culture as including a process of selective inattention paralleling more explicit or consciously articulated constructions of reality, and I see this socially constructed inattention as both constructing and confirming individual processes of inattention. On possible connections between individual personality and cultural construction, see Bruner 1951, 1957.

12. I prefer "techniques of self," to the more common "technologies of self," which I find mystifies the notion unnecessarily and erases useful if problematic distinctions between material and symbolic technologies. The term "technologies of self" was popularized by Foucault (e.g., 1988), but I prefer the preliminary but seminal work of M. Mauss (1936), who in speaking of cultural techniques of the body seems to me to have a more elegant model for understanding this aspect of the work of culture. I also see interesting connections between these notions and the way in which Erikson (1985) and Lorenz (1973) see intellectual pursuits and ideologies as extensions of processes of ritualization that are grounded in evolutionary and ego-development processes involving a mind-body unit.

13. The term "pseudospeciation" is borrowed from Erikson (1975), but I assume that the human tendency to perceive one's own group as a distinct species, or as the only truly human subspecies, is not only pervasive, but an integral part of the work of culture. Erikson (1975: 75–77) considers pseudospeciation as a common, but nonetheless pathological, aspect of human behavior. I see the process of pseudospeciation as ethically suspect, but not necessarily pathological. Erikson's views are, of course, heavily influenced by the work of Konrad Lorenz (especially Lorenz 1963). One may speak of this process of identity formation as "negative identity" (identity defined through exclusion) or as "adversary identity" (See French 1989).

14. In this essay I adopt a moderately generous definition of what may have been "his work," that is, the product of a single person: namely, the author of the *Madhyamaka-Kārikās*. In this definition I include *Vigrahavyāvartanī*, *Śūnyatāsaptatī*, *Yuktiṣaṣṭikā*, *Ratnāvalī*, *Catuḥstava*, *Suhṛllekha* and, of course, the *Vaidalyaprakaraṇa*, which

of what we know of Buddhist Indian *śāstric* literature, it is fair to assume that Nāgārjuna was a religious specialist and a monastic. Our capacity to know exactly what it meant to be religious in the presumed context of his work (the polemic and academic roles of his writing) is restricted by the paucity of materials. Furthermore, our understanding of Nāgārjuna's own personal predilections and habits is even more limited (if not totally inexistent). We will never know if most of his energies went into philosophical debate or if he spent most of his time in ritual and meditation—or, for that matter, if his life centered around any one of the many other possible scenarios of a human life.

The role of the intellectual monastic agrees with the moralistic tone of key passages in *Ratnāvalī* and *Suhṛllekha*. But these passages do not tell us much as to what was the focus of Nāgārjuna's daily life. We have no way even of guessing at his personal hierarchy of interests and commitments—whether or not Nāgārjuna the person was committed to a life of teaching, debate, and speculation more than to some other form of the bodhisattva-monastic vows or some other sort of religious aspiration. I would volunteer provisionally that he most likely belonged to a class of religious specialist (known to us in various contemporary settings) who acted as if the preservation and propagation of particular forms of discourse (a theological discourse) is in fact the most important function of the bodhisattva-monk.[15]

---

is not referred to in the present essay. Even a more conservative definition of authorship that would discard the *Ratnāvalī*, *Catuḥstava*, and *Suhṛllekha* would give us a similar doctrinal picture. Although I cannot accept Lindtner's (1982b) much broader conceptions of the authorship and authenticity of the "Nagarjunian" corpus, I see enough continuities among the above six works to argue that the traditional attribution is most likely correct—or, to express it as accurately as possible, that these are the works of a single author, and therefore they are the work of the author of the *Madhyamaka-Kārikās*, whoever he might have been, and at whatever time he might have lived. However, I would argue that even a minimalist view of the authorship of the Nagarjunian corpus (a view that accepts only the *Madhyamaka-Kārikās* and the *Vigrahavyāvartanī* as his) demands that we account for obvious religious meanings (e.g., of chapters 24–25 of the *Kārikās*). Additionally, I am also willing to concede that some works of doubtful attribution are most likely the work of the same author or one of his immediate disciples, such is the *Bodhicittavivaraṇa*. For more on dating and authorship, see Ruegg 1981, 1982. Some of these problems, especially those relating to the composition of the *Yuktiṣaṣṭikā*, are taken up in Tola and Dragonetti 1983.

15. This model is proposed partly in hope that our scholarly understanding of religion will someday restore the role of doctrinal speculation and debate to its proper place among the many forms of religious practice. The Indian Buddhist doctrinal reflections that have survived represent the thought of a privileged few, and whatever data (or ideal representation) we have on the ritual life of ancient

Truths and Orders

The two truths are indeed about the nature of truth and reality in the abstract, but they are at the same time about distinctions of social prestige and intellectual competence and about the construction of public and private experience.[16] The truth of *paramārtha* is the truth of the *ārya*, and *saṁvṛti* is the realm of the world (*loka*). Unavoidably, this has implications for the attribution of privilege, authority, and judgements of esteem and competence.[17] These are, of course, not the only implications of this discourse and its metaphors, as I expect to show below.[18] The distinction between ultimate and noble on the one hand and conventional and common on the other has many meanings, some social and some of a different order. For instance, the distinction is also that between the theological expert (using the term loosely to include the ideal *yogī* and buddhas and bodhisattvas, as well as the monk-scholar) and the ignorant or the unbeliever (the distinction between these last two being often very diffuse). This often coincided (and coincides) with distinctions of class, but it does not have to.[19] Additionally, it is a distinction of spheres of discourse and practice (e.g., ritual versus the acceptance of

---

Indian Buddhists may very well represent the religious life of only a few. Yet, this is religious material, human religious material. Moreover, we cannot assume, prima facie, that this elite religion did not affect other dimensions of Buddhist religious life. Taking elite religious discourse as religious data does not diminish the importance of the doctrinal reflections of those who are not privileged enough to have access to the most prestigious and literate forms of religious speculation. Those reflections deserve our attention, and we should not lose sight of the fact that all strata of the hierarchies of literacy engage in doctrinal reflection. The study of religious *practices of thought and discourse* among the non-literate or the marginally literate could throw much light on the nature of religion generally. For a charming and insightful study of a tragic case, see Ginzburg 1976.

16. I use the concept of construction in the weaker sense used by Bruner (1986, 1990), with no intention whatsoever of implying reduction by elimination, cultural relativism, or the absolute primacy of language over other dimensions of experience (e.g., biological substrata).

17. This is tacitly recognized by J. Takakusu in terms that must be qualified as a caricature, although they were most likely not intended to sound this way. Takakusu (1944: 96–98) suggested that Nāgārjuna was proposing a dialectic to reconcile popular belief or opinion with scientific truth. Popular belief he qualifies as the opinions of the uneducated masses. He believes that the doctrine of the two truths in Nāgārjuna proposes some sort of dialectic between "popular" and "scientific" belief, whereby one affects the other in some sort of progressive succession.

18. I have discussed the polyvalence or polysemy of some Buddhist metaphors of nobility in Gómez forthcoming.

19. Contestation of truths occurs at many levels (Scott 1990), and power can be exerted, of course, top down or top up (de Certeau 1988).

the truth "behind" ritual). In this sense it is also about the distinction between religious practice and two elusive and problematic (therefore, powerful) concepts: experience (in traditional terms: "yogic direct perception") and foundational meaning (in traditional terms: the ultimate).

Furthermore, the two truths reflect a classical religious maneuver of claiming ineffability for foundational beliefs, and thus shifting authority from public argument to a hidden, protected realm of unquestioned authority. The *ārya*'s silence is "aryan" because it is authoritative silence, but, insofar as it is silent, it is unassailable.[20]

At the social level, one may say that *saṁvṛti* is the Buddhist equivalent of the contemporary critical notion of false consciousness, and as such, it is of one piece with the modern intellectual's fantasy of correcting the mistakes of others: the world others see is a false world, only the critical thinker sees the world as it truly is. The concept of *saṁvṛti* presupposes a certain degree of deception that is traditionally understood as "error," and entails a hierarchy of competence: the few who see through the veil of convention and the many who blindly persist in it. Insofar as this error is partly moved by desire (and animosity), one can posit that it involves a certain degree of self-deception: wanting to see the object of our desire as we imagine it, whether it is real or not.

However, this is only one aspect of the dichotomy, because *saṁvṛti* is also the vehicle that leads to truth, as stated in the *Madhyamaka-kārikās* (MK xxiv.10ab): "Without having recourse to convention, the ultimate goal cannot be taught."[21] Religious doctrines, beliefs, and arguments may be extensions of the ultimate truth, they may point at it or manifest it, but they are still *saṁvṛti*. They belong to a

20. Consider the following passage from the *Prasannapadā* (p. 57): "[Objection:] 'If no such assertions are made [by you], then how can you establish with such certainty your proposition that any entity whatsoever arises from itself, or from another, or from both, or from without a cause?' [Reply:] 'It is said [in our teachings] that this proposition has been established by a reasoning acceptable to the world, not by the arguments (*upapatti*) of Noble Ones (*ārya*).' [Objection:] 'Now, is it then that the Noble Ones do not have any arguments (*upapatti*)? Who then says that [reality] is neither being nor non being?' [Reply:] 'Since the ultimate truth is the silence of the Noble Ones (or, 'the ultimate truth is something about which Noble Ones keep silent'), where in this [silence] can discriminating discourse (*prapañca*) arise so that they could have a thesis or a non-thesis (*upapattir anupapattir vā*)?"

21. Henceforth, references to the *Madhyamaka-Kārikās* are given with the common abbreviation MK. All passages are translated from the Sanskrit in L. de la Vallée Poussin's edition of *Prasannapadā*. The *Kārikās* were also edited separately by de Jong 1977.

type of public discourse claiming to be grounded on an ineffable truth, which, in turn, is privately known but publicly displayed.

Roy Rappaport (1974, 1976) suggested that concepts of an ineffable or numinous absolute serve as the unquestionable grounding for religious propositions that sanctify social relations. If this hypothesis is applied to the doctrine of the two truths, one may say that *paramārtha* serves as one such unquestionable grounding, whereas *saṁvṛti* has the dual value of untruth by virtue of not being *paramārtha*, and the value of truth by virtue of being both what leads to *paramārtha* and what expresses *paramārtha*. In other words, the doctrine of the two truths can be seen as an instance of a type of mystification, rationalization, and sanctification of religious propositions and institutions seen in other traditions under other forms of religious rhetoric. One may say that the interaction between the two is functionally equivalent to carrying the host in a monstrance in a procession that is led by church hierarchs with princes, dukes, and counts following closely behind. In the doctrinal context of this essay, one may say that the analogue is Nāgārjuna's dialectic creating the space for the unsayable that will carry in its train the vast and complex retinue of Buddhist doctrines, practices, and institutions.[22]

Bridging a Chasm

However, this is not all that is at play here. Religious truths carry conviction also because they are somehow true. That is to say, the apparent withdrawal of truth into the safe niche of the ineffable is not merely an attempt to protect religious dogma, it is also an extension of certain cognitions and affective states that accompany religious thought, conviction, and commitment.[23] The manner in which such thoughts and feelings are reworked and made accessible and intelligible is that part of the "work of religion" that makes it religious, rather than merely one aspect of secular culture.

22. On discourse and authority, see Bourdieu 1977a, 1977b, and Bourdieu and Passeron 1977. On the authority of narrative and interpretation, see, e.g., Cain 1980 and Fraser 1987.

23. Hallisey (1994) follows a similar line of argument, exploring the role of the doctrine of the two truths in pedagogy, communication, and persuasion in a Singhalese case. A much more radical variant of this take on Mādhyamika is found in the work of Huntington (1989, 1992), but his views are rooted in a particular way of reading the doctrine of the two truths that is, in my view, too narrow, as it fails to raise the issue of religious meanings.

This type of discourse is the second dimension of the doctrine of the two truths that I wish to highlight in this essay. My interest here is not in false consciousness or authority, or the way in which the work of religion accomplishes certain social or institutional ends, but the way in which the construct of the two truths reflects a type of religious "argument," or "narrative" expressive of an understanding that is characteristic of religious discourse, specifically the religious discourse of wisdom. I propose to summarize this understanding in a simple statement: the mystified restatement of a problem appears as the solution to the problem.

An example from a narrative text may clarify this point. The daughter of a poor family from the city of Śrāvastī, Kisā Gotamī, married the son of a rich merchant.[24] She conceived a child with him, but the child died soon after it was born. The bereft mother wandered the streets of Śrāvastī looking for a medicine that would restore her child to life. She was finally directed toward the incomparable physician, the Buddha. The Buddha "cured" her pain by asking her to bring to him a pinch of the medicine he recommended: a single mustard seed obtained from a house where "no son or daughter nor any one else has yet died." Kisā Gotamī wandered from village to village, but nowhere could she find a house untouched by death. Finally she realized there was no refuge from death, no cure for it—and with this she was enlightened. In other words, the realization that the prescribed medicine did not exist was her cure.[25]

Paradoxical therapy? Perhaps. But unquestionably the story also captures the site of religious authority and its rhetorical order. The realization is nothing else but a restatement of Kisā Gotamī's original experience: death is, and it is inevitable. The realization that brings about the cure is, admittedly, an intensified and generalized version of the initial experience of grief. In its abstraction the second experience (Kisā's realization of the inevitability of death) is somehow weaker

24. A number of characters in canonical narrative go by the name of Kisā Gotamī (also transcribed Kisāgotamī). The story referenced here is that of Kisā Gotamī Therī, who the Buddha is said to have considered foremost among the hermit nuns (*Aṅguttara Nikāya*, PTS i.25). She is the *arhantī* whose story is narrated in the *Apadāna* (PTS ii.564–566) and in the *Therīgāthā-aṭṭhakathā* (PTS pp. 174–176 —although the story in the commentary does not seem to match the corresponding verses in the *Therīgāthā*, namely stanzas 213–223). Here I follow mostly *Dhammapada-aṭṭhakathā* (PTS ii.270–275).

25. Readers wishing to read the story in full may consult the English version by Burlingame (1969), 2.257–260. Burlingame also offers useful references to parallel versions of the story (257, n. 1).

(and perhaps, hence, a cure or inoculation), but it is nevertheless a restatement of the original understanding.

It is no accident that the story depends on the literary conceit that Kisā Gotamī "had never seen death before."[26] In this way the narrative can proceed as if Kisā does not understand that death is final—another way, perhaps, of telling us she refuses to accept the obvious. This primary ignorance or denial is removed only by a repetition of the experience: death is lived again, in a different, healing modality.

We are familiar with similar uses of rhetoric in religious discourse. The logical incomprehensibility of the doctrine of the Trinity is lived as a powerful mystery, and thus incomprehensibility is turned into truth. The initial puzzlement turns into conviction. The absurdity of the human predicament of evil is attributed to an equally puzzling original evil event: original sin. Displaced into the realm of origins, an inconceivable, if not absurd, proposition becomes meaningful belief. Incomprehensible, experienced evil events are relived, replaced or displaced by the acceptance of a myth that repeats the incomprehensible.

Similarly, *paramārtha* is another way of recognizing that sacred and profane do not meet. The dialectics of *saṁvṛti-paramārtha* restate *paramārtha* and restate the obvious; they do not solve the mystery, but intensify it. Yet, because *paramārtha* stands above all duality and predication, it is both beyond reason and unassailable. Hence, recognizing its non-rationality, one is convinced of its truth.

However, the nonrationality of the ultimate truth is in good measure due to the fact that it is ground, point of departure, and goal. It is also possible to see the ineffable absolute as the end of a dialectic process that includes the acceptance of the point of departure (e.g., death and impermanence), its realization by acceptance, its presence as that which is left after the relative is consumed by its own contradictions, and as the goal (*paramārtha*) of a religious practice. The ineffable is to the believer much more than the object of a belief; at the very least it is the ground of meaning for a practice, but it is also the distant goal. Even as it is rehearsed, therefore, the one ultimate truth becomes what it was to begin with: two truths.

---

26. Also of interest is the use of this story to illustrate *Dhammapada* 114 (or the use of *Dhammapada* 114 as a commentary to the story). The stanza reads:

> Better than living for a hundred years never seeing the deathless would be to live for a single day seeing the deathless.

This adds another layer of meaning to the realization of death: the realization of death results in or is identical with liberation from death.

Do We Really Need Two Truths?

Western preconceptions about truth would seem to dictate an exegesis of the two truths that would show that they are somehow not two. This, as we shall see presently, is not only a Western desideratum. But it is definitely a problem of interpretation if we assume that this is the case before we have examined the complex rhetoric involved in the doctrine of the two truths.

The problem with having only one truth is that it tends to erase what multiple truths have to teach us about the nature of religious authority: namely, that truth is not one, insofar as (a) there are diverse and conflicting claims on "truth," (b) the notion of "truth" is far from being transparent, and is constantly challenged by the incomprehensible, and (c) multiple truths is the normal way to speak, for it is the only way one can account, however tentatively, for the fragmentation and confusion of the world as it is given to us.

The advantage of having only one truth (or the primary need to think of truth as only one) is that it satisfies our need for unified experience. Yet, even a single truth, once stated, is many. This is the axiom behind many philosophies of non-duality, and the reason why ultimate religious truths are often mysteries in which contradictions coexist in a formula that is understood as transcending the contradictions (or, if you prefer, in which truth is a coincidentia oppositorum).[27] The ineffability of the absolute truth is a necessity, perhaps a psychological necessity, but, as argued by Rappaport, possibly a social and symbolic necessity.

When we seek one truth, we seek a way out of the multiplicity of truth. We are in fact agreeing with the desire implied in the passage from *Suttanipāta* quoted in the epigraph of this paper (*Suttanipāta* 886):[28]

---

27. See, for instance, the summary statement in *Ratnāvalī*, stanzas 50–51 (Hahn, pp. 20–23): (50) "When he understands that effects arise from their causes in this manner, he does not assert the thesis of non-existence, for he asserts this world's view of how things come to be, [knowing that such a] view originates in discriminating discourse."— *evaṁ hetuphalotpādaṁ dṛṣṭvā nopaiti nāstitāṁ* | *abhyupetyāsya lokasya yāthābhūtyaṁ prapañcajaṁ* | |. (51) "Because he is one who has understood that cessation occurs when there is no more discriminating discourse, he does not assert the thesis of existence. Therefore, he is liberated when he relies only on the non-dual."— *nirodhaṁ cāprapañcotthaṁ yāthābhūtyād upāgataḥ* | *na upayāty astitāṁ tasmān mucyate 'dvayaniśritaḥ* | |. Notice that the two stanzas seem to suggest that there are two kinds of *yāthābhūtyaṁ*; hence the passage appears to be once more trapped by the distinction between the two levels of truth. On the so-called correspondence or mutual implication of contraries, see May 1959, nn. 68 and 773.

28. Translated from the edition of Andersen and Smith. A slightly more stilted

> For there are not many and diverse truths, other than the notions [people] of the world have about permanent things. They construct arguments for these views and proclaim two realities: the true and the false.

In this passage, the Buddhist twist is to assume that permanence is the culprit that creates multiple truths. But implicit in this passage is the hope that truth about impermanence will somehow transcend the duality of truth and untruth, and hence, the multiple truths that confuse all of us.

The paradox in this passage is that the many views of truth are all about a single truth: that which is permanent. Somehow, clinging to the notion of a single permanent reality precludes the possibility of a unifying truth, of a truth that is superordinate to multiple truths and to the duality between the true and the false. With this rejection of the two and assertion of the one, we are left, of course, with a new double truth. But multiple truths also create problems, because holding multiple truths leads to a slippery or wriggly claim on authority.

And the same can be said of having no truth at all, because such claims, when they do not imply defiance, hide an authority that is secret, as it were, or that simply postpone a commitment to truth, with a promise of delivery after commitment. In other words, the Mādhyamika's famous claim to have "no thesis" is indeed still an authority claim. The problem is in the implicit (and unavoidable) truth claim behind the silence. This is suggested by the second quotation in the epigraph (*Suttanipāta* 911):[29]

---

imitation of the word order and structure of the original is possible, and may help summarize my thinking in translating these passages [henceforth such explanations will be announced with the abbreviation "Lit.", which stands for the unscientific but common notion of "literal translation"]. For the first stanza one can imagine an English *chāyā* along the lines of: "For in fact there are not many diverse truths, other than the permanent things [imagined/created] by means of conception in the world. Giving shape to arguments (speculations) based on views, they speak of a thing (reality, truth = *dhamma*) that is a duality: namely, true and false."—*na h'eva saccāni bahūni nānā, aññatra saññayā niccāni loke* | *takkañ ca diṭṭhīsu pakappayitvā, saccaṁ musā 'ti dvayadhammaṁ āhu* | |. In *Suttanipāta* dialogues the responses can often be read as a single unitary text, hence my reading of *h'eva* as a reason for, or expansion of, the statements found in 884, rather than a simple "indeed" in response to the question in 885.

29. Translated from the edition of Andersen and Smith The quotation can be rendered lit.: "The Brahmin, shaping no concepts, does not engage in them, or hold a view as the gist and kernel, nor is he relative or companion of knowledge(s). Understanding commonplace agreements [about what is true or acceptable], he is indifferent to them. Others seize [accept, and hold on to] them."—*na brāhmaṇo kappaṁ upeti saṁkhaṁ, na diṭṭhisārī na pi ñāṇabandhu* | *ñatvā ca so sammutiyo puthujjā, upekhati uggahaṇanta-m-aññe* | |.

> The [true] Brahmin does not construct and adopt conceptualizations, or hold as essential any view, nor is he a follower of [any special] knowledge. Understanding commonplace conventions and opinions, he is indifferent to them, while others latch on to them.

If this is to be taken to mean that the Buddha simply accepts things as they are, then one must ask, Why do we need the authority of the Buddha for this? Only two answers are possible, both supposing that "things as they are" is not a simple given or our everyday experience: (a) that the Buddha accepts things as they are but knows of a special meaning to/in "things as they are," or (b) that no one except him really knows the truth that is other than things as they are. Either way, a secret hides behind his "acceptance" of all conventional truth, a surplus of meaning to which only he has access. I propose that Buddhists waver between these two possibilities.

This wavering or ambivalence is what allows for a rich use of a rhetoric of truth that states the obvious in ways that appear not obvious. This is what we see normally outside of philosophy in stories like that of Kisā, or in our efforts to make sense of the "wisdom" of the Noble Truths. One can read statements like *sabbā saṅkhārā aniccā* as tautologies or restatements of the obvious.

Yet, statements of this kind seem to encapsulate a wisdom of sorts. What is it that makes this statement mean so many different things, like a novel read many times, like a prayer heard or uttered many times? I am not suggesting that there is somehow a knowledge that is radically nonverbal, unbounded by the culture and tradition of discourse. But, with recent psychological literature on "wisdom," I would go as far as claiming that a restatement of the obvious may occur after a second sort of cognition, one of familiarity and acceptance, which derives its power in part from the fact that they do impart knowledge that is processed or integrated at a nonverbal level. It is not simply, however, a matter of gaining a direct and immediate intuition, because often the trick is in a rehearsal or a repetition, and often it depends on a certain genre of rhetoric. But, as in the case of the story of Kisā, the rehearsal is not a simple repetition, but an intensification that changes the meaning of the original separation. The rhetoric and the rehearsal make the many into one, or what is conceptually disjointed into a whole experience.

The Two and the One

But, the two truths are a special case of this mode of discourse that I have called restatements of the obvious, because in this case it appears that what should be one is reformulated as two. Of course, in a certain manner of speaking, the ultimate truth is in itself an attempt to hold together the many as one. This attempt has more than one meaning. It is, as already noted, an attempt to secure a firm ground for the authority of religious discourse. But it is also a shorthand for an epistemic-ontological issue. In other words, it hides a complex set of questions about what we can know and about a presumed object of that knowledge.

The many is not false by necessity, but it appears confusing: the heterogeneous seems to have built in itself the seeds of contradiction. But the tradition that saw in the diversity of opinion (*dṛṣṭi*) proof that opinions and theses cannot be valid seems to ignore that every "true opinion" pretends to be homogeneous with itself and heterogeneous with the world. In this sense, homoglossia is the basis for *doxa*, the fruit of heteroglossia. Speaking with one consistent voice is only the precondition for speaking with many contradictory voices.

Both in Asia and in the West, two traditions seem to clash on this issue.[30] In India, Buddhism, for all its claims to metaphysical pluralism, always sought the one voice that would silence all voices—even when it spoke of this voice as silence itself.[31] This is not an erasure that creates equality; rather it is one that creates a necessary hierarchy: the sharp distinction between the one real and the many unreal generates a split universe.

Two truths, two realities? How many realities we can tolerate is the question, and it is a psychological as well as a social question. For the one truth is also a reflection of a presumed single self, of a reintegration of all opposites. Stated in Buddhist terms, the quest for a single reality is inseparable from attachment to a single, unitary and controlling self.

Be that as it may, the higher truth, the one, has to be theoretically formulated; it is an abstract truth. To sustain this notion of truth one can take a number of paths, among which the Buddhists appear to have taken two positions, which are not mutually exclusive. First, the higher truth can be conceived as a "theoretical truth" (a purely mental cognition) that is higher than the sensory and the factual. Second, one can assume that the truth derives from the teachings of a sage (preferably an omniscient sage) whose direct apprehension of reality shows that the world as we know it is not what it seems to be.

---

30. For a summary of the Western issue see Heimsoeth 1953.

31. Cp. *Prasannapadā*, p. 57, translated in n. 20, above.

It is possible to hold both of these views simultaneously, or hold them ambivalently. But, either way, in order to maintain this delicate balance one must simultaneously hold to one truth and to many truths. The *Bodhicaryāvatāra*, for instance, affirms on the one hand that there are only two, mutually exclusive, truths (*Bodhicaryāvatāra* ix.2–3):[32]

> We admit these two truths: the relative and the ultimate. That which is beyond the ken of intellection (*buddhi*) is the [ultimately] real; intellection [itself] is the relative. (2)
>
> On this point the world is divided in two: the uncultivated, and the [cultivated] yogi. The knowledge of those persons who are yogis sublates (*bādhate*) that of the common folk. (3)

But, on the other hand, the text appears to establish a hierarchy within the higher apprehensions of truth (*Bodhicaryāvatāra* ix.4):

> Moreover, yogis sublate other yogis, each according to his intellectual competence (*dhīviśeṣeṇa*), although they do not quarrel about the goal of their practice (*kāryārha*), as set by a common set of similes (*dṛṣṭānta*). (4)

The Hindu critics of Buddhism had already noted the problems inherent in this appeal to yogic authority (e.g., *Ślokavārttika*): that one person can cognize what others do not, and thereby claim to have access to a higher truth.[33] It is this sense of "sublating," or, literally, "overpowering" (*bādhate*) that is most problematic, because it is ultimately a matter of authority, the yogi's experience being superior to that of the common person only by dint of a doctrinal preference, for why should everyday experience not sublate yogic claims to extraordinary perceptions? The inherent claim to authority is at the root of the notion of *saṁvṛti* as "covering," insofar as non-yogic experience can be a covering only if we accept, a priori, the superiority of the yogi.

But by usage the meaning of *saṁvṛti* is hardly "covering." In fact even etymologically such meaning has only a restricted value. The word is most likely a simple Sanskritic form of Middle Indic *saṁmuti* (= Sanskrit *saṁmati*), "consensus, convention." This reconstruction would trace the word to the root *saṁ√man* (to agree on).[34] The other

---

32. Translated from the Sanskrit in La Vallée Poussin 1914.

33. Kumārila's critique is found in the Nirālambanavāda section of his *Ślokavārttika*, stanzas 90ff. The arguments are summarized with a fair degree of neutrality in Śāntarakṣita's *Tattvasaṅgraha*, chapter XXVI (see Shastri 1968). A useful modern summary is found in Sinha 1938: 98ff. Many of the same arguments have been recast in modern philosophical languages by Matilal 1971a, 1971b, 1973.

34. A Middle Indic *saṁmuti* would easily be Sanskritized (or as the technical term

common term for the "relative truth," *vyavahāra*, also denotes "consensus," in its meanings of "commercial transaction, business, and negotiation." If the relative truth is like the truths of market exchange or commercial transaction, it is "false," but only in the sense that it is not unconditionally true; yet it is true in the sense that convention is a practical sense that allows for human relations and human actions. The need to account for both the falsity and the truth of convention is in fact part of the problem inherent to the notion of an absolute truth.

Two Jars on Two Tables

The absolute presents us with the need to regard with suspicion the very same object that appears obvious to conventional discourse. A jar, for instance, will then be both real (conventionally) and unreal (absolutely). Exactly how Nāgārjuna addresses this problem might be clarified by a quick look at a different Buddhist tradition of the two truths. Vasubandhu, in the *Abhidharmakośa* (kārikā VI.4 and *Bhāṣya*), addresses the issue of the jar as follows:[35]

> The Blessed One proclaimed the Four Truths, but he also taught another two truths: the conventional (*saṁvṛti*) and the ultimate (*paramārtha*). What are the defining characteristics of these two?
>
> > [An entity is said to be] existing in a conventional sense if the mental percept of [the entity (*tad-buddhi*)] disappears when the [entity] is broken down [into its component parts], or if one can mentally (*dhiyā*) abstract [and remove all] other [attributes] (*anyāpoha*) from [this entity]—for instance, as in the cases of [respectively] a jar of water. Otherwise [the entity is regarded as] existing in an ultimate sense. (4)
>
> If the idea (*buddhi*) of a thing disappears when that thing is broken into its component parts, that thing exists [only] conventionally (*saṁvṛti-sat*). For instance, a jar: The idea of a jar disappears when it is reduced to

---

goes "hypersanskritized") into *saṁvṛti* This analysis is now widely accepted in the field. The point is summarized in Nagao 1954 (1991: 13). This is a contemporary analysis. Candrakīrti assumes that the Sanskrit form of the term represents its true etymology, yet affirms its meanings of "relational truth" and "convention" (*Prasannapadā*, p. 492):

> "*Saṁvṛti*" means the action and effect of covering something completely. For ignorance is called "covering" because it conceals from all sides the reality of all entities (*sarva-padārtha-tattva*). Or, the word can be taken to refer to interdependent arising in the sense of mutual dependence of one thing on another. Or, likewise, "*saṁvṛti*" can also mean "symbol" (*saṁketa*), "worldly discourse and exchange" (*lokavyavahāra*). And this [worldly discourse] is defined as signification and signified, cognition and cognized."

35. Shastri 1973: 3.889–890. All four volumes are paginated continuously.

its pieces. And, if the idea of a thing disappears when one abstracts with the mind [all] other qualities and entities (*dharma*), then that thing also must be regarded as existing relatively. For instance, water: for, if one abstracts the elements (*dharmas*) [that constitute] water, such as color, etc., the idea of water disappears.

Then, Vasubandhu acknowledges the split:[36]

With reference to these same entities one constructs conventional designations (*saṁvṛti-saṁjñā*), so that when people say, in agreement with conventional usage (*saṁvṛtivaśāt*), "here is a jar, here is the water," they are speaking nothing but the truth (*satyam eva*), they do not speak falsely. Consequently this is called conventional truth (*saṁvṛti-satya*).

What is the opposite of this [conventional truth] is the ultimate truth. If the mental percept of [an entity] persists even after that [entity] is broken down, or even if one abstracts with the mind other qualities and entities (*dharma*), that [is an entity that] exists in an ultimate sense (*paramārthasat*). Such is the case with, for instance, [the *dharma* constituting the *skandha* of] form (*rūpa*), because even if it is broken down into atoms, or even if one abstracts with the mind the *dharmas* [associated with form], such as the *dharma* of taste, the essential reality (*svabhāva*) of form remains, and the mental percept remains. One should regard in the same way sensation (*vedanā*) and the other [*skandhas*]. Because [such an entity] exists as an ultimate object, it is called ultimate truth.

But if this is the case, then can I see a jar (the very same jar) as two different things? One is the jar as it appears to me, the other one the jar as ultimate truth. In Vasubandhu's explanation of the difference between the two truths, the higher truth appears to be accessible to all. One need not be an omniscient buddha to see the jar after it is decomposed by breakage.

One can object that the whole passage is nothing but an authority move: the absolute is what the buddha taught. One can also ask why one could not say that the *skandhas* disappear just like the water—if not more quickly. One can perhaps see why Vasubandhu the Buddhist would state the distinction in these terms, but one can also have a less generous reading: that he is simply saying what is expected of him.

He of course derives part of his authority from the belief, shared by his audience, that some human beings have a type of knowledge that is supramundane or extraordinary:[37]

The ancient masters (Sautrāntikas?) say that this [ultimate truth] is the truth of an ultimate object as apprehended by a supramundane knowledge (*lokottara-jñāna*) or by knowledge derived from a supramundane knowledge

36. *Op. cit.*, p. 890.

37. *Op. cit.*, p. 890-891.

> (*pṛṣṭhalabdha-jñāna*) or through a mundane knowledge (*laukika-jñāna*), whereas the conventional truth is known through a different [act of knowing].
>
> But how then is the vision of this [ultimate truth attained]? This needs to be explained. Therefore, [the *kārikā*] discusses [this question], beginning with the initial practice:
>
>> A person who is firmly grounded on [moral] conduct, who has studied and is learned about [these truths], and has reflected and thought [them] through, will apply himself to the cultivation [of truth] through meditation. (5ab)
>
> The one who wants to perceive the truths first of all applies himself to guarding moral conduct, then he hears, [memorizes, and studies the doctrines] that lead gradually and naturally (*anuloma*) to the perception of the truth, or he hears the meaning [of this truth], and, once he has heard and learned it, he reflects on it, and having reflected on it [with an understanding that is] free from error, he applies himself to cultivation, that is, to *samādhi*. [That is to say,] relying on the discernment consisting in learning, he gains the discernment consisting in proper reflection, and relying on the discernment consisting of reflection, he is able to practice the discernment consisting in proper cultivation.

One should not lose sight of the fact that the argument from (and for) authority is only one of the issues raised by the passage. Vasubandhu is also struggling, like Nāgārjuna, with the question of what it means to posit a reality other than what is conventional. And, like Nāgārjuna, he believes that the fissure that separates these two is bridged by practice more than by theory.

Nevertheless, for all the discussion of the right means to know the ultimate truth and the practice of the path, Vasubandhu appears to consider the jar known through conventional knowledge as distinct (or even discontinuous) from the jar known to absolute knowledge. One is a real jar, the other is a deconstructed jar.

Eddington (1928: ix ff.) argued that the scientific model of matter (he was, coincidentally also referring to an atomic model) bifurcates our world into a consensual world of what we perceive and a theoretical world of what the percepts "really" are.[38] Thus, a scientific model seems to suggest that every time I see a table, I should be seeing two tables: the one I actually see (or believe I am seeing) and the atomic table that the table "really is." This is a simpler, and in my view more elegant, formulation of the scientific aporia that James Jeans expressed in terms of appearance and reality (1948: 92–95). Yet, the

---

38. My argument here is an extension of Schwartz's (1991) critique of Eddington. Therefore, I do not intend to imply that the coexistence of two models is an eliminative reduction.

issue of appearance and reality is still the underlying philosophical issue.

Naturally, a crucial question is the extent to which one can continue to posit the conventional table (or Vasubandhu's conventional jar) after one has known that there is a second reality, or, if you will, a second, true conception of the object which is different from the first, untrue or illusory conception of the same object.

In other words, do we then have two jars? For, this sort of religious-metaphysical rhetoric, whether it is meant to justify authority or explain some sort of "experience," raises the same issues that are raised by scientific reductionism. The two truths, then would not be a solution to any problem, but the simple statement of a fundamental split generated by philosophical argument (and, I would argue, religious claims generally). This is the split created by two competing claims: (1) an empirical given—we still live in the world of tables and jars, and (2) a theoretical given—an ontology believed to represent the true state of affairs. But the split is reinforced precisely by the religious model that is supposed to solve it: a foundational truth that is beyond the world of practice, and the practical truths of religion as a system of behavior regulation.[39]

Two Truths One Commitment

The relative position of the two classes of claims and demands (empirical and practical on the one hand, and theoretical or absolute on the other) are a fundamental issue for most, if not all, of the śāstric literature of the Great Vehicle. Even if we limit our observations to a few passages attributed to Nāgārjuna, it is not difficult to see that the question of the relative position of these two discourses (absolute, conventional) has much to do with the question of religion and its relationship to the ontological issues raised in Nāgārjuna's writings.

This brings us back to the beginning of this essay and the question of the religious meanings of a doctrine that appears to be, prima facie, an ontology. The problem is, of course, finding the proper niche for religion, understood broadly, in Nāgārjuna's thought. Trad-

---

39. Notice how Vasubandhu makes the connection also by making the second claim a step towards the first, that is, religious praxis is a cause for the apprehension of the uncaused. The same strategic move is made by Nāgārjuna, as we shall see below. I am referring, of course, to religious philosophy as ontological model, not to the sort of issue discussed in Yob 1992.

itionally, four approaches have been followed or tacitly assumed. First, there is what I call the simple statement of fact: he was a Buddhist and a Buddhist monk, so his thought is ipso facto religious. Second, one may appeal to Mahāyāna categories: Nāgārjuna's references to the vows and to the noble truths, for instance, indicate unambiguously that he was "a religious person." Or, third, one may use an argument based on certain assumptions regarding what is "religious" in philosophical discourse: his dialectic is understood as "negative theology"—the apophatic counterpart of a positive doctrine of liberation and sainthood. This is closely related to the fourth approach: Nāgārjuna's thought is seen as a type of so-called "mysticism."[40] This carries both the implication that his rhetoric is somehow mystical and that his ultimate claims are based on some sort of personal experience.

Provisionally let me propose that these solutions or approaches have a number of common elements, some of which lead to suggestive ways around the problem of the two truths and some of which are highly problematic. The first, commendable point is that it is reasonable to assume that Nāgārjuna was in fact religious and that he was in fact a Mahayanist (pace Warder 1973). This would presumably connect him to issues of "mysticism" and to issues of language, insofar as we expect from every Mahayanist thinker some degree of constructivism, that is, we expect this thinker to be something of a *prajñaptivādin*.

The problematic point is that being a member of a religious organization does not necessarily predict a person's philosophical preferences. Furthermore, the appellative "Mahayanist" is only a starting point that has very limited significance as long as we are unable to understand what sort of Mahayanist he was.

I have here attempted a different approach. Taking from the above what can be salvaged, I have argued that Nāgārjuna engages in a religious rhetoric that is more narrative than mystical.[41] This is the strategy of intensification outlined above: the restatement of a profane

---

40. The term "mysticism" is problematic in most contemporary contests (philosophical, historical, psychological). Its continued usage, however, requires that we revisit and reexamine the term. Off the beaten track and insightful were the long neglected philosophical remarks of Matilal 1977, 1982. See also Stafford 1983, Bronkhorst 1993, and Yandel 1993.

41. The assumption that such rhetoric is by necessity "mystical" is one of those assumptions that have acquired the force of axiomatic truths in the western literature on the subject. There is really no formal, logical, or historical reason for assuming such a connection; and, moreover, apart from this rhetoric itself, it is hard to see what "mystical" means in a Madhyamaka context.

fact in a sacred context transforms the ambiguous or puzzling into unquestioned and illuminating truth.[42] I have exemplified this process with the story of Kisā and have outlined the parallel process I detect in the rhetoric of the two truths.

We may now ask which religious truths are the object of this sacrilizing representation in Nāgārjuna. Nāgārjuna saw *paramārtha* in light of the sutra texts that stated that this was the point of view of the Buddha himself: thus, the *Madhyamaka-Kārikās* state that "when buddhas teach the Dharma they resort to two truths" (MKxxiv.8)—that is, buddhas themselves accept a truth that conforms to the conventions of the world, and a truth that agrees with the ultimate goal of the path.

But the second of these truths is the nameless, of which *Lokātītastava* (stanza 27) says:[43]

> You have taught that there can be no liberation without gaining access to the signless (*animitta*). This is why you have taught it in full (*sākalyena*) in the [teachings of the] Great Vehicle.

The second sentence is significant, because this truth that cannot be defined in any way, the "unmarked" (*animitta*), is in fact explained *in all its parts* (*sākalyena* < *sakala*), *in detail* by the Buddha. In fact, only the Buddha knows it in full detail.

It seems that Nāgārjuna believes there is a state of being, or a cognitive event, or an object of cognition that can be accurately described as "unmarked" (*animitta*), and that such a state is (or gives access to) the highest meaning (*paramārtha*, which also can be interpreted to mean, "the highest goal," and "the highest object"). Nāgārjuna also seems to imply that the condition of *ānimitta* or *paramārtha*, although unmarked and unassailable, is one that can be explained, and that the explanation (and therefore presumably its object) has many parts to it. And this is not at all surprising, since his own work stands as a not so silent witness to the fact that he also believed that it could be defined, or established by some sort of rational argument.

Hence, in the *Kārikās paramārtha* is, on the one hand, that to which one gains access when one understands *pratītyasamutpāda*, and on the other, a dictum of the Buddha. Similarly, *paramārtha* appears as something altogether other (it is *lokātīta*), that is to say, somehow

42. The strategy is, of course, not only used in religion. But it is characteristically used in religious contexts, and it is preferentially used when there is need for the sanctifications of truth.

43. This translates *animittam anāgamya mokṣo nāsti tvam uktavān | atas tvayā mahāyāne tat sākalyena deśitam | |*. References to the Sanskrit text as edited by Lindtner 1982b.

discontinuous with the world. And yet the truth of the Buddha's words, and his very presence, must necessarily abide in the world: "Without having recourse to convention, the ultimate goal cannot be taught" (MK xxiv.10). The ultimate goal is somehow located in conventional discourse.

Two forms of assertion are in tension. On the one hand, the ultimate teaching is a denial of the reality of what is of the world, the mind, and language. On the other hand, this denial is considered to somehow reassert the reality of the world, and the value of convention seems to be reasserted in stating that it is a necessary precondition for the attainment of the ultimately real.[44] The tension comes to light if one compares statements of the first kind with statements of the second type. On the one hand, the conventional similes of mirage, foam, bubble, dream, and the like describe accurately every thing that is (*Śūnyatāsaptatī* 66), while on the other hand, the Buddha does not contradict what others say about the *dharmas* of the world, and he teaches nothing about *dharmas* (*Śūnyatāsaptatī* 70).[45] In what is arguably the most famous lines of the *Kārikās* we read (MK xxv.19):

> There is no difference whatsoever between *saṁsāra* and *nirvāṇa*. There is no difference whatsoever between *nirvāṇa* and *saṁsāra*.[46]

We are also told that *nirvāṇa* is nothing but the understanding of becoming (*bhāva*—*Yuktiṣaṣṭikā* 6cd): "the full understanding of becoming and nothing else is what one calls *nirvāṇa*."[47] Yet MK xxiv.40 states that in understanding conditioned arising one is only understanding the Four Truths: suffering, its arising, its cessation, and the path that leads to its cessation.[48] How are we to understand, then, the relationship of *paramārtha* to the Four Truths?

---

44. Contrast the way in which the presumed interdependence is construed in the *Bodhicittavivaraṇa* stanzas 67–69, discussed below in the main body of the essay.

45. References to the *Śūnyatāsaptatī* are to the Tibetan text as edited by Lindtner 1982b, or to the surviving Sanskrit fragments, also edited by Lindtner 1982b.

46. Lit. "Saṁsāra has nothing to distinguish it from nirvāṇa; nirvāṇa has nothing to distinguish it from saṁsāra— *na saṁsārasya nirvāṇāt kiṁcid asti viśeṣaṇam* | *na nirvāṇasya saṁsārāt kiṁcid asti viśeṣaṇam* | | (MK xxv.19). Cp. *Yuktiṣaṣṭikā*, stanzas 5–6, discussed below.

47. Preserved in Sanskrit as *parijñānaṁ bhavasyaiva nirvāṇam iti kathyate*. References to the *Yuktiṣaṣṭikā* are to the Tibetan text as edited by Lindtner 1982b. His edition includes the Sanskrit fragments and offers cross-references to the sources in which these fragments have been found.

48. Lit. "He who sees conditioned arising sees this, and nothing else: suffering, arising, cessation, and the path as well"— *yaḥ pratītyasamutpādaṁ paśyatīdaṁ sa paśyati* | *duḥkhaṁ samudayaṁ caiva nirodhaṁ mārgam eva ca* | | (MK xxiv.40).

The location of MK xxiv.8 in the chapter on the two truths (*āryasatya*) suggests that the two truths are meant either as a gloss of the four noble truths or as a statement of a higher order, because the two truths are introduced as an argument in defense of the Noble Truths in spite of the doctrine of emptiness. Thus the statement of MK xxiv.8 must refer to the Four Noble Truths as conventional truth:

> When buddhas teach the Dharma they resort to two truths: the truth that is the world's conventions, and a truth referring to the highest goal.[49]

At first blush we seem to be reading a statement on the equal value of statements of transcendence and those of immanence (for lack of better terms). But as it turns out, there is a clear and sharp hierarchy. Thus MK xxiv.9 states:

> Those who do not understand the difference between these two truths do not understand what the buddhas in fact teach.[50]

It is in view of this simple, but pointed, statement that we must understand the value attributed subsequently to the conventional truth (MK xxiv.10):

> Without having recourse to convention, the ultimate goal cannot be taught. Without access to the ultimate goal, nirvāṇa will not be attained.[51]

This places the highest goal in a privileged, but dangerously isolated, position. This is a position held almost universally by all Buddhist

---

49. Lit. "The teaching of Dharma by the buddhas uses two truths: a truth that is the consensual truth of the world, and a truth that reflects the highest attainment." The expression *paramārthataḥ* is of course not at all transparent. Streng (1967) renders the compound as "the truth which is the highest sense." His rendering of *saṁvṛti* as "world-ensconced" is of course grammatically and philosophically unacceptable. The traditional interpretation (e.g., in Candrakīrti, *Prasannapadā*, 492) is that it is like a veil or covering (*varaṇa*) that covers everything completely (*samantāt*). This interpretation evidently suggests the "world-ensconcing."

50. Lit. "Those who do not understand the difference between these two truths do not understand the profound reality contained in the teaching of the buddhas"—*ye 'nayor na vijānanti vibhāgaṁ satyayor dvayoḥ* | *te tattvaṁ na vijānanti gambhīraṁ buddhaśāsane* | |. The choice of the word *tattva* suggests that there is an object or a way of understanding that encompasses both *saṁvṛti* and *paramārtha*. One could interpret the second line as meaning that such persons do not understand the meaning of a buddha preaching the Dharma, or why buddhas preach the Dharma.

51. Lit. "Without having recourse to conventional transactions, the ultimate goal is not shown. Without access to the ultimate goal, nirvāṇa is not attained"—*vyavahāram anāśritya paramārtho na deśyate* | *paramārtham anāgamya nirvāṇaṁ nādhigamyate* | |. Cp. this statement with *Lokātītastava*, stanza 27, quoted above, n. 43.

scholastics, because once nirvāṇa was conceived as "uncaused" and perfectly pure, it could no longer remain in the realm of the conventional—that is, in the realm of our world.

On Having No Views

Returning to a passage referred to above (*Śūnyatāsaptatī* 70) we are faced with a peculiar claim:

> 70ab. The Buddha does not contradict the teachings of the world, and he has not taught a Dharma in any real sense (*yang dag nyid du*, *tattvataḥ*?).

The Tibetan text is admittedly ambiguous.[52] The ostensible claim is that the Buddha never contradicts the *dharma*s of the world, and that he has no *dharma* of his own. A similar notion is stated in a passage the first line of which was quoted in the epigraph to this essay, and which parallels one of the *Suttanipāta* passages also quoted in the epigraph:[53]

> "Monks, I do not quarrel with the world. The world quarrels with me. Why is this so? Monks, one who speaks the Dharma does not quarrel with the world. That which wise men of the world say is [the case], that is what I say is [the case].... That the body is an impermanent, painful, changing thing—this wise men of the world say is the case.[54]

---

52. The Tibetan of *Śūnyatāsaptati*, 70ab reads: *'jig rten pa yi chos bstan mi 'jig cing* | | *yang dag nyid du nam yang chos bstan med* | |. This is the Tibetan translation of Gzhon-nu-mchog, et al. The translation of Jinamitra and Ye-shes-sde reads: "[He] does not contradict the assertions of the world, and ultimately [has] no teaching of Dharma whatsoever" *'jig rten pa yi bstan mi 'jig* | | *yang dag chos bstan ci yang med* | |. The second half of the stanza makes it clear that the issue is not primarily rhetorical (following Gzhon-nu-mchog, "Those who misunderstand the words of the Tathāgata, are therefore afraid of this unblemished teaching"— *de bzhin gshegs pas gsungs pa ma rigs pas* | | *de las dri med brjod pa 'di las skrag* | |). This passage comes close to Huntington's (1989, 1992) reading of Mādhyamika as a rhetoric of persuasion, but the dialectic is more complicated than that, as seen from similar points made in the *Bodhicittavivaraṇa*, stanza 67, and in MK xxiv.8–10, discussed above.

53. Translated from the Chinese text of the *Samyuktāgama*, in Taishō 99 (II) 8b16–18. The Pāli (*Saṁyutta Nikāya*, PTS, iii.138–139) differs slightly: "Monks, I have no quarrel with the world, but the world quarrels with me. Monks, a speaker of Dharma has no quarrel with anyone in the world. That which wise men of the world agree to consider as non-existent, I too declare to be non-existent. That which wise men of the world agree to consider as existent, I too declare to be existent"— *nāhaṁ bhikkhave lokena vivadāmi* | *loko ca mayā vivadati* | | *na bhikkhave dhammavādī kenaci lokasmiṁ vivadati* | | *yaṁ bhikkhave natthi[-]sammataṁ loke paṇḍitānaṁ ahaṁ pi tam natthīti vadāmi. yaṁ bhikkhave atthi[-]sammataṁ loke paṇḍitānaṁ ahaṁ pi tam atthīti vadāmi* | |.

54. The *Saṁyutta* and *Saṁyukta* sutras go on to explain, disappointingly, that what is meant by the opinion of the world is the opinion of those wise men who agree that the *skandha*s are impermanent, etc. The same passage is quoted in Sanskrit in

The key phrase is of course "wise men of the world" (世間智者 = Pāli, *loke paṇḍitānaṁ*). These wise men are by necessity Buddhists, followers of the wisest among all sentient beings, the Buddha.[55]

There is very little room for doubt as to where Nāgārjuna stood on the matter of who are the wise and who are the unwise. One need only read the harsh words he reserves for the unwise (*Ratnāvalī*, stanzas 119–120):[56]

> If it is not properly understood, this teaching (*dharma*) will destroy the unwise, because they will sink into the mire of nihilistic views.[57] (119) Likewise, because of his misunderstanding of this [teaching], the fool that believes himself wise will fall head first into the Avīci hell, having destroyed himself by his own obduracy. (120)

Moreover, a wise person is most likely not just any Buddhist, but one who can speak for or as the Buddha. It is a friend of the good, who delights in compassion, a strict sense of ethics, and the discernment that destroys delusion and mental turmoil (*Ratnāvalī*, 492); but he is also one who knows the doctrine that transcends being and nonbeing, a doctrine that is not known to the followers of other teachers,

---

Prasannapadā, p. 370: *loko mayā sārdhaṁ vivadāmi* | *nāhaṁ lokena sārdhaṁ vivadati* | *yal loke 'sti saṁmatam tan mamāpy asti saṁmatam* | *yal loke nāsti saṁmatam mamāpi tan nāsti saṁmatam* | |. Huntington, translating the Sanskrit version quoted by Candrakīrti, appears to follow the philosophical interpretation suggested by the second half of the Pāli quotation: "that which is considered to exist in the context of the world," etc. (Huntington 1983b). Personally, I find it more natural to read the last two sentences as saying, "That which is accepted in the world, that has my acceptance as well. That which is not accepted in the world, that does not have my acceptance either." In following the Chinese, I have tried to bring out this more nuanced rendering that sees the second half of the section quoted by Candrakīrti as a gloss of the first half, and not as a philosophical expansion. Needless to say, part of the problem with these passages is the parsing of the phrase "*mama ... asti sammatam*," in its various manifestations in the parallel versions.

55. Also consider Candrakīrti's use of the *Samādhirāja Sūtra* at *Prasannapadā* 135 and 270, as well as his use of the locus classicus from *Mahāvastu*, *Lalitavistara*, etc.: "Not long after the Blessed One had attained full awakening, he thought: 'I have understood a profound truth (*dharma*), deeply luminous, not to be reasoned, not to be discussed by reason, subtle, understandable only to the wise and learned. If I were to reveal this to others, they would fail to understand me, and that would be tiring and vexing for me....'" (*Prasannapadā*, p. 498). Cp., for example, *Ratnāvalī*, stanzas 117–118; scriptural text in *Mahāvastu* III.314 (ed. Senart).

56. Although this section as a whole is a criticism of all misconceptions about the non-dual, the particular passage quoted above is directed primaily at those who think emptiness means non-existence (cp. MK xxiv.11; *Prasannapadā*, p. 496). In this context the need to create a negative identity responds to a need to distance Buddhism from accusations of nihilism in an ethical sense as well as ontological nihilism.

57. The original is in the singular, but a plural seemed more natural to me in the English.

which is the ambrosia of the Buddhas (*Ratnāvalī*, 61–62). Appeal to the wise means appeal to buddhas and bodhisattvas, or to the doctrines attributed to them. We may then paraphrase the *Tattvasaṅgraha* (3323–3324): any wise person who can know and teach without error the highest truth must by definition be a buddha.[58]

Here agreement between the Buddha and the world is not acceptance of the world, but transformation of the world. The wisdom and insight of the Buddha teaches the emptiness without which a substantial being would render "not only the worldly but also the supramundane as totally absurd" (*Prasannapadā*, p. 524).

This is not the teaching of the world generally. Conformity with the world and convention, then, ends up being nothing but Buddhist doctrine—a disappointing turn of events. Tradition will insist that "the buddhas have taught no dharma whatsoever."[59] Yet, under the realities of Buddhism as an institution and the realities of Buddhist doctrine, this silence of the Buddha will also turn out to be nothing but Buddhist doctrine a thousand times over.

But is it not the case that these texts are actually claiming that the Buddhist doctrine is, ultimately, nothing but silence? After all, we read more than one passage stating unambiguously that the Buddha had no teaching.[60] Or, in even stronger terms, MK xviii.8 states:[61]

> Nothing is true (*tathya*), nor not true, nothing is both true and untrue, nothing is both not true and not untrue—this is the teaching of the Buddha.

---

58. The context in the *Tattvasaṅgraha* is a discussion of omniscience, and the argument is that if anyone else agrees completely with the Buddha and is able to have a direct experience of his *dharmas*, that person is by definition omniscient, like the Buddha.

59. Accordingly, when the speaker, as the spokesperson of the Buddha, asserts that he has no thesis of his own, he mimics, as it were, the Buddha's silence. Cp. the often quoted lines from *Vigrahavyāvartanī*, 29: "If any thesis whatsoever were to be present in this [argument of mine], then that could be [held] against me as an error [in my argument]. But I hold no thesis. Therefore, no error [can be attributed] to me" *yadi kācana pratijñā tatra syād, eṣa me bhaved doṣaḥ | nāsti ca mama pratijñā, tasmān naivāsti me doṣaḥ | |*. For a useful compilation of the standard, though dated, Western editions, see Bhattacharya 1978; the kārikās were re-edited in Lindtner 1982b. The thesis of no thesis recurs in Nāgārjuna and his heirs; see, for example, *Yuktiṣaṣtikā*, stanzas 50 and 58; *Ratnāvalī*, stanza 60; *Catuḥśatka*, stanza 400 (XVI.25); *Prasannapadā*, p. 16–19; *Madhamakāvatāra*, VI.119 (= pp. 232–233); more references in May 1959, nn. 761 and 773.

60. I have looked at these assertions from a slightly different perspective in Gómez 1998.

61. *Sarvaṁ tathyaṁ na vā tathyaṁ tathyaṁ cātathyam eva ca | neivātathyaṁ naiva tathyam etad buddhānuśāsanaṁ | |*.

Yet, as a comment to this same passage Candrakīrti quotes two stanzas from Āryadeva's *Catuḥśataka* (stanzas 60 and 194) that reveal the complexities that accompany such claims. Since the Buddha does recommend specific teachings and practices, one must assume that when the Teacher addresses his disciple (*Catuḥśataka*, stanza 60)[62]

> He must at first do and say only that which will be agreeable to the [disciple]. For there is no way to turn into a true vessel of the Good Dharma a person that has been antagonized [by the teaching].

Passages like this one seem to imply that "agreement with the word" is only a temporary, and at best a patronizing, concession to the beliefs of the world. This impression is reinforced by a stanza appearing later in the text (*Catuḥśataka*, stanza 194):[63]

> Just as it is impossible to communicate with a barbarian in a language other [than his own], it is impossible to make people of the world understand without reference to worldly things.

As a gloss to this quotation and a further gloss to Nāgārjuna's stanza, Candrakīrti then quotes the Sanskrit version of the first passage of the epigraph:[64]

---

62. Āryadeva's *Catuḥśataka*, stanza 60 (numbered V.10 in Lang's 1986 edition): *yad yad yasya priyaṁ pūrvaṁ tat tat tasya samācaret | na hi pratihataḥ pātraṁ saddharmasya kathaṁ cana | |*.

63. Āryadeva's *Catuḥśataka*, stanza 194 (numbered VIII.19 in Lang's edition). This is part of a short set of three stanzas, 192–194 (numbered VIII.17–19 in Lang's edition) that should be read together: (192) "The Tathāgatas counsel devotion to virtuous behavior (*dharma*) to those who desire heaven. They repudiate this same [attachment when speaking] to those who seek liberation. How much less [would they recommend to them] attachment to anything else?" *chos chags de bzhin gshegs rnams kyis | mtho ris 'dod pa rnams la gsungs | thar pa 'dod rnams la de nyid | smad 'gyur gzhan du smos ci dgos | |*. (193) "The person who seeks to gain merit should not speak of emptiness all the time: Isn't it the case that an herbal balm that is applied to the wrong spot can be noxious?" *śūnyatā puṇyakāmena vaktavyā naiva sarvadā | nanu pratyaktam asthāne jāyate viṣam auṣadham | |*. (194) "Just as it is impossible to communicate with a barbarian in a language other [than his own], it is impossible to make people of the world understand without reference to worldly things" *nānyayā bhāṣayā mlecchaḥ śakyo grāhayituṁ yathā | na laukikam ṛte lokaḥ śakyo grāhayituṁ tathā | |*. References to Sanskrit sources are found in Lang, pp. 84–85. The translation of M. Winternitz (1930: 69) highlights this division even more: (192) "Die *Liebe zur Religion* wird von den Tathāgatas für diejenigen gelehrt, welche nach dem Himmel verlangen; *hingegen* wird für diejenigen, welche Erlösung suchen, die höchste Wahrheit gelehrt." (193) "Wer *religioses Verdienst* zu erwerben wünscht, *kann nicht immer* von Leerheit reden. Wird nicht eine unrichtig angewendete Medizin zu Gift?" (194) "Wie man *einem Barbaren* eine Sache nicht anders als in seiner Sprache verständlich machen kann, so kann man *den gewöhnlichen Leuten* nichts ohne den Gebrauch der gewöhnlichen Sprache verständlich machen."

64. Here translated from the Sanskrit text of Candrakīrti (*Prasannapadā*, p. 370): *tathā ca bhagavatoktaṁ | loko mayā sārdhaṁ vivadati nāhaṁ lokena sārdhaṁ vivadati | |*

> And, as the Blessed One has said in the Āgama: "The world quarrels with me; I do not quarrel with the world. Whatever is acceptable to the world, I too accept; whatever is not acceptable to the world, I too do not accept."

It turns out, then, that the texts speak with more than one voice. At times it appears that, in fact, the Buddha agrees with the world. The vision from the final goal (*parama-artha*) only sanctifies the world (*saṁsāra* is *nirvāṇa*). In fact, the two views appear to be interdependent (*Bodhicittavivaraṇa* stanzas 67–68):[65]

> If one speaks of things as they truly are, this causes no break in conventional usage; and apart from conventional usage, there is no apprehension of the real. (67)
> One says that convention is emptiness; emptiness is nothing but convention; because in the absence of the one, the other surely does not arise, like the constructed and the impermanent [are mutually dependent]. (68)

One would think that this means that both convention and ultimate reality must remain as an integral part of a plan of liberation. Yet, we have also been told that buddhas speak the language of the world, only because the world would otherwise not understand. And, what is more, we also discover that the world of conventions is irredeemably flawed (*Bodhicittavivaraṇa* stanza 69):[66]

> Convention arises from the karmic activity of the afflictions (*kleśa-karma*), [such] activity arises from the mind, the mind is constituted by an accumulation (*bsags*) of past habitual tendencies (*bag chags rnams: vāsanā*); freedom from [such] habitual tendencies is bliss.

A full appraisal of Nāgārjuna requires that we take into account these apparent contradictions—not that we try to solve them, but that we take them into account in imagining the religious ideals of a forever-incomplete human being in fluid historical and psychological locations.

---

yal loke 'sti saṁmataṁ tan mamāpyasti saṁmataṁ | yal loke nāsti saṁmataṁ mamāpi tan nāsti saṁmataṁ ity āgamāc ca | |. My translation assumes that the final *ca* is a scribal error. See also n. 34 above.

65. *Bodhicittavivaraṇa*, from the Tibetan, *Byang chub sems 'grel ba*, Lindtner 1982b: *de nyid ji bzhin bshad pas na* | | *kun rdzob rgyun ni 'chad mi 'gyur* | | *kun rdzob las ni tha dad par* | | *de nyid dmigs pa ma yin te* | | *kun rdzog stong pa nyid du bshad* | | *stong pa kho na kun rdzog yin* | | *med na mi 'byung nges pa'i phyir* | | *byas dang mi rtag ji bzhin no* | |.

66. *Bodhicittavivaraṇa*, from the Tibetan, *Byang chub sems 'grel ba*, Lindtner 1982b: *kun rdzob nyon mongs las las byung* | | *las ni sems las byung ba yin* | | *sems ni bag chags rnams kyis bsags* | | *bag chags bral na bde ba ste* | |.

Conclusion

In this essay I have first attempted a reading of Nāgārjuna's two truths from a perspective usually associated with the social sciences. Nāgārjuna's doctrine of the two truths belong to a family of human endeavors aimed at making and sustaining "claims to religious truth, logical validity, sure knowledge."[67] But I have not dealt with the two truths only "in conditions of philosophical purity;" I have tried to bring some suspicion to the doctrine's apparent propositional purity. I have looked at the ways in which it could have emerged "from within heterogeneous social contexts of verbal exchange and contestation." I have tried to imagine alternatives to "the coherence of dogma" in the coherence of a "community on the ground within which conversation" could have taken place. In this way I have suggested ways in which the two truths may have functioned within the lives of a religious philosopher.

These reflections suggest that the doctrine of the two truths is an *abstract formulation* of a hierarchy of privilege and competence, of a common theme in religious thought—the restatement of the division between the sacred and the profane, transcendence and immanence—and of the conviction that the source of religious authority is an ineffable, unassailable whole that is nevertheless coextensive with the believer's universe.

In the specific form of the two truths, these religious themes serve not only as a consecration of the distinction between the truth of the experts and the truth of the ignorant, but a sacralization of the human profane as well, albeit a reluctant and conflicted sacralization. In formulating the doctrine of the two truths, Nāgārjuna engages in both the process of consecrating the distinction between the truth of the experts and the truth of the ignorant and that of making the profane sacred. It is to Nāgārjuna's credit to have done so unambiguously and boldly. But this does not justify us in assuming that his restatement of the division or the reduction of all conventional reality to an absolute has in fact solved the problem. The interdependence of *saṁvṛti* and *paramārtha* is a given, and their ranking appears to be a formal necessity. A clear statement of these facts is not the solution to the social and metaphysical quandary in which they are embedded: in particular it is a restatement of the contradiction presented by

67. This and the following sentences contain short extracts and paraphrases are from Wendy James's Introduction to James 1995: 11. Her remarks are addressed at anthropologists but can be construed (mutatis mutandis) as a constructive criticism of some of the efforts of the textual scholar.

experiences of transcendence in the midst of necessarily historical and culturally specified doctrinal discourses.

Because the doctrine of the two truths is much more than an ontology, it both embodies the inconsistencies of religious life on the ground and attempts to address them, as expected, with mixed success. The doctrine at times sanctifies orders of human relationships. At times it seems to require that we transcend such orders and hierarchies. And at times (or even at the same time) it intensifies the distance between the ideal of spiritual liberation and the reality of the conventional.

Bibliography

Abhidharmakośa, Kārikās and Bhāṣya (Abhidharmakośa-bhāṣya) by Vasubandhu, references to chapter and verse number or to volume and pages in the ed. of S. D. Shastri 1973.

Andersen, Dines, and Helmer Smith. 1965. *Sutta-Nipāta*. New Edition. Pali Text Society. London: Published for the Pali Text Society by Luzac and Co., Ltd., 1965 (reprint of the original ed. of 1913). This edition is called "new edition" in contrast to Fausbøll's *editio princeps* of 1885.

Āryadeva's *Catuḥśataka*. References to Tibetan text and Sanskrit fragments in the ed. of Lang 1986. See also H. Shastri 1914, Vaidya 1923, and V. Bhattacharya 1926 and 1931.

Bhattacharya, Kamaleswar. 1978. *The Dialectical Method of Nāgārjuna: Vigrahavyāvartanī*. Translated by Kamaleswar Bhattacharya; text critically edited by E. H. Johnston and Arnold Kunst (Delhi: Motilal Banarsidass).

Bhattacharya, V., (ed.). 1926. "The Catuḥśataka of Āryadeva, chapter VII, with extracts from the commentary of Candrakīrti, reconstructed from the Tibetan version with an English translation." *Proceedings and Transactions of the Fourth Oriental Conference* 2 (Allahabad): 831–871.

———, (ed.). 1931. *The Catuḥśataka of Āryadeva*. Sanskrit and Tibetan texts with copious extracts from the commentary of Candrakīrti, reconstructed and edited, Part II (Calcutta). Only Part II was published.

Bourdieu, Pierre. 1971. "Genèse et structure du champ religieux." *Revue française de sociologie* 12: 295–334.

———. 1975. "Le langage autorisé: Note sur les conditions sociales de l'efficacité du discours rituel." *Actes de la recherche en sciences sociales* 5–6: 183–190.

———. 1977a. "Symbolic power." Eng. trans. C. Wringe. In D. Gleeson, ed., *Identity and Structure: Issues in the Sociology of Education* (Driffield, England: Nafferton Books): 112–119. Also in Bourdieu 1991: 163–170.

———. 1977b. *Outline of a Theory of Practice.* Translated by Richard Nice. Cambridge Studies in Social Anthropology, no. 16 (Cambridge and New York: Cambridge University Press). Translation with revisions of *Esquisse d'une théorie de la pratique.*

———. 1980. *Le sens pratique* (Paris: Éditions de Minuit). English: *The Logic of Practice*, translated by Richard Nice (Cambridge: Polity Press, in association with Basil Blackwell, 1990).

———. 1991. *Language and Symbolic Power.* Ed. and introd. by John B. Thompson; trans. by G. Raymond and M. Adamson (Cambridge: Harvard University Press).

Bourdieu, Pierre, and Jean-Claude Passeron. 1977. *Reproduction in Education, Society and Culture.* Eng. trans. by R. Nice (Beverly Hills, CA: Sage Publications).

——— and Monique de Saint Martin. 1994. *Academic Discourse: Linguistic Misunderstanding and Professorial Power.* With contributions by Christian Baudelot and Guy Vincent; translated by Richard Teese (Cambridge [England]: Polity Press). Translation of *Rapport pedagogique et communication.*

Boyer, Pascal. 1994. *The Naturalness of Religious Ideas: A Cognitive Theory of Religion* (Berkeley, CA: University of California Press).

Bronkhorst, Johannes. 1993. Review of Ilkka Pyysiäinen 1993, *Beyond Language and Reason: Mysticism in Indian Buddhism*, in *Asiastische Studien/ Études Asiatiques* 47 (4): 709–715.

Bruner, Jerome S. 1951. "Personality dynamics and the process of perceiving." Chapter 5 in R. R. Blake and G. V. Ramsey, eds., *Perception: An approach to personality* (New York: Ronald Press): 121–147. Repr. in Bruner 1973: 89–13.

———. 1957. "On Perceptual Readiness." *Psychological Review* 64: 123–152. Repr. in Bruner 1973: 7–42.

———. 1973. *Beyond the Information Given: Studies in the Psychology of Knowing.* Selected, edited, and introduced by J. M. Anglin (New York: W. W. Norton and Co.).

———. 1986. *Actual Minds, Possible World.* (Cambridge: Harvard University Press).

———. 1990. *Acts of Meaning. The Jerusalem–Harvard Lectures* (Cambridge, MA, and London: Harvard University Press).

Buddhaghosa. *Dhammapada-aṭṭhakathā.* See Norman 1906–1915.

Burke, Kenneth. 1950. *A Rhetoric of Motives.* 1st. ed. (New York: Prentice-Hall).

———. 1961. *The Rhetoric of Religion: Studies in Logolog.* (Boston: Beacon Press).

———. 1973. *The Philosophy of Literary Form: Studies in Symbolic Action.* 3d ed. (Baton Rouge: Louisiana State University Press, 1941; reprint: Berkeley: University of California Press).

Burlingame, Eugene Watson. 1969. *Buddhist Legends.* Translated from the original Pali text of the Dhammapada Commentary. 3 vols. (London:

Luzac and Company, Published for the Pali Text Society). Originally volumes 28–30 of the Harvard Oriental Series (Cambridge, MA: Harvard University Press, 1921).

Cain, William E. 1980. "Authors and Authority in Interpretation." *Georgia Review* 34: 617–634.

Certeau, Michel de. 1988. *The Practice of Everyday Life.* Translated by Steven Rendall (Berkeley: University of California Press; from the French *Arts de faire*, Paris, 1984).

Eddington, Arthur Stanley. 1928. *The Nature of the Physical World.* The Gifford Lectures, 1927 (New York: The Macmillan Company; Cambridge University Press, 1929 [Copyright 1928]).

Erikson, Erik H. 1977. *Toys and Reasons: Stages in the Ritualization of Experience* (New York: H. H. Norton).

———. 1985. *The Life Cycle Completed: A Review* (New York: H. H. Norton. First pub. 1982).

Foucault, Michel. 1988. "Technologies of the Self." In Luther H. Martin, Huck Gutman, and Patrick H. Hutton, eds. *Technologies of the Self: A Seminar with Michel Foucault* (Amherst: University of Massachusetts Press): 16–49.

Fraser, John. 1987. "Playing for Real: Discourse and Authority." *University of Toronto Quarterly* 56: 416–434.

French, Hal W. 1989. "The Psychodynamics of Adversary Identity." *Studies in Religion/Sciences religieuses* 18 (3): 261–272.

Ginzburg, Carlo. 1976. *Il formaggio e i vermi: Il cosmo di un mugnaio del 1500.* Torino: G. Einaudi. English: *The Cheese and the Worms: The Cosmos of a Sixteenth-century Miller.* Translated by John and Anne Tedeschi (Baltimore: Johns Hopkins University Press, 1980).

Gómez, Luis O. 1998. "Words of Silence: Liberation from Language and the Language of Liberation in Buddhism." Forthcoming in C. Jan Swearingen, ed., *The Word: Studies in the Language of Religion and the Religious Meaning of Language* (University of Arizona Press).

———. Forthcoming. "Noble Lineage and August Demeanor: Religious and Social Meanings of Aryan Virtue." To appear in a special volume of *Études asiatiques/Asiatische Studien*, edited by Johannes Bronkhorst.

Hahn, Michel. 1982. *Nāgārjuna's Ratnāvalī.* Vol. 1, The Basic Texts (Sanskrit, Tibetan, Chinese). Indica et Tibetica 1 (Bonn: Indica et Tibetica Verlag).

Hallisey, Charles. 1994. "In Defense of a Rather Fragile and Local Achievement: Reflection on the Work of Gurulugomi." In Frank E. Reynolds and David Tracy, eds., *Religion and Practical Reason: New Essays in the Comparative Philosophy of Religions* (Albany: State University of New York Press): 121–162.

Heimsoeth, Heinz. 1954. *Die sechs grossen Themen der abendlandischen Metaphysik und der Ausgang des Mittelalters.* 3. durchgeschene Aufl. (Stuttgart: W. Kohlhammer). English: *The Six Great Themes of Western Metaphysics and the End of the Middle Ages.* Translated with a critical introduction by Ramon J. Betanzos (Detroit: Wayne State University Press, 1994).

Huntington, C. W., Jr. 1983a. "A 'Nonreferential' View of Language and Conceptual Thought in the Work of Tsoṅ-kha-pa." *Philosophy East & West* 33: 325–339.

———. 1983b. "The System of the Two Truths in the *Prasannapadā* and the *Madhyamakāvatāra*: A Study in Mādhyamika Soteriology." *Journal of Indian Philosophy* 11: 77–106.

———. 1989. *The Emptiness of Emptiness: An Introduction to Early Indian Mādhyamika.* With Geshe Namgyal Wangchen (Honolulu: University of Hawaii Press).

———. 1992. "The Theatre of Objectivity: Comments on José Cabezón's Interpretations of mKhas grub rje's and C. W. Huntington, Jr.'s Interpretations of the Tibetan Translation of a Seventh Century Indian Buddhist Text." *Journal of the International Association of Buddhist Studies* 15/1: 119–133.

James, Wendy, (ed.). 1995. *The Pursuit of Certainty: Religious and Cultural Formulations* (London and New York: Routledge).

Jeans, James Hopwood, Sir. 1948. *Physics and Philosophy* (Cambridge University Press. Reprinted, Ann Arbor: University of Michigan Press, 1958).

Jha, Ganga Nath, (trans.). 1983. *Ślokavārttika.* Translated from the original Sanskrit, with extracts from the commentaries "Kāśika" of Sucarita Miśra and "Nyayarathākara" of Partha Sarathi Miśra, [by] Ganga Nath Jha. 2nd ed. (Delhi: Sri Satguru Publications, 1983. Reprint of the original edition of Calcutta, 1900).

Jong, J. W. de, (ed.). 1977. *Mūlamadhyamakakārikāḥ.* Nagarjuna. Adyar Library series 109 (Madras: Adyar Library and Research Centre).

Kumārila Bhaṭṭa. (Seventh century). *Ślokavārttika* (Śabarasvāmin. Mīmāṁsābhāṣya Ślokavārttika). See Musalgaonkar 1979, and Jha 1983.

Lang, Karen, (ed./trans.). 1986. *Āryadeva's Catuḥśataka: On the Bodhisattva's Cultivation of Merit and Knowledge.* Indiske Studier 7 (Copenhagen: Akademisk Forlag).

La Vallée Poussin, Louis de, (ed.). 1903–1913. *Mūlamadhyamakakārikās (Mādhyamikasūtras) de Nāgārjuna, avec la Prasannapadā commentaire de Candrakīri.* Bibliotheca Buddhica, IV (Original ed. published in fascicles in St. Petersburg, 1903–1913; reprint Osnabrück: Biblio Verlag, 1970).

———, (ed.). 1907–1912. *Madhyamakāvatāra par Candrakīrti.* Tibetan text (only complete version extant). Bibliotheca Buddhica IX (Original ed. published in fascicles in St. Petersburg, 1907–1912; reprint Osnabrück: Biblio Verlag, 1970).

———, (ed.). 1914. *Bodhicaryāvatārapañjikā. Prajñākaramati's Commentary on the Bodhicaryāvatāra of Śāntideva.* 7 fascicles. Bibliotheca Indica: A Collection of Oriental Works, published by the Asiatic Society of Bengal, New Series 983, 1031, 1090, 1126, 1139, 1305, and 1399 (Calcutta: Baptist Mission Press; published by the Asiatic Society, 1901, 1903, 1904, 1906, 1907, 1912, and 1914).

Lindtner, Chr. 1982a. *Nāgārjunas filosofiske værker: Nāgārjunīyaṁ Madhyamakaśāstram. Oversat og indledet af Chr. Lindtner.* Indiske Studier 2 (Copenhagen: Akademisk Forlag).

———. 1982b. *Nagarjuniana: Studies in the Writings and Philosophy of Nāgārjuna*. Indiske Studier 4 (Copenhagen: Akademisk Forlag). Originally presented as the author's doctoral thesis, University of Copenhagen, 1982.

Lorenz, Konrad. 1963. *Das sogenannte Böse: Zur Naturgeschichte der Aggression* (Vienna: G. Borotha-Schoeler).

———. 1973. *Die Ruckseite des Spiegels: Versuch einer Naturgeschichte menschlichen Erkennens* (Munich: R. Piper).

Madhyamakāvatāra of Candrakīrti. References are to the edition of Louis de la Vallée Poussin 1912.

Matilal, Bimal Krishna. 1971a. *Epistemology, Logic and Grammar in Indian Philosophical Analysis*. Janua Linguarum, Series Minor 111 (The Hague/Paris: Mouton).

———. 1971b. "Negation and the Mādhyamika dialectic." Chap. 5 in Matilal 1971a: 146–167.

———. 1973. "A critique of the Mādhyamika position." In Mervyn Sprung, ed., *The Problem of the Two Truths in Buddhism and Vedānta* (Dordrecht and Boston: Reidel): 54–63.

———. 1977. *The Logical Illumination of Indian Mysticism*. Inaugural Lecture delivered before the University of Oxford, 5 May (Oxford: Clarendon Press).

———. 1982. *Logical and Ethical Issues of Religious Belief.* Stephanos Nirmalendu Ghosh Lectures on Comparative Religion, 1978 ([Calcutta]: University of Calcutta).

Mauss, Marcel. 1936. "Techniques of the body." *Economy and Society* 2/1: (1973): 70–88. Repr. in Ben Brewster, *Sociology and Psychology: Essays, Marcel Mauss.* Translated [from the French] by Ben Brewster (London and Boston: Routledge and Kegan Paul, 1979): 95–123. Originally published 1936 in *Journal de psychologie normale et pathologique* 32 (3–4): 271–293.

May, Jacques. 1959. *Candrakīrti, Prasannapadā Madhyamakavṛtti*. Collection Jean Przyluski II (Paris: Adrien-Maisonneuve).

Musalgaonkar, Gajanan Shastri, (ed.). 1979. *Mīmāṁsādarśanam:* Tatra Śrīkumārilabhaṭṭa-viracitam *Mīmāṁsāślokavārtikam*, tacca *Śabarabhāṣyeṇa, Nyāyaratnākaravyākhyāya-ṭippanna* [*sic*] ca samvalitam. Śrīmaj-Jaiminīmunipraṇitam; sampadakaḥ Musalagamvakaropanama Gajananasastri (Varanasi: Bharatiya Vidya Prakasana).

Nagao, G. M. 1954. "An Interpretation of the Term Saṁvṛti (Convention) in Buddhism." *Silver Jubilee Volume of the Zinbun Kagaku Kenkyusyo* (Kyoto: Kyoto University): 550–561. Reprinted in Nagao 1991: 13–22.

———. 1955. "The Silence of the Buddha and Its Madhyamic [*sic*] Interpretation." In G. M. Nagao and J. Nozawa, eds., *Studies in Indology and Buddhology Presented to Professor Susumu Yamaguchi on the Occasion of His Sixtieth Birthday* (Kyoto: Hōzōkan): 137–151. This is an English translation of the Japanese original, which appeared also in 1955, in *Tetsugaku Kenkyū* 430 (37/8). The English version was reprinted in Nagao 1991: 35–50.

———. 1989. *The Foundational Standpoint of Mādhyamika Philosophy.* Translated by John P. Keenan (Albany: State University of New York Press).

———. 1991. *Mādhyamika and Yogācāra: A Study of Mahāyāna Philosophies.* Collected papers of G. M. Nagao. Translated by Leslie S. Kawamura (Albany: State University of New York Press).

Norman, Harry Campbell, (ed.). 1906–1915. *Dhammapada-aṭṭhakathā: The Commentary on the Dhammapada.* 5 vols. Pali Text Society Publications, 59, 64, 68, 71,74, 78 (London: Published for the Pali Text Society by H. Frowde. Reprinted, London: Published for the Pali Text Society by Luzac, 1970).

Pradhan, Prahlad, (ed.). 1975. *Abhidharmakośa-bhāṣyam of Vasubandhu.* 2nd ed., revised with introduction and indices by Aruna Haldar. Tibetan Sanskrit Works Series VIII (Patna: K. P. Jayaswal Research Institute).

Rappaport, R. A. 1974/1979. "The obvious aspects of ritual." *Cambridge Anthropology* 2/1: 3–69. Rev. and exp. in Rappaport 1979: 173–221.

———. 1976/1979. "Liturgies and lies." *International Yearbook for the Sociology of Knowledge and Religion* 10: 75–104. Rev. as "Sanctity and lies in evolution," in Rappaport 1979: 223–246.

———. 1979. *Ecology, Meaning and Religion* (Richmond, CA: North Atlantic Books).

Ruegg, David Seyfort. 1981. *The Literature of the Madhyamaka School of Philosophy in India* (Wiesbaden: Otto Harrassowitz).

———. 1982. "Towards a Chronology of the Madhyamaka School." In L. A. Hercus, et al., eds., *Indological and Buddhist Studies. Volume in Honour of Professor J. W. de Jong on His Sixtieth Birthday* (Canberra: Faculty of Asian Studies): 505–530.

Schwartz, Justin. 1991. "Reduction, Elimination, and the Mental." *Philosophy of Science* 58: 203–220.

Scott, James C. 1990. *Domination and the Arts of Resistance: Hidden Transcripts* (New Haven: Yale University Press).

Shastri, Dwarikadas (Swami), (ed.). 1968. *Tattvasaṁgraha of Ācārya Śānta-rakṣita, with the Commentary of Śrī Kamalaśīla.* Bauddha Bharati Series 1–2 (Varanasi: Bauddha Bharati).

———, (ed.). 1973. *Abhidharmakośa & bhāṣya of Ācārya Vasubandhu with Sphuṭārthā commentary of Ācārya Yaśomitra.* 4 vols. Bauddha Bharati Series 5–7, 9 (Varanasi: Bauddha Bharati, [1970–1973]).

Shastri, Hariprasad, (ed.). 1914. "Catuḥśatika by Āryadeva." *Memoirs of the Asiatic Society of Bengal* 3/8: 449–514.

Sinha, Jadunath. 1938. *Indian Realism* (London: Kegan Paul, Trench, Truebner and Co., Ltd.).

Stafford, Betty L. 1983. "Nāgārjuna's Masterpiece—Logical, Mystical, Both, or Neither?" *Philosophy East and West* 33/2: 123–138.

Streng, Frederick J. 1967. *Emptiness: A Study in Religious Meaning* (Nashville: Abingdon Press).

Sullivan, Harry Stack. 1953. *The Interpersonal Theory of Psychiatry* (New York: W. W. Norton).

Takakusu, Junjirō. 1944. "Buddhism As a Philosophy of 'Thusness.'" In Charles A. Moore, ed., *Philosophy—East and West* (Princeton: Princeton University Press): 69–108.

Tola, Fernando, and Dragonetti, Carmen. 1983. "The Yuktiśaṣṭikā of Nāgārjuna." *Journal of the International Association of Buddhist Studies* 6/2: 94–123.

Vasubandhu. *Abhidharmakośa, Kārikās and Bhāṣya (Abhidharmakośa-bhāṣya).* References are to chapter and verse number or to volume and pages in the edition of S. D. Shastri 1973.

Warder, A. K. 1973. "Is Nāgārjuna a Mahāyānist?" In Mervyn Sprung, ed., *The Problem of the Two Truths in Buddhism and Vedānta* (Dordrecht and Boston: Reidel): 78–88.

Williams, Paul. 1991. "On the Interpretation of Madhyamaka Thought." *Journal of Indian Philosophy* 19/2: 191–218. Review of Huntington 1989.

Winternitz, Moritz, (ed./trans.). 1930. *Der Mahāyāna-Buddhismus, nach Sanskrit- und Prākrittexten.* Religiongeschichtliches Lesebuch, Vol. 15, (Tübingen: J. C. B. Mohn).

Yandell, Keith E. 1993. *The Epistemology of Religious Experience* (Cambridge: Cambridge University Press).

Yob, Iris M. 1992. "Religious Metaphor and Scientific Model: Grounds for Comparison." *Religious Studies* 28: 475–485.

Dignāga's Theory of Meaning

An Annotated Translation of the *Pramāṇasamuccayavṛtti* Chapter V: *Anyāpoha-parīkṣā* (I)

Masaaki Hattori

Introduction

The fifth chapter of Dignāga's *Pramāṇasamuccayavṛtti* is devoted to the study of the problem of meaning, which constituted an important topic of philosophical inquiry in classical India.[1] Criticizing the theories maintained by different schools which admit that a word is denotative of an objective reality, either an individual or a universal or something else, Dignāga sets forth the doctrine of *anyāpoha* (differentiation from others, exclusion of others) in this chapter. The basic idea of this doctrine is that a word, having no direct reference to any real entity, functions merely to differentiate an object from other things. According to Dignāga, a real thing is an indivisible unity of innumerable aspects, and no single word is effective to denote it in its totality. It is grasped only by means of perception, and it can never be expressed by a word. A word expresses only one aspect of the object by differentiating it from other things. For example, the word *palāśa* functions to differentiate the directly perceived object from non-*palāśa*s, such as *khadira*, but it does not express the object with its innumerable aspects: height, shape, and so on. The same object is referred to by the word *vṛkṣa* (tree) when it is to be differentiated from non-trees. Though the object is one and the same, the two words applied to it are not synonymous with each other, because they are related to different aspects of the object. Dignāga states with this observation that a word refers to that portion of the object which is differentiated from other things. Since the object itself is an indivisible entity, the portion for which a word stands is nothing other than the product of mental construction. It is a concept formed through the mental process of *anyāpoha*, and as such is devoid of objective reality. The doctrine of *anyāpoha* thus expounded by Dignāga formed a subject of discussion among the post-Dignāga Bauddha logicians and their opponents.

---

1. The first paragraph is quoted with a slight change from the introduction to my edition of the *Pramāṇasamuccayavṛtti*, Chapter V, mentioned below.

The text used for this translation is:

"The *Pramāṇasamuccayavṛtti* of Dignāga, with Jinendrabuddhi's Commentary. Chapter Five: Anyāpoha-parīkṣā. Tibetan Text with Sanskrit Fragments." Edited by M. Hattori. *Memoirs of the Faculty of Letters*, Kyoto University 21 (1982): 101–224 (abbrev.: Hattori [1982]).

The section numbers in the translation are in accordance with those in the text.

By constantly referring to both K (Kanakavarman's version) and V (Vasudhararakṣita's version) and also to *PST* (Jinendrabuddhi's *Pramāṇasamuccayaṭīkā*), I have freely adopted the reading which I have considered to be most appropriate.

The sections translated here are reconstituted into Sanskrit by Muni Jambuvijaya in *Dvādaśāram Nayacakram of Ācārya Śrī Mallavādī Kṣamāśramaṇa with the Commentary Nyāyāgamānusāriṇī of Śrī Siṁhasūri Gaṇi Vādi Kṣamāśramaṇa*, Part II (5–8 Aras), ed. with Critical Notes by Muni Jambūvijayajī (Bhavnagar: Jain Atmanand Sabha, 1976): 607–608. I have derived much help from this work for my translation. A tentative Japanese translation of these sections was published in M. Hattori, "Uddyotakara ni hihan sareru *Apoha*-ron" (The *Apoha*-theory as criticized by Uddyotakara), *Bukkyōgaku Ronbunshū* (Papers on Buddhist Studies): Professors S. Ito and J. Tanaka Felicitation Volume, edited by the Seminar for Buddhist Studies, Kōyasan University (Tōhō Shuppan, 1979): 117–131. An English translation with annotations of these sections is contained in Richard P. Hayes, *Dignāga on the Interpretation of Signs* (Dordrecht/Boston/London: Kluwer Academic Publishers, 1988): 252ff., (abbrev.: Hayes [1988]). Ole Pind is preparing a complete English translation of Chapter five of the *Pramāṇasamuccayavṛtti*. S. Katsura also is making, with the collaboration of some other scholars, an attempt to translate into Japanese the whole chapter with Jinendrabuddhi's commentary. So far a translation of sections 1 and 2 has been published. Since the two Tibetan versions of the *Pramāṇasamuccayavṛtti* are both deficient, the translations by different scholars may be useful for a proper understanding of this important text.[2]

---

2. In the footnotes the following abbreviations are used:
   NV: *Nyāyavārttika* of Uddyotakara. Kāshī Sanskrit Series 33 (Benares, 1916).
   Pāṇ: *Aṣṭādhyāyī* of Pāṇini. Ed. in O. Böhtlingk, *Pāṇini's Grammatik* (Leipzig, 1887).
   PS(V): *Pramāṇasamuccyavṛtti* of Dignāga.

Translation

1. Two means of cognition have been explained. Some hold that the cognition derived from word (*śābda*) also is a separate means of cognition.

> v.1.[3] That [means of cognition] which is based on word is not an [independent] means of cognition other than inference. Because it [viz., a word][4] expresses its own object through the exclusion of the other [things], just as [the inferential mark (*liṅga*)] "*kṛtakatva*" (producedness) or the like [establishes the object to be proved through the exclusion of what is not a possessor of that inferential mark].

When a word is applied to a certain thing, [the word] is connected with a part of that [object] through an inseparable relationship (*avinābhāva*), and it denotes [only] that [part of the object] through the exclusion of other [things], just as [the inferential mark] "*kṛtakatva*" [indicates the possessor of that mark (*liṅgin*), which is necessarily connected with it, through the exclusion of what is not a possessor of that mark].[5] Therefore, [the cognition derived from word] is not distinguished from inferential cognition.[6]

PST: *Viśālāmalavāti Pramāṇasamuccayaṭīkā* of Jinendrabuddhi (in Hattori [1982]).
ŚVT: *Ślokavārt(t)ikaṭīkā (Śarkarikā)* of Bhaṭṭaputra-Jayamiśra. Ed. C. Kunhan Raja. Madras University Sanskrit Series 17 (Madras, 1946).
TSP: *Tattvasaṁgrahapañjikā* of Kamalaśīla. Ed. with *Tattvasaṁgraha* of Śāntarakṣita by Dwarikadas Shastri. Vol. 1. Bauddha Bharati Series 1 (Varanasi, 1968).
VP: *Vākyapadīya* of Bhartṛhari. Ed. in W. Rau, *Bhartṛharis Vākyapadīya.* Abhandlungen für die Kunde des Morgenlandes XLII, 4 (Wiesbaden, 1977).

3. This verse is quoted in *TSP*, p. 539.17–18 as follows:
na pramāṇāntaraṁ śābdam anumānāt tathā hi saḥ |
kṛtakatvādivat svārtham anyāpohena bhāṣate | | .

4. Though there is no mention of the thing to be indicated by the pronoun *saḥ* in pāda b, it is understood from the context that *saḥ* refers to a word (*śabda*). Cf. PST, D237b.5/P268b.8: *de źes pa śugs kyis thob pa sgra la sbrel lo.*

5. TSP, p. 540.3–4: *tat kṛtakatvādivad arthāntaravyavacchedena dyotayati.*

6. Cf. *PS(V)*, II, k. 13 and *Vṛtti*. The Tibetan text and a Japanese translation are given in H. Kitawaga, *Indo-koten-ronrigaku no Kenkyū—Jinna no Taikei* (A Study of Indian Classical Logic: Dignāga's System) (Tokyo: Suzuki Research Foundation, 1965): 462, 112. The main portion of *PS(V)*, II is translated into English in R. P. Hayes, "Dignāga's view on Reasoning (*svārthānumāna*)," *JIPh* 8 (1980): 219–277. Cf. also E. Frauwallner, "Dignāga, sein Werk und seine Entwicklung," *WZKSO* 3

2. There are some who hold that a *jāti-śabda* (a word referring to a universal) expresses all particulars (*bheda, viśeṣa)* subsumed under the universal without exception (*eva*), [but] a *bheda-śabda* (a word referring to a particular) is [still used] for the purpose of restricting (*niyama*) [the object of reference to a specific one] among the particulars expressed [by the *jāti-śabda*].[7] To them the [following] answer is given:

v.2a. A *jāti-śabda* is not [a denoter] of particulars.[8]

[The word] "denoter" (*vācaka)* [which is to be supplied here] will be mentioned below [in v.2c]. First of all, a *jāti-śabda*, for example "*sat*," is not a denoter of [particulars, such as] a substance (*dravya)*, etc.

v.2b_1. Because [particulars are] innumerable (*ānantya*).

Since particulars are innumerable, it is impossible to establish the relation [of each of them] to a word. And it is not reasonable that an object is expressed by the word of which the relation [with the object] is not established. [Such a] word simply makes people understand its own form (*svarūpa*).[9]

3. Furthermore,

(1959): 102; M. Hattori, "*Apoha* and *Pratibhā*," *Sanskrit and Indian Studies: Festschrift in Honor of Daniel H. H. Ingalls* (Dordrecht and Boston: D. Reidel, 1980): 61. The close relation of Dignāga's doctrine of *anyāpoha* to his theory of *anumāna* is discussed in detail in S. Katsura, "Gainen—*apoha*-ron wo chūshin ni (Concept: with a focus on the *apoha*-theory), *Iwanami-kōza, Tōyō-shisō* (Eastern Thought), v. 10: *Indo-Bukkyō* (Indian Buddhism) 3 (Tokyo: Iwanami Shoten, 1989): 135–159.

7. Cf. *PST*, D239b.4–6/P271a.1–4. In the statement *brāhmaṇo na hantavyaḥ*(One should not kill a brāhmaṇa), the word "brāhmaṇa" refers to all individuals grouped under the brāhmaṇa-class. When there is need for restricting the object of reference to Kauṇḍinya among the brāhmaṇas, the word referring to that particular person is used in the form: *ehi brāhmaṇa kauṇḍinya* (Come! brāhmaṇa Kauṇḍinya!)

8. Cf. *ŚVT*, p. 49.22, 25, etc. (cf. Hattori [1982]):
na jātiśabdo bhedānām ānantyavyabhicārataḥ |
vācako yogajātyor vā bhedārthair apṛthakśruteḥ | | *k.* 2

9. Cf. *VP*, III.3 (Saṁbandhasamuddeśa). 1: *jñānaṁ prayoktur bāhyo 'rthaḥ svarūpaṁ ca pratīyate* | *śabdair uccaritais* ... | |
By the words which are uttered the idea of the speaker, an external object and the own form [of words] are understood.
PST, D240a.6–7/P271b.5–6 gives the following example: When an Aryan hears a word spoken by a foreigner (*mleccha*), he understands its own form (*svarūpa*), but not its object of reference, because he is not familiar with the relation between the word and its object of reference.

v.2b_2. Because of deviation (*vyabhicāra*).

Since the word "*sat*" occurs not only in respect to a substance but also in respect to a quality and so on, there is deviation [in denotation]. Therefore, a doubt may arise [as to what is denoted by the word "*sat*"]. [The word which produces a doubt is] not a denoter.

4. Some people maintain the following view: [A *jāti-śabda* denotes] just a universal (*jāti-mātra*) or the relation (*saṁbandha*) [of the universal to a particular], because, [since the universal or the relation is not differentiated,] it is easy to relate [a word to it] (*saṁbandha-saukarya*) and because there is no deviation [in denotation]. They are not right either.

v.2c–d. [A *jāti-śabda* is not] a denoter of the universal or of the relation [of the universal to a particular], because it is heard without a difference [in case-ending] with the words referring to particulars (*bhedārtha*).

[Their view does not hold good,] because [the *jāti-śabda* "*sat*"] would [then] not be in the relation of co-reference (*sāmānādhikaraṇya*) with such words as "*dravya*," etc., which denote particulars, and there would not be such expressions as "*sad dravyam*," "*saṅ guṇaḥ*" and "*sat karma*." However, this is observed [in common usage]. The universal "*sattā*" or the relation [of *sattā* to *dravya*, etc.] is not [identical with] a *dravya* nor [with] a *guṇa*, but it is [a property] *of dravya* (*dravyasya*) or *of guṇa* (*guṇasya*).
[Bhartṛhari] also says: "Two words expressive of a qualifier (*guṇa*) and a qualified (*guṇin*) have different case-endings in accordance with a restrictive rule. Between two words referring to [the same] substance (*dravya-śabda*) the relation of co-reference is established."[10]

5. v.3. The relation (*saṁbandha*) also is denoted here [only] as what is to be expressed (*vācya*) by a property of its relata (*saṁbandhin*). Thus it is expressed after being made an action (*bhāva*), and the action is related to something else [viz., the possessor of the action].

---

10. *VP*, III. 14 (Vṛttisamuddeśa). 8:
vibhaktibhedo niyamād guṇaguṇyabhidhāyinoḥ |
sāmānādhikaraṇyasya prasiddhir dravyaśabdayoḥ | |
This verse is not quoted in K nor in *PST*. It is doubtful whether this was originally in *PSV*.

The relation means the act of relating (*saṁbandhana*).[11] It is related to [something] other [than itself], just as color (*rāga*) [viz., the act of coloring], etc. Inasmuch as the relation is expressed by a property of its relata, there is no word which denotes the relation by its own property.[12] Therefore, it does not stand to reason that it (= the relation) is the meaning of a *jāti-śabda*.

6. Some people maintain as follows: "What it is intended to express [by a *jāti-śabda*] is only that which possesses the universal (*jātimat*), [viz., a particular qualified by the universal,] because [the *jāti-śabda* "*sat*" is] co-referential with the words referring to particulars (*viśeṣa-śabda*), [such as "*dravya*," etc.] and because it is easy to relate [the word to the object of reference], and also because there is no deviation [in denotation]." For them [we argue as follows].

> v.4a. [A *jāti-śabda*] is not [a denoter] of a [particular] possessing that [universal] (*tadvat* = *jātimat*), because [it is] not independent [in denoting that object].[13]

In that case also, the word "*sat*" expresses a substance (*dravya*) which has only the universal (*jāti*) and the word's own form (*svarūpa*) as qualifiers, but does not [express the substance itself] directly. Therefore, it has no implicit reference (*ākṣepa*) to the particulars, a pot and so on, subsumed under that [substance]. Accordingly, [a pot, etc. are] not the particulars of that [substance as qualified by the universal and a word's own form], and therefore there would be no co-referential relation [of "*sat*" with "*ghaṭa*," etc.].[14] When there is no pervasion

---

11. The meaning of the term *saṁbandha* (*sam*-√*bandh* + *ghañ*) is explained on the basis of *Pāṇ*, III.3.18: *bhāve* (*ghañ*). The *Kāśikā* on this sūtra mentions *rāga* as an example.

12. Cf. *VP*, III.3.4:
nābhidhānaṁ svadharmeṇa saṁbandhasyāsti vācakam |
atyantaparatantratvād rūpaṁ nāsyāpadiśyate | |
There is no word which denotes the relation by its (= relation's) own property. Since it [viz., relation] is absolutely dependent [on something else], its [own] form cannot be indicated.
The term *saṁbandha* in this verse means the relation between a word and its object of reference. Dignāga applies the idea expressed in this verse to the case of the relation between a particular and the universal.

13. *ŚVT*, p. 60.3, etc. (cf. Hattori [1982] p. 109) *tadvato nāsvatantratvāt.*

14. *TSP*, p. 382.6–8: *sacchabdo jātisvarūpopasarjanaṁ dravyam āha na sākṣād iti tadgataghaṭādibhedānākṣepād atadbhedatve sāmānādhikaraṇyābhāvaḥ*. Cf. *NV*, p. 320. 23–25.

(*vyāpti*) [of a particular object by a word, that word is] not co-referential [with the word denoting that particular object]. For example, since the word "white" (*śukla*) expresses the substance as qualified only by its own object of reference, i.e., the quality of white (*śuklaguṇa*), it does not implicitly refer to [other qualities, such as] "sweet" (*madhura*), etc., although these [qualities] are residing in the [same substance]; therefore, they are not particulars of that [substance qualified by "white"]. The same would apply in this case.[15]

7. Furthermore, [granted that a *jāti-śabda* expresses a *tadvat* (viz., a particular possessing the universal) through ascription of identity between the universal and a *tadvat*,]

> v.4b$_1$. Since it is a figurative expression, [a *jāti-śabda* is not truly the denoter of a *tadvat*].

The *jāti-śabda* "*sat*" expresses in the true sense of the word its own form (*svarūpa*) or the universal (*jāti*)[*sattā*]. The word which is [primarily] applied to it is applied to a *tadvat* [only] figuratively.[16] When a word is applied to a certain thing in a figurative sense, it does not truly express that thing.[17]

8. [A word can be figuratively applied to a certain object only when this object has similarity (*sārūpya*) to the primary meaning of the word. However, [the similarity of a *tadvat* to the universal] is also

---

15. In his *Mīmāṁsāślokavārttika*, Apohavāda vv. 120–122, Kumārila utilized Dignāga's argument put forward in this section for the refutation of the *apoha*-theory. Dharmakīrti gives an answer to Kumārila's refutation. Cf. M. Hattori, "Discussions on *jātimat* as the Meaning of a Word," *Shri Niwas Shastri Commemoration Volume* (forthcoming).

16. *ŚVT*, p. 61.20–21: *sacchabdo 'pi bhūtārthena svarūpaṁ jātiṁ vāha, tatra pravṛttas tadvaty upacaryamāṇo gauṇaḥ syāt.* Cf. *NV*, p. 321.1–2, 325.4–5.

17. *PST*, D244a.2/P275b.7 makes reference to *VP*, III.14.348:
mañcaśabdo yathādheyaṁ mañceṣv eva vyavasthitaḥ |
tattvenāha tathā jātiśabdo dravyeṣu vartate | |

> Just as the word *mañca*, which is determined to mean "bench," expresses really what is on it, so does a word referring to a universal denote the substances [subsumed under the universal].

Helārāja gives an example as *mañcāḥ krośanti* (the benches cry out). For this example, cf. D. H. H. Ingalls, J. M. Masson, and M. V. Patwardhan (trans.), *The Dhvanyāloka of Ānandavardhana with the Locana of Abhinavagupta*, HOS 49 (Cambridge, Mass. / London: Harvard University Press, 1990): 572, n. 9.

v.4b_2. impossible. [Hence a *jāti-śabda* is not a denoter of a *tadvat* even in the figurative sense.]

For a *tadvat* the similarity in quality (*guṇa-sārūpya*)[18] [to the universal] either (1) through the transfer of notion (*pratyayasaṁkrānti*) or (2) through the help of a qualifier (*guṇopakāra*) is impossible.[19]

9. If you ask why [the similarity through] the transfer of notion is impossible, [we answer as follows:] Because, in the case of figurative expression,

v.4c-d. the form of cognition (*buddhirūpa*) is different; as in the case of the figurative application of the word "king" to a servant.

For example, when the word "king" (*svāmin*) is [figuratively] applied to a servant in the form "He who is a servant is a king (*svāmin*)," the [form of] cognition with respect to the king and that with respect to the servant are not the same. A *jāti-śabda* is also figuratively applied to *tadvat.*
[Therefore, there must be a difference in the form of idea with respect to the universal and to *tadvat*. Thus there is no similarity between the two.]

10. v.5a-b. Also because [the universal and a *tadvat* are] not mentioned in succession, as in the case of the whiteness of a jasmine flower and of a conch shell, [there is no similarity between them].

When there occurs the same notion [in respect to some similar objects], it is observed that [these objects are] mentioned in succession; for example, [we use the expression] "the whiteness of a jasmine, of a water-lily, and of a conch shell." [That is to say, the notion "whiteness" is transferred from jasmine to water-lily, and then to conch shell]. Since the word ["*sat*"] is applied to the universal and to a *tadvat* simultaneously, there is no similarity based on the transfer of notion [between the two].

---

18. For example, sovereignty (*ādhipatya*), which is a quality (*guṇa*) of a king, is observed in a servant, who appears like a conqueror (*jitakāśin*), cf. *NV-tātparyaṭīkā* (in *Nyāyadarśanam*, Calcutta Sanskrit Series 18): 673.20.

19. For sections 8–10 and 12, cf. *NV*, p. 321.4–7: *tadvati ca na guṇasārūpyāt pratyaya-saṁkrāntiḥ* | *yathā svāmiśabdasya bhṛtye* | | *na guṇoparāgāt* | *yathā nīlaḥ sphaṭika iti* | | *kramavṛttyabhāvāt* | *yugapadasaṁbhavāc ca* | | *ayathārthajñānotpattiprasaṅgāc ca* | | .

11. v.5cd. If [the *tadvat* is considered to possess] the nature [of the universal] through the help of the qualifier (*guṇa*) [viz., the universal], there would be [the cognition of] the superiority of quality (*guṇa-prakarṣa*) without the cognition [of the superiority of quality of the qualifier].[20]

If [it is assumed that] by the help of the qualifier [viz., the universal] the *tadvat* comes to take the form of the qualifier (= the universal), just as the crystal [comes to have the red color by the help of the *lākṣā*], then, in respect to the substance [viz., a *tadvat*], there would be the cognition of the superiority of quality without depending on the cognition of the [superiority of quality of the] qualifier.[21] Because, with reference to a crystal, the occurrence of the idea of "red" (*rakta*) does not depend upon the cognition of the [red] *lākṣā*, for [it is observed that], in regard to impure crystals, [such as violet quartz,] there do not occur different cognitions [of the crystal and the material for coloring].[22]

12. Furthermore, [if it were admitted that by the help of the qualifier a *tadvat* comes to assume the form of the qualifier,][23]

v.6ab. Since [all cognitions derived from word are] of the form of that which is combined (*saṁsargin*) [with the object, viz., a qualifier

---

20. *ŚVT*, p. 66.3: *guṇopakāratādrūpye prakarṣaḥ syād vinā dhiyā.*
Cf. *PST*, D 246b.2/P 278b.2: *blo med kyaṅ* (*vinā dhiya*) *źes pa yon tan rab tu gyur ba'i blo med par yaṅ ṣes pa'i don to.*

21. The superiority (*prakarṣa*) is a property which is expressed by the affix *taraP* /*tamaP* added to bases. When a piece of cloth is recognized as "more blue" (*nīlatara*) than another piece of cloth, this is due to the cognition of the superiority of the quality "blue" which is a qualifier of the piece of cloth. A piece of cloth is neither superior nor inferior by itself. Cf. *PST*, D246b.2–4/P278b.2–4.

22. If it is assumed that the cognition of a *tadvat*, viz., a particular, is obtained without depending on the cognition of the qualifier, viz., a universal, then it would follow that a man who indistinctly perceives an object in twilight would have a clear notion of "cow" in reference to that object. Cf. *PST*, D247a.3–5/P279a.3–6.

23. Tib., *'dres pa.* Cf. *PST*, D247a.7/P279b.1: *'dres pa'i khyad par ni yon tan ṣes pa don gcig pa'o*; *VP*, III.5.1:

saṁsargi bhedakaṁ yad yat savyāpāraṁ pratīyate |
guṇatvaṁ paratantratvāt tasya śāstra udāhṛtam | |
Whatever is combined with [a thing], differentiates [a thing from other things], and is understood as functional, it is, [as] called in the *śāstra*, a quality, since it is dependent on [something else].

of the object], there would be, in respect to any [object], a wrong cognition.

With respect to an object, all cognitions derived from word are mediated by the form of that which is combined [with the object, viz., the qualifiers, such as the universal, etc.]. Therefore, [all cognitions] would not conform to the thing in itself (*ayathārtha*), just like the cognition of the crystal [appearing red, etc.].[24]

24. By a cognition derived from word, an object is apprehended as, for example, a "pot" (*ghaṭa*), that is to say, as a *dravya* qualified by the universal "potness" (*ghaṭatva*). The cognition of this type does not conform to the object itself which is not split into the qualifier and the qualified. If the *tadvat* is conceived as being of the nature of the qualifier, it would never be perceived as it is.

Śāntarakṣita and Bhāviveka as Opponents of the Mādhyamika in the *Madhyamakāloka**

Masamichi Ichigō

The main project of Kamalaśīla's *Madhyamakāloka* (MĀ) is to explain that all *dharmas* are in reality empty and that there is ultimately only one vehicle. The ultimate purpose of the treatise is to enable one to cut off one's afflictions by understanding the treatise.

The MĀ is composed of eighty-three *pūrva-pakṣas* and corresponding *uttara-pakṣas*. The first three of them examine the position which holds that the claim "all *dharmas* have no intrinsic nature" cannot be proved by Scripture (*āgama*).[1] The opponent selects twelve passages from seven sūtras exhibiting ideas which appear to contradict the notions of non-intrinsic nature (*niḥsvabhāva*) and non-production (*anutpāda*) of the Mādhyamika. The opponent maintains that the teaching of non-intrinsic nature or non-production is merely taught with a certain intention (*saṁdhi*), but that the intention is not always directed to prove the teaching.

Then in the *uttara-pakṣas* Kamalaśīla elucidates the true intention expressed in the passages and shows that the expressions are not opposed to the Mādhyamika standpoint. It is possible, therefore, to prove by Scripture that all dharmas have no intrinsic nature.

In this context, Kamalaśīla introduces the views of two unnamed scholars, whom I will provisionally label (A) and (B), who seem to be treated as the opponents of the Mādhyamika or Kamalaśīla, since (A) maintains that from the point of view of the conventional truth mind exists, and (B) again holds that from the point of view of conventional truth both mind and even the external object exist.

Kamalaśīla, however, having investigated the intention of the two scholars, holds that there is no evidence to suggest that they maintain the existence of intrinsic nature on the basis of the canonical passages in question.

This paper discusses the identity of these two scholars, suggesting

---

* I would like to express my gratitude for the painstaking effort of computerizing my manuscript undertaken by Mr. Satoshi Beppu, which I will never forget.

1. Ichigō 1992: 204.

that (A) is Śāntarakṣita and (B) is Bhāviveka according to the identification by the Mongolian commentator on the MĀ, bsTan-dar.[2]

This paper consists of three parts: The first presents the Tibetan text which contains the views of the two scholars and Kamalaśīla's standpoint. The second is a translation of this Text. In the third part, the author confirms bsTan-dar's identification and the historical existence of the Yogācāra-Mādhyamika school to which Śāntarakṣita belongs, and summarizes its central tenet.

I. Text

[A] (C 157a6; D 157a6; N 162a2; P 171a5)

(1) gźan dag na re

sems tsam ni raṅ gis rab tu grub pa'i ṅo bo ñid yin pa'i phyir kun rdzob tu gnas pa kho na yin la | phyi'i don ni kun rdzob tu yaṅ mi gnas te | sems kyi rnam pa las ma gtogs par de grub pa med pa'i phyir ro | de'i phyir de rab tu bstan pa'i ched du bcom ldan 'das kyis dṅos po[a] rnams sems tsam ñid du bstan gyi | don dam par yod pa ñid ni ma yin te (D157b) | mdo gźan las de yaṅ ṅo bo ñid (b med pa ñid b) du bstan pa'i phyir te |

(2) ji skad du *'phags pa saṅs rgyas thams cad kyi yul la*[c] *'jug pa ye śes snaṅ ba'i rgyan* las

saṅs rgyas rnams kyis nam yaṅ ni | |
gtan du chos rnams thams cad daṅ | |
sems ma brñes śiṅ chos mkhyen pa | |
dmigs mi mṅa' la phyag 'tshal bstod | |[3]

ces gsuṅs pa lta bu'o

(3) *'phags pa dkon mchog brtsegs pa* las kyaṅ

'od sruṅs sems ni yoṅs su btsal na mi (P171b) dmigs so | (d gaṅ mi dmigs pa de ni ñe bar mi dmigs so d) | gaṅ ñe bar mi dmigs pa de ni 'das pa yaṅ ma yin | ma 'oṅs pa yaṅ ma yin | da ltar byuṅ ba yaṅ ma yin no | gaṅ 'das pa ma yin | ma 'oṅs pa ma yin | da ltar byuṅ ba ma yin pa de ni dus gsum las 'das pa yin no | gaṅ dus gsum las 'das pa 'di ni yod pa yaṅ ma yin med pa yaṅ ma yin no | gaṅ yod pa yaṅ ma yin med pa yaṅ ma yin pa de ni ma skyes pa'o | gaṅ ma skyes pa de la ni ṅo bo ñid med do | gaṅ la ṅo bo ñid med pa de la skye ba med do | gaṅ la skye ba med pa de la 'gag pa med do | gaṅ la 'gag pa med pa de la 'bral ba med do | gaṅ la 'bral ba med pa

---

2. Ichigō 1992: 196.

3. *Sarvabuddhaviṣayāvatārajñānālokālaṁkāra-nāma*, P [28] 768, 328b6, 大正 12, 359, 263a9–10: *saṅs rgyas rnams kyi lan 'ga' yaṅ | | sems daṅ chos kun gtan mi dmigs | | chos rnams thams cad kun mkhyen pa | | mi rten khyod la phyag 'tshal lo | |*. 智者於心無所得 是中亦復畢竟無 於一切法正遍知 無所緣尊今讚礼.

de la 'gro ba yaṅ med | 'oṅ ba yaṅ med | 'chi 'pho ba[e] yaṅ med | skye ba yaṅ med[f] | gaṅ la 'gro ba yaṅ med | 'oṅ ba yaṅ med | 'chi 'pho ba yaṅ med | skye ba yaṅ med pa de la 'du byed ci yaṅ med do | gaṅ la 'du byed ci yaṅ med pa de ni 'dus ma byas so | gaṅ 'dus ma byas pa de ni 'phags pa rnams kyi rigs so[4]

źes rgyas par gsuṅs so | des na yaṅ *de ñid* las

'od sruṅs rtag ces bya ba 'di ni mtha' gcig go | 'od sruṅs mi rtag ces bya ba 'di ni mtha' gñis pa'o | [5] 'od sruṅs de bźin du yod ces bya ba 'di ni mtha' gcig go | 'od sruṅs med ces bya ba 'di ni mtha' gñis pa'o | [6] mtha' 'di gñis kyi dbus gaṅ yin pa de[g] ni brtag tu med pa | bstan du med daṅ | thogs pa med pa | mi gnas pa | snaṅ ba med pa | rnam par rig pa med pa | (hgnas pa med pah) ste 'di ni chos rnams kyi dbu ma'i lam la yaṅ dag par so sor rtog pa (D158a) źes bya'o[7]

źes gsuṅs pa yin te | de ni dbu mar gyur ba | dṅos por yod pa rnam par śes pa'i ṅo bo yod pa ñid du sgrub par byed pa ma yin gyi | 'on kyaṅ chos kyi dbyiṅs mtha' gñis po thams cad daṅ bral ba | chos ma lus pa ṅo bo ñid med pa'i mtshan ñid (P172a) spros pa med pa rjod par byed pa yin no |

chos kyi dbyiṅs de yaṅ bdag ñid kyis 'di 'o de 'o źes brtag par mi nus pa'i phyir brtag tu med pa'o | gźan dag la bstan par mi nus pa'i phyir bstan du med pa'o | naṅ gi khams daṅ skye mched kyi ṅo bor mi gnas pa'i phyir mi gnas pa'o | phyi'i khams daṅ | skye mched ltar snaṅ bar mi 'gyur ba'i phyir snaṅ ba med pa'o | mig gi rnam par śes pa la sogs pa'i khams kyi raṅ bźin las 'das pa'i phyir rnam par rig pa med pa'o | 'dod chags la sogs pa ñon moṅs pa mtha' dag gi gnas ma yin pa'i phyir gnas pa med pa źes bya'o |

gal te dbu ma la sems kyi raṅ gi ṅo bo bdag ñid kyi dṅos po don

---

4. KP p. 149, §102: *cittaṁ hi kāśyapa parigaveṣamāṇaṁ na labhyate 30 yan na labhyate tan nopalabhyate tan nātītaṁ nānāgataṁ na pratyutpannaṁ | yan nātītaṁ nānāgataṁ na pratyutpannaṁ tatradhvasamatikrāntaṁ yatryadhvasamatikrāntaṁ | tan naivāsti neva nāsti | yan naivāsti na nāsti | tad ajātaṁ yad ajātaṁ | tasya nāsti svabhāvaḥ yasya nāsti svabhāvaḥ tasya nāsty utpāda | yasya nāsty utpādaḥ tasya nāsti nirodhaḥ yasya nāsti nirodhaḥ tasya nāsti vigamaḥ avigamas tasya na gatir nāgatir na cyutir nopapattiḥ yatra na gatir nāgatir na cyutir nopapattiḥ tatra na kecit saṁskārāḥ yatra na kecit saṁ- skārāḥ tad asaṁskṛtaṁ | tad āryāṇāṁ gotra.*

5. KP p. 86, §56,1–2: *nityam iti kāśyapa ayam eko ntaḥ anityam iti kāśyapa ayaṁ dvitīyo ntaḥ.*

6. KP p. 90, §60,1: *astīti kāśyapa ayam eko ntaḥ nāstīty ayaṁ dvitīyo ntaḥ.*

7. KP p. 86, §56,2–4: *yad etayor dvayo nityānityayor maddhyaṁ tad arūpy anidarśanam anābhāsam avijñaptikam apratiṣṭham aniketam iyam ucyate kāśyapa madhyamā pratipad dharmāṇāṁ bhūtapratyavekṣā* |. The Sanskrit and Chinese words corresponding to *brtag tu med pa* (not examined) and *thogs pa med pa* (not hindered) are not found in the KP. The term *arūpin* (無色) in the KP has no corresponding word in the Text.

dam pa ci yaṅ ruṅ ba źig yod par gyur na ni de'i tshe de la yod pas rtag go źes bya ba'am | mi rtag go źes bya bar mṅon par źen pa yaṅ ji ltar mthar 'gyur te | dṅos po'i de kho na ñid [i] ji lta ba bźin gyi rjes su soṅ źiṅ tshul bźin yid la byed pa ñid ni lhuṅ ba'i gnas so źes bya bar rigs pa ma yin no | rtag pa la sogs pa'i ṅo bo ñid las ma gtogs pa dṅos po'i ṅo bo ñid du gyur pa dṅos po'i rnam pa gźan ni mi srid do |

gal te dbu ma la dṅos po'i raṅ gi ṅo bo med na med do źes bya bar 'dzin pa yaṅ mthar mi 'gyur ro sñam du sems na | de yaṅ rigs pa ma yin te | (j med do źes bya bar 'dzin pa yaṅ rigs pa ma yin te j) | med do źes bya bar 'dzin pa yaṅ yod par 'dzin pa med na med pa yin pa'i phyir ro | yul med pa'i dgag pa ni yod pa ma yin te | de bas na gdon mi za bar gaṅ la med par 'dzin pa yod pa de la yod par 'dzin pa de yaṅ yod pas mtha' 'di gñi gar 'gyur ro |

gal te dbu ma la dṅos po yod na de'i tshe de la yod par 'dzin pa gaṅ gis bzlog par 'gyur | *'phags pa tiṅ ṅe 'dzin gyi rgyal po* (P172b) las dbu mar yod pa don dam pa pa'i dṅos po la gnas pa dgag pa'i phyir gsuṅs pa gaṅ yin pa de (D158b) daṅ yaṅ 'gal bar 'gyur te |

> yod ces med ces gñis ga'ṅ mtha' |
> dag daṅ ma dag 'di yaṅ mtha' |
> de phyir mtha' gñis rnam spaṅs nas |
> mkhas pa dbus la'ṅ gnas mi byed | [8]

ces gsuṅs pa gaṅ yin pa'o |

mdo'i don ni brten par bya ba dbu mar yod pa'i dṅos po'i raṅ gi ṅo bo 'ga' yaṅ med na ni mkhas pa dbus la'ṅ[k] gnas mi byed ces bya ba ruṅ bar 'gyur ro źes bya ba yin no | dṅos po źig yod na ni ji ltar na de la mkhas pa gnas par[l] byed par mi 'gyur | *'phags pa 'jig rten las 'das pa'i le'u* las kyaṅ

> kye rgyal ba'i sras dag gźan yaṅ khams gsum sems tsam du 'jug ste | dus gsum yaṅ sems daṅ 'dra bar rtogs par byed la | sems de yaṅ mtha' daṅ dbus med pa ñid du 'jug go[9]

źes gsuṅs te | mdo'i don ni skye ba daṅ 'jig pa'i mtha' daṅ | gnas pa'i mtshan ñid kyi dbus don dam par med pa'i phyir sems mtha' daṅ dbus med pa la 'jug par 'gyur | rtogs par 'gyur[10] źes bya ba yin no źes zer ro | |

---

8. SR IX.27; Cüppers1990: 43, 98: *astīti nāstīti ubhe pi antā śuddhī aśuddhīti ime pi antā | tasmād ubhe anta vivarjayitvā madhye pi sthānam na karoti paṇḍitaḥ* | |.

9. BA, P [26] 74,1,8–2,1; DBh, Vaidya ed. 32,9: *uktaṁ cāryalokottaraparivartate "punar aparaṁ, bho jinaputra,cittamātraṁ traidhātukam avatarati tac ca cittam anantamadhyatayāvatarati" iti* | |. 大正 10, 279, 288c5–6 菩薩摩訶薩知三界唯心。三世唯心。而了知其心無量無辺. This is cited in MAV 296, 2–5; I BhK 217, 9–11.

[B]

gźan dag na re

(1) (a)

kun rdzob tu rnam par śes pa daṅ 'dra bar phyi'i don yaṅ gnas pa yin no | de lta ma yin na *'phags pa sa bcu pa* las | sa brgyad pa la byaṅ chub sems dpa' 'jig rten gyi khams su gtogs pa'i rdul phra rab kyi graṅs la sogs pa yoṅs su śes par gsuṅs pa gaṅ yin pa de daṅ 'gal bar 'gyur te | ji skad du

> de rdul phra rab phra mo yaṅ rab tu śes la | chen por gyur pa daṅ | tshad med pa daṅ | rnam par phye ba yaṅ rab tu śes so | rdul phra rab kyi rnam par phye ba tshad med pa la mkhas par yaṅ rab tu śes so | 'jig rten gyi khams gaṅ na sa'i khams kyi rdul phra rab ji sñed pa [(m]yod pa[m)] yaṅ rab tu śes la | de bźin du chu'i khams (P173a) daṅ | me'i khams daṅ | rluṅ gi khams kyi yaṅ rab tu śes so[11]

źes rgyas par gsuṅs pa lta bu'o |

(b) rnam par śes pa bźin du phyi'i don yaṅ grags pa'i phyir grags pas gnod pa yaṅ[n] yin te | rigs pas rnam par dpyad na ni gñi ga yaṅ brtag pa'i khur mi bzod pa ñid kyis dṅos po'i gnas mi thod[12] la | tha sñad kyi bden par ni dṅos (D159a) po gñi ga yaṅ gnag rdzi'i chuṅ ma yan chad la grags pa ñid do |

(2) (a) sems tsam du gsuṅs pa'i 'bras bu ni gźan gyis kun brtags pa byed pa po daṅ za ba po dgag pa yin te[13] | tha sñad du yaṅ sems las[o] ma gtogs pa'i byed pa po la sogs pa gźan rab tu ma grub pa'i phyir ro |

(b) yaṅ na sems ni chos thams cad kyi sṅon du 'gro ba yin pa'i phyir chos thams cad la bltos[p] nas sems gtso bor[14] bsgrub pa'i phyir ro |

gaṅ yaṅ

---

10. Cf. MAV 296, 6–8 ; I BhK 217, 11–13: *antayor utpādabhaṅgalakṣaṇayoḥ sthitilakṣaṇasya ca madhyasyābhāvād anantamadhyaṁ cittam* |. This passage is Śāntarakṣita's commentary on the BA cited above.

11. DBh Vaidya ed. 44, 18–21; Kondō ed. 139, 1–6: *paramāṇurajaḥsūkṣmatāṁ ca prajānāti, mahadgatatāṁ ca apramāṇatāṁ ca vibhaktitāṁ ca prajānāti* | *apramāṇaparamāṇurajovibhaktikauśalyaṁ ca prajānāti* | *asyāṁ ca lokadhātau yāvanti pṛthivīdhātoḥ paramāṇurajāṁsi tāni prajānāti* | *yāvanti abdhātoḥ* ... . | *tejodhātoḥ* ... . | *vāyudhātoḥ* .... |.

12. This word cannot be identified in dictionaries. Japanese scholars render it into Japanese in the sense of "obtaining." Matsumoto 1984: 154 b.23, Moriyama 1991: 94,14.

13. TJ ad MH V.28.

14. MAv VI. 87. Cf. Matsumoto 1984: 155a 12.

don yod ma yin sems ñid de | | [15]

źes bya ba daṅ | de bźin du

bag chags kyis ni dkrugs pa'i sems | |
don du snaṅ bar rab tu 'byuṅ | | [16]

źes bya ba la sogs pa gsuṅs pa der yaṅ rnam pa med pa'i sems kyis ji ltar yaṅ yul 'dzin par mi ruṅ bas de'i phyir gdon mi za bar de rnam pa daṅ bcas pa ñid du khas blaṅ dgos so | de bas na sems kyi rnam pa las ma gtogs pa don gyi rnam pa[q] mi snaṅ ba'i phyir de bkag pas[r] sems rnam pa daṅ bcas pa ñid du bstan pa 'ba' źig tu zad kyi | de las phyi rol gyi don med par rtogs par 'gyur ba ni ma yin no |

(c) yaṅ na bdag la sogs pa yod pa la sogs par bstan pa bźin du de lta bus 'dul ba'i skye bo la bltos[s] nas sman pa rnams nad pa ji lta ba bźin gso bar byed pa daṅ 'dra bar saṅs rgyas bcom ldan 'das rnams kyi chos bśad pa sna tshogs rab tu 'jug ste | de skad du *'phags pa laṅ kar gśegs pa* las kyaṅ

nad pa daṅ ni nad pa la | |
sman pas rdzas[t] byin ji lta bar | | (P173b)
de bźin saṅs rgyas sems can la | |
sems tsam ñid du gsuṅs pa yin | | [17]

źes gsuṅs so |

gźan dag la bslu[u] ba yaṅ ma yin no[v] | de lta bus 'dul ba'i skye bo la phan pa daṅ bde ba thob par byed pas bśad pa don yod pa'i phyir ro | pha rol la gcig du phan pa ñid bden pa yin pa'i phyir bcom ldan 'das rnams la brdzun gsuṅ ba yaṅ mi mṅa' ste | ji skad du

bslu[w] daṅ ldan pa bden ma yin | |
don gyi dgoṅs pa med pa'ṅ min | |
gźan la gcig tu phan pa bden | |
phan pa med phyir cig[x] śos min | | [18]

źes gsuṅs pa lta bu'o
źes brjod do | |

---

15. LA X.153cd: *bāhyārthadarśanaṁ mithyā nāsty arthaṁ cittam eva tu* |. Cited in MAV 126.

16. LA X.155ab: *vāsanair lulitaṁ cittam arthābhāsaṁ pravartate* |.

17. LA X.406: *āture āture yadvad bhiṣagdravyaṁ prayacchati* | *buddhā hi tadvat sattvānāṁ cittamātraṁ vadanti te* | |. Cited in MAvBh 196, 8–11.

18. RĀ 11.35 (cf. Hahn 1982: 52–53): *slu*[a] *ba med*[b] *ldan bden min te* | *sems pas*[c] *bsgyur ba don du min* | *gźan la gcig tu phan pas bden* | *mi phan phyir ni cig*[d] *śos min* | [a: *bslu* P; b: *mi* N.P; c: *dpas* N, P; d: *gcig* N, P]. *nāvisaṁvādavat satyaṁ* [*na bhā*]*vodbhavam arthataḥ*| *paraikāntahitaṁ satyam ahitatvān mṛṣetarat* | |. 大正 32.496b9–10: 実意起無違 流靡能利他 是説名実語 翻比為妄言.

[C]
de ltar na kun (D159b) rdzob tu phyi rol gyi don yaṅ yod dam | sems tsam ñid kyaṅ bla ste | the tshom med par dṅos po'i ṅo bo ñid yaṅ dag pa pa[y] phra rab kyaṅ sgrub par 'gyur ba gaṅ yin pa de lta bu'i yid ches pa'i bka' ni rnam pa thams cad du med do |

a: om. in P. b: om. in P. c: om. in P. d: om. in P. e: om. in P.
f: *med do* D. g: om. in D. h: om. in P. i: om. in P. j: om. in D.
k: *la* P. l: *pa* P. m: om. in P. n: *ma* Matsumoto [1984: 154 b.21].
o: om. in P. p: *ltos* D. q: *par* P. r: *pa* P. s: *ltos* D.
t: *rjes* P. u: *slu* D. v: *to* P. w: *slu* D. x: *gcig* C.
y: om. in D.

II. Translation

[A]

(1) A certain (scholar) seems to claim as follows: Since "Mind-only" has an intrinsic nature which is self-established, it is definitely settled from the point of view of conventional (truth). But an external object is not settled even from the point of view of conventional (truth), because (the external object) is not established separately from the image of mind. Therefore, to elucidate it, the Blessed One says that things are nothing but mind. But this does not mean that (mind) really exists from the point of view of ultimate (truth), because in the other scripture (mind) also is said to be of non-intrinsic nature.

(2) As the *Sarvabuddhaviṣayāvatārajñānālokālaṁkāra* (*sūtra*) says:

> Buddhas never grab hold of all dharmas and the mind, and pay homage and praise those who understand dharma and do not take hold of objects of perception.

(3) Also, in the *Ratnakūṭa* (*sūtra*) in detail:

> Kāśyapa, when mind is totally searched, it is not obtained. The one which is not obtained is not possessed. The one which is not possessed does not exist in the past, the present and the future, either. The one which does not exist in the past, the present and the future, either, transcends the three times. The one which transcends the three times is neither existence nor non-existence. The one which is neither existence nor non-existence is non-arising. The one which is non-arising is without inherence. The one which is without inherence is without arising. The one which is without arising is without ceasing. The one which is without ceasing does not pass. The one which does not pass, neither goes nor comes nor passes away nor is born. The one which neither goes nor comes nor passes away nor is born, is without disposition at all. The one which is without disposition at all is the unconditioned. The unconditioned is the innate inherence possessed by the Sages.

Therefore, in the same (sūtra):

> To uphold the idea of permanence—this, Kāśyapa, is one extreme. To uphold the idea of impermanence—this, Kāśyapa, is a second extreme.[19] The middle between these two is neither examined nor shown nor hindered nor marked nor appeared nor known nor grounded. This is spoken of as the Middle Way, as true comprehensive examination of things.

This (passage) does not bear testimony that the middle exists as substance, has mind as its inherence, but explains that (the middle) is the realm of truth (*dharma-dhātu*) separate from all pairs of extremes, has characteristic marks of non-intrinsic nature of all *dharma*s, and is free from the manifold fiction of human ideas (*prapañca*). Moreover the realm of truth is not examined, because it can not be examined by itself as this or that. (It is) not shown, because it can not be shown to others. (It is) not marked, because it is not marked as the inherence of inner domain (*dhātu*) and department (*āyatana*). (It has) not appeared, because it has not appeared as outer domain and department. (It is) unknowable, because it transcends the intrinsic nature of the sense realm of the eye and the rest. (It is) not grounded, because it is not the ground of all defilements such as lust and the rest.

If the middle were to possess some ultimate substance whose intrinsic nature is mind, then in that case [the middle] would exist and therefore how would it be an extreme to uphold the idea of permanence or the idea of impermanence? It is not acceptable to say that (the middle) into which one may fall is a correct way of thinking which conforms to true reality, (because) there is no other mode of being of a thing having the intrinsic nature of a thing other than the intrinsic nature of permanence and the rest.

If (the opponent) thinks that when the middle has no intrinsic nature of a thing, attachment to the concept of "non-existence" also does not become an extreme, this (position) is not reasonable either, because attachment to "non-existence" also is not reasonable, and there is no attachment to non-existence when there is no attachment to existence. Negation can not be applied to what is without objective existence. Therefore, since necessarily where there is attachment to non-existence there is also attachment to existence, this extreme is a pair.

If the middle were to have (the intrinsic nature of) a thing, then who would (be able to) prevent attachment to the idea of its existence? (If the middle were to have the intrinsic nature of a thing, then,) it

---

19. Quoted from the draft manuscript translation of J. Silk and G. Nagao.

would contradict what is taught in the *Ārya-Samādhirāja-sūtra* which negates taking the existence of the middle as an ultimate existence. (The sūtra runs as follows):

> "There is" and "there is not" are both extremes;
> "Pure" and "impure," these are also extremes;
> Therefore the wise man avoids the two extremes,
> And takes no stance, not even in the middle.

The meaning of the sūtra is that it is right that the wise man takes no stance even in the middle because there is no intrinsic nature of a thing at all which exists as the middle to be relied on. If anything at all were to exist, how could the wise man not take a stance in it?

Also, it is taught in the *Lokottara-parivarta*:

> Oh! sons of the Victor, further, it is understood that the three-worlds are mind-only. It is understood that the three times also are similar to mind and the mind is without extremes or middle.

The meaning of the sūtra is that since the (two) extremes of birth and destruction and the middle characterized by subsistence do not exist from the point of view of ultimate (truth), mind is understood and comprehended as being without extremes and middle.

[B]

Another (scholar) seems to claim as follows:

(1) (a) From the point of view of conventional (truth), an external object also exists in a way similar to the way consciousness exists. Otherwise, it would contradict what is taught in the *Holy Ten Stages*, namely that the Bodhisattva knows at the eighth stage the number of the atoms belonging to a world-region (*loka-dhātu*), and so on. That is, the sūtra runs in detail as follows:

> He (the Bodhisattva) knows that the atom is a small (quantity), a large (quantity), innumerable and divided, too. (He) knows that he is well informed about the innumerable divisions of the atom. He knows even how many atoms of earth-element (*pṛthivī-dhātu*) exist in the world-region. Likewise, (he) knows how many atoms of the water-element, the fire-element and the air-element exist (in the world-region), too.

(b) Since (the existence of) the external object also, like consciousness, is known (to common people), (the opposite view) is disproved (*bādhita*) by what is known. When logically investigated, both (consciousness and the external object) do not stand up to the burden of the investigation, and so (they) cannot obtain the place of existence, but from the point of view of empirical truth, both existences are well known up to the wife of the cowherd.

(2) (a) What is taught as mind-only results in repudiating the subject of action (*kartṛ*) and the enjoyer of its fruits (*bhoktṛ*) which are conjured up by the opponent, because even from the point of view of empirical truth, the other subjects of actions, etc., except for mind, are not established.

(b) Or, (the reason why mind-only is taught) is that mind is established as a chief with regard to all *dharmas*, because mind is set forth as a premise of all *dharmas*.

Furthermore, even when the following are taught (in the sūtra):

> Only mind exists without (an external) object,

and likewise,

> mind which is disturbed by latent impression (*vāsanā*) appears as (the external) object,

since mind without the image (*nirākāra*) can never seize the object, therefore (mind must be) understood by all means as having the image. Therefore, since the image of the (external) object does not appear except as the image of mind, by rejecting it (i.e., the mind without image), it is said only that mind possesses the image (as its object). So from those (passages in the above-quoted sūtras), you should not understand that the external object dose not exist.

(c) Furthermore, just as it is said that *ātman*, etc. are real existence, etc., in the same way conforming to the people who are to be led just as a physician prepares medicines according to (the illness of) the patient, the Buddhas, Blessed Ones, preached, various types of teachings.

In the *Holy Laṅkāvatāra-sūtra*, too, it is taught as follows:

> Just as a physician gives medicine to each sick person, so the Buddha taught the "mind-only" (theory) to sentient being.

(This) is not meant to deceive other people either, because the sermons have as their objective to make the people who are to be led obtain benefit and bliss by that means.

Since (the sermon) which earnestly gives benefit to others is true, the Blessed Ones cannot teach a false (sermon) at all. As taught by Nāgārjuna:

> (The sermon) with deception is not truth. (The sermon) without the intention to do (others) good is not truth, either.
> (The sermon) which earnestly gives benefit to others is truth. The other (sermon which does not give benefit to others) is not (truth), either, because of non-benefit.

[C]
As above-mentioned, from the point of view of conventional (truth), it does not matter whether there exists an external object or mind-only. Undoubtedly, there is not in any way any teaching at all to (enable one to) believe in such (a view) that even a bit of real intrinsic nature of a thing is to be established.

III. Commentary

(1) bsTan-dar considers the description of (A)'s view in the Text as the gist of kārikā 91 of MA and its commentary.[20] According to bsTan-dar, the aim of (A)'s view is to describe two subjects: the first is that [Pratijñā] Mind-only exists from the point of view of conventional truth, [Hetu] because it has the nature of being realized by itself, [Dṛṣṭānta] like knowledge in a dream, and so on. The second is that [P] Color-form, etc., are not established as the external object even in the sense of practical experience (*vyavahārataḥ*), [H] because they are not established as substance separate from the image of mind, [D] like the color-form in a dream, and so on.

Furthermore, according to bsTan-dar,[21] the theory which expresses the gradual progress of repudiating the existence of the external object, entering the mind-only, and going beyond even the mind-only is demonstrated by Kamalaśīla by means of quoting the three well-known verses of the LA (X 256–258) in the MĀ,[22] and it is Śāntarakṣita's MAV[23] which proves by means of quoting verses of the LA (11.138 = X 85) and the YṢ (34) that the theory can be traced back to Nāgārjuna.

These comments by bsTan-dar seem to strongly support my understanding concerning the tenets of Śāntarakṣita and the Yogācāra-Mādhyamika school. Their tenets can be understood as follows: Theoretically, conventional truth (*saṁvṛti-satya*) is nothing but mind-only, that is self-cognition (*svasaṁvedana*), and mind-only is bereft of intrinsic nature in reality. From the viewpoint of religious practice, they can be taken as a progressive development to enlightenment from the mind-only theory to the Mādhyamika, and the mind-only theory is considered as a means to attain the ultimate stage of emptiness (*śūnyatā*).

---

20. MĀS 686, 1–687, 2.
21. MĀS 687.5–688.1.
22. Mā D.157a4–6; P 171a2–4.
23. MAV 302 2–8; MAP 303, 6.

Their tenets can be elucidated through understanding two sets of verses, 64–66 and 91–92 of the MA.[24] We can confirm what the central tenet of the Yogācāra-Mādhyamika school is through the following passage of Haribhadra:[25]

> Basing oneself on external objects by repudiating ātman, etc.; (1) afterwards depending on the understanding that the triple realm is mind-only because of the teaching of the imagined, dependent, and consummate self-natures; (2) then [investigating] the two conventional truths by distinguishing between true and untrue, conforming and not conforming (respectively) to (their) real causal efficiency, and showing that what is agreeable and tacitly accepted only as long as it is not investigated critically depends on its own successive former causes; (3) based on true conventional truth (you) must practice giving and the rest according to (worldly) appearance as (if you were) a magically created person, (4) and (you) must (mentally) cultivate (the notion of) nonproduction from the point of view of ultimate truth. You must thus gradually penetrate the Perfection of Wisdom.

The expression "what is agreeable and tacitly accepted only as long as it is not investigated critically depends on its own successive former causes" in the above passage is equivalent to the content of verse 65 of the MA. The expression "its own successive former causes" (*pūrva-pūrvasvakāraṇa*) can be compared with the expression "Because it is said that the cause of conventional truth is the former-former beginningless," commented upon by Kamalaśīla just before verse 65 of the MA.[26] Here "its own successive former causes" must mean the beginningless stream of consciousness. Then it is understood that the definition of conventional truth,"what is agreeable and tacitly accepted only as long as it is not investigated critically," is ascribed to consciousness. This means that conventional truth is nothing but consciousness.

---

24. See the verses at the end of this paper.

25. AAA 594, 18–25: *ātmādinirākaraṇena bāhye'rthe pratiṣṭhāpya,paścāt kalpitaparatantrapariniṣpannasvabhāvakathanena traidhātukacittamātrāvagame niyojya, tadanu samyagarthakriyāsu yogyam ayogyaṁ tathyātathyabhedena saṁvṛtisatyadvayaṁ*[a] *avicāraikaramyaṁ*[b] *pūrvapūrvasvakāraṇādhīnaṁ nirdiśya, tathyasaṁvṛtau sthitvā yathādarśanaṁ māyāpuruṣeṇeva dānādy ācaritavyaṁ, paramārthato 'nutpādaś ca bhāvayitavyaḥ ity evaṁ krameṇa prajñāpāramitāyām avatārayitavyaḥ.*
(a) After *-dvayam* a word equivalent to Tib. *rnam par dpyod do* should be supplied. Cf. P, vol. 90, 171, 1, 1. (b) Wogihara's edition has *-ramya-pūrva-*, but his MS C reads *-ramyaṁ*. Tib. has *ma brtags na nyams dga'ba tsam du*.
The word "[investigating]" is added on the basis of the Tibetan *rnam par dpyod do.*

26. MAP 211, 8–9.

At this point we should note that Matsumoto Shirō has cast some doubt on the historical existence of the Yogācāra-Mādhyamika school and on Śāntarakṣita as one of the representative scholars belonging to the school.[27] On the other hand, he admitted that the view of scholar (A) in the above-quoted MĀ clearly corresponds to the theory which holds that mind-only exists from the point of view of conventional truth and the theory holding that there is not an external object even from the point of view of conventional truth. He furthermore accepts that the view of scholar (A) is the same as that mentioned in verse 91 of MA and its commentary, MAV.[28]

If we rely on Haribhadra's passage quoted above, we can easily notice that both the mind-only theory and even the theory that the mind-only theory is a means to attain the ultimate goal of emptiness of the Mādhyamika coexist in one system.

Here, I would again[29] like to suggest the following arrangement of the thought of the Yogācāra-Mādhyamika school:

i. First of all, it is an important phase in the theory of the Yogācāra-Mādhyamika that conventional truth is attributed to mind-only and self-cognition.

The expression of MA 91ab, "that which is cause and effect is nothing but mind-only," really seems to exemplify this phase. Further, the following materials also seem to prove the fact:

> Conventional truth is that which is as it appears. (Jñānagarbha, SDVK 3)
> This body of color-form, etc., undefiled by the evils of conceptualization, is by nature dependent on others, and is an appearance only in knowledge. (Nevertheless) it cannot be rejected, and if one were to reject it one would certainly undermine (the validity of) direct perception, etc. (Jñānagarbha, SDV-V D.12b 2–3)

Śāntarakṣita comments on this passage as follows:

> [Question]: And what is ("the body of color-form, etc.")?
> [Answer]: Its "nature is to be dependent on others," since it arises conditioned by causes and conditions.
> [Question]: Why is the body not defiled by the evils of conceptualization?
> [Answer]: Because "it is an appearance only in knowledge." This means the appearance of knowledge which is detached from concept. The word "only" implies that it rejects the accompanying concept. Since such things as color-form, etc., are the self-cognized, (the phrase) "it cannot be rejected" connects with "and if one were to reject it one would certainly undermine . . . ."

27. Matsumoto 1984: 141a 1–3.

28. Matsumoto 1984: 154b 6–11.

29. Cf. Ichigō 1982, 1985, 1987, 1989.

[Question]: Undermine what ?
[Answer]: "Direct perception, etc." The word "etc." implies inference, etc. (SDV-P, P[100] 300, 1^{6}–2^{1})

By combining all the above passages of Jñānagarbha and Śāntarakṣita, we can easily understand the following expressions as synonyms of conventional truth:

Conventional truth = that which is as it appears = direct perception = knowledge bereft of conception = appearance of mind-only = self-cognition = that which cannot be rejected.

Therefore, it is no wonder that Kamalaśīla comments "it describes mind-only from the point of view of conventional truth" when he quotes the verses of LA (11.35 = X.85) and YṢ (34) in the MAP commenting on verse 92 of MA,[30] because the theory which states that mind-only exists from the point of view of conventional truth can already be found in Śāntarakṣita's view.

Thus, Śāntarakṣita states that conventional truth is self-cognized, which means of course that he repudiates the existence of the external object even from the point of view of conventional truth.

ii. Our next problem is the definition and content of conventional truth. According to Matsumoto, it is the common understanding of ordinary people (*loka-pratīti* 世間極成), it should not be the understanding of the academic school, and it is "appearance" (顕現).[31] "Appearance" seems simply to imply the appearance of mind. When we remember the equivalence of conventional truth and appearance, as mentioned above, we can recognize that the theory which states that mind-only is admitted from the point of view of conventional truth is already implied.

Who are the ordinary people? When we find in the Text [B.1.b] the deliberate expression, "well known up to the wife of the cowherd," *loka-pratīti*, as far as the level of intelligence is concerned, it seems to imply a common understanding of ordinary people, including all those from academic scholars to female cowherds.

Moriyama orders conventional truth into two kinds by investigating the opinions of Jñānagarbha, Śāntarakṣita, Kamalaśīla, and Haribhadra.[32] One kind is conventional truth as common knowledge held by ordinary people, and the other is conventional truth relating to religious practice by a Yogin. Thus, he analyzed the practical difference

30. MAP 303, 1.

31. Matsumoto 1984: 145a, 156a.

32. Moriyama 1991: 51, 59, 70, 72–73.

between the Yogin and ordinary people, and concluded that the term "conventional truth" has a broad application in this way.

According to bsTan-dar,[33] three kinds of conventional truth are shown in verse 64 of MA in which, according to Matsumoto,[34] Śāntarakṣita's view of conventional truth is totally explained: a) general conventional truth (*spyir kun rdzob*), b) conventional truth of what is produced (*'dus byas kyi kun rdzob*), c) true conventional truth (*yaṅ dag kun rdzob*). These are respectively explained as follows: a) all *dharmas* which are unreal are conventional truth, because they are the objects which are grasped by proper knowledge (*rigs śes*) which investigates the domain of ordinary verbal usage; b) what is produced is conventional truth, because it is characterized by arising and decay; c) objects such as blue, yellow, etc., are true conventional truth, because they have causal efficiency just as they appear in knowledge which perceives them (blue, yellow, etc.) in its presence. So, according to this explanation of bsTan-dar, that which is agreeable and tacitly accepted as long as it is not investigated critically—the expression of MA 64—is the common understanding of ordinary people (*loka-pratīti*), corresponding to general conventional truth (a). Accordingly, *loka-pratīti* has as its content the object which is grasped by "proper knowledge" which investigates the domain of ordinary verbal usage, and which is percieved broadly by common people including female cowherds, although the content of "proper knowledge" is obscure.

iii. In my understanding, which differs from that of Matsumoto,[35] it is one of the characteristics of the Yogācāra-Mādhyamika doctrinal system that the mind-only theory is evaluated as being admitted on the level of conventional truth from the philosophical point of view and as a means to attain the ultimate stage of emptiness from the religious or practical point of view.

My understanding, like that of bsTan-dar, results from the fact that I recognize verse 91 of MA as showing Śāntarakṣita's standpoint and understand verses 91 and 92 of MA as co-relative. Such an understanding seems reasonable even from the way Kamalaśīla comments on verses 91 and 92 of MA.

The expression of verse 91ab of MA, "that which is cause and effect is nothing but mind-only," is what Matsumoto refers to in

33. MĀS 693, 1–5.

34. Matsumoto 1984: 143b.

35. Matsumoto 1984: 149b, 152b.

holding that the dependent nature is mind-only.[36] Since it is clear from the passages of SDV-V and SDV-P quoted above that the dependent nature is characteristic of conventional truth, MA 91ab shows that conventional truth is nothing but mind-only. Then, since a question, "Is mind-only recognized as real?" is anticipated, according to Kamalaśīla,[37] the MAV states as follows: when mind is investigated from the point of view that it is possessed of a singular or a plural nature, it is not proved as real, because it has no substance in reality.[38]

Further, Kamalaśīla comments that Śāntarakṣita offers verse 92 in order to explain that the view put forward in verse 91, that conventional truth is nothing but mind-only, is reasonable, because it is applicable to penetration of reality.[39]

As long as we follow Kamalaśīla's comments, we cannot but consider verses 91 and 92 as one. It seems that the contents of verses 91 and 92 are parallel to those of verses 64 to 66. To wit, the cause of conventional truth explained in verse 64 is sought in its own successive former cause, that is, the beginingless series of consciousness in verse 65. And the ultimate reality of the stream of consciousness which is the cause of conventional truth is rejected in verse 66. So this development coincides with that of verses 91 and 92, that conventional truth is attributed to mind-only, and that which is mind-only is made bereft of intrinsic nature.

iv. Matsumoto emphasizes that verse 91 of MA expresses the *Sākāra-vijñānavāda*, based on the commentary, *raṅ gis grub pa'i ṅo bo bor nas śes pa'i ṅo bo gźan rtog pa med do*, found in the begining of MAV on MA 91.[40] He found in AAA[41] the Sanskrit expression *svataḥ-siddha-rūpa* as an equivalent to the Tibetan translation *raṅ gis grub pa'i ṅo bo*. He then takes the word *rūpa* (*ṅo bo*) in the same meaning as *ākāra* (*rnam pa*), and he translates the sentence as follows: [自己認識によって] 自立的に成立している形象を捨てて、別な、知の形象を想定することはできない. On the other hand, I take the *ṅo bo* in the sense of "nature" (性質) or "way" (あり方), not as equivalent to *rnam pa*, and translate as follows: [対象なくして] 自ら成立しているというあり方を別にして知識のあり方は考えられない. An English version of this

36. Matsumoto 1984: 143b.

37. MAP 295, 1.

38. MAV 294, 1–3.

39. MAP 295, 8–9.

40. MAV 292, 6.

41. AAA 626, 9–10.

might run: "There can be no other way of knowledge apart from the way independently self-established [without external object]."

I confess that I am not aware of the usage of *ṅo bo* (*rūpa*) in the same meaning as *rnam pa* (*ākāra*), but I still cannot agree with Matsumoto. My reasons are as follows:

1. We come across the expression *sṅon po la sogs pa'i rnam pa* just six lines below that of the MAV passage just mentioned.[42] Why did not the Tibetan translator use the word *ṅo bo* instead of *rnam pa*, or vice versa? If *ṅo bo* (*rūpa*) and *rnam pa* (*ākāra*) have the same meaning, why did Śāntarakṣita use a different word in such closely related sentences? This phenomenon is also found in a passage in the Text [[A] (1)]. Here the former, "nature" (性質), is a translation of *ṅo bo* and the latter,"image" (形象), is a rendering of *rnam pa*. And both words stand quite close to each other, but Matsumoto here again takes them both in the meaning of "image."

2. Do we need to take the word *ṅo bo* here in the sense of *ākāra*? The sentence of MAV here seems to me a commentary on MA 91cd, *raṅ gis grub pa gaṅ yin pa* | *de ni śes par gnas pa yin*. Kamalaśīla also comments only as follows: this says that the external object is totally not perceived.[43]

3. The expression of verse 91d, *śes par gnas pa yin*, is rendered by Matsumoto "知において存在しているのである."[44] I do not agree with this. My translation is, "it is established that (that which is self-validated) is knowledge."

As seen above, concerning the understanding of the thought of the Yogācāra-Mādhyamika school Matsumoto and I disagree. His understanding seems to result chiefly from the description of the *dBu ma rnam ṅes* of Śākya mchog ldan, who was a leading opponent to Tsoṅ-kha-pa.[45] As long as Haribhadra's passage quoted above is not repudiated, however, I will believe in the historical existence of the Yogācāra-Mādhyamika school in India and in Śāntarakṣita as a representative scholar belonging to that school.

(2) Now, let us proceed to examine whether the description of (B)'s view can be Bhāviveka's. (B)'s basic argument is that even the external object, in addition to mind, exists from the point of view of

---

42. MAV 292, 12.

43. MAP 293, 5–6.

44. Matsumoto 1984: 143, a-b.

45. Matsumoto 1984: 157b.

conventional truth. In order to prove this point the discussion is developed as follows:

i. The existence of external objects from the point of view of conventional truth is:

a) supported by the sentence which speaks of the existence of the atom at the eighth stage of the DBh, by means of scripture (*āgama*);

b) granted by the common understanding of ordinary people, by means of reasoning (*yukti*).

ii. But, the argument is contradictory to the passage "the triple world is nothing but mind-only," found in the sixth stage of the same sūtra. Then, the investigation into mind-only is made:

a) the word "only" of mind-only has a negative aspect, because it repudiates the existence of a soul which is conjured up by non-Buddhist philosophers as the subject of actions;

b) the word "only" also has an affirmative aspect, because it is affirmed that mind plays a role of leading function in all dharmas;

c) mind-only is taught as a means to altruism (*parārtha*).

Moriyama identifies the positions in (B) with three scholars: Bhāviveka, Candrakīrti, and Śubhagupta.[46] The reason seems chiefly to be that the standpoint of these three scholars against the Vijñānavādins is the same.

Matsumoto, on the other hand, identifies (B) with Bhāviveka, though with some hesitation.[47] The grounds for his arguments are that the description (B) contains an explanation just the same as that in TJ commenting on the sūtra passage which states that triple world is nothing but mind-only, and that (B) also states the view of the Sautrāntika,[48] by which the identification seems to be appropriate. But Matsumoto's hesitation comes from the fact that we find in a passage of the Text[49] the expression "mind plays a role of leading function," which is equivalent to an expression in MAv VI.87 of Candrakīrti.

In this regard, we may note that bsTan-dar clearly states that (B) is Bhāviveka, a person other than Śāntarakṣita.[50] Whether this assertion is appropriate or not depends on whether we can identify the passages

46. Moriyama 1991: 93 (303).

47. Matsumoto 1984: 154–155, 159 (25).

48. Text [B] (2) (a).

49. Text [B] (2) (b).

50. MĀS 701, 4–5.

in the Text which seem to express his view with those in Bhāviveka's works. Let us look into the question.

i. a. The sentence "A bodhisattva knows the number of atoms belonging to a world-region," seen in DBh, is a suitable scriptural testimony to the theory which holds the existence of external objects from the view point of conventional truth, because it states the existence of atoms. But unfortunately, we cannot find this expression so far in Bhāviveka's works.

b. We can confirm that it is Bhāviveka's standpoint that it is the common understanding of ordinary people that external objects as well as mind exist from the point of view of conventional truth, by reference to verse 17 of MH, which has been indicated by Moriyama,[51] and by the following sentence in the *Prajñāpradīpa*:[52]

> If [the Yogācāra school] states that consciousness arises from the point of view of conventional truth without depending on external conditions, this is opposed to the common understanding of ordinary people.

ii. a. The sentence "Oh! son of the Victorious One, the triple world is nothing but mind-only" seen in DBh is an inconvenient scriptural reference for those who admit the existence of an external object, such as Bhāviveka. But, Bhāviveka protects his standpoint by explaining the meaning of the sūtra as follows:

(i) "Mind-only" is taught in the sūtra to repudiate the existence of a soul which is conjured up by non-Buddhist philosophers as the subject of action (*kartṛ*) and the enjoyer of its fruits (*bhoktṛ*).[53]

(ii) In order to repudiate the existence of a subject of action and the enjoyer of its fruits, different from consciousness, which is conjured up by the opponents, the Heretics, the Buddha, the Bodhisattva, taught mind-only, but not to negate the existence of the external object.[54]

(iii) It should be noted that "only" (of mind-only) implies not the negation of the external object but that of the subject of action, its non-existence.[55]

We can recognize that these passages of Bhāviveka are quoted in the Text by Kamalaśīla.[56]

---

51. Moriyama 1991: 81.

52. *Prajñāpradīpa*, D 245a8–b1.

53. MH V.28.

54. TJ D. 207 b5–6.

55. *Prajñāpradīpa*, D 245 b7.

56. Text [B] (2) (a).

It is not only Bhāviveka, however, but also Candrakīrti who understands the meaning of "mind-only" as the negation of the subject of action. MAv runs as follows:

> The victorious teaches only mind as the subject of actions in the world, not *pudgala*, etc., taught by the Heretics in their own treatises. (VI.86)

Thus, we can see both Bhāviveka and Candrakīrti mention that the expression "mind-only" in the sūtra has the meaning of negation which implies the negation of the subject of action which is conjured up by the Heretics.

b. Further, we should also realize that "mind-only" can have the meaning of affirmation. "Affirmation" here implies that mind plays an important or leading role in terms of all *dharmas*. We realize, first, that Candrakīrti had such an understanding on the basis of MAv V1.87:

> Just as the (word) Buddha is implied by "truth" or "the extended," the sūtra means by "mind-only" that mind indeed plays an important role (*gtso*) in the world. (So) here it is not implied by the sūtra that the negation of (the existence of) external materials is taught in that way.

Candrakīrti's understanding can be proved by the following statement of Tsoṅ-kha-pa:

> Thus, when you depend on the description of DBh that the subject of actions and the enjoyer of its fruits do not exist, (you can understand that) the word "only" (of mind-only) states the negation of the subject except for (mind). And also when you depend on the description that all twelve members of the links of conditioned co-production are based on one mind, (you can understand that) the word "only" emphasizes the importance (*gtso*) of mind. The former description is made from the negative aspect (*dgag phyogs*) and the latter from the affirmative (*sgrub phyogs*).[57]

Further, concerning the explanation that the expression "mind-only" has the negative connotation that it means not the negation of external objects but the negation of the subject except for mind, conjured up by the Heretics, Tsoṅ-kha-pa says:

> That (explanation) had been made by Bhāviveka, and depending on it, it was followed by Candrakīrti, too.[58]

Thus it is clear that Candrakīrti follows Bhāviveka concerning the explanation that "mind-only" has a negative aspect, which is already shown in MH V.28.

---

57. Ogawa 1988: 212, 10–15.

58. Ogawa 1988: 207, 12–13.

So, depending on Tsoṅ-kha-pa's statement we can confirm that Candrakīrti also admits the explanation of "mind-only" having an affirmative aspect.

But, did this explanation originate with Candrakīrti, not Bhāviveka? If so, the view seen in the Text[59] would show Candrakīrti's standpoint and prove that the scholars whose views are expressed in (B) include even Candrakīrti. On this matter, Tsoṅ-kha-pa's account is not clear. However, bsTan-dar suggests the following in the context of commenting on the scholar (B)'s view:

> ("Mind-only") is taught in that way, from the negative aspect (*dgag phyogs*) (to negate the subject of actions) and, from the affirmative aspect (*sgrub phyogs*), to prove that mind plays an important or leading role in terms of all dharmas including defilement and purity, because mind is presupposed by all dharmas including both defilement and purity, which are its own fruits.[60]

Since this statement of bsTan-dar shows us that there were two aspects to the explanation of mind-only, it is certain that Bhāviveka had such an understanding.

Our next problem is whether or not we can discover in Bhāviveka's works any passage which states the importance of mind. To begin with, the importance of mind is traditionally a basic idea of Buddhist thought, as shown in the following sentence:

> The world is led by mind and afflicted by it. Everything follows the one, mind.[61]

So it is natural that the idea of the importance of mind can be found in Bhāviveka's works as well. For example, Bhāviveka speaks as follows:

> [Pratijñā] (Mind) must be the subject of actions,[Hetu] (Because it) produces different things, [Dṛṣṭānta] Like the bell (which produces sound).[62]

Therefore, the understanding that the "only" of mind-only has two meanings, a negative and affirmative aspect, was already found in Bhāviveka and taken over even by Candrakīrti. This means that the interpretations of "mind-only" by Mādhyamika scholars are consistently the same, in contrast to those of the Yogācāra-vādins. Recognizing such details, Kamalaśīla seems to introduce Bhāviveka's view in the Text. Thus, it seems to me that we can imagine that both

---

59. Text [B] (2) (b).

60. MĀS 705, 5–6.

61. *Saṁyutta-Nikāya* 1. 39. Cf. *Dhammapada* 1.

62. MH III, 55cd.

Tsoṅ-kha-pa and bsTan-dar made their statement about "mind-only" following Kamalaśīla's description found in the Text.

In conclusion, we can say that bsTan-dar's idenfication of scholar (B) with Bhāviveka is correct.

It is a valuable contribution that Moriyama discovered[63] the same description seen in the Text[64] in Śubhagupta's *Bāhyārthasiddhikārikā*. But I think it would be better to understand that Śubhagupta adopted in his work Bhāviveka's view as that of the teacher of his own academic school.

Verses from MA:

64. *ma brtags gcig pu nyams dga' zhing* | |
skye dang 'jig pa'i chos can pa | |
don byed pa dag nus rnams kyi | |
yang bzhin kun rdzob pa yin rtogs | |

64. One should understand that conventional (truth) is in essence (1) that which is agreeable and tacitly accepted only as long as it is not investigated critically; (2) that which is characterized by arising and decay; and (3) whatever has causal efficiency.

65. *brtags pa ma byas nyams dga' ba'ang* | |
bdag rgyu snga ma snga ma la | |
brten nas phyi ma phyi ma yi | |
'bras du de 'dra 'byung ba yin | |

65. Even that which is agreeable and tacitly accepted only as long as it is not investigated critically implies the production of similar successive effects conditioned by their own successive causes.

66. *de phyir kun rdzob rgyu med na* | |
rung min zhes pa'ang legs pa yin | |
gal te 'di yi nyer len pa | |
yang dag yin na de smros shig | |

66. Therefore, it is also correct to say that it would be impossible for conventional truth to be causeless. But if (you claim that) its substratum (*upādāna*) is real, you have to explain what it is.

---

63. Moriyama 1991: 80.

64. [B] (1)(a).

91. *rgyu dang 'bras bur gyur pa yang* | |
shes pa 'ba' zhig kho na ste | |
rang gis grub pa gang yin pa | |
de ni shes par gnas pa yin | |

91. That which is cause and effect is nothing but knowledge. It is established that knowledge is that which is self-validated.

92. *sems tsam la ni brten nas su* | |
phyi rol dngos med shes par bya | |
tshul 'dir brten nas de la yang | |
shin tu bdag med shes par bya | |

92. Based on [the standpoint of] mind-only one must know the nonexistence of external entities. Based on this standpoint [of the lack of intrinsic nature of all dharmas] one must know that there is no self at all even in that (which is mind-only).

Abbreviations and Bibliography

AAA *Abhisamayālaṁkārāloka* of Haribhadra, Skt. ed., Wogihara Unrai 1932.

BA *Buddhāvataṁsakasūtra.* See DBh.

I BhK *Bhāvanākrama* of Kamalaśīla, Skt. ed., G. Tucci., *Minor Buddhist Texts*, Part II, Serie Orientale Roma IX, 2, 1958.

BST Buddhist Sanskrit Texts.

C Cone edition.

Cüppers, Christoph. 1990. *The IXth chapter of the Samādhirājasūtra.* Alt- und Neu-Indische Studien, Band 41, herausgegeben vom Institut für Kultur und Geschichte Indiens und Tibets an der Universität Hamburg, Stuttgart: Franz Steiner Verlag.

D Derge edition.

DBh *Daśabhūmikasūtra*, Kondō ed. (reprint, Kyoto: Rinsen, 1983); Vaidya ed. BST 7, 1967.

Hahn, Michael. 1982. *Nāgārjuna's Ratnāvalī.* Indica et Tibetica 1. Bonn.

Ichigō Masamichi. 1982. "Yugagyōchūganha." In *Kōza Daijō Bukkyō* 7, *Chūganshisō*. Tokyo: Shunjūsha.

———. 1985. *Madhyamakālaṁkāra of Śāntarakṣita with his own commentary or Vṛtti and with the subcommentary or Pañjikā of Kamalaśīla* (Kyoto: Bun'eidō).

———. 1987. "Yugagyōchūganha no shisō." In *Bukkyōgaku Seminar* 45.

———. 1989. "Śāntarakṣita's Madhyamakālaṁkara," *Studies in the Literature of the Great Vehicle, Three Mahāyāna Buddhist Texts*, ed. by L. O. Gómez and J. A. Silk, Michigan Studies in Buddhist Literature 1.

———. 1992. "On the DBU MA SNAṄ BA'I BRJED THO," *Asiatische Studien / Études Asiatiques*, XLVI. 1.

KP *The Kāśyapaparivarta, A Mahāyānasūtra of the Ratnakūṭa Class, edited in the Original Sanskrit, in Tibetan and in Chinese*, Baron A. von Staël-Holstein, 1926.

LA *Saddharmalaṅkāvatārasūtra*, Skt. ed., Vaidya P. L., BST 3, 1963.

La Vallée Poussin, L. de. 1907. *Madhyamakāvatāra par Candrakīrti*, traduction tibétaine, Biblio. Bud. 9, St. Petersburg.

Lindtner, Chr. 1982. *Nagarjuniana, Studies in the Writings and Philosophy of Nāgārjuna*. Copenhagen.

MA *Madhyamakālaṁkāra* of Śāntarakṣita, cf. Ichigō 1985.

MĀ *Madhyamakāloka* of Kamalaśīla.

MAP *Madhyamakālaṁkāra-pañjikā* of Kamalaśīla, cf. Ichigō 1985.

MĀS *Dbu ma snaṅ ba'i brjed tho* of bsTan-dar, Śata-piṭaka Series 291.

MAV *Madhyamakālaṁkāra-vṛtti* of Śāntarakṣita, cf. Ichigō 1985.

MAv *Madhyamakāvatāra* of Candrakīrti, cf. La Vallée Poussin 1907.

MAvBh *Madhyamakāvatāra-bhāṣya* of Candrakīrti, cf. La Vallée Poussin 1907.

MH *Madhyamaka-hṛdaya* of Bhāviveka.

Matsumoto Shirō. 1984. "Kōkichūganha no kūshisō, Yugagyōchūganha ni tsuite." *Risō* 610: 140–159.

———. 1986."Kōkichūganshisō no kaimei ni mukete, Ichigō Masamichi shi, Chūkanshōgonron no kenkyū wo chūshin ni," *Tōyō gakujutsu kenkyū* XXV-2.

Moriyama Seitetsu. 1991. "Kōkichūganha no Yuishinsetsu to Nitai-setsu—Sanshu no yuishin kaishaku (shōgi, yoga gyōja no sezoku, bonbu no sezoku)." *Bukkyō daigaku kenkyū kiyō* 75: 47–96.

Ogawa Ichijō. 1988. Kūshō shisō no kenkyū II, Text (*Dbu ma dgoṅs pa rab gsal* of Tsoṅ-kha-pa, Gelug pa Student's Welfare Committee Central Institute of Higher Tibetan Studies, Varanasi, India 1973) and its Japanese translation (Kyoto: Bun'eidō).

om. omit [ted].

P Peking edition.

Rā *Ratnāvalī*, cf. Hahn 1982.

RM *Ratnamegha sūtra*, Tib: P[35] (897) *dzu* l–121a3, Ch. T. XIV 489, XVI 658, 659, 660.

SDVK *Satyadvayavibhaṅga-kārikā* of Jñānagarbha, ed. M. D. Eckel, *Jñānagarbha's Commentary on the Distinction between the Two Truths* (Albany: State University of New York Press, 1987).

SDV-V *Satyadvayavibhaṅga-vṛtti* of Jñānagarbha, D. (3882) sa 3b3–15b1.

SR *Samādhirāja-sūtra*, cf. Cüppers 1990.

T Taishō shinshū daizōkyō.

TJ *Madhyamakahṛdayavṛtti-tarkajvālā* of Bhāviveka.

YṢ *Yuktiṣaṣṭikā-kārikā* of Nāgārjuna, ed. Lindtner 1982.

The Buddha and His Teachings

J. W. de Jong

1.1. A previous paper discussed some of the problems which arise when one attempts to recover the original message of the Buddha or, less ambitiously, to try to know the earliest Buddhist doctrines (de Jong 1993). In the past, scholars such as Mrs. Rhys Davids and Schayer maintained that the canonical texts do not give a true picture of early Buddhism and that it is necessary to reconstruct a pre-canonical Buddhism. Their theories have found little approval and have fallen into abeyance. However, in recent years several scholars have attempted to establish stages of doctrinal development by means of a comparative study of canonical texts. There is no doubt that the canonical texts, i.e., the Nikāyas and the Āgamas and the older Vinayas, contain older and newer elements. However, as these texts have been transmitted orally for centuries there is no objective criterion which helps us to distinguish older and newer elements. Bareau selected a small number of texts belonging to the Sūtra and Vinaya sections of the canon and compared their different versions in the Pāli canon and in the Chinese Tripiṭaka. However, in selecting these texts Bareau already greatly determined in advance the results of his critical examination. His choice of texts depended on his opinion as to which elements in the teachings of the texts are more original than others. It is difficult to see how one can avoid this vicious circle. One either selects some texts which are considered to reflect the earliest Buddhist doctrines, or one assumes that some doctrines are the original ones and tries to trace their development in the canonical texts. In both cases the point of departure is determined by a subjective decision. One may object that the Buddhist tradition itself has preserved the earliest teachings of the Buddha in its accounts of the first sermons of the Buddha. However, how reliable is the Buddhist tradition? Moreover, the tradition is not without contradictions. For instance, in his examination of the first sermon of the Buddha Bareau showed that there are divergent traditions concerning the contents of the first sermon (de Jong 1993: 19).

1.2. Much can be learned about the background of early Buddhism from the study of the Jain scriptures. There is a great similarity in much of the religious terminology used by the Buddhists and the Jains. Terms such as Buddha, Tathāgata, Jina, and Nirvāṇa are common to both schools. Of particular importance is the term *āsrava* which has been studied by Enomoto (Enomoto 1978, 1979, 1983) and recently by Lambert Schmithausen (Schmithausen 1992: 123–129). Buddhists and Jains share not only many terms but also some important doctrines such as the *ahiṁsā* doctrine and the rejection of ritual purity (de Jong 1993: 25–26). Last but not least the same verses occur in the scriptures of both religions and are found in the oldest parts of their canonical texts. It would, however, not be justified to draw the conclusion that these similarities have to be explained by the fact that the Buddhists borrowed these terms and doctrines from the Jains on the ground that Jainism is older than Buddhism. It is obvious from the Jain and Buddhist scriptures that at the time of the Mahāvīra and the Buddha there were many ascetics who propounded a great variety of doctrines and ideas. These ascetics have left no scriptures and their teachings are only known from references in the Jain and Buddhists scriptures. Probably the terms and doctrines which were common to Buddhists and Jains were shared by many groups of wandering ascetics of which the teachings have disappeared. It is only in religions such as Jainism and Buddhism which transmitted their teachings through the establishment of a *saṁgha* that the doctrines ascribed to their founders were preserved orally for centuries and, finally, committed to writing.

2.1. In recent years several scholars have tried to reconstruct the doctrines of the earliest stage of Buddhism on the basis of the older verses in the Pāli canon. There is a general consensus that, for instance, in the *Suttanipāta* the last two *vagga*s (*Aṭṭhakavagga* and *Pārāyanavagga*) and the *Khaggavisāṇasutta* belong to the oldest parts of the Buddhist canon. In 1980 Aramaki Noritoshi distinguished five strata (cf. de Jong 1991: 6; in line 14 correct *Suttanipāta* to *Saṁyuttanikāya*). According to him the oldest stratum of the Buddhist scriptures consists of the proto-*Dharmapada*, the *Aṭṭhakavagga*, and the *Pārāyanavagga* of the *Suttanipāta*. In a recent article he proposes a different stratification:

> I. The *Aṭṭhakavagga* of *Suttanipāta* (Sn); II. The *Pārāyanavagga* of Sn; III. The *Devatāsaṁyutta* and the *Devaputtasaṁyutta* of the *Sagāthavagga* (Sg) of *Saṁyuttanikāya* (SN) and the proto-*Dharmapada* (Dhp); IV. The remaining *vagga*s of Sn, the remaining *saṁyutta*s of Sg of Sn and *Udāna* (Ud); V. The strata of prose *sūtra*s and *vinaya*s (Aramaki 1993: 33).

2.2. Different methods have been applied to distinguish older verses from more recent ones in Jain and Pāli texts. Warder made a study of the Pāli metre in order "to be able to arrange our texts in chronological order, using a criterion more objective than any proposed hitherto" (Warder 1967: 224). Warder distinguishes six periods of composition to which he assigns approximate dates (*op. cit.* p. 225). Norman is much more careful and remarks that "if the criteria normally adopted for dating texts on metrical grounds have any validity at all, they can only be used to date texts relatively" (Norman 1991: 161; 1992: XXIX). Undoubtedly old are verses written in the old *āryā* metre. Alsdorf mentions fourty-six verses written in this metre (Alsdorf 1965: 60). Another four hundred verses are written in the classical *āryā* metre (Alsdorf 1966: 233). Only three chapters of the whole Jain canon are written in the old *āryā* metre: *Uttarajjhāyā* 8, *Āyāraṅga* I,9 and *Sūyagaḍaṅga* 1,4 (Schubring 1926: 3). However, the relative chronology of verses written in other metres is not yet definitely established, and it would be hazardous to rely too much on metrical grounds for distinguishing older and newer verses. The texts which are considered to be the seniors of the Jain and Buddhist canons, i.e., *Āyāraṅga*, *Sūyagaḍaṅga*, *Uttarajjhāyā*, *Dasaveyāliya*, and *Isibhāsiyāiṁ* (Alsdorf 1965: 28); *Suttanipāta*, *Dhammapada*, *Thera-*, and *Therīgāthā* (Bollée 1983: I) contain verses of different origin and date.

2.3. Of great importance for the study of early Buddhism and Jainism is the existence of the same verses (or *pādas*) in both canons as has been pointed out by several scholars (Bollée 1980, 1983; Nakamura 1983). Parallel verses, especially verses proclaiming ethical doctrines, are also found in the *Mahābhārata* and other texts (Rau 1957; Murakami 1980, 1981). Already in 1908 Winternitz drew attention to the presence of what he called *Asketendichtung* (ascetic poetry) in the *Mahābhārata* (Winternitz 1908: 267; 1927: 320). Winternitz remarked: "Viele moralische Erzählungen und Sprüche, welche unser *Mahābhārata* enthalt, gehören der Asketendichtung an, aus welcher vom 6. Jahrhundert v. Chr. an auch Buddhisten und Jains geschöpft haben" (Winternitz 1908: 403; 1927: 474). It would be very useful to publish in one volume all the verses which can be recognized as common to Jain, Buddhist, and epic texts.

2.4. Many parallels to Pāli verses are found in the Chinese translations of Buddhist texts and much important work in identifying these verses has been done by Japanese scholars. In the first place one must mention here the contribution made by Mizuno Kōgen, for instance, in his studies of the *Suttanipāta* and the different recensions of the *Dhammapada* (Mizuno 1981; 1982a, b; 1990, 1991, 1992). The study of parallel verses in Chinese texts can be very helpful in distinguishing older and newer layers in metrical texts, but much work has still to be done making use of the available materials for a critical analysis of early Buddhist verses.

3.1. The problem which poses itself is the importance of the older verses for the study of early Buddhism. Nobody assumes that the Buddha himself spoke in verses. Nakamura refers to Oldenberg and writes that, originally, the Buddha's teachings were delivered in prose but that, after having been repeated hundred of times, their main contents were conveyed in the form of verses (Nakamura 1971: 274). This is perhaps the case of some later verses in the canon but it is impossible to suppose that the great majority of the verses in the canon, and especially those which are considered to belong to the oldest parts of the canon, were originally formulated in prose. Furthermore, it is obvious that the older verses do not give an adequate picture of the Buddhist doctrines. Nakamura himself remarks that technical terms which are specifically Buddhist are not to be found in the verses and he even goes so far as to state that they contain only terms which occur in Brahmanical and Jain texts (Nakamura 1971: 273).

3.2. Undoubtedly the oldest verses contain teachings which are also found in the prose parts of the canon, i.e., the first four Nikāyas and the Āgamas. The difficulty in studying these verses is the fact that they contain three different elements: pre-Buddhist, non-Buddhist, and Buddhist. Some teachings were taken over by Buddhism. They may originally have belonged to the Jains or to some other school or have been the common property of different groups of ascetics. Other teachings were rejected by the Buddhists, and their presence in some of the oldest verses is due to their incorporation into the Buddhist canon at some stage in the development of the canon. Finally, typically Buddhist teachings are found in a number of verses. However, in the case of the *Suttanipāta*, for example, which in recent years has been often quoted by many scholars as one of the most reliable and oldest sources for the study of early Buddhism, Nakamura remarked that in the verse parts there are almost no specific Buddhist doctrines (Nakamura 1984: 442). At the same time he writes that the *Suttanipāta* is the oldest among the many Buddhist texts and is a collection of verses which are closest to the words of the Gotama Buddha as historical person (*ibid.*: 433). The conclusion which forces itself on the reader is that what the Buddha taught was not Buddhism!

4.1. The oldest verses are not a reliable source for the knowledge of early Buddhism. In order to understand the Buddhist teachings, one has to consult the discourses of the Buddha and his disciples. We will never be able to know the contents of the teachings of the Buddha himself. In the canonical writings we find the doctrines which the compilers of the canon considered to have been preached by the Buddha. This does not mean that we find a unified system of belief in the canon. In recent times scholars have attached much importance to inconsistencies in the transmission of Buddha's word (Vetter 1985: 68) and have tried to explain their existence by the development of the Buddhist doctrine as reflected in successive textual layers. However, the compilers of the canon did not worry about these inconsistencies and it is only when the schools with their doctrinal differences developed that the transmitted teachings were subjected to a closer scrutiny. The compilers of the canon brought together the discourses of the Buddha which were orally transmitted by the monks and did not bother too much about differences between the teachings as long as they were considered to be emanating from the Buddha (de Jong 1993: 23–24).

Even though there are inconsistencies in the Buddhist canon, the dominating ideas of early Buddhism which differentiate it from other contemporary schools can easily be discerned. It is not always possible to trace the origin of those ideas which existed already before the time of the Buddha. Just as the Buddha took over technical terms from Jainism and gave them a new meaning (Norman 1993: 133, n. 4; pp. 264–270), in the same way Buddhism took over existing doctrines and filled them with a new content. On the other hand, we encounter in early Buddhism ideas which are not found elsewhere and may have been developed for the first time by the Buddhists. In the absence of sources for the many schools of ascetics which existed before or at the time of the Buddha it would be hazardous to claim absolute originality for those ideas. However, the question of priority is of secondary importance. No religion arises in an absolute void, but it becomes a new religion when it distinguishes itself by the nature of its principal doctrines.

4.2. One of the fundamental doctrines of Buddhism is that of the act and its fruit. The doctrine of karma is already foreshadowed in the Upaniṣads but no detailed explanation is to be found in them. More is known about the karma doctrine of the Jains. According to them karma matter flows into the soul and must be annihilated by austerities (*tapas*). This doctrine is referred to several times in Buddhist texts (Fujita 1979: 144, n. 20), cf. *Aṅguttara-nikāya* i.220: *so purāṇānaṁ kammānaṁ tapasā vyantibhāvaṁ paññāpeti, navānaṁ kammānaṁ akaraṇā setughātaṁ*; *Majjhima-nikāya* i.93: *purāṇānaṁ kammānaṁ tapasā byantibhāvā navānaṁ kammānaṁ akaraṇā*.... For the Jains the sins of the body are more blamable, for the Buddhists the sins of the mind, cf. *Majjhima-nikāya* i.372: *kāyadaṇḍaṁ Nigaṇṭho Nātaputto mahāsāvajjataraṁ paññāpeti pāpassa kammassa kiriyāya*; ibid.: 373: *manokammaṁ mahāsāvajjataraṁ paññāpemi pāpassa kammassa kiriyāya* (cf. T. 26 [I] 638c7–8, b28). For the Buddhists the act is essentially a mental act, cf. *Aṅguttara-nikāya* iii.415: *cetanāhaṁ bhikkhave kammaṁ vadāmi; cetayitvā kammaṁ karoti kāyena vācāya manasā* (for corresponding Chinese texts, cf. Fujita, *op. cit*: 104). It is obvious that the Jain concept of the act is more archaic than the Buddhist one. The existence of doctrines of the act in both religions indicates that there must have been one or several doctrines concerning the act and its fruit in India before the time of the Mahāvīra and the Buddha. Probably the Jain theory is closer to the earlier doctrines.

4.3. Another important doctrine of early Buddhism is that of "dependent origination" (*pratītyasamutpāda*). Although this expression is not used by the Jains in their older scriptures, the idea is not unknown to them, cf. for instance, *Uttarajjhāyā* 32.7: "Love and hatred are caused by Karman, and they say that Karman has its origin in delusion; Karman is the root of birth and death, and birth and death they call misery." (Jacobi 1895: 185). However, in Jainism the doctrine of dependent origination has not been developed, whereas in Buddhism it is found in many different forms. Much has been written on this topic and attempts have been made to discern different stages in the development of the doctrine of dependent origination. However, there is general agreement that its definitive form has been reached in the doctrine of dependent origination in twelve members, beginning with ignorance (*avijjā, avidyā*). Here again as in the doctrine of the act one sees that for the Buddhists the mind and its activity are of primordial importance. The right insight and the right view are essential, not austerities or other physical activities.

4.4. The doctrine of dependent origination implies that no state of existence is permanent. The idea of impermanence (*anicca, anitya*) is characteristic of Buddhism. In comparing Jainism with Buddhism Jacobi remarked: "But the metaphysical principles of Buddhism are of an entirely different character, being moulded by the fundamental principle of Buddhism, viz. that there is no absolute and permanent Being, or, in other words, that all things are transitory" (Jacobi 1914: 465b). According to brahmanical doctrine the true reality is the identity of ātman and Brahman, a static state, whereas for the Buddhist nothing ever remains the same. The fact that everything is impermanent implies that everything is suffering (*dukkha, duḥkha*). In an article on impermanence, suffering, and non-self in early Buddhism Mori Shōji made an exhaustive inventory of the occurrence of these three concepts in the Nikāyas and the Āgamas. There are variations in the formulae in which they are mentioned. In the Pāli texts one finds in several instances as third item *vipariṇāmadhammaṁ* (*yaṁ panāniccaṁ dukkhaṁ vipariṇāmadhammaṁ*, *Majjhima-nikāya* i.138) instead of *anattā* (*yad aniccaṁ taṁ dukkhaṁ, yaṁ dukkhaṁ tad anattā*, *Saṁyutta-nikāya* iii.22). A later development is a series of four items, void being added between suffering and non-self. This series is not found in Pāli texts but only in the Āgamas (Mori 1974: 137). However, in the majority of cases the three concepts mentioned are impermanence, suffering, and non-self. It is obvious that in early Buddhism impermanence and suffering imply the non-existence of the self as a permanent entity. These three concepts are insolubly linked together and constitute a basic doctrine of early Buddhism. With regard to the doctrines of karman and of dependent origination there are indications that such doctrines were not unknown in India before the time of the Buddha. However, in early Buddhism these doctrines were developed in a specific way. The combination of the idea of impermanence with the ideas of suffering and non-self seems peculiar to Buddhism.

4.5. Another basic doctrine is that of the four noble truths. It proclaims the fundamental idea of suffering which is the dominating theme of Buddhist teachings. Typical also for Buddhism is the temporal aspect: suffering arises, it is destroyed, and there is a way leading to its destruction. Buddhism in its essence stresses always the changeability of everything. Nothing is permanent, nothing remains as it is.

5.1. When one considers some of the basic ideas of early Buddhism, two aspects strike one as distinguishing Buddhism: the primacy given to the activity of the mind and the insight into the impermanence of everything. These two aspects are not isolated from each other. It is through insight that one arrives at the idea of impermanence. However, early Buddhism is not a philosophical system. Buddhism teaches the way to deliverance from impermanence, which is seen as identical with suffering. The importance of the role of the mind does not mean that one arrives at insight by a process of reasoning. For instance, the teaching about impermanence, suffering, and non-self is often followed by the declaration that one must see everything as it is by right insight, *yathābhūtaṁ sammappaññāya daṭṭhabbaṁ* (*Majjhima-nikāya* i.139). This leads to disregard (*nibbinda*) and disregard results in dispassionateness (*virāga*) through which one becomes delivered

(Mori 1984: 117, n. 4). Repeatedly the texts speak about *prajñā* for which it is difficult to find a good English equivalent. It is an insight obtained by an inner vision, not a rational knowledge obtained by reasoning.

5.2. For the supreme state of being the Buddhists use the word Nirvāṇa, a concept which is also known to Jainism. However, it is impossible to describe the state of Nirvāṇa. Many words are used to indicate Nirvāṇa and it has been remarked that some of these words or similar words are also used to express the absolute reality, Brahman, in the Upaniṣads (Kumoi 1955). However, this did not create any problem for the Buddhists who were well aware of the fact that whatever word one used it was impossible to express the real nature of Nirvāṇa. With the rise of Mahāyāna the situation became different. As remarked before, for the Buddhists the world was impermanent, suffering, and non-self. The early Buddhists did not oppose to this world of impermanence a world of permanence, bliss, and self but it is not surprising that these notions penetrated into Buddhism in later times. This is, however, a topic which is beyond the scope of this paper which is concerned only with early Buddhism.

6. As mentioned above, the teachings of the Jains and the Buddhists have been preserved due to the fact that they were transmitted by the congregation (*saṁgha*). It has been shown convincingly by Fujita and Norman (Norman 1991: 233–249) that the concept of the pratyeka-buddha predates Buddhism and Jainism. The praise of pratyeka-buddhas in such texts as the *Khaggavisāṇa-sutta* of the *Suttanipāta* clearly refers to a period in which, as de La Vallée Poussin remarked, there existed "the old ideal of a solitary and silent life—an ideal that was flourishing before Śākyamuni came" (de La Vallée Poussin 1918: 153b). As Norman pointed out, both the Jain and Buddhist traditions show the same ambivalence about whether pratyeka-buddhas teach or not (Norman 1991: 245). Probably there were ascetics who lived a solitary life and others who followed a charismatic leader whose word was authoritative for his followers. Such groups tend to disintegrate with the death of the leader and his teachings become lost. Remarkable in the case of both Jainism and Buddhism is not only the creation of a *saṁgha* which preserved the teachings of the founder but also the express command to spread the teaching. As far as we know Jainism and Buddhism are the first missionary religions in the world. In the *Āyāraṅga* it is said: "A saint with right intuition, who cherishes compassion for the world, in the east, west, south, and north, should preach, spread, and praise (the faith), knowing the

sacred lore" (Jacobi 1884: 60). In the *Mahāvagga* the monks are urged to proclaim the doctrine: "Let not two go together. Monks, teach the doctrine which is good at the beginning, good at the middle, good at the end, in the spirit and in the letter" (de Jong 1979: 79, 647).

7.1. It is certainly possible to obtain a true picture of early Buddhism from the prose texts, i.e., the first four Nikāyas, the Āgamas, and the early Vinayas. This does not mean that one has to neglect the verses which contain important materials for the study of early Buddhism. However, one must take into account the fact that they contain materials of different origin. Some Buddhist doctrines are already found in the verses such as, for example, the doctrine of the four noble truths. Norman has suggested that the original form did not contain the word *ariyasaccaṁ* and had the following wording: *idaṁ dukkhaṁ*, *ayaṁ dukkha-samudayo*, *ayaṁ dukkha-nirodho*, *ayaṁ dukkha-nirodha-gāminī paṭipadā* (Norman 1991: 219). The doctrine of the four noble truths is clearly enunciated in verse 726 of the *Suttanipāta* although the terminology is different:

ye ca dukkhaṁ pajānanti atho dukkhassa sambhavaṁ
yattha ca sabbaso dukkhaṁ asesaṁ uparujjhati
tañ ca maggaṁ pajānanti dukkhūpasamagāminaṁ

Nakamura quotes this and similar verses in order to show that the standard formula of the four truths is not found in verses. He concludes that it does not belong to the very oldest period and consequently is very (*hijō-ni*) new compared to the statements found in verses (Nakamura 1971: 18). It is difficult to agree with Nakamura. It is true that the standard formula occurs only in prose texts, but even there different formulae occur (Norman 1991: 210–215). It is not surprising that the verses do not use the same expressions as found in the formulae used in prose texts. An idea found more or less in a standard form in prose texts can be formulated in different ways in verses which are subjected to the exigencies of metre. There is no valid reason for assuming that the formulation of the four truths as found in *Suttanipāta* 726 is older than the standard formula (or rather formulae) of the prose texts.

7.2. For the study of early Buddhism it is necessary to analyse in the first place the principal doctrines as found in the prose texts because they reflect the main tradition. The verses belong to a different tradition as they contain pre-Buddhist and non-Buddhist ideas. It is possible that by combining different methods of research one will in due course be able to distinguish older and newer elements in the verses. This will certainly be of great help in obtaining a better insight into the background and origins of Buddhism. However, such insight can not be gained without knowledge of the basic doctrines of early Buddhism as found in the prose texts.

Bibliography

Alsdorf, Ludwig. 1965. *Les études Jaina. État présent et tâches futures* (Paris).

———. 1966. "Āryā Stanzas in Thera-Therī-Gāthā." *Thera- and Therīgāthā* (London: Pali Text Society): 233–250.

Aramaki, Noritoshi. 1993. "The Development of the Term "Pātimokkha" in Early Buddhism." *Premier Colloque Étienne Lamotte* (Louvain-la-Neuve): 33–49.

Bollée, W. B. 1980. *The Pādas of the Suttanipāta with Parallels from the Āyāraṅga, Sūyagaḍa, Uttarajjhāyā, Dasaveyāliya and Isibhāsiyāiṃ* (Reinbek).

———. 1983. *Reverse Index of the Dhammapada, Suttanipāta, Thera- and Therīgāthā Pādas with Parallels from the Āyāraṅga, Sūyagaḍa, Uttarajjhāyā, Dasaveyāliya and Isibhāsiyāiṃ* (Reinbek).

Enomoto, Fumio. 1978. "Āsrava ni tsuite." *Indogaku bukkyōgaku kenkyū* 27/1: 158–159.

———. 1979. "Āsrava (ro) no seiritsu ni tsuite (omo-ni Jaina kosōkyōten ni okeru)." *Bukkyō shigaku kenkyū* 22/1: 17–42.

———. 1983. "Shoki butten ni okeru āsrava (ro)." *Nanto bukkyō* 50: 17–28.

Fujita Kōtatsu. 1979. "Genshi bukkyō ni okeru gōshisō." *Gōshisō kenkyū* (Kyoto): 99–144.

Jacobi, Hermann. 1884. *Jaina Sutras.* Part I (Oxford).

———. 1895. *Jaina Sutras.* Part II (Oxford).

———. 1914. "Jainism." *Encyclopaedia of Religion and Ethics*, Vol. VII (Edinburgh): 465a–474a.

Jong, J. W. de. 1979. *Buddhist Studies* (Berkeley).

———. 1991. "Buddhist Studies (1984–1990)." *Chūō gakujutsu kenkyūjo kiyō* 20: 1–60.

———. 1993. "The Beginnings of Buddhism." *The Eastern Buddhist* N.S. XXVI/2: 11–30.

Kumoi Shōzen. 1955. "Nehan no dōgi igo ni tsuite." *Yamaguchi hakase kanreki kinen: Indogaku bukkyōgaku ronsō* (Kyoto): 47–54.

La Vallée Poussin, Louis de. 1918. "Pratyekabuddha." *Encyclopaedia of Religion and Ethics*, Vol. X (Edinburgh): 152b–154b.

Mizuno, Kōgen. 1981. *Hokkukyō no kenkyū* (Tokyo).

———. 1982a. "Bongo Hokkukyō (SDhp) no kenkyū." *Bukkyō kenkyū* 11: 1–47.

———. 1982b. "Shohokkukyō no ge no shinko ni tsuite." *Bukkyō kenkyū* 12: 1–29.

———. 1990. "Bongo Hokkukyō (SDhp) no kenkyū (sono 2)." *Bukkyō kenkyū* 19: 1–29.

———. 1991. "'Pāri Hokkukyō' ge no taiōhyō." *Bukkyō kenkyū* 20: 1–66.

———. 1992. "'Suttanipāta' no ge ya kyō no taiōhyō." *Bukkyō kenkyū* 21: 1–50.

Mori, Shōji. 1974. "Genshi bukkyō ni okeru 'mujō-ku-muga' setsu ni tsuite." *Ōkurayama ronshū* 11: 105–154.

Murakami, Shinkan. 1980. "Muyoku to mushou—Mahābhārata to bukkyō (1)." *Tōhoku daigaku bungaku-bu kenkyū nempō* 29: 140–213; English abstract: 248–244.

———. 1981. "Mujōkan to shukke shikō—Mahābhārata to genshi bukkyō." *Bukkyō kenkyū* 10: 51–74.

Nakamura, Hajime. 1971. *Genshi bukkyō no shisō*. Vol. 2 (Tokyo).

———. 1983. "Common elements in early Jain and Buddhist literature." *Indologica Taurinensia* XI: 303–330.

———. 1984. *Budda no kotoba. Suttanipāta* (Tokyo).

Norman, K. R. 1991. *Collected Papers*. Vol. II (Oxford).

———. 1992. *The Group of Discourses (Sutta-nipāta)*. Vol. II (Oxford).

———. 1993. *Collected Papers*. Vol. IV (Oxford).

Rau, Wilhelm. 1959. "Bemerkungen und nicht-buddhistische Sanskrit-Parallelen zum Pāli-Dhammapada." *Jñānamuktāvalī: Commemoration Volume in Honour of Johannes Nobel* (New Delhi): 159–175.

Schmithausen, Lambert. 1992. "An Attempt to Estimate the Distance in Time between Aśoka and the Buddha in Terms of Doctrinal History." *The Dating of the Historical Buddha*, Part 2 (Göttingen): 110–147.

Schubring, Walther. 1926. *Worte Mahāvīras* (Göttingen-Leipzig).

Vetter, T. E. 1985. "Recent Research on the Most Ancient Form of Buddhism. A Possible Approach and its Results." *Buddhism and Its Relation to Other Religions: Essays in Honour of Dr. Shozen Kumoi on His Seventieth Birthday* (Kyoto): 67–85.

Warder, A. K. 1967. *Pali Metre: A Contribution to the History of Indian Literature* (London).

Winternitz, Moriz. 1908. *Geschichte der indischen Literatur*. Vol. 1 (Leipzig).

———. 1927. *A History of Indian Literature*. Vol. I (Calcutta).

Abbreviation

T *Taisho shinshū daizōkyō*, edited by Takakusu and Watanabe, 55 vols. (Tokyo, 1924–1929).

Buddhist Cosmology as Presented in the *Yogācārabhūmi*

Yūichi Kajiyama

The *Yogācārabhūmi* contains in the first part of the *Manobhūmi* a description of Buddhist cosmology, which, however, covers a wide range of topics concerning sentient beings as well as the material world. Here in this paper I translate the portion including the descriptions of (1) a cycle of the transmigrating world, (2) the *kalpa* (world-age) of preservation of the world, (3) the three great disasters in the *kalpa* of world destruction, (4) the *kalpa* of empty space, (5) the *kalpa* of regeneration of the world, and (6) a *trisāhasra-mahāsāhasra-lokadhātu* (that is, a galactic system), which forms a field of a Buddha's teaching.

The Sanskrit text of the portion in question is found on pp. 30,21–44,14 of the *Yogācārabhūmi*, Part I, edited by V. Bhattacharya (below, S), which corresponds to Hsüan-tsang's Chinese translation, Taishō 1579 (XXX) 285b19–288a25 (below, C). A Tibetan translation of the same portion is found in the Derge edition (Tōhoku 4035) *Tshi*, 15b3–22a4 (below, T).

The Buddhist cosmology in our text is important and valuable, because no other Sanskrit text regarding this cosmology is extant, except chapter 3 of the *Abhidharmakośa* with its *Bhāṣya* and *Vyākhyā*, although we have many materials in Chinese and Tibetan translations. As will be seen, moreover, the cosmology as presented in the *Yogācārabhūmi* shows a transmission different from that in the *Abhidharmakośa*. It gives many particular accounts which we do not find in the *Abhidharmakośa*, although the two are in general similar.

Although collation of all the available Tibetan texts of our cosmology should precede a translation, I am, being abroad, not in a position to present such a collation at this time. Thus, my present translation is in this sense tentative. However, I have noted the chief variant readings in the Sanskrit, Tibetan (Derge ed. and partly Peking ed.), and Chinese versions. Numbers at the beginnings of paragraphs refer to the pages and lines in the Sanskrit edition. I have added the section titles denoted by roman numerals.

Corrections to the Sanskrit edition

31,16 *viśatim* → *viṁśatim*
31,17 *eca* → *eva*
32,4 *catvāriśad-* → *catvāriṁśad-*

32,13 *niyāṇa* → *niryāṇa*
33,1 *vikarṣati* → *virakṣati* (cf. n. 7)
33,1 MS *nisthāmaḥ* → *niḥsthāmānaḥ* (editor's correction)
33,9 *hīyamānās* → *āyuṣā hīyamānās* (cf. n. 8)
34,7 *bhojanānāṁ magryo* → *bhojanānām agryo*
35,2 *yāvadvitīyaṁ* → *yāvad dvitīyaṁ*
35,9 *apareṣā sūrya-* → *apareṣāṁ ṣaṇṇāṁ sūrya-* (cf. n. 9)
35,13 *ku*... (?)*mahā*...*drā* (?) → *kuvilvāni mahāvilvāni ca* (?) (cf. n. 11)
36,5 *viśatiś ca* → *viṁśatiś ca*
36,15 *viṁśātam* → *viṁśatim*
37,15 *tāsāmaram*... → cf. n. 18
38,5 *saṁmūrchayāṁta* → *saṁmūrchayanti*
39,1–2 cf. n. 24
39,2 *narakāṇāṁ* → (T / C) *śītanarakāṇāṁ*
39,14 *śakrasya devendrasya balaṁ* should be placed at the beginnng of line 13 (before *te*) (cf. n. 25)
40,14 *śataparivārā pañcaśataparivārā*. T/C seem to read: *puṣkaraṇī-pañca-śata-parivārā* (cf. n. 30).
41,13 *śalmalī* → *śālmalī*
43,1 *candramaṇḍasya* → *candramaṇḍalasya*
43,9 *kṣipram astagamanaṁ* → *kṣipraṁ* [*ciraṁ vā*-]*stagamanaṁ* (cf. n. 37)
43,14 *param* → *paramāṇām* (editor)
44,1 *lohādayo* → (T / C) *loha-tāmrādayo*
44,10 *varṣādhāre* → **īṣādhāre* (cf. n. 47)
44,14 *etāvad* → *etad* (cf. n. 48)

An English Translation

I General Description of a Cycle of the World

(30,21) How then do the destruction (*saṁvarta*) and regeneration (*vivarta*) of the external objects occur? [They occur] because of sentient beings' karma conducive to the destruction or regeneration[1] [of the world]. If a karma conducive to destruction is present, it, with [the cooperation of] external conditions, comes to destroy those [external objects]. But [the external objects are destroyed] not as internal [or spiritual] things [of sentient beings] are destroyed due to the abandonment of life, because the external objects are material, gross, made of the four great elements [i.e., earth, water, fire, and wind], and motionlessly continuing (*sthāvarasantatayaḥ*), whereas the internal

1. S *saṁvarta-vivarta-saṁvartanīyena karmaṇā*. T 15b3: *sems can rnams kyi*, as well as C 285b19: 諸有情, "of sentient beings," add **sattvānām* before the above phrase.

things are not so. The karma conducive to the regeneration of those material [objects][2] projects a definite world-age (*niyataṁ kalpākṣepakam*)[3] as the period during which it abides, and which is neither longer nor shorter [than that period]. A being enumerated among sentient beings, however, has no definite length of lifetime, because those [beings] make various karmas. Therefore, their lifetime is sometimes longer than a *kalpa*, sometimes shorter than that, even less than ten[4] years.

(31,9) It should also be known that there are three kinds of destructions of the world: (1) the destruction by fire, which destroys all things beginning with the Avīci hell through the Brahmaloka world [i.e., the first *dhyāna* heaven]; (2) the destruction by water, which destroys everything up to the second *dhyāna* heaven; (3) the destruction by wind, which destroys all things up to the third *dhyāna* heaven. However, in the fourth *dhyāna* heaven [there is no destruction at all]. Those gods inhabiting the fourth *dhyāna* are born together with their palaces, and die together with their palaces. Therefore they do not suffer from destruction, nor do they have the cause of destruction. There are three upper realms (*śīrṣa*)[which are saved from the three destructions]: the second *dhyāna* heaven [is saved from the destruction by fire], the third *dhyāna* heaven [is saved from the destruction by water], and the fourth *dhyāna* heaven [is saved from the destruction by wind].

(31,15) This world is destroyed (*saṁvartate*) during the period of twenty intermediate *kalpas* (*antarakalpa*), remains as it is destroyed (*saṁvṛttas tiṣṭhati*) [i.e., remains as empty space] during that of twenty intermediate *kalpas*, is regenerated (*vivartate*) during that of twenty intermediate *kalpas*, and continues in the regenerated state (*vivṛttas tiṣṭhati*) during that of twenty intermediate *kalpas*. These periods cover [in total] eighty intermediate *kalpas*; and the period [of eighty intermediate *kalpas*] is called a great *kalpa* (*mahākalpa*) in the agreement of calculation (*saṁkhyā-prajñaptitaḥ*). Here [in this world, gods] in the Brahma world (*brahmaloka*) have the life-span of one *kalpa*. And [during the time of destruction the Brahma world] is the last of all to be destroyed, and it is also the first of all to be regenerated [during the time of regeneration].

---

2. Here *teṣām bhājānām* = *bhājanaloka*.

3. A world-age (*kalpa*) here means "twenty intermediate *kalpas*," during which the regeneration of the world is completed.

4. S = T: "ten years," but C 285b26 alone has "one year" instead.

(32,3) Regarding the [life-span of the gods of the Brahma world], we should know a different way of determining it. One *kalpa* as the life-span of the Brahmakāyika gods is so determined, being considered to actually mean twenty intermediate *kalpa*s; one *kalpa* as the life-span of the Brahmapurohita gods is so determined, being considered to actually mean forty intermediate *kalpa*s; one *kalpa* of the Mahābrahma gods is so determined, being considered to actually mean sixty intermediate *kalpa*s.

II The Age of the Preservation of the World Preceding the Age of the Destruction of the World

(32,7) What is the destruction by fire (*tejaḥsaṁvartanī*)? [Preceding the period of the destruction of the world], there is a period during which sentient beings with infinite life-span begin to degenerate with respect to life-span until they live only for eighty thousand years. Furthermore, their life-span, due to their acceptance of immorality (*akuśalānāṁ dharmānām samādānahetoḥ*), continues to decrease down to the life-span of ten years. When people get disgusted (*saṁvega-prāpta*) [with worldly life, or obtain the desire of emancipation], however, they begin to increase in life-span because they obtain good morals (*kuśalāṇāṁ dharmāṇāṁ samādānahetoḥ*) until they again come to live for eighty thousand years. Putting together both the time of decreasing [life-span] and that of increasing [life-span], we call [the period covering the two times] an intermediate *kalpa*, for the sake of establishing calculation.

(32,12) The intermediate *kalpa* passes away[5] with three kinds [of small disasters] called famine (*durbhikṣa*), disease (*roga*), and battle (*śastra*). The famine takes place when human beings have the life-span of thirty years. Things such as the following occur over and over again. They try to support life (*yātrāṁ kalpayati*)[6] by boiling even old bones. When they happen sometimes and somehow to find grains of barley, rice, black pepper, pulse, and sesame, they protect[7] them, putting them in a casket as if they were jewels. These beings have mostly lost energy, fallen down, and are lying on their backs on the

---

5. S *niyāṇa* should be corrected into *niryāṇa*. T 16a7: *thal bar 'gyur ro*. Cf. P. Pradhan, *Abhidharmakośabhāṣya* (Patna: K.P. Jayaswal Research Institute, 1967): 187,24.

6. T 16b1: *srog zungs su byed de* = S. C 285c20, however, reads 共爲讌會, "arrange a feast together." *Yātrā* can be understood as "feast, dinner party."

7. S *vikarṣati* should be *virakṣati*. T 16b2: *srung bar byed do*, as well as C 285c21, 守護, read "protect."

ground, unable even to stand up. Most of the people die through this kind of famine. The famine, however, lasts as long as seven years, seven months, and seven days and nights, and after the period it is said to come to an end. Then the beings gather together and unitedly obtain a lower kind of disgust (*mṛdukaṁ saṁvegam*) [with worldly life]. On this ground and for this reason, their life-span stops decreasing, and the famine also ceases.

(33,8) When human beings come to have a life-span of twenty years, and [the life-span][8] continues to decrease due to disappearance of their disgust, then many kinds of plague, misfortune, and suffering occur. People fall prey to many diseases, and most of them lose their lives. This disease of theirs lasts as long as seven months and seven days and nights, and after that it is said to be over. Then the beings are possessed of middle disgust (*madhya-saṁvega*), and on this ground and for this reason, their life-span does not decrease any more, and they do not suffer from diseases.

(33,14) Also, when human beings have the life-span of ten years and their life-span is decreasing due to the disappearance of disgust, then they, looking at one another, become filled with fierce murderous intention. Thus, if they grasp a stalk, pebble, or stone, they turn these into pointed, well sharpened weapons, with which they murder one another. This [battle] continues as long as seven days, and after that it is said to come to an end.

(34,4) At that time the beings suffer from three kinds of extreme misfortunes, that is to say, the misfortune of life-span, that of body and that of means of subsistence. Of them, the misfortune of life-span means that it becomes ten years at the most. The misfortune of body is that the measure of their bodies is no more than a *vitasti* (9 inches) or a *muṣṭi* (the breadth of a fist). The misfortune of means of subsistence is that *kodrava* (foxtail millet) is the best of foods, a blanket of hair is the best of clothes, a weapon is the best of decorations, and all the five flavors—that is, the flavor of ghee (*sarpis*), the flavor of honey (*madhu*), the flavor of oil (*taila*), the flavor of molasses (*ikṣuvikāra*), and the flavor of salt (*lavaṇa*)—completely disappear. Thus, these beings become excessively disgusted (*adhimātra-saṁvega*) [with worldly life], and they never lose the disgust. Moreover, abandoning the

---

8. S *saṁvegasya punar vigamād dhīyamānās tadā* .... T and C follow S. Considering S 33,14: *saṁvegasya vigamād āyuṣā hīyamānās*, and T 16b6: *skyo ba de nyid med par gyur pas tshe 'grib par gyur ba de'i tshe*..., however, we should read S 33,8–9 inserting *āyuṣā* between *vigamād* and *hīyamānās*.

evil qualities that impair their life-span, they engage in collecting good qualities that strengthen life-span. They meet one another and gather together, and their life-span again increases. They also continue to progress in complexion, [strength,] happiness, superhuman powers (*aiśvarya*), and influence until their life-span becomes eighty thousand years.

III The Disappearance of Sentient Beings

(34,15) In this way, [as an intermediate *kalpa* in the age of preservation of the world consists of the time of decreasing life-span and that of increasing life-span, the age of preservation consisting of twenty intermediate *kalpas*] has twenty times of decreasing life-span and twenty times of increasing life-span. When forty times of decreasing and increasing life-spans have passed by, [the destruction of the world begins] at the very last time of increasing life-span. Then, sentient beings die in hell (*naraka*) and are not born [again there]. When all of them are dead, their world is said to have been destroyed (*saṁvṛtta*) by the destruction of hell (*naraka-saṁvartanī*). Just as the destruction of hell, just so happen the destruction of the animal world (*tiryak-saṁvartanī*) and the destruction of the world of hungry ghosts (*preta-saṁvartanī*).

(34,19) On the other hand, a certain person among human beings, having understood the true nature of all things (*dharmatā*), attains as far as the second *dhyāna* [heaven], and passes time there. Following his example, other sentient beings also understand the true nature of all things, and having attained as far as the second *dhyāna*, live there. Having died here [on the ground], they are born among the group of heavenly beings in the Ābhāsvara heaven [or the highest of the second *dhyāna* heavens]. Then, this world is said to have been destroyed by the destruction of human beings (*manuṣya-saṁvartanī*). Just as [the world is destroyed] by the destruction of human beings, so [it is destroyed also] by the destruction of heavenly beings (*deva-saṁvartanī*).

IV Destruction of the World by Fire, Water, and Wind

(35,5) When even a single sentient being is not found at [any] place in the worlds of five kinds of living beings (*pañcagatika*, i.e., denizens of hell, hungry ghosts, animals, humans, and gods), then there is no means of subsistence available either. When no means of subsistence is available, even rains do not fall. When it does not rain, grasses, plants, and trees on this great earth dry up. Without being controlled by timely rains the disk of this sun (*sūryamaṇḍala*) increases its heat more and more. Six[9] suns other than [the present one] come to appear because of the dominance[10] of six kinds of things to be burnt, that is to say, due to the power of sentient beings' karma leading to the destruction [of the world]. Moreover, these [six new] suns have burning power four times stronger than that of this [present] sun. Thus, [the suns] will become seven in number and burn seven times stronger.

(35,13) What are the six kinds of things? (1) Small or large lakes and marshes,[11] which are dried up by the second sun; (2) small rivers and great rivers, which are dried up by the third sun; (3) Anavatapta the great lake, which is dried up by the fourth sun; (4) the great ocean, which is dried up by the fifth sun and a part of the sixth sun; (5) Mount Sumeru and the earth (*mahāpṛthivī*), having very hard bodies, are burnt down by [a part of] the sixth sun and the seventh sun; (6) thereafter the rays, being moved by wind, continue to burn until they reach as far as the Brahma world (that is, the first *dhyāna* heaven).

(35,19) Again, all the things stated above are [summarized into the following] three points: (1) things born out of water such as grasses and so forth which are dried up by the first [sun]; (2) things which are in essence water [lakes, rivers, and Anavatapta the great lake] and which are dried up by the other five [suns, that is, from the second to the sixth suns]; (3) immovable and hard bodies [Mount Sumeru and the great earth] which are burnt down by the two [suns, or the sixth and the seventh suns].

(36,3) As is taught in detail in Buddhist sūtras,[12] when all places of the world are burnt and blown, even soot[13] is not found, nor are ashes[14] known. To that extent the world is destroyed by what is called the destruction of the material world (*bhājana-saṁvartanī*),

---

9. *ṣaṇṇāṁ* should be inserted after *pareṣāṁ*, as both T 17b3 and C 286b1 have "six suns."

10. S *ṣaṭ prakāra-dāhyavastv-adhikārataś ca*. T 17b3: *bsreg par bya ba'i dngos po rnam pa drug yod pa'i phyir* (as there are six kinds of things to be burnt). C 286a29-b1: 依六種所焼事, "depending on six kinds of things to be burnt."

11. MS illegible, as noted by the editor. T 16b4: *lteng ka chung ngu dang | lteng ka chen po.* C 286b4: 小大講坑, "small and large lakes or marshes." Skt. could read: *kuvilvāni mahāvilvāni ca*. For *vilva*, see *Mahāvyuttpatti* 4172.

12. Cf. *Pitṛputrasamāgama*, quoted in the *Śikṣāsamuccaya* (ed. Bendall) 246.9ff.

13. S *masi* = *maṣi*. T 18a1 has *dud pa* = smoke.

14. S *chārikā*. T 18a1: *thal ba'i lhag ma* = **bhasma-śeṣa* (remnants of ashes). C 286b13–14 reads: 灰墨及與餘影, "ashes, soot and other things."

and twenty intermediate *kalpa*s [of the age of destruction] pass away. The world destroyed in this way remains [as empty space] for another twenty intermediate *kalpa*s [of the age of empty space].

(36,7) What is the destruction by water (*apsaṁvartanī*)? When the destruction by fire [which occurs once at every *mahākalpa*] has happened seven times and been completed, then in the second dhyāna [heaven] is produced the element of water which has been innate (*sahaja*) [to the second *dhyāna*]; and the element of water dissolves the material world just as water melts salt. The element of water disappears together with the material world. [The world] that has been destroyed in this way remains [as empty space] for twenty intermediate *kalpa*s.

(36,11) What is the destruction by wind (*vāyusaṁvartanī*)? When the destruction by water has been repeated seven times, the destruction by fire follows once more.[15] Immediately after it, the element of wind, which is innate [to the third *dhyāna*], is produced in the third *dhyāna* [heaven]. The wind, drying up the material world, causes it to disappear, just as wind causes limbs of the body [to disappear as it desiccates a corpse]. The wind also disappears together with that [material world]. For instance, we see that when someone is buffeted by the element of wind he is emaciated until all that is left is bones. [The material world that has been] destroyed [into emptiness] remains in that state for twenty intermediate *kalpa*s. In this way the world is destroyed.

V Regeneration of the World

(36,19) What is the regeneration (*vivarta*) [of the world]? It should be known that after those twenty intermediate *kalpa*s [of the age of empty space] have passed by, the age of regeneration (*vivarta-kalpa*) [of the world] begins again because of the influence (*ādhipatyāt*) of sentient beings' karma [conducive to] the regeneration [of the world]. In this case, the third *dhyāna* [heaven] first of all evolves in empty space (*ākāśa*), that is to say, [it is created] by means of the regeneration of the material world (*bhājana-vivṛtti*). And as the third *dhyāna*, so the second and the first [*dhyāna* heavens are also made in due order].

(36,22) From the upper realm (*śīrṣa*) of the third destruction [by wind, i.e., from the fourth *dhyāna* heaven], sentient beings, having

15. S and T 18a4 say "destruction by fire follows once more," but C 286b21 says, 復七火災, "destruction by fire follows seven times." C agrees with the description in the *Abhidharmakośa*.

died of the exhaustion of their life-span and merits,[16] are reborn in the third *dhyāna* heaven. This is to be understood in connection with all the other heavens. [Gods in the third *dhyāna* heaven, which is] the upper realm of the second destruction [by water, having died there], are reborn in the second *dhyāna* heaven. This again is to be understood in connection with all the other heavens. A certain heavenly being in [the second *dhyāna* heaven, which is] the upper realm of the first destruction [by fire, having died there] due to the exhaustion of life-span up to that of merits, is reborn in the first *dhyāna* heaven, i.e., in the Brahma heaven.

(37,4) He [who has been reborn in the first *dhyāna* heaven] becomes there a Brahmā called the great Brahmā.[17] As he is quite alone he is not pleased and feels longing, "Oh, may other beings also be born here!" Because of the working of his mind, other beings also, having died in the [second] *dhyāna* heaven due to the exhaustion of life-span through the exhaustion of merits, are born in the first *dhyāna* heaven.

(37,8) The three *dhyāna* heavens [i.e., the third, second, and first *dhyāna* heavens] are regenerated in this way, that is to say, again by means of the regeneration of sentient beings (*sattva-vivartanī*). And then the palaces of the groups of gods in the four worlds of desire (*caturṇāṁ kāmāvacarāṇāṁ devanikāyānām ... vimānāni*) are manifested in space. It should be regarded that all of their palaces in space are produced [all of a sudden] in the same way as an apparition (*nirmāṇa*) is manifested. The rebirth in these [palaces] of sentient beings who have died from the group of gods of Ābhāsvara heaven [or the highest of the second *dhyāna* heavens] is to be understood as above (*pūrvavat*).

(37,12) Thereafter a whirlwind as large as the Trisāhasra-mahāsāhasra [world] arises here and becomes the support of the Trisāhasra-mahāsāhasra [world] as well as of sentient beings having no palaces [i.e., gods of the two lowest worlds of desire and sentient beings on and under the earth]. It is of two kinds: the whirlwind stretching itself upwards and that stretching itself on the flank of the world, which prevent water [on the wind] from leaking out downwards and sideways.[18] And then clouds containing gold appear above these [whirl-

16. T 18a7: *tshe zad pa dang, las zad pa dang, bsod nams zad pa* (the exhaustion of their life-span, that of karma, and that of merits). C 286c2 agrees with T.

17. T 18b2: *tshangs pa'i nang na tshangs pa'i chen por 'gyur la* (he becomes the great brahmā among brahmās). C 286c6: 梵世界中爲最大梵, "he becomes the greatest brahmā in the brahmā world."

18. S *yena tāsāmaraṁ tiryagvimānaḥ adhaś cāyatanaṁ* is, as the editor says, not clear.

winds] by the influence of [sentient beings'] karma. Rains fall from the [clouds]. The water [of the rains] is sustained on the whirlwind. Then, wind blows and condenses and hardens[19] the water. It is called[20] the earth made of gold as it withstands upward and downward agitations[21] of water.

(38,3) When the [earth] is regenerated, clouds containing various kinds of elements are produced above the earth by virtue of the influence of karma [made by sentient beings]. Rains fall from the clouds, and the water stays on the golden earth. Again, in the same way [as above] wind condenses and hardens [the water]. In this case, however, [the best] elements, which are extremely pure, prominent, superior, and perfect, produce, with the help of the drawing power of wind, Mount Sumeru, made of four kinds of jewels—gold, silver, crystal, and cat's eye.

(38,8) There is also the middle class of elements (*madhyo dhātus*), from which are produced seven mountain ranges made of gold, that is to say, Yugandhara, Vinataka, Aśvakaraṇagiri, Sudarśana, Khadiraka, Īṣādhara, and Nimindhara.[22] They are situated surrounding the Sumeru in this order [from inside to outside].

(38,11) As to the measure of Mount Sumeru, it is eighty thousand *yojana*s in height as well as in width, and dives under water as deep as eighty [thousand *yojanas*]. Yugandhara is half [of Sumeru] in size. The other [six] golden mountain ranges beginning with Vinataka and ending with Nimindhara are to be known to reduce one after another their size to half of the preceding one. The tops of these [seven] mountain ranges seem to resemble the shapes of different things respectively after which they are named [as e.g., Aśvakarṇa is so named as its top is of the shape of a horse's ears].

T 18b6: *des chu de dag thad kar yang mi 'bo la, thur du yang mi 'dzag go*. C 286c17–18: 由此持水令不散墜, "By this water is sustained without falling asunder." I follow T and C.

19. The editor corrects *saṁkarchayanti* in the manuscript into *sammūrchayanti*. T 18b7: *kun du 'thas pa dang sra bar byed de*. C 286c19: 次復起風鼓水令堅, "Then is produced wind again, which beats water and hardens it."

20. S *bhavati*, but T 18b7 *zhes bya'o*, as well as C 286c20 此即名爲, say "it is called."

21. S *vimarṣya* is corrected by the editor into *vimarda*. T 18b7: *'khrug pa* = agitation. C 286c20–21: 上堪水雨之所激注。下爲風飇之所衝薄, "pouring of water and impact of wind."

22. Note that the order in the *Abhidharmakośa* differs: Yugandhara, Īṣādhara, Khadiraka, Sudarśana, Aśvakaraṇagiri, Vinataka, and Nimindhara.

(38,16) Out of the inferior elements (*hīnāt ... dhātoḥ*) [are produced], on the four sides of Mount Sumeru and outside the [seven] golden mountain ranges, four great continents (*catvāro dvīpāḥ*), eight mid-islands (*antardvīpa*),[23] and Cakravāḍa Mountain. The size [of the Cakravāḍa] is half of the Nimindhara mountain range. The four continents are surrounded by that Cakravāḍa Mountain. The palaces of Asuras (evil spirits) are located in the water under Mount Sumeru. The Snowy Mountain (*himavat*) borders on the Anavatapta Lake. Underneath [Jambūdvīpa] there are the worlds of Great Hells (*mahānarakasthāna*),[24] [that is to say,] Eight kinds of Hells, Individual Hells (*pratyekanaraka*), Cold Hells (*śīta-naraka*), and Border Hells (*sāmantakanaraka*).[25] There are also the abodes of some animals and hungry ghosts.

(39,3) The four continents are namely Jambūdvīpa, Pūrvavideha, Avaragodānīya, and Uttarakuru. Of them, Jambūdvīpa is of the form of a carriage. Pūrvavideha is of the form of a half moon. Godānīya is circular, and Uttarakuru is quadrangular. Jambūdvīpa is six thousand five hundred *yojana*s in size. Pūrvavideha is seven thousand *yojana*s in size. Avaragodānīya is seven thousand five hundred *yojana*s in size. Uttarakuru is eight thousand *yojana*s in size.

(39,9) Waters existing between the seven golden mountain ranges are endowed with the eight kinds of meritorious properties (*aṣṭāṅgo-peta*). Each [of them] is an inland sea, in which there are palaces of serpent-demons (*nāga*). These serpent-demons are of eight kinds, live for a *kalpa*, and are [called] earth-bearers (*dharaṇindhara*). They are Nanda, Upananda, Aśvatara, Mucilinda, Manasvī, Dhṛtarāṣṭra, Mahākāla, and Elapatra. With the strength of Śakra the lord of gods,[26] they join and fight a battle with gods and asuras.

---

23. Two mid-islands are located in the neighorhood of each of the four continents, thus totaling eight. T 19a6 renders *antardvīpa* by *gling phran* (little island). Edgerton in his *Buddhist Hybrid Sanskrit Dictionary* s.v. explains *antaradvīpa* (Skt. *antardvīpa*) as "island in the midst (of a body of water)." *Antar* or *antara* here does not refer to the middle in size between large and small, as the Chinese (C 287a5 中洲) and Japanese (which follows Chinese) translations may mean.

24. S *narakasthānāni*. T 19a7 *sems can dmyal ba chen po rnams kyi gnas*, as well as C 287a9 大那落迦處, suggest **mahā-naraka-sthānāni*.

25. S *aṣṭau narakasthānāni, mahānarakāṇāṁ pratyekanarakāṇāṁ ca, narakāṇāṁ sām-anta[ka]narakāṇāṁ ca*. T 19a7 enumerates as follows: **mahānarakasthānāni, aṣṭanara-kāṇāṁ, pratyekanarakāṇāṁ, śītanarakāṇāṁ, sāmantakanarakāṇāṁ*. C 287a9–10: **aṣṭau mahānaraka-sthānāni, mahānarakaṇāṁ*. . . . I translate in the order of T.

26. Here the order of the Skt. text is disrupted. T 16b4: *de dag kyang lha'i dbang po brgya byin gyi dpung yin te*. C 287a21 是諸龍王由帝釋力 agrees in meaning with T.

(39,14) The serpent-demons are classified into four races: those born from eggs (*aṇḍaja*), from wombs (*jarāyuja*), from moisture (*saṁsvedaja*), and by spontaneous generation (*aupapāduka*). Garuḍas (*suparṇin*) are [also] of four kinds: those born from eggs, from wombs, from moisture, and by spontaneous generation.

(40,1) The water located outside the inland seas is the open sea, [whose bed is formed of] four layers extended out from the root of Mount Sumeru. The first [or lowest] layer protrudes from Sumeru to the length of sixteen thousand *yojana*s. Each of the other [three layers] is reduced in length to a half of the preceding one in regular order. (Yakṣas called) Karoṭapāṇi ("holding up a cup in the hand") live on the first layer, Rudhirapāṇi ("holding blood in the hand") on the second, Sadāmada[27] ("always intoxicated") on the third, and Mālādhara ("holding a wreath") on the fourth.

(40,5) There are four peaks with the height of five hundred *yojana*s on the four corners of the flat land at the top of [Su-]Meru. There [on these peaks] live Yakṣas named Vajrapāṇi ("Thunderbolt-handed").

(40,7) On the four flanks of Yugandhara the mountain range there are [four] royal residences of the great kings (*mahārāja*). They are Dhṛtarāṣṭra, Virūḍhaka, Virūpākṣa, and Vaiśravaṇa, living in the east, west, south, and north respectively. Also on all the golden mountain ranges there are villages, towns, and districts of the great kings.

(40,10) In the neighborhood of Himavat, the king of mountains, there is a slope made of gold and named "Asura's Flank" (*asura-pārśva*)[28] which is fifty *yojana*s in length and width. This is the residence of Supratiṣṭha the king of elephants (*nāgarāja*). And it is also a battlefield (*saṅgrāmāvacara*)[29] of Śakra, the lord of gods. Here there is Supratiṣṭhita, the king of trees, being surrounded by seven rows of palm trees. There is also here [a lotus pool named] Mandākinī which is surrounded by [five] hundred [small] lotus pools.[30] It is a playground

---

27. The MS reading Sadāmatta is often found, and may be correct. See *Divyāvadāna* 218. *Abhidharmakośabhāṣya* 167.7 says: *sadāmadāḥ sadāmattāḥ*. See also BHSD s.v.

28. S *sura-pārśva*. But both T 20a3: *lha ma yin gyi ngos*, and C 287b5 非天脅, have *asura-pārśva* instead.

29. C 287b6–7 alone reads 又天帝釋時來遊幸, "Śakra sometimes comes for a pleasure outing."

30. S *puṣkaraṇī-śata-parivārā*. However, both T 20a 4 *rdzing bu lnga brgyas bskor ba* and C 287b8–9 五百小池以爲眷屬 read: "surrounded by five hundred [small] lotus pools."

of Supratiṣṭha[31] [the king of elephants]. Here he [Supratiṣṭha], assuming any shape at will (*kāmarūpin*), enjoys lotus fibers, tearing them off out of the lotus pool. He is surrounded by five hundred female elephants.

(40,17) In the neighborhood of that [Mandākinī] there is the great lake, Anavatapta, which is fifty *yojana*s deep and fifty *yojana*s wide. [Its bed is] strewn with golden sands; it is possessed of water endowed with eight kinds of meritorious properties; and it is beautiful, attractive, and pleasant. From it branch out four great rivers, that is to say, Gaṅgā, Sindhu, Sītā, and Vakṣu.

(41,3) In the flat land [on the top] of Mount Sumeru there is the divine castle [of Śakra and dependent gods] measuring ten thousand *yojana*s in length as well as in width. In other places there are villages, cities and districts belonging to these gods. Sumeru has four sides, facing which there are the four continents beginning with Jambūdvīpa. It [= Mount Sumeru] has four flanks, of which the flank facing Jambūdvīpa is made of cat's eye, that facing Pūrvavideha is made of silver, that facing Avaragodānīya is made of gold, and that facing Uttarakuru is made of crystals.

(41,9) In the neighborhood of Jambūdvīpa there is a golden avenue of a sovereign of the world (*cakravartin*) which is submerged in the great ocean just as the knees of beings belonging to the four great kings (*caturmahārājakāyikasattva*)[32] are sunk [in water]. When the sovereign of the world appears, so much water in the great ocean as up to his knees dries up.

(41,12) In a region south of the Anavatapta lake there is a great black plum tree (*jambū*) after which this continent is named Jambūdvīpa. In the northern part there is a great cotton plant (*kūṭaśālmalī*),[33] in which four [kinds of] garuḍas (= *suparṇin*) live. To each of the four

---

31. S *supratiṣṭhita* seems to be a confusion for Supratiṣṭha, the king of elephants. Or both names could be one and the same.

32. S: some words between *caturmahārājakāyikasattva*...and *mahāsamudranimagnas tiṣṭhati* are missing. They are complemented by T 20b2: *rgyal chen bzhi'i ris kyi sems can gyi pus mo'i tshad kyi pus nub tsam zhig rgya mtsho chen po na nub cing*..., and C 287b21–22: 如四大王天有情膝量沒住大海, "the avenue is sunk in the ocean as deep as up to the knees of sentient beings of the heaven of the four great kings."

33. S *mahatī kūṭa-śalmalī* (*śālmalī*). Kūṭa-śālmalī is explained by Monier-Williams s.v. as "a fabulous cotton plant with sharp thorns (with which the wicked are tortured in the world of Yama)". But our text is talking neither of the world of Yama nor of hell. T 20b4: *shing shal ma li rtse mo shin tu mtho ba* (śālmalī tree whose points are

continents belong two mid-islands (*antaradvīpa*). One of them is an island in which malignant demons (*rākṣasa*) live.

(41,17) When the material world (*bhājanaloka*) has been accomplished in this way, beings among the heavenly class of Ābhāsvara die there and are born here [in this world], as stated before, because of their karma which should be recognized as leading to (*saṁvedanīya*), the first *kalpa* [of the regeneration of the world]. It is the superior, first, excellent karma belonging to the world of desire (*kāmāvacara*), and the karma completes its effect only at this time [when the world is regenerated], and not at other times. And those sentient beings in this very time are called "belonging to the first *kalpa*" (*prathamakalpaka*). They have beautiful forms and are "made of will" (*manomaya*). All of this is described according to Buddhist sūtras.

(42,1) At this time no houses, residences, villages, nor abodes exist. All the earth is simply even and flat. Then the earth nectar (*bhūmirasa*) appears for sentient beings, and in the same way appear successively thin paper-like dried cakes (*parpaṭaka*) [edible mushrooms?], forest creepers (*vanalatā*), and rice growing without being tilled and sown, which is free from bran and husk. After that, however, bran and husk overgrow rice grains (*taṇḍulaphala*); and next, paddies stand in thickets and underbrush (?).[34] Thereupon those sentient beings are seen seizing [these foods]. Then, due to their consumption of [earth] nectar and the rest, those sentient beings become ugly (*daurvarṇya*), and their supernatural powers disappear. The more one eats, the uglier he becomes, and the heavier his body gets. Thus, one sentient being tends to despise another. Due to the fact that they perform immoral deeds (*akuśalānāṁ dharmānāṁ*), more and more foods such as [earth] nectar and the others disappear. The conditions are as described in detail in the sūtras.

(42,9) Then, they gaze at each other eye to eye, and they become enamored. Then, because of their karma conducive to either femaleness or maleness, some of them acquire female organs and others male organs, and they transgress by means of copulation (*dvayadvaya-samāpatti*). Therefore, they are blamed by others (*vijugupsya-*

---

very tall?). C 287b25: 設拉末梨大樹叢林, "a forest of great śālmalī trees." C seems to understand *kūṭa* as "a multitude" or "forest."

34. S *tataḥ ṣaṇḍāvaṣaṇḍe tiṣṭhate śāliḥ*. The word *avaṣaṇḍa* is not found in any Skt. dictionary. T 20b7: *de'i 'og tu sā lu tho rtser skye bar 'gyur ro*. I cannot understand the word *tho rtse*. C 287c8 renders 粳稻叢生, "rice plants grow gregariously."

nte).[35] For that reason, they have houses built [in order to hide themselves]. And in order to secure rice, they also secure possession of fields. As a result of that, theft (*adattādāna*) and [fighting one another by] pulling and drawing (*ākarṣaṇa-parākarṣaṇa*) begin. Because of that, they establish a king as a preventer [of crimes and fighting], and he becomes the "highly honored" (*mahāsammata*). In this way the group (*maṇḍala*) of Kṣatriya as well as the groups of Brāhmaṇa, Vaiśya, and Śūdra appear in the world, as described in the sūtras.

(42,18) Darkness covers the world due to the disappearance of the light that was present in the sentient being's body. Thereafter, the sun, moon, and constellations appear in the world. The measure of the disk of the sun is fifty-one *yojana*s, and that of the disk of the moon is fifty *yojana*s. Of them, the disk of the sun is made of fire-crystal (*tejaḥ-sphaṭika*), and the disk of the moon is made of water-crystal (*udaka-sphaṭika*). Of the two, the disk of the moon is to be known as moving very fast or as moving with indefinite speed. Moreover, the sun spreads light on two continents simultaneously, and darkens two simultaneously. Thus, it makes the midday in one continent, the sunrise in the second, the midnight in the third, and the sunset in the fourth. The whole group of the moon, sun, and constellations all roll on (*gatisaṁcāra*) [in their courses] around halfway up Mount Sumeru, in other words, as high as the Yugandhara mountain. When they (or the sun)[36] roll(s) on adhering closely to Sumeru it is known as the summer season, and when they (or the sun) move(s) on far away from Sumeru it is known as the winter season. For this very reason, it should be known that [the sun] sets quickly [in winter and slowly in summer].[37] Also when the upper part of the disk of the moon becomes a little crooked,[38] a half moon is seen. [The moon] becomes invisible when the other side (*parabhāga*) [of the moon] is concealed by this side (*arvāgbhāga*).[39] The more crooked the moon

---

35. T 21a4: *de nas gzhan dag gis rnam par smad par 'gyur ro* (Thus they are blamed by others). C 287c15–16: 遂爲他人之所訶起, "They are scolded by other people."

36. Only C 287c29 has "the sun" instead of "they."

37. S *kṣipraṁ astagamanaṁ veditavyaṁ* seems to be incomplete. T 21b2: *myur du nub pa dang ring zhig nas nub par 'gyur bar rig par bya'o.* C 288a2: 即由此故沒有遲速, "There are the late and early settings [of the sun]."

38. T 21b3 has *steng du 'dzur ba na* . C 288a3 於上稍欹 agrees with T.

39. The meanings of *parabhāga* and *arvāgbhāga* are not clear to me. T 21b3 : *des pha rol gyi ngos de tshu rol gyi ngos kyis sgribs pa'i phyir mi snang ste.* C 288a3–4, however, says: 由彼餘分障其近分遂令不見, "As this side is concealed by the other side, [the moon] becomes invisible [at last]." I follow T in this translation. Considering

becomes, the more close to full it appears. In a waning moon (*kṛṣṇa-pakṣe*), on the contrary, the lower its head moves down, the more diminished it appears. When the reflections of fish, turtles, and so on in the great ocean appear [on the moon], dark color[40] is seen on the middle of the moon. As to the size of the constellations, the greater ones[41] are eighteen *krośa*s in size, middle ones are ten *krośa*s, and small ones are four *krośa*s.

(43,15) When the four castes (*varṇa*) have been created, [sentient beings] begin to create karmas, agreeable or disagreeable, which are to be felt as [one of the] five kinds of existences (*pañcagati-vedanīya*). In this manner, a certain being is born [in the hells][42] as King Yama due to his defiled karma conducive to overlordship (*saṁkliṣṭenādhipatya-saṁvartanīyena karmaṇā*). Thereupon hell guards are born as are magical creations (*nirmitopama*). Iron, copper, and so on, with which torment and torture are performed, and the fires of hell[43] appear. Then sentient beings, following karmas they have made, are born there [in hell] or in other states of existence.

VI The Field of a Buddha

(44,3) In this way, a billion (*koṭiśata*) worlds, each of which includes the four continents (*cāturdvīpaka*), a billion Sumerus, a billion groups of gods belonging to the world of desire, and a billion Brahma worlds are regenerated or destroyed at the same time in a world system of a triple thousand great thousand worlds.[44] They are also [classified into] three kinds of world systems: (1) a small world system consisting of one thousand worlds (*sāhasrikaś cūḍika*s) is so called when a thousand moons, a thousand suns, and [everything else in a system] on up to a thousand Brahma worlds are heaped together into one system; (2) a middle world system consists of the square of a small world system

---

T and C, the Sanskrit should be understood as: *yadā tasya parabhāgo 'rvāgbhāgāvṛto tadā candramaṇḍalaṁ na dṛśyate*.

40. S *śyāmatā*, with which C 288a7 黒相 agrees. T 21b4, however, has instead *ri ri po*, which is not known to me.

41. S *parama* should be corrected into *paramāṇām* as the editor suggests. T 21b4 reads not *nang gi tshe* as the editor notes, but *nang gi che ba*.

42. T 21b5 *sems can dmyal ba rnams na*, and C 288a 11 生那落迦中作靜息王, suggest the addition.

43. S should be read following the Tibetan understanding the editor mentions in his note: *yātanā-kāraṇā-nirvartakā loha-tāmrādayo nārakaś cāgniḥ*.

44. A world system consisting of the cube of one thousand small worlds.

(*dvisāhasro madhyamaḥ*,[45] square of one thousand worlds); (3) a thousand of a thousand middle world systems form a world system of a triple thousand great thousand worlds (*trisāhasra mahāsāhasra lokadhātu*, i.e., cube of a small world system).

(44,9) In this way, worlds are destroyed and regenerated in the eastern direction, southern, western, [northern],[46] upper and lower directions without end and without limit. Just as when the god Īṣādhāra sends rain[47] there are no interruptions nor intervals in the showers falling in all the directions, so worlds are destroyed and regenerated without end and without limit in all the directions.

(44,14) This[48] triple thousand great thousand world system is called the field of a Buddha (*buddhakṣetra*), and there Tathāgatas are born and perform the deeds of the Buddha (*buddhakarman*) in infinite worlds.

---

45. The editor suggests the emendation of *madhyaḥ* into *madhyamaḥ*.

46. S lacks "northern," which both T 22a2 and C 288a20 have.

47. The text is to be emended. The reading at 44.10, *varṣādhāre*, is evidently wrong. T 22a22 has *char pa gshol mda' tsam 'bab pa na*, and C 288a21 天雨注如車軸. *Śikṣāsamuccaya* (ed. Bendall) 247.7 has *īṣādhāro devo varṣati*, which the Tibetan translation (Derge 136b1) renders *gshol mda' tsam gyi char gyi rgyun 'bab po*. Note also that in the *Abhidharmakośabhāṣya* Hsüan-tsang renders the name Īṣādhāra 滴如車軸.

48. Both T 22a3 *de ni* and C 288a3 此 support reading *etad* for the edition's *etāvad*.

Nāgārjuna and the Tetralemma (*Catuṣkoṭi*)*

Shōryū Katsura

In a previous paper[1] I have tried to explain the logical structure of the Tetralemma (*catuṣkoṭi*) by using Venn diagrams, relying mainly upon the materials found in the *Abhidharmasamuccayabhāṣya*. The aim of the present paper is to apply the same analytical method to Nāgārjuna's uses of the Tetralemma in his main work, the *Mūlamadhyamakakārikā* (below, MMK).

It is my great pleasure to contribute a paper to this Festschrift for Prof. Nagao, who initiated me into the deep and vast ocean of Buddhist studies when I was a student at Kyoto University. Since my student days I have been mainly interested in how Indian Buddhists developed their logical thinking, which Prof. Nagao, if I am not wrong, did not seem to regard as an essential part of Buddhism. Today, in order to suggest to him that there is a place for logic in Buddhist philosophy, I would like to show him how even a great Buddhist philosopher like Nāgārjuna, who was at heart anti-"logic-of-his-times," can be placed in the history of development of Indian logic.

1. In the early Buddhist literature Tetralemma-forms of arguments often appear in the context of the so-called ten or fourteen "unexplicated points" (*avyākṛtavastu*). Just for the sake of convenience I quote the more or less standard versions from the *Prasannapadā* [446.9–14].

(1) "The world is eternal." *śāśvato lokaḥ.*
(2) "The world is non-eternal." *aśāśvato lokaḥ.*
(3) "The world is both eternal and non-eternal." *śāśvataś cāśāśvataś ca lokaḥ.*
(4) "The world is neither eternal nor non-eternal." *naiva śāśvato nāśāśvataś ca lokaḥ.*

(5) "The world is finite." *antavān lokaḥ.*

---

* An early version of this paper was presented at the annual meeting of the Japanese Association of Indian and Buddhist Studies held at Musashino Women's College on May 22, 1994. I would like to thank those who offered me their comments on that presentation.

1. Katsura 1993.

(6) "The world is infinite." *anantavān lokaḥ.*
(7) "The world is both finite and infinite." *antavāṁś cānantavāṁś ca lokaḥ.*
(8) "The world is neither finite nor infinite." *naivāntavān nānantavāṁś ca lokaḥ.*

(9) "The Tathāgata exists after death." *bhavati tathāgataḥ paraṁ maraṇāt.*
(10) "The Tathāgata does not exist after death." *na bhavati tathāgataḥ paraṁ maraṇāt.*
(11) "The Tathāgata both exists and does not exist after death." *bhavati ca na bhavati ca tathāgataḥ paraṁ maraṇāt.*
(12) "The Tathāgata neither exists nor does not exist after death." *naiva bhavati na na bhavati ca tathāgataḥ paraṁ maraṇāt.*

(13) "The soul is identical with the body." *sa jīvas tac charīram.*
(14) "The soul is different from the body." *anyo jīvo 'nyac charīram.*

Not only the well-known episodes of Māluṅkyaputta and Vacchagotta,[2] but also that related to Sañjaya-Velaṭṭhaputta in the *Sāmaññaphalasutta*,[3] seem to suggest that those fourteen unexplicated points are "questions put to various religious leaders by disputants as ready reckoners of each system."[4] At least some of the points might well have been held by non-Buddhist teachers of the Buddha's time, for the *Brahmajālasutta* refers to and criticizes sixty-two such speculative views (*diṭṭhi*s) held by non-Buddhists.

The first three sets of four propositions can be called a "Tetralemma" and be formally restated as follows:

(a) "x is A,"
(b) "x is non-A,"
(c) "x is both A and non-A," and
(d) "x is *neither* A *nor* non-A."

The last two points, (13) and (14), which can be called a "Dilemma" (*dvikoṭi*), were not expanded into four probably because the notions of identity and difference were considered to be complementary,

---

2. Andersen, *A Pāli Reader* (Copenhagen, 1917): 92–95.
3. *Dīgha Nikāya* i.58–59.
4. Gunaratne 1986:229.

which prohibited the Buddhist exegetes from constructing the possible third and fourth points:

*(15) "The soul is both identical with and different from the body," and

*(16) "The soul is neither identical with nor different from the body."

These must have been regarded as contradictory or meaningless.

This in turn seems to indicate that the third formula of the Tetralemma, "x is A and non-A," should not be discarded as contradictory as some modern scholars have done. Consequently, the fourth formula, too, must be regarded as meaningful. As Jayatilleke [1967:78–79] and others have noted, one can avoid the contradiction in the third formula by interpreting it as "x is partly A and partly non-A" or "x is A in one sense and non-A in another." For example, the *Brahmajālasutta*[5] explains point (7) above by suggesting that someone might conceive that "the world is finite vertically and infinite horizontally." As Ruegg [1977: 21] points out, Nāgārjuna himself alludes to and rejects such an interpretation of the third formula (MMK 27.17, 25). Now, as long as the third formula does not involve any contradiction, the fourth formula can be interpreted rationally. Either subject "x" is empty or it is incapable of being predicated by A or non-A. In any case, the fourth formula has a perfectly independent and legitimate meaning.

In this connection I would like to propose another solution to the riddle by applying the theory of two types of negation developed by Indian grammarians. The grammarians have two concepts of negation expressed by the negative particle (*na/a-/an-*), namely *Paryudāsa* and *Prasajya-pratiṣedha*. Although modern writers have given various interpretations to these two terms, in this connection, I believe, it is sufficient to mention that the *Paryudāsa* negation ("non-A"), which always implies the affirmation of something other than that which is negated (A), presupposes the complementary relation between A and non-A and hence it does not permit the third possibility (A and non-A/neither A nor non-A), while the *Prasajya* negation, which is considered to be a mere negation (*nivṛttimātra*) without any positive implication, does not presuppose such a relation and consequently allows the third and more possibilities.

5. *Dīgha Nikāya* i.23.

When the negative particle is used in a Sanskrit sentence, we must be careful to judge whether it is used in a *Paryudāsa* or in a *Prasajya-pratiṣedha.* If it is used in the former sense, the Laws of Non-Contradiction, Double Negation, and Excluded Middle are safely presupposed. But if it is used in the latter sense, these three Laws are not necessarily presupposed. Thus, the third formula "x is both A and non-A" becomes contradictory if the negation involved is *Paryudāsa*; it is not so if the negation is *Prasajya-pratiṣedha*. In the former case, the Tetralemma should be reduced to the Dilemma as in points (13) and (14) above. In the latter case one can have a legitimate Tetralemma, whose fourth formula refers to a part of our universe of discourse, as Jayatilleke [1967: 80] says. As far as the interpretation of the Tetralemma formulae found in the early Buddhist literature is concerned, I agree with Jayatilleke [1967: 70] who considers that the four propositions are mutually exclusive and together exhaustive; in this regard I would also like to mention my high respect for the results of the analysis given by Gunaratne [1980].

Thus, if we take the negation of "non-A" as *Prasajya-pratiṣedha*, the Tetralemma can be reformulated as follows:

(a′) "x is A but *not* non-A,"
(b′) "x is *not* A but rather non-A,"
(c′) "x is both A and non-A," and
(d′) "x is *neither* A *nor* non-A."

The italicized negatives in the above formulae should be interpreted as *Paryudāsa*. If we symbolize *Paryudāsa* negation by "~" and *Prasajya-pratiṣedha* by "-," then we can further reformulate the above four propositions as follows:

(a″) "x is A&~-A,"
(b″) "x is ~A&-A,"
(c″) "x is A&-A," and
(d″) "x is ~A&~-A."

It is to be noted that the Law of Double Negation does not apply in the expressions like "*not* non-A" and "*nor* non-A" (= ~-A). As I mentioned above, the Law applies only in the case: ~~A = A. Furthermore, the expression "A&-A" does not violate the Law of Contradiction because the negation should be taken in the sense of *Prasajya-pratiṣedha*. The four predicates of the above formulae, namely {A&~-A, ~A&-A, A&-A, and ~A&~-A}, together make up the four compartments of a Venn diagram:

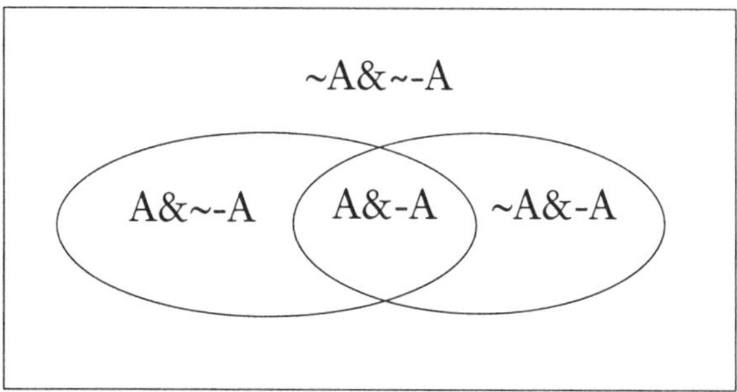

The Tetralemma is a method to enumerate all the theoretically or logically possible propositions or views (*dṛṣṭi*) with regard to a pair of concepts, such as eternity or non-eternity, finity or infinity, and existence or non-existence after death. In any case, the Buddha is said to have remained silent when he was questioned about those fourteen propositions, probably because he thought them to be unessential and even unhelpful to the Buddhist goal of enlightenment. It is to be noted in this connection that he never used the Tetralemma positively in order to express or explain his own views or teachings.

2. If we turn to the Vinaya, Abhidharma, or Yogācāra literatures, we will find that the Tetralemma is used for the purpose of enumerating all the possible relations between two terms or concepts. For example, with respect to eyes (A) and ears (B), people can be divided into four groups, namely (a) those who have eyes but not ears (+A-B), (b) those who have ears but not eyes (-A+B), (c) those who have both eyes and ears (+A+B), and (d) those who have neither eyes nor ears (-A-B). These four predicates {+A-B, -A+B, +A+B, -A-B} respectively occupy the four compartments of a Venn diagram.[6]

In this connection I would like to call the Tetralemma-type of analysis a "Method of Enumeration" by which one can enumerate all the possible combinations of two items. When one of the four combinations is impossible because of doctrinal or some other reasons, we will have a Trilemma (*trikoṭi*), and when two of them are impossible, we will have a Dilemma (*dvikoṭi*).

It may be interesting to note in passing that, in order to analyze the relations among dharmas, the Abhidharma exegetes often employ pairs (*dvika/duka*) or trios (*trika/tika*) of topics, whose lists are called

6. For more details, see Katsura 1993.

"*Mātṛkā/Mātikā.*" The Theravāda's *Dhammasaṁgani* lists one hundred such pairs headed by "cause and non-cause" (*hetu/na hetu*) and "defilement and non-defilement" (*kilesa/na kilesa*) and twenty-two trios headed by "good, bad and neutral" (*kusala/akusala/avyākata*).[7] The Sarvāstivādin's *Prakaraṇa*[8] also has a similar list of pairs, such as "material and non-material"(*rūpin/arūpin*), "visible and invisible" (*sanidarśana/anidarśana*), "with resistance and without resistance" (*sapratigha/apratigha*), "defiled and undefiled" (*sāsrava/anāsrava*), and "conditioned and unconditioned" (*saṁskṛta/asaṁskṛta*), and of trios, such as "good, bad and neutral." It also contains a list of sets of four topics, such as the Four Noble Truths, and those of five or more topics.

One of the main endeavors of the Abhidharma exegetes is to try to analyze and classify various dharmas mentioned in the early canon in accordance with those *Mātṛkā*s. As a matter of fact, the idea of classifying dharmas according to numbers goes back to the *Saṅgītiparyāya* and the *Dasottarasuttanta*. I wonder whether the *Mātṛkā* might have given a stimulus to the rise of what I call the Method of Enumeration among the Buddhist exegetes. Anyway, such a topic-wise analysis of dharmas can easily be formulated into the Dilemma, Trilemma, Tetralemma, and so on. Before moving on to Nāgārjuna, I would like to reemphasize that in the Vinaya, Abhidharma, and Yogācāra literatures the Tetralemma is used positively in order to analyze their universes of discourse and to enumerate all the possible relations between two items.

3.1. Generally speaking, Nāgārjuna seems to follow the Buddha's attitude towards the fourteen unexplicated points.[9] While the Buddha remained silent in the face of those questions, Nāgārjuna outright rejected them. For instance, MMK 25.17 reads:

> It should not be conjectured that the Blessed One exists after cessation (i.e., death). Nor should it be conjectured that He does not exist or both [exists and does not exist] or neither [exists nor does not exist after the cessation].
>
> *paraṁ nirodhād bhagavān bhavatīty eva nohyate*[10] |
> *na bhavaty ubhayaṁ ceti nobhayaṁ ceti nohyate* | |

---

7. Warder 1961.

8. Taishō 1542 (XXVI) 711b–713c.

9. Cf. Nagao 1955.

10. de Jong's edition of MMK reads: *nājyate* instead of *nohyate* in *padas* b & d.

Nāgārjuna also refers to and criticizes in MMK, chapter 27, speculative views similar to those found in the *Brahmajālasutta*.

Nāgārjuna's main aim in composing MMK seems to have been to criticize the Ābhidharmikas' interpretation of the Buddha's teaching of "dependent origination" (*pratītiyasamutpāda*), as we learn from the MMK's *maṅgalaśloka*, and to reinterpret dependent origination through his philosophy of "emptiness" (*śūnyatā*) (MMK 24.18). For that purpose he usually tries to enumerate all the theoretically possible positions with regard to a certain philosophical or doctrinal concept. Naturally he resorts to the Tetralemma, Trilemma, and Dilemma as the Method of Enumeration. Then Nāgārjuna rejects all positions by means of *reductio ad absurdum* (*prasaṅga*).

The best example of Nāgārjuna's logical argument is found in MMK, chapter 25, where he examines whether Nirvāṇa is existence (*bhāva*) or non-existence (*abhāva*). In this connection he is clearly assuming the following four positions:

(17) "Nirvāṇa is existence [but *not* non-existence],"
(18) "Nirvāṇa is [*not* existence but rather] non-existence,"
(19) "Nirvāṇa is both existence and non-existence," and
(20) "Nirvāṇa is *neither* existence *nor* non-existence."[11]

Positions (17) and (18) may represent the Sarvāstivādin and the Sautrāntika, respectively, for the former takes Nirvāṇa to be an "unconditioned" (*asaṁskṛta*) dharma which is by definition real (*paramārthasat*) and the latter considers the unconditioned dharma to be unreal.

Nāgārjuna rejects the above four positions one by one by applying a *reductio ad absurdum*. It runs as follows:

[I] First of all, it is not the case that Nirvāṇa is **existence**. [If it were existence,] it would follow (*prasajyeta*) that [Nirvāṇa was] characterized by old age and death. For there is no existence without old age and death.

bhāvas tāvan na nirvāṇaṁ jarāmaraṇam |
prasajyetāsti bhāvo hi na jarāmaraṇaṁ vinā | | 25.4

And if Nirvāṇa were existence, it would be conditioned [by cause and conditions]. For there is no unconditioned existence anywhere.

---

11. Cf. *Prasannapadā* 524.10–11: *ye tu sarvakalpanopaśamarūpaṁ nirvāṇam apratipadyamānā bhāvābhāvatadubhayānubhayarūpaṁ nirvāṇaṁ parikalpayanti tān praty ucyate* | |

bhāvaś ca yadi nirvāṇaṁ nirvāṇaṁ saṁskṛtaṁ bhavet |
nāsaṁskṛto hi vidyate bhāvaḥ kva cana kaś cana | | 25.5

Furthermore, if Nirvāṇa were existence, how could it be independent (*anupādāya*)? For there is no existence independent [of something else].

bhāvaś ca yadi nirvāṇaṁ anupādāya tat katham |
nirvānaṁ nānupādāya kaścid bhāvo hi vidyate | | 25.6

[II] How can Nirvāṇa become **non-existence**, if it is not existence? For there is no non-existence with reference to that of which there is no existence.

yadi bhāvo[12] *na nirvāṇam abhāvaḥ kiṁ bhaviṣyati* |
nirvāṇaṁ yatra bhāvo na nābhāvas tatra vidyate | | 25.7

And if Nirvāna were non-existence, how could it be independent? For there is no non-existence which is independent [of something else].

yady abhāvaś ca nirvāṇam anupādāya tat katham |
nirvāṇaṁ na hy abhāvo 'sti yo 'nupādāya vidyate | | 25.8

[III] If Nirvāṇa were **both existence and non-existence**, Liberation (*mokṣa*) would be both existence and non-existence. But that is not reasonable.

bhaved abhāvo bhāvaś ca nirvāṇam ubhayaṁ yadi |
bhaved abhāvo bhāvaś ca mokṣas tac ca na yujyate | | 25.11

If Nirvāṇa were both existence and non-existence, it would not be independent. For both [existence and non-existence] are dependent [on something else].

bhaved abhāvo bhāvaś ca nirvāṇam ubhayaṁ yadi |
nānupādāya nirvāṇam upādāyobhayaṁ hi tat | | 25.12

How could Nirvāṇa be both existence and non-existence? [For] Nirvāṇa is unconditioned, while both existence and non-existence are conditioned.

bhaved abhāvo bhāvaś ca nirvāṇam ubhayaṁ katham |
asaṁskṛtaṁ ca[13] *nirvāṇaṁ bhāvābhāvau ca saṁskṛtau* | | 25.13

How could both existence and non-existence belong to Nirvāṇa? For both cannot exist in one and the same place as in the case of light and darkness.

bhaved abhāvo bhāvaś ca nirvāṇa ubhayaṁ katham |
tayor abhāvo hy ekatra prakāśatamasor iva[14] | | 25.14

12. de Jong reads: *bhāvo yadi*.

13. de Jong reads *hi*, which may be a better reading.

14. de Jong provides this second line, which was missing in the MSS consulted by La Vallée Poussin.

[IV] The assertion that Nirvāṇa is **neither existence nor non-existence** is proven only when both existence and non-existence are proven.

naivābhāvo naiva bhāvo nirvānam iti yāñjanā |
abhāve caiva bhāve ca sā siddhe sati sidhyati | | 25.15

If Nirvāṇa exists as neither existence nor non-existence, how can it be [actually] asserted that it is neither existence nor non-existence?

naivābhāvo naiva bhāvo nirvāṇaṁ yadi vidyate |
naivābhāvo naiva bhāva iti kena tad ajyate | | 25.16

I am not going to discuss the contents of the above argument. I just want to show the structure of Nāgārjuna's argument. If we represent Nirvāṇa by "N," existence by "A," and non-existence by "B," we can simplify the arguments in the following manner:

[I] If N were A(&~B), then F (i.e., false); therefore, N is not A.
[II] If N were (~A&)B, then F; therefore, N is not B.
[III] If N were A&B, then F; therefore, N is not A&B.
[IV] If N were ~A&~B, then F; therefore, N is not ~A&~B.

It is clear that Nāgārjuna rejects propositions (17), (18), (19), and (20) by means of *reductio ad absurdum*. His goal is to prove that Nirvāṇa cannot be predicated by any ontological concept, such as existence and non-existence. Moreover, Nirvāṇa is beyond any conceptual construction or it is of the nature of cessation of every kind of conceptual constructions (*sarvakalpanākṣayarūpam eva nirvāṇam*).[15] In this sense, it is said that Nirvāṇa is "neither existence nor non-existence" (*na bhāvo nābhāvo nirvāṇam*),[16] which should not be taken to be contradictory to Nāgārjuna's negation of proposition (20).[17]

3.2. A Japanese logician, Masao Yamashita, once argued that various philosophical thoughts could be classified into two groups, namely, Conceptualism (分別主義) which respects the value of "structure" (構造) and Non-conceptualism (無分別主義) which respects the value of "non-structure." He suggested that Nāgārjuna's philosophy of emptiness may belong to the second group. However, as Yamashita concluded, "philosophy of non-structure cannot exist by itself; it can exist only with reference to some well-established structure."[18] Yamashita's analysis seems to be supported by Nāgārjuna's uses of the

---

15. *Prasannapadā*:524.6.
16. MMK 25.10cd.
17. See Ruegg 1977:16–18.
18. Yamashita 1984:266.

Tetralemma. For, in order to prove that reality (*tattva*), either mundane or supermundane, is free from our conceptual constructions, Nāgārjuna should be able to grasp the structure of our universe of discourse by means of the Tetralemma and other techniques.

It is often the case in MMK that the structure assumed by Nāgārjuna represents different positions of the opponents of his time. For example, MMK 1.1 reads:

> There is nothing whatsoever anywhere which has arisen from itself, from others, from both, or from no cause.
>
> *na svato nāpi parato na dvābhyāṁ nāpy ahetutaḥ* |
> *utpannā jātu vidyante bhāvāḥ kva cana ke cana* | |

More precisely, the above verse can be put into the following four negative propositions:

(21) "It is not the case that there is something somewhere which has arisen from itself." (*na svata utpannā jātu vidyante bhāvāḥ kva cana ke cana.*)

(22) "It is also not the case that there is something somewhere which has arisen from others." (*nāpi parato utpannā jātu vidyante bhāvāḥ kva cana ke cana.*)

(23) "It is not the case that there is something somewhere which has arisen from both itself and others." (*na dvābhyām utpannā jātu vidyante bhāvāḥ kva cana ke cana.*)

(24) "It is also not the case that there is something somewhere which has arisen from non-cause." (*nāpy ahetuta utpannā jātu vidyante bhāvāḥ kva cana ke cana.*)

It is clear that these propositions are the negation of the following four positions, if we may put them in a little simpler form:

(25) "Something has arisen from itself [but *not* from others]."

(26) "Something has arisen from others [but *not* from itself]."

(27) "Something has arisen from both itself and others."

(28) "Something has arisen from no cause (i.e., *neither* from itself *nor* from others)."

If we change the subject of the above four propositions from "something" to "everything," (25) corresponds to the Sāṁkhya view of causation, i.e., *satkāryavāda*, and (26) to the Vaiśeṣika view of *asatkāryavāda*; (27) seems to correspond to the traditional Buddhist view found in the Abhidharma literature, while (28) may refer to the views of those who deny causation altogether, such as the *svabhāvavāda* of the Lokāyata according to whom everything occurs naturally through its own-nature (*svabhāva*) and without any particular cause.

If we symbolize "having arisen from itself" by "A" and "having arisen from others" by "B," the predicates of (25), (26), (27), and (28) will be represented by {A&~B, ~A&B, A&B, and ~A&~B} which occupy the four compartments of a Venn diagram. Thus, logically speaking, they exhaust all the possible modes of arising; consequently, we can say that the above four propositions represent all the possible theories of causation.

In the following verses of MMK chapter 1 Nāgārjuna does not give the *reductio ad absurdum* type of argument against the above four positions; instead he goes on to criticize the Abhidharma theories of four "conditions" (*pratyaya*). Let us reconstruct the probable *reductio ad absurdum* with the help of Candrakīrti.

(I) If something arose from itself, it would follow that there was no merit in arising. It is in fact incorrect that what has already arisen arises again.[19]

(II) If something arose from others, it would follow that anything arose from anything else as darkness from a lamp, which is absurd.[20]

(III) If something arose from both itself and others, it would follow that there resulted both defects mentioned with reference to the above two propositions.[21]

(IV) If something arose from no cause, it would follow that everything arose from everything all the time.[22]

Thus it is demonstrated that nothing is predicated by any possible mode of arising. Therefore, it is concluded that there is no arising (*nāsty utpādaḥ*)[23] or nothing arises in the ultimate sense (*paramārthataḥ*).

3.3. Only twice in MMK did Nāgārjuna use the Tetralemma or Trilemma positively in order to sum up the various teachings of the Buddha found in the early canon. Concerning the concepts of "Self" (*ātman*) and "non-Self" (*anātman*), Nāgārjuna states as follows:

> On the one hand, the Buddhas have tentatively stated that there is Self; and on the other hand, they have taught that there is non-Self; they have also taught that there is neither Self nor non-Self whatsoever.

---

19. *Prasannapadā*: 13.7–8.
20. *Ibid.*: 36.6 ff.
21. *Ibid.*: 38.1.
22. *Ibid.*: 38.10–11.
23. *Ibid.*: 39.6.

ātmety api prajñapitam anātmety api deśitam |
buddhair nātmā na cānātmā kaścid ity api deśitam | | (18.6)

The following Trilemma is presupposed here:

(29) "There is Self [but *not* non-Self]."
(30) "There is [*not* Self but rather] non-Self."
(31) "There is *neither* Self *nor* non-Self."

If we follow Candrakīrti,[24] Nāgārjuna is proposing here that there are three different levels in the teachings of Buddhas concerning "Self." Namely, towards ordinary people who deny even the conventional truths, such as existence of the other world (*paraloka*) and fruition of the results of human actions (*karmaphalavipāka*), in order to deny their wrong views, Buddhas may say that there is Self, so that those people can easily understand, for example, the doctrine of transmigration. Towards those who have strong attachment to themselves and their possessions even after having been initiated into religious life, in order to deny their wrong belief in a real Self (*satkāyadṛṣṭi*), the Buddhas may teach that there is non-Self, i.e., there is no Self. And finally, towards those who are highly qualified disciples, Buddhas may teach from the ultimate point of view that there is neither Self nor non-Self. This is the middle path between the two extreme views of Self and non-Self. In this connection it is to be noted that the usual third lemma, namely, *"There is both Self and non-Self," is missing, probably because such a proposition presents a mere contradiction, for the two concepts, namely, Self and non-Self, are in a complementary relationship.

Furthermore, concerning the concept of "all" (*sarva*), Nāgārjuna states as follows:

> All is true (*tathya*); or [all is] untrue (*atathya*); [all is] both true and untrue; [all is] neither true nor untrue—this is the teaching of the Buddhas.

sarvaṁ tathyaṁ na vā tathyaṁ tathyaṁ cātathyam eva ca |
naivātathyaṁ naiva tathyam etad buddhānuśāsanam | | (18.8)

The following Tetralemma can be reconstructed:

(32) "All is true [but *not* untrue]."
(33) "All is [*not* true but rather] untrue."
(34) "All is both true and untrue."
(35) "All is *neither* true *nor* untrue."

---

24. *Ibid.*: 356–358.

This is again a sort of graded presentation of the Buddhas' teachings. According to Candrakīrti,[25] (32) represents the Buddhas' teachings of the Five Groups, Twelve Spheres, Eighteen Elements, and so on, which accord well with the conventional truths, and (33) may correspond to the doctrine of Momentariness which from the Buddhist point of view denies the common belief in lasting entities. (34) involves no contradiction, if we interpret it according to Candrakīrti,[26] namely, the Buddhas have taught to ordinary people (*bālajana*) that all is true and to the sages (*āryajana*) that all is untrue or false (*mṛṣā*). (35) is meant for those who have already practiced the true insight for a long time but have not yet removed the obstacles completely. Therefore, it can be said that (35) represents the highest level of the Buddhas' teachings.

For a more detailed discussion of the above two verses, one may refer to the discussions of Ruegg [1977:5–9]. I just want to point out that Nāgārjuna, too, used the Tetralemma and Trilemma in a positive way in order to list all the possible teachings of the Buddha in a certain context. In other words, if I may repeat, the Tetralemma is used as the Method of Enumeration.

3.4. Now let us glance at Nāgārjuna's use of the Trilemma. MMK 2.1 gives a good example. It reads as follows:

> First of all, the "traversed" (*gata*) is not being traversed (*gamyate*). The "untraversed" (*agata*) is not being traversed. The "being traversed" (*gamyamāna*) independent of the "traversed" and the "untraversed" is not being traversed.
>
> *gataṁ na gamyate tāvad agataṁ naiva gamyate* |
> *gatāgatavinirmuktaṁ gamyamānaṁ na gamyate* | |

It is clear that the following three propositions are negated in the above verse:

(36) "The 'traversed' is being traversed." (*gataṁ gamyate*)
(37) "The 'untraversed' is being traversed." (*agataṁ gamyate*)
(38) "The 'being traversed' is being traversed." (*gamyamānaṁ gamyate*)

---

25. *Ibid.*: 370–371.

26. *Ibid.*: 371.8–9: *keṣāṁ cit sarvam etat tathyaṁ cātathyam eva ceti deśitaṁ* | *tatra bālajanāpekṣayā sarvam etat tathyaṁ* | *āryajñānā(sic!)pekṣayā tu sarvam etan mṛṣā* | *tair evam anupalambhād iti* | |

The subjects of the propositions correspond to the three divisions of time, namely, past, future, and present. (36) and (37) can be rejected simply because they both involve some sort of incompatibility (*virodha*). The "traversed" or the path that has been traversed in the past cannot be said to be being traversed at present, nor can the "untraversed" or the path that has not yet been traversed. The present act of traversing is incompatible with the past and future paths of traversing. (38) does not involve such incompatibility but the verse seems to reject the very notion of the "being traversed." Nāgārjuna seems to insist that there is no third possibility of the path being traversed independent of the traversed and untraversed paths. Such an argument is quite possible, if one takes the negative particle of the compound "*agata*" (untraversed) in the sense of a *Paryudāsa* negation, as I discussed above.[27]

In this connection it is to be noted that if one takes the negative particle in the sense of *Prasajya-pratiṣedha*, there arises the possibility of the present-tense expression, which accords very well to our linguistic convention. If we use the vocabulary of the Indian grammarians,[28] past, future, and present may be characterized by "existence" (*sat*), "non-existence" (*asat*), and "both existence and non-existence" (*sadasat*). The last compound does not necessarily involve a contradiction, if one takes the negative particle in the sense of *Prasajya-pratiṣedha*.

As to proposition (38), Nāgarjuna gives a *reductio ad absurdum* type of argument. For example, he points out that if the "being traversed" were actually being traversed, it would follow that there were two acts of traversing, one of which was supposed to justify the nominal expression "the path being traversed" (*gamyamāna*) and the other to justify the verbal expression "is being traversed" (*gamyate*).[29] He goes on to discuss other concepts involved in the act of traversing, such as "traverser" (*gantṛ*) and "starting and stopping." He concludes as follows that no concepts can describe the actual act of traversing:

---

27. See Cardona 1991 and Ogawa 1991 for a detailed discussion of the above propositions from the viewpoint of Pāṇinian grammar and presentation of the subsequent arguments given by both Nāgārjuna and Candrakīrti. As they point out, opponents' arguments similar to Nāgārjuna's are found in *Mahābhāṣya* ad P.3.2.123, *Nyāyasūtra* 2.1.37, and *Vākyapadīya* III.kālasamuddeśa–85.

28. See, e.g., Helārāja ad *Vākyapadīya* III. kāla.85: *sādhyamānāvasthā kriyā bhaṇyate* | | *tatra ca yaḥ kṣaṇo'tītaḥ* | *sa san siddhasvabhāva iti kriyā tatrātītā* | | *yaś cāsan* | *sa sādhyaḥ* | *sa bhāvī kṣaṇa iti tatra bhaviṣyadupādhikā kriyā* | | *na cānyo'sti kaścit kṣaṇaḥ sadasadubhayarūpaḥ* | | *viruddhasvabhāvasyaikatvavirodhāt* | |

29. MMK 2.5.

An existent (i.e., past) traverser does not make (lit. traverse) the three kinds of traversing (namely, past, future, and present traversing).[30] A non-existent (i.e., future) traverser does not make the three kinds of traversing, either.
A both-existent-and-non-existent (i.e., present) traverser does not make the three kinds of traversing. Therefore, there is not an act of traversing, nor a traverser, nor a path to be traversed.

sadbhūto gamanaṁ gantā triprakāraṁ na gacchati |
nāsadbhūtao 'pi gamanaṁ triprakāraṁ sa gacchati | | (2.24)
gamanaṁ sadasadbhūtaḥ triprakāraṁ na gacchati |
tasmād gatiś ca gantā ca gantavyaṁ ca na vidyate | | (2.25)

The argument that nothing is established or relevant if analyzed in terms of the three divisions of time, namely, past, future, and present (*traikālyāsiddhi*), comes to be recognized by Nāgārjuna himself as the standard means of rejecting opponents' positions,[31] and there are many instances of similar Trilemma throughout MMK. It is to be noted in passing that the Indian logicians who compiled the *Nyāya-sūtra* seem to have sensed the danger of such an argument and classified it as one of the sophistical refutations (*jāti*) named "*ahetusama*," which is to be avoided by sincere disputants.[32]

Finally, let me give an instance of the Dilemma. Concerning the relation between the cause and the effect, Nāgārjuna states:

When X (i.e., a result) exists depending upon Y (i.e., a cause), X is *neither* identical with *nor* different from Y. Therefore, Y is neither annihilated nor eternal.

pratītya yad yad bhavati na hi tāvat tad eva tat |
na cānyad api tat tasmān nocchinnaṁ nāpi śāśvatam | | (18.10)

The above argument presupposes the following Destructive Dilemma:

(39) "If the result were identical with the cause, it would follow that the cause was eternal, which is improper; therefore, the result is not identical with the cause."

(40) "If the result were different from the cause, it would follow that the cause was annihilated, which is improper; therefore, the result is not different from the cause."

---

30. Cf. *Prasannapadā* 107.11: *tatra sadbhūto gantā sadbhūtam asadbhūtaṁ sadasadbhūtaṁ triprakāraṁ gamanaṁ na gacchati* | |

31. See, e.g., MMK, chapters 8 and 10.

32. *Nyāyasūtra* 5.1.18: *traikālyāsiddher hetor ahetusamaḥ.*

In short, "The result is neither identical with nor different from the cause." So, the "neither~ nor~ " formula should sometimes be understood as a shortened form of the Destructive Dilemma.

4. By now it should be clear that Nāgārjuna's way of argument is based on two strategies, namely, the Method of Enumeration and the *reductio ad absurdum*. He enumerates all the possible theoretical or doctrinal positions by means of the Tetralemma, Trilemma, or Dilemma and examines them one by one in order to find some error in every case and to reject all of them; consequently, he can suggest that reality is beyond our conceptual structures or, in other words, that everything is empty (*sarvaṁ śūnyam*).

The above procedure of argument, in fact, is not peculiar to Nāgārjuna. For example, the *Vaiśeṣikasūtra* (below, VS) uses the Method of Elimination (*pariśeṣa*) in order to prove the existence of "air" (*vāyu*) and "ether" (*ākāśa*) which are by definition invisible.[33] It is also recorded that one of the lost works of the Sāṁkhya school called the *Ṣaṣṭitantra* employed—in order to prove that all the manifested material beings (*vyakta*) come from the unmanifested (*avyakta*), hence invisible, Primordial Material (*pradhāna*)—a sort of indirect proof called *avīta* which consists of the Method of Elimination supported by *reductio ad absurdum*.[34]

The best example of an actual application of the Method of Elimination may be found in Pakṣilasvāmin's *Nyāyabhāṣya* ad *Nyāyasūtra* 1.1.5:

> [One of the three types of inference called] *Śeṣavat* is the Method of Elimination. It is a firm conviction in the remaining [possibility] (*śiṣyamāna*) when [some] theoretical possibilities (*prasakta*) are rejected and there is no other possibility (*aprasaṅga*). As for example sound (*śabda*) is differentiated from universal (*sāmānya*), particular (*viśeṣa*), and inherence (*samavāya*) by the common characteristics of substance (*dravya*), quality (*guṇa*), and action (*karman*), which are [mentioned in VS 1.1.7 as] being existent (*sat*), non-eternal (*anitya*), and so on. Then a doubt arises whether it (i.e., sound) is substance, action, or quality. [In such a case, we eliminate as follows:] it is not a substance because it possesses a single substance [as its inherent cause] (=VS 2.2.27), and it is not an action because it is the cause of another [subsequent] sound. Then it is what is remaining and thus sound is known to be a quality.[35]

---

33. VS 2.1.8–14, 2.1.24–28.

34. See Hadano 1944 and Frauwallner 1958.

Both Vaiśeṣikas and Naiyāyikas admit only the six kinds of categories, namely, substance (A), quality (B), action (C), universal (D), particular (E), and inherence (F), and they hold that anything existent, knowable, and namable, should belong to one of those six categories. A question arises concerning to which category an item called "sound" (S) belongs. Now the Method of Elimination works as follows:

(41) "If sound were universal, particular, or inherence, it would follow that it was eternal; however, it is not eternal by definition. Therefore, sound is not universal, nor particular, nor inherence."

(42) "If sound were a substance, it would follow that it either possessed many substances (*anekadravya*) like a pot, or possessed no substance (*adravya*) as its inherent causes like an atom or ether; however, sound possesses a single substance (*ekadravya*), i.e., ether, as its inherent cause. Therefore, sound is not a substance."

(43) "If sound were an action, it would follow that it could not produce another sound because an action could not result in another similar action;[36] however, it in fact results in a series of similar sounds. Therefore, sound is not an action.

(44) "Consequently, sound must belong to the only remaining category, that is, quality."

Here the universe of discourse consists of {A, B, C, D, E, and F}. Since S (i.e., sound) is demonstrated by the *reductio ad absurdum* not to belong to A, C, D, E, or F, it must belong to the only remaining possibility, B (i.e., quality). It is needless to mention that the Method of Elimination works very well within a closed ontological system, such as the six categories (*padārtha*) of the Vaieśeṣika and the twenty-five principles (*tattva*) of the Sāṁkhya.

I believe that the Method of Elimination briefly described above shares a common logical structure with Nāgārjuna's method of argument discussed in this paper. Both of them either presuppose or enumerate all the possible answers to a question, examine them one

35. *Nyāyabhāṣya* ad NS 1.1.5: *śeṣavan nāma pariśeṣaḥ* | *sa ca prasaktapratiṣedhe 'nyatrāprasaṅāc chiṣyamāne sampratyayaḥ* | *yathā sad anityam evamādinā dravyaguṇakarmāṇām aviśeṣeṇa sāmānyaviśeṣasamavāyebhyo vibhaktasya śabdasya* | *tasmin dravyakarmaguṇasaṁśaye* | *na dravyam* | *ekadravyatvāt* | *na karma* | *śabdāntarahetutvāt* | *yas tu śiṣyate so 'yam iti śabdasya guṇatvapratipattiḥ* | |. Cf. Chattopadhyaya and Gangopadhyaya 1967: 63–64.

36. Cf. VS 1.1.10.

by one through the *reductio ad absurdum*, and come to a conclusion. The only difference lies in the fact that the Method of Elimination comes up with one positive answer, while Nāgārjuna rejects all possible answers in order to indicate that every concept is empty of reality.

In conclusion I would like to point out Nāgārjuna's contribution to the development of Indian logic. One of his small treatises called *Vaidalyaprakaraṇa* is devoted to a refutation of the definitions of the sixteen categories of the Naiyāyikas, and another treatise called *Vigrahavyāvartanī* contains a severe criticism of the Naiyāyika theory of valid means of knowledge (*pramāṇa*). This clearly indicates that Nāgārjuna was very well aware of the rising danger of the realistic system of logic represented by the Naiyāyikas.

In order to refute these opponents Nāgārjuna did not resort to the common method of direct proof or counter-proof which consisted of the five statements, namely, thesis (*pratijñā*), reason (*hetu*), example (*dṛṣṭānta*), application (*upanaya*), and conclusion (*nigamana*). Instead he adopted the Method of Enumeration, such as the Tetralemma, which he inherited from the early Buddhist exegetes, and developed a new way of argument which resembled the Method of Elimination employed by the Vaiśeṣikas and Sāṁkhyas.

The essence of Nāgārjuna's argument is *reductio ad absurdum* (*prasaṅga*). It is not certain who first applied the *reductio ad absurdum* in Indian debates. However, the fact that Nāgārjuna often uses the expression "it (i.e., the undesirable consequence) would follow that ..." (*prasajyeta*) in his works may suggest that he was the one who gave formal expression to a type of the argument, which was to be called "*prasaṅga*(-*āpatti*)" or "*tarka*" by later logicians.

The compilers of the *Nyāyasūtra* must have been well aware of the destructive nature of Nāgārjuna's arguments. They record several debates with Buddhists, some of which are clearly criticisms against Nāgārjuna. Furthermore, as I mentioned above, the Naiyāyikas rejected some of the typical *prasaṅga* arguments offered by Nāgārjuna, considering them to be simply sophistical refutations (*jāti*).[37] As a matter of fact, orthodox Indian logicians like the Naiyāyikas regarded the *reductio ad absurdum* type of argument not as leading to true knowledge but as something supplementary to the direct five-membered proof.[38]

---

37. For more detailed discussion on the relationship between Nāgārjuna and *Nyāyasūtra*, see Kajiyama 1984 and 1991.

Though despised or disregarded by most Indian logicians, the *reductio ad absurdum* continued to be utilized in actual doctrinal debates in India as the most effective means to refute opponents. Not only the direct followers of Nāgārjuna, that is the Buddhist Mādhyamikas, but also non-Buddhists, such as the Cārvākas, Jainas, Vaiśeṣikas, Sāṁkhyas, and even Naiyāyikas, employed it either explicitly or implicitly to refute their opponents.

As far as the debate is concerned, I think, Indian logic should be considered to have taken two lines of development, namely, the development of direct proof by the five statements and that of indirect proof by *reductio ad absurdum*. Nāgārjuna played quite an important role in the history of Indian logic, by initiating the method of argument which was in essence *reductio ad absurdum*, and he stimulated both his successors and opponents to further develop his methodology. Perhaps he was at heart anti-logic, but he was certainly quite logical in his actual arguments.

Bibliography

Cardona, George. 1991. "A Path still taken: Some early Indian arguments concerning time." *Journal of the American Oriental Society* 111/3: 445–464.

Chattopadhyaya, Debiprasad, and Mrinalkanti Gangopadhyaya. 1967. *Nyāya Philosophy, Literal Translation of Gautama's Nyāyasūtra & Vātsyāyana's Bhāṣya along with a free and abridged translation of the Elucidation by Mahāmahopadhyāya Phaṇibhūṣaṇa Tarkavāgīśa* (Calcutta: Indian Studies Past & Present).

Dīgha Nikāya, ed. by T. W. Rhys Davids and J. E. Carpenter (Pali Text Society, 1890; reprint, 1975).

Frauwallner, Erich. 1958. "Die Erkenntnislehre des Klassischen Sāṁkhya-Systems." *Wiener Zeitschrift für die Kunde Sud- und Ostasiens* 2: 84–139.

Gunaratne, R. D. 1980. "The logical form of Catuṣkoṭi: A new solution." *Philosophy East and West* 30/2: 211–239.

———. 1986. "Understanding Nāgārjuna's catuṣkoṭi." *Philosophy East and West* 36/3: 213–235.

Hadano Hakuyū 羽田野伯猷. 1944. "Surongakuha no ronrisetsu: *vīta/avīta* ni tsuite" 数論学派の論理説、ヴィータ・アヴィータについて [*Vīta* and *avīta*, a logical theory of the Sāṁkhya school]. *Bunka* 文化 11/3: 177–219, 11–4: 300–326.

38. See *Nyāyabhāṣya* ad NS 1.1.40.

Jayatilleke, K. N. 1967. "The Logic of Four Alternatives." *Philosophy East and West* 17: 69–83.

Jong, J. W. de, ed. 1977. *Nāgārjuna's Mūlamadhyamakakārikāḥ* (Madras: The Adyar Library and Research Centre).

Kajiyama Yūichi 梶山雄一. 1984. "Bukkyō chishikiron no keisei" 仏教知識論の形成 [The formation of Buddhist logic and epistemology]. In Y. Kajiyama, ed., *Kōza Daijō Bukkyō 9—Ninshikinron to Ronrigaku* 講座大乗仏教 9 認識論と論理学 (Tokyo: Shunjūsha 春秋社): 1–101.

———. 1991. "On the authorship of the Upāyahṛdaya." In E. Steinkellner, ed., *Studies in the Buddhist Epistemological Tradition* (Wien: Österreichische Akademie der Wissenschaften): 107–117.

Katsura, Shōryū. 1993. "Tetralemma (*catuṣkoṭi*) Explained by Venn Diagrams." In Egaku Mayeda, ed., *Genshi Bukkyō to Daijō Bukkyō* 原始仏教と大乗仏教 (Kyoto: Nagata Bunshōdō 永田生慈文昌堂): 91–110.

Nagao Gadjin 長尾雅人. 1955. "Budda no chinmoku to sono chūganteki igi" 仏陀の沈黙とその中観的意義. *Tetsugaku Kenkyū* 哲學研究 430. An English version is available, "The Silence of the Buddha and its Madhyamic Interpretation." In G. M. Nagao and J. Nozawa, eds., *Yamaguchi Festshrift* (Kyoto, 1955: 137–151). This is reprinted in *Mādhyamika and Yogācāra*, ed. by L. Kawamura (Albany: State University of New York Press, 1991): 35–49.

Nyāyadarśanam with Vātsyāyana's Bhāṣya, ed. by Taranatha Nyaya-Tarkatirtha et. al., 2 vols. (Calcutta, 1936–1944; reprint: Kyoto: Rinsen, 1982).

Ogawa Hideyo 小川英世. 1991. "Gamyate, Gamyamāna, Gata, Agata—『中論』II. kk. 1–6 の一考察" [Gamyate, gamyamāna, gata, agata—A study of MMK, II. kk.1–6]. *Indogaku Bukkyōgaku Kenkyū* 印度学仏教学研究 39/2: 167–172.

Prasannapadā of Candrakīrti, ed. by Louis de La Vallée Poussin, *Bibliotheca Buddhica* IV (Reprint: Osnabrück, 1970).

Ruegg, D. Seyfort. 1977. "The Uses of the Four Positions of the *Catuṣkoṭi* and the Problem of the Description of Reality in Mahāyāna Buddhism." *Journal of Indian Philosophy* 5/1: 1–71.

Warder, A. K. 1961. "The Mātikā." *Mohavicchedanī*, PTS.

Yamashita Masao 山下正男. 1984. "Kū no ronrigaku" 空の論理学 [The logic of emptiness]. *Risō* 理想 610: 253-266.

The Middle Path According to the *Kāśyapaparivarta-sūtra*

Leslie Kawamura

It is a Buddhist view that the highest level of attainment (*pratipatti*) that one can gain by practicing the dharma in a proper way is the middle path (*madhyamapratipad*). It is known as the middle path because, in accomplishing it, one goes beyond all extreme views (*anta*). This paper will attempt to elucidate this central concern of Buddhism in the light of the discussion on the middle path found in the *Kāśyapaparivarta-sūtra*, a Mahāyāna-sūtra of the Ratnakūṭa class.

The *Kāśyapaparivarta-sūtra* was first brought to the attention of the scholarly world by Baron A. von Staël-Holstein when he edited and published in 1929 the only extant Sanskrit manuscript of the sūtra that was found near Khotan in Chinese Turkestan some thirty years earlier.[1] This Sanskrit manuscript found its way to the Leningrad Academy of Sciences and was later housed there when Mr. Petrovsky, the then Russian Consulate at Kashgar, sent the manuscript to the Academy. It was at the Academy that Staël-Holstein studied and prepared it for publication. Staël-Holstein's edition is particularly useful for research because it has, together with the Sanskrit text, four Chinese translations designated by him as the Han 漢 (the oldest text, attributed to Lou-chia-ch'an 婁迦讖 and translated during the second century C.E. in the Later Han), the Tsin 晉 (made between 265 and 420 C.E.; translator unknown), the Ch'in 秦 (made during the Ch'in dynasty 350 to 431 C.E.; translator unknown), and the Sung 宋 (made during the last decade of the tenth century in the Sung dynasty; translator Shih-hu 施護) and one Tibetan translation found in the *bka'-'gyur* section of the Tibetan Tripiṭaka made by the well-known Lotsa-bas Jinamitra, Silendrabodhi, and Ye-shes-sde, who lived in the ninth century.

The great Buddhist savant, Sthiramati (510–570), who precedes Candrakīrti (600–650), the well-known advocate of the *prasaṅga* method of the Madhyamaka, wrote a commentary (*ṭīkā*) which has been transmitted to us through a translation into Chinese by Bodhiruci

1. A. von Staël-Holstein, 大宝積経迦葉品梵蔵漢文六株種対照 *Kāśyapaparivarta, a Mahāyānasūtra of the Ratnakūṭa Class, edited in the Original Sanskrit, in Tibetan, and in Chinese* (Shanghai: Commercial Press, 1926). Hereafter, Staël-Holstein Sūtra.

(flourished circa 520 C.E.) and through a translation into Tibetan by a translator whose name is unknown.[2] In examining Bodhiruci's Chinese translation, it becomes obvious that his use of technical terms is based upon the Ch'in (秦) translation. The Tibetan and Chinese texts of Sthiramati's *ṭīkā* do not always agree.

In more recent years, Friedrich Weller's translation into German, *Zum Kāśyapaparivarta* (Berlin, 1965) and his research on the text in *Mitteilungen des Instituts für Orientforschung*, XII–4, 1966 have appeared.[3] I was unable to consult these works, as they are not readily available in Calgary. Gadjin M. Nagao has translated the sūtra into Japanese in the series, *Daijō Butten*,[4] edited by him. There is also an English translation in *A Treasury of Mahāyāna Sūtras: Selections from the Mahāratnakūṭa Sūtra.*[5]

In his edition, Staël-Holstein divided the manuscript into 166 sections. In his translation into Japanese, Nagao grouped and arranged those sections into thirteen major chapters containing forty-five topics in accordance with the Tibetan translation of Sthiramati's commentary. The relationship between Staël-Holstein's 166 sections and Nagao's thirteen chapters [roman numerals I–XIII] consisting of forty-five topics is as follows:

Contents of the *Kāśyapaparivarta-sūtra*

I. The Eight Erroneous and Eight Correct Practices of a Bodhisattva

Sections

1–2 1. Practices that diminish and that increase a Bodhisattva's understanding.

3–4 2. Practices that obstruct and that aid the occurrence of a mind bent towards enlightenment.

---

2. A. von Staël-Holstein, *A Commentary to the Kāśyapaparivarta edited in Tibetan and in Chinese* (Peking: The National Library of Peking and the National Tsinghua University, 1933). Hereafter, Staël-Holstein Commentary. See p. x: "Our Tibetan codices give us no information as to who translated the commentary into Tibetan, but all our Chinese codices contain the following note: 後魏北印度三蔵菩提流支譯."

3. For this information, see G. Nagao and H. Sakurabe, trans., "Hōshakubu kyōten" 宝積部経典 [Mahāyāna Sūtras of the Ratnakūṭa Class], in G. M. Nagao and Y. Kajiyama, eds., *Daijō Butten* 大乗仏典 9 (Tokyo: Chūōkōronsha, 1974): 6, n. 3.

4. *Ibid.*

5. *A Treasury of Mahāyāna Sūtras: Selections from the Mahāratnakūta Sūtras.* C. C. Chang, General Editor (University Park: Pennsylvania State University, 1983).

5–6 3. Practices that impede and that advance positive qualities.
7–8 4. Practices that warp the mind and that keep it aligned.
9–10 5. Practices that exhaust and that refresh discipline.
11–12 6. Practices that trip one and that support one on the path.
13–14 7. Practices of selecting bad companions or good companions.
15–16 8. Practices that are artificial and that are genuine.

17–22 II. Virtues that Result from Correct Practices

III. The Thirty-two Defining Characteristics of the Bodhisattva

23 1. Five practices that are superior to those of a śrāvaka.
23–24 2. Ten practices that are attentive to the principle of equality.
24–25 3. Six perfections that constitute positive qualities.
25 4. Eleven practices that solidly establish appropriate actions.
26–28 5. Summation of the thirty-two in verse form.

IV. Twenty-two Similes that Define Characteristics of the Bodhisattva

29–32 1. The Bodhisattva as the place where a seed is planted and nourished.
33–35 2. A Bodhisattva as becoming accomplished himself and as bringing others to fruition.
36–39 3. A Bodhisattva as neither attached to Nirvāṇa nor afflicted by saṁsāra.
40–51 4. A Bodhisattva as one who sees the benefiting aspects of afflictions.

V. The Hub of the Bodhisattva Practice—The Middle Path

52–55 1. The Middle Path as contrasted to the path of the outsiders and the śrāvakas.
56–60 2. The Middle Path in view of the error of taking existence as non-existent and non-existence as existent.
61–62 3. The *dvadaśāṅgapratītyasamutpāda* and the Middle Path.
63 4 The Middle Path as the seven kinds of knowledge.
64–65 5. *Śūnyatā*- and *ātma-dṛṣṭi*—simile of medicine and illness.
66–67 6. Those who fear *śūnyatā*.
68–71 7. *Śūnyatā* and its actuality.

VI. The Bodhisattva as Superior to the Śrāvaka

72–75 1. The bodhisattva, flower that blooms from the mire of affliction.
76–79 2. The bodhisattva's positive qualities are greater than those of the śrāvakas.
80–83 3. Similes of the Cakravartin's family lineage and attributes.
84–92 4. Various similes regarding the Bodhisattva.

VII. Actualization of the Practice of Benefiting Others

93–96 1. The bodhisattva practice of remaining in the mire of the everyday world.

97–102 2. An investigation of mind by means of trans-worldly knowledge.
103–104 3. The bodhisattva family (*gotra*).

VIII. How are the Śrāvakas to Enter the Mahāyāna?

105–110 1. Simile of a dog that chases a rock.
111–120 2. Various points to be considered by a śramaṇa.

IX. Inauthentic Śramaṇa and Authentic Śramaṇa

121 [Introductory words]
122–124 1. Three kinds of disreputable śramaṇas.
125 2. Reputable śramaṇa.
126 3. Verses regarding the four kinds of śramaṇa.
127–133 4. Various unworthy and worthy virtues.

X. The Ill-behaved and the Well-conducted

134 1. The four ill-behaved not worthy of imitating.
135 2. The bodhisattva, the well-conducted worthy of imitating.
136–137 3. Verses in summary.

XI. The Parable of Five-hundred Bhikṣus who Could Not Attain Realization

138–140 1. The five-hundred bhikṣus who left while the Bhagavan was reciting those verses.
141–144 2. The Bhagavan approaches the five-hundred bhikṣus through appropriate actions.

XII. The Mysterious Instruction Beyond Words

145–149 1. Dialogue between Subhūti and the five-hundred bhikṣus.
150–154 2. Instructions to Samantāloka.
155–156 3. The immediate acquisition of higher knowledge.

XIII. The Virtues and Benefits Accrued through this Sūtra

157 1. Kāśyapa asks the Bhagavan what virtues and benefits accrue from hearing this sūtra.
158–160 2. Explanation of the virtues and benefits as numerous as the sands of the Ganges.
161–162 3. Explanation of the ten pure bodily acts.
163 4. Explanation of the ten pure mental acts.
164–165 5. Summary of the ten pure bodily and mental acts in verse.
166 6. Conclusion.

The discussion that follows will concentrate on the contents of "V. The Hub of the Bodhisattva Practice—The Middle Path," as it is the intention of this paper to discuss the idea of the Middle Path as expressed in this Sūtra. According to Staël-Holstein's division, the discussion on the Middle Path takes place between sections 52 and 71. These sections have been discussed by Nagao in view of the seven divisions outlined above. Sthiramati gives a summary of each of the sections one at a time and then he gives an expanded explanation in which he discusses the contents of sections 52–71 under the following thirteen headings.[6]

	Headings	Sections
1.	An explanation on how the personality (*pudgala*) is *śūnyatā*.	52
2.	An explanation on how the personality is non-substantial (*anātman*).	
3.	An explanation on how the entity of reality (*dharma*) is *śūnyatā*.	53–55
4.	An explanation on how the entity of reality is non-substantial.	55
5.	An explanation on the extreme of over-evaluation (*samāropa*).	56–59
6.	An explanation on the extreme of denial (*apavāda*).	60
7.	An explanation on how to concentrate (*abhinirūpaṇa*) on an entity of reality.	61–62
8.	An explanation on how experiential knowledge (*anubhāva*) transforms into Mahābodhi.	
9.	An explanation on how the mind is not taken over by conflicting emotions (*kleśa*) and by frustrations (*duḥkha*) when it is transformed into Mahābodhi.	63
10.	An explanation on the specific differences (*viśeṣa*) resulting from turning to (*abhimukha*) the two kinds of non-substantialities.	64–67
	i. Superior in seeing	64
	ii. Superior to those who think small	64–65
	iii. Superior in view of clearing away error	66
	iv. Superior in view of being freed from erroneous thinking	67
11.	An explanation that a former non-substantiality is a cause for a later non-substantiality.	68–69
12.	An explanation on how *śūnyatā* is the consummated accomplishment (*niṣṭha*).	70
13.	An explanation on how *śūnyatā* is just that.	71

I have translated the term *pudgala* (Tib. *gang zag*) by "personality" rather than by "self," because the term *pudgala* refers to the dynamics of being and not to an ontological principle underlying existence itself.[7] Because a personality can shift from one mode of being into another, it characterizes how a person is, but it need not be, as a consequence, an explanation of what a person is. In other words, the term "personality" is used to characterize the dynamics of "be-ing" but this does not mean that "be-ing" is a thing-as-such. This very dynamic of "be-ing" is expressed by the term *śūnyatā*.

I have rendered *anātman* as "non-substantiality" instead of the usual "no-self," because it seems evident, at least for me, that the

6. Staël-Holstein Commentary, pp. 132–152. For headings 1 and 2: 132; 3 and 4: 133; 5: 135; 6 and 7: 140; 8 and 9: 143; 10 and 10i: 144; 10ii: 146; 10iii: 148; 10iv and 11: 149; 12: 151; 13: 152.

7. See, for example, Y. Takeda, ed., Vinītadeva, *Sum cu pa'i grel bshad* (Kyoto: Shojiya Shoten, 1938) and Tibetan Tripitaka (Otani University), vol. 114, no. 5571.

intention of Buddhism is neither to prove nor to disprove an ontological principle. Instead, Buddhism systematically clarifies what is entailed in a mistaken notion of substantiality. That is, according to its own doctrine, there is no underlying, eternal, unchanging substance at the basis of existence that makes existence what it is. In other words, it is reasonable for Buddhism to accept the notion of people, ego, self, etc., as a view of existence, but it is unreasonable to accept that view of existence as exemplifying an inherent, eternal, unchanging substratum or foundation of existence-as-such. The Buddhist avoids (rejects) a belief in any extreme view, because within the domain of impermanency, a belief in permanence or impermanence or a belief in substance or non-substance as the definitive view (position) will lead to frustration. In short, the term *anātman* is a shorthand expression for negating any kind of belief in an inherent, eternal, unchanging substratum or foundation be it permanent or impermanent or substantive or non-substantive.

Thirdly, I have intentionally left the term *śūnyatā* untranslated in most cases, because I trust that the discussion in the text and the references to Sthiramati's commentary will articulate and clarify the meaning of this term within the context in which it appears.

Sthiramati's commentary on Sūtra sections 52–71 consists of a summary of the contents of each of the sections and an expanded explanation of them, in which he discusses the contents under the thirteen headings stated above. He begins by informing us that the content of the proper attainment (*samyakpratipatti*) attained on the spiritual path of the Bodhisattva is the Middle Path. He states:

> The natural state (*svabhāva*) of that proper attainment has been taught by the Bhagavan as the Middle Path (*madhyamapratipad*).[8]

Here, reference is made to the Sūtra (52) which reads:

> ... Oh Kāśyapa, the Bodhisattva wishing to learn the discourse on the Mahāratnakūṭa should practice the dharma in a proper way. Oh Kāśyapa, what is the practice of the dharma by a Bodhisattva? ... That is the Middle Path, the observation of reality just-as-it-is.[9]

8. Staël-Holstein Commentary: 119.2–4: *yang dag par sgrub pa'i rang bzhin ni ma bshad do | | de ni dbu ma'i lam gyis ston te | mtha' gnyis yongs su spangs pas dbu ma'i lam du rig par bya'o | |.*

9. Staël-Holstein Sūtra: 52: *tasmin tarhi kāśyapa iha mahāratnakūṭe dharmaparyāye śikṣitukamena bodhisattvena yoniśo dharmaprayuktena bhavitavyaṁ | tatra kāśyapa katamo yoniśadharmaprayogaḥ ... kāśyapa madhyamā pratipad dharmāṇāṁ bhūtapratyavekṣā |.*

Here it is made clear that the Middle Path refers to the observation of reality-as-it-is. From his expanded explanation, we learn further that in this context, the Middle Path should be understood to refer to a systematization of training which firmly establishes a Bodhisattva in the proper practice of dharma. In Sthiramati's words,

> When a Bodhisattva dwells in the dharma, he accepts as *śūnyatā* the method by which the *modus operandi* of the conventional truth (*saṁvṛtti-satya*) is established and he does not accept [the sūtras of] provisional meaning (*neyārtha*) in accordance with the [written] words. Because of these two reasons, a Bodhisattva does not follow the sūtras held by those on the spiritual path of the Listener (*śrāvaka*). Because [a Bodhisattva] has gone beyond [the Listener's spiritual level], he is accustomed to their [ways]; consequently, he apprehends the methods by which the deep and profound teachings of the Mahāyāna are established or not established as being coterminous with *śūnyatā*, and thus his expertise becomes the foundation for the definitive meaning (*nitārtha*) by virtue of the fact that it exhibits the expanse of the dharma (*dharmadhātu*) as the unity of the *modus operandi* of the conventional truth and the higher truth. For that very reason, [a bodhisattva] is said to practice the dharma in a proper way and thus enter on the Middle Path.[10]

With this introduction, in order to clarify further the meaning of the term Middle Path, the Sūtra (sections 52–62) discusses what are conventionally termed the external and internal worlds or the physical and psychological worlds with the following kinds of statements:

> Oh Kāśyapa, what is the Middle Path, the observation of reality just-as-it-is? It is where no self (*nātma*), no being (*na-sattva*), no soul (*na-jīva*), no nourisher (*na-poṣa*), no individual personality (*na-pudgala*), no man (*na-manuja*), no son of Manu (*na-manava*) is realized. Oh Kāśyapa, this is called the Middle Path, the observation of reality as-it-is.[11] (section 52)

---

10. Staël-Holstein Commentary: 130–31: *byang chub sems dpa' chos la gnas pa ni kun rdzob kyi bden pa'i tshul du bshad pa rnam par bzhag pa'i bden pa'i tshul ston pa dang* | *drang ba'i don la sgra ji bzhin du mi 'dzin te* | *rgyu de gnyis kyis nyan thos kyi theg pa dang rab tu ldan pa'i mdo sde'i phyir mi 'brang ste* | *'das nas de la yang sbyang bar byas mkhas par bya ste* | *de la theg pa chen po dang rab tu ldan pa'i chos zab mo stong pa nyid dang rab tu ldan par bzhag pa dang* | *rnam par ma bzhag pa'i bden pa'i tshul bsdus pa'i phyir kun rdzob dang don dam pa'i bden pa'i tshul bstan pa'i chos kyi dbyings tshul gcig tu ston pas nges pa'i don gyi gzhir gyur mkhas par gyur te* | *rgyu de nyid kyi phyir 'brang bar sbyor bas tshul bzhin du rab tu sbyor ba zhes bya'o* | |.

11. Staël-Holstein Sūtra: 52. Here I have translated from the Tibetan text which is constructed with the question "Oh Kāśyapa, what is the Middle Path, the observation of reality just-as-it-is?" (*'od srung dbu ma'i lam chos rnams la yang dag par so sor rtog pa gang zhe na* |). The Sanskrit text is constructed differently as it asks the question, "Oh Kāśyapa, what is observation of reality just-as-it-is?" (*katamā … kāśyapa sarva-dharmāṇāṁ bhūtapratyavekṣā*) to which the Sūtra, after giving the list (i.e., *nātma-*

and

> Oh Kāśyapa, if you say, "Mind is real," this is one extreme. If you say, "Mind is unreal," this is one extreme. Oh Kāśyapa, where there is no motivation (*na cetanā*), no intellectualization (*na manas*), no perception (*na vijñāna*), this, Oh Kāśyapa, is called the Middle Path, the observation of reality as-it-is.[12] (section 58)

In the discussion on the physical and psychological worlds (sections 52 to 62), the Middle Path is highlighted by the explanation of what constitutes each aspect of the two extreme views to be avoided. From section 63, the Sūtra takes a different approach in its discussion. That is, from section 63 to section 71, the Middle Path is discussed in view of *śūnyatā*.

In section 63, we are introduced to how great awakening (*mahābodhi*) becomes ripened (*pariṇāmana*) when one investigates the teaching in a proper manner. In this context, what constitutes an investigation of the teaching in a proper manner is discussed in view of various ways of reflecting upon reality-as-it-is, but the ways of reflecting upon reality-as-it-is differ in number in the Sanskrit text from those in the Tibetan translations. That is, although the Sūtra passage here in Sanskrit discusses ten ways to reflect upon reality-as-it-is, the Tibetan translation of this Sūtra passage lists seven and the Tibetan translation of Sthiramati's commentary states that there are seven statements to be made in reference to this topic.[13] The Sūtra passage in the Tibetan translation reads:

---

pratyavekṣā nasatva-najīva-napoṣa-napudgala-namanuja-namānava-pratyavekṣā), responds by stating, "Oh Kāśyapa, this is called the Middle Path, the observation of reality as-it-is" (*iyam ucyate kāśyapa madhyamā pratipad dharmāṇāṁ bhūtapartyavekṣā*).

12. Staël-Holstein Sūtra: 58: *bhūtacittam iti kāśyapa ayam eko 'ntaḥ abhūtacittam iti kāśyapa ayaṁ dvitiyo 'ntaḥ yatra kāśyapa na cetanā na mano na vijñānam* | [Skt. no *daṇḍa*] *iyam ucyate kāśyapa madhyamā pratipad dharmāṇāṁ bhūtapratyavekṣā*.

13. The ten ways of reflecting upon reality-as-it-is listed are presented in the Sūtra in a fixed pattern. Only the first one will be given in detail and the others will be abbreviated.

1.	Sūtra:	*na śūnyatāyā dharmā śūnyā karoti dharmā eva śūnyā*
	Tib. trans.:	*gang stong pa nyid kyis chos rnams stong par mi byed de* | *chos rnams nyid stong pa*
	Sthiramati:	*stong pa nyid kyis chos rnams stong par mi byed*
2.	Sūtra:	*nānimittena dharmā animittān karoti*, etc.
	Tib. trans.:	*gang mtshan ma med pas …*
	Sthiramati:	*smon pa med pas…*
3.	Sūtra:	*nāpraṇihitena dharmāpranihitān karoti*, etc.
	Tib. trans.:	*gang smon pa med pas…*
	Sthiramati:	*mtshan ma med pas …*

Again, Kāśyapa, the Middle Path, the observation of reality-as-it-is [means to observe in the following way]:

1. It is not the case that there exists some kind of a *śūnyatā* (open-ness) by which entities of reality are made to be *śūnya* (devoid of an inherent nature); entities of reality are simply *śūnyatā*.
2. It is not the case that there exists some kind of sign-less nature (*animitta*) by which entities of reality are made to signless; entities of reality simply are not objects-as-such.
3. It is not the case that there exists some kind of wishless nature (*apraṇihita*) by which entities of reality are made to be not wished for; entities of reality simply do not have the nature of being wished for.[14]
4. It is not the case that there exists some kind of non-motivation (*anabhisaṁskara*) by which entities of reality are made not to be motivated; entities of reality simply do not motivate.
5. It is not the case that there exists some kind of non-arising (*anutpāda*) by which entities of reality are made not to arise; entities of reality simply do not arise (i.e., come into being).
6. It is not the case that there exists some kind of non-birth (*ajāti*) by which entities of reality are made not to be born; entities of reality are simply not born (i.e., not a product)....

4.	Sūtra:	*nānabhisaṁskareṇa dharmānabhisaṁskaroti*, etc.
	Tib. trans.:	*gang mngon par 'du byed med pas ...*
	Sthiramati:	*mngon par 'du mi byed pas ...*
5.	Sūtra:	*nānupādena*, etc.
	Tib. trans.:	*gang ma skyes pa ...*
	Sthiramati:	*mi srid pa can gyi las dang skyes ba'i rgyun ...*
6.	Sūtra:	*nājatā*, etc.
	Tib. trans.:	*gang ma byung bas ...*
	Sthiramati:	*skad cig gis skye ba'i rgyun ...*
7.	Sūtra:	*na agrāhya*, etc.
8.	Sūtra:	*anāsravā*, etc.
9.	Sūtra:	*n[ā]svabhāvena*, etc.
10.	Sūtra:	*na svabhāvena*, etc.
	Tib. trans.:	*gang ngo bo med pas ...*
	Sthiramati:	*ngo bo med pas ...*

Here we should note that Sthiramati's text has nos. 2 and 3 reversed, and that nos. 4, 5, and 6 are embedded within the sentence: *mngon par 'du mi byed pas mi srid pa can gyi las dang skye ba'i rgyun dang | skad cig gis skye ba'i rgyun dang | 'du byed thams cad ngo bo nyid med pas mya ngan las 'das pa dang | 'khor ba'i rgyun te | ....*

14. These first three—open-ness, signless, and wishless—refer to the three kinds of meditations or gates to liberation. E. Conze refers to these as the three Doors to Liberation for which see his *Buddhist Thought in India*, pp. 59–61 for "emptiness," pp. 61–66 for "signless," and pp. 67–69 for "wishless."

10. It is not the case that there exists some kind of self-nature (*svabhāva*) by which entities of reality are made to be devoid of self-nature; entities of reality are simply without a nature of their own.[15]

Oh Kāśyapa, to investigate in that manner, that is called the Middle Path, observation of reality-as-it-is.

These passages illustrate the means by which a belief in an inherent, eternal, unchanging substratum or foundation underlying existence is removed. To understand that reality has no such underlying substance is to understand reality-as-it-is, and in the above passage that understanding has been discussed in view of those ten [or seven] topics. In his notes (nos. 34–35), Nagao states that the first three refer to the three kinds of meditations that have been systematized as the three gates to liberation; further, he claims that the three not mentioned above, i.e., non-seizing (Skt. no. 7 *agrahya*), non-defilements (Skt. no. 8 *anāsrava*), and no-self-nature (Skt. no. 9 *asvabhāva*), are later interpolations, and thus concludes that the seven, i.e., nos. 1–6 and 10, constitute the original list.[16]

According to Sthiramati's commentary,[17] the first one, *śūnyatā*, is an antidote against all biased opinions. The second, the signless, is an antidote against the occurrence of the characteristic of cupidity (*lobha*), anger (*dveṣa*), and darkness (*moha*). The third, the wishless, is an antidote against the wish for a future life. The fourth, non-motivation, is an antidote against the motivation of the activities of

15. The item expressed here is numbered 10 intentionally, because in accordance with the Sūtra, this is the tenth way to reflect upon reality-as-it-is.

16. See Nagao and Sakurabe, *op. cit.*, p. 318. In n. 35, Nagao informs us that in discussing the original seven as the "seven kinds of two-fold extremes," the *Madhyānta-vibhāga-bhāṣya* and Vasubandhu and Sthiramati give seven kinds of knowledges that correspond to these seven and use this Sūtra passage to substantiate their discussion.

17. Staël-Holstein Commentary: 125–126: *de la mi mthun pa'i phyogs rnam pa bdun gyi gnyen por rig par stong pa zhes bya ba nas | ngo bo nyid med ces bya ba'i bar du'o | |*
1) *mi mthun pa'i phyogs bdun las lta ba de'i gnyen po ni stong pa nyid do | |*
2) *dod chags dang | zhe sdang dang | gti mug gi mtshan ma skye ba de'i gnyen po ni mtshan ma med pa'o | |*
3) *yang srid par smon pa de'i gnyen po ni smon pa med pa'o | |*
4) *yang srid pa'i las mngon par du byed pa de'i gnyen po ni mgnon par du mi byed pa'o | |*
5) *de'i bras bu skye ba de'i gnyen po ni skye ba med pa'o | |*
6) *skyes nas bde ba dang sdug bsngal byung ba de'i gnyen po ni 'byung ba med pa'o | |*
10) *stong pa nyid mthong bas nga'o snyam pa'i nga rgyal de'i gnyen po ni chos nyid kyi ngo bo nyid med ces bya'o | |*
de la bdag med par so sor rtogs pas ni gang zag med pa la gang zag tu 'dzin pa bkag go | | rnam pa gnyis su dbyer med ces bya ba'i bar du lhag ma rnams kyis chos med pa la chos su 'dzin pa bkag go | |

the future life. The fifth, non-arising, is an antidote against the arising of their results. The sixth, non-birth, is an antidote against the pleasures and pains of existence. The tenth, "devoid of self-nature," is an antidote against the belief that "I am something because I understand *śūnyatā*." These seven are observations that remove an attachment to the belief that the personality (*pudgala*) is a substantive-self (*ātman*), because these observations clarify the non-substantiality of reality-as-it-is (*pudgalanairātmya*). The remaining ones remove an attachment to the belief in the existence of what, in essence, is non-existent, that is, they remove the two extremes of denial (*apavāda*) and over-evaluation (*samāropa*).

In section 64, it is made clear that one should not take refuge (*pratisaraṇa*) in *śūnyatā* for the purpose of destroying the idea of a self-as-such. That is, the idea of a self-as-such and the belief in the existence of things-as-such are to be negated simply because they do not exist in and of themselves. In other words, *śūnyatā* does not contextually establish a belief by negation. According to the Sūtra passage (64):

> Oh Kāśyapa, *śūnyatā* is not meant for the purpose of destroying the idea of a self-as-such, but *śūnyatā* is itself *śūnya* [i.e., devoid of any possibilities of being illustrated, of being explained, and of being a response]. It is initially *śūnya*, it is *śūnya* in the middle, and it is finally *śūnya*. In such a *śūnyatā*, Oh Kāśyapa, take refuge.[18]

Sthiramati states that this passage explains that *śūnyatā* is accepted as perfection for those who are at the stages of an ordinary being (*pṛthagjana*), a student (*śaikṣa*), or a teacher (*aśaikṣa*) because these people claim that *śūnyatā* exists in that manner.[19] In other words, they think that because they do not postulate what is to be known, they will comprehend the essence of Nirvāṇa at some future time because they have a direct experience of reality-as-it-is in the present time owing to having seen at a previous time the non-substantiality of entities, beliefs, propositions as being subsumed under *śūnyatā*. In regard to this idea, the Sūtra (section 64) goes on to say:

---

18. Staël-Holstein Sūtra: 64: *na khalu punaḥ kāśyapa pudgalabhāvavināśāya śūnyatā pudgalaś caiva śūnyatā śūnyatā caiva śūnyatā | atyantaśūnyatā | purvāntaśūnyatā | aparānta-śūnyatā pratyutpannaśūnyatā | śūnyatā kaśyapa pratisaratha.*

19. Staël-Holstein Commentary: 127: *stong pa nyid de'i yongs su grub pa de yod par bstan pa'i phyir sngon gyi mtha' stong zhes rgya cher gsungs te | so so'i skye bo dang slob pa dang mi slob pa'i dus na dus thams cad du de bzhin du yod par yongs su ston pa'i phyir ro | |.*

> Those who have taken refuge in *śūnyatā* by becoming attached to it, I call "impaired." Oh Kāśyapa, it is rather better to have a belief in individuality as big as Mt. Meru, rather than the view of *śūnyatā* that these arrogant people hold![20]

The view of these arrogant people is next explained by the analogy of medicine (section 65).[21] Illness can be cured if medicine is taken in and dissolved by the stomach. But if the medicine is taken and kept within the stomach without being dissolved, then the illness will not be cured. In the same manner, one who becomes attached to the view that *śūnyatā* derives from some kind of view (*dṛṣṭigata*) is everywhere and always attached to non-existence and, hence, incurable.

However, in case one may think that *śūnyatā* can be grasped if one grasps the reality of no-change (*avikṛti*), that is, grasp the non-changingness of *śūnyatā*, the Bhagavan cites the example of the sky (section 66). The sky, when gradually unobstructed by clouds, is thought by someone to be breaking open and that person becomes afraid that the sky is falling apart. However, there is no distinction between cloud and sky. In the same manner, when one realizes that one's life is *śūnyatā*, there is no need to fear it.[22]

---

20. Staël-Holstein Sūtra: 64: *tān ahaṁ kāśyapa naṣṭapranaṣṭān iti vadāmi ito pravacanāt varaṁ khalu puna kāśyapa sumerumātrā pudgaladṛṣṭir āśritā na tv evādhimānikasya śūnyatādṛṣṭim ālinā.*

21. Staël-Holstein Sūtra: 65: *tad yathāpi nāma kāśyapa kaścid eva puruṣo glāno bhavet | tasmai vaidyo bhaiṣajyaṁ dadyāt tasya tad bhaiṣajyaṁ sarvadoṣān ucālya koṣṭhagata na nirgacchet | tat kim manyase kāśyapa api nu sa glānapuruṣas tasmād glānyā parimukto bhavet | yasya tad bhaiṣajyam sarvakoṣṭhagatā doṣān uccālya koṣṭhagatam na niḥsaret | āha no bhagavān | gāḍhataraś ca tasya puruṣasya tad gelānyaṁ bhavet | yasya tad bhaiṣajyaṁ sarvadoṣān ucālya sakoṣṭhagataṁ na niḥsaret | bhagavān āha | evam eva kāśyapa sarvadṛṣṭigatānāṁ śūnyatā niḥsaraṇa, yasya khalu punaḥ kāśyapa śūnyatādṛṣṭis tam aham acikitsyam iti vadāmi |.*

22. There is no Sanskrit text available for section 66. See Staël-Holstein Sūtra: 99. The Tibetan passage reads: *'od srung 'di lta ste | dper na mi la la zhig nam mka' 'jigs skrag nas brang rdung zhing ngu ste | nam mkha' 'di sol | nam mkha' 'di sol zhes de skad ces zer na | od srung 'di ji snyam du sems | nam mkha' de bsal bar nus sam | gsol pa | bcom ldan 'das de ni rngo mi thog lags so | bcom ldan 'das kyis bka' stsal pa | od srung de bzhin du dge sbyong dang | bram ze gang dag stong pa nyid kyis skrag rab tu skrag na | de dag ni sems 'khrugs pa chen por 'gyur ro zhes nas bshad do | de ci'i phyir zhe na | 'od srung de dag ni stong pa nyid la spyod la de nyid kyis skrag pa'i phyir ro |.*

Jñānasārasamuccaya kk° 20–28

Mise au point with a Sanskrit Manuscript

Katsumi Mimaki

I. Introduction

Twenty years ago I had an occasion to edit the Tibetan version of the *Jñānasārasamuccaya* kk° 20–28,[1] exposing the doctrinal positions of the four main Buddhist schools. I tried then to put the Sanskrit text side by side with whatever portions of these verses were found as citations in other treatises. Since then several other verses in Sanskrit have been found and reported, as I shall describe below. Recently I have had the good fortune to come across the Sanskrit manuscript of the *Jñānasārasamuccaya*.[2] The present article is therefore a reexamination of these nine verses only. I shall leave the task of editing the whole *Jñānasārasamuccaya* to a later work.

The *Jñānasārasamuccaya* of the Second Āryadeva (eighth century)[3] is a small text consisting of thirty-eight verses. It belongs to the genre of Indian doxographical works (*siddhānta*), and it is well known as a model of Tibetan doxography (*grub mtha'*), exposing the doctrinal position of the Buddhist and Non-Buddhist schools. The text has only been available up to now in Tibetan translation,[4] and we know of the existence of a commentary (*Jñānasārasamuccaya-nibandhana*)[5] by Bodhibhadra (tenth–eleventh century)[6] in the Tibetan *bsTan 'gyur*

1. K. Mimaki, *La réfutation bouddhique de la permanence des choses (sthirasiddhidūṣaṇa) et la preuve de la momentanéité des choses (kṣaṇabhaṅgasiddhi)* (Paris, 1976): 186–189.

2. I would like to express my sincere thanks to Prof. Jiang Zhongxin and Dr. Hu Haiyan von Hinüber, who kindly helped me to consult a copy of this important and indispensable material. I thank also my old friend, Christian Lindtner, who gave me valuable information regarding this manuscript several years ago.

3. See my article, "Āryadeva," in *The Encyclopedia of Religion*, Mircea Eliade et al., eds. (New York, 1987): 1.431a–432a.

4. *Ye śes sñiṅ po kun las btus pa*, C *tsha* 26a4–27b6, D (3851) *tsha* 26b2–28a3, N (3242) *tsha* 25a6–26b6, P [95] (5251) *tsha* 29a5–31a3.

5. *Ye śes sñiṅ po kun las btus pa źes bya ba'i bśad sbyar*, C *tsha* 27b6–45b4, D (3852) *tsha* 28a3–45b4, N (3243) *tsha* 26b6–44b4, P [95] (5252) *tsha* 31a3–53b3.

6. Newman mentions that his name is probably Bhadrabodhi, based on the colophons to P [47] (2081), P [81] (4608), and P [86] (5004): cf. John Newman, "Buddhist

and one by 'Jam mgon 'Ju Mi pham rgya mtsho (1846–1912),[7] as far as I know the only commentary on this text extant in the collection of Tibetan extra-canonical works.

There have been several works on the *Jñānasārasamuccaya*. First of all, Susumu Yamaguchi published the Tibetan text of all thirty-eight verses, based seemingly only on the Peking edition and accompanied by a Japanese translation.[8] Then Yūichi Kajiyama, in his English translation of the *Tarkabhāṣā* of Mokṣākaragupta,[9] identified a considerable number of verses in Sanskrit. The present writer edited the Tibetan text of the *Jñānasārasamuccaya* kk°20–28, based on the sDe dge, sNar thaṅ, and Peking editions, together with the commentary *Jñānasārasamuccaya-nibandhana* by Bodhibhadra, and translated them into French.[10] He also did research on Mi pham's commentary[11] and edited the entire Tibetan text.[12] It was Yasunori Ejima who pointed out for the first time the parallel relation between the *Jñānasārasamuccaya* kk°21–28 and the *Sugatamatavibhaṅgakārikā* of Jitāri (elev-

---

Siddhānta in the Kālacakra Tantra," *Wiener Zeitschrift für die Kunde Südasiens* 36 (1992): 227–234; p. 229 n. 5. But, concerning our author, we should not forget that his name is transcribed as Bo dhi bha dra in such treatises as Tāranatha's *rGya gar chos 'byuṅ* (ed. Schiefner 197.9, 197.12), Sum pa mkhan po's *dPag bsam ljon bzaṅ* (ed. Das 122.7) and Atiśa's *rNam thar rgyas pa* (ed. Eimer, 2.10 = 018, 22–23 = 034 A 17b1, M 8b6).

7. *Collected Writings of 'Jam-mgon 'Ju Mi-pham-rgya-mtsho*, by Sonam Topgay Kazi, Ngagyur Nyingmay Sungrab, vol. 60–74 (15 vols.), Gangtok, 1972–1979, vol. 11: 297–323. The section of the Mādhyamika and its colophon is edited and translated into French in K. Mimaki, "Le commentaire de Mi pham sur le *Jñānasārasamuccaya*," *Indological and Buddhist Studies*, Volume in Honour of Professor J.W. de Jong on his Sixtieth Birthday (Canberra, 1982): 353–376.

8. S. Yamaguchi, *Chūkan Bukkyō Ronkō* (Essays on Mādhyamika Buddhism) (Kyoto, 1944; reprinted, Tokyo, 1965): 263–345.

9. Y. Kajiyama, "An Introduction to Buddhist Philosophy," *Memoirs of the Faculty of Letters (Kyoto University)* 10 (1966): 1–173 (reprinted in Y. Kajiyama, *Studies in Buddhist Philosophy (Selected Papers)* [Kyoto, 1989]: 189–360). See also S. Katsura, "Dharmakīrti no Jikoninshiki no Riron" (Dharmakīrti's Theory of *svasaṁvedana*), *Nanto Bukkyō* 23 (1969) : 8–9.

10. Mimaki 1976: 183–207.

11. K. Mimaki, "Mi pham no Chishinzuishū-chū" (Mi pham's commentary on the *Jñānasārasamuccaya*), *Journal of Indian and Buddhist Studies (Indogaku Bukkyōgaku Kenkyū)* 27/1 (1978): 194–195; K. Mimaki, *op. cit.* (*supra* n. 7) .

12. K. Mimaki, "The *Ye śes sñiṅ po kun las btus pa'i mchan 'grel mu tig gi phreṅ ba* of 'Jam mgon 'Ju Mi pham rgya mtsho," *Kyōryōbu no Kenkyū* (Research on Sautrāntika) (Kyoto, 1986): 1–29.

enth century).[13] The latter is composed of only these eight verses, which are almost identical with *Jñānasārasamuccaya* kk°21–28. Kenjō Shirasaki is continuing his research on Jitāri's auto-commentary, the *Sugatamatavibhaṅgabhāṣya*, of which he has published a critical edition and a Japanese translation.[14] Finally, John Newman discovered that these eight verses are cited in the *Vimalaprabhā*, a commentary on the *Kālacakratantra*.[15] Thus, except for k° 20, all of the *Jñānasārasamuccaya* verses in question are found cited in other Sanskrit texts. The following is a table of these correspondences:[16]

JSS	k°	20	
JSS	k°	21:	TBh (61.1–2; 63.15–16), VP
JSS	k°	22:	VP
JSS	k°	23:	VP; *pāda* ab TBh (63.19)
JSS	k°	24:	VP
JSS	k°	25:	TBh (68.12–13), VP
JSS	k°	26:	SS (389.5–6), VP; *pāda* ab TBh (69.4)
JSS	k°	27:	TBh (70.4–5), SS (389.7–8), VP
JSS	k°	28:	BCAP (174.11–12), SS (389.9–10), SSS (III k°9), TRat (5.6–7), VP

As far as the Sanskrit manuscript of the *Jñānasārasamuccaya* is concerned, we owe its discovery in the first place to Rāhula Sāṅkṛtyāyana, who made in total four expeditions to Tibet from 1929 to

13. Y. Ejima, *Chūkan Shisō no Tenkai* (Development of Mādhyamika thought) (Tokyo, 1980): 255, n. 60 (pp. 215–226, nn. 32–62 = his earlier article published in *Shūkyō Kenkyū* [Journal of Religious Studies] 220 [1974]: 25–43, n. 32). It is very interesting to notice that the colophon of Mi pham's commentary already recognizes this parallel relation and indicates that those who want a more detailed explanation of the *Jñānasārasamuccaya* should refer to the *Sugatamatavibhaṅgabhāṣya*. Cf. Mimaki, *op. cit.* (n.7) pp. 364–365.

14. In particular, at the beginning of his article, "The *Sugatamatavibhaṅgabhāṣya* of Jitāri (I)," *Kōbe Joshi Daigaku Kiyō* 17/1 (1984): 77–107, which consists of an edition and Japanese translation of the Sautrāntika and Yogacāra sections, three versions of the text in the Peking edition of the *Sugatamatavibhaṅgakārikā* kk°1–8 are ennumerated and are of great use for comparison. For convenience, we shall nevertheless present, as an appendix to the present article, a critical edition of these verses based on four canonical editions.

15. Newman, *op. cit.* (*supra* n. 6), pp. 230–231. Cf. also Jagannatha Upadhyaya (ed.), *Vimalaprabhāṭīkā of Kalki Śrī Puṇḍarīka on Śrī Laghukālacakratantrarāja by Śrī Mañjuśrīyaśa*, vol.1 (Sarnath, Varanasi: Central Institute of Higher Tibetan Studies, 1986): 266–267.

16. Cf. Mimaki 1976: 186, 188; Mimaki 1982, *op. cit.* (*supra* n. 7) pp. 358–359; Newman, *op. cit.* (*supra* n. 9) pp. 230–232.

1938.[17] The manuscript of the *Jñānasārasamuccaya* was kept in the monastery of sPos khaṅ,[18] and Rāhula Sāṅkṛtyāyana found it on his second expedition (4.4.–10.11, 1934). His description of the manuscript is as follows:

X.1. 37. *Jñānasārasamuccaya* T Āryadeva Vartula 20.2/3 × 2
3 folios Complete

T means that there is a Tibetan translation. The manuscript is written in Vartula script. The size is indicated in inches. The manuscript consists of three folios and is complete.

As is well-known, the microfilms taken by Rāhula Sāṅkṛtyāyana are preserved in the Kashi Prasad Jayaswal Reseach Institute at Patna. But surprisingly enough, the *Jñānasārasamuccaya* is not found among them. It is possible that he did not photograph it, thinking that this manuscript, consisting of only three folios, was not important, or it is possible that the microfilm was lost for some reason. But, fortunately, we know now that certain manuscripts from Tibet were rediscovered and were at some point deposited in the Cultural Palace of Nationalities in Peking. A catalogue was prepared,[19] and our *Jñānasārasamuccaya* is listed in it as number 146. Unfortunately, the readings of this manuscript are not always satisfactory. We are sometimes obliged to emend them on the basis of the Tibetan versions, or of citations in other texts. But in any case, the rediscovery of the Sanskrit manuscript is the most valuable and reliable basis for our *mise au point* of the original form of this important text.

17. Cf. Rāhula Sāṅkṛtyāyana, "Sanskrit Palm-leaf Mss. in Tibet," *Journal of Bihar and Orissa Research Society* XXI/1 (1935): 21–43; "Second Search of Sanskrit Palm-leaf Mss. in Tibet," *id.* XXIII/1 (1937): 1–57; "Search for Sanskrit Mss. in Tibet," *id.* XXIV/4 (1938): 137–163; "Chart of letters in Sanskrit Mss. from Tibet," *id.* XXV/1 (1939): 64–65.

18. Rāhula Sāṅkṛtyāyana, 1935, p. 30.

19. *Minzu Tushuguan Zang Fanwen Beiyejing Mulu* (Catalogue of the Sanskrit Manuscripts in Palm-leaves preserved in the Library of the Cultural Palace of Nationalities), Wang Sen, ed. (Beijing, 1985).

II. *Jñānasārasamuccaya* kk°20–28

[Introduction]

[20] buddhaiś catur-vidho[1] dharmo[2] dṛṣṭaḥ pūrvaṁ[3] manīṣibhiḥ।
Vaibhāṣikâdayo mārgā bhāṣitās ta*ttva[4]-sādhane।। (*Ms.3b2)

1 caturvvidho Ms. 2 dharmā Ms. 3 pūrvva Ms. 4 tatva Ms.

saṅs rgyas chos ni rnam pa bźir।।
yid 'dod rnams kyis sṅon mthoṅ ste[1] ।।
Bye brag smra la sogs pa'i lam[2] ।।
bśad pas de ñid bsgrub[3] pa 'o।।

1 de DNP 2 las N 3 sgrub CD

Those who accept the mind[20] observe that the Law [taught] previously by the Buddhas is of four kinds. The paths of the Vaibhāṣika and other [schools] are explained in order to establish reality.[21]

[Vaibhāṣika]

[21] ākāśaṁ dvau[1] nirodhau ca nityaṁ trayam asaṁskṛtaṁ (।)
[2-]saṁskṛtaṁ[-2] kṣaṇikaṁ sarvaṁ[3] ātma-śūnyam[4] akartṛkaṁ[5] ।।

1 dvau TBh, VP; vyaumā (?) Ms. 2 om. Ms. 3 sarvvaṁ Ms.
4 ātmanaṁ śūnyam Ms.; ātma-śūnyam TBh, VP
5 °aṁ Ms.; °am TBh, VP

nam mkha' 'gog pa gñis dag ste[1] ।।
'dus ma byas gsum po ni rtag।।
'dus byas bdag gis kun stoṅ la।।
byed pa po med skad cig ma।।

1 daṅ NP

20. The normal sense of the term *manīṣin* is something like "intelligent," "wise," etc., but according to the *Jñānasārasamuccaya-nibandhana* of Bodhibhadra, it is someone who maintains that deliverance is not possible by body or speech, but that deliverance and bonds are due to the force of the mind: *lus daṅ ṅag gis grol ba mi 'thad kyi। grol ba daṅ 'chiṅ ba sems kyi dbaṅ las so।। źes 'dod pa rnams ni yid 'dod rnams te।*... (cf. Mimaki 1976, pp. 190–191).

21. According to the Tibetan, "As the paths of the Vaibhāṣika and other [schools] are explained, reality is established."

The three unconditioned [factors]—space and the two extinctions—are permanent. All the conditioned [factors] are void of self, without agent-creator, momentary.

[22] akṣajā dhīr anākārā[1] sākṣād vedâṇu-sañcayaṁ |
[2-]dhīmatām[3] iti Kāśmīra[-2]-Vaibhāṣika-mataṁ mataṁ ||

1 anākārā VP; ānākārā Ms. 2 syāt Kāśmīramatâmbhodhi VP
3 dhīmatyām Ms.

mig las skye blo rnam[1] med ciṅ ||
mṅon sum rig pa rdul gyi tshogs ||
blo ldan źes bya Kha che yi ||
Bye brag smra ba'i gźuṅ du bśad ||

1 rnams NP

For the wise persons the consciousness born from the visual organ does not have the form [of each atom]. One perceives directly the mass of atoms. This is considered to be the thought of the Vaibhāṣika of Kaśmīr.

[Sautrāntika]

[23] sākāra[1]-jñāna-ja*nakā dṛśyā nêndriya-gocarāḥ | (* Ms. 3b3)
vandhyāsuta-samaṁ vyoma nirodhau vyoma-sannibhau[2] ||

1 cf. svâkāra TBh 2 sammabhau (?) Ms., sannibhau VP

mthoṅ ba dbaṅ po'i yul min te ||
śes pa rnam pa bcas pa skye ||
nam mkha' mo gśam bu 'dra la ||
'gog pa nam mkha' daṅ 'dra 'o ||

The objects which give birth to the consciousness endowed with the form [of the objects] are not the domain of the faculties. Space is the same as the son of a barren woman. The [two] extinctions resemble space.

[24] saṁskārā na jaḍāḥ santi traikālyânugamo na ca |
asan na saṁcitaṁ rūpaṁ[1] iti Sautrāntikā viduḥ ||

1 asad apratigha-rūpam Ms., asad apratighaṁ rūpam VP [Our reading is a reconstruction from the Tibetan version. See n. 22].

'dus byas bems po yod min la | |
dus gsum dag kyaṅ khas mi len | |
bsags pa'i gzugs med min źes pa | |
mDo sde pa ni mkhas rnams so | |

The conditioned [factors] do not exist as inert [things of the external world]. One does not admit the three times either. [But] assembled matter is not nonexistent.[22] Thus know the Sautrāntika.

[Yogācāra]

[25] na sann avayavī[1] nāma na santaḥ[2] paramâṇavaḥ (|)
*pratibhāso nirālambaḥ svapnânubhava-sannibhaḥ[3] | | (*Ms. 3b4)

1 āvayavī Ms. 2 santaḥ Ms. VP, santi TBh
3 °nubhavasannibhaḥ TBh VP, °nubhavāsannibhaḥ Ms.

cha śes can źes bya med ciṅ | |
phra rab rdul rnams med pa daṅ | |
so sor snaṅ ba dmigs med daṅ | |
ñams su myoṅ ba rmi lam 'dra | |

[Except for consciousness] the 'whole' does not indeed exist. Atoms do not exist [either]. The [diverse] apparition [in consciousness] does not have an object [outside consciousness] and resembles experience in a dream.[23]

---

22. *asan na saṁcitaṁ rūpaṁ* is a reconstruction from the Tibetan version, but it is confirmed by the commentary of Bodhibhadra: *rnam par śes pa las gud na rdul phra rab bsags pa'i goṅ bu'i gzugs med pa ni min no źes 'dod pa ste* (JSSN 196.15–17 = P 49a7–8). On the other hand, the reading of the manuscript *asad apratigha-rūpaṁ* (non-resistant matter [= *avijñapti*] is nonexistent) corresponds with the *Sugatamata-vibhaṅgakārikā* of Jitāri (*thogs bcas gzugs min yod ma yin*) and his auto-commentary confirms this reading: *thogs pa med pa'i gzugs yod min źes gsuṅs so | | thogs pa ste raṅ gi yul du gźan 'byuṅ ba'i gegs byed pa rnam par rig byed ma yin pa źes bya ba'i gsugs gaṅ la med pa de yaṅ yod pa ma yin te* | (SMVBh 94.25–96.1 = P 322b4–5). The verse cited in the *Vimalaprabhā* has almost the same form as Jitāri's. I do not know for the moment how to analyse correctly what happened with the manuscript of the *Jñānasārasamuccaya*.

23. The Tibetan translation of the JSS for this *pāda* does not seem correct. That of the *SMVK* (*rmi lam ñams su myoṅ ba bźin*, ed. Shirasaki [1984]: 79) is much better.

[26] grāhya-grāhaka-nirmuktaṁ[1] vijñānaṁ[2] paramārthasat[3] |
Yogācāra-matâmbhodhi-pāragair iti gīyate ||

1 °grāhakanirmuktaṁ TBh SS, °grāhyakavinirmuktaṁ Ms., °grāhaka-vaidhuryāt VP 2 °naṁ Ms. Tbh, °nam SS 3 paramā° TBh SS VP, pāramā° Ms.

gzuṅ daṅ 'dzin pa las grol ba'i ||
rnam śes dam pa'i don du yod ||
blo mtsho'i pha rol phyin pa yi ||
rNal 'byor spyod pa'i gźuṅ du bsgrags ||

Consciousness free from subject-object [dichotomy] is the absolute existence. This is related by the Yogācāra, who reached the other shore of the sea of intelligence.[24]

[Mādhyamika]

[27] nêṣṭaṁ tad api dhīrāṇāṁ[1] vijñānaṁ pāramārthikaṁ[2] |
ekâneka-vicāreṇa vi*yogād[3] gaganâbja-vat || (* Ms. 4a1)

1 dhīrāṇā Ms., dhīrāṇāṁ TBh SS 2 pāramārthikaṁ Ms. SS, pāramārthikam TBh, paramārthasat VP 3 -vicāreṇa viyogā Ms., -svabhāvena viyogād TBh VP

rnam śes dam pa'i don ldan pa ||
de yaṅ brtan[1] rnams mi 'dod de ||
gcig daṅ du ma'i raṅ bźin daṅ ||
bral phyir nam mkha'i pa dma bźin ||

1 brtan NP, brten CD

Even that consciousness [existing] in absolute reality, [which the Yogācāra proclaim,] is not admitted by the [Mādhyamika who are] steady. For, [it is] deprived of [a single or a plural nature] in consequence of an examination[25] of whether it has a single or a plural [nature], as, for example, the sky-lotus.

---

24. For *pāda* cd, the Tibetan translator translates the same word *mata* twice, namely as *blo* and *gźuṅ*. The Tibetan translation of the SMVK (*rNal 'byor spyod gźuṅ rgya mtsho yi* || *pha rol phyin rnams de skad smra* ||, ed. Shirasaki [1984]: 80) is closer to our Sanskrit.

25. The reading of the TBh and VP (*ekâneka-svabhāvena viyogād*) corresponds better to the Tibetan version of the JSS.

[28] na san nâsan na sadasan na câpy anubha[1]yâtmakaṁ[2] |
catuṣkoṭi-vinirmuktaṁ[3] tattvaṁ[4] Mādhyamikā[5] viduḥ ||

1 amubha° Ms., anubha° SS BCAP TRat
2 °kaṁ Ms. SS, °kam BCAP TRat
3 vinimuktaṁ Ms., vinirmuktaṁ SS BCAP TRat
4 tatvaṁ Ms. 5 Mādhyami Ms., Mādhyamikā SS BCAP TRat

yod min med min yod med min||
gñis ka'i bdag ñid kyaṅ min pas||
mtha' bźi las grol dBu ma pa||
mkhas pa rnams kyi de kho na'o||

Neither existence [as in the case of the consciousness of the Yogācāra], nor nonexistence [as postulated by the Lokāyata, etc.], nor [the third category which is the affirmation of both, namely] existence and nonexistence, nor [the fourth category, which has] the nature of the negation of both, are [admitted].[26] The Mādhyamika know reality which is free from these four extremes.[27]

III. Appendix: *Sugatamatavibhaṅgakārikā*

The location of the text in the *bsTan 'gyur* is as follows:

C a7b6–8a5
D (3899) a 7b5–8a4
N[1] (3287) ha 59a6–b6
N[2] (3452) gi 199b3–200a2
N[3] (5859) ño 268a4–b4
P[1] [101](5296) ha 64b2–65a1

---

26. There is a slight difference in the Sanskrit and Tibetan versions of *pāda* b. The Sanskrit version is easier to understand, whereas we need a somewhat acrobatic interpretation in order to understand the Tibetan version. That is what Bodhibhadra and Mi pham do in their commentaries. The third and the fourth categories of the *catuṣkoṭi* usually are the same as they are in our translation. But the commentaries of Bodhibhadra and Mi pham make the third category the negation of existence and nonexistence, and the fourth category the affirmation of the both (cf. JSSN 204.32–206.6 = P 51b1–3; JSSMip, ed. Mimaki 19.19–23). In the SMVK, the Tibetan text of *pāda* b is exactly the same as in *JSS*.

27. The Tibetan version of *pāda* cd is not very precise. The SMVK has also the same reading.

P[2] [103](5461) gi 208b8–209a8
P[3] [146](5867) ño 283a2–b2

SMVK k°1 'dus ma byas gsum rtag pa ste||
nam mkha' daṅ ni 'gog pa gñis||
'dus byas thams cad skad cig ma||
bdag med byed pa po yod min||

SMVK k°2 rnam par śes pa dbaṅ skyes blos||
mṅon sum du[1] ni phra bsags rig||
Kha che[2] Bye brag smra ba yi||
gźuṅ 'di yin par mkhas rnams bźed||

1 N[1] P[1] om. du 2 phye N[2] P[2]

SMVK k°3 raṅ gi rnam par śes pas[1] rig||
dbaṅ po'i[2] yul du snaṅ ba min[3] ||
nam mkha' mo gśam[4] bu daṅ mtshuṅs||
'gog pa gñis[5] kyaṅ nam mkha' bźin||

1 pa N[2] P[2] 2 gi N[1] N[3] P[1] P[3], gis CD
3 yin SMVK, min BSGT, cf. SMVBh P 321a2: dbaṅ po'i spyod yul snaṅ ruṅ min
4 śam N[1] P[1], bśam N[2] N[3] P[2] 5 ñid P[1]

SMVK k°4 sems daṅ mi ldan 'du byed med||
dus gsum du ni rjes 'jug med||
thogs bcas gzugs min yod ma yin||
mDo sde pa yin mkhas źes bya||

SMVK k°5 cha śes źes byar yod min phyir||
phra rab rdul yaṅ yod ma yin||
snaṅ ba dmigs su yod min te||
rmi lam ñams su myoṅ ba bźin||

SMVK k°6 gzuṅ[1] daṅ 'dzin pa las grol ba'i||
śes pa dam pa'i don du yod||
rNal 'byor spyod gźuṅ rgya mtsho yi||
pha rol phyin rnams de skad smra||

1 gzuṅs N[3] P[3]

SMVK k°7 rnam śes don dam yin pa ru | |
de yaṅ mkhas rnams mi bźed de[1] | |
gcig daṅ du ma'i raṅ bźin bral | |
dṅos med[2] nam mkha'i pa dma bźin | |

1 do N[3] P[1] P[3] 2 miṅ (?) P[1]

SMVK k°8 yod min med min yod med min | |
gñis kyi bdag ñid du yaṅ med | |
mtha' bźi dag las ṅes grol ba[1] | |
dBu ma de ñid mkhas pa 'dod | |

1 ba'i N[3] P[3]

Abbreviations

BSGT: *Blo gsal grub mtha'* by dBus pa blo gsal. K. Mimaki, ed. (Kyoto, 1982).

BCAP: *Bodhicaryāvatārapañjikā* by Prajñākaramati. P. L. Vaidya, ed. (Darbhanga, 1960).

C: Co ne edition.

D: sDe dge edition.

Das: S. C. Das, ed., *dPag bsam ljon bzaṅ* (Calcutta, 1908; reprint: Kyoto, 1984).

Eimer: H. Eimer, *rNam thar rgyas pa*. 2 vols. (Wiesbaden, 1979).

JSS: *Jñānasārasamuccaya* by Āryadeva.

JSSN: *Jñānasārasamuccayanibandhana* by Bodhibhadra. K. Mimaki, ed. (Paris, 1976): 183–207. (See n. 1).

JSSMip: Mi pham's commentary on the *Jñānasārasamuccaya*. (See n. 7).

Ms.: Manuscript.

Mimaki (1976): see n. 1.

N: sNar thaṅ edition.

P: Peking edition.

Schiefner: A. Schiefner, *Tāranāthae de Doctrinae Buddhicae in India Propagatione* (Petropoli, 1868; reprint: Tokyo, 1963).

Shirasaki (1984): See n. 14.

SMVBh: *Sugatamatavibhaṅgabhāṣya* by Jitāri, ed. K. Shirasaki (1984).

SMVK: *Sugatamatavibhaṅgakārikā* by Jitāri.

SS: *Subhāṣitasaṁgraha*, ed. C. Bendall, *Le Muséon* (1903): 375–402.

SSS: *Sarvasiddhāntasaṁgraha*, ed. L. de La Vallée Poussin and F. W. Thomas, *Le Muséon* (1902): 402–412.

TBh: *Tarkabhāṣā* by Mokṣākaragupta. R. Iyengar, ed. (Mysore, 1952).

TRat: *Tattvaratnāvalī* by Advayavajra. H. Ui, ed., in *Nagoya Daigaku Bungakubu Kenkyūronshū* 3 (1952): 1–31.

VP: *Jñānasārasamuccaya* verses cited in the *Vimalaprabhā*. J. Newman, ed.: 230–231. (See n. 6).

On Three *Yogācārabhūmi* Passages Mentioning the Three *Svabhāvas* or *Lakṣaṇas**

Lambert Schmithausen

In my study on *ālayavijñāna*[1] I reasserted my view, already expressed in an earlier paper,[2] that the *Maulī Bhūmi*[3] (*MauBh*) or "Basic Section" of the *Yogācārabhūmi* (*Y*) does not, on the whole, give the impression that it knows, or presupposes the existence of, the *Saṁdhinirmocanasūtra* (*Saṁdh*), or, for that matter, of the *Viniścayasaṁgrahaṇī* Section

---

* Abbreviations:

Ālayav.	=	L. Schmithausen, *Ālayavijñāna. On the Origin and Early Development of a Central Concept of Yogācāra Philosophy.* Studia Philologica Buddhica, Monograph Series IVa and IVb (Tokyo: The International Institute for Buddhist Studies, 1987)
BoBh	=	*Bodhisattvabhūmi*
BoBhD	=	*Bodhisattvabhūmi*, ed. N. Dutt (Patna, 1966)
CiBh	=	*Cintāmayī Bhūmi*
MauBh	=	*Maulī Bhūmi*
Saṁdh	=	*Saṁdhinirmocanasūtra*, ed. E. Lamotte (Louvain-Paris, 1935)
SavBh	=	*Savitarka-savicārādi-bhūmi*
ŚrBhm	=	*Śrāvakabhūmi* manuscript (copy recopied from a copy [Univ. of Göttingen] of the photos kept in the K. P. Jayaswal Research Institute, Patna)
ŚruBh	=	*Śrutamayī Bhūmi*
VinSg	=	*Viniścayasaṁgrahaṇī*
Y	=	*Yogācārabhūmi*
YB	=	*Yogācārabhūmi* of Ācārya Asaṅga, ed. V. Bhattacharya (Univ. of Calcutta, 1957)
Yc	=	Hsüan-tsang's Chinese translation of *Y* (T 1579)
Ym	=	*Yogācārabhūmi* manuscript (copy of the photos kept in the K. P. Jayaswal Research Institute, Patna)
Yt	=	Tibetan translation of *Y*: Peking Tanjur, mDo-'grel, vols. dzi ff.

1. *Ālayav.*, §§1.6.3–6.

2. L. Schmithausen, "Zur Literaturgeschichte der älteren Yogācāra-Schule," *Zeitschrift der Deutschen Morgenländischen Gesellschaft*, Supplementa I.3 (1969): 822f.

3. Cp. K. Matsuda in *Report of the Japanese Association for Tibetan Studies (Nihon Chibetto Gakkai Kaihō)* 34 (1988): 18. The designation "*Maulī Bhūmi*" is found only in the *Viniścayasaṁgrahaṇī* (cp. Sh. Suguro, *Shoki-yuishiki-shisō no Kenkyū (Studies on Early Vijñaptimātra Philosophy)* [Tokyo, 1989]: Engl. summary, p. 11) and was hence probably given by the compiler(s) of the latter.

(*VinSg*).[4] I had, however, to admit that there are occasional exceptions,[5] but I held that these could not shake the assumption that the compilation of *MauBh* precedes that of *Saṁdh*, let alone *VinSg*, because it can be rendered probable in other cases that the text of *MauBh* was occasionally modified or supplemented not only in the process of its own compilation,[6] but even after the compilation of *VinSg*.[7] Thus, it would not be merely arbitrary to also regard the passages which seem to presuppose *Saṁdh* and/or *VinSg* (very few only, as far as I can see) as later additions. Yet, I admit that this is merely a possibility, and that resorting to it looks very much like clinging to a preconception at any cost. In order to turn possibility into probability, it would be necessary to discover some additional evidence, or palpable traces of later redaction or interpolation in, or in the context of, these passages. This is what I already tried, provisionally, in the case of the most spectacular of these passages.[8] But now I think that my former attempt is not entirely convincing and that the evidence may require a somewhat different interpretation. In the present paper, I shall therefore offer a reconsideration of this passage and, in addition, discuss two others which unfortunately I did not take into consideration in my previous study.

1.

The passage which I briefly discussed in my previous study (and which had already been pointed out by A. Mukai)[9] is found in the *Śrutamayī Bhūmi* (*ŚruBh*) of *MauBh*. The passage belongs to an exposition of *saṁjñā-prabheda-prajñapti-vyavasthāna* ("establishing discourse with reference to different [dogmatic] concepts, or technical terms") and explains *pada*, which seems to mean something like "key term" (cp. Ch. 句) or "basic concept" (cp. Tib. *gnas*). Since, as far as I know, the original of the passage has not been published so far, I shall first give the Sanskrit text on the basis of *Ym*:[10]

---

4. This does not, of course, exclude that *Saṁdh* and *VinSg* may occasionally contain materials that predate the compilation of *MauBh*.

5. *Ālayav*. §1.6.7 and n. 132.

6. Cp. *Ālayav*. ch. 6.

7. Cp. *Ālayav*. §6.2.1–4.

8. *Ālayav*. n. 132.

9. "On the Compilation of the Yogācārabhūmi and the Dates of Asaṅga," *Indogaku Bukkyōgaku Kenkyū* 29/2 (1981): 680ff., esp. 683f.

padaṁ katamat । tadyathā

[A.] [01.] ṣaḍāyatanaṁ apramāṇaviṣayam apramāṇadeśam apramāṇakālaṁ ।

[02.] trayo dhātavaḥ । kāmadhātuḥ rūpadhātuḥ ārūpyadhātuś ca ⟨ । ⟩

[03.] apare trayo[11] dhātavaḥ । sāhasrikaś cūḍikaḥ, dvisāhasro madhyaḥ ⟨,⟩ trisāhasrama*[2]*hāsāhasraś ca ।

[04.] catvāraś ca pakṣāḥ ⟨ । ⟩ gṛhipakṣaḥ pravrajitapakṣaḥ upāsakapakṣaś ca, amanuṣyapakṣaś ca ⟨ । ⟩

[05.] tisro vedanāḥ ⟨ । ⟩ sukhā duḥkhā aduḥkhāsukhā ca ।

[06.] trayo ⟨'⟩dhvānaḥ ⟨ । ⟩ atītaḥ anāgataḥ pratyutpannaś ca ।{।}

[07.] trīṇi ratnāni । buddharatnaṁ, dharmaratnaṁ, saṁgharatnaṁ ca ।

[08.] trayo{ḥ} dharmā⟨ḥ⟩ ⟨।⟩ kuśalā akuśalā avyākṛtā⟨ḥ⟩ ।{।}

[09.] trayaḥ saṁkleśāḥ । kleśasaṁkleśaḥ karmasaṁkleśaḥ janma*[3]*saṁkle⟨śa⟩ś ca ।

[10.] catvāry āryasatyāni । duḥkhaṁ samudayo nirodho mārgaś ca ।

[11.] navānupūrvasamāpattayaḥ । prathamaṁ dhyānaṁ yāvat saṁjñāvedayitanirodhaḥ ।

[12.] saptatriṁśad bodhipakṣyā dharmāḥ ⟨।⟩ smṛtyupasthāna-samyakprahāṇa-ṛddhipādêndriya-bala-bodhyaṅga-mārgā⟨ṅ⟩gā{ṁ}ni ।

[13.] catvāri śrāmaṇyaphalāni ⟨।⟩ srotaāpattiphalaṁ, sakṛdāgāmiphalam, anāgāmiphalam ⟨,⟩ agraphala*[4]*m arhat⟨t⟩–vam ।

[14.] saṁbahulā vaiśeṣikāḥ guṇāḥ ⟨,⟩ tadyathā apramāṇāni vimokṣâbhibhvāyatana-kṛtsnāyatanāni, araṇā praṇidhijñānaṁ pratisaṁvidaḥ ṣaṭ cābhijñāḥ ⟨ । । ⟩

---

10. *Ym* 84a1-b2; *Yt* dzi 184a6–185b6; *Yc* 345b4-c16. Paragraphs mine. Variation of the punctuation signs is also mine; the ms. has *daṇḍa* in all cases except those given in angular brackets ⟨ ⟩, which are my additions. { } means "to be deleted"; ⟨ ⟩ marks additions to the wording of *Ym*; italics indicate conjectures. Numbers in italics and square brackets within the text point to the beginning of a new (folio or) line of *Ym*. I have not normalized sandhi, etc., but reproduced the ms. as it stands. The sign °\ is transcribed as *m/* (or *m,*).

11. Part of this word concealed by a drawing pin.

[B.] [00.] vaipulyaṁ vā punaḥ adhikṛtya

[01.] paṁca vastūni। nimittaṁ nāma vikalpaḥ tathatā samyagjñānaṁ ca।

[02.] dvividhā śūnyatā ⟨।⟩ pudgalaśūnyatā, dharmaśūnyatā ca।

[03.] dvividhaṁ nairātmyam। pudgalanairātmyam, dharma-[5]nairātmyañ ca।

[04.] antadvayavivarjitā madhyamā pratipat। samāropāntavivarjitā apavādāntavivarjitā ca।

[05.] caturvidhaṁ ta⟨t⟩tvam। lokaprasiddhaṁ ⟨yuktiprasiddhaṁ⟩[12] kleśāvaraṇa-viśuddhi-jñāna-gocaraḥ jñeyāvaraṇa-viśuddhi-jñāna-gocaraḥ।

[06.] catasraḥ paryeṣaṇāḥ ⟨।⟩ nāma-paryeṣaṇā vastu-paryeṣaṇā svabhāva-prajñapti{।}-paryeṣaṇā viśeṣa-prajñapti{।}-paryeṣaṇā ca।

[07.] catvāri yathā[6]bhūta-parijñānāni। nāma-paryeṣaṇā-gataṁ yathābhūta{ṁ}-parijñānaṁ, vastu-paryeṣaṇā-gataṁ ⟨,⟩ svabhāva-prajñapti-paryeṣaṇā-gataṁ, viśeṣa-prajñapti-paryeṣaṇā-gatañ ca yathābhū⟨ta⟩-parijñānaṁ।

[08.] trividhaḥ svabhāvaḥ ⟨।⟩ pari{n}niṣpannaḥ svabhāvaḥ ⟨,⟩ paratаṁtraḥ ⟨,⟩ parikalpitaś ca svabhāvaḥ।

[09.] trividhā niḥsvabhāvatā ⟨।⟩ lakṣaṇa-niḥsvabhāvatā ⟨,⟩ utpatti-[13]niḥsvabhāvatā, paramārtha-niḥsvabhāvatā ca।

[10.] [7]pañcākārā mahābodhiḥ ⟨।⟩ tadyathā svabhāvataḥ śaktitaḥ upāyataḥ{।} pravṛttito nivṛtt⟨it⟩aś ca ⟨।⟩

[11.] pañcākāram{।} mahāyānaṁ ⟨।⟩ bījam ⟨,⟩ avatāraḥ, kramaḥ ⟨,⟩ samyakpratipattiḥ ⟨,⟩ samyakpratipatti-phalaṁ ca।

[12.] [a] tathā prathamaś cittotpādaḥ ⟨,⟩ sattveṣu karuṇā, pāramitā-saṁgrahavastubhiḥ sva-para-santati-paripākaḥ ⟨।⟩
[b] paṁcâprameya-saṁjñā⟨ḥ⟩ ⟨।⟩ sat⟨t⟩vadhātv-aprameyatāyāṁ saṁjñā, lokadhātu-dha[84b1] [14]rmadhātu-vineyadhātu-vinayopāyadhātv-aprameyatāyāṁ ca{।} saṁjñā ⟨।⟩
[c] tat⟨t⟩vārthānugamaḥ—sarvvāsv aprameyatāsv a[15]nugatā yā tathatā, tatra ca yaj jñānaṁ ⟨– ,⟩ aciṁtya-

12. Supplied acc. to Tib. and Ch.; cp. *BoBhD* 25,6f. and 25,17.

13. Ms. *upapatti-*.

14. Ms. is very indistinct in the beginning (ca. thirty *akṣara*s) of this and the following lines.

15. *sva* inserted in the lower margin.

prabhāv⟨*at*⟩ā ⟨,⟩ *vimuktiḥ*[16] ⟨,⟩ anāvaraṇaṁ jñānaṁ ⟨,⟩ [d] dvātriṁṣan mahāpuruṣalakṣaṇāni, aśīty anuvyaṁjanāni ⟨,⟩ catasraḥ sarvākārāḥ pariśuddhayaḥ, daśa balāni ⟨,⟩ catvāri vaiśāradyāni ⟨,⟩ trīṇi smṛtyupasthānāni, trīṇy arakṣyāṇi ⟨,⟩ mahā[2]karuṇā ⟨,⟩ asaṁmoṣadharmatā ⟨,⟩ vāsanāsamudghātaḥ, sarvākāra[17] -vara-jñānaṁ ca ⟨ | | ⟩

[C.] tad evam[18] abhisamasya dvividhaṁ padaṁ bhavati | śrāvakayāna-nirddeśa-padaṁ ca, mahāyāna-nirddeśa-pada{ṁ}ñ ca ⟨ | | ⟩

As was already pointed out by A. Mukai,[19] this passage mentions and enumerates several fundamental concepts which are, totally or on the whole,[20] alien to *MauBh*: not only the threefold "own-being" or "essence" or "nature" (*svabhāva*: B.08)[21] and the threefold "lack of

---

16. Ms. *aciṁtyaprabhāvādhimuktiḥ*; both Tib. (*mthu bsam gyis mi khyab pa la mos pa*) and Ch. confirm *adhimukti*, but it seems difficult to justify *adhimukti* at this point in what is quite obviously a sequence of items referring to ever higher stages of Mahāyāna soteriology. For, *adhimukti* (conviction and appreciation) is the attitude of persons who have not yet directly experienced Truth or have not yet themselves acquired the supranormal powers. It is rather the *bodhisattva* on the lower stages who is advised to believe in and appreciate the unimaginable power of the Buddhas and [advanced] *bodhisattva*s (*adhimukti-bahulo bhavati … buddha-bodhisattva-prabhāve*: *BoBhD* 67,13+15; cp. also 119,19f., where *adhi-muc* refers to both *tattvārtha* and *prabhāva*). Therefore, an item *acintyaprabhāvādhimuktiḥ* ought to *precede* the item "gnosis of True Reality" (*tattvārthajñāna*) and is entirely unexpected between this and *anāvaraṇaṁ jñānam* which stands for the gnoseological aspect of the highest *bodhi* (*BoBhD* 62,5–7). What does fit in between these two is the actual attainment or *possession* of such unimaginable power ([*acintya*]*prabhāva*[*tā*]: cp. *BoBhD* 193,9f. [see n. 26]). My suggestion is therefore that °*dhimuktiḥ* is an old corruption for *vimuktiḥ*, which would correspond to *prahāṇa* in *BoBhD* 62,3–5 (cp. 64,6!) and thus perfectly fit in with the sequence of concepts in *BoBh* (see n. 26). The only alternative I can think of is to understand *acintyaprabhāvâdhimuktiḥ* in the sense of *BoBhD* 42,1ff., i.e., not as a compound but as two words in the sense of "[transforming things by an act of] firm will+conviction of unimaginable power"; but I think that this specific supranormal power is far too insignificant to be included in a comparatively concise list of the central key-terms of Mahāyāna.

17. Ms. adds 3 illegible (deleted?) *akṣara*s.

18. Ms. has a (deleted?) *akṣara* after °*va*°. Tib. *de dag kyaṅ* = *tac caitad*? Ch. 如是 probably represents *evam*.

19. See n. 9.

20. I.e., with the exception of the two passages to be discussed in §§2 and 3, which contain equivalents to B.08 and B.08+09, respectively.

21. It should be noted that the sequence of the three *svabhāva*s is reversed as compared with the standard one already found in *Saṁdh* and *VinSg*.

own-being" or "essencelessness" (*niḥsvabhāvatā*: B.09), but also the five entities (*vastu*: B.01), the fivefold Great Awakening (*mahābodhi*: B.10), and perhaps also the twofold emptiness (*śūnyatā*: B.02) which, as far as I can see, does not occur elsewhere in *MauBh* either.

Since these terms are, apart from the twofold emptiness, anything but self-explanatory, their mere enumeration in this passage would seem to presuppose that the reader already has the supplementary information required to make this enumeration intelligible. As far as I can see, only the three *svabhāva*s and *niḥsvabhāvatā*s occur in *Saṁdh*,[22] but all the five categories can be found, along with definitions, in the *Bodhisattvabhūmi* of *VinSg*.[23]

If we assume that, when the present passage was written, *VinSg* (or the materials it contains) were not yet in existence except in the head of the author or group of authors (understood to have conceived, from the outset, the whole *Y* as we have it), one would expect him (or them) to have referred the reader to a later section of the text for a detailed explanation. But there is no such reference, and in contrast to copious cross-references to other chapters and portions of *Y*, there is, as far as I know,[24] none at all to *VinSg* in the whole *MauBh* (or, for that matter, in the other sections like the *Vastusaṁgrahaṇī*). Since, on the other hand, *VinSg* refers to *MauBh* quite often, the easiest assumption is that *VinSg* came to be compiled after the (more or less) final redaction (including cross-references) of *MauBh*, not as a supplement planned from the very outset but as a collection of materials which had arisen, or become available, only after *MauBh* had been finished. In this case, however, it would seem difficult to explain the occurrence of typical *VinSg* concepts in the present *MauBh* passage, unless this passage is regarded as a later addition. But, as stated above, such an assumption would be more convincing if traces of some revision of the text could be pointed out.

Actually, as I have already indicated in the above-mentioned study,[25] the compositional structure of the passage is somewhat irregular.

---

22. In the case of the three *svabhāva*s, the key paragraphs of *Saṁdh* on the subject prefer, however, the term *lakṣaṇa*; their designation as *svabhāva*s is found only in *Saṁdh* VII.10 and 13 and in later chapters. Cp. Åke Boquist, *Trisvabhāva* (Univ. of Lund, 1993): 28f.

23. **B.01**: *Yt* zi 302b2ff.; *Yc* 696a1ff.; **B.02**: *Yt* 'i 124b1f. and 4ff.; *Yc* 742c22f. and 743a4ff.; cp. also *Yt* zi 245a7f.; *Yc* 672b5–7; **B.08**: *Yt* 'i 19b6ff.; *Yc* 703a24ff.; **B.09**: *Yt* 'i 17b8ff.; *Yc* 702b17ff.; **B.10**: *Yt* 'i 30a5ff.; *Yc* 707a1ff.

24. Cp. also Suguro, *op. cit.* [see n. 3], 265; 267; Engl. summary p. 11.

25. *Ālayav.*, n. 132.

For, on the one hand, it concludes with the remark that the enumerated concepts may be subsumed under a twofold [set of] key term[s]: one describing Śrāvakayāna, and another describing Mahāyāna. Yet only the set of key terms referring to Mahāyāna (B) is explicitly introduced by the phrase "Or, on the other hand, with reference to the 'Extensive [Tradition]': ... " (*vaipulyaṁ vā punaḥ adhikṛtya* ...). But there is no such introduction to the list of Śrāvakayāna key terms (A). Nor is there any indication in the beginning of the passage that *two* sets of key terms will be listed. This, as I argued in my previous study, gives the impression that there was, originally, just one homogeneous set of *traditional* key terms, and that this set was *afterwards* augmented by another set of specifically Mahāyāna key terms. But this may, of course, already have happened when the *ŚruBh* was compiled, or even before. Such a possibility deserves serious consideration because it may well be that it is only the final sentence (C) that was added by the compiler. This is even more probable in view of the terminological difference: *mahāyāna* in C against *vaipulya* in B.00. In this case, however, the structure of the preceding text (A and B) hardly contains any significant incoherence anymore; for it would then merely consist of a list of common traditional key words to which a list of specific *vaipulya* key terms expressly marked as such was appended as a kind of supplement, possibly, but by no means necessarily, by a second author.

But even in this case the key terms which are unexpected for *MauBh* and seem to presuppose *VinSg* (or at least *VinSg* materials) need not have formed part of the *vaipulya* list from the outset but may well have been added later on to an earlier form of the list containing only key terms derived from, or at any rate consistent with, the *Bodhisattvabhūmi* of *MauBh* (*BoBh*).[26] Actually, the key terms

---

26. **B.3**: *BoBhD* 190,16ff. (+ def.); **B.4**: 27,5f.; def.: cp. 30,26ff.; **B.5**: 25,5ff. (+ def.); **B.6**: 3613ff. (+ def.); 199,20ff.; **B.7**: 36,20ff. (+ def.); 200,1ff.; **B.11**: see below; **B.12.a**: cp. 197,12 (*prathamaś cittotpādaḥ* | *sattveṣv anukampā*) and 156,5f. (*pāramitābhir adhyātmaṁ buddhadharmaparipākaḥ* | *saṁgrahavastubhiḥ sarvasattvaparipākaḥ*); cp. also 197,21ff.; for *prathamaś cittotpādaḥ* also 8,2ff. (+ def.); *sattveṣu kāruṇyam*: 10,12 (as *hetu* of *cittotpāda*; but 14,2f. *sattvānām antike karuṇācittatā* as one of its beneficial effects); *pāramitā*s and *saṁgrahavastus*: ch. I.ix-xiv and xv; *paripāka/paripācana*: 15,7f. and 10f.; ch. I.vi; **B.12.b**: 200,5–201,11; **B.12.c**: 193,9f. (°*tattvārthānupraveśaḥ*, *acintya-prabhāvatā ca*; cp. also the preceding reference to *vineya* and *vinayopāya*, reminding one of the end of B.12.b) and probably (i.e., if my conjecture *vimuktiḥ* for [*a*]*dhimuktiḥ* is right) 62,5–7 (*bodhi* = twofold *prahāṇa*, viz., of the two *āvaraṇa*s, and twofold *jñāna* free from these *āvaraṇa*s, the second being expressly called *anāvaraṇaṁ jñānam*); cp. also the sequence of chapters in *BoBh*: I.iv *Tattvārtha* (referring to *tathatā* and the

which seem to presuppose *VinSg* seem to disturb the pattern of arrangement of the other key terms of list B. For, if we exclude the unexpected ones, we get a sequence of key terms arranged in such a way that those comprising fewer items precede those which comprise more.

To be sure, this holds good only for the first part of the list; towards the end (B.12), the situation becomes somewhat obscure,[27] and it may, moreover, not be the only principle of arrangement. For, in the case of the Śrāvakayāna key terms (list A), we have a similar situation. Here too, if we ignore two (probably apparent) exceptions,[28] the list starts with key terms comprising three items only and then moves on to key terms with four, nine, and thirty-seven items.

---

gnosis [*jñāna*] by which it is cognized [e.g., 26,11–13; 28,9–14]), I.v *Prabhāva*, I.vii *Bodhi*; **B.12.d** (expressly presented as one group called the 140 *āveṇika-buddha-dharmas*): 62,22ff. (i.e., shortly after *anāvaraṇaṁ jñānam*!); cp. 259,4ff. (+ def.).—The only key-term for which I have not found a more or less literal parallel in *BoBh* is **B.11**; but there is no doubt that *bīja* represents *gotra* with which it is identified at *BoBhD* 2,7f.; *avatāra* would seem to correspond to (the first) *cittotpāda* (8,18; 202,19 and 22); *krama* (cp. 8,21?) and *samyakpratipatti* remain somewhat vague but may refer to the gradation of the *bodhisattva* Path (cp. *Daśabhūmikasūtra*, ed. J. Rahder, p. 42 (C): *°bodhisattva-bhūmi-krama°*) and its actual practice (cp. *BoBhD* 203,15+17: *bodhisattvacaryāsu samyak pratipadyante* = *bodhisattvaśikṣāsu śikṣante*; 147,6f.: *svaparārtha-pratipatti*), or to the preliminary and to the higher stages (cp. 253,9?), respectively. *Samyakpratipatti-phala* is most probably the attainment of Buddhahood. But I admit that (unless I have overlooked better parallels) this set of terms, though compatible with *BoBh*, lacks significant features clearly pointing to *BoBh* as its source.

27. If *pāramitā-saṁgrahavastubhiḥ sva-para-santati-paripākaḥ* is counted as three items (cp. *Yc* 345c6f.), B.12.a would form another set of five, just as B.12.b explicitly does. Likewise, B.12.c+d may also be taken as a set of five if *sarvāsv ... yā tathatā tatra ca yaj jñānam* which is clearly an explanation of *tattvārthānugama* is ignored and if the 32 *mahāpuruṣa-lakṣaṇas*, etc., are taken to stand for a single concept, viz., the 140 *āveṇika-buddhadharmas* (cp. *BoBhD* 62,22ff.; 259,3ff.). But it is also possible that B.12.a-d is merely another, not numerically fixed (cp. A.14!) pattern of subdividing the key-term *mahāyāna*.

28. Viz., A.1 (*ṣaḍ-āyatana*) and A.4 (*catvāraḥ pakṣāḥ*). But the first one is specified into *three* items, and in the case of the four *pakṣas* the quite unexpected *ca* after the third item would seem to indicate that the fourth item has been *added* to an original set of *three*, the more so since the fourth item is somewhat heterogeneous also from the point of view of contents and may have been added to a division of *human* beings in order to transform it into a pattern comprising *all* possible followers of the Dharma; cp. *Yt* yi 58b6ff. (*Yc* 750c22ff.): *gṛhasthas* and *pravrajitas* (58b8), humans and non-humans (59a3) as addressees of preaching; cp. also the case of Nāgas (i.e., *amanuṣyas*) trying (albeit unsuccessfully) to receive ordination (*Vin* I 87; *Yc* 592b8–16) and the well-known presence of non-human beings among the audience of Mahāyāna sūtras.

However, the last but one key term (A.14: *śrāmaṇyaphala*) definitely disturbs the numerical pattern since it comprises four items only. The reason is that the list is obviously *also* arranged according to a principle of *contents*, starting from concepts referring to the mundane sphere or to a comprehensive analysis of existence, then moving on to elements decisive for spiritual pollution and purification, and culminating in liberation and the spiritual qualities it entails.

There is good reason to assume that the Mahāyāna key terms were originally arranged according to a similar principle: arrangement according to the number of items comprised, superseded by an arrangement according to a principle of contents: basic concepts concerning the analysis of existence followed by key terms referring to the Path, and finally elements of Buddhahood.

Now, it is precisely the unexpected key terms that do not fit in with at least one of these two principles of arrangement. The five *vastus* (B.01), the three *svabhāvas* (B.08), and the three *niḥsvabhāvatās* (B.09) disturb the numerical pattern. The fivefold *mahābodhi* (B.10), on the other hand, does not, to be sure, disturb the numerical pattern but ought not to precede the fivefold *mahāyāna* (B.11) which, primarily at least, refers to the Path; being the final result of the Path, the fivefold *mahābodhi* rather ought to have been placed somewhere at or towards the end of the list, like other concepts referring to Buddhahood, viz. *vimukti* and *anāvaraṇaṁ jñānam* (B.12.c) and the thirty-two *mahāpuruṣalakṣaṇas*, etc. (B.12.d). And even the position of the three *svabhāvas* (B.08) and the three *niḥsvabhāvatās* (B.09) would be somewhat odd unless the four *paryeṣaṇās* and *yathābhūta-parijñānas* are taken as key terms referring to the analysis of existence rather than to the Path. The only key term that seems to be unusual in *MauBh* and taken from *VinSg* but fits in with both principles of arrangement is the twofold *śūnyatā* (B.02), preceding as it does the twofold *nairātmya* (similarly as, by the way, in *VinSg*).[29] But I think that the irregular position of the other four key terms is conspicuous enough to support the suspicion that they may have been added later.

In view of the central importance of at least three of the concepts under discussion (B.01, B.08, and B.09), it is easy to understand that when they had arisen and become known they were considered indispensable in a list of key terms of Mahāyāna and hence inserted

29. Cp. n. 23. At *Yt* zi 245a7f., the two *śūnyatās* precede the two *nairātmyas*. At *Yt* 'i 124b1f. and 4ff., *pudgala-* and *dharma-śūnyatā* precede *pudgala-* and *dharma-nairātmya*, respectively.

(though I have to admit that I cannot convincingly explain why they were added exactly where they are).[30] The crucial question is, of course, to decide when this insertion may have taken place. The most convenient solution would be the one I suggested in my previous study, viz., after the compilation of *VinSg*. But this hypothesis is argued against by the fact that the treatment of the fivefold *mahābodhi* in *VinSg* is introduced by an explicit reference to the occurrence of this concept "in the *Śrutamayī Bhūmi* [of *MauBh*] on the occasion of summarizing the Mahāyāna,"[31] i.e., in our passage. Therefore, the conclusion appears inevitable that at least this key-word, and thus probably also the other unexpected ones, were inserted *before* the compilation of *VinSg*. In view of the fact that, as stated above, the bare key terms in *ŚruBh* presuppose or require additional information but are not accompanied by a reference to *VinSg* for further elucidation, I presume that they were added at a time when the compilation of *MauBh* was already finished or at least in its very final stage, and some of the materials that were collected in *VinSg* afterwards had already arisen and/or become known to the compiler(s) or redactor(s) of *MauBh*.

2.

Three "characters" (*lakṣaṇa*) equivalent to the three *svabhāva*s are also mentioned in a passage of the *Savitarka-savicārādi-bhūmi* of *MauBh* (*SavBh*). This passage aims to refute the erroneous view that "everything is non-existent in every regard (lit., in the form of every character)" (*sarvaṁ sarvalakṣaṇena nāsti*),[32] a view described as based on a misunderstanding and misinterpretation of the profound Sūtras preached by the Buddha with reference to the inexpressible true essence of things (*nirabhilapya-dharmatām ārabhya*).[33] The adherent of this erroneous view is refuted by the following argument:[34]

---

30. E.g., the redactor may have had assembled a set of additional key-terms in a definite sequence (slightly different, however, from their occurrence in the *Bodhisattvabhūmi* of *VinSg*) and may have then decided to insert them before the item *mahāyāna* (which he might have taken to continue up to the end), but found that the twofold *śūnyatā* should precede the twofold *nairātmya* and therefore separated the first two key-terms of his set from the rest and prefixed it to the already existing list. But this is less than even a guess.

31. *Yt* 'i 30a5f. (= *Yc* 707a1ff.): *Thos pa las byuṅ ba'i sar theg pa chen po bsdus pa'i skabs su "byaṅ chub ni rnam pa lṅa ngo bo ñid daṅ | mthu daṅ | thabs daṅ | 'jug pa daṅ | ldog pa las rig par bya'o" źes ji skad du bstan pa de'i rab tu dbye ba gaṅ yin |.*

32. *Y* 151,21; *Yt* dzi 89a4; *Yc* 311a20f.

That [person] should be given the following rejoinder: Do you accept an entity [having] a perfect character, a dependent character, an imagined character? If [an entity having any such character] exists, then it is unreasonable [to assert] that everything is non-existent in the form of every character (i.e., in every regard). If [however such an entity] does not exist, then [even] a wrong view does not exist, [and hence] neither pollution nor purification exists.[35] Thus, [on this assumption, too, your position turns out to be] unreasonable.

sa idaṁ syād vacanīyaḥ | kaccid icchasi pariniṣpannalakṣaṇaṁ dharmaṁ, paratantralakṣaṇaṁ, parikalpitalakṣaṇaṁ | [36] *saced asti, tena sarvaṁ sarveṇa lakṣaṇena nāstīti na yujyate | sacen nāsti, tena nāsti viparyāso nāsti saṁkleśo nāsti vyavadānam iti na yujyate | |*

For this passage, too, the same argument holds good as in the case of the *ŚruBh* passage discussed in §1, viz., that the three *lakṣaṇas* are hardly self-explanatory and that therefore referring to them without explanation would seem to presuppose some knowledge of them on the part of the reader. Now, in view of the use of the term *lakṣaṇa*, not *svabhāva*, the most probable assumption would then be that the present passage presupposes chapter 6 of *Saṁdh* where these concepts are in fact introduced and defined using the same terminology, i.e., as *lakṣaṇas*, not as *svabhāvas* as in *VinSg*. To be sure, in *Saṁdh* the order is the opposite one (viz., *parikalpita*, *paratantra*, *pariniṣpanna*), but the present passage may have reversed it in order to achieve a sequence of ever less real forms of existence to be negated (which means ever more radical negation). Besides, in *Saṁdh* VII.20 we even find the three *lakṣaṇas* in the same context as in our *SavBh* passage. Here, too, reference is to persons who take the profound Sūtras propounding the emptiness and essencelessness of all *dharmas* (cp. also *Saṁdh* VII.19) literally and adopt, on this basis,

33. *Y* 153,2–6; *Yt* dzi 89b7–90a1; *Yc* 311b16–21.—The extreme position that all is non-existent is, of course, already mentioned in the canon, e.g., *SN* II 17: *sabbaṁ natthīti ... anto*. But the reference to *nirabhilapya-dharmatā* in our passage clearly points to *BoBh* where the sūtras alluded to are doubtless Mahāyāna-sūtras like the *Prajñāpāramitā* (cp. *Ālay*. n. 114).

34. *YB* 154,11ff.; *Yt* dzi 90b2–4; *Yc* 311c15–19.

35. Since the opponent is a (Mahāyāna) Buddhist, the defendent thinks that this consequence must be undesirable for him. And it certainly is so if intended to apply not only to the ultimate but also to the conventional level.

36. The editor has changed the text in accordance with Tib. to *asti pariniṣpannalakṣaṇo dharmaḥ paratantralakṣaṇaḥ parikalpitalakṣaṇo nāsti vā* , but I prefer to follow the ms. since its text makes perfect sense and is syntactically unobjectionable. Tib. (and Ch.) have merely translated the passage in a more explicit way.

with regard to all *dharmas* the wrong view that they do not exist (*med par lta ba = nāstidṛṣṭi*?)[37] and that they have no character (*mtshan ñid med par lta ba*), and thus deny [the existence] of everything in the form of every character (i.e., in every regard) (*mtshan ñid thams cad kyis = sarvalakṣaṇena*). These persons are, indirectly, refuted in a way similar to that of our *SavBh* passage, namely by showing that their denial extends to all the three *lakṣaṇa*s, including the Imagined one (*parikalpita*), because even the Imagined character can be conceived (*rab tu śes par 'gyur = prajñāyate*) only if the Perfect (*pariniṣpanna*) and the Dependent one (*paratantra*) exist.

There is a similar passage in the *Maitreya Chapter* of (some versions of) the *Larger Prajñāpāramitā*.[38] But this text does not introduce the three *lakṣaṇa*s in this passage; when it does so in another place, it employs a different terminology,[39] and can thus hardly have been the source of our *SavBh* passage. On the other hand, the related passages of *BoBh*,[40] which may well have been the basis for *Saṁdh* VII.20, seem to be reflected in the terminology of the description, in our passage, of the *motives* of the wrong view that every thing is non-existent, when it declares (*Y* 153,4) the inexpressible nature of things (*nirabhilapya*[41]*-dharmatā*) to be the real purport of the profound Sūtras.[42] On the other hand, the key concept of the three *lakṣaṇa*s is totally absent in *BoBh* and thus, if in fact presupposed by our *SavBh* passage as known to the reader, must come from elsewhere, i.e., probably *Saṁdh*, perhaps (though this may need more solid proof)[43] *Saṁdh* VII.19–20.

---

37. Cp. *Y* 153,5.

38. Ed. E. Conze and Sh. Iida in *Mélanges d'Indianisme à la mémoire de Louis Renou* (Paris, 1968): 236 (§23–26).

39. *Op. cit.*, 286 (§§37–41): *parikalpitaṁ rūpam*, *vikalpitaṁ rūpam*, *dharmatā-rūpam*.

40. *BoBhD* 31,10ff. and 180,16ff.

41. Thus (and not °*lā*°) ed. and *Ym*; similarly, the Patna ms. of *BoBh* has, at least in the *Tattvārtha* chapter, °*la*° in almost all occurrences of the term. Cp. n. 62.

42. Cp. *BoBhD* 180,23ff., esp. 181,5, 12 and 17; 30,1ff.; 31,1; etc. The concept is not alien to *Saṁdh*; it is a central concept in I and II (cp. esp. I.2: *brjod du med pa'i chos ñid*, probably = *nirabhilapya-dharmatā*), but it does not seem to play any role in VI and VII, and at any rate does not occur in *Saṁdh* VII.19–20 .

43. One would have to exclude the possibility that our *SavBh* passage is based only on *BoBh* and *Saṁdh* VI or a nucleal version of *Saṁdh* VI–VII not yet containing VII.19–20, and that these latter paragraphs, on the contrary, were created on the basis of our *SavBh* passage.

Yet, in the case of our *SavBh* passage, too, the exceptional occurrence of concepts possibly borrowed from *Saṁdh* does not necessarily invalidate the conclusion, drawn from the almost complete lack of such concepts in the large corpus of *MauBh* as a whole, that the bulk of the material contained in *MauBh* is earlier than, or at least not influenced by, *Saṁdh*. Still less so if some evidence could be discovered that this passage, too, may be a later addition. For this purpose, a closer look at the compositional structure of the whole text portion, i.e., the refutation of "nihilism" (*nāstikavāda*: *YB* 151,19–155,5), is required.

At first glance, the composition of the text looks, to be sure, quite harmonious, with a *pūrvapakṣa* (*YB* 151,19–21) containing two erroneous "nihilist" views: firstly the traditional, canonical "nihilist" view denying [the moral value and transcendent effect of] gift, sacrifice, etc.,[44] and secondly the "nihilist" view we are concerned with, viz., the one denying existence of anything in any regard.[45] Then the motives for the two erroneous views are laid bare (152,1–153,2 and 153,2–6, respectively). Thereupon, the two views are refuted one after the other (153,7–154,10 and 154,11–155,2, respectively); and finally (155,3–5), the refutation is summed up by catch words exactly corresponding to the sections of the actual refutation.

Yet, on closer inspection, the structure of the passage turns out to be less consistent. For when the motives why some people adopt the two types of the "nihilist" view are described, the superficial symmetry of treatment is disturbed by the fact that only the second view is introduced by a *specific* question: "For what reason does [a person] have such a view and advocate such [a position], *viz.*, *that everything is non-existent in every regard*?"[46] One would, of course, expect the first, viz., the canonical, "nihilist" view to be introduced by an analogous *specific* question, but actually there is only a *general* one: "For what reason does [a person] have such a view and advocate such [a

44. *YB* 151,19f.: *yathāpīhaikatyaḥ śramaṇo vā brāhmaṇo vaivaṁdṛṣṭir bhavaty evaṁvādī: "nāsti dattaṁ nāstīṣṭam" iti vistareṇa yāvan "na santi loke 'rhanta" iti*| (*Ym* is very indistinct from °*van na* onward; there may be one more *akṣara* after *nna*).

45. *YB* 151,21 (corrected acc. to *Ym*): *evaṁdṛṣṭir vā punar bhavaty evaṁvādī: "sarvaṁ sarvalakṣaṇena nāstī"ti*|. The photo is very indistinct up to °*tyevaṁvādī*, but there are definitely three *akṣara*s looking like *rvāpuna*. This is, moreover, confirmed by Tib. (*yaṅ*) and Ch. 復. For *vā punaḥ*, cp. also *YB* 152,14; 15; 16; 17 (ms. *vā punaḥ* instead of *vā*).

46. *kena kāraṇenaivaṁdṛṣṭir bhavaty evaṁvādī: "nāsti sarvaṁ sarvalakṣaṇene"–ti?*

position]?"[47] This introductory phrase doubtless creates the impression that there was *only one* "nihilist" view, the motives for adopting which are going to be explained, viz., the traditional, canonical one. For in this case—and only then—it would have been quite natural not to specify the view itself again (since this had already been done immediately before), as is in fact the case in most of the other erroneous positions, treated in this chapter of *SavBh*, that contain only one wrong view.[48] But if, as in the present case, the erroneous position comprises two *different* wrong views, and if also the motives for adopting them are different—as they in fact are—[49] it would seem necessary to introduce the motives for *both* of them, and not only those for the second view, by *specific* questions. Hence, the fact that the motives for the first "nihilist" view are introduced only in a general way, just as if there were only this one, is strange and looks very much like a trace of an incomplete redactional change. It would in fact be easily explicable on the assumption that the passage *originally* consisted of a treatment of the canonical "nihilist" view only, and that the second, Mahāyāna "nihilist" view was *added later*. The only thing one would have to assume in addition is that the redactor failed to notice that, after he had inserted this second "nihilist view along with an appropriately introduced separate paragraph pointing out the motives behind it, the original introductory question, now no longer introducing the motives for *the* "nihilist" view but those of the first only, would have required specification.

It is difficult to decide when exactly the treatment of the Mahāyāna "nihilist" view was added. Theoretically, this might have happened even before the compilation of *MauBh*, but equally well during the compilation process, or even later. In view of the fact that the refutation makes use of the three *lakṣaṇa*s absent in *MauBh* except for the three passages discussed in this paper, and totally absent in what seem to be the older layers, like *BoBh* and *Śrāvakabhūmi*, I for one consider the first alternative (viz., before the compilation of *MauBh*) extremely unlikely. As for the other alternatives, I shall return to the question

47. *kena kāraṇenaivaṁdṛṣṭir bhavaty evaṁvādī?*

48. Cp. *YB* 123,2; 129,7f. (read, with ms., *kena kāraṇena sa evaṁ°*); 143,5; 144,10; 146,1f.; 151,4; 155,11; 159,16.

49. The *śuddhivāda* (*YB* 156,19ff.) comprises, to be sure, three different wrong views, but there is no difference with regard to the motives for adopting them, hence no need for specific introductions to the description of these motives.

at the end of my investigation of the third passage to be discussed in this paper.

3.

This passage is found in the beginning of the *Cintāmayī Bhūmi* of *MauBh* (*CiBh*). Here we find the three *lakṣaṇa*s (in the same inverted sequence as in the *SavBh* passage treated in §2) as the first three items of a set of five kinds of "being existent" (*astitā*).[50] This set is paralleled by a set of five kinds of "being non-existent" (*nāstitā*),[51] the first three of which correspond to the three *niḥsvabhāvatā*s, once again in inverted sequence, although the terminology is somewhat different.

> Which one is the fivefold "being existent"? [1] being existent [in the sense of] the Perfect Character; [2] being existent [in the sense of] the Dependent Character; [3] being existent [in the sense of] the Imagined Character; [4] being existent [in the sense of] a specific character; [5] being existent [as something having] an incommunicable character.
>
> *pañcavidhā astitā katamā* | *pariniṣpanna-lakṣaṇâstitā, paratantra-lakṣaṇâstitā, parikalpita-lakṣaṇâstitā, viśeṣa-lakṣaṇâstitā, avaktavya*[52]*-lakṣaṇâstitā ca* |
>
> ...
>
> Which one is the fivefold "being non-existent? [1] being non-existent [in the sense of lacking] the character of highest reality;[53] [2] being non-existent [in the sense of lacking] the character of [being] independent; [3] being non-existent [in the sense] of entirely [lacking] a character of its own; [4] being non-existent [in the sense of] lacking a specific character; [5] being non-existent [in the sense of] lacking a communicable character.[54]
>
> *pañcavidhā nāstitā katamā* | *paramārtha-lakṣaṇa-nāstitā, svatantra-lakṣaṇa-nāstitā, sarveṇa sarvaṁ sva-lakṣaṇa-nāstitā, aviśeṣa-lakṣaṇa-nāstitā, avaktavya-lakṣaṇa-nāstitā ca* |

In the case of this passage, however, it is not so easy to decide whether the concepts have been borrowed from somewhere else

---

50. *Ym* 104b3f.; *ŚrBhm* 3A4,5; *Yt* dzi 234b7–235a1; *Yc* 362c21–24.

51. *Ym* 104b6–105a1; *ŚrBhm* 3B4–1; *Yt* dzi 235b2f.; *Yc* 363a8–10.t

52. *ŚrBhm: avyakta.*

53. A simpler rendering would be: "the fact that [something] lacks the character of ...."

54. Tib. (*brjod par bya ba'i mtshan ñid med pa ñid*) = "non-existence (or: lack) of a communicable character" (i.e., *vaktavya*-°). Similarly Ch.

because at least in the case of the three *lakṣaṇa*s the text adds short definitions:[55]

> Among these [five kinds of "being existent"], the first [refers to] the character belonging to the highest reality. Next, the second [refers to] the character of what has arisen in dependence [on causes and conditions]. Next, the third [refers to] the character of [linguistic] convention.
>
> *tatra prathamā pāramārthikaṁ*[56] *lakṣaṇaṁ* | *anu dvitīyā pratītyasamutpannaṁ*[57] *lakṣaṇaṁ* | *anu*[58] *tṛtīyā saṁketalakṣaṇaṁ* |

To be sure, the corresponding three kinds of "being non-existent" are not expressly defined in our text, but this might be accounted for by the fact that their meanings are more or less self-explanatory in view of their close correspondence to the three kinds of "being existent."

On the other hand, the combination of the three *lakṣaṇa*s and their negative counterparts, as forms of "being existent" and "being non-existent," with two more *lakṣaṇa*s which, at least as far as I can see, are not organically related to them, may indicate that even this passage has borrowed them from somewhere else and extended them, for external reasons (i.e., compulsion to numerical symmetry), into a pattern of five items.

Actually, such a reason is easily discernable. For our passage forms part of a larger section explaining the "analysis of what may, or should, be object of knowledge" (*jñeya-pravicaya*).[59] What may or should be object of knowledge is defined as "what is to be investigated" (*parīkṣyo 'rthaḥ*), and this is stated to comprise the existent and the non-existent, to be investigated (and understood) *as* existent and non-existent, respectively (*sac ca sataḥ, asac câsataḥ*). The existent (*sad vastu*) to be investigated is then, in its turn, said to be regarded as *fivefold*: existent in the sense of its own character (*sva-lakṣaṇa-sat*), existent in the sense of a common character (*sāmānya-lakṣaṇa-sat*), existent in the sense of a conventional character (*saṁketa-lakṣaṇa-sat*), existent as what has the character of cause (*hetu-lakṣaṇa-sat*), and existent as what has the character of effect (*phala-lakṣaṇa-sat*),[60] all of which are extensively explained. Likewise, the non-existent (*asad vastu*)

---

55. *Ym* 104b4; *ŚrBhm* 3A4,5f.; *Yt* dzi 235a1f.; *Yc* 362c24f.

56. *Ym*: °*ka*°.

57. *ŚrBhm*: °*nna*°.

58. *ŚrBhm*: °*ṇamanu*.

59. *Ym* 102b6–105a1; *ŚrBhm* 3B2,6 - 3B4,1; *Yt* dzi 231a3–235b3; *Yc* 361c1–363a10.

60. *Ym* 102b6–103a1; *ŚrBhm* 3B2,6f.; *Yt* dzi 231a4–6; *Yc* 361c4–6.

to be investigated is also *fivefold*: non-existent because not yet arisen (*anutpannâsat*), non-existent because it has ceased to exist (*niruddhâsat)*, mutually non-existent (*itaretarâsat*, i.e., not being identical with each other), non-existent in the sense of the highest reality (*paramārthâsat*), and absolutely non-existent (*atyantâsat*), like the son of a barren woman.[61] These too are briefly explained. Thereafter, the passage on the fivefold "being existent" (*astitā*) and "being non-existent" (*nāstitā*) is appended by means of an introductory phrase (*api khalu pañcavidhā astitā, pañcavidhaiva nāstitā* |). It is obvious that this additional specification of existence and non-existence is intended as an alternative explanation of the fivefold existent and non-existent constituting the *jñeya* and that there is hence in fact a strong formal motive why a pre-existing pattern of three concepts might have been supplemented so as to become five.

In addition, the change of terminology (*astitā* and *nāstitā* instead of *sad* [*vastu*] and *asad* [*vastu*]) would seem to suggest that the whole passage from *api khalu* onward is an addition to a textual structure that is entirely complete without it. This first and main part of the *jñeya-pravicaya* chapter does not, as far as I can see after an admittedly preliminary inspection, contain any significant terminology one would not expect to find in *MauBh*. Similar to the bulk of the *vaipulya* key terms in the *ŚruBh* passage, it merely makes use of characteristic ideas of *BoBh*, especially the idea of the highest reality as the inexpressible reality in all *dharmas* which is the object of supramundane gnosis (*paramārtha-lakṣaṇaṁ katamat* | *yo nirabhilapyo*[62] *'rthaḥ sarva-dharmeṣu lokottara-jñāna-gocaraḥ* ...),[63] whereas the own-being or essence established by means of the ordinary, everyday application of language is non-existent from the point of view of highest reality (*paramārthâsat katamat* | *vyāvahārikeṇa svabhāva-prajñapti-vādena yaḥ svabhāvo vyavasthāpitaḥ* |)[64].[65] It seems that to this self-contained textual unit the passage on the five kinds of *astitā* and *nāstitā* was added with the intention to include, into the treatment of the existent and non-existent that has to be investigated and understood as such, the new

61. *Ym* 104b2 (two items missing); *ŚrBhm* 3A4,3; *Yt* dzi 234b3f. = *Yc* 362c14–16.

62. Thus (and not °*lā*°) at least *ŚrBhm*; *Ym* indistinct. Cp. n. 41.

63. *Ym* 103a1; *ŚrBhm* 3B2,7; *Yt* dzi 231a7; *Yc* 361c8–10.

64. *Ym* 104b3: *ŚrBhm* 3A4,4–5; *Yt* dzi 234b6; *Yc* 362c19f.

65. Cp. *BoBhD* 26,11–13; 26,27; 28,9–11; 30,1–5 and 7f., etc.; 187,15f.; 188,16ff.; 190,19f., etc.

and more differentiated pattern of the three *lakṣaṇa*s and their negative counterparts.[66]

This does not, of course, by itself, exclude the possibility that the concept of the three *lakṣaṇa*s is an invention of our *CiBh* passage.[67] But if I am right in taking the fact of their being combined with two other, hardly homogeneous, concepts into a set of five to indicate that our *CiBh* passage took over the concept of the three *lakṣaṇa*s from somewhere else, *Saṁdh* VI would, just as in the case of the *SavBh* passage discussed in §2, seem to be the most likely candidate. Actually, the definitions given by our passage are compatible with those given by *Saṁdh*,[68] and those of the *paratantra-* and the *parikalpita-lakṣaṇa* even look like abbreviations of their *Saṁdh* counterparts. On the other hand, our *CiBh* passage differs from *Saṁdh* by using *lakṣaṇa* instead of *svabhāva* also in the case of the three negative counterparts, called the three *niḥsvabhāvatā*s in *Saṁdh* VII. It would thus have unified the non-uniform terminology of *Saṁdh* in favor of *lakṣaṇa* (in contrast to *VinSg* which consistently uses *svabhāva*). Besides, the fact that different specific designations are used in the case of two items of the negative set (viz., *svatantra-* and *sarveṇa sarvaṁ sva-lakṣaṇa-nāstitā* against *utpatti-* and *lakṣaṇa-niḥsvabhāvatā* in *Saṁdh* VII.3–5) may indicate that the concepts had not yet become firmly rooted, i.e., that they were quite new, perhaps not yet there—or not yet available to the compiler/redactor of our *CiBh* passage—in a fixed literary form.

In view of the fact that both the *SavBh* passage and the *CiBh* passage enumerate the *lakṣaṇa*s in the same unusual sequence differing from that of *Saṁdh* (and most other sources)[69] by exchanging *parikalpita* and *pariniṣpanna*, it is reasonable to assume that either one of these passages has made use of the other or, more probably, both have been inserted into *MauBh* by the same person (or team). Since this

---

66. The deviance of the *CiBh* passage on the fivefold *astitā* and *nāstitā* is also underlined by the reference to the "incomprehensible *dharmakāya* of the Tathāgatas" (*Ym* 104b5; *Yt* 235a7; *Yc* 363a3); the term *dharmakāya* is very rarely used in *MauBh* (as far as I know, only at *Ym* 129a4 = *Yt* dzi 289b7 = *Yc* 382c20, in contrast to *rūpakāya*).

67. In this case, the present passage would, of course, also suffice to explain the occurrence, in the same sequence, of the three *lakṣaṇa*s in the *SavBh* passage discussed in §2.

68. Viz., *Saṁdh* VI.4–6.

69. An exception is the *Mahāyānasaṁgraha* where we find (II.1; Prast. 3.2) the *paratantra* preceding *parikalpita* and *pariniṣpanna*.

same sequence is also found in the case of the three *svabhāvas* in the *ŚruBh* passage,[70] this too would seem to have some connection with (at least one of) the two others, but the divergent terminology (*svabhāva* instead of *lakṣaṇa*) and the fact that in the case of the three *niḥsvabhāvatās* the sequence is the usual one indicates that the *ŚruBh* passage is based on additional material or information.

To sum up: In the case of all the three passages examined in this paper, which contain concepts unexpected in *MauBh* (like the three *svabhāvas* / *lakṣaṇas*), traces or indications suggesting that something was added to older materials can be discerned. Yet, even in the case of the *ŚruBh* passage (§1), which even seems to presuppose *VinSg* materials probably later than *Saṁdh* VI-VII, the addition must have taken place *before* the compilation of *VinSg*. Hence, the same is possible also in the case of the other two passages, the more so if I am right in concluding from the inverted sequence of the three *svabhāvas* in the *ŚruBh* passage that it presupposes (at least one of) them. My conclusion is therefore that these passages were probably added after or at least towards the very end of the compilation of *MauBh*, but before the compilation of *VinSg* had started (hence no reference to it). At this time, some information on *Saṁdh* VI-VII (or the ideas to be developed there) and, in the case of the *ŚruBh* passage, on some materials later included in *VinSg* would have reached the compiler(s) (or a redactor) of *MauBh*, but they were, for whatever reason,[71] only made use of in a few places and not included systematically. I admit that this is nothing but a hypothesis, but I hope that at least the materials and observations presented in this paper may contribute to future clarification.

---

70. Cp. n. 21.

71. One possibility is that the compilation process had already reached a stage that did not allow the inclusion of the new materials more fully; or perhaps more probably the ideas were quite new and had not yet assumed, or become available in, a fixed literary form. Unfortunately, we have no first hand information about how, precisely, literary works like *Saṁdh* (or *Y*, for that matter, or the materials used for its compilation) were produced.

The *Yogācāra Bhikṣu*[*]

Jonathan A. Silk

It is never easy to understand any Indian Buddhist text. Every volume—sometimes it seems like every line on every page—is filled with terms and ideas foreign to us, obscure, part of a jigsaw puzzle-like world many of whose pieces we have not yet discovered or correctly identified. Yet, we can sometimes uncover continuities in ideas or usages that may, especially when put into a broader context of Buddhist thought, yield significant insights into the tradition as a whole, allowing us to gradually discern the outlines and underlying structures of the system. Professor Gadjin M. Nagao, the great scholar to whom this volume is dedicated, has shown us by his example how careful consideration of individual words may deepen our understanding of Buddhist thought, enhance our ability to read a variety of Buddhist texts with greater precision, and gradually work toward a more comprehensive appreciation of old Indian Buddhist world-views. In the following I would like to offer to Prof. Nagao what I believe to be, although small, a potentially important piece of this large puzzle.

The term *yogācāra bhikṣu* appears several times in the relatively early Mahāyāna sūtra *Kāśyapaparivarta*, of which Prof. Nagao and I are preparing a new translation, and again more regularly in the probably somewhat later text upon which I focussed my doctoral thesis, the *Ratnarāśisūtra*.[1] Although both of these sūtras certainly

---

* This is a substantially revised version of part of chapter 4 of my doctoral dissertation, Silk 1994: 97–142.

I would like to thank Nobuyoshi Yamabe for his generous assistance, criticism, and discussion over the years on the specific and general problems dealt with here. I was also fortunate enough to receive a detailed and lengthy critique of an earlier draft from Prof. Lambert Schmithausen, which has dramatically improved the paper. In addition, for their many corrections and for much information I am indebted to Professors Jens-Uwe Hartmann, Harunaga Isaacson, Seishi Karashima, Shōryū Katsura, Gadjin Nagao, and Gregory Schopen. I thank also Prof. Madhav Deshpande for his remarks on Sanskrit grammar, and Kaoru Onishi and Klaus Wille for their kindness in sending me materials. None of the above are, of course, responsible for any of the shortcomings of the paper.

1. See Silk 1994. I am preparing a new edition of the Indic text of the *Kāśyapaparivarta*, a critical edition of the Tibetan and Chinese translations and, together with Prof. Nagao, an English translation. We hope to publish the complete results of our study before too long.

contain a large amount of obviously problematic vocabulary, my attention was nevertheless drawn to the perhaps not so clearly troublesome term *yogācāra bhikṣu*. I gradually realized that although I thought I could translate the term adequately, I did not actually clearly understand it. The present paper, then, represents one attempt to investigate this term, primarily as it is used in so-called Mainstream Buddhism and early Mahāyāna literature, but with some attention also given to its use in the later and more systematic śāstric literature.[2]

When the word *yogācāra* is defined by dictionaries of Classical Sanskrit, its primary sense is given as "the practice or observance of Yoga."[3] It is thus understood as a genitive *tatpuruṣa*. The word appears to be rare in Classical Sanskrit, although it does occur in several technical works.[4] The form *yogācāra* apparently does not occur in either of the two Epics, the *Mahābhārata* or *Rāmāyaṇa*, but a related term, *yogācārya*, appears several times in the former.[5]

---

2. I do not know whether, and if so how, the term is used in Buddhist logical or tantric literature, fields in which I have no competence.

3. Apte 1957, s.v., without citation. Monier-Williams 1899 s.v. also cites the term as equivalent to *yogin*, again without reference. Böhtlingk and Roth 1855–1875 s.v. define it as "die Observanz des *Joga*," as well as "Titel einer Schrift über den Joga," citing for the second sense Mallinātha's commentary on *Kumārasambhava* 3.47, but the latter is apparently an error. The text I have been able to check has instead *Yogasāra* (Thakkur 1987).

4. The last verse of Praśastapāda's *Padārthadharmasaṁgraha* (Jetly and Parikh 1991: 698) reads: *yogācāravibhūtyā yas toṣayitvā maheśvaram* | *cakre vaiśeṣikaṁ śāstraṁ tasmai kaṇabhuje namaḥ* | |. "Homage to Kaṇabhuj who, having pleased Maheśvara (i.e., Śiva) by the richness of his practice of yoga, created the Vaiśeṣika *śāstra* (i.e., *Vaiśeṣika-sūtra*-s)."

In Vācaspatimiśra's *Tātparyaṭīkā*, glossing Pakṣilasvāmin's *Nyāyabhāṣya* ad *Nyāya-sūtra* 4.2.46 (Taranatha Nyaya-Tarkatirtha and Amarendramohan Tarkatirtha 1936–1944), he explains *yogācāra* as: *ekākitā āhāraviśeṣaḥ ekatrānavasthānam ityādi yati-dharmoktam*. "*Yogācāra* is the practice of renouncers comprising solitude, [eating only] special foods, not staying in one place, and so on."

In both examples, the term is clearly a *tatpuruṣa*. I owe these references entirely to the kindness of Dr. Harunaga Isaacson.

5. Thanks to the invaluable computer data of the complete critical editions of the two Epics, input by Prof. Muneo Tokunaga and his students, I was able to easily check the entire corpus. I have found the following occurrences: *Mahābhārata* 1.60.42 (with regard to Bhṛgu) reads: *yogācāryo mahābuddhir daityānām abhavad guruḥ* | *surāṇāṁ cāpi meghāvī brahmacārī yatavrataḥ* | |. Nīlakaṇṭha comments: *yogācārya iti cāpī vyastau* | *surāṇām api ca gurur iti saṁbandhaḥ* | *devānāṁ gurur eva yogācāryo yogabalena kāyadvayaṁ kṛtvā devānām apy ācāryo bhavad ity arthaḥ* | . . .; 12.59.91: *adhyāyānām sahasreṇa kāvyaḥ saṁkṣepam abravīt* | *tac chāstram amitaprajño yogācāryo mahātapāḥ* | |; 16.5.23: *tato*

In Buddhist texts in Sanskrit we find nearly exclusively the form *yogācāra*, with the feminine form *yogācārā*.[6] Sometimes the word is explicitly coordinated with *bhikṣu* (or in the feminine with *bhikṣuṇī*), but often it is not. I have never encountered the form **yogācārin*, which should perhaps be considered a ghost word,[7] and have so far found the term *yogācārya* only a very few times in Buddhist texts.[8] The term *yogācāra* often appears coordinated with *yogin*, and indeed in some cases the terms appear to be used as synonyms.[9] In late canonical and post-canonical Pāli we find what seems to be an

---

rājan bhagavān ugratejā nārāyaṇaḥ prabhavaś cāvyayaś ca | *yogācāryo rodasī vyāpya lakṣmyā sthānam prāpa svaṁ mahātmāprameyam* | |. See also the prose passage at 12.185.1.2.

The term seems not to occur in the *Rāmāyaṇa*. Note however that my search takes into account only the computer data of the critically established texts, and does not consider variants (which are often considerable).

The term *yogācārya* also appears in other similar texts, for example in the *Bhāgavata Purāṇa* 9.12.3. According to Monier-Williams 1899 s.v., *yogācārya* is sometimes wrongly written for *yogācāra* but, again, he gives no reference (but the *Mahābhārata* passages obviously intend *yogācārya*).

The term *yogācārya* is relatively easy to understand, being a *tatpuruṣa* constructed from *yoga* and *ācārya*, apparently in a genitive relation, and it seems to mean just what we would expect: "master of yoga." The exact meaning of the term *yoga* is of course not thereby clarified, but with the proviso that *yoga* itself may remain not fully determined, the compound is basically clear.

6. For the feminine, see below n. 64.

7. The form *yogācārī bhikṣuḥ* is printed several times in Bendall's edition of the *Śikṣāsamuccaya* (Bendall 1897–1902: 55.13–18). However, the manuscript is perfectly clear in all cases in reading *yogācāro bhikṣuḥ*; see below n. 55. Perhaps the most plausible explanation is that in reading the early sheets of the proofs, being as he confesses (Wogihara 1904: 97, n. 1) unfamiliar with the St.-Petersburg type, Bendall failed to notice the misprint. Although somewhat similar in modern *devanāgarī*, *ī* and *o* are written entirely differently in the script of the *Śikṣāsamuccaya* manuscript (Cambridge Add. 1478). A new edition of the *Śikṣāsamuccaya* is now in preparation by Jens Braarvig and myself.

8. Once in Schlingloff 1964: 128R2, and once in the *Abhidharmadīpa* (Jaini 1977: 337.2): *yogācāryasya khalv abhi///* [subsequent text lost]. I have not found any indication of equivalents of *yogācārya* in Tibetan translations of Indic works. Bhattacharya 1982: 388 suggested that the Buddha is called *yogācārya* in the *Śivapurāṇa* II.5.16.11. The verse reads (edition Shri Venkateshvara Press, Bombay, 1965): *namas te gūḍha-dehāya vedaniṁdākarāya ca* | *yogācāryāya jaināya bauddharūpāya māpate* | |. (I owe the Sanskrit to the kindness of Prof. Georg von Simson.) While Bhattacharya is probably right that *yogācārya* is meant to qualify the Buddha, strictly speaking it refers to Viṣṇu in his *avatāra* as the Buddha, and it is not impossible that it is Viṣṇu who is here being called the "yoga master," rather than, or at least as much as, the Buddha.

9. See below for citations of *yogācāra* and *yogin* used appositionally.

equivalent term, *yogāvacara*.[10] The standard Tibetan equivalent of the Sanskrit, *rnal 'byor spyod pa*, fully supports the form *yogācāra*.[11] When we come to Chinese sources, however, we do not encounter the same precision.

The least equivocal Chinese rendering of *yogācāra* is *yuqieshi* 瑜伽師. The Chinese exegete Kuiji 窺基, the chief disciple of Xuanzang, has attempted a grammatical analysis of this term in his *Cheng Weishi-lun shuji* 成唯識論述記. He writes:[12] "'A master of *yoga*' is a *tatpuruṣa*.

---

10. On the Pāli evidence, see Silk 1997. The only canonical use of the term in Pāli is in the late *Paṭisambhidāmagga*.

11. Harunaga Isaacson has kindly drawn my attention to the word *yogacaryā*, which occurs, for example, in *Hevajratantra* I.vi.15 (Snellgrove 1959). Interestingly, it too is there rendered *rnal 'byor spyod pa*. I have not noticed this Sanskrit word in other Buddhist texts I have examined, but according to Isaacson it occurs in the *Mahābhārata* as well.

12. T. 1830 (XLIII) 272c6–14: 瑜伽之師、即依士[though often so read, likely a mistake for 主]釋。師有瑜伽名瑜伽師、即有財釋. La Vallée Poussin 1928–1929: I.46, note 1, in reference to this passage says that "Kuiji signals the variant Yogācāra." Mukai 1978: 268 also seems to understand the reference as *yogācāra*. Miyamoto 1932: 780–81, however, thinks that Kuiji is thinking of *yogācārya*. Although not without problems, we should probably assume that 瑜伽之師 as a *tatpuruṣa* is intended to refer to a compound analyzed as **yogasya + ācārya*. The *bahuvrīhi* is especially hard to understand in its Chinese guise, but the reading 師有瑜伽 *could* support **yogācāra*, which as a *bahuvrīhi* certainly means 瑜伽師, but the 師 would be problematic. If we understand 師 to directly represent one of the members of the compound, **ācāra* would be ruled out. This would lead to the conclusion that here too **yogācārya* is intended, even though as a *bahuvrīhi* this is probably impossible. So far the *Cheng Weishi-lun shuji*. However, Nobuyoshi Yamabe has brought to my attention T. 1861 大乘法苑義林章 (XLV) 255b, in which in a rather confused argument the same Kuiji suggests that 成唯識論 = *Vijñaptimātratāsiddhi* is not only a *tatpuruṣa* but also a *bahuvrīhi*. The crucial sentence seems to be 255b15–16: 此論以唯識爲所成。名成唯識論。亦有財釋, "This treatise takes mere cognition (**vijñaptimātra*[*tā*]) as what is to be proved (**sādhya*), and thus it is called *Vijñaptimātratāsiddhi*, which is a *bahuvrīhi*." Actually, if I understand the passage at 255a23–25 correctly, Kuiji also seems to suggest that the term is a *karmadhāraya*! As Yamabe suggested to me, it is possible to speculate that since Kuiji knows that the treatise itself is not equivalent to Vijñaptimātratāsiddhi, that is, he knows that the treatise *explains* the establishment of mere cognition but is not that establishment *itself*, he feels the term must somehow be a *bahuvrīhi*. All of this would strongly suggest that Kuiji was not quite at home with Sanskrit grammatical analysis.

We might just notice here the remarks of the Chinese Faxiang (Yogācāra) monk Huizhao 慧沼, in his sub-commentary on Kuiji's commentary (T. 1832 [XLIII] 696a14–15): "There is an explanation that [*yogācāra* should be analyzed] as a *tatpuruṣa*: 'a teacher of yoga.' Or as a *bahuvrīhi*: 'a teacher who possesses yoga (?).' This is also a *tatpuruṣa*, and not a *bahuvrīhi*." 有說瑜伽之師、即依士釋。師有瑜伽師、即有財

'A master who possesses *yoga*' is called a *yuqieshi* 瑜伽師; this is a *bahuvrīhi*." This led some scholars, such as Louis de La Vallée Poussin, to suggest that what Kuiji had in mind here was the term **yogācārya*, perhaps since it does not seem possible to translate *yogācāra* as a *tatpuruṣa* with *yuqieshi*.[13] However, Kuiji's knowledge of Sanskrit grammar is suspect, and the interpretation of his Korean colleague Toryun 遁倫 (better Tullyun 道倫?)[14] may, in this regard at least, be more correct. In his own voluminous commentary on the *Yogācārabhūmi*, Toryun seems well aware that *shi* 師 represents *ācāra*.[15] Other Chinese renderings, which we will discuss below, while valuable from the point of view of the *meaning* of *yogācāra*, do not contribute to our *grammatical* understanding of the term.

In agreement with what the Chinese sources seem to indicate, it has been usual for modern scholars, too, to interpret the primary

---

釋。此亦依主、而非有財. (There appears to be something wrong with the expression 師有瑜伽師, from which the final 師 should perhaps be deleted, although the expression is quoted with the same reading in T. 2266 [LXVII] 175a8–9. Prof. Schmithausen suggests that 師有瑜伽師 may be due to an understanding something like "a person who has *yoga* as his *ācāra*," but with 師 being used for *both* "person" and "*ācāra*.")

13. Kuiji is commenting on *Cheng Weishi-lun* T. 1585 (XXXI) 4b29, 瑜伽師, which La Vallée Poussin 1928–1929: I.46 rendered as "Yogācārya." The problem was already alluded to by Sylvain Lévi in 1911: *16, n. 1.

14. See Mochizuki 1932–1936: 4924b.

15. See T. 1828 (XLII), the 瑜伽論記. At 312c10–11 we find: 梵言。阿遮羅。此云師. How Miyamoto 1932: 780 gets *ācār(ya)*, 1933 [1985]: 178 *ācār(y)a*, out of this mystifies me. (Without referring to Miyamoto, Ui 1958: 29 unequivocally rejects *ācārya* here.) Further, Miyamoto 1932: 783 is fairly insistent that 師 must reflect Sanskrit *ācārya*, although he is clearly aware (and even more so in 1933) that *yogācāra* may be a *bahuvrīhi*. All of this, however, should not necessarily suggest that Toryun understood Sanskrit well. In his T. 1828 (XLII) 313a3–6, following a lengthy section which is a recapitulation and gloss on T. 1580 (XXX) 884, is what appears to be a somewhat garbled version of Kuiji's T. 1829 (XLIII) 2b4–8, in which the term *Yogācārabhūmi* is discussed as follows: 師有瑜伽即財釋。瑜伽之師。依主釋也。瑜伽師之地。亦依主釋。瑜伽即地。二體無別。地是所詮。能詮即論。瑜伽師地之論。亦依主釋。合爲瑜伽師地論有三釋. We may translate this: "[If we interpret the compound *yogācāra* in the sense that] the master possesses yoga, then it is a *bahuvrīhi*. [If we interpret it to mean] a master of yoga, then it is a *tatpuruṣa*. [Then, we can interpret the compound *yogācārabhūmi* in the sense of] the bhūmi of a *yogācāra*, which again is a *tatpuruṣa*. [But] yoga and bhūmi are entirely identical. [Therefore, the compound may also be an appositional *karmadhāraya*]. Bhūmi is what is explained, and what explains is a *śāstra*. [Therefore, the *Yogācārabhūmi-śāstra*] means the *śāstra* of the *Yogācārabhūmi*; this also is a *tatpuruṣa*. Altogether, three types of compounds [*bahuvrīhi*, *tatpuruṣa*, *karmadhāraya*] are involved in interpreting the [compound] *Yogācārabhūmi-śāstra*." I thank Nobuyoshi Yamabe for his help with this passage.

usage of *yogācāra* in Buddhist literature as a *bahuvrīhi*, literally "one who has yoga as his practice" or "one who carries out his practice through yoga," and thus "a practitioner of yoga."[16] A recent article by Hajime Nakamura, however, has suggested another interpretation. Nakamura raised the possibility that the compound should be understood according to Pāṇini III.2.1 (*karmaṇy-aṆ*).[17] According to the explanation of Madhav Deshpande, this rule allows the derivation of a compound with *ācāra* as an agentive final member, namely *yogaṁ ācarati iti yogācāraḥ*.[18] Without test forms such as **yogācāraka*, we cannot then be certain whether the term should actually be understood as a *bahuvrīhi*.[19] It is, however, as Prof. Deshpande further pointed out, so understood in the *Abhidhānarājendra* (s.v. *jogāyāra*), *yogena ācāraḥ yasya*: *yoga* + *ā* + *car* + *ghañ*. While it is, then, worthwhile being cautious in this regard, it might not be too rash to suggest that in its ordinary Buddhist usage *yogācāra* is probably an exocentric compound. Moreover, this usage seems to be particularly Buddhist, in so far as I have been able to determine.

In addition to the guidance we get from etymological considerations and from examining actual context and usage, Chinese translations of Indian Buddhist terms often provide what amounts to another interpretation which can also guide us in our own attempts to understand the term. But this very fact conceals a danger: how can we know that a given Chinese term in fact represents a given Indic term? Below we will examine a number of texts which we possess in either Sanskrit and Chinese or Tibetan and Chinese, and occasionally in all three. In the case of the term *yogācāra*, the virtually complete standardization of the Tibetan rendering allows us to set the Tibetan and Chinese translations side by side. And what we discover through this process is disturbing.

---

16. Matsunami 1954: 158, for example, explicitly calls it a *bahuvrīhi*.

17. Nakamura 1993 actually refers to the *Sarvadarśanasaṁgraha* (Abhyankar 1978: 293.3–94.12 = XIII.59–82, in the chapter *Pāṇinidarśana*), and only tangentially to Pāṇini and Patañjali. The *Sarvadarśanasaṁgraha* translation of Cowell and Gough 1904: 207 seems to be based on a slightly different text. The relevant discussion in the *Mahābhāṣya* is found in Kielhorn 1965: 95.21–96.4. For the grammatical discussion which follows I am entirely indebted to the kind explanations of Prof. Madhav Deshpande.

18. The feminine of such a compound should (according to P. IV.1.15) be **yogācārī*. Kātyāyana, however, (*vārttika* 7) suggests an alternative, namely that rather than *-aṆ* the suffix be understood as *-Ṇa*, this yielding a feminine in *-ā*.

19. And since of course we have no accented instance of the term.

As an example, while *zuochan biqiu* 坐禪比丘 seems very often to correspond to *yogācāra bhikṣu*, *zuochan* itself at least more often certainly does *not* render *yogācāra*. A famous expression is that naming Revata the first among meditators, those who engage in *dhyāna*, which of course is very often rendered *zuochan* 坐禪.[20] The same Chinese term may also render other Sanskrit terms.[21] In his translation of the *Abhidharmakośa* Paramārtha, who is known for his inconsistency, renders the Sanskrit text's *yogācāra* once with *guanxingshi* 觀行師, then the term *dhyāyin* with *guanxingren* 觀行人, and then again another *yogācāra* with the same *guanxingren* 觀行人.[22] Here Xuanzang's translation is entirely consistent, with *yogācāra* both times rendered with the transcription-cum-translation *yuqieshi* 瑜伽師.[23] Would that things were only this simple! What is truly distressing is that even this term which we might have felt with some confidence to systematically represent *yogācāra* in Chinese, *yuqieshi* 瑜伽師, does not always and necessarily do so. When we encounter this rendering in one version of the *Laṅkāvatāra*, for instance, it clearly does *not* render *yogācāra*.[24] So perhaps it is only lesser translators than Xuanzang who falter?

On the whole, Xuanzang is certainly among the more consistent of the Chinese translators, and in fact he is often consistent even to

---

20. See, for example, the *Śūraṁgamasamādhi* T. 642 (XV) 643c18–19, in which we have 坐禪第一如離婆多, which is in Tibetan (Derge 132, *mdo sde*, *da*, 305b4) *la la na ni nam gru bzhin du bsam gtan par gyur.*

In the *Samādhirājasūtra*, chapter 28 (Dutt 1939–59: II.163.1), *daśeme kumāra ānuśaṁsā dhyānādhimuktasya bodhisattvasya mahāsattvasya* ... appears in Chinese (T. 639 [XV] 584c24) as 菩薩摩訶薩與禪相應, and (T. 640 [XV] 621a11) as 坐禪菩薩.

21. Again in the *Śūraṁgamasamādhi* 643c19–20 we find: 入諸城邑聚落乞食 ... 說法 ... 坐禪. Here the Tibetan (Derge 132, *mdo sde*, *da*, 305b6) has ... *yang dag par 'jog par snang ste* |, which Lamotte 1975: 60 reconstructs into *pratisaṁlīna* (although this equivalent seems to me problematic). In any case, the Tibetan suggests neither *yogācāra* nor *dhyāna* here.

22. See Nagao 1994: I. xii. The passages cited are found at Pradhan 1975: 197.5–8, ad IV.4ab = T. 1559 (XXIX) 227a7–14.

23. T. 1558 (XXIX) 69b1–12.

24. See the *Laṅkāvatāra*, T. 672 (XVI) 591b24–25: 云何修行進。云何修行退。瑜伽師有幾。令人住其中. Compare the corresponding passage in T. 671 (XVI) 520a1–2, very similar to T. 672 except for *pada* c: 何因修行退。何因修行進。教何等人修。令住何等法. However, in the corresponding Sanskrit text (Nanjio 1923: 27 [II.41]), *yogācāra* is not the term that is actually found: *kathaṁ vyāvartate yogāt kathaṁ yoga pravartate* | *kathaṁ caivaṁvidhā yoge narā sthāpyā vadāhi me* | |. The sense of people who practice yoga is certainly expressed here, but despite the appearance of the Chinese term 瑜伽師 the Sanskrit technical term *yogācāra* does not occur.

the extent of sacrificing clarity for consistency.[25] But, alas, this is not always and universally the case. In Xuanzang's translation of an *Abhidharmakośabhāṣya* passage quoted below, three types of *yogācāra* are rendered with two terms, *yuqieshi* 瑜伽師 and *guanxingzhe* 觀行者.[26] In another spot, *yuqieshi* 瑜伽師 renders *yogin*.[27] In Xuanzang's translation of the *Mahāyānasaṃgraha* we find *yuqieshi* 瑜伽師 once each in prose and in verse (at I.60), and *yuqiezhe* 瑜伽者 once in verse. At II.11 we find *guanzhe* 觀者 once, in verse. All of these terms refer, according to the Tibetan translation, to *rnal 'byor pa* = **yogin*.[28] This illustration that even the generally consistent Xuanzang was far from entirely systematic and mechanical in his renderings must, I think, seriously shake our confidence in the utility of Chinese translations for sensitive terminological investigations. One of the implications of this fact is that we should be very careful about using, or even refrain entirely from relying upon, passages in Chinese which we cannot confirm with Indic or Tibetan parallels.[29] But of course the key to understanding any term is not primarily etymology or translation equivalents, but use.

All students of Indian thought are at least superficially familiar with the word Yogācāra since it, along with Madhyamaka, is used to

---

25. See the remarks in Nagao 1994: I.xi, xiv.

26. Pradhan 1975: 338.2–5 = T. 1558 (XXIX) 117c1–3.

27. Pradhan 1975: 456.20 = T. 1558 (XXIX) 151c5.

28. Actually, the verse occurrence of 瑜伽師 in I.60 is not confirmed by Tibetan, since this verse is not found in the Tibetan translation. See Nagao 1982: 261, n. 5. My remarks here on the *Mahāyānasaṃgraha* are based on the texts found in Nagao 1982. See now also Nagao 1994, s.v. yogin. It is, of course, not absolutely certain that the occurrence in prose of 瑜伽師 could not refer to an original *yogācāra*, and the different rendering in verse could have been intended to differentiate the rendering from that of *yogin*, a form suggested as more likely by metrical constraints (it being less likely that a form in four syllables would be used when an equivalent in two was available), but the Tibetan translation does not support this interpretation.

29. I mean this stricture to apply only to investigations of Indic *terminology* in texts, not to the study of Buddhist literature or thought in general.

As an example of a passage to which we might otherwise want to refer, see the **Ādiviśeṣavibhāgasūtra* 分別緣起初勝法門經 (T. 717 [XVI] 843b6–9): "What is **samyak-smṛti*? The Blessed One said: Energetic cultivation of **śamatha* and **vipaśanā* (止觀). The **yogācāras* (? 諸瑜伽師) rely on the three marks (? 三相). They always concentrate on those three marks and are not distracted and careless (**pramāda*)...." Another version, T. 716 (XVI) 836a29, does not have the term 瑜伽師 / **yogācāra*, but it is probable that 合相應 is meant to represent the same term. See Silk 1997 for further references to Chinese passages unconfirmed by parallels.

refer to one of the two main schools of Mahāyāna philosophy; in this sense the term Yogācāra-Vijñānavāda is also used.[30] Whether this is the *same* word as that we are investigating here is a vexing question. Several scholars have investigated the term in this context, and sought to trace the antecedents of the Yogācāra-Vijñānavāda school through earlier uses of the term *yogācāra*.[31] Here I am not directly concerned

---

30. This meaning of Yogācāra as a Buddhist philosophical school is naturally also noted by the dictionaries. Ronald Davidson has emphasized to me in personal communication his opinion that there existed no Yogācāra-Vijñānavāda school per se prior to Bhāvaviveka. I will not use the word in such a strict sense, however, but rather to point to the developing tradition of the *Yogācārabhūmi*, and of the thinkers Asaṅga, Vasubandhu, and so on.

31. These include Davidson 1985, and the forthcoming work of Nobuyoshi Yamabe. Several Japanese scholars have also addressed the origins of the Yogācāra-Vijñānavāda school in this light. Mukai 1978: 269, 270 suggests that the term Yogācāra as a school name is directly (直接的に) based on the śāstra called *Yogācārabhūmi*, in the same way that, he asserts, the school called Vaibhāṣika is based on the (*Mahā*-) *Vibhāṣā*, the Sautrāntika on the sūtras, and the Madhyamaka on the *Mūlamadhyamaka kārikā*s. What he means is that as Vaibhāṣikas study the *Vibhāṣā*, Yogācāras study the *Yogācārabhūmi*, thence their name. Other Japanese scholars cited by Mukai suggest instead a connection with the practice of yoga (*yogācāra* as a *tatpuruṣa*). As far as I can tell, none of these scholars took a serious look at the history of the term. (Mukai mentions none of the important studies of the term, such as Miyamoto 1932 or Nishi 1939.) Although there is evidence (for example, in Yaśomitra's *Abhidharma-kośavyākhyā* [Shastri 1971: 15]) for the naming of the Vaibhāṣika and Sautrāntika, the application of the same logic to the Madhyamaka at least seems to me to be in error. Prof. Schmithausen (personal communication) seems open to the idea that such a logic might apply in the case of the Yogācāra, although he does not commit himself.

Ui 1958: 34 suggested that the origins of the *Yogācārabhūmi* lie with the *yogācāra*s discussed in the **Abhidharma-Mahāvibhāṣā* (see too Ui 1965: 372), which is apparently also the view of Mizuno 1956: 228–29, of Fukuhara 1975: 406, and of La Vallée Poussin 1937: 189–190, note 1, who wrote that *yogācāra* designates "a member of a school known by the Vibhāṣā and the Kośa, which continues in the schools which are connected with Asaṅga." Takasaki 1966: 96 wrote that "*yogācāra*s are monks who concentrated mainly on the practice of meditation (*zenkan* 禅観)," and contrasted them with Ābhidhārmikas. He went on to suggest that the origins of the Yogācāra school are to be sought with Sarvāstivādin *yogācāra*s who gave special attention to the practice of the *Avataṁsaka* sūtra's "mind only." I do not know if he has developed this view at length elsewhere.

Another approach has been taken by Deleanu, who states (1993: 9–10): "Even if we accept that they originated from a common tradition, which is not totally excluded, we must conclude that the Vijñānavādins split from the Śrāvakayāna *yogācāra*s branch at an early date and evolved in a quite unique way." Deleanu, however, seems not to distinguish between *yogin*s and *yogācāra*s, and apparently identifies these practitioners as those whose ideas and practices are exposed in early

with the sense of *yogācāra* as denoting "the Yogācāra-Vijñānavāda school of Buddhist doctrinal speculation." I am, moreover, not able to enter into the question of the possible connections, if any, of the *yogācāra bhikṣu* with the rise of that school. These seem to me interesting problems, but ones I will leave to others to address.[32] Here my main goal is to try to understand who the *yogācāra bhikṣu* is, most especially in Mahāyāna sūtra literature.

I am, to be sure, not the first to have become interested in this term. One of the earliest modern scholars to examine the meaning of the term *yogācāra* was Miyamoto Shōson.[33] Working without reference to Tibetan materials and at a time, more than sixty years ago, before many of the Sanskrit texts now published were available, Miyamoto nevertheless was able to make many important discoveries. He recognized the equivalence of the Chinese transcription-cum-translations *zuochan biqiu* 坐禪比丘 and *yuqieshi* 瑜伽師 as renderings of *yogācāra* (*bhikṣu*),[34] and pointed out many of the most important relevant passages in Chinese texts, including the *Śrāvakabhūmi* of the *Yogācārabhūmi*, now available in Sanskrit but accessible to Miyamoto only in Chinese. Miyamoto's questions centered around an exploration of the history of Buddhist "practice" and the origins of the Yogācāra-Vijñānavāda school, and in that context he examined the question of who the *yogācāra bhikṣus* were, and why they might be important. He offered the opinion that the term *yogācāra* seems to refer primarily to meditative monks in general (the *zuochan biqiu*), and suggested that groups of these monks were connected for the most part with Northwestern India, Kashmir, and Gandhāra.[35] Miyamoto's paper made a very auspicious start on the problem. Unfortunately, perhaps because of its uninviting title, which gives no hint as to its true contents, his

---

Yogācārabhūmi texts such as those of Saṅgharakṣa and Dharmatrāta (T. 606 and T. 618). I am not sure why Deleanu groups together those who hold such ideas and advocate such practices as "*yogācāras*."

Another study which devotes considerable attention to the issue of Buddhist yoga and the *yogācāra* is Yin 1988: 611–645. I regret that I have not been able to make full use of this work.

32. I hope not to imply that I believe there to be anything illegitimate in speculating on the connection between the *yogācāra bhikṣu* and the Yogācāra-Vijñānavāda school; this is simply not the task I have set for myself here. For one attempt in this direction, see Hotori 1980.

33. Miyamoto 1932, slightly revised in 1933.

34. Miyamoto 1932: 770.

35. Miyamoto 1932: 773.

research has not been widely influential.[36] At least one scholar, however, appreciated and used the work of Miyamoto, namely Nishi Giyū.

Nishi investigated the place of the *yogācāra* in, primarily, the **Abhidharma Mahāvibhāṣā*.[37] His detailed studies seek to identify the particular doctrinal position of the *yogācāra* and to situate him within the world of Abhidharma philosophy, in addition to clarifying the meaning of the term. The highly architectonic, systematic, and self-referential nature of the Abhidharma literature makes any attempt to understand only a portion of it in isolation probably doomed from the outset. Moreover, my own insufficient familiarity with the system makes it impossible for me to present Nishi's discoveries in a simpler form. While I will refer below to what I understand the *Vibhāṣā* to say about the *yogācāra*, here I will merely cite one of Nishi's conclusions,[38] namely that "The *yogācāra* is, in India, a meditator (禅定行者), and should be seen as the precursor of the Chan masters of China."

Another scholar to contribute to the question has been Nishimura Minori who observed, based primarily on some instances of the term in the vinaya literature, and especially the *Abhisamācārikā* of the Mahāsāṁghika Vinaya, that *yogācāra bhikṣu* does not seem to refer to a specialization, as it were, so much as to those monks who are, by the by, engaged in yogic praxis.[39] The *yogācāra bhikṣus* "belong to the same monastic community [as the monks whose behavior annoys them], but they are by no means specialists in practice; it is clear that they are monks who happen to be engaged in yogic practice at the time [the incidents cited took place]." For Nishimura, the Mahāsāṁghikas had the general custom of referring to those monks engaged generally in yogic practice as *yogācāra bhikṣus*.[40]

---

36. Demiéville 1954: 340, n. 2, referred to Miyamoto's paper, but offered no corollary studies of his own. Nishimura 1974, Mukai 1978, and Kodama et al. 1992–1993 appear to be ignorant of Miyamoto's work. (Kodama et al. 1992–1993, however, do refer to a large number of studies, including: Nishi 1939, 1974, Ui 1965, Fukuhara 1975, and Matsunami 1954.)

37. The titles of Nishi's 1939 and 1974 papers refer to the place of the *yogācāra* in Sectarian Buddhism, but in practice he refers almost exclusively to the voluminous commentary on the Abhidharma, the *Vibhāṣā* T. 1545.

38. Nishi 1974: 361; see also 370.

39. Nishimura 1974: 916.

40. Nishimura 1974: 917.

Western scholars have also noted the term. La Vallée Poussin, for example, remarked as follows:[41]

> The Pāli scriptures recognize and admit, alongside of monks of strict observance, an ill-defined category of ascetics (yogins, yogāvacaras, later yogācāras), who are at the same time saints and irregulars, schismatics or heretics. They are referred to as men of the forest (*āraṇyaka*) or of cemeteries (*śmāśānika*s).[42] Doing away with the novitiate and communal living, stringent in their practice of the rigorous rules of asceticism, they are professional solitaries and penitents, and thus thaumaturges.

The use of the term *yogācāra* in the *Yogācārabhūmi* and other, primarily Abhidharmic, texts has been treated by Ronald Davidson in the context of his study of the early Yogācāra school:[43] "Probably the oldest use of the term 'Yogācāra' ... indicates simply a 'yogin' and should be considered identical with that term." Finally, in his study of the Mahāsāṁghika *Bhikṣuṇī-Vinaya*, Gustav Roth concludes as follows:[44]

---

41. La Vallée Poussin 1909: 356. In this regard he offered a note and commented on the passage from the *Mahāvastu* discussed below, and on occurrences of the term *yogāvacara* in Pāli, remarking: "I think that in the Mahāvastu ... the Yogācāras, who are spoken of with disfavor, are not the adherents of the doctrine of the Vijñānavāda but rather ascetic thaumaturges." It is rare that one will want to disagree with any conclusion of the great scholar, but as we will see, there does not seem to be any evidence to uphold the claim that *yogācāras* are "ascetic thaumaturges." For a discussion of what might characterize Buddhist "wonder working," see Gómez 1977.

42. The text prints *śāṁśanika*s, but this is probably an error.

43. Davidson 1985: 126. On page 184 he says:

> The other element in establishing the nature of the fundament and its transformation—or 'replacement'—is the definition surrounding the four-fold purification (*pariśuddhi*) found within the **Revatasūtra* and given by Asaṅga in the *Śr*[*āvaka*]*Bh*[*ūmi*] as the canonical source for fundamental transformation. There the question is posed concerning the manner of a *yogācāra* becoming one practicing unobstructed meditation (*anirākṛtadhyāyī*). The answer is that a *yogācāra* who practices diligently the correct meditative activity will obtain, touch and come face to face with a) the purity of fundament (*āśrayapariśuddhi*) from the cleansing of all hindrances (*sarvadauṣṭhulyānāṁ pratipraśrabdher*), with b) the purity of objective support (*ālambanapariśuddhi*) through the inspection of the objects of knowledge (*jñeyavastupratyavekṣatayā*), with c) the purity of mind (*cittapariśuddhi*) through the elimination of desire (*rāgavirāgāt*), and with d) the purity of gnosis (*jñānapariśuddhi*) through the elimination of ignorance (*avidyāvirāgāt*).

Such a portrayal of the *yogācāra* is, of course, highly systematized and must represent a stage of development subsequent to, or at least distinct from, that represented in the bulk of the sūtra literature.

44. Roth 1970: XLIV.

As the designation of a monk as *yogācāra* or *yogācārin* is not at home in the old Vinaya text of the Hīnayāna trend we can conclude that this term has entered our text from later strata of Buddhist tradition not belonging to the ancient Vinaya. The well confirmed occurrence of *bhikṣur yogācāra* in the Mahāyānistic Kāśyapaparivarta as well as the traceability of *yogācāra* in Abhidh[arma]k[ośa] indicates that it has its origin in the early strata of Mahāyāna Buddhism during the period of transition from Hīnayāna to Mahāyāna.

Setting aside the problem of the Mahāyāna/Hīnayāna dichotomy,[45] I think we will see in the following that Roth's conclusion concerning the origins of the term, that it is a Mahāyānistic term evidently, as I understand him, borrowed from Mahāyāna circles by "Hīnayāna" authors, is almost certainly wrong. But he is certainly right about the appearance of the term in one of the oldest Mahāyāna sūtras, the *Kāśyapaparivarta*.

To begin our own investigation, then, let us first take a look at the passages which spawned this study to begin with, those from the *Kāśyapaparivarta* and the closely related *Ratnarāśisūtra*.

The *Kāśyapaparivarta* uses the term in two places:[46] "when a *yogācāra* monk contemplates any object whatsoever, all of them appear to him absolutely void. They appear hollow, empty, without essence." And again:[47] "everywhere a *yogācāra* monk sees perturbations of mind, he practices in order to hold them in check. He holds his mind in check in such a way that it never again leaps out of control." The Chinese versions have a variety of renderings, none of which, at least at first glance, seem to be especially helpful to us in determining the precise meaning of the word, since they all point in the general direction of "practice."[48] As we will see as we go on, however, it may be precisely this lack of precision which is a vital element of the signification of the term *yogācāra bhikṣu*. Finally, the term is not remarked upon in

45. On this issue, see Silk 1994: 1–52.

46. Staël-Holstein 1926: §68: *yogācāro bhikṣur yad yad evālambanaṁ manaskaroti tat sarvam asya riktakam eva khyāti* (**tucchaka, śūnyaka, asāraka*). The last three terms are suggested on the basis of the Tibetan, as the quotation of the passage (*Madhyānta-vibhāgaṭīkā*, Yamaguchi 1934: 247.12–16), which is missing in the *Kāśyapaparivarta* Sanskrit manuscript, does not contain the sentence.

47. Staël-Holstein 1926: §108: *yogācāro bhikṣur yatra yatraiva cittasya vikāraṁ paśyati tatra tatraivāsya nigrahāya pratipadyate sa tathā tathā cittaṁ nigṛhṇāti yathā na puna prakupyate.*

48. T. 351 (Jin): §68, §108 修行比丘; T. 659 (Maṇḍalasena): §68 行道沙門, §108 行者; T. 310 (Qin): §68 行道比丘, §108 行者; T. 352 (Song): §68 相應行比丘, §108 相應比丘.

the *Kāśyapaparivarta* commentary, and although this is not necessarily significant, it is possible to speculate that the term was well enough known, or unproblematic enough, that no explanation was required.[49] What little we can gather from the context of the *Kāśyapaparivarta* passages suggests that *yogācāra* monks are those involved in meditative contemplation.

The *Ratnarāśisūtra* treats the term—which appears in the form *yogācāra* and *yogācāra bhikṣu* (*dge slong rnal 'byor spyod pa*)—at somewhat greater length.[50] It appears in four passages. First of all:[51]

> Monks, ... for that intent monk, *yogācāra*, who practices what I have taught, having enjoyed the robes, begging bowl, sleeping mat, and medicaments—that is to say, the personal belongings—[obtained] from donors and benefactors, who sees the faults of saṁsāra, sees the impermanence in all conditioned things, understands that all conditioned things are suffering, zealously applies himself to the [fact that] all dharmas lack a self, and comprehends that nirvāṇa is calm, even though he consumes mouthfuls [of food] as great as Mount Sumeru [given as] a gift of faith, those offerings of that [gift of faith] are still completely and totally pure.[52]

---

49. On the other hand, commentaries as a rule often "explain" what requires little explanation, while sometimes overlooking the truly problematic, which is why I say the omission here is not necessarily significant.

50. The Chinese translation of the term in this text presents a very interesting problem, which I discuss in Silk 1997.

51. I translate the Tibetan (nearly identical in the sūtra text from the Kanjur and the *Śikṣāsamuccaya* text from the Tanjur), which I quote from the text established in my edition, Silk 1994: 408–409: *dge slong dag de la dge slong ldan pa rnal 'byor spyod pa nga'i bstan pa la zhugs pa gang zhig sbyin pa po dang | sbyin bdag las chos gos dang | bsod snyoms dang | mal cha dang | na ba'i gsos sman dang | yo byad rnams yongs su spyad nas 'khor ba'i skyon mthong | 'du byed thams cad mi rtag par mthong | 'du byed thams cad sdug bsngal bar rig | chos thams cad la bdag med par mos | mya ngan las 'das pa zhi bar rtogs pas ni ri rab tsam gyi kham dag gis dad pas byin pa yongs su spyad kyang de'i yon shin tu yongs su dag par 'gyur ro | | sbyin pa po dang sbyin bdag gang dag las dad pas byin pa yongs su spyad pa de las de dag gi bsod nams kyi rnam par smin pa 'byor pa chen po dang | phan yon chen por 'gyur ro | | de ci'i phyir zhe na | dge slong dag rdzas las byung ba'i bsod nams bya ba'i dngos po rnams las | gang byams pa'i sems la snyom par 'jug pa de mchog yin pa'i phyir ro | |*.

The corresponding Sanskrit is quoted in the *Śikṣāsamuccaya* (Bendall 1897–1902: 138.3–8 = MS 68b7–69a1): *yadi bhikṣavo bhikṣur yukto yogācāro mama śikṣāyāṁ pratipannaḥ sarvvasaṁskāreṣv anityadarśī sarvvasaṁskāraduḥkhaviditaḥ sarvvadharmeṣv anātmādhimuktiḥ śāntanirvāṇābhikāṁkṣī sumerumātrair ālopaiḥ śraddhādeyaṁ bhuñjītātyantapariśuddhaiva tasya sā dakṣiṇā bhavati | yeṣāñ ca dāyakānān dānapatīnāṁ sakāśāc chraddhādeyaṁ paribhuktaṁ tatas teṣān dāyakadānapatīnā[ṁ] maharddhikaḥ puṇyavipāko bhavati mahādyutikaḥ | tat kasmād dhetoḥ | agram idam aupadhikānāṁ puṇyakriyāvastūnāṁ yeyaṁ maitracittasamāpattiḥ |*.

52. Or the clause may mean: "the offerings made to him are still completely and

> When [that monk] enjoys a gift of faith from donors and benefactors, the maturation of merit from that [gift] for those donors and benefactors has great power, and the benefit [to them] is great. Why? Because, monks, the attainment of a friendly attitude is the best of the material objects related to meritorious action.

Here again we would suspect that the *yogācāra* monk is a meditator, and also—perhaps even merely by virtue of that status—a special source of merit as a recipient of alms. The latter point is emphasized in a further passage:[53]

> When this teaching had been preached, five-hundred *yogācāra* monks thought: "It would not be right if we were to enjoy the gift of faith while our keeping of the precepts is not completely pure," and they fell [away from the precepts] and returned to the home life. Then, a few other monks criticized them saying: "It is very bad that these *yogācāras*, heroic (**māhātmya*)[54] monks, have fallen away from the teaching."

It is interesting that it is not meditation that is emphasized here, but rather strict adherence to the monastic rule that produces merit rendering one fit to receive alms. But in the following passage, meditation is obviously an integral part of the *yogācāra*'s practice. That the *yogācāra* monk requires quiet and perhaps even special treatment is stressed as follows:[55]

---

totally pure." The referent of the pronoun *tasya/de'i* is not clear. The Chinese translation is not strictly parallel; see Silk 1994: 566.

53. Silk 1994: 435: *bstan pa 'di bshad ba na dge slong rnal 'byor spyod pa lnga brgyas bdag cag tshul khrims yongs su ma dag bzhin du dad pas byin pa spyad par gyur na mi rung zhes nyams par byas te slar khyim du dong ngo | | de la dge slong gzhan dag cig 'di skad du dge slong che ba'i bdag nyid can rnal 'byor spyod pa 'di dag bstan pa las nyams pa ni shin tu ma legs so zhes 'phya'o | |.*

54. It is not clear to me what the qualification **māhātmya* indicates here, and the translation, which was kindly suggested by Gregory Schopen, is provisional.

55. Again I translate the Tibetan, Silk 1994: 439–440: *'od srung de la dge slong rnal 'byor spyod pa gang yin pa de dag la dge slong zhal ta byed pas 'thun pa'i 'tshog chas dang | na ba'i gsos sman dang | yo byad rnams sbyin par bya'o | | dge slong rnal 'byor spyod pa des phyogs ga la gnas pa'i sa phyogs der dge slong zhal ta byed pa des sgra chen po dang | skad drag po mi dbyung zhing byed du yang mi gzhug go | dge slong zhal ta byed pas dge slong rnal 'byor spyod pa de bsrung zhing mal cha yang sbyar bar bya'o | | kha zas bsod pa dang | yi gar 'ong ba dang | rnal 'byor spyod pa'i sa dang 'thun pa'i bza' ba dang bca' ba rnams sbyin par bya'o | | dge slong de la dge slong 'di ni de bzhin gshegs pa'i bstan pa rton pa'i phyir gnas pa yin te | de la bdag gis rjes su 'thun pa'i yo byad thams cad mang du sbyar bar bya'o snyam du shin tu phangs pa'i 'du shes bskyed bar bya'o | |.*

The corresponding Sanskrit is found in Bendall 1897–1902: 55.13–18 (= MS 32b7–33a2; see above n. 7): *tatra kāśyapa yo bhikṣur yogācāro bhavati | tasya tena vaiyāvṛtyakareṇa bhikṣuṇā 'nulomikāny upakaraṇāny upasaṁharttavyāni glānapratyaya-bhaiṣajyapariṣkārāś ca | yasmiṁś ca pradeśe sa yogācāro bhikṣuḥ prativasati tasmin pradeśe*

> Now, Kāśyapa, the superintending monk should give to those who are *yogācāra* monks appropriate paraphernalia, medicine to cure the sick, and personal belongings. In whatever place that *yogācāra* monk is dwelling the superintending monk should not cry aloud and yell nor permit [others] to do so. The superintending monk should protect that *yogācāra* monk and also provide him with a bed. He should give him sumptuous food, savories and hard food and soft food suitable for [one in] the stage of the practice of yoga (*yogācārabhūmi*).[56] It occurs to that [superintending] monk: "This [*yogācāra*] monk lives in order to promote the Tathāgata's teaching. I should generously provide him with all the appropriate personal belongings," and he should think him very dear.

We will see below that at least one vinaya text confirms the impression one receives from this passage about the conditions under which a *yogācāra* would flourish. Finally, the yogic aspects of the *yogācāra* monk's practice are emphasized in the following:[57]

> If one truly comprehensively reflects on this body as a disadvantage, he correctly comprehends. And making his mind single-pointed he will become mindful and constantly attentive, and thus the stage of generating the first Concentration will be his. Having obtained the Concentration, if he desires the bliss of Concentration he dwells for the space of one day, or two days, or from three days up to seven days with the bliss of Concentration as his food. If, even entered into yoga, he is not able to generate the Concentration, then gods, nāgas, and yakṣas renowned for their superior knowledge will offer food to that *yogācāra* monk, striving in that manner, who dwells in the Teaching.

The monks characterized in the *Ratnarāśi* as *yogācāra* monks are clearly intent upon their practice. That these monks engage in meditative cultivation is explicitly stated in the passage just quoted, in which we find a discussion of the importance of the first Concentration (*dhyāna*).

Now, while we can certainly feel confident at this point that we more or less understand the term, since its etymology and the uses

---

noccaśabdaḥ karttavyaḥ | *rakṣitavyo vaiyāvṛtyakareṇa bhikṣuṇā yogācāro bhikṣuḥ* | *śayyāsanopastambhanāsya karttavyā* | *praṇītāni ca saṁpreyāṇi yogācārabhūmyanukūlāni khādanīyabhojanīyāny upanāmayitavyāni* | |.

56. On this important term, see Silk 1997.

57. Silk 1994: 483: *de lus 'di la skyon du yang dag pa ji lta ba bzhin du so sor rtog pa na tshul bzhin la zhugs pa de* | *sems rtse gcig tu 'gyur zhing dran pa dang ldan la* | *shes bzhin dang ldan pas bsam gtan dang po bskyed pa'i gnas gang yin ba de yod par 'gyur te* | *des bsam gtan thob nas bsam gtan gyi bde ba 'dod pa na* | *nyi ma gcig gam* | *nyi ma gnyis sam* | *nyi ma gsum nas nyi ma bdun gyi bar du bsam gtan gyi bde ba'i zas kyis gnas so* | | *gal te 'di ltar rnal 'byor la zhugs pa bsam gtan bskyed par mi nus na* | *de ltar brtson zhing rnal 'byor spyod pa'i dge slong chos la gnas pa de la mngon par shes pa mngon par shes pa'i lha dang* | *klu dang* | *gnod sbyin dag kha zas 'bul bar 'gyur ro* | |.

we have discovered seem to be in accord, we still do not have a good appreciation of the term's scope and importance. For it is a word which appears in many different genres of Buddhist literature, and may indeed be more important than it might at first have seemed.

In default of any reliable chronology of Indian Buddhist literature, I will survey the available materials genre by genre.[58] The first important fact we must note is that there do not appear to be any references at all to the term *yogācāra* (with or without *bhikṣu/bhikkhu*) in the canonical Āgama/Nikāya corpus.[59] The word *yogācāra* appears in fact to be missing entirely from the Pāli canon,[60] the only canonical corpus complete in an Indic language, and as far as I know our term never appears in Indic language fragments of canonical material from,

---

58. Of course, there *is* some sort of implicit relative chronology hiding in the wings which motivated the ordering of the following discussion, but neither the absolute nor the relative chronology of our sources will be critical for what follows. Therefore, whatever problems there are with chronology are not of primary concern in this context.

59. It is very difficult if not impossible to state categorically that the term does not appear in the Chinese Āgamas. We have, first of all, no comprehensive index to these materials, and second of all, even if we did, we would not know with any certainty whether a given Chinese term should correspond to the Indic *yogācāra*. The stricture that the term is missing from the canonical Āgama/Nikāya corpus, then, must be understood with this proviso.

In this context we should take note of a passage in the *Vibhāṣā* T. 1545 (XXVII) 533a23–b2 which seems to quote "a sūtra" in which the interlocutor Anāthapiṇḍada asks the Buddha a question about *yogācāras* (瑜伽師). However, as far as I know, the passage has not been identified, and it cannot, at this point, be accepted as a genuine Āgamic use of the term. A passage from Vasumitra's **Vibhaṅga* (分別論) including the term 瑜伽師 and explaining the sūtra quotation is also quoted at 533b9.

60. The only exceptions to this absence of *yogācāra* and the like in canonical Pāli seem to be due to wrong writings for the term *yoggācariya*, a term apparently equivalent to *yogyācārya* and meaning something like "groom, trainer." See AN iii.28,17, reading *yoggācariyo*, with variant *yogācariyo*. MN iii.97,8 reads *yogācariyo* without variant, and MN iii.222,29, SN iv.176,18, and Thag 1140 read *yoggācariyo* without variants. It should be noted, of course, that the PTS editions are not critical editions, and the absence of a variant reading cannot be taken too seriously. In Sanskrit the term *yogyācārya* appears in *Arthaśāstra* 2.30.42 in the sense of "trainer."

It is also extremely interesting that the term appears already in the Second Minor Rock Edict of Aśoka in the form *yŭg[y]ācariyāni.* (A careful synoptic version is found in Andersen 1990: 120.) For some comments on this term, see Bloch 1950: 151, n. 18. Norman 1966: 116–117 = 1990: 80–81 suggested that the word in MRE II means "teacher of yoga," but this seems to me quite unlikely.

I have discussed a parallel term which occurs in late Pāli, namely *yogāvacara*, in Silk 1997. To this paper please make the following corrections: n. 3: *acara* → *avacara*. n. 61: *Abhidhammathasaṅghaha* → *Abhidhammatthasaṅgaha*.

for example, Central Asia.[61] Given the absence of the relevant term in the canonical Āgama/Nikāya corpus, let us begin our genre-wise survey with the vinaya literature.

While it is entirely absent from the Pāli Vinaya,[62] we do find the term *yogācāra bhikṣu* in the *Abhisamācārikā*, a portion of the Mahāsāṁghika Vinaya for which we have an extant Indic text. The Chinese translation generally understands this term as "meditating/meditator monk," *zuochan biqiu* 坐禪比丘,[63] or even and perhaps more literally, "monk engaged in/dedicated to seated meditation." It is evident that those referred to in the *Abhisamācārikā* as *yogācāra bhikṣu* are those who require a quiet and undisturbed atmosphere for their meditative practice. But we have raised a crucial point here, alluded to above in discussing Nishimura's views: which of the two possibilities apparently inherent in *zuochan biqiu* 坐禪比丘 (which is after all an *interpretation* of *yogācāra bhikṣu*) is preferable? Is this to be understood as a vocational designation—meditator monk—or as a specification of a state—a

---

61. But see below nn. 78 and 136. Since these Central Asian manuscript fragments are as yet unidentified, there does exist some possibility, however small, that they belong to Āgamic texts.

62. Schopen has several times (for example, 1992: 2; 1995: 108) remarked that this vinaya seems in many ways to be remarkable and *not* characteristic of vinaya literature in general.

63. As pointed out by de Jong 1974: 65. We may refer to the following instances (Sanskrit from the edition of Jinananda 1969): 106.9–107.11 = T. 1425 (XXII) 506b28–c10. At 106.9–12 = 506b28–c1 we have: *aparo dāni bhikṣuḥ yogācāro vaidehake parvate niṣaṇṇo cittaṁ samādhayiṣyāmīti | aparo dāni bhikṣuḥ āgacchiya tasya purato sthito | tasya dāni tena nīvaraṇena cittaṁ samādhānaṁ na gacchati | etaṁ prakaraṇaṁ so yogācāro bhagavato ārocaye |* .... = 爾時、比丘在帝釋石室山邊坐禪。時、有比丘在前立住。坐禪比丘心不得定。諸比丘以是因緣往白世尊. These *yogācāra bhikṣus* are annoyed by other monks standing in front of them and disturbing their meditations. The same grammatical constructions are found in 107.13–109.3 = T. 1425 (XXII) 506c19–507a3, where the *yogācāra bhikṣus* are disturbed by flapping sandals (*tālapāduka*). At 203.5 (disturbed by smells of extinguished lamps), 213.3–4 (disturbed by sounds of meditation mats being folded), and 219.1 (disturbed by sounds of sneezing) = T. 1425 (XXII) 512c14, 513b9, and 513c4, *yogācārā bhikṣū* = 諸坐禪比丘. However, at 215.1–2 (disturbed by sounds of sandals being knocked together), 217.8 (disturbed by sounds of coughing), 220.15 (disturbed by sounds of scratching), and 222.9 (disturbed by sounds of yawning) = T. 1425 (XXII) 513b18, b26, c12, and c21, *yogācārā bhikṣū* = 諸比丘. The occurrence of the term in Sanskrit at 226.4 (disturbed by sounds of flatulence) is apparently not rendered in Chinese, which is somewhat more terse than the Indic text at this point. (I am aware that the reliability of Jinananda's edition is suspect, but in the absence of any alternative I have accepted his readings as they stand.) On these and the Mahāsāṁghika *Bhikṣuṇī-Vinaya* passages, see Nishimura 1974.

monk engaged (perhaps temporarily) in meditational activities? This is a question that we will have to consider, while keeping in mind that there need not be only one correct answer.

Our term also appears in another text of the same Mahāsāṁghika school, the *Bhikṣuṇī-Vinaya*. Gustav Roth discusses the term, and quotes it from *Bhikṣuṇī-Vinaya* in the context of a story of the group of six nuns who attend a theatrical performance. Roth translates the relevant sentence:[64] "They (the nuns) stand silently, like *those whose conduct emanates from disciplined concentration*." The Chinese translation has 默然似如坐禪人.[65] Clearly *zuochanren* 坐禪人 is intended here as a translation of *yogācārāḥ*. Both Roth and the more recent student of the *Bhikṣuṇī-Vinaya*, Édith Nolot, then, have understood *yoga* here as meaning "disciplined concentration" and *yogācārā* as "nonnes à la conduite réfléchie," respectively. The Chinese translation, however, apparently takes the term to refer explicitly to the practice of seated meditation. An exact parallel to this passage in the Mahāsāṁghika Vinaya has the group of six monks watch a musical performance "like *zuochan biqiu* 坐禪比丘."[66]

The same term, *yogācārā*, is found in another passage in the same vinaya, where it is used to contrast good with ill-behaved nuns. As Roth has pointed out, corresponding to *yogācārā bhikṣuṇī* the Chinese has only "good nuns."[67] In yet another passage we have the same equivalence in Chinese.[68] Roth suggests that "No doubt the nuns are not characterized here as the followers of the *yogācāra* system." This is quite correct, I believe, if by "the *yogācāra* system" Roth intends to

---

64. Roth 1970: XLIII–XLIV. §238 *tāyo dāni tūṣṇīkās tiṣṭhanti yogācārā iva*. Roth's translation is similar to that of Nolot 1991: 299, "elles restaient silencieuses comme des *nonnes à la conduite réfléchie*." (Emphasis added to both quotations. Strictly speaking, Nolot should of course have placed "nonnes" within brackets, since no such word occurs in the text.) Does Roth's translation imply that he understands *yogācāra* as a *bahuvrīhi* based on an ablative *tatpuruṣa*?

65. T. 1425 (XXII) 540b22. Hirakawa 1982: 344 rendered this: "(the bhikṣuṇīs) kept their mouths closed, and sat as if they were meditating." This translation must be corrected in light of the Indic text.

66. T. 1425 (XXII) 494a9. There does not seem to be any similar expression in the other parallel passages cited by Sasaki 1991 in his valuable study of vinaya rules on monks and musical performances.

67. Roth 1970: §243. Chinese at T. 1425 (XXII) 541c2 has 善比丘尼. See the translation in Nolot 1991: 308.

68. Roth 1970: §248. Chinese at T. 1425 (XXII) 542c18. See the translation in Nolot 1991: 316.

refer to the philosophical school of that name, the Yogācāra-Vijñānavāda. He continues, "In the Vinaya context, *yogācāra* qualifies nuns of mentally well disciplined conduct." At least some of our evidence, however, suggests that we might be somewhat more precise.

Since we lack corresponding Sanskrit materials for other sections of the vinaya of this school, we cannot suggest with the same degree of confidence that the same Chinese terminology in additional passages in Mahāsāṁghika Vinaya texts represents the same Indic technical terms. But if we assume that the correspondences are more or less standard within the same translation, then we also have several other references to *yogācāra bhikṣus* in the same vinaya.[69] When we turn to an examination of the Vinayas of other schools, however, we are faced with a more serious problem. We have access to most of these materials only in Chinese. Now, the term *zuochan biqiu* 坐禪比丘 and similar expressions *do* occur, but in default of any Indic language (or Tibetan) materials with which to compare the Chinese translations, we are unable to clarify whether that translation represents the terminology in question. Moreover, it would be mere circularity to adduce the Chinese term *zuochan biqiu* in support of the hypothesis that *yogācāra bhikṣu* means a meditating or meditation monk. I have pointed out above the danger of relying on unconfirmed Chinese evidence in terminological studies, and therefore refrain from discussing the exclusively Chinese vinaya evidence here.[70]

A final example of the designation *yogācāra* in a vinaya or vinaya-like text is found in an anomalous passage in the *Mahāvastu*. There the spiritual aspirant is advised to avoid *yogācāras*:[71] "If they are endowed

69. In the Mahāsāṁghika Vinaya, T. 1425 (XXII) 268b1, we find 坐禪比丘, who apparently meditate in darkness. At 468c7 the meaning is not clarified. At 482b3–5 we have monks walking about in wooden shoes disturbing meditating monks, 坐禪比丘.

70. In Silk 1997 I point out some passages from Chinese vinaya texts in which the term 坐禪比丘 appears.

71. Senart 1882: i.120.7–9: *caturbhi bho jinaputra ākārair dhuta*[*guṇa*]*dhara bodhisatvā bodhāye ye praṇidhenti paṁcamāyāṁ bhūmau vartamānāḥ ṣaṣṭhyāṁ bhūmau vivartanti* | *katamehi caturhi* | *samyaksaṁbuddhānuśāsane pravrajitvā yogācārehi sārdhaṁ sambhuvaṁ kurvanti* |. [Read *saṁstavaṁ* for *sambhuvaṁ*, with BHSD s.v. saṁbhuva (and as suggested already by Senart 1882: i.469)?]

Jones 1949: i.94 rendered: "O son of the Conqueror and my pious friend, there are four ways in which Bodhisattvas who have made a vow to win enlightenment in the fifth *bhūmi* lapse and fail to reach the sixth. What are the four ways? Though the Bodhisattvas have taken up the religious life in the Buddha's instruction, they yet join forces with the Yogācāras."

with four characteristics, Son of the Victor [Mahākāśyapa], upholder of the dhuta ascetic purification practices,[72] bodhisattvas in the fifth stage who make a vow to attain awakening turn back from the sixth stage. What are the four? 1) Having renounced the world in the instruction of the perfectly awakened buddha, they associate together with *yogācāras*." This passage contrasts rather sharply with the usual positive representations of *yogācāras*, and has occasioned much discussion. As indicated above, La Vallée Poussin thought the reference was to wonder-working ascetics, while Davidson has suggested that "From this use we see the graduation to the usage of *yogācāra* indicating a Buddhist *yogin*, specifically a monk."[73] It seems therefore that Davidson thinks the meaning of the term in the *Mahāvastu* (and other earlier materials?) is that of a non-Buddhist yogin. Yet other scholars, undoubtedly wrongly, have viewed the *Mahāvastu* passage as a reference to the Yogācāra-Vijñānavāda school.[74] However, we should keep several things in mind. First, the text does not specify that these

---

Leumann and Shiraishi 1957: 93 have: "Auf vier Arten, mein lieber Siegersohn(!), machen o du in den Dhuta-Tugenden Erprobter, die Bodhisattva's, welche zur (Erlangung der) Bodhi (ihren) Praṇidhāna(-Wunsch) äußern (und) sich auf der fünften Stufe befinden, von der sechsten Stufe Rückschritte (d.h. auf vier Arten gelangen die Bodhisattva's durch Rückschritte aus der sechsten Stufe in die fünfte). Auf welche vier (Arten)? (1) Nachdem sie in der Unterweisung der (oder eines) Vollerleuchteten als Mönche eingetreten sind, pflegen sie Umgang mit den Yogācāra(-Anhängern)."

72. The text's reading *dhutadharmadhara*, which I have emended, is troublesome. However, given the parallel usages at Senart 1882: i.66.16, 71.12, 105.3, and 120.11, the term must clearly be a vocative. Prof. Schmithausen (to whom I owe these references) suggests the possibility that we should read instead **dhutaguṇadhara*, as an epithet of Mahākāśyapa, which would indeed be quite fitting, and which I have adopted.

73. Davidson 1985: 127.

74. Senart 1882: i.469 remarked: "The general sense of the portion of the sentence *yogācārehi* and so on is not uncertain: communication, joining together with the Yogācāras is represented as if criminal and as bringing about a downfall in the spiritual life." Senart goes on, however, in a way which indicates that he understood the term Yogācāra to refer to the philosophical school of that name. Jones 1949: i.94, note 1, also seems to have thought so, as did Edgerton in BHSD s.v. yogācāra. This understanding was already explicitly rejected by Shāstrī 1931: 837. Miyamoto 1932: 790–791 stated that while it is clear that the passage does *not* refer to followers of the Yogācāra-Vijñānavāda, he was unsure whether the reference was to "old *yogācāras*" or to non-Buddhist *yogins*, although he tended toward the opinion that the text is thinking of groups of *yogācāras* related to Dārṣṭāntikas, for reasons having to do with the doctrinal contents of the other three points mentioned in the passage. Nishimura 1974: 917 also seems to follow this approach, since he understands the

yogācāras are monks, or even that they are Buddhists.[75] Second, it is certainly possible that this text is expressing a dissenting view about meditation or about specialists in meditation (if indeed this is how *yogācāra* is to be understood). Since this negative attitude seems to be unique in the texts I have examined, it is difficult to draw any immediate conclusions, but we should be sensitive to the anomalous nature of this passage.

Let us turn now to the Abhidharma literature, in which again the term occurs fairly frequently, particularly in the **Abhidharma Mahāvibhāṣā*. The occurrences of the term in this text have been extensively studied by Nishi Giyū, and perhaps more accessibly for Western scholars, noted by Davidson.[76] For the *Vibhāṣā*, a *yogācāra* may be a śrāvaka, pratyekabuddha, or buddha, a *śaikṣa* or *aśaikṣa*,[77] and indeed even a *pṛthagjana* may be a *yogācāra*.[78] The same idea is found in Saṅgharakṣa's *Yogācārabhūmi*.[79] Apparently *yogācāras* may be found

---

reference to be to the same sort of practice mentioned in item three of the passage, *śamathavipaśyanābhāvanā*.

75. To be sure, it would, however, be even more interesting if the reference were not to Buddhists since, as I have indicated, I know of no evidence that the term *yogācāra* is ever used to refer to non-Buddhist practitioners.

It is worth mentioning one suggestion which, as far I know, has not been offered before. Prof. Nagao has tentatively asked whether one might read not *pravrajitvā yogācārehi*, but rather *pravrajitvā-ayogācārehi*. Aside from the fact that the term **ayogācāra* seems to be otherwise unattested, I see no prima facie reason why this should not be possible.

76. Nishi 1939, 1974. Combining the references in Davidson 1985: 128 (which seem to be based on the entries in the published index to the Taishō edition) with those of Nishi 1939 and 1974, and adding a few of my own observations, the following *partial* list of occurences of the term 瑜伽師 in the *Vibhāṣā* may be offered: T. 1545 (XXVII) 13ab, 38b25–27, 47a22, 186a7, 205b11ff., 223c14, 237a27, 238c19–21, 276a10, 289a10–15, 316c–318a, 338b–339a, 341a15–16, 385a24-b7, 404b17, 25, 407a4-b15, 414c25, 417c12–18a1, 422b6, 423b1, 433a3, 433b2, 439b11–12, 512c28, 527c16–20, 528a14, 529b1–6, 533a29-b8, 534a19ff., 536a29, 537b6, 540c11, 704c1–705b11, 775b3, 766b2–24, 816c1–3, 832a22, 834c11, 840a1–13, 842b4, 879c23–26, 880b14, 898a7, 899b8, 905b10–18, 938b14–22, 939a–40c. (Matsunami 1954: 159 says the term appears in more than 60 places in the text, but he provides no list.) Davidson also refers to the *Saṁgītiparyāya* T. 1536 (XXVI) 446a1.

77. T. 1545 (XXVII) 417c12–14, and 534ab, Miyamoto 1932: 768, and Nishi 1939: 227–28. In the first passage, the "three *yogācāras*" 三瑜伽師 are referred to; in the old *Vibhāṣā* T. 1546 (XXVIII) 313b16–18, the same term is rendered "three types of practitioner" 三種行人.

78. T. 1545 (XXVII) 341a15–21, Nishi 1939: 228–30, 1974: 364. It is possible that the same thing is being said in an unidentified Turfan collection Sanskrit manuscript

anywhere.[80] Those who perform the *aśubha* meditations and contemplate the unsatisfactoriness of saṁsāra are referred to as *yogācāra*,[81] but in general the term seems to be used generically for "practitioner." In fact, at least in some passages it seems to occur in free variation with *xingzhe* 行者 ("practitioner"), *xiuguan xingzhe* 修觀行者 ("one who practices the cultivation of visualization/contemplation"), and *xiudingzhe* 修定者 ("one who cultivates concentration").[82] Davidson suggests that in almost all the occurrences of the term *yogācāra* in the *Vibhāṣā* it means "master meditator," although he also adduces three cases in which he suggests it refers to the Yogācāra-Vijñānavāda school.[83] It would seem, however, that since even a *śaikṣa* and *pṛthagjana* might be a *yogācāra*, "master meditator" is not really an apt rendering, given that mastery implies some sort of rather high attainment. There are clear indications that this is not how the term is being used in the *Vibhāṣā*. Since one of any degree of attainment, from the rank beginner up to and including a buddha himself, may be styled *yogācāra*, the generic rendering "practitioner" or the simple "meditator" is much more likely to be accurate.

---

fragment (Waldschmidt 1971: 139, SHT 889, a.B.v), in which one partial line reads: ///[ta]tra yo yogācāraḥ [p]ṛ[th]agjanaḥ śaikṣa . . ///.

79. T. 606 (XV) 182c3 = T. 607 (XV) 231b4–5: *yogācāra*s may be *pṛthagjana*, *śaikṣa*, or *aśaikṣa*. See Demiéville 1954: 398–399.

80. T. 1545 (XXVII) 704b28-c1 refers to southern, northern, and ubiquitous *yogācāras*: 北方諸瑜伽師, 南方諸瑜伽師, and 一切處諸瑜伽師. I doubt, however, that we should go so far as Fukuhara 1975: 404, who suggests identifying these "southern *yogācāra*s" with the *yogāvacara*s of the *Yogāvacara's Manual* and the *Visuddhimagga* (two texts in which, in any case, the respective uses of the term *yogāvacara* may have considerably different referents; see Silk 1997).

81. T. 1545 (XXVII)839b–840a, Nishi 1939: 238. It seems likely that here and in some other passages the *aśubha* meditation is intended to be emblematic for all meditation practice.

82. T. 1545 (XXVII) 404b–405a. Nishi 1939: 225–226 suggests that there is in fact no essential difference between these terms, and that they may all stand for either *yogācāra* or *yogin.* At T. 1545 (XXVII) 938b 瑜伽師 is apparently equivalent to 修行者, used in the context of the four *smṛtyupasthāna*s. See Nishi 1939: 238.

83. Davidson 1985: 128. The three cases in which the term refers to the school he locates as T. 1545 (XXVII) 815c11, 682b2, 795c9–12. Nishi 1939: 261 does not seem to take the final passage, at least, in this meaning, and at 682b2 (Nishi 1939: 262–263) he opposes the *yogācāra*s to Ābhidhārmikas. Further on (263–264) Nishi is reluctant to speculate on the relationship between the *yogācāra*s whose opinions are referred to in the *Vibhāṣā* and the Yogācāra-Vijñānavāda school. For Matsunami 1954: 160, on the other hand, "The *Vibhāṣā*'s *yogācāra* is a sect (派) connected to mainly yogic practice."

When we turn to the *Abhidharmakośabhāṣya*, we find what may be a somewhat more precise or restricted usage. For example, we read:[84]

> In that regard the *yogācāra*s say: A *rūpa* that is the object of *samādhi* is produced for the meditator (*dhyāyin*) by the force of his *samādhi.* It is invisible because it is not within the domain of the visual sense. It is without resistance because it does not obstruct space. You may think: Now, how [can] that be *rūpa*? This is the same as in the case of the *avijñapti.* As for what was said [at *Abhidharmakośa* IV.4a, namely] that [*avijñapti* exists as a substance], because [a sūtra] speaks of a *rūpa* which is free from the depravities, the *yogācāra*s say that this very *rūpa* in question here, produced through the power of *samādhi*, is free from the depravities when it is [produced] in a *samādhi* which is free from the depravities.

Yaśomitra's *Abhidharmakośavyākhyā* comments on this passage:[85]

> The *yogācāra* who is actualizing the [noble] path acquires such a mental intention and physical basis that he acquires a morality free from the depravities just like [his] correct view. When he is in that state he dwells in a state of natural morality. Or: those masters maintain that even in *samādhi* without depravities there is such a type of *rūpa*.

As La Vallée Poussin remarks, "It turns out from the *Vyākhyā* that the term Yogācāra does not refer here to the adept of a certain philosophical school, but simply to the ascetic."[86]

---

84. Pradhan 1975: 197.5–8, ad IV.4ab: *tatra yogācārā upadiśanti | dhyāyināṁ samādhiviṣayo rūpaṁ samādhiprabhāvād utpadyate | cakṣurindriyāviṣayatvāt anidarśanam | deśānāvaraṇatvād apratigham iti | atha matam | katham idānīṁ tat rūpam iti | etad avijñaptau samānam | yad apy uktam anāsravarūpokter iti tad eva samādhiprabhāvasaṁbhūtaṁ rūpam anāsrave samādhāv anāsravaṁ varṇayanti yogācārāḥ |*. Cp. *Dīghanikāya* (PTS ed.) iii.217,23–24. My translation is deeply indebted to the help I received from Nobuyoshi Yamabe and Prof. Schmithausen.

85. Shastri 1971: 583–584: *mārgaṁ sammukhīkurvāṇo yogācāras tadrūpam āśayaṁ cāśrayañ ca pratilabhate yat samyagdṛṣṭivad anāsravaṁ śīlaṁ pratilabhate | yasmin sati prakṛtiśīlatāyāṁ santiṣṭhate | athavā anāsrave 'pi samādhau tad evaṁvidhaṁ rūpaṁ ta ācāryā icchanti |*.

86. La Vallée Poussin 1923–1931: iv.18, n. 1. In the same note La Vallée Poussin further remarks that Saeki Kyokuga 1887 has a long note on the term *yogācāra* (*kan* 13.7a–8a, reprint 557–559). In fact, although I do not know if this has been pointed out before, the note consists almost entirely of quotations from the following: 瑜伽論記 T. 1828 (XLII) 311c12–19, 312c10–12, 成唯識論述記 T. 1830 (XLIII) 272c6–15, 瑜伽論略纂 T. 1829 (XLIII) 2b3–5 (? paraphrase?), 大毘盧遮那成佛經疏 T. 1796 (XXXIX) 601c28–29, and finally two references to the first and third *juan* of the same text. Note that the opinion of La Vallée Poussin, that here *yogācāra* does not refer to the Yogācāra-Vijñānavāda, is contradicted by Griffiths 1986: 173, n. 1. In fact, Prof. Schmithausen suggests the possibility that the doctrine being referred to in this passage might actually be one upheld by some Yogācāras, referring to Schmithausen 1976: 239, with n. 5, and Bhattacharya 1957: 68.14.

Another and perhaps more important passage occurs later in the *Abhidharmakośabhāṣya*:[87]

> The *yogācāra* who cultivates this [contemplation on] the disgusting is said to be of three types: a beginner, a master,[88] and one who has gone beyond mental reflection. ...
>
> First of all, the *yogācāra* who wants to cultivate the [contemplation on] the disgusting fixes his mind on a limb of his body, on his big toe, his forehead, or wherever it pleases him to do so. By progressive zealous application of attention there [on that respective limb, he visualizes] the putrefaction and dropping off of his flesh [from the bone], and so purifies the bone [until finally] he sees [his body] as entirely a collection of bones. And in just the same way, in order to extend his zealous application of attention he zealously applies his attention to [visualize] a second [skeleton], until he progressively zealously applies his attention [to visualize his] monastery, the park [around it], the region, and [finally] the whole earth, surrounded by the sea, as filled with skeletons. And yet again, he contracts [his attention] until he zealously applies his attention to [visualize] himself alone as a collection of bones, in order to concentrate his mind. After so much time, it is said, [the contemplation on] the disgusting will come to be perfected. This is the beginner *yogācāra*....
>
> And again, in order to further concentrate his mind, leaving aside [from his visualization] the bones of the feet of that collection of bones, he contemplates the rest. In this way gradually he [continues] until, leaving half of his skull aside he contemplates [only the top] half of his skull. This one is a master....

---

87. Pradhan 1975: 338.2–20 (VI.10–11ab; I omit the verses in the following): *sa punar ayam aśubhāṁ bhāvayan yogācāras trividha ucyate | ādikarmikaḥ kṛtaparijayo 'tikrāntamanaskāraś ca | ... aśubhāṁ bhāvayitukāma ādito yogācāraḥ | svāṅgāvayave cittaṁ nibadhnāti pādāṅguṣṭhe lalāṭe yatra [v]āsyābhiratiḥ | sa tatra māṁsakledap[ā]tādhimokṣa-krameṇāsthi viśodhayan sakalām asthisaṁkalāṁ paśyati | tathaiva ca punar dvitīyām adhimucyate yāvad vihārāramakṣetrakrameṇa samudraparyantāṁ pṛthivīm asthisaṁkalā-pūrṇām adhimucyate 'dhimokṣābhivardhanārtham | punaś ca saṁkṣipan yāvad ekām eva svām asthisaṁkalām adhimucyate cittasaṁkṣepārtham | iyatā kila kālenāśubhā pariniṣpannā bhavati | ayam ādikarmiko yogācāraḥ | ... sa punaḥ cittasaṁkṣepaviśeṣārthaṁ tasyām asthiśaṁkalāyāṁ pādāsthīni hitvā śeṣaṁ manasikaroti | evaṁ krameṇa yāvat kapālasyā-rdhaṁ hitvā 'rdhaṁ manasikaroti [| ayaṁ] kṛtaparijayaḥ | ... so 'rdham api kapālasya muktvā bhruvor madhye cittaṁ dhārayati | ayaṁ kilāśubhāyām atikrāntamanaskāro yogācāraḥ |*. [The emendation of °*pīta*° to °*pāta*° is based on Tib. *sha myags shing zag par mos pa* and Xuanzang's 皮肉爛墮. I owe this emendation, as the other corrections in this and the following passage, and numerous corrections of my translations of the *Abhidharmakośa* texts, to Prof. Schmithausen. Harunaga Isaacson has also given me valuable advice about this passage.]

For a French translation, see La Vallée Poussin 1923–1931: vi.150–51. This passage is commented upon in the **Abhidharma Mahāvibhāṣā* T. 1545 (XXVII) 205b10ff. See n. 89 for Yaśomitra's remarks.

88. See BHSD s.v. parijaya.

And again, leaving aside even the half-skull [as an object of contemplation], one places his attention between the eyebrows. This is the *yogācāra* who has gone beyond mental reflection on the disgusting.

Yaśomitra's commentary does not add much to the above discussion.[89] It is clear that in this conception of the *yogācāra*, he is a meditator who devotes himself to cultivation of the contemplation of the disgusting. It is not specified, however, whether this should be treated as a vocational designation.

Before we turn to an examination of Mahāyāna sūtra materials, we should note several other Sanskrit texts in which the term occurs. The Sanskrit "Yogalehrbuch" published by Dieter Schlingloff, a text which seems to be closely related to Central Asian meditative practices, uses the term many times. Schlingloff consistently renders *yogācāra* with Yogin (treating the latter as a German word), although in fact *yogin* also appears in the same text numerous times (but the two never appear side by side). While provisionally it is best not to treat the two terms as identical, despite their obvious relation, in this text at least there does seem to be little difference. Since in some sense it can be argued that the subject of the entire "Yogalehrbuch" is the *yogācāra*, as indeed the text has been read by D. S. Ruegg, it would be difficult to refer to passages of particular importance.[90] Ruegg in fact goes so far as to suggest that this text "virtually identifies the Yogācāra with the Bodhisattva ... when it remarks that at the end of his meditation the Yogācāra's *āśraya* becomes radiant with the Marks and Signs of the *mahāpuruṣa* ...; in fact the Yogācāra is destined one day to become a Bhagavat, a Samyaksaṁbuddha, and a Guide of all living beings ...."[91] While it is obvious that the *yogācāra* here is a

---

89. Shastri 1971: 896–897: *atra samāsato 'śubhāyāṁ vartamāno yogācāras trividhaḥ — ādikarmikaḥ kṛtaparijayaḥ atikrāntamanasikāraś ca* | *tatra saṁkṣepacitta ādikarmiko yogācāra ekasmin pādāṁguṣṭhe mana upanibadhya pādāṁguṣṭhaṁ klidyamānaṁ paśyati* [**apeta*]*māṁsam* [|] *evaṁ yāvat sarvaṁ śarīram asthiśaṅkalam adhimucyate* | *kṛtaparijayas tu tathaiva yāvat kapālārdham* | *atikrāntamanasikāras tathaiva yāvad bhruvor madhye cittaṁ dhārayati* | *vistaracittas tu āsamudrāsthivistārasaṁkṣepād ādikarmikaḥ ity evam-ādis trividha iti.*

90. See Schlingloff 1964. In the interests of space, I will not quote the text but merely the folio numbers on which the relevant passages begin. See the following: 127V6-R1; 128V4; 130R3; 131V6; 131R2; 136V2; 146V5; 152V6; 159V6, 160V5; and 165R1. In the following locations we find *yogācārāśraya*, but due to the fragmentary nature of the text the sense is unclear: 121R6, 123V6, 124R1, 128V2, 130V2, 131R1, 135R2, 139R3, 144R1. In addition, at 127V3 we find the compound *yogācārapādatalaiḥ*. At 165V1 we have *yogācārasya*.

91. Ruegg 1967: 162. In fact, however, the passages to which Ruegg refers do not

meditator, I do not think we can obtain any clue as to whether he is a "professional," rather than simply anyone who happens to be involved in meditation. In any case, this text, if only as a representative of an important genre of "meditation manuals," provides interesting evidence for one use of the term.

Finally, we may note two interesting occurrences of the Sanskrit term in the relatively early *Saundarananda* of Aśvaghoṣa.[92] At XIV.19 we find the following:[93] "So the *yogācāra* gives food to his body only in order to suppress hunger, not out of lust [for food] or to show favor [to the body]." And again, in XV.68:[94] "Just as here in this world a smith melts in a fire gold, pure through progressive washings with water, separated from its impurities, and smelts it repeatedly, just so here in this world the skilled *yogācāra*, separated from his faults, purified of his defilements, calms and concentrates his mind." The *Saundarananda* is undoubtedly an important text for the study of Buddhist yoga, but at least explicitly the term or concept of the *yogācāra* does not seem to play a big role in the work as a whole.

Above I discussed the *Kāśyapaparivarta* and the *Ratnarāśi*, both Mahāyāna sūtras which belong to the *Mahāratnakūṭa* collection. Although there is reason to believe that these two and the other forty-seven texts in the same collection were grouped together at a relatively late date, and perhaps only in seventh century China, some of them also contain the term *yogācāra*, and it might be convenient to cite them together here. In a passage from the *Bhadramāyākāravyākaraṇa*, the term seems to refer generally to practitioners, without any specification of their practice:[95]

---

say *exactly* what he suggests they do, partly because they are fragmentary and the last (152V5), at least, largely a creation of the editor (according to the discussion of the meaning of round parentheses in the "Vorbemerkungen zum Text" in Schlingloff 1964: 58.)

92. The yoga in the *Saundarananda* has been extensively studied by Matsunami 1954.

93. Text from Johnston 1928. In addition, my translation is indebted to that of Johnston 1932. *yogācāras tathāhāraṁ śarīrāya prayacchati* | *kevalaṁ kṣudvighātārthaṁ na rāgeṇa na bhaktaye* | |. I confess I do not understand well the force of *bhakti* here; my translation owes something to Prof. Schmithausen's suggestion.

94. *krameṇādbhiḥ śuddhaṁ kanakam iha pāṁsuvyavahitaṁ yathāgnau karmāraḥ pacati bhṛśam āvartayati ca* | *tathā yogācāro nipuṇam iha doṣavyavahitaṁ viśodhya kleśebhyaḥ śamayati manaḥ saṁkṣipati ca* | |. La Vallée Poussin 1937: 190, note, remarks that the *yogācāra* here "achieves his purification after respiratory exercises," obviously referring to the preceding XV.64, which mentions *ānāpānasmṛti*.

95. Régamey 1938: §102: *bzang po bzhi po* | *'di dag ni byang chub sems pa rnams kyi*

> These four things, Bhadra, are the bodhisattva mahāsattva's generation of incorrect aspiration, which must be eliminated. What are the four? ... 2) To not have faith (**adhimukti*) in *yogācāras*....

Here we have in some ways an exact contrast to the passage from the *Mahāvastu* we encountered above, in which one is warned away from the *yogācāra*. On the other hand, there is certainly no need for the two texts to agree in their respective attitudes toward the *yogācāra*.

In the *Ugradattaparipṛcchā* we find a list of designations of monks. The Tibetan version lists the designations as: **bahuśruta*, *dharmabhāṇaka*, *vinayadhara*, *mātṛkādhara*, *bodhisattvapiṭakadhara*, *āraṇyaka*, *paiṇḍapātika*, *pāṁśukūlika*, *alpeccha*, *saṁtuṣṭa*, *pravivikta*, *yogācāra*, *dhyāyin*, *bodhisattvayānika*, *navakarmika*, *vaiyāpṛtyakara*, and *dpon sna byed pa*. We should note that *yogācāra* and *dhyāyin* are clearly distinguished, at least in the Tibetan version of this list,[96] but this of course does not mean that they point to mutually exclusive categories, as other items in the list suggest.[97] Another *Mahāratnakūṭa* text, the *Acintyabuddhaviṣayanirdeśa*, says: "Blessed One, the *yogācāra* who pursues emptiness separately from lust, hatred and delusion is one who does not practice (**√car*) yoga; he is not a yogin. Why? Blessed One, emptiness is not to be sought separately from lust, hatred and delusion.

---

tshul bzhin ma yin pa'i sems skye ba zlog par bya ba yin te | *bzhi gang zhe na* | ... *rnal 'byor spyod pa dag la ma mos pa* | .... (The text is from Régamey's edition, but the translation is my own.) The Chinese at T. 310 (XI) 490c9–10 has item 2 as 於所修行不生信受. I am not sure, but in T. 324 (XII) 35b8, item 3 seems to correspond: 於安隱無所造立. I say this not because I understand this expression, but only because I suspect that 安隱 is meant for **yogakṣema*. If *adhimukti* is here at all, I cannot detect it, and by the same token I am puzzled by 所造立 (= **abhisaṁskṛta*?). (Prof. Schmithausen wonders whether 無所造立 might be meant for **asaṁsthitatā*, pointing out that Pāli *santiṭṭhati* can be used in a sense close to *adhimukti*.)

96. The Tibetan is found at Peking *zhi* 317b5–7 = Derge *nga* 274a5–7 = sTog *ca* 28a7-b3, the Chinese at T. 310 (19) (XI) 477a1–4, T. 322 (XII) 19a28-b3, T. 323 (XII) 27a20–25, T. 1521 (XXVI) 63a2–8. A very helpful comparative list of the three Chinese translations of the sūtra, the quotation in the **Daśabhūmivibhāṣā*, and the Tibetan translation is found in Hirakawa 1990: 130–131. The text is translated in Nagao and Sakurabe 1974: 278. The Han dynasty translation of the sūtra has 思惟者 and 道行者, corresponding I suspect to the two terms *yogācāra* and *dhyāyin*, in reverse order, while Saṅghavarman has, respectively, 修行 and 坐禪. Dharmarakṣa and the **Daśabhūmivibhāṣā* both have only 坐禪者 in the place of the two terms.

97. That is, one might well, for example, be both *alpeccha* and *saṁstuṣṭa*. Therefore, to say that the Tibetan "clearly distinguishes" *yogācāra* and *dhyāyin* does not imply that they were necessarily thought of as mutually exclusive categories; I mean only that the *terms* are distinguished.

Blessed One, lust, hatred and delusion *are* emptiness."[98] In the *Akṣobhyatathāgatavyūha*, the term appears in a fairly nonspecific sense.[99]

Such references in Mahāyāna sūtras are not, of course, limited to the *Mahāratnakūṭa* collection. In both the *Aṣṭasāhasrikā Prajñāpāramitā* and *Pañcaviṁśatisāhasrikā Prajñāpāramitā* we find the following in almost identical words:[100] "By way of example, Kauśika: When a *yogācāra* monk has arisen from meditative trance, since his mind is saturated with concentrated attention, he does not feel a strong attraction to food; his thoughts about food are few." Haribhadra, commenting on the *Aṣṭasāhasrikā*, says:[101] "*yogācāra* means 'intent on the practice of (a) particular kind(s) of meditative trance.'" Here the Chinese translations of the sūtra are interesting: Lokakṣema renders *biqiu*

98. Tibetan: sTog *ca* 442a5–7; Peking *zi* 283a7-b1; Derge ca 268b7–269a2: *bcom ldan 'das rnal 'byor spyod pa gang 'dod chags dang | zhe sdang dang | gti mug las gud du stong pa nyid tshol ba de ni rnal 'byor la mi spyod pa lags te |* [P *lags so | |*] *rnal 'byor ma lags* [P *legs*] *pa'o | | de ci'i slad du zhe na | bcom ldan 'das 'dod chags dang | zhe sdang dang | gti mug las gud du stong pa nyid btsal bar bgyi ba ma mchis te | bcom ldan 'das 'dod chags dang | zhe sdang dang | gti mug nyid stong pa lags so | |*. Chinese is found at T. 310 (35) (XI) 566c17–20: 世尊、若觀行者離於煩惱而求性空、則不相應。云何別有性空異於煩惱。若觀煩惱即是性空、爲正修行. "Blessed One, if a practitioner (**yogācāra*) seeks emptiness separately from the defilements, then this is not appropriate (**na yujyate*?). How can there be emptiness distinct from the defilements? If one contemplates the defilements, [one finds that] they are nothing but emptiness; this is correct cultivation."

Following a suggestion of Jens-Uwe Hartmann, I have understood *rnal 'byor ma lags pa'o* to mean "he is not a yogin." However, the corresponding Chinese 不相應 seems to suggest that its translators took the Indic expression as something like **na yujyate*.

99. sTog 11 (6), *dkon brtsegs, kha*, 27b3, Peking 760 (6), *dzi* 21b6: *rnal 'byor spyod pa'i dge slong rdzu 'phrul dang ldan pa*. The Chinese versions have T. 310 (6) (XI) 104b28 比丘諸神足, T. 313 (XI) 754c24 神通比丘, omitting **yogācāra*. Dantinne 1983: 119 and 174, n. aw, completely ignores **yogācāra* in the Tibetan. I owe the reference to this passage to the kindness of Jan Nattier.

100. *Aṣṭa*: Mitra 92 = Wogihara 1932–1935: 262.15–17: *tad yathāpi nāma kauśika bhikṣor yogācārasya samādher vyutthitasya manasikāraparişyanditena cittena na balavaty āhāre gṛddhir bhavati | mṛdukā cāsyāhārasaṁjñā bhavati |*. *Pañcaviṁśati*: Kimura 1986: 86.26–28: *tad yathāpi nāma kauśika yogācārasya bhikṣoḥ samādher vyutthitasya manasikārasaṁtarpitena cittena na balavaty āhāre gṛddhir bhavati |*. We might recall here the idea referred to above in the *Ratnarāśi*, namely that the bliss created by the Dhyānas serves as food for the meditator, so material nourishment is not necessary.

101. Wogihara 1932–1935: 263.7: *yogācārasyeti samādhiviśeṣānuṣṭhānaparasya |*. *samādhiviśeṣa* may also mean "the most excellent meditative trance."

dechan 比丘得禪,[102] Zhi Qian has just *biqiu* 比丘,[103] Kumārajīva has *zuochan biqiu* 坐禪比丘,[104] Xuanzang renders *yuqieshi rushengmiaoding* 瑜伽師入勝妙定,[105] *Mokṣala offers *xixing biqiu* 習行比丘,[106] and *Dānapāla has *xiu xiangyingxing pichu* 修相應行苾芻.[107] While Lokakṣema renders "a monk who has attained concentration," Zhi Qian has avoided the issue altogether, rendering merely "monk." Kumārajīva offers what in some contexts at least, such as that of the Mahāsāṁghika Vinaya,[108] seems to be the standard rendering, "meditating/meditation monk," while Xuanzang has also given what is his usual (though apparently not invariant) equivalent. *Mokṣala has merely "the monk who cultivates practice," while the latest, Song dynasty, translation of *Dānapāla has gone the farthest, rendering "the monk who cultivates yogic practice." The Chinese translations of the two sūtras (or two versions of the same sūtra?) generally agree well.

The renderings of Kumārajīva are also, like those of Xuanzang, not always consistent. In the Sanskrit *Saddharmapuṇḍarīka* we find the following:[109] "Those monks and nuns, male and female lay disciples,

102. T. 224 (VIII) 435b22 = T. 226 (VIII) 517b9.

103. T. 225 (VIII) 485b4.

104. T. 227 (VIII) 545a15–16, and T. 223 (VIII) 290a15–16. Actually the latter reads 比丘坐禪, which seems to be a misprint or miscopy. It is hard to imagine what could be intended here by 比丘坐禪, while 坐禪比丘 would be easily understandable.

105. T. 220 (2) (VII) 161b1–2 = T. 220 (4) (VII) 781a20 = T. 220 (5) (VII) 877b14. Compare also Xuanxang's T. 220 (VII) 1016c20–22.

106. T. 221 (VIII) 51a22.

107. T. 228 (VIII) 601b18–19.

108. It is possible that the translators of the Mahāsāṁghika Vinaya, who worked shortly after the time of Kumārajīva, adopted the rendering selected by him. I do not know if there are any studies of the translation equivalents in the Chinese Mahāsāṁghika Vinaya, and whether on the whole these equivalents agree with the terminology found in the works of Kumārajīva.

109. Kern and Nanjio 1908–1912: 6.11–12: *ye ca teṣu buddhakṣetreṣu bhikṣubhikṣuṇy-upāsakopāsikā yogino yogācārāḥ prāptaphalāś cāprāptaphalāś ca te 'pi sarve saṁdṛśyate sma.* (Kashgar and Gilgit are identical.) Tibetan (Peking 4b1–2): *sangs rgyas kyi zhing de dag na dge slong dang dge slong ma dang | dge snyen dang | dge bsnyen ma dang | rnal 'byor can dang | rnal 'byor spyod pa gang dag 'bras bu thob pa dang | 'bras bu ma thob pa de dag thams cad kyang snang ngo | |*. The syntax of the Sanskrit has been understood strangely in Matsunami et al. 1975: 12: それらの仏陀の国土には比丘・比丘尼、信男・信女の修行者たちがいて、瑜伽行を修め、その結果を得たものもあれば、まだ得ないものもあるが、彼らもまたすべて見えた. I frankly think this cannot be correct. Note that the Tibetan translation does not support this rendering. Compare the translations in Burnouf 1852: 4, and Kern 1884: 7.

yogins and *yogācāras*, who had attained the fruit and who had not attained the fruit, also all appeared in those buddha fields." The Chinese translation of Kumārajīva has, corresponding to *yogino yogācārāḥ prāptaphalāś cāprāptaphalāś ca*, 諸修行得道者.[110] It is at least possible that this should be understood as more or less equivalent to *yogācārāḥ* and *prāptaphalāḥ*, although a recent English rendering has more naturally understood the Chinese phrase as one (apparently causal) expression: "those who had practised and achieved the path."[111]

The *Ratnamegha*, a very interesting text, actually makes some attempt to, as it were, "define" the term *yogācāra* (although of course one should not confuse this type of listing with true definition):[112]

> If, gentle son, bodhisattvas possess ten qualities they are *yogācāras*. What are the ten? [They are] (1) Amply cultivating [the contemplation on] the disgusting (**aśubhabhāvanā*). (2) Amply cultivating [the contemplation on] friendliness (**maitrī°*). (3) Amply cultivating [the contemplation on] dependent arisal (**pratītyasamutpāda°*). (4) Being amply expert concerning faults.[113] (5) Amply cultivating [the contemplation on] emptiness (**śūnyatā°*). (6) Amply cultivating [the contemplation on] the signless

---

The identical expression in the Sanskrit text of the *Karuṇāpuṇḍarīka* (Yamada 1968: II.5.2–21) is due to the fact that, the beginning of the Sanskrit original having been lost at some point, the *Karuṇāpuṇḍarīka* manuscripts were suppleted from the *Saddharmapuṇḍarīka* (Yamada 1968: I.22).

110. T. 262 (IX) 2b21. Exactly the same is found at T. 264 (IX) 135b28.

111. Kubo and Yuyama 1991: 3. It is also so understood by Watson 1993: 6: "who had carried out religious practices and attained the way." This is also a traditional Japanese reading (Nakada 1989: 14): もろもろの修行し得道するもの.

Dharmarakṣa's version, T. 263 (IX) 63c12–13, has: 修行獨處者逮得徳果一切表露. Here *yogin* and *yogācāra* seem to have been understood as 修行獨處者, a translation which we might have understood otherwise as equivalent to **yogācāra* and **āraṇyaka* (?).

It is worth remarking that, the syntax notwithstanding, it is unlikely that the text means to imply that male or female lay disciples might be *yogācāras*.

112. Derge Kanjur 231, *mdo sde, wa*, 90a6-b1: *rigs kyi bu chos bcu dang ldan na byang chub sems dpa' rnal 'byor spyod pa rnams yin no* | | *bcu gang zhe na* | *'di lta ste* | (1) *mi sdug pa bsgom pa mang ba rnams yin* | (2) *byams pa bsgom pa mang ba rnams yin* | (3) *rten cing 'brel par 'byung ba bsgom pa mang ba rnams yin* | (4) *skyon la mkhas pa mang ba rnams yin* | (5) *stong pa nyid bsgom pa mang ba rnams yin* | (6) *mtshan ma med pa bsgom pa mang ba rnams yin* | (7) *rnal 'byor bsgom pa mang ba rnams yin* | (8) *rgyun tu bsgom pa mang ba rnams yin* | (9) *'gyod pa med pa rnams yin* | (10) *tshul khrims phun sum tshogs pa rnams yin* |. The Chinese versions of this passage are found as follows: T. 489 (XIV) 740b22–28, T. 658 (XVI) 232c28–233a2, T. 659 (XVI) 269b1–6, T. 660 (XVI) 318b23–29.

113. The sense is not entirely clear to me. Two of the Chinese versions seem to suggest "completely eliminating all faults and transgressions," T. 489 於諸過患善能

(**animitta*°). (7) Amply cultivating [the contemplation on] yogic practice (**yoga*°). (8) Amply engaging in continual cultivation. (9) Being without remorse (**kaukṛtya*). (10) And completely upholding the precepts.

Here there can be no question that it is the meditative cultivation of the *yogācāra* which is felt to define him, although we should not overlook the mention in item (10) of the precepts.

The *Brahmaviśeṣacintiparipṛcchā* contains a reference to the *yogācāra* in a widely quoted passage:[114]

Those deluded people, Blessed One, who having renounced the world into the well-known community are fallen into the speculative views of the heretics and seek nirvāṇa as a real existent—just as [people seek to

---

除斷 and T 658 多修離過患法; another two support "expert," T. 659 善識汚心之法 and T. 660 於諸過患常修善巧.

114. In his edition of the first *bam po* of the sūtra, Goshima Kiyotaka has traced multiple quotations of the passage. In this unfortunately not very accessible edition, Goshima 1981: 31–32, and appendix pages 9–13, the passage is critically edited on the basis of a number of sources. For reference see the Derge Kanjur 160, *ba*, 33b, and Peking 827, *phu*, 34b4, and in Chinese T. 585 (XV) 4c7–13; T. 586 (XV) 36c28–37a4; T. 587 (XV) 66c16–21. The Sanskrit for the passage is available in the *Prasannapadā* of Candrakīrti, although quoted there under the odd name *Tathāgatavāgguhyaparivarta* = *de bzhin gshegs pa'i gsang ba bstan pa'i le'u.* (No such name appears in the list of alternative titles found at the end of the sūtra itself.) See La Vallée Poussin 1903–1913: 540.12–541.5: *tad ime bhagavan mohapuruṣā ye svākhyāte dharmavinaye pravrajya tīrthikadṛṣṭau nipatitā nirvāṇaṁ bhāvataḥ paryeṣate tadyathā tilebhyas tailaṁ kṣīrāt sarpiḥ | atyantaparinirvṛteṣu bhagavan sarvadharmeṣu te nirvāṇaṁ mārganti tān aham ābhimānikān tīrthikān iti vadāmi | na bhagavan yogācāraḥ samyakpratipannaḥ kasyacid dharmasyotpādaṁ vā nirodhaṁ vā karoti nāpi kasyacid dharmasya prāptim icchati nābhisamayam iti vistaraḥ* | |. The Tibetan translation of this passage is found in the Derge Tanjur 3860, *dbu ma*, *'a*, 182a1–5. According to Goshima's edition, the passage is also found in the *Prajñāpradīpa* of Bhāvaviveka, Peking Tanjur, *dbu ma*, *tsha*, 311b7–312a5, Chinese T. 1566 (XXX) 131b2–8, and in Avalokitavrata's *ṭīkā*: Peking, *dbu ma*, *za*, 360b7–361a5. In all cases the Tibetan versions of the sūtra and its quotations in the śāstras have *yogācāra samyakpratipanna* as *rnal 'byor spyod pa yang dag par zhugs pa*. The Chinese versions, however, show a considerable variation: T. 585 修行者; T. 586 and T. 587 正修道者; and *Prajñāpradīpa* 成就行者. Although not mentioned by Goshima, the final portion of the quotation is also found in the 瑜伽師地論釋 T. 1580 (XXX) 884a3–6, and there the term is rendered with Xuanzang's (nearly) habitual 瑜伽師. The Tibetan equivalent of this text is the **Yogācār(y)abhūmivyākhyā*, Tōh. 4043 (Derge Tanjur, *sems tsam*, *'i*, 69b4), in which we read: *tshangs pas zhus pa chen po'i mdo las kyang | bcom ldan 'das rnal 'byor spyod pa'i sa la yang dag par zhugs pa ni chos gang skye ba'am 'gag par mi bgyid do zhes bya ba la sogs pa gsungs so* | |. The rendering *rnal 'byor spyod pa'i sa* suggests, however, an understanding of **yogācārabhūmi*. Does this imply that we should imagine something like **yogācārabhūmau samyakpratipanna*, i.e., "one who is perfected in his practice in the stage of the practice of yoga"? (On the relation between Tōh. 4043 and T. 1580, see Mukai 1979: 42, and 61, n. 10.)

> obtain real] oil from [real] sesame seeds, [real] ghee from [real] milk—are seeking, Blessed One, after nirvāṇa among all things which are already completely passed into nirvāṇa.[115] I call those people misguided heretics. The *yogācāra*, Blessed One, who is correctly perfected in his practice does not cause the arisal or destruction of anything at all, nor does he wish for the acquisition of anything, nor its realization.

Here the authors of the sūtra use the term *yogācāra* to refer to the type of practitioner of whose behavior and views they approve; he is in fact a sort of touchstone of orthodoxy against which the heterodox are to be contrasted. If we are to so understand the *yogācāra*s as those practitioners whose views are correct, in contrast to the deluded, then it seems to be implied that they too are monks, those who have "renounced the world into the well-known community." It is interesting here too to note that this passage clearly refers to orthodoxy, not orthopraxy, as one might expect if the defining characteristic of the *yogācāra* were his practice itself.

Hints that the *yogācāra* may be more than a mere monk appear in several places. The *Ratnamegha* contains the following passage:[116] "Gentle son, if people are endowed with ten qualities they are noble bodhisattvas (**ājāneyabodhisattva*). ... 1) [If they] are *yogācāra*s who abundantly contemplate emptiness...." In the *Gaṇḍavyūha* we find the expression:[117] "[The Tathāgata's body] makes fall for the *yogācāra*

---

115. It is possible we should read this, as Jens-Uwe Hartmann has suggested to me, as a locative absolute: "when all things are already completely passed into nirvāṇa." The point is that it is a mistake to regard such things as real, and seek to obtain from them something real.

116. The passage in Tibetan reads (Derge Kanjur 231, *mdo sde, wa* 58a4): *rigs kyi bu chos bcu dang ldan na byan chub sems dpa' cang shes pa rnams yin no* | | *bcu gang zhe na* | *'di lta ste* | (1) *stong pa nyid la sgom pa mang bas rnal 'byor spyod pa rnams yin* |. The Chinese translations render the crucial expression: T. 660 (XVI) 305c4 得瑜伽師; T. 489 (XIV) 726c12–13: 雖修定行而常觀空; T. 659 (XVI) 257a6–7: 坐禪攝心; T. 658 (XVI) 222b18: 雖行禪定恒修空相.

117. Suzuki and Idzumi 1949: 94.13–14: *yogācārāṇāṁ bodhisattvānāṁ sarvadharmasvabhāvatalanirghoṣaṁ nāma dharmameghavarṣaṁ abhipravarṣamāṇān*. The Chinese versions have the critical term as T. 278 (IX) 696c18: 修行菩薩; T. 279 (X) 342a4: 修行位諸菩薩; T. 293 (X) 691c7–8: 修行相應位諸菩薩. They do not offer much help, however, with the word *tala*. The translation of Kajiyama et al. 1994: I.166 has avoided the problem of interpreting the difficult compound by merely quoting the Chinese rendering of T. 293. Takasaki 1974: 554, n. 54 suggested that the list in which the item quoted here appears is presented in descending order of importance, namely: *bodhimaṇḍavaragata bodhisattva*, *abhiṣekaprāpta b°*, *mahādharmayauvarājyābhiṣeka b°*, *kumārabhūta b°*, *avivartya b°*, *śuddhādhyāśaya b°*, *pūrvayogasaṁpanna b°*, *janmaja b°*, *yogācāra b°*, *ādikarmika b°*, *prathamacittotpādika b°*, etc. The same list

bodhisattvas rain from the cloud of the teaching which is called the cry of the base (?) of the intrinsic nature of all things." I confess that this remains rather unclear to me, but taken together with the *Ratnamegha* passage it is interesting that both point explicitly to the *yogācāra* as a bodhisattva. As noted above, Ruegg pointed out that the "Yoga-lehrbuch" seems to take a similar view of the *yogācāra* as a bodhisattva.

Another important, although quite obviously not early, Mahāyāna sūtra, the *Laṅkāvatāra*, has the following passage:[118]

---

appears in several other texts, there limited to ten members, however. (See Yamada 1959: 256–57.) See for example T. 1487 (XXIV) 1033a26-b4, where *yogācāra* is transcribed 喩阿闍, and the almost identical text at T. 283 (X) 454c4, 455a11–18, where the term is 瑜阿闍, and ten qualities of the *yogācāra* are listed.

118. Nanjio 1923: 248.8–14: *śmaśānikānāṁ ca mahāmate araṇyavanaprasthāny amanuṣyāvacarāṇi prāntāni śayanāsanāny adhyāvasatāṁ yogināṁ yogācārāṇāṁ maitrīvihāriṇāṁ vidyādharāṇāṁ vidyāsādhayitukāmānāṁ vidyāsādhanamokṣavighnakaratvān mahāyānasaṁprasthitānāṁ kulaputrāṇāṁ kuladuhitṝṇāṁ ca sarvayogasādhanāntarāyakaram ity api samanupaśyatāṁ* (?) *mahāmate svaparātmahitakāmasya māṁsaṁ sarvam abhakṣyaṁ bodhisattvasya.*

The Tibetan text in the Derge Kanjur 107, *mdo sde*, *ca*, 154a6–b1, reads: *blo gros chen po dur khrod pa rnams dang | dgon pa nags 'dab mi ma yin pa rgyu ba bas mtha'i mal stan la gnas pa'i rnal 'byor pa | rnal 'byor la spyod pa byams pa la gnas pa rnams dang | rig sngags 'chang ba | rig sngags grub par 'dod pa rnams kyi rig sngags sgrub pa dang | thar pa la bgegs byed pa'i phyir theg pa chen po la zhugs pa'i rigs kyi bu dang | rigs kyi bu mo rnams kyi rnal 'byor sgrub pa thams cad kyi bar chad byed par 'gyur bar rjes su mthong nas bdag dang gzhan gyi lus la phan par 'dod pa'i byang chub sems dpas sha thams cad mi bza'o | |.*

My translation of the Sanskrit is guided by my understanding of the Tibetan translation. This is especially so with regard to the insertion of conjunctions; the Sanskrit appears to intend several classes, cemetery dwellers, *yogin*s, upholders of spells, etc., in apposition, while the Tibetan translation conjoins them. I follow the latter understanding. The Chinese translation T. 672 (XVI) 623b27-c2 appears to have an equivalent for *yogācāra* with 寂靜修行, but the equivalence is problematic. I am very grateful to Prof. Schmithausen for his remarks on this and the following *Laṅkāvatāra* passage, and to Prof. Nagao for his suggestion on the first quotation. Prof. Nagao, in fact, would translate this passage as follows:

> And moreover, Mahāmati, because for those who dwell in cemeteries, and for those yogins and *yogācāra*s, who dwell in wilderness areas, realms frequented by demons, and border regions, and who dwell in friendliness, and for those upholders of spells, who wish to completely command spells, it (meat eating) creates an obstacle to the perfection of spells and to liberation,—and also for those gentle sons and gentle daughters who, observing that this causes obstruction to all the perfections of yoga, just set out in the Mahāyāna, (the same is true)—Mahāmati, the bodhisattva who desires his own and others' benefit should not eat any meat at all.

I confess that despite the assistance of these two great scholars I still cannot clearly construe the construction of the whole passage. (Prof. Schmithausen suggests

And moreover, Mahāmati, because [meat eating] creates an obstacle to the perfection of spells and to liberation for those who dwell in cemeteries, and for yogins, *yogācāras*, who dwell in wilderness areas, realms frequented by demons, and border regions, who dwell in friendliness, and for the upholders of spells, those who wish to completely command spells, and observing that this causes obstruction to all the perfections of yoga for those gentle sons and gentle daughters just set out in the Mahāyāna, Mahāmati, the bodhisattva who desires his own and others' benefit should not eat any meat at all.

Here again *yogācāra* seems to be virtually synonymous with *yogin*, and may or may not be considered as an avocation parallel to dwelling in cemeteries or dwelling in wilderness areas.[119] I think we have virtually the same implications a bit later in the same sūtra:[120]

---

that *vidyādharāṇāṁ vidyāsādhayitukāmānāṁ vidyāsādhanamokṣavighnakaratvān* may be an intrusion, pointing to *Hastikakṣyasūtra* T. 814 [XVII] 787a11, Peking 873, *mdo, tsu*, 115a3.)

119. One of the many powers of a *dhāraṇī* described in the *Sūryagarbhasūtra* is that it makes the *yogācāra* delight in wilderness dwelling. At least this is the understanding of the Chinese text: T. 397 (XIII) 250b12 令坐禪人樂阿蘭若, 258b22 能令坐禪人樂阿蘭若, and 264a17 坐禪行人樂阿蘭若. The Tibetan, however, reads somewhat differently (Derge Kanjur 257, *mdo sde*, *za*, 137b7, 158a3, and 172a3): *rnal 'byor spyod pa rnams mngon par dga' bar bgyi ba* (or: *byed pa*['*o*]). Should we emend *mngon par* to **dgon par*? (In the first place, of course, the reading of these passages in other Kanjurs must be confirmed; I regret that at the moment I lack access to any Kanjur other than the Derge.)

120. Nanjio 1923: 254.8–16: *yadi tu mahāmate anujñātukāmatā me syāt kalpyaṁ vā me śrāvakāṇāṁ pratisevituṁ syān nāhaṁ maitrīvihāriṇāṁ yogināṁ yogācārāṇāṁ śmaśānikānāṁ mahāyānasaṁprasthitānāṁ kulaputrāṇāṁ kuladuhitṝṇāṁ ca sarvasattvaikaputrakasaṁjñābhāvanārthaṁ sarvamāṁsabhakṣaṇapratiṣedhaṁ kuryāṁ* | *kṛtavāṁś cāsmi* <Edition: *kuryāṁ kṛtavāṁś ca asmin*> *mahāmate dharmakāmānāṁ kulaputrāṇāṁ kuladuhitṝṇāṁ ca sarvayānasaṁprasthitānāṁ śmaśānikānāṁ maitrīvihāriṇām āraṇyakānāṁ yogināṁ yogācārāṇāṁ sarvayogasādhanāya sarvasattvaikaputrakasaṁjñābhāvanārthaṁ sarvamāṁsapratiṣedham.*

The Tibetan text in the Derge Kanjur 107, *mdo sde, ca*, 156a6–b2, reads: *blo gros chen po gal te ngas gnang bar bya bar 'dod dam* | *nga'i nyan thos rnams kyis bsnyen par rung ba zhig yin na ni* | *byams pas gnas pa'i rnal 'byor can dur khrod pa rnams dang* | *theg pa chen po la yang dag par zhugs pa'i rigs kyi bu dang* | *rigs kyi bu mo rnams la sems can thams cad bu gcig bzhin du 'du shes bsgom pa'i phyir sha thams cad za ba gcod par yang byas so** | | *blo gros chen po ngas ni rigs kyi bu dang rigs kyi bu mo chos 'dod pa theg pa thams cad la rab tu zhugs pa rnams dang* | *dur khrod pa byams pa la gnas pa dgon pa pa rnal 'byor la spyod pa rnams kyi rnal 'byor thams cad sgrub pa dang sems can thams cad bu bzhin du 'du shes bsgom pa'i phyir* | *sha thams cad gcod par yang byas so* | |. *Something is very odd here in the Derge text: a negation seems to be missing from the final verb in this sentence. I regret I have not been able to check other editions, but Prof. Schmithausen informs me it is missing in the Peking edition too.

My translation of the Sanskrit was guided by the Tibetan translation and Prof.

But if, Mahāmati, I had wanted to allow [meat-eating], or if I were to judge it as acceptable for my auditors to indulge in [meat eating], then I would not make the prohibition of all meat-eating, in order for yogis, *yogācāras*, who dwell in friendliness, who dwell in cemeteries, and[121] for gentle sons and gentle daughters who are set out in the Great Vehicle, to cultivate the idea that all beings are like their only child. But, Mahāmati, I have [in fact] made the prohibition on all meat, so that gentle sons and gentle daughters who desire the teachings, who are set out in any vehicle, who dwell in cemeteries, who dwell in friendliness, who dwell in wilderness areas, who are *yogins*[122] and *yogācāras*, might cultivate the idea that all beings are like their only child so that they may perfect all the yogas.[123]

Finally, in the *Saṁdhinirmocana*, also of unknown date but certainly not early, the term seems to be used, as we have seen it before, in a quite nonspecific sense:[124]

Again, Subhūti, the *yogācāra* monk, understanding the true nature of one skandha as the ultimate selflessness of dharmas, does not seek out individually the ultimate characterization of absence of self of other skandhas, dhātus, āyatanas, dependent arisal, nourishments, truths, foundations of mindfulness, exertions, bases of magical power, powers, strengths, limbs of awakening, and the eight-fold noble path. Rather, relying on the non-dual knowledge which conforms to true reality, he ascertains and correctly understands the characteristic of the same flavor

---

Schmithausen's comments; the emendation is also his. Equivalents in the Chinese translations are found at T. 671 (XVI) 563c4–12, with 如實行者, and T. 672 (XVI) 624a22–26 with 修觀行者. On terminology close to 如實行者, and its relation to *yoga/yogin*, see Takasaki 1993.

121. The conjunction is indicated by Tibetan, but absent in Sanskrit, which appears to be appositional.

122. Tibetan omits *yogins*.

123. Tibetan has: "so that they might cultivate the perfection of all yogas and the idea that all beings are like their only child." This seems to give a somewhat better sense.

124. Lamotte 1935: IV.9: *rab 'byor gzhan yang dge slong rnal 'byor spyod pa ni phung po gcig gi de bzhin nyid don dam pa'i chos bdag med pa rab tu rtogs nas yang de las gzhan pa'i phung po rnams dang | khams rnams dang | skye mched rnams dang | rten cing 'brel par 'byung ba dang | zas rnams dang | bden pa rnams dang | dran pa nye bar bzhag pa rnams dang | yang dag par spong ba rnams dang | rdzu 'phrul gyi rkang pa rnams dang | dbang po rnams dang | stobs rnams dang | byang chub kyi yan lag rnams so so dang | 'phags pa'i lam yan lag brgyad pa so so la de bzhin nyid don dam pa bdag med pa yongs su tshol bar mi byed kyi de bzhin nyid kyi rjes su 'brang ba gnyis med pa'i shes pa la rten pa de nyid kyis don dam pa thams cad du ro gcig pa'i mtshan nyid nges par 'dzin pa dang | mngon par rtogs pa kho nar byed de | rab 'byor rnam grangs des kyang khyod kyis 'di ltar thams cad du ro gcig pa'i mtshan nyid gang yin pa de don dam pa yin par rig par bya'o ||*. The Chinese versions are found at T. 675 (XVI) 668c11–16, and T. 677 (XVI) 714b1–10. Both render **yogācāra bhikṣu* with 修行比丘.

in all ultimate truth. Through this teaching, Subhūti, you must understand that what is characterized by the same flavor in everything is the ultimate truth.

As mentioned above, the term does not seem to have received quite the attention in the śāstric literature one might have expected. In the *Yogācārabhūmi* of Saṅgharakṣa, in genre somewhat similar to the "Yogalehrbuch" published by Schlingloff, both *yogācāra* and *yogācārabhūmi* are defined. However, the definitions are not entirely clear. We possess two versions of the text in Chinese, one by Dharmarakṣa, and the other (partial) version by An Shigao. The former at least seems to understand *yogācāra* as a *tatpuruṣa*,[125] "practicing what is to be cultivated and following it." Unfortunately the following definition of *yogācārabhūmi* is not entirely clear.[126] This is not a Yogācāra text. However, the term *yogācāra* does appear in the works of the Yogācāra-Vijñānavāda school proper, although apparently again (and surprisingly?) without special emphasis.[127] In the portion of the *Śrāvakabhūmi* published by Wayman, for instance, we find the word several times. In the fourth *Yogasthāna* the term *yogācāra* seems to be used synonymously with *yogin*, and the specification *ādikarmika yogācāra*, which we saw above in the *Abhidharmakośabhāṣya*, is found.[128] The fact that this term refers to one involved in mental, meditative cultivation is made clear in a subsequent passage.[129] The word appears also in other *Śrāvakabhūmi* materials studied by Sakuma, also fortunately preserved in Sanskrit.[130] Especially important is a lengthy quotation

---

125. T. 606 (XV) 182b29-c1, with variant 16. The version of An Shigao T. 607 (XV) 231b3 is not helpful in this regard. See Demiéville 1954: 398.

126. T. 606 (XV) 182c1–2, T. 607 (XV) 231b5–6; see Demiéville 1954: 398, and 343.

127. The term seems to be likewise rare in Madhyamaka texts. For example, despite its title (the precise meaning of which is not clear to me), the *Bodhisattvayogācāracatuḥśatakaṭīkā*, Candrakīrti's commentary to Āryadeva's *Catuḥśataka*, appears, according to Suzuki's index (1994b: 265, s.v. yogācāra) to use the term only once (Suzuki 1994a: 154.9 [ad VIII.24]), and then in a rather generic way. It is interesting that the Tibetan translation here renders *yogācāra* with *rnal 'byor pa* (but this Tibetan version differs from the extant Sanskrit on many points).

128. Wayman 1961: 125, and see also Shukla 1973: 437. This expression also occurs in Pāli in the form *ādikammiko yogāvacaro*, on which see Silk 1997, n. 26.

129. Wayman 1961: 130, and see also Shukla 1973: 470.

130. I refer to the critical edition of Sanskrit, Tibetan, and Chinese (with German translation) in Sakuma 1990. For the Sanskrit see also the editio princeps of Shukla 1973: 197–200. The passage below was already noticed (in Chinese) by Miyamoto 1932: 772.

from what might be an as yet unidentified sūtra source.[131] I refer to this material in the context of śāstric rather than sūtra sources because I am not certain that the "quotation" has a genuine source older than the śāstra.[132] In any case, the term here is juxtaposed with *bhikṣu* and *yogin* in one set expression, *bhikṣur yogī yogācāraḥ*.[133] It is clear from the context that the monk who is a *yogin* and *yogācāra*[134] is considered to be one engaged in meditative cultivation. The apparent quotation begins:[135]

---

131. See Sakuma 1990: i.16. He refers there to Shukla 1973: 197, n. 1.

132. That is, we might keep in mind the possibility that the author(s) or compiler(s) of the *Yogācārabhūmi* may have made up the sūtra reference him- or them-selves as a way of legitimating his or their ideas. (Note that there is actually no reference to a sūtra in Sanskrit, Tibetan, or Chinese. The Sanskrit begins: *yathoktaṁ bhagavatā āyuṣmantaṁ revatam ārabhya*. The implication, however, is that the following was spoken in a sūtra.) In regard to the source of the quotation, although the case is obviously quite different and the evidençe as yet weak, we might recall Nagao's discussion concerning the **Abhidharma-mahāyāna-sūtra*, quoted often in the works of Asaṅga. Nagao 1982: 28–33 considers in detail the facts concerning this **Abhidharma-mahāyāna-sūtra*, concluding (p. 33) in a cautious manner, but clearly implying that the author of the "quoted" passages may well have been Asaṅga himself. Notice that our "sūtra quotation" has been studied from an entirely different point of view by Schmithausen 1976: 239–242. Schmithausen does not mention any doubts about the authenticity of the source, merely referring to it as "an unknown Sūtra." Davidson 1985 seems to assume that what he calls the **Revatasūtra* is a legitimately old work, since he cites it together with the *Aṣṭasāhasrikā* and the *Kāśyapaparivarta*. And on p. 131 he makes his assumption explicit by calling it "probably the oldest *sūtra* base for the doctrine of *āśraya-parivṛtti* under the guise of *āśraya-viśuddhi*." At 194, n. 9, he says "The actual title of this sūtra is unknown, but Revata as a figure and the material in this sūtra appear to have been specific sectarian developments within the Kashmīr-Gandhāra area." I have pointed out above that Revata is important in canonical sources as the first among those dedicated to *dhyāna*.

133. I am not certain that this form is invariant, however, and wonder whether we must agree with Sakuma 1990: ii.9 n. 43 (§A.2.1) who restores *yogī*, missing in the Sanskrit manuscript and Tibetan translation. He suggests that it is found in the Chinese translation, which has 比丘勤修觀行是瑜伽師, its habitual translation of the complete set *bhikṣur yogī yogācāraḥ*. In other nearby passages, *yogin* alone is indeed regularly rendered 修觀行者. While it is therefore likely that the Chinese text does in fact represent the whole phrase, the entire question is a relatively minor one, and especially in view of this, given the agreement of the Tibetan translation with the Sanskrit text, I would prefer not to emend the latter solely on the basis of the Chinese.

134. Tibetan supports the understanding of the expression as an appositional phrase, so perhaps even better: "a *yogin*, a *yogācāra*."

135. Sakuma 1990: ii.9–10 (§A.2.1–2): *kiyatā bhadanta bhikṣur yogācāra ālambane cittam upanibadhnāti* | *katamasminn ālambane cittam upanibadhnāti* | *kathaṁ punar ālambane*

In how many ways, Reverend, does a monk who is a *yogācāra* fix his mind on an object? On what object does he fix his mind? And how is his mind fixed on its object that it comes to be firmly fixed? ... Now, Revata, a monk who is a *yogin* and *yogācāra* and wants to purify his practice, or wants to produce expertise [in the skandhas, and so on], or wants to free his mind from the depravities, fixes his mind on a suitable object, and fixes it exactly correctly on a corresponding [object], and he is an assiduous meditator devoted to that [object].

It is clear from this passage and the passages that follow it that the *yogācāra* monk, who is considered simultaneously to be a *yogin*, is here a meditator. This is quite in concert with what other sources suggest.[136]

I noted at the outset that I did not initially see any serious problem in finding an appropriate translation for *yogācāra*, thinking one would not go far wrong with "practitioner of yoga." But this actually begs several questions. What we really need to understand is the specific reference or references of the term. Is the *yogācāra* a meditator or a meditation specialist? Or again, is he (or she) merely a generic "practitioner"? What does "*yoga*" signify here? Does it signify the same thing in every text in which the term appears? Our survey above seems to suggest that, in the majority of cases, the reference of *yogācāra* does not in fact seem to be specific at all. On the contrary, it is rather generic. Certainly in most cases the *yogācāra* or *yogācāra bhikṣu* seems to be a meditative practitioner, although there are several

---

cittam upanibaddhaṁ sūpanibaddhaṁ bhavati | ... *iha Revata bhikṣur yogī yogācāraḥ caritaṁ vā viśodhayitukāmaḥ kauśalyaṁ vā kartukāmaḥ āsravebhyo vā cittaṁ vimocayitukāmaḥ anurūpe cālambane cittam upanibadhnāti pratirūpe ca samyag eva copanibadhnāti tatra cānirākṛtadhyāyī bhavati* |. The corresponding Tibetan text is found on pages 43–44 (Derge 4036, 77a1ff.; Peking 5537, 92b5ff.), Chinese on 79–80 (T. 1579 [XXX] 427c27ff.). Sakuma offers the following translation (pages 105–106): "Auf wieviele [Weisen] (oder: Aufgrund von wieviel[en Motiven(?)]) fixiert der Yoga-Praxis übende Mönch seinen Geist auf den [Übungs]gegenstand? Auf welchen [Übungs]-gegenstand fixiert er seinen Geist? Wie, ferner (oder: anderseits), muss der Geist auf den [Übungs]gegenstand fixiert [sein, um] gut fixiert [zu sein]? ... Wenn da ein Mönch, der ein Yogin ist, der die Yoga-Praxis übt, sein Verhalten läutern, Versiertheit erwerben oder seinen Geist von den "üblen Einflüssen" befreien will, so fixiert er seinen Geist auf den (jeweils) angemessenen [Übungs]gegenstand, auf einen entsprechenden (/ähnlichen) [Gegenstand], [fixiert ihn] in genau der richtigen Weise, und ist unermüdlich der darauf [gerichteten] versenkungsmäßigen Betrachtung gewidmet."

136. A further reference from what is perhaps a sūtra commentary is worth mentioning. Waldschmidt 1965: 294 (SHT 649 R3–4) has: *evaṁ yogī yogācāraḥ pañcaskandhāṁ duḥkhān iti paśya*[*ti*]. Nothing further in the manuscript fragment clarifies what is meant by *yogācāra* here, but its conjuction with *yogin* does not seem unusual.

cases in which even meditation seems not necessarily to be involved. If we are to understand the Chinese renderings at their face value, they often suggest that *yogācāra* refers to the practice of seated meditation ("zazen"), but even this term does not imply anything specific about the actual mental content of the practice. By the same token there is also a considerable number of cases in which the term has been rendered into Chinese with a generic term seeming to indicate nothing more precise than what we might mean in contemporary English by "practitioner."

When we can tell (and usually there is no indication), the term *yogācāra* does not seem to be used to distinguish advanced from beginning practitioners; some of our sources (and there may be interesting commonalities between diverse sources in this regard) are in fact quite explicit about the application of the term to one at *any* stage of the path. Likewise, the specific doctrinal content or orientation of the meditation undertaken by the *yogācāra* (when indeed meditation comes into the question) does not seem to be specified; the term seems to be widely used with reference to different varieties of meditative practice, or even more usually with reference to meditative practice generically understood. This supports the observation that the label may be applied equally to beginning and advanced practitioners. It has not been possible to determine with certainty whether the term points more to a vocation or career than an avocation—in other words, whether the *yogācāra* is a professional meditator, or rather more simply a monk who happens to be engaged in meditative practice (however this is understood) at a given time. But certainly the generic usages documented above argue forcefully against the strong reading of "meditation monk" in the sense of one who devotes himself especially to meditative cultivation as a vocation. This also raises the question of the importance of the term *bhikṣu* here. Indeed, while we do frequently find the collocation *yogācāra bhikṣu*, we also find *yogācāra* alone, and there are even some indications that a *yogācāra* need not necessarily be a monk (or nun). On the other hand, there is no indication that the term *yogācāra bhikṣu* need indicate anything more specific or precise than does *yogācāra* alone.

The frequent coordination of *yogācāra* with *yogin* suggests that the two terms are, at least sometimes, if not usually, thought to be near or virtual synonyms.[137] If this be the case, we might suppose *yogācāra*

---

137. Although this is only corollary evidence at best, it is interesting to note that it appears that Uigur translators of Tibetan texts often, even systematically, rendered

to be the more restricted term, since it appears to be found, in this sense (rather than as a *tatpuruṣa* meaning "the practice of yoga"), only in Buddhist literature, whereas *yogin* is, of course, a common term in almost all genres of Sanskrit literature.

The appearance of the term *yogācāra* in vinaya literature might suggest a relatively early origin for the term. (We should remember, however, that we have little solid information upon which to base *any* absolute chronology of Indian Buddhist literature, and without further specification a word like "early" is not terribly meaningful, and even potentially misleading.) We cannot say, since we are so poorly supplied with Buddhist texts in Indic languages, whether the term was favored by one school more than another. Although absent, to be sure, from almost all Pāli canonical literature, the apparently related term *yogāvacara* does appear rather often in post-canonical Pāli literature.[138] Since we can positively identify the term *yogācāra* or *yogāvacara* in texts of at least the Theravāda, Mahāsāṁghika, and Sarvāstivāda (and possibly Sautrāntika)[139] schools, at least at this point it is not possible to assign its use alone any special sectarian significance. To the extent that *yogācāra* is a technical term, it seems possible that

---

yogin (rnal 'byor pa) with *yogačari*. De Jong 1982: 204 quotes *rnal 'byor nyams kyi snang ba la* as *yogačari-nïng tüzülmäklig köngül-dä*. The German translators render this with Yogācārya. The same is true in Kara and Zieme 1976: 47 (360, and note), 63 (9), 102, and 1977: 36 (100, with note), where again *yogačari* is rendered Yogācārya. But in 1977: 49 (287) the same authors render it with *yogācārin*. The Tibetan-Uigur vocabulary in 1977: 75 quotes for *rnal 'byor gyi dbang phyug* the Uigur *yogačarilar iligi*, but the Uigur glossary 1977: 147 quotes *yogačari* twice, once as equivalent to *yogācāra*, once to *yogācārya*, without explanation. Jan Nattier has informed me that Indic short final *a* is normally rendered in Uigur with *i*, and therefore the form *yogačari* does not support the form **yogācārin*, but rather suggests that the translators had in mind *yogācāra*.

We may note that the same term appears also as a loan in Tocharian. At Sieg and Siegling 1949: 18 (9b5) of the text we find *yogācā///*, explained by the glossary (p. 158 of the translation and glossary) as representing the nominitive plural *yogācāri*. See also p. 15 and n. 13 of the translation. This text is an *Udānālaṅkāra*. In an Abhidharma text in Thomas 1964: 44 (XIII.29) we find *yogācāres*, translated in the glossary (p. 131) as "Yogabeflissener." I owe the indication of these sources to Davidson forthcoming, n. 29. I do not know if the word *yogācāra* or any similar or related form appears in Khotanese.

138. See Silk 1997 for a study of these materials.

139. Depending on how one understands the doctrinal standpoints of Vasubandhu and Aśvaghoṣa. Honjō has recently maintained that Aśvaghoṣa belonged to the Sarvāstivāda sect, and the Sautrāntika school (Honjō 1993: 28).

it is pan-Buddhist, although further studies will be required to clarify this impression.

In some ways these may seem rather bland conclusions. But one aspect of their importance lies precisely in this lack of specificity. One ramification of this lack of specificity may be that, if we wish to identify particular sectarian origins for the Mahāyāna sūtra or śāstra sources in which the term *yogācāra* appears or, even further, trace the origins of the Yogācāra-Vijñānavāda school, the results of the investigation undertaken above suggest that we probably cannot look to an analysis of the term *yogācāra* for help. The term seems to be too common, too generalized to be of assistance in this regard. This in turn suggests that, contrary to what some scholars have suggested, there may be no particular connection at all between the *yogācāra bhikṣu* per se and the Yogācāra-Vijñānavāda school, although this is far from a foregone conclusion. It is perfectly possible to imagine a group drawing particular inspiration from a pan-Buddhist notion and giving it special attention and emphasis. This is in fact a usual pattern in the development of schools.[140] We cannot, it therefore seems, pinpoint specific sources for the Yogācāra-Vijñānavāda based on the appearance of the term *yogācāra* in any given text or text-group. Probably only a painstaking investigation of Yogācāra-Vijñānavāda literary sources themselves, coupled with a survey of the scriptural sources appealed to by early Yogācāra-Vijñānavāda writers, can provide solid clues to the intellectual origins of the school.

Bibliography

Abhyankar, Vasudev Shastri. 1978. *Sarva-darśana-saṁgraha of Sāyaṇa-Mādhava.* Government Oriental Series, class A, no. 1. Third edition (Poona: Bhandarkar Oriental Research Institute).

Andersen, Paul Kent. 1990. *Studies in the Minor Rock Edicts of Aśoka I: Critical Edition* (Freiburg: Hedwig Falk).

Apte, Vaman Shivaram. 1957. *The Practical Sanskrit-English Dictionary* (Poona. Reprint: Kyoto: Rinsen Book Company, 1978).

140. Compare in this regard Gregory Schopen's 1977 investigations of the pan-Mahāyāna nature of the Sukhāvatī cult with the later rise of a specific "Pure Land Buddhism."

Bendall, Cecil. 1897–1902. *Çikshāsamuccaya: A Compendium of Buddhistic Teaching Compiled by Çāntideva, Chiefly from Earlier Mahāyāna-sūtras.* Bibliotheca Buddhica 1 (St. Petersburg: Imperial Academy. Reprint: Osnabrück, Biblio Verlag, 1970).

Bhattacharya, Ram Shankar. 1982. "Buddha as Depicted in the Purāṇas." *Purāṇa* 24/2: 384–404.

Bhattacharya, Vidhushekhara. 1957. *The Yogācārabhūmi of Ācārya Asaṅga: The Sanksrit Text Compared with the Tibetan Version* (Calcutta: The University of Calcutta).

BHSD Edgerton 1953.

Bloch, Jules. 1950. *Les Inscriptions d'Asoka: traduites et commentées.* Collection Emile Senart (Paris: Société d'Édition «Les Belles Lettres»).

Böhtlingk, Otto, and Rudolph Roth. 1855–1875. *Sanskrit-Wörterbuch* (St. Petersburg: Kaiserlichen Akademie der Wissenschaften). 7 volumes.

Burnouf, Eugène. 1852. *Le Lotus de la Bonne Loi* (Paris: Imprimerie Nationale. Reprint: Adrien Maisonneuve, 1989).

Cowell, Edward Byles, and A. E. Gough. 1904. *The Sarva-Darsana-Saṁgraha, or: Review of the different systems of Hindu philosophy* (Reprint: New Delhi: Cosmo Publications, 1976).

Dantinne, Jean. 1983. *La Splendeur de l'Inébranlable (Akṣobhyavyūha).* Publications de l'Institut Orientaliste de Louvain 29 (Louvain: Université Catholique de Louvain).

Davidson, Ronald Mark. 1985. "Buddhist Systems of Transformation: *Āśraya-parivṛtti/-parāvṛtti* Among the Yogācāra." Doctoral dissertation, University of California at Berkeley.

———. Forthcoming. "Prolegomenon to Paracanon: Category Construction and Textual Bundles in Three Meditative Traditions." To appear in C. Wedemeyer, ed., *Intercultural Transmission and Interpretation.*

Deleanu, Florin. 1993. "Śrāvakayāna Yoga Practices and Mahāyāna Buddhism." *Waseda Daigaku Daigakuin Bungaku Kenkyūka Kiyō Bessatsu: Tetsugaku, Shigakuhen* 早稲田大学大学院文学科研究紀要別冊: 哲学・史学編 20: 3–12.

Demiéville, Paul. 1925. "Les Versions Chinoises du Milindapañha." *Bulletin de l'École Française d'Extrême-Orient* 24: 1–258.

———. 1954. "La *Yogācārabhūmi* de Saṅgharakṣa." *Bulletin de l'École Française d'Extrême-Orient* 44/2: 339–436.

Dutt, Nalinaksha. 1939–1959. *Gilgit Manuscripts.* 4 vols. in 9 pts. (Srinagar and Calcutta: J. C. Sarkhel at the Calcutta Oriental Press).

Edgerton, Franklin. 1953. *Buddhist Hybrid Sanskrit Grammar and Dictionary.* 2 vols. (New Haven: Yale University Press).

Fukuhara Ryōgon 福原亮厳. 1975. *Bukkyō Gairon* 仏教概論 (Kyoto: Nagata Bunshōdō 永田文昌堂).

Gómez, Luis Oscar. 1977. "The Bodhisattva as Wonder-worker." In Lewis Lancaster, ed., *Prajñāpāramitā and Related Systems: Studies in honor of Edward Conze.* Berkeley Buddhist Studies Series 1 (Berkeley: Berkeley Buddhist Studies Series): 221–261.

Goshima Kiyotaka 五島清隆. 1981. *The Tibetan Text of the Brahmaparipṛcchā (Brahmaviśeṣacintiparipṛcchā)*. Vol. I (Tib. bam po daṅ po) (Takatsuki-shi, Japan: Goshima Kiyotaka).

Griffiths, Paul J. 1986. *On Being Mindless: Buddhist Meditation and the Mind-Body Problem* (La Salle, Illinois: Open Court).

Hirakawa Akira 平川彰. 1982. *Monastic Discipline for the Buddhist Nuns: An English Translation of the Chinese Text of the Mahāsāṁghika-Bhikṣuṇi-Vinaya*. Tibetan Sanskrit Works Series 21 (Patna: Kashi Prasad Jayaswal Research Institute).

———. 1990. *Shoki Daijō Bukkyō no Kenkyū* 初期大乗仏教の研究 II. Hirakawa Akira Chosakushū 平川彰著作集 4 (Tokyo: Shunjūsha 春秋社).

Honjō Yoshifumi 本庄良文. 1993. "Memyō no Gakuha ni kansuru Senkō-gakusetsu no Ginmi: Jonsuton-setsu" 馬鳴の學派に關する先行學説の吟味—ジョンストン説—[E. H. Johnston's Arguments on the School Affiliation of Aśvaghoṣa]. In Egaku Mayeda 前田恵学 ed., *Watanabe Fumimaro Hakase Tsuitō Kinen Ronshū: Genshi Bukkyō to Daijō Bukkyō* 渡邊文麿追悼記念論集・原始仏教と大乗仏教 (Kyoto: Nagata Bunshōdō 永田文昌堂): II.27–43.

Hotori Rishō 阿理生. 1980. "Yugagyō to Yuishikisetsu" 瑜伽行と唯識説 [Yogācāra and the Consciousness-only theory]. In Nihon Bukkyō Gakkai 日本仏教学会, ed., *Bukkyō ni okeru Shugyō to sono Rironteki Konkyo* 仏教における修行とその理論的根拠 (Kyoto: Heirakuji Shoten 平楽寺書店): 73-85.

Ishihama, Yumiko, and Yoichi Fukuda. 1989. *A New Critical Edition of the* Mahāvyutpatti. Studia Tibetica 16. Materials for Tibetan-Mongolian Dictionaries 1 (Tokyo: The Toyo Bunko).

Jaini, Padmanabh S. 1977. *Abhidharmadīpa with Vibhāṣāprabhāvṛtti*. Tibetan Sanskrit Works Series 4 (Patna: Kashi Prasad Jayaswal Research Institute).

Jetly, J. S., and G. C. Parikh. 1991. *Nyāyakandalī, being a Commentary on Praśastapādabhāṣya, with three sub-commentaries*. Gaekwad's Oriental Series 174 (Baroda, India: Oriental Institute).

Jinananda, B. 1969. *Abhisamācārikā (Bhikṣuprakīrṇaka)*. Tibetan Sanskrit Works Series 9 (Patna: Kashi Prasad Jayaswal Research Institute).

Johnston, Edward Hamilton. 1928, 1932. *The Saundarananda of Aśvaghoṣa* (London. Reprint: Delhi: Motilala Banarsidass, 1975).

Jones, John James. 1949–1956. *The Mahāvastu* (Reprint: London: Pali Text Society, 1973–1978).

de Jong, Jan Willem. 1974. "Notes on the *Bhikṣuṇī-Vinaya* of the Mahāsāṁghikas." In L. Cousins, ed., *Buddhist Studies in Honour of I. B. Horner* (Dordrecht: D. Reidel): 63–70. Reprinted in *Buddhist Studies by J. W. de Jong*. Gregory Schopen, ed. (Berkeley: Asian Humanities Press, 1979): 297–304.

———. 1982. Review of Peter Zieme and György Kara, *Ein uigurisches Totenbuch*. Asiatische Forschungen 63 (Wiesbaden: Otto Harrassowitz, 1979). *Indo-Iranian Journal* 24: 162–166. Reprinted in J. W. de Jong, *Tibetan Studies*. Indica et Tibetica 25 (Swisttal-Odendorf, Germany: Indica et Tibetica Verlag, 1994): 198–205. (I refer to the reprint.)

Kajiyama Yuichi 梶山雄一, et al. 1994. *Satori e no Henreki: Kegonkyō Nyūhokkaibon* さとりへの遍歴・華厳経入法界品 [The *Gaṇḍavyūhasūtra*] (Tokyo: Chūōkōronsha 中央公論社). Two volumes. [Translated by Kajiyama, Tanji Teruyoshi 丹治昭義, Tsuda Shin'ichi 津田真一, Tamura Chijun 田村智淳, and Katsura Shōryū 桂紹隆.]

Kara, Georg, and Peter Zieme. 1976. *Fragmente tantrischer Werke in uigurischer Übersetzung*. Schriften zur Geschichte und Kultur des alten Orients: Berliner Turfantexte VII (Berlin: Akademie Verlag).

———. 1977. *Die uigurischen Übersetzungen des Guruyogas "Tiefer Weg" von Sa-sakya Paṇḍita und der Mañjuśrīnāmasaṁgīti*. Schriften zur Geschichte und Kultur des alten Orients: Berliner Turfantexte VIII (Berlin: Akademie Verlag).

Kern, Hendrik. 1884. *The Saddharma-pundarîka, or The Lotus of the True Law*. Sacred Books of the East 21 (Oxford: Clarendon Press. I have used a reprint of 1909).

Kern, Hendrik, and Bunyiu Nanjio. 1908–1912. *Saddharmapuṇḍarīka*. Bibliotheca Buddhica 10 (St. Petersburg: Imperial Academy. Reprint: Osnabrück: Biblio Verlag, 1970).

Kielhorn, Lorenz Franz. 1965. *The Vyākaraṇa-Mahābhāṣya of Patañjali. Adhāyas III, IV, and V*. Vol 2. 3rd ed., rev. by Kashinath Vasudev Abhyankar (Poona: Bhandarkar Oriental Institute). First published in 1883.

Kimura, Takayasu. 1986. *Pañcaviṁśatisāhasrikā Prajñāpāramitā II - III* (Tokyo: Sankibō Busshorin Publishing).

Kodama Daien 小玉大圓, Nakayama Masaaki 中山正晃, and Chokkai Gentetsu 直海玄哲. 1992, 1993. "Yugashi to Zenkyōten no Kenkyū: Denshō no Mondaiten to Beunseki o chūshin ni" 瑜伽師と禅経典の研究・伝承の問題点と分析を中心に [Yogācāra and meditation sūtras]. 2 parts. *Ryūkoku Daigaku Bukkyō Bunka Kenkyūjo Kiyō* 龍谷大学佛教文化研究所紀要 31: 115–134, and 32: 166–179.

Kubo, Tsugunari, and Akira Yuyama. 1991. *The Lotus Sutra: The White Lotus of the Marvelous Law*. BDK English Tripitaka 13–1 (Tokyo and Berkeley: Bukkyō Dendō Kyōkai).

Lamotte, Étienne Paul Marie. 1935. *Saṁdhinirmocana Sūtra: L'Explication des Mystères*. Université de Louvain, Recueil de travaux publiés par les membres des Conférences d'Histoire et de Philologie 2e Série, 34e Fascicule (Louvain: Bureaux du Recueil/Paris: Adrien Maisonneuve).

———. 1975. *La Concentration de la Marche Héroïque (Śūraṁgamasamādhisūtra)*. Mélanges chinois et bouddhique 13 (Bruxelles: Institut Belge des hautes Études Chinoises).

La Vallée Poussin, Louis de. 1903–1913. *Mūlamadhyamakakārikās (Mādhyamikasūtras) de Nāgārjuna avec la Prasannapadā Commentaire de Candrakīrti*. Bibliotheca Buddhica 4 (St. Petersburg: Imperial Academy. Reprint: Osnabrück: Biblio Verlag, 1970).

———. 1909. *Bouddhisme: Opinions sur l'Histoire de la Dogmatique*. Études sur l'Histoire des Religions 2 (Paris: Gabriel Beauchesne & Cie.).

———. 1923–1931. *L'Abhidharmakośa de Vasubandhu* (Paris: Geuthner. Reprint: *Mélanges chinois et bouddhiques* 16, Brusells: Institut Belge des hautes Études Chinoises, 1971).

———. 1928–1929. *Vijñaptimātratāsiddhi: La Siddhi de Hiuan-Tsang*. Buddhica Première série: Mémoires, Vol. 1, 5 (Paris: Librairie Orientaliste Paul Geuthner). 2 vols.

———. 1937. "Musīla et Nārada: Le chemin du nirvāṇa." *Mélanges chinois et bouddhiques* 5: 189–222.

Leumann, Ernst, and Shiraishi Shindō 白石眞道. 1957. "Mahāvastu, Heft II." *Yamanashi Daigaku Geigakubu Kiyō* 山梨大學藝學部紀要/*Proceedings of the Faculty of Liberal Arts and Education, Yamanashi University* 2: 1–133. Reprinted in *Shiraishi Shindō Bukkyōgaku Ronbunshū* 白石眞道・仏教学論文集 [The Collected Papers of Shiraishi Shindō]. Shiraishi Hisako 白石寿子 (ed.) (Sagamihara-shi, Japan: Kyōbi Shuppansha 京美出版社, 1988): 79–208. It is stated: "übersetzt von Prof. Dr. Ernst Leumann ... in Verbindung mit Shindō Shiraishi."

Lévi, Sylvain. 1911. *Mahāyāna-Sūtrālaṁkāra: Exposé de la Doctrine du Grand Véhicule, Selon le Systéme Yogācāra.* Vol. II: Traduction—Introduction—Index. Bibliothèque de l'École des Hautes Études: Sciences Historiques et Philologiques 190 (Paris: Librairie Honoré Champion. Reprint: Kyoto: Rinsen Book Company, 1983).

Matsunami Seiren 松濤誠廉. 1954. "Yugagyōha no So toshite no Memyō" 瑜伽行派の祖としての馬鳴 [Aśvaghoṣa as a partriarch of the Yogācāra school]. *Taishō Daigaku Kenkyū Kiyō* 大正大学研究紀要 39: 191–224. Reprinted in Matsunami 1981: 158–181, to which I refer.

———. 1981. *Memyō: Tansei naru Nanda* 馬鳴・端正なる難陀 (Tokyo: Sankibō Busshorin 山喜房仏書林).

Matsunami Seiren, et al. 1975. *Hokekyō* 法華経 I [The *Saddharmapuṇḍarīka-sūtra*]. *Daijō Butten* 大乗仏典 4 (Tokyo: Chūōkōronsha 中央公論社).

Miyamoto Shōson 宮本正尊. 1932. "Shin, Shiki, Funbetsu to Konpon Funbetsu" 心・識・分別と根本分別 [*citta*, *vijñāna*, *vikalpa* and *mūla-vikalpa*]. *Shūkyō Kenkyū* 宗教研究 9/5 (new series): 759–794.

———. 1933. "Konpon Funbetsu no Kenkyū" 根本分別の研究 [The *mūla-vikalpa*]. In *Tokiwa Hakase Kanreki Kinen: Bukkyō Ronsō* 常盤博士還暦記念・佛教論叢 (Tokyo: Kōbundo 弘文堂): 353–498 (esp. 376–409). Reprinted in Hirakawa Akira 平川彰, Saigusa Mitsuyoshi 三枝充悳, and Takasaki Jikidō 高崎直道, eds., *Miyamoto Shōson Hakase Bukkyōgaku Ronshū: Bukkyōgaku no Konpon Mondai* 宮本正尊博士仏教学論集・仏教学の根本問題 (Tokyo: Shunjūsha 春秋社, 1985): 162–180, 191–197.

Mizuno Kōgen 水野弘元. 1956. *Genshi Bukkyō* 原始仏教. Sāra sōsho サーラ叢書 4 (Kyoto: Heirakuji Shoten 平楽寺書店).

Mochizuki Shinkō 望月信亨. 1932–1936. *Bukkyō Daijiten* 佛教大辭典 (Tokyo: Sekai Seiten Kankō Kyōkai 世界聖典刊行協会).

Monier-Williams, Monier. 1899. *A Sanskrit-English Dictionary: Etymologically and Philologically Arranged with Special Reference to Cognate Indo-European Languages* (Oxford: The Clarendon Press).

Mukai Akira 向井亮. 1978. "Yōgācyāra (yugagyō)-ha no Gakuhamei no Yurai" ヨーガーチャーラ (瑜伽行) 派の学派名の由来 [The origins of the name of the Yogācāra school]. *Sanzō* 三蔵 153: originally distributed with the reprint edition of the *Kokuyaku Issaikyō, Ronshūbu* 國譯一切經・論集部 6. Reprinted in *Kokuyaku Issaikyō Indo Senjutsubu Geppō: Sanzōshū* 國譯一切經印度撰述部月報・三藏集 4 (Tokyo: Daitō Shuppan 大東出版, 1978): 267–273.

———. 1979. "*Ken'yō shōgyō-ron* to *Yuga shiji-ron*" 『顕揚聖教論』と『瑜伽師地論』 [On the *Śāsanodbhāvana* and the *Yogācārabhūmi*]. *Bukkyōgaku* 佛教學 8: 39–68.

Mvy. *Mahāvyutpatti*. See Sakaki 1916, and Ishihama and Fukuda 1989.

Nagao Gadjin 長尾雅人. 1982, 1987. *Shōdaijōron: Wayaku to Chūkai* 摂大乗論・和訳と注解 [The *Mahāyānasaṁgraha*: Japanese Translation and Commentary]. Indo Koten Sōsho インド古典叢書. 2 vols. (Tokyo: Kōdansha 講談社).

———. 1994. *An Index to Asaṅga's Mahāyānasaṁgraha*. Studia Philologica Buddhica, Monograph Series 9. 2 vols. (Tokyo: The International Institute of Buddhist Studies).

Nagao Gadjin and Sakurabe Hajime 桜部健. 1974. *Hōshakubu Kyōten* 宝積部経典 [*Mahāratnakūṭa* texts]. *Daijō Butten* 大乗仏典 9 (Tokyo: Chūō Kōronsha 中央公論社).

Nakada Norio 中田祝夫. 1989. *Myōichi Kinenkan-bon Kanagaki Hokekyō* 妙一記念館本・仮名書き法華経 (Tokyo: Reiyūkai 霊友会).

Nakamura Hajime 中村元. 1993. "Yogācāra: 'yugagyō' ka? 'yugashi' ka?" Yogācāra・「瑜伽行」か？「瑜伽師」か？ [Yogācāra: yoga practice or practitioner of yoga?]. *Tōhō* 東方 9: 72–75.

Nanjio, Bunyiu. 1923. *The Laṅkāvatāra Sūtra*. Bibliotheca Otaniensis 1 (Reprint: Kyoto: Otani Univeristy Press, 1956).

Nishi Giyū 西義雄. 1939. "Buha Bukkyō ni okeru Yugashi to sono Yakuwari" 部派仏教に於ける瑜伽師とその役割 [The yogācāra in Sectarian Buddhism and his role]. *Bukkyō Kenkyū* 佛教研究 3/1. Reprinted in Nishi 1975: 219–265, to which I refer.

———. 1974. "Buha Bukkyō Kyōdan Gojisha toshite no Yugagyōsha no Jissen" 部派仏教教団護持者としての瑜伽行者の実践 [The practice of the yogācāra as a protector of the Sectarian Buddhist community]. Extracted from the latter half of "Datsuma Izen no Indo no Denryū Kenkyū Josetsu" 達磨以前のインドの伝流研究序説, in *Zenbunka Kenkyūjo Kiyō* 禅文化研究所紀要 6. Reprinted in Nishi 1975: 351–374, to which I refer.

———. 1975. *Abidatsuma Bukkyō no Kenkyū* 阿毘達磨仏教の研究 [Studies in Abhidharma Buddhism] (Tokyo: Kokusho Kankōkai 国書刊行会).

Nishimura Minori 西村実則. 1974 "Daishubu-Setsushussebu ni okeru Yōgācyāra" 大衆部・説出世部におけるヨーガーチャーラ [Yogācāra in the Mahāsāṁghika-Lokottaravāda]. *Indogaku Bukkyōgaku Kenkyū* 印度学仏教学研究 32/2: 915–918.

Nolot, Édith. 1991. *Règles de Discipline des Nonnes Bouddhistes*. Collège de France, Publications de l'Institut de Civilisation Indienne 60 (Paris: Collège de France).

Norman, Kenneth Roy. 1966. "Middle Indo-Aryan Studies VI." *Journal of the Oriental Institute* (*Baroda*) 16: 113–119. Reprinted in *Collected Papers: Volume I* (Oxford: The Pali Text Society, 1990): 77–84.

Pradhan, Prahlad. 1975. *Abhidharmakośabhāṣyam of Vasubandhu*. Tibetan Sanskrit Works 8 (Patna: K. P. Jayaswal Research Institute).

Régamey, Konstanty. 1938. *The Bhadramāyākāravyākaraṇa: Introduction, Tibetan Text, Translation and Notes.* The Warsaw Society of Sciences and Letters, Publications of the Oriental Commission Nr. 3 (Warsaw: Nakładem Towarzystwa Naukowego Warswzawskiego Wydano z Zasilku Funduszu Kultury J. Piłsudskiego).

Roth, Gustav. 1970. *Bhikṣuṇī-Vinaya: Manual of Discipline for Buddhist Nuns.* Tibetan Sanskrit Works Series 12 (Patna: K. P. Jayaswal Research Institute).

Ruegg, David Seyfort. 1967. "On a Yoga Treatise in Sanskrit from Qïzïl." *Journal of the American Oriental Society* 87/1: 157–165.

Saeki Kyokuga 佐伯旭雅. 1887. *Kandō Abidatsuma Kusharon* 冠導阿毘達磨俱舍論. 3 vols. (continuous pagination) (photo reprint of woodblock edition: Kyoto: Hōzōkan 法蔵館, 1978).

Sakaki Ryōsaburō 榊亮三郎. 1916. *Mahāvyutpatti* (Kyoto: Kyōto Teikoku Daigaku Bunka Daigaku Sōsho 京都帝國大學文科大學叢書 3. Numerous reprints.)

Sakuma, Hidenori S. 1990. *Die Āśrayaparivṛtti-Theorie in der Yogācārabhūmi.* Alt- und Neu-Indische Studien 40. 2 vols. (Stuttgart: Franz Steiner).

Sasaki Shizuka 佐々木閑. 1991. "Biku to Gigaku" 比丘と伎楽 [Monastic worship of stūpas with music and dance in vinaya texts]. *Bukkyō Shigaku Kenkyū* 佛教史學研究 34/1: 1–24.

Schlingloff, Dieter. 1964. *Ein Buddhistisches Yogalehrbuch.* Sanskrittexte aus den Turfanfunden 7 (Berlin: Akademie-Verlag).

Schmidt, Richard. 1928. *Nachträge zum Sanskrit-Wörterbuch in Kürzer Fassung von Otto Böhtlingk* (Leipzig: Otto Harrassowitz. Reprint: Tokyo: Meicho-Fukyukai, 1983).

Schmithausen, Lambert. 1976. "On the Problem of the Relation of Spiritual Practice and Philosophical Theory in Buddhism." In *German Scholars on India* II (Bombay: Nachiketa Publications): 235–250.

Schopen, Gregory. 1977. "Sukhāvatī as a Generalized Religious Goal in Sanskrit Mahāyāna Sūtra Literature." *Indo-Iranian Journal* 19: 177–210.

———. 1992. "On Avoiding Ghosts and Social Censure: Monastic Funerals in the Mūlasarvāstivāda-vinaya." *Journal of Indian Philosophy* 20: 1–39.

———. 1995. "Monastic Law Meets the Real World: A Monk's Continuing Right to Inherit Family Property in Classical India." *History of Religions* 35/2: 101–123.

Senart, Émile Charles Marie. 1882–1897. *Le Mahāvastu.* Sociéte Asiatique, Collection d'Ouvrages Orientaux, Seconde Série. 3 vols. (Paris: Imprimerie National. Reprint: Tokyo: Meicho Fukyūkai, 1977).

Shāstrī, Haraprasād. 1931. "Chips from a Buddhist Workshop." In Bimala Churn Law, ed., *Buddhistic Studies* (Calcutta: Thacker Spink. Reprint: Delhi/Varanasi: Indological Book House, 1983): 818–858.

Shastri, Swami Dwarikadas. 1971. *Abhidharmakośa & Bhāṣya of Acharya Vasubandhu with Sphutārthā Commentary of Ācārya Yaśomitra.* Bauddha Bharati Series 6 (Varanasi: Bauddha Bharati).

Shukla, Karunesha. 1973. *Śrāvakabhūmi of Ācārya Asaṅga.* Tibetan Sanskrit Works Series 14 (Patna: K. P. Jayaswal Research Institute).

Sieg, Emil, and Wilhelm Siegling. 1949. *Tocharische Sprachreste: Sprache B. Heft 1: Die Udānālaṅkāra-Fragmente* (Göttingen: Vandenhoeck & Ruprecht).

Silk, Jonathan Alan. 1994. "The Origins and Early History of the *Mahāratnakūṭa* Tradition of Mahāyāna Buddhism, with a Study of the *Ratnarāśisūtra* and Related Materials." Ph.D. dissertation, The University of Michigan.

———. 1997. "Further remarks on the *yogācāra bhikṣu.*" In *Dharmadūta: Mélanges offerts au Vénérable Thích Huyên-Vi à l'occasion de son soixante-dixième anniversaire.* Bhikkhu Pāsādika and Bhikkhu Tampalawela Dhammaratana, eds. (Paris: Éditions You Feng): 233–250.

Snellgrove, David L. 1959. *The Hevajra Tantra: A Critical Study.* Part II: Sanskrit and Tibetan Texts. London Oriental Series 6 (London: Oxford University Press).

Staël-Holstein, Alexander Wilhelm, Baron von. 1926. *The Kāçyapaparivarta: A Mahāyānasūtra of the Ratnakūṭa Class: Edited in the Original Sanskrit in Tibetan and in Chinese* (Shanghai: Commercial Press).

Suzuki, Daisetz Teitaro, and Hokei Idzumi. 1949. *The Gandavyuha Sutra* (Kyoto: The Society for the Publication of Sacred Books of the World. Originally published 1934).

Suzuki, Kōshin. 1994a. *Sanskrit Fragments and Tibetan Translation of Candrakīrti's Bodhisattvayogācāracatuḥśatakaṭīkā.* (Tokyo: The Sankibo Press).

———. 1994b. *Index to the Sanskrit Fragments and Tibetan Translation of Candrakīrti's Bodhisattvayogācāracatuḥśatakaṭīkā.* Sanskrit-Tibetan (Tokyo: The Sankibo Press).

T. *Taishō Shinshū Daizōkyō.*

Takasaki Jikido 高崎直道. 1966. *Bukkyōshi Gaisetsu—Indo-hen* 仏教史概説・インド篇 [History of buddhism—India] (Kyoto: Heirakuji shoten平楽寺書店). The book is co-authored with Sasaki Kyōgo 佐々木教悟, Inokuchi Taijun 井ノ口泰淳, and Tsukamoto Keisho 塚本啓祥.

———. 1974. *Nyoraizō Shisō no Keisei: Indo Daijō Bukkyō Shisō Kenkyū* 如來藏思想の形成・インド大乗仏教思想研究 [Formation of the Tathāgatagarbha Theory]. (Tokyo: Shunjūsha 春秋社).

———. 1993. "Giyaku *Nyūryōgakyō* no "Nyojitsu Shūgyō' to *Kishinron*" 魏訳『入楞伽経』の「如実修行」と『起信論』 [The term *rushi xiuxing* in the Wei translation of the *Laṅkāvatāra-sūtra* and the *Awakening of Faith*]. In Tsukamoto Keishō Kyōju Kanreki Kinen Ronbunshū Kankōkai 塚本啓祥教授還暦記念論文集刊行会, eds., *Tsukamoto Keishō Kyōju Kanreki Kinen*

Ronbunshū: Chi no Kaikō—Bukkyō to Kagaku 塚本啓祥教授還暦記念論文集・知の邂逅—仏教と科学 (Tokyō: Kōsei Shuppansha 佼成出版社): 223–238.

Taranatha Nyaya-Tarkatirtha and Amarendramohan Tarkatirtha. 1936–1944. *Nyāyadarśanam with Vātsyāyana's Bhāṣya, Uddyotkara's [sic] Vārttika, Vācaspati Miśra's Tātparyaṭīkā & Viśvanātha's Vṛtti.* Calcutta Sanskrit Series nos. 18 and 19 (Calcutta: Metropolitan Printing & Publishing House Limited. Reprint: Delhi: Munshiram Manoharlal, 1985).

Thakkur, Kanaklāl. 1987. *Kumārasambhavaṁ-Mahākāvyam of Mahākavi Kālidāsa with Sañjīvinī and Śiśuhitaiṣiṇī Commentaries by Mallinātha and Sītārām Kavi.* Kashi Sanskrit Series 14 (Varanasi: Chaukhambha Sanskrit Sansthan).

Thomas, Werner. 1964. *Tocharisches Elementarbuch. Band II: Texte und Glossar* (Heidelberg: Carl Winter Universitätsverlag).

Ui Hakuju 宇井伯壽. 1958. *Yugaron Kenkyū* 瑜伽論研究. Daijō Bukkyō Kenkyū 大乘佛教研究 II (Tokyo: Iwanami Shoten 岩波書店).

———. 1965. *Indo Tetsugaku Kenkyū* 印度哲學研究 I (Tokyo: Iwanami Shoten 岩波書店).

Waldschmidt, Ernst. 1965. *Sanskrithandschriften aus den Turfanfunden I.* Verzeichnis der orientalischen Handschriften in Deutschland X, 1 (Wiesbaden: Franz Steiner Verlag).

———. 1971. *Sanskrithandschriften aus den Turfanfunden III*. Verzeichnis der orientalischen Handschriften in Deutschland X, 3 (Wiesbaden: Franz Steiner Verlag).

Watson, Burton. 1993. *The Lotus Sutra* (New York: Columbia University Press).

Wayman, Alex. 1961. *Analysis of the Śrāvakabhūmi Manuscript*. University of California Publications in Classical Philology 17 (Berkeley and Los Angeles: University of California Press).

Wogihara Unrai. 1904. "Bouddhisme. Notes et Bibliographie: Contributions to the study of the Śikṣāsamuccaya derived from Chinese sources (1) (Continuation) and (end)," *Le Muséon* (New Series) 5: 96–103, 209–215, 7: 255–261.

———. 1932–1935. *Abhisamayālaṁkārāloka Prajñāpāramitāvyākhyā*. Tōyō Bunko Publications Series D, 2 (Tokyo: The Tōyō Bunko. Reprint: Tokyo: Sankibō Busshorin, 1973).

Yamada, Isshi. 1968. *Karuṇāpuṇḍarīka*. 2 vols. (London: The School of Oriental and African Studies).

Yamada Ryūjō 山田龍城. 1959. *Daijō Bukkyō Seiritsuron Josetsu* 大乗佛教成立論序說 (Kyoto: Heirakuji Shoten 平樂寺書店).

Yamaguchi, Susumu. 1934. *Madhyāntavibhāgaṭīkā: Exposition Systématique du Yogācāravijñaptivāda.* Tome I–Texte. Suzuki Research Foundation Reprint Series 7 (Nagoya: Librarie Hajinkaku. Reprint: Tokyo: Suzuki Gakujutsu Zaidan, 1966).

Yin Shun 印順. 1988. *Shouyiqieyoubuweizhu de Lunshu yu Lunshi zhi Yanjiu* 說一切有部爲主的論書與論師之研究 (Taipei: Zhengwen Chuban 正聞出版).

Manuscript Fragments, Texts, and Inscriptions in the Temple of Tabo

An Interim Report with Bibliography*

Ernst Steinkellner

Tabo[1] monastery in the Spiti valley of the Indian Himalayas was founded in 996 C.E. That it survived and can give us an idea today of the minds which created it is a miracle of history.[2] The manuscript fragments remaining at Tabo are a part of this miracle, and are of far-reaching import for Tibetan philology and Kanjur studies in particular. This treasure of Tabo as such is, in fact, just the visible tip of an iceberg, to whose hidden bulk I would compare the still unidentified remains of an independent western Tibetan manuscript tradition which lasted from its beginnings in the tenth century until the advance of central Tibetan traditions in the seventeenth century. Despite the fact that this western Tibetan manuscript tradition has so far only been verified and exemplified by the Tabo collection, I venture to assert that its value for the history of the transmission of Tibetan canonical literature is in all probability second only to the Tibetan holdings of the Dunhuang library cave. Yet the unveiling of this treasure has taken nearly a hundred years, or three generations of scholars: first A. H. Francke in 1909, then Giuseppe Tucci and Eugenio Ghersi in 1933, and finally a small Italian-Austrian group who visited in 1991. Two world wars and two Tibetan catastrophes—the exile of

---

* Paper delivered at the annual meeting of the Nihon Chibetto Gakkai, Nov. 1, 1997, at Kyoto University. The presence of Prof. Nagao Gadjin and his kind interest in the subject are my reasons for offering it to this volume in his celebration.

Gratefully I acknowledge the help received from Cristina Scherrer-Schaub and Paul Harrison, as well as the support of the Austrian Fund for the Promotion of Science for the research on the Tabo literary heritage.

1. The proper old spelling of modern Tabo and the etymology of the name are unclear. The name can hardly be Tibetan. Several different etymologized spellings such as *lta*, *rta*, *sta* can be found, and the variations *po/pho/bo* are also attested in inscriptions and manuscripts. For the sake of convenience, we earlier followed the proposal of Klimburg-Salter to use the spelling Ta pho (1987: n.9). At the last meeting of the Tabo research group in Vienna (January 19–20, 1996) it was decided to abstain in future from this or similar differentiations, and to return to the modern spelling "Tabo."

2. For a comprehensive introduction to this cultural treasure cf. D. Klimburg-Salter, *Tabo—a Lamp for the Kingdom*, Milan, 1997.

the monastic intelligentsia and the destruction that occurred during the so-called Cultural Revolution—together with the fascination of the Dunhuang finds have respectively impeded and deflected the curiosity of the scholars concerned for the best part of a century.

In the following report I shall try to give an overview of (1) the object of this research and its import, (2) the history of previous research, (3) of research in progress, and (4) of the results achieved so far.

(1) While the enormous task of working on the surviving Tibetan and Sanskrit manuscript collections in Tibet proper is waiting to be taken up by future generations of scholars, the collection in Tabo has been accessible for some time. The reason that nobody bothered to look into the matter must probably lie in the fact that the full range of its import remained unrecognized despite the fact that both Francke and Tucci had already clearly indicated this in general terms.

What exactly is the import of this material? The history and stemmatic distribution of the transmission of the Tibetan Canon has only recently become clearer through the work of scholars such as Helmut Eimer and Paul Harrison.[3] But since Michael Hahn's examination of two texts from the seventeenth century manuscript Kanjur in Phudrag (Phug brag), Ladakh, we have known of a textual tradition in western Tibetan areas which constitutes an "independent" line of transmission for the old Tibetan translations, i.e. ,"independent" in the sense that it did not enter the work of mainstream compilations started in early fourteenth century Central Tibet.[4] Another testimony for this independent regional transmission may emerge from the

---

3. Cf. Eimer 1992.

For a methodological summary of practical use to the critical philologist, cf. Harrison 1992: XLVIII–L. Other modern editions in the same spirit of critical awareness are Schoening 1995, Silk 1994a, Braarvig 1993, Schneider 1993 and 1995, Skilling 1994a. Their editorial observations are worthy of note, Silk's contribution being a useful general introduction to the related problems.

Newly investigated manuscript Kanjurs and Kanjur catalogues have meanwhile also been drawn into the circle of these materials, from Tawang (Jampa Samten 1994), from Mustang (Eimer 1994), and Batang (Skilling 1994b: 769). Further, Harrison 1994 gives a survey of our present knowledge of the Kanjur sources, and in his recent pioneering contribution P. Skilling tried to weave the various threads of information on the gradual formation of early pre-Kanjur groupings of canonical texts into a first comprehensive picture of textual history (cf. Skilling 1997). For a succinct survey of this process, cf. also Harrison 1996.

4. This "independent" character of at least parts of the Phug brag Kanjur has meanwhile also been recognized from the study of other texts (cf. Harrison 1992: XXXV f., Hartmann 1996, Schoening 1995: 168, Dietz 1996: 14f., Silk 1994a: 26f.).

materials still extant (?) in Tsaparang and Tholing.[5] In short, an assumption which in 1991 was still hypothetical, is now already an established fact: the Tabo collection contains a considerable amount of fragmentary texts which represent a version of the translations that never entered the mainstream tradition of the Tibetan canonical transmission. This means that here we have the remains of an independent textual tradition derived from proto-canonical collections, which goes back in part to the same original translations dating to the period of the great revision of translation methods in the early ninth century, but which was made use of neither in the 1351 Tshal pa revision of the Old Narthang manuscript (represented by the editions, e.g., of Peking, Lithang, Cone) nor in the 1431 *Them spang ma* manuscript edition (represented by editions like Stog, Tokyo, London), nor, of course, in their conflations (represented by Derge, Narthang, Lhasa, and others).[6]

(2) A first report with notes on the history of the collection's discovery, a description of the state of the collection in 1991, together with brief remarks on its contents, some of its external features, and its possible genesis was published in 1994.[7] I will just briefly summarize some of the information given in this report on previous work with regard to the Tabo documents.

The first description of the manuscript collection in Tabo was given by the Moravian missionary A. H. Francke in the report on his visit to Tabo in 1909 (1914: 37–43). Francke found two piles of manuscripts consisting of "loose and disarranged leaves." He noticed the high quality of the handwriting and identified the contents of *Prajñāpāramitā* texts. He assigned the "manuscript" to Rin chen bzaṅ po's own times on the basis of its orthography and deduced its period from the orthography's relation to that of the inscription in the temple which commemorates the renovation under Byaṅ chub 'od. Finally, he clearly recognized the great significance of these manuscript materials for the history of textual transmission in Tibet: "The value of such a manuscript for critical purposes is enormous. Works like the *Prajñāpāramitā* have up to the present been known only from modern manuscripts or woodblock prints. Here, on the other hand,

5. Cf. Eimer 1995, as well as Eimer 1991, Silk 1989: 160, and Pritzker 1996: 47.

6. Cf. Harrison 199? (A12).

7. E. Steinkellner, "A Report on the 'Kanjur' of Ta pho," *EW* 44/1 (1994): 115–136.

we obtain a text, as it was known in the translator's own days." Of course, as we now know, the enthusiasm of this statement was exaggerated, but in the general terms of its scholarly vision it is still quite true.

Giuseppe Tucci visited Tabo with Eugenio Ghersi in 1933, and a whole section in his *Indo-Tibetica III.I*, "La biblioteca di Tabo" (1935: 86–89, pls. XLIV–XLV) is the result of his more experienced investigation. In this chapter, Tucci turns his attention to the possible history of the library's devastation and to the difficulty of distinguishing between ancient original manuscripts and later copies, and he emphasizes the great importance of these various copies for a critical edition of the Tibetan translation of the *Prajñāpāramitā* in its different versions, and of other canonical texts.

Tucci thought that the core of the library consisted of manuscripts and copies of West Tibetan origin and contained translations made by Rin chen bzaṅ po or his collaborators and their schools; that the work of copying was continued in Tabo for a considerable time and strongly supported by the lay people who would donate the means to cover the costs of copying; and that this cultural tradition had a lasting effect, producing a sort of conservatism, even after the general cultural assimilation with the main centers of central Tibet had taken place.

As possible times for the devastation of the temple and its library, Tucci proposed the raid by the Dogra general Zorawar Singh's soldiery during his campaign to crush the rebellion in Zangs dkar in 1837, or the Dogra expedition against Tibet of 1849.[8]

In more recent times, my colleague Deborah Klimburg-Salter mentioned the manuscripts again in the reports on her visits to Tabo in 1978 (with Chaya Bhattacharya) and 1989. She also whetted my curiosity; and in 1991, at the invitation of Tabo's abbot, the Venerable Geshe Sonam Wangdu, I was able to inspect these materials together with a small team of philologists.

This team—we call it "philological" to distinguish its activities from the art-historical team working in Tabo under the guidance of D. Klimburg-Salter[9]—consisted of Elena De Rossi Filibeck (IsMEO, Rome), Jampa L. Panglung (Bayerische Akademie der Wissenschaften, Munich), Helmut Tauscher, and myself (ITB, University of Vienna).

---

8. For some additional observations on the library's fate, cf. Steinkellner 1994: 130–133.

9. A description of the work of this latter team is available in the introduction to Klimburg-Salter 1997, as well as all related bibliographical data.

What we found in 1991 was a total of approximately 35,500 folios assembled in sixty huge bundles.[10] These folios were written between the end of the tenth and the seventeenth century, a considerable proportion in the eleventh and twelfth centuries, and were in an unbelievable state of disorder. No further serious evaluation of the collection being possible, the need to reconstitute any original units was seen to be the most urgent task. It also soon became evident that there is not a single complete manuscript left in this collection, that we have only fragments and remains. There are hardly any beginnings and ends—with some most valuable exceptions. In a rough calculation based on the remains, P. Harrison estimates that only about 20 percent of the original complete state of the manuscripts is all that is left now, with often no more than a single folio of a complete unit surviving.[11] Irrespective of the collection's value as a source of texts is its value for Tibetan paleography, orthography, manuscript writing styles and ornamentation, systems of pagination, paper production, and so on and so forth, in short for all the material features of these manuscripts. Together with the Dunhuang manuscripts, the Tabo manuscripts are a new and invaluable source for the development of "Tibetan Codicology" as a new research discipline initiated by C. Scherrer-Schaub on a comparative basis which makes full use of the new data from the Tabo collection (cf. A15).

As far as I can see, the various expeditions to Spiti by Japanese scholars from Naritasan in 1978 and 1986 and from Kōyasan in 1982 concentrated on investigating the art and religious traditions of Tabo and the Spiti valley, but ignored the "library" at Tabo.[12]

(3) In 1992 I presented a paper on the above to the Tibetological Seminar at Fagernes which stimulated the immediate interest of two leading specialists in the field of Kanjur studies, Cristina Scherrer-Schaub and Paul Harrison, who have collaborated on this enterprise since then. Meanwhile, a considerable number of scholars has joined

10. Cf. Steinkellner 1994: fig. 1–3. The bundles are now kept in new closed bookcases whose construction was made possible by a generous donation from Tenzing N. G. Ronge in 1992 and commissioned by Geshe Sonam Wangdu, abbot of Tabo, in the same year.

11. Cf. Harrison 199? (A12) and Harrison–Scherrer-Schaub 1996(A8): 49 (uncensored version!)

12. Cf. *Spiti no hibutsu*. Daihonzan Naritasan Shinshōji—Naritasan Bukkyō Kenkyūsho (Narita, 1987); Y. Miyasaka, "Spiti no bukkyō," *Journal of the Naritasan Institute for Buddhist Studies* 15 (1992): 447–493, Kōyasan Daigaku, *Chibetto bukkyō bunka chōsadan hōkokusho* 4 (Kōyasan, 1983).

this research on Tabo, working in different times and different ways. Some worked "only" in the field: H. Lasic (Vienna), I. Onians (Oxford). Most worked in the field and did research on smaller or larger parts of the collection, or on particular texts: Ch. Cüppers (Lumbini), E. De Rossi Filibeck (Rome), P. Harrison (Christchurch), U. Pagel (Seattle), J. S. Panglung (Munich), C. Scherrer-Schaub (Lausanne), H. Tauscher (Vienna), T. Tomabechi (Lausanne). Some have already made or are making use of Tabo copies available for their own ongoing studies of canonical texts: H. Eimer (Bonn), J.-U. Hartmann (Berlin), K. Kōda (Kyoto), B. Otokawa (Kyoto), A. Saito (Mie), G. Schopen (Austin), J. Silk (New Haven), Michael Zimmermann (Hamburg).

The work of preparing an inventory of the fragments was started jointly by Scherrer-Schaub and Harrison. This inventory will cover only that part of the whole collection which consists of fragments of texts other than the *Prajñāpāramitā*. The presence of *Prajñāpāramitā-sūtra* manuscripts in the Tabo library is breathtaking. The sheer number of copies is awe-inspiring, and the sensitive observer cannot fail to be inspired with profound reverence for the spiritual aspirations and efforts of donors and scribes to which these often damaged but nonetheless beautiful leaves bear witness. The most elegant calligraphy (almost all of it *dbu can*) and papers of fine quality distinguish the productions of the former scriptoria at Tabo and its region. All versions of the venerable scripture are extant: the mighty one of 100,000 lines (*'Bum*), the one of 25,000 (*Ñi khri*), of 18,000 (*Khri brgyad*), of 10,000 (*Khri pa*), and the one of 8,000 lines (*brGyad stoṅ*).

These manuscripts constitute about 75 percent of the "library," and compiling a detailed inventory of them remains a distant dream given the constraints of academic reality: only short summer periods of work in Tabo being possible, financial support more and more difficult to secure, and research priority not necessarily given to archival enterprises. From among these *Prajñāpāramitā* holdings we shall try to catalogue only those fragments which are believed to belong to the earliest period of copying; at a rough estimate only 7 percent of these fragments will be taken into consideration at the moment. However, we are planning to reconstitute the original units of the whole collection in the future.

Thus the inventory will cover approximately a third of the "library." It will give detailed lists and descriptions of mainly Mahāyāna sūtras which occur either separately (e.g., *Myaṅ 'das*) or in larger groups (e.g., *mDo sde*, *dKon brtsegs*, *Phal chen*, *gZuṅs*). Tantra are also extant, as well as Vinaya texts and a number of Tanjur texts. In general, even minute holdings in this "library," such as various single folios, are and will be providing sensational surprises. There are no Sanskrit texts in this "library"; almost all Tibetan texts are translations belonging to what we now refer to as the Tibetan Canon with its two parts, Kanjur and Tanjur. When the partial inventory is completed, the fragments dealt with will also have been photographed and will be available at the ITB for research purposes.

(4) The research conducted on the texts in this collection so far is best considered under different aspects relative to whether the texts in question are already well-known from the classical canonical versions, or whether they have been unknown so far. Our primary concern in the beginning, one which naturally remains a focus of our research, was to investigate the character of transmissional "independence." This is done, basically, by observing the presence or absence of significant variant readings[13] in the texts investigated, or of particular arrangements in the case of collections of texts. Really new "canonical" finds have also been made, albeit still at random. Moreover, it also seems that a small number of indigenous Tibetan religious texts were added to the collection.

(a) The character of "independence" has meanwhile been established for almost all texts examined so far in detail, either with regard to their significant variant readings, or to their variant arrangements:

1. *Pañcaviṁśatikā Prajñāpāramitā* fragment examined by E. De Rossi Filibeck (cf. A3).
2. Translation of Dharmakīrti's *Sambandhaparīkṣā* with its *Vṛtti* and Vinītadeva's *Ṭīkā* examined by H. Tauscher (cf. A5).
3. Collection of *dhāraṇī* texts (*gZuṅs 'dus*) examined by P. Harrison (cf. A7).
4. Some Tantra (*Guhyasamāja*) and tantristic texts (*Pradīpoddyotanā*, *Pañcakrama*) examined by T. Tomabechi (cf. A17).
5. Various Mahāyāna sūtras (*Pratyutpannabuddhasaṁmukhāvasthitasamādhi-sūtra*, *Drumakinnararājaparipṛcchā*, *Ajātaśatrukaukṛtyavinodanā*, *Lokānuvartanā*) examined by P. Harrison (cf. A12).
6. *Bodhisattvacaryāvatāra* examined by A. Saito (cf. A14).[14]
7. **Bodhimaṇḍālaṅkāra* examined by C. Scherrer-Schaub.[15]

---

13. "Significant variant readings" of the kind called "recensional" as distinct from "transmissional" by P. Harrison (cf. 1992: XXV f.).

14. Saito was able to show that the Tabo copy is of the version first translated by Rin chen bzaṅ po (958–1055) but prior to the revision by Blo ldan śes rab (1059–1109).

15. "The version transmitted by the canonical editions was translated from the

No significant variants are to be found (possibly because of a too limited material basis) in:

8. A leaf from the *Mahāparinirvāṇasūtra* examined by H. Eimer (cf. A11).
9. Some leaves from the *Ratnarāśi* examined by J. Silk (cf. A6)
10. A leaf from Kamalaśīla's *Bhāvanākrama I* examined by C. Scherrer-Schaub (e-mail August 8, 1997).
11. Data is also inconclusive for the *Samādhirājasūtra*, part of which (Chap. 9) was examined by P. Harrison (cf. A12).

We already have indisputable proof, therefore, of the value of these Tabo fragments for the history of the transmission of the Tibetan canonical translations. Some of these translations were already made by the early ninth century, while some go back to the activities of Rin chen bzaṅ po. Thus, in Tabo we have been able to identify copies of the oldest Buddhist literature in Tibetan.

Because their "independence" has been established, the Tabo fragments, as far as they are available, will then have to be used in all future critical work on Tibetan canonical texts. Luckily (in fact because it was the only letter left, although I am inclined to interpret this as a recognition of the great value of this library), in the convention recently agreed upon by Tibetologists for the sigla to be used in future for the extant canonical prints and manuscripts, the letter **A** was assigned to the Tabo material (cf. Harrison-Eimer 1997), for "Tabo Ancient Monastery," the name given by its present abbot, Geshe Sonam Wangdu.

(b) Important as the Tabo collection is for all these reasons, it also contains some really new material that even merits the attribute "sensational," e.g.,

12. Ten folios of a text called *rNal 'byor chen por bsgom pa'i don* ("Meaning of the practice consisting in Mahāyoga") and examined by B. Otokawa (cf. A13), which is a collection of citations from various sūtras in response to a series of questions. This text played an eminent role in the "debate of bSam yas" and is commonly alluded to by later authors as a "rDzogs chen" text. It is unknown in any of the canonical versions, but there is a Dunhuang manuscript (PT 996), which contains the biography of its author (sPug Ye śes dbyaṅs, 771–850 C.E.), and we

---

Chinese by mGon po skyabs in the eighteenth century (however, close examination reveals that he must have seen at least a fragmentary copy of the "old" translation). The Tibetan translation made from the Sanskrit is kept in the Dunhuang and in the Tabo collections. This version is quite close to the Phug-brag version, although better transmitted" (e-mail August 8, 1997).

also have a fragmentary Dunhuang manuscript (PT 818 and ST 705) which partly overlaps with the Tabo manuscript.

13. During the course of our very first inspection, in 1991, we were lucky to find two folios (*ka* and *a*) of what looked like a dictionary. Panglung Rimpoche later identified them as two separate parts of the famous etymological dictionary *sGra sbyor bam po gñis pa* (*Madhyavyutpatti*). Fortunately, the beginning, consisting of an introduction and an annalistic note, has survived. It provides the guidelines for establishing Buddhist terms and for translating from Sanskrit, has the formal aspects of an edict issued under royal orders, and is considerably shorter than the one previously known to us. Panglung Rimpoche was able to show (cf. Panglung 1994 [A4]) that the "great revision" of Buddhist terminology and translation under the king Khri lDe sroṅ btsan (alias Sad na legs), which was confirmed by a royal edict in 814/815 C.E, was not the first one. The first revision can now be assigned—only on the basis of the Tabo fragment—to 795 C.E., within the reign of Khri Sroṅ lde btsan. The well-known Tanjur version is an extended version of the edict we have from Tabo, and "must be taken as a confirmation by Khri lDe sroṅ btsan of the earlier edict of his father" (Panglung 1994 [A4]: 171).

14. Examining the small number of colophons and scribal annotations to be found in Tabo, Scherrer-Schaub (cf. A16) discovered a single folio, probably the last of a *Śatasāhasrikā* manuscript, with a short text added that "may be qualified as a complex *deyadharma* formulation." The text, using the diplomatic phraseology of the Old Tibetan documents known from Dunhuang, gives the name of the scribe, one "Klu mgon sgra of sÑel 'or," of the donor, the king, styled as "dPal lha btsan po Byaṅ chub sems dpa'," evidently Ye śes 'od, and the person to consecrate the manuscript and thus the recipient of the donation, "Ratnagarbha of Graṅ." Furthermore, a date is given: *lug gi lo*, a sheep year.[16]
A dGe sloṅ Ratnagarbha of Graṅ is, however, also recorded in the captions to the pictorial representations of the sGo khaṅ of Tabo which commemorate the persons involved in the temple's foundation together with Ye śes 'od and his two sons.[17] Thus we are in all probability confronted with the remains of a manuscript produced at Tabo and "the sheep year in question might be 1007 or 1019" (A16).

At Tabo there is also a relatively small number (about sixty) of illustrated folios, half of them belonging to a single fine *Pañcaviṁśatisāhasrikā* manuscript.[18] A first survey of the illustrated folios has

16. This might be [995], 1007, 1019, and [1031] if one considers the two possibilities for Ye śes 'od's dates.

17. Cf. Luczanits 199? (C6).

18. Cf. Harrison 199?(A12), and Harrison–Scherrer-Schaub 1996(A8): 50.

related them to others found in the area and clearly confirms an early date for these productions, on art-historical grounds as well.[19] *Gser yig* manuscripts are also present, but again their number is disproportionately small.

*

Finally I would like to mention another kind of textual treasure in the temple of Tabo: the two inscriptions[20] containing the *Gaṇḍavyūhasūtra* and a long quotation from the *Kṣitigarbhasūtra*. Both inscriptions can be safely dated to the period of renovation in 1042 C.E.[21]

The inscriptional text of the *Gaṇḍavyūhasūtra* edited by myself (cf. C1) is, in fact, the earliest known surviving version of the Tibetan translation made two centuries earlier in Central Tibet and mentioned in the catalogue of translations in the lHan kar royal palace ("*Denkarma*"). It is, however, what I call a "redactional text" of the sūtra. This redaction had the aim of reproducing the "complete" text of the sūtra on the temple's walls.

The wish to reproduce the complete sūtra text on the one hand and the limited space on the other demanded some form of abbreviation. The solution arrived at was a redaction of the text which did not change it in any way, but merely abbreviated it by means of omission. In general it can be said that this redactional text was prepared by a person (or team) who had an excellent grasp of the sūtra's contents, who judiciously tried to preserve the main points of the chapters, and who left the retained sūtra text unaltered and was remarkably adept at transferring the "complete" sūtra onto the small space on the walls. What is crucial in the redactional character of this text is that while the sūtra's text has been shortened, it has not at all been tampered with as such, by changing or transforming it into some other literary form, for example by transmitting the contents rather than the exact words. As is to be expected of this text, it shares

---

19. Cf. Klimburg-Salter: 1994b (B2), also 1994a, 1994c (B3), and 199? (B4).

20. Except for the *Gaṇḍavyūhasūtra* inscription (cf. C1), all inscriptions of the main temple will be published in a volume edited by L. Petech and C. Luczanits (C3). Some generalising remarks on these inscriptions are made in Thakur 1997: 973–975, with specimens of transcriptions and translations. Thakur forthcoming is to contain a chapter entitled "Surviving Epigraphic Evidence," which will also give "a complete list of inscriptions" (Thakur 1997: 970).

The only inscription dealt with so far is the "Renovation inscription," which was edited and translated by G. Tucci (cf. Tucci 1935: 195–204, and C4 for a new treatment of the same).

21. Cf. Steinkellner 199? (C9).

with the hitherto investigated manuscripts from Tabo the character of "independence" in relation to the canonical versions, and is thus another example of the import of Tabo's texts for the early Tibetan canonical transmission.

The same is true of the second sūtra text on the walls of the 'Du khaṅ, the *Kṣitigarbhasūtra*, which is contained in the "Admonitory Inscription" on the southern front of the wall separating the main hall from the apse. The general meaning of this inscription is quite different: it is a warning to everybody not to molest any monk irrespective of his moral status.

Without an introductory address, this inscription starts with a simple statement to the effect that everybody, be he king, minister, lord, or layman, by physically harming or verbally abusing a monk, whether the latter be immoral or moral, will accumulate immeasurable bad karma.

Then follows a question: "How/why is such (a fact) known/evident?" (*de ltar ci mṅon źe na/*), and the answer is: "In this way it is known from the Mahāyāna-sūtra called '*Ārya-Daśacakrakṣitigarbha*.'" In the quotation which follows we find five passages from the third chapter of the sūtra. The contents of the five passages quoted from the *Kṣitigarbhasūtra* are all of a kind that supports the initial statement, namely that a monk of whatever moral status and behavior may not be touched, even if this were to be in accordance with worldly law, and that even the wearing of a monk's robe is sufficient to make the wearer sacrosanct.

The sūtra text in this inscription has one conspicuous feature in common with the sūtra text in the Sudhana frieze: the parts of the sūtra quoted have not been changed in their textual form. The differences are also evident: no completeness is intended, and the purpose of the quotation is clear from the introductory question. This inscription has been edited by H. Tauscher (cf. C5).

Since inscriptional texts like these are rare in Tibetan temples (some other cases are known from the 'Du khaṅ in Alchi, the gSer khaṅ of Shalu, and may be inferred for bSam yas in its dBu rtse chen mo), I have tried to answer the simple question which naturally arises with regard to their purpose (cf. Steinkellner C9). Here I would only like to summarize my working hypothesis concerning the function of these two texts: they serve as the necessary evidence in a proof from the scriptures. In the same way as the passages quoted from the *Kṣitigarbhasūtra* are the evidence adduced for the truth of the initial statement, the *Gaṇḍavyūhasūtra* inscription is the evidence adduced, as a document of scripture, for proving that what is depicted in the painted scenes is truly authentic Buddhist teaching. In other words, it is attached to the scenes as authentication.

Of course, all these written documents, whose individual nature and historical significance have for the most part yet to be determined in detail, are part of a larger cultural unit the most prominent aspects of which have long been studied by specialists in the art and ritual representations to be found in the Tabo main temple.[22]

Let me end this short and elliptic survey of our work on the Tabo manuscripts and textual treasures with a word of gratitude. Gratitude first of all to the abbot of Tabo, Geshe Sonam Wangdu. Without his openness of mind and interest in scholarly pursuits, and without his continuous hospitality, we would not have achieved as much as we did in this short time. This remarkable man, although from a native place far from this remote valley,[23] seems to us like the embodiment of the spirit of devotion to the Word of the Buddha which must have ruled over Tabo monastery from its earliest beginnings up to our own times. He is also the strongest guarantee for the future safety of this "Kanjur" in the Tabo temple, notwithstanding the unavoidable curiosity and other less favorable instincts that may threaten to disturb its peace in the future as a result of our work.

Gratitude is also due to all our colleagues who devoted considerable effort in terms of physical strength, time, financial resources, untiring diligence, and intellectual acumen to develop the various lines of research necessary. Above all, I would like to thank Deborah Klimburg-Salter, who has been working on the art and history of Tabo for more than eighteen years and stimulated my curiosity in the first place, as well as Cristina Scherrer-Schaub, Paul Harrison, and, last but not least, Helmut Tauscher, who shared my belief in the great value of this treasure. These friends and colleagues are and will continue to be the guarantees for the successful continuation of this research on the Old Tibetan manuscripts at Tabo and adjacent West Tibetan areas.

---

22. For a comprehensive description of the different phases of the artistic and ritual context present in this temple cf. Klimburg-Salter 1997.

23. For a short biography of "Geshela" cf. "Tabo Today: Interview with Geshe Sonam Wangdü" in Klimburg-Salter 1997: 39–41.

Bibliography

All publications related to the Tabo "library," consequent to its recent opening in 1991, to "illuminated mss.," and to "inscriptions" in Tabo are listed separately and identified for easier reference by the signatures A, B, C respectively, with running numbers in parentheses.

Abbreviations

BISt	*Berliner Indologische Studien*
EW	*East and West*
IeT	Indica et Tibetica
IsIAO	Istituto Italiano per l'Africa e l'Oriente
IsMEO	Istituto Italiano per il Medio ed Estremo Oriente
ITB	Institut für Tibetologie und Buddhismuskunde der Universität Wien
JIABS	*The Journal of the International Association of Buddhist Studies*
PIATS	Proceedings of the Seminar of the International Association for Tibetan Studies
SBB	Sacred Books of the Buddhists
SOR	Serie Orientale Roma
WSTB	Wiener Studien zur Tibetologie und Buddhismuskunde
ZSt	*Zentralasiatische Studien*

Publications of Relevance

Braarvig, Jens. 1993. *Akṣayamatinirdeśasūtra.* 2 vols. (Oslo: Solum Forlag).

Dietz, Siglinde. 1996. "Four stanzas from the Lokaprajñaptiśāstra," in Michael Hahn, Jens-Uwe Hartmann, Roland Steiner, eds., *Suhṛllekhāḥ: Festgabe für Helmut Eimer.* IeT 28 (Swisttal-Odendorf): 7–15.

Eimer, Helmut. 1991. "Einige Bemerkungen zu Handschriftenfunden aus Guge/Westtibet," *ZSt* 22: 244–255.

———. 1992. *Ein Jahrzehnt Studien zur Überlieferung des tibetischen Kanjur.* WSTB 28 (Vienna). ["Zum Stand der Kanjurforschung," p. IX- XL]

———. 1994. "Preliminary Notes on Ṅor chen's Kanjur Catalogue," in Per Kvaerne, ed., *PIATS Fagernes 1992* (Oslo): Vol.1, 230- 236.

———. 1995. "Zwei in Tsaparang gefundene Fragmente aus dem tibetischen Vinaya," *ZSt* 25: 7–27.

Francke, A. H. 1914. *Antiquities of Indian Tibet. Part I: Personal Narrative* (Calcutta).

Hahn, Michael. 1988. "Bemerkungen zu zwei Texten aus dem Phudrag-Kanjur," in H. Eimer, ed., *Indology and Tibetology* (Bonn): 53–80.

Harrison, Paul. 1992. Druma-kinnara-rāja-paripṛcchā-sūtra. *A Critical Edition of the Tibetan Text (Recension A) based on Eight Editions of the Kanjur and the Dunhuang Manuscript Fragment.* Studia Philologica Buddhica, Monograph Series 7 (Tokyo).

———. 1994. "In Search of the Source of the Tibetan bKa' 'gyur: A reconnaissance Report," in Per Kvaerne, ed., *PIATS Fagernes 1992* (Oslo): Vol.1, 295–317.

———. 1996. "A Brief History of the Tibetan Kanjur," in José Cabezon and Roger Jackson, eds., *Tibetan Literature: Studies in Genre* (New York): 70–94.

Harrison, Paul, and Eimer, Helmut. 1997. "Kanjur and Tanjur Sigla: A Proposal for Standardisation," in H. Eimer, ed., *Transmission of the Tibetan Canon. PIATS Graz 1995*, Vol. III (Vienna): XI-XIV.

Hartmann, Jens-Uwe. 1996. "Notes on Two Texts in the Phug brag Kanjur," in Michael Hahn, Jens-Uwe Hartmann, Roland Steiner, eds., *Suhṛllekhāḥ: Festgabe für Helmut Eimer.* IeT 28 (Swisttal-Odendorf): 69–78.

Klimburg-Salter, Deborah E. 1982. *The Silk Road and the Diamond Path: Esoteric Buddhist Art on the Trans-Himalayan Trade Routes* (Los Angeles: UCLA Art Council).

———. 1987. "Reformation and Renaissance: A Study of Indo-Tibetan Monasteries in the Eleventh Century," in G. Gnoli, L. Lanciotti, eds., *Orientalia Iosephi Tucci Memoriae Dicata.* SOR LVI,2 (Rome): 683–702.

———. 1990. "Tucci Himalayan Archives Report, 1: The 1989 Expedition to the Western Himalayas, and a Retrospective View of the 1933 Tucci Expedition," *EW* 40: 145–171.

———. 1994a. "Tucci Himalayan Archives Report, 2: The 1991 Expedition to Himachal Pradesh," *EW* 44: 13–82.

———. 1997. *Tabo—a Lamp for the Kingdom: Early Indo-Tibetan Buddhist Art in the Western Himalayas* (Milan).

Pritzker, Thomas J. 1996. "A Preliminary Report on Early Cave Paintings of Western Tibet," *Orientations* 27/6: 26–47.

Samten, Jampa. 1994. "Notes on the bKa'-'gyur of O-rgyan-gling, the Family Temple of the Sixth Dalai Lama (1683–1706)," in Per Kvaerne, ed., *PIATS Fagernes 1992*, (Oslo): Vol. 1, 393–402.

Schneider, Johannes. 1993. *Der Lobpreis der Vorzüglichkeit des Buddha. Udbhaṭasiddhasvāmins Viśeṣastava mit Prajñāvarmans Kommentar.* IeT 23 (Bonn).

———. 1995. "Der Buddha als der wahre Śiva. Udbhaṭasiddhasvāmins Sarvajñamaheśvarastotra," in *BISt* 8: 153–187.

Schoening, Jeffrey D. 1995. *The Śālistamba Sūtra and its Indian Commentaries.* 2 vols. WSTB 35,1–2 (Vienna).

Silk, Jonathan A. 1989. "A Note on the Opening Formula of Buddhist *Sūtras*," *JIABS* 12: 158–163.

———. 1994a. *The Heart Sūtra in Tibetan. A Critical Edition of the Two Recensions Contained in the Kanjur.* WSTB 34 (Vienna).

Skilling, Peter. 1994a. *Mahāsūtras: Great Discourses of the Buddha*. Vol. I: Texts. SBB 44 (Oxford).

———. 1994b. "Kanjur Titles and Colophons," in Per Kvaerne, ed., *PIATS Fagernes 1992* (Oslo): Vol. 2, 768–780.

———. 1997. "From bKa' bstan bcos to bKa' 'gyur and bsTan 'gyur," in H. Eimer, ed., *Transmission of the Tibetan Canon. PIATS Graz 1995*, Vol. III (Vienna): 87–111.

Thakur, Laxman S. 1997. "Tibetan Historical Inscriptions from Kinnaur and Lahaul-Spiti: A Survey of Recent Discoveries,"in H. Krasser, M. T. Much, E. Steinkellner, H. Tauscher, eds., *Tibetan Studies II. PIATS Graz 1995*, Vol. II (Vienna): 967–979.

———. Forthcoming. *Tabo Monastery Revisited: An Interplay of Mantra, Mudrā, and Maṇḍala*. (The New Indo-Tibetica 1).

Tucci, G. 1935. *Indo-Tibetica III. I templi del Tibet Occidentale e il loro simbolismo artistico. Parte I. Spiti e Kunawar* (Rome).

Studies on Tabo Manuscripts

(A1) Steinkellner, Ernst. 1994. "A Report on the 'Kanjur' of Ta pho," *EW* 44,1: 115–136.

(A2) Jackson, D. 1994. "Note on a Leaf from a Xylographic Edition of the *Lam rim chen mo* Recently Located in Spiti," in (A1): 134–135.

(A3) De Rossi Filibeck, Elena. 1994. "A Study of a Fragmentary Manuscript of the *Pañca-viṁśatikā* in the Ta pho Library," *EW* 44,1: 137–159.

(A4) Panglung, Jampa L. 1994. "New Fragments of the *sGra-sbyor bam-po gñis-pa*," *EW* 44,1: 161–172.

(A5) Tauscher, Helmut. 1994. "Tanjur Fragments from the Manuscript Collection at Ta pho Monastery. *Sambandhaparīkṣā* with Its Commentaries *Vṛtti* and *Ṭīkā*," *EW* 44,1: 173–184.

(A6) Silk, Jonathan. 1994b. *The Origins and Early History of the Mahāratnakūṭa Tradition of Mahāyāna Buddhism, with a Study of the Ratnarāśisūtra and Related Materials*. Ph.D. dissertation, The University of Michigan.

(A7) Harrison, Paul. 1996. "Preliminary Notes on a *gZungs 'dus* Manuscript from Tabo," in Michael Hahn, Jens-Uwe Hartmann, Roland Steiner, eds., *Suhṛllekhāḥ: Festgabe für Helmut Eimer*. IeT 28 (Swisttal-Odendorf): 49–68.

(A8) Harrison, Paul (and) Scherrer-Schaub, Cristina. 1996. "A Brief Description of the Tabo Manuscripts," in *Tabo Bauddha Vihāra Sahasrābdī* (Shimla: Antarrāṣtrīya Samāroha): 49–52. [Copies of a corrected and uncensored version of this paper can be obtained from ITB.]

(A9) Scherrer-Schaub, Cristina, and Steinkellner, Ernst (eds.). 1999. *Tabo Studies II: Manuscripts, Texts, Inscriptions, and the Arts*. (48 plates) SOR 87 (Rome).

(A10) De Rossi Filibeck, Elena. 1999. "A Manuscript of the 'Sūtra of Golden Light' from Western Tibet," in (A9): 191-204.

(A11) Eimer, Helmut. 1999. "A Fragment of the Tibetan *Mahāparinirvāṇasūtra* found in Tabo," in (A9): 163-174. (Plates XIII–XIV.)

(A12) Harrison, Paul. 1999. "Philology in the Field: Some Comments on Selected *mDo mang* Texts in the Tabo Collection," in (A9): 37-54.

(A13) Otokawa, Bun'ei. 1999. "New Fragments of the *rNal 'byor chen por bsgom pa'i don* from Tabo," in (A9): 99-161.

(A14) Saito, Akira. 1999. "Remarks on the Tabo Manuscript of the *Bodhisattvacaryāvatāra*," in (A9): 175-189.

(A15) Scherrer-Schaub, Cristina. 1999. "A Methodology for the Study of Old Tibetan Manuscripts: Dunhuang and Tabo," in (A9): 3-36. (Plates I–XII.)

(A16) Scherrer-Schaub, Cristina. 1999. "Was Byaṅ chub sems dpa' a Posthumous Title of King Ye śes 'od? Evidence of a Tabo Colophon," in (A9): 207-225.

(A17) Tomabechi, Toru. 1999. "Selected Tantra Fragments from Tabo Monastery," in (A9): 55-98.

(A18) Scherrer-Schaub, Cristina. 199?. "Establishing a Typology of the Old Tibetan Manuscripts." [Paper presented to the International Dunhuang Project at the British Library, Workshop "Forgeries of Dunhuang Manuscripts in the Early Twentieth Century," to appear in the British Library Special Series.]

(A19) Bonani, G., and Scherrer-Schaub, C. 199?. "Radiocarbon Dating of Tibetan Mss of Tabo." [To appear in *Radiocarbon*.]

(A20) De Rossi Filibeck, Elena. 1996. "Note on a Manuscript from the Tucci Collection in the IsIAO Library," *EW* 46: 485–487.

(A21) Tauscher, Helmut. 1999. "Here in La ri, in the valley where the ten virtues convene ... A Poem of Dedication in the 'Tabo Kanjur,'" in (A9): 227–242.

(A22) Pagel, Ulrich. 1999. "Three Bodhisattvapiṭaka Fragments from Tabo: Observations on a West Tibetan Manuscript Tradition," *JIABS* 22/1.

Studies on Illustrated Manuscripts in Tabo and Beyond

(B1) Cf. Klimburg-Salter. 1994a.

(B2) Klimburg-Salter, Deborah E. 1994b. "Indo-Tibetan Miniature Painting from Himachal Pradesh," in Per Kvaerne, ed., *PIATS Fagernes 1992* (Oslo): Vol.1, 441–453.

(B3) Klimburg-Salter, Deborah. 1994c. "A Decorated Prajnaparamita Manuscript in Poo," *Orientations* 25/6: 54–60.

(B4) Klimburg-Salter, Deborah. 1996. "Style in Western Tibetan Painting: The Archaeological Evidence," *EW* 46/3–4: 319–336

Studies on Tabo Inscriptions

(C1) Steinkellner, Ernst. 1995. *Sudhana's Miraculous Journey in the Temple of Ta pho. The inscriptional text of the Tibetan Gaṇḍavyūhasūtra edited with introductory remarks.* SOR 76 (Rome).

(C2) Steinkellner, Ernst. 1996. *A Short Guide to the Sudhana Frieze in the Temple of Ta pho.* Published on the occasion of the monastery's millennium (Vienna). [An epitome of (C1) for the general visitor.]

(C3) Petech, Luciano, and Christian Luczanits, (eds.). 1999. *Inscriptions From the Tabo Main Temple. Texts and Translations.* (26 plates.) SOR 83 (Rome).

(C4) Steinkellner, Ernst, and Christian Luczanits. 1999. "The Renovation Inscription of the Tabo gTsug lag khaṅ. New Edition and Translation," in (C3): 9-28 (plates 1–8).

(C5) Tauscher, Helmut. 1999. "The 'Admonitory Inscription' in the Tabo 'Du khaṅ," in (C3): 29–94.

(C6) Luczanits, Christian. 1999. "Minor Inscriptions and Captions in the Tabo gTsug lag khaṅ," in (C3): 95–187 (plates 9–20).

(C7) De Rossi Filibeck, Elena. 1999. "Later Inscriptions in the Tabo gTsug lag khaṅ," in (C3): 189–206 (plates 21–26).

(C8) Steinkellner, Ernst, and Christian Luczanits. 1997. "A New Translation of the Renovation Inscription," in Klimburg-Salter (1997): 257–259. [Version of (C4) for the general reader.]

(C9) Steinkellner, Ernst. 1999. "Notes on the Function of Two 11th-Century Inscriptional Sūtra Texts in Tabo: *Gaṇḍayavyūhasūtra* and *Kṣitigarbha-sūtra*," in (A9): 243-274.

Saṁsāra eva nirvāṇam

Jikidō Takasaki

1.

The *Shushōgi* 修證義 (The Significance of Practice and Realization), the basic holy text of the Sōtō 曹洞 sect in Japan,[1] begins with the following sentences:

> To realize what is life and to realize what is death is the biggest motive for Buddhists. When there is a buddha in Samsaric life, then the latter will be no more. Keeping in mind that Samsaric life is nothing but Nirvāṇa (**saṁsāra eva nirvāṇam*), one should feel neither disgust with Samsaric life nor wish for Nirvāṇa. (When one is able to fulfill this condition,) then one will for the first time be free from Samsaric life.

These sentences are originally found in the *Shōbōgenzō* 正法眼藏 of Dōgen 道元,[2] the founder of the Sōtō sect in Japan. Thus we realize that Dōgen's teaching is fundamentally established on the basis of the idea of the unity of Saṁsāra and Nirvāṇa.

Not only Dōgen or the Sōtō sect but almost all Japanese Buddhist sects also believe in this doctrine of the unity of Saṁsāra and Nirvāṇa, regarding it as the quintessence of Mahāyāna Buddhism.[3]

What is the significance of this doctrine and where is its origin in Mahāyāna scriptures? The following article is a note on these points.

2.

In our Japanese Buddhist tradition, the Chinese translations of the Tripiṭaka have been used as the sacred canon throughout the ages. In the context of the idea of the unity of Saṁsāra and Nirvāṇa, the origin of the phrase *shêng szŭ tsi nieh p'an* 生死即涅槃 should be sought for first of all in the Chinese Tripiṭaka. In spite of its popularity, however, the first appearance of this phrase has not yet been clarified.

---

1. The *Shushōgi* 修證義 was originally compiled by Ōuchi Seiran 大内青巒 and recognized with some revision as one of its holy texts by the Sōtō sect in 1890.

2. The first sentence is taken from the section on *shoakumakusa* (諸悪莫作), and the other three from the section on *shōji* (生死). See Mizuno Kōgen 水野弘元, *Shushōgi kōwa* 修証義講話 (Tokyo: Sōtōshū Shūmuchō 曹洞宗宗務廳, 1968): 45.

3. This idea was often misunderstood under the influence of the doctrine of original enlightenment (*hongaku hōmon* 本覚法門) to mean that there is no use practicing to attain enlightenment. Dōgen corrected this misunderstanding with this statement.

Even modern Buddhist scholars have not been able to clarify the source. For example, the *Mochizuki Bukkyō Daijiten*, referring to the phrase under the item *shōji soku nehan*, mentions a passage in Paramārtha's translation of the *Mahāyānasaṁgraha* as its source, and offers an explanation with the help of Vasubandhu's Bhāṣya on the same text.[4] (I will refer to this passage in detail below.) But there is no direct reference to any sūtra sources. Other sources referred to by Mochizuki are Chinese works such as the *Wang sheng lun chu* 往生論注 of T'an luan 曇鸞, the *T'ien t'ai szŭ chiao i* 天台四教儀 and the *Ma ho chih kuan* 摩訶止觀 of Chih-i 智顗, and among Japanese sources, Shinran's 親鸞 works. Oda's *Bukkyōjiten*[5] mentions, besides an apparently erroneous reference to a verse of the *Mahāsaṁnipāta-sūtra*, the *Ma ho chih kuan* as the first source, while the *Bukkyōgo jiten*[6] of H. Nakamura mentions Japanese sources only (the *Ippen goroku* 一遍語録 and the *Shōshinge* 正信偈), referring in addition to Sanskrit phrases of similar import such as *saṁsāraśānty-ekarasa* from the *Mahāyānasūtrālaṁkāra*.[7]

Generally speaking, in the Buddhist tradition when we meet a phrase consisting of a pair of concepts contrary to each other, we are easily reminded of the doctrine of the entrance into non-duality of the *Vimalakīrtinirdeśa*. And in fact, we find in the *Wang sheng lun chu* just referred to the following passage:

> The one way (一道) means the unobstructed way. Here "unobstructed" means to know that Saṁsāra is nothing but the Nirvāṇa. In this way the doctrine of the entrance into non-duality as such has the characteristics of nonobstruction.[8]

In the *Vimalakīrtinirdeśa*, however, we cannot find exactly the same phrase, although there is a passage expressing a similar meaning. In the chapter called "The doctrine of the entrance into non-duality," we find the following as the words of Bodhisattva Sumati (善意):

> Here "the two" means Saṁsāra and Nirvāṇa. If one sees the nature of Saṁsāra, then to him there is no Saṁsāra. There is neither bondage nor

4. Mochizuki Shinkō 望月信亨, *Bukkyō Daijiten* 佛教大辭典 (Tokyo: Sekai Seiten Kankō Kyōkai 世界聖典刊行協会): 3. 2621a.

5. Oda Tokunō 織田得能, *Bukkyō Jiten* 佛教辭典 (New Corrected Edition: Tokyo: Daizō Shuppan 大藏出版, 1974): 780a. See now the Addendum to this paper.

6. Nakamura Hajime 中村元, *Bukkyōgo Daijiten* 仏教語大辞典 (Tokyo: Tōkyō Shoseki 東京書籍): 1.707d (s.v. Shōji soku nehan) and 708a (s.v. Shōji-nehan).

7. The *Mahāyānasūtrālaṁkāra*, ed. by Sylvain Lévi (Paris: Librairie Honoré Champion, 1907): 9 (v. II, 3). See below, n. 30.

8. 往生論註, *Taishō* vol. 40, 843c.

release, nothing is born and nothing perishes. To understand in this way is called entrance into the doctrine of non-duality.[9]

In this way we realize that the non-duality of Saṁsāra and Nirvāṇa is established through an understanding of the nature of Saṁsāra as of no reality, and that this understanding is nothing but the attainment of Nirvāṇa. This passage should be regarded as one of the Mahāyāna scriptural sources of the concept in question here, although it does not state the idea literally.

3.

Prior to entering into an investigation of the original text of the passage of the *Mahāyānasaṁgraha* referred to above and its meaning, let us look at the development of the idea in question in those Mahāyāna works which we may suppose to have been composed before the days of Asaṅga and Vasubandhu.

The *Ta chih tu lun* 大智度論 in one hundred volumes, translated by Kumārajīva, is the greatest source book in the Chinese Tripiṭaka of not only Mahāyānistic but also Abhidharmic concepts and doctrines as well. In spite of its encyclopedic character, however, there are rather few references to the idea of the unity of Saṁsāra and Nirvāṇa. Only the following three examples have been found so far.

1. (Bodhisattvas) are fearless, having accumulated the powers of immeasurable wisdom and compassion. As is said in the stanzas:

If one could destroy evils, even the smallest ones,
For him, being of great virtue, there would be no wish unfulfilled.
This person of great wisdom would have no sufferings in the world,
Therefore, for one like him, Saṁsāra and Nirvāṇa are but one
(生死涅槃一). (*Taishō* vol. 25, 101a)

2. And again Bodhisattvas, having known the characteristics of things, do not regard defilements as evils, nor regard virtuous qualities as excellent. And so they do not feel disgust for defilements, nor feel affection for virtuous qualities. Due to this power of wisdom, they are able to practise patience (*kṣānti*). As is said in the stanzas:

The Bodhisattva has cut off the evils as far as those of atomic size without residue,
His virtues and merits are measureless, actions created by him are never undone.

9. 維摩詰所説經 trans. by Kumārajīva, *Taishō* vol. 14, p. 551a.

Due to his power of wisdom the Bodhisattva can not suffer from defilements,
Therefore he knows the characteristics of things: Saṁsāra and Nirvāṇa are one and non-dual (生死涅槃一無二). (*ibid.* 169b–c)

The stanzas quoted in the two examples above are probably from some canonical works, but I have so far been unable to identify them.

3. And next, in the teachings for Disciples and Self-enlightened ones, it is not taught that the world (Saṁsāra) is Nirvāṇa. Why? Because (their) wisdom cannot penetrate deep into dharmas. (On the contrary) in the teachings for Bodhisattvas, it is taught that the world (Saṁsāra) is Nirvāṇa, because their wisdom penetrates deep into dharmas. As the Buddha told Subhūti:

> Matter is nothing but emptiness. Emptiness is nothing but matter. (In the same way) sensation, conception, volitions, and cognition are nothing but emptiness. Emptiness is nothing but sensation, conception, volitions, and cognition. (In the same way as far as) emptiness is nothing but Nirvāṇa, Nirvāṇa is nothing but emptiness.

Also it is said in the *Madhyamaka-śāstra*:

Nirvāṇa is not different from the world (Saṁsāra), the world is not different from Nirvāṇa,
Because the extreme of Nirvāṇa and the extreme of the world (Saṁsāra) are the same and of no difference. (*ibid.* 197c–198a)

Of the two quotations above, the first one seems to be from the *Prajñāpāramitā*. In Kumārajīva's translation of the *Larger Prajñāpāramitā*, a similar passage is found in the chapter on Māyā (*Taishō* vol. 8, p. 240b). A parallel passage in the *Pañcaviṁśati Prajñāpāramitā* reads as follows:[10]

> *punar aparaṁ, Subhūte, bodhisattvo mahāsattvaḥ prajñāpāramitāyāṁ carann evaṁ pratyavekṣate: na rūpaśūnyatayā rūpaṁ śūnyaṁ, rūpam eva śūnyatā, śūnyataiva rūpam| na vedanaśūnyatayā ... na vijñānaśūnyatayā ... (yāvat) buddhadharmā eva śūnyatā śūnyataiva buddhadharmāḥ|*

Here *dharmas* are mentioned in a series as far as the eighteen qualities exclusive to Buddhas. But there is no reference to Nirvāṇa, although in so far as it is a concept Nirvāṇa is a *dharma*, and hence it too is logically to be identified with emptiness.

The original Sanskrit verses of the second quotation of the *Madhyamakaśāstra* are as follows:

10. N. Dutt, ed., *Paṁcaviṁśatisāhasrikā Prajñāpāramitā* (London: Luzac & Co., 1934): 155, 15–22.

Na saṁsārasya nirvāṇāt kiṁcid asti viśeṣaṇam |
na nirvāṇasya saṁsārāt kiṁcid asti viśeṣaṇam ||
nirvāṇasya ca yā koṭiḥ koṭiḥ saṁsārasya ca |
na tayor antaraṁ kiṁcit susūkṣmam api vidyate || (XXV.19–20)[11]

From these verses, we understand that the Chinese term *shih hsien* (世間) in Kumārajīva's translation is equivalent to Sanskrit *saṁsāra.* On this basis we are able to suppose that the phrase *shih hsien tsi shih nieh p'an* (世間即是涅槃) is identical in meaning to *shêng szŭ tsi nieh p'an* (生死即涅槃).

As for the subject of the third example, namely that the very idea of the unity of Saṁsāra and Nirvāṇa is the teaching exclusively for Bodhisattvas, i.e., Mahāyāna, the *Ta chih tu lun* refers to it later again in terms of the superiority of Bodhisattvas' wisdom over that of Disciples and Self-enlightened Ones. Here I will freely translate the passage:

> 4. Through two reasons Bodhisattvas are superior to Disciples and Self-enlightened Ones. Firstly they understand through emptiness that all *dharma*s are empty, and still never perceive this emptiness. (They regard) emptiness as equal to, one with, and not different from non-emptiness. Secondly they, with this wisdom (i.e., of emptiness), wish to release all sentient beings (from Saṁsāra) and cause them to attain Nirvāṇa. The wisdom of Disciples and Self-enlightened Ones only perceives the emptiness of all dharmas, but cannot perceive that Saṁsāra and Nirvāṇa are but one. For example, there may be two kinds of persons coming out of a prison. One, after making a hole in the wall, himself alone would come out and be released. Another, having himself been released, would destroy the prison, break chains, and release many others from that prison (兼濟衆人). (*Taishō* vol. 25, p. 320a)

Here is emphasized the altruistic attitudes of Bodhisattvas in relation to their perception of the unity of Saṁsāra and Nirvāṇa.

On the basis of the *Ta chih tu lun*, we know that the idea of the unity of Saṁsāra and Nirvāṇa belongs exclusively to the Mahāyāna, which aims at the salvation of all sentient beings, whose agency is the Bodhisattvas, and that this idea is motivated by the Bodhisattva's desire to work for the salvation of others.

The *Ta chih tu lun* is traditionally attributed to Nāgārjuna, but modern scholarship has expressed doubts about this attribution and is inclined to view Kumārajīva's participation in the composition of

---

11. The *Prasannapadā*, ed. L. de La Vallée Poussin (St. Petersburg: Imperial Academy, 1903–1913): 535; 中論, trans. by Kumārajīva, *Taishō* vol. 30, p. 36a: 涅槃與世間 無有少分別 世間與涅槃 亦無分別 涅槃之實際 及與世間際 如是二際者 無毫釐差別.

this treatise as crucial. In the present case, however, we cannot deny the identity of the treatise's position with Nāgārjuna's view, as is shown in the stanzas of the *Madhyamakaśāstra* quoted above.

Besides the two verses in the chapter on the Investigation of Nirvāṇa (chap. XXV) mentioned above, there is another verse that expresses the same idea in the chapter on the Investigation of Bondage and Release (chap. XVI). Namely:

na nirvāṇasamāropo na saṁsārāpakarṣaṇam |
yatra kas tatra saṁsāro nirvāṇam kiṁ vikalpyate || (XVI.10)[12]

Where there is neither superimposition of Nirvāṇa nor diminution of Saṁsāra,
What Saṁsāra, and what Nirvāṇa, could be constructed in thought there?

*Piṅgala's commentary in Kumārajīva's translation of the *Madhyamakaśāstra* explains this in the following way:

> In the ultimate meaning which represents the reality of *dharmas*, no elucidation of Nirvāṇa as being apart from Saṁsāra is possible. As is said in the scripture: Nirvāṇa is nothing but Saṁsāra, Saṁsāra is nothing but Nirvāṇa. (涅槃即生死 生死即涅槃). The reality of *dharmas* being thus, how can one definitely say that this is Saṁsāra, this is Nirvāṇa? (*Taishō* vol. 30, p. 21b)

Unfortunately again, the sūtra passage that expresses the very phrase in question has not yet been identified.

4.

Let us now return to the passage of the *Mahāyānasaṁgraha* mentioned at the beginning of section 2 of this paper, *Mahāyānasaṁgraha* IX.3.

1. In Paramārtha's translation the passage runs as follows:

In Saṁsāra and Nirvāṇa, when there arises the knowledge of equality,
Then Saṁsāra is (identified with) Nirvāṇa, since of the two no (distinction of) this or that is observed.
Therefore, of Saṁsāra there should be neither abandonment nor non-abandonment.
Of Nirvāṇa, too, (there should be) neither attainment nor non-attainment.[13]

---

12. 中論: 不離於生死 而別有涅槃 實相義如是 云何有分別, *Taishō* vol. 30, p. 21b.

13. *Taishō* vol. 31, p. 129b: 於生死涅槃 若智起平等 生死即涅槃 二無此彼故 是故於生死 非捨非非捨 於涅槃亦爾 無得無不得. Cf. Hsüan-tsang's translation: 於生死涅槃 若起平等智 爾時由此證 生死即涅槃 由是於生死 非捨非不捨 亦即於涅槃 非得非不得.

These two stanzas are probably a quotation of some unknown scripture. They are quoted as a source authority for the doctrine of the unstable Nirvāṇa (*apratiṣṭhitanirvāṇa*), whose terminology was newly established by the Yogācāras. The same idea was, however, already transmitted in the *Prajñāpāramitā* as an ideal state of the Bodhisattva in terms of *susthito 'sthāna-yogena* (well standing in a manner of no standing).[14] In the *Mahāyānasaṁgraha* the unstable Nirvāṇa is defined as the result of a Bodhisattva's abandonment of defilements, which is otherwise characterized as the transformation of the basis (*āśraya-parivṛtti*).[15] Commenting on these verses, Vasubandhu says the following:

---

14. The first use of this phrase is perhaps in the *Aṣṭasāhasrikā* (ASP), p. 8.3 in Mitra's edition: *bodhisatvo mahāsatvaḥ prajñāpāramitāyāṁ veditavyaḥ sthito 'vinivartanīyāyāṁ bodhisatvabhūmau susthito 'sthānayogena.*

This sentence is located at the end of a passage in which a bodhisattva's perception of all *dharmas* by means of *prajñāpāramitā* is elucidated and understood by Subhūti to be that no *dharma* exists, so even a bodhisattva is non-existent and is appellation only (*nāmadheyamātra*), and what is appellation only is neither abiding nor not abiding (*na sthitaṁ nāsthitaṁ na viṣṭhitaṁ nāviṣṭhitaṁ*) because it is not existent, and that if a bodhisattva has no fear but has faith with a deep mind when this *prajñāpāramitā* is taught, then he is to be known as abiding in the irreversible stage of a bodhisattva standing firm in perfect wisdom in the manner of non-standing (ASP, 7.9–8.3). Cf. Kumārajīva's translation, *Taishō* vol. 8, p. 537c: 住無所住 for the phrase.

The same passage is considerably enlarged in the *Pañcaviṁśatisāhasrikā* (PVP), pp. 123.14–128.1 in N. Dutt's edition, by enumerating various kinds of *dharmas*, among which is found the pair *saṁsārika* and *nairvāṇika* (126.11–12). Cf. Kumārajīva's trans. (Larger PP), *Taishō* vol. 8, pp. 234a–235a: 住不住法故 for the phrase. There is no direct reference to Saṁsāra and Nirvāṇa there.

Besides this passage, the PVP adds a passage in which this idea of "standing in the *prajñāpāramitā* in the manner of non standing" is taught, and locates it, probably with the idea of emphasizing the importance of this concept, towards the head of the main part of the sūtra, i.e., immediately after the introductory part: *iha, Śāriputra, bodhisattvena mahāsattvena prajñāpāramitāyāṁ sthitvā 'sthanayogena dānapāramitā paripūrayitavyā aparityāgayogena deyadāyakapratigrāhakānupalabdhitām upādāya*। (18.7–10). Cf. the Larger PP, *Taishō* vol. 8, 218c: 以不住法住般若波羅蜜中.

The *dānapāramitā* is followed by other *pāramitās*, and next by the thirty-seven *dharmas* as the means for the attainment of *bodhi*, etc., up to the eighteen qualities exclusive to the Buddha and compassion. It is with reference to just these passages that the *Ta chih tu lun* explains these *dharmas* in detail (139a–257c), among which are the references to the unity of Saṁsāra and Nirvāṇa discussed above.

15. The stanzas referred to here are located at the end of the chapter on the result of annihilation, or attainment of Quiescence as the result of a bodhisattva's practices, being the ninth subject of the text. In this chapter, the main topic is the *āśrayaparivṛtti*.

> (Both Saṁsāra and Nirvāṇa are products of thought-construction. They are but one and the same suchness. If one attains the non-discriminative wisdom, then equality is established between them.)
>
> The impure part of the dependent nature (*paratantra-svabhāva*) is called Saṁsāra, while the pure part is called Nirvāṇa. (To understand) the non-reality of Saṁsāra and non-substantiality of ego and *dharma*s is nothing but Nirvāṇa. If one, attaining non-discriminative wisdom, perceives the non-existence of Saṁsāra, then he perceives the non-existence of Nirvāṇa. Therefore there is no distinction between the two. Then what is the merit of this wisdom? ... Though he perceives non-substantiality (of Saṁsāra), he never retires from Saṁsāra. This is the meaning of non-abandonment. Though staying in Saṁsāra, he always perceives non-substantiality. This means non-non-abandonment. ... As he obtains no Saṁsāra, then he obtains no Nirvāṇa. This means non-attainment. The point that he perceives supreme quietude in Saṁsāra, this is the meaning of non-non-attainment.[16]

As for the phrase *shêng szŭ tsi nieh p'an* (生死即涅槃) in the former stanza, Hsüan-tsang's translation uses the same expression, while the equivalent Tibetan translation is *ḥkhor ñid mya ṅan ḥdas par ḥgyur.*[17]

There are some other passages in the *Mahāyānasaṁgraha* where the same idea is expressed in similar phrases.

2. In the chapter on the objects of knowledge (*jñeya*), the second subject out of ten and which elucidates the *trisvabhāva* doctrine, Asaṅga discusses the meaning of the idea of the non-distinction of Saṁsāra and Nirvāṇa with reference to the character of the Dependent nature. A summary of the passage (II.28) runs as follows:

> Q: In the *Brahmaparipṛcchā* the Bhagavat taught that the Tathāgata does not see Saṁsāra, or Nirvāṇa. What was his hidden intention in this teaching?
>
> A: The Dependent nature is in one respect the Constructed nature, and is in another respect the Perfect nature. Therefore there is no difference between Saṁsāra and Nirvāṇa (*ḥkhor ba daṅ mya ṅan las ḥdas pa ñid bye brag med pa*). This is the hidden meaning. Thus the Dependent nature is

---

16. *Taishō* vol. 31, p. 249a-b, according to Paramārtha's translation.

17. Tibetan translation, sDe dGe (D), *Ri* (*sems tsam* 12), 37a2–3. The two stanzas are as follows:

ḥkhor ba daṅ ni mya ṅan ḥdas | | *mthuṅs par śes pa nam kye ba* | |
de tshe de phyir de la ni | | *ḥkhor ñid mya ṅan ḥdas par ḥgyur* | |
de yi phyir na ḥkhor ba ni | | *gtoṅ ba ma yin mi gtoṅ min* | |
de phyir mya ṅan ḥdas pa yaṅ | | *thob pa ma yin mi thob min* | |

It is difficult for me to restore the Sanskrit of these verses. A hypothetical sentence for the fourth *pada* of the first verse, which is equivalent to the third *pada* of Paramārtha's translation, would be *saṁsāro nirvṛtir bhavet* | | (*nirvṛti* for *nirvāṇa*, *causa metrica*).

in Saṁsāra due to its part of the Constructed nature, the same is in Nirvāṇa when its part of the Perfect nature is realized.[18]

The Dependent nature is represented by the *ālayavijñāna* and the latter is otherwise characterized as the beginningless basis (*anādikāliko dhātuḥ*), the basis for both paths of Saṁsāra, and attainment of Nirvāṇa.[19]

The quoted scripture, otherwise called the *Brahmaviśeṣacinti-paripṛcchā*, is also found among Kumārajīva's translations, and we should add this sūtra to the list of sources of the idea in question.[20]

3. In the same chapter, there is another passage (II.30) in which the Buddha's teaching concerning pairs of concepts contrary to each other, such as *nitya* and *anitya*, is discussed in relation to the Trisvabhāva doctrine (*ibid.* 121a). Among the list of such pairs, we find *shêng szŭ nieh p'an wu er* (生死涅槃無二), which we suppose to be equivalent to Sanskrit *saṁsāra-nirvāṇādvaya*. The term is reconstructed (by Nagao) from Tibetan, *ḥkhor ba daṅ mya ṅan las ḥdas pa daṅ gñis su med*, which means "Saṁsāra, Nirvāṇa, and the Non-dual" representing the Constructed, the Perfect, and the Dependent nature, respectively.[21] This may be called the Yogācāra interpretation of the doctrine of entering non-duality.

4. In the last chapter of the *Mahāyānasaṁgraha* on the Buddha's wisdom, we find the following stanza (X.28A[12]):

thabs chen rnams daṅ ldan pa la|| ñon moṅs byaṅ chub yan lag ḥgyur||
ḥkhor ba'aṅ shi baḥi bdag ñid de|| de phyir de bshin gśegs bsam yas||[22]

For one who has accomplished the great means (for salvation),
Defilements become components of enlightenment,

---

18. D *ibid.* 19b4–5; Paramārtha, *Taishō* vol. 31, p. 120c–121a. For the phrase mentioned in Tibetan, Paramārtha has: 生死爲涅槃依無差別義.

19. The term appeared in a quotation of the *Abhidharma-Mahāyānasūtra* at the beginning of chap. 1, on *jñeyāśraya*, as its synonym.

20. The passage is in *Taishō* no. 586 思益梵天所問經, vol. 15, p. 36c. The sūtra explains the reason for the Buddha's statement by saying that Nirvāṇa is only an appellation and is not perceived (但有名字而有不可得).

21. The Sanskrit reconstruction of the phrase is correct from a doctrinal viewpoint, but D here (20b1) has the reading: *ḥkhor ba daṅ mya ṅan las ḥdas pa dag kyaṅ gñis su med pa*, instead of Nagao's reading. See Gadjin Nagao, *Shōdaijōron: Wayaku to Chūkai* 摂大乗論・和訳と注解. Indo Koten Sōsho インド古典叢書 (Tokyo: Kōdansha 講談社, 1982, 1987): 1.382 (§II.30).

22. D *ibid.* 40b1–2; Paramārtha, *ibid.* 131b: 諸惑成覺分 生死爲涅槃 得成大方便故佛難思議. H. *ibid.*150c: 煩惱成覺分 生死爲涅槃 具大方便故 諸佛不思議.

And Saṁsāra becomes Quiescence itself;
Therefore the Tathāgata is inconceivable.

This verse is quoted in the *Madhyāntavibhāga-ṭīkā* of Sthiramati, and as most of the verse except for the first four syllables was missing in the Sanskrit manuscript, it was restored into Sanskrit by Yamaguchi, the editor, in the following way:

kleśo bodhyaṅga *āpanno mahopāyaprayoginaḥ* |
saṁsāro 'py upaśāntyātmā tato 'cintyas tathāgataḥ ||[23]

Both Chinese translations of Paramārtha and Hsüan-tsang locate the first *pada* of the Tibetan translation (equivalent to *mahopāya-prayoginaḥ*) in the third *pada* without showing any sign of case relations, thus making it very difficult for us to understand the verse. (Paramārtha's 得成大方便 is better than Hsüan-tsang's 具大方便故. 故 is to be located at the head of the fourth *pada*, as Paramārtha has it.)[24]

The same stanza is quoted in the *Fo sing lun* (佛性論), attributed to Vasubandhu and translated by Paramārtha. The passage in which it is quoted is as follows:

> Because of this real way of the reasoning of the essence of *dharma*s (如實法界道理門), what is Nirvāṇa is nothing but Saṁsāra (即是涅槃即是生死), and it is impossible to distinguish them. And thus one is able to enter the doctrine of non-duality. And again, both are neither one nor two, as they abide in instability (住無住處故). In other words, one does not stay in Saṁsāra due to his destruction of defilements, nor does he abide in Nirvāṇa due to his previous vow. By means of wisdom he is able to destroy defilements, and by means of compassion he is able to complete his previous vow. So it is taught in a verse of the Sūtra of the Inconceivable (不可思量經—**Acintyatā-sūtra*):
>
> Defilements become components of enlightenment,—(and so on).[25]

The scripture whose name is mentioned above has not yet been identified.

According to modern scholarship, the *Fo sing lun* is to be regarded as a different version of the *Ratnagotravibhāga*, the basic text for the so-called Tathāgatagarbha doctrine, or rather as a text composed

---

23. *Sthiramati Madhyāntavibhāgaṭīkā*, ed. Susumu Yamaguchi (Nagoya: Librarie Hajinkaku, 1934): 98. Cf. Nagao *Shōdaijōron*, 2.401–3.

24. Nagao's correction of the third *pada* into "*-prayuktataḥ*" is not necessary. Tibetan ~ *daṅ ldan pa* may mean "one who is possessed of ~," and *la* may be used here for the genitive case.

25. *Taishō* vol. 31, p. 799c. The translation of the verse in Paramārtha is as follows: 諸惑成覺分 生死成涅槃 修習大方便 諸佛叵思議. (叵 = 不可).

under the influence of the latter.[26] And in fact we find in the *Ratnagotravibhāga* an equivalent of part of this passage:

> *tad anena dharmadhātunayamukhena paramārthataḥ saṁsāra eva nirvāṇam ity uktam* |
>
> That by this introduction to the theory of the essence of *dharmas*, it is taught that from the ultimate standpoint Saṁsāra is nothing but Nirvāṇa.[27]

In the *RGV* this passage belongs to the section on the eternity of the embryo of the Tathāgata from the result aspect as representing the Dharma body and is elucidated as commenting on the latter half of the verse I.38: *nityaḥ saṁsāranirvāṇasamatāprativedhataḥ*. The sentence mentioned above is immediately followed by an explanation of the Unstable Nirvāṇa[28] similar to that in the *Fo sing lun*. As for the verse quoted in the *Fo sing lun*, however, the *RGV* lacks it, and instead has the following verse:

> *chittvā snehaṁ prajñayātmany aśeṣaṁ*
> *sattvasnehān naiti śāntiṁ kṛpāvān* |
> *niḥśrityaivaṁ dhīkṛpe bodhyupāyau*
> *nopaity āryaḥ saṁvṛtiṁ nirvṛtiṁ vā* || 39
>
> The saint, being full of mercy, does not approach
> Quiescence because of his affection towards sentient beings.

---

26. See J. Takasaki, *A Study on the Ratnagotravibhāga (Uttaratantra)* (Rome: Istituto Italiano per il Medio ed Estremo Oriente, 1966): 47–49. (§2. *Buddhagotraśāstra*). I received the suggestion first from Prof. G. Nagao in 1955. I suppose the translator Paramārtha himself was the real author of the text.

27. *Ratnagotravibhāga Mahāyānottaratantraśāstra*, ed. E. H. Johnston (Patna: Bihar Research Society, 1950): 35.3 (hereafter *RGV*).

28. The whole passage is in *RGV* 34.18–35.16. The direct reference to the unstable Nirvāṇa following after the sentence mentioned above runs as follows:

> (That is) because he has realized the unstable Nirvāṇa in which both (Saṁsāra and Nirvāṇa) are not discriminated (*ubhayathāvikalpanāpratiṣṭhitanirvāṇa-sākṣātkaraṇataḥ*). — Now, in the world, the Bodhisattva is not entirely involved among all living beings because he has completely rejected all tendencies of desire by means of Wisdom. (At the same time) he is not remote from them owing to his great compassion. This is the means for the acquisition of Supreme Enlightenment, of which the instability is the essential nature (*apratiṣṭhitasvabhāva ... samyaksambodhi*). Owing to wisdom, indeed, the bodhisattva ... having deep intention towards Nirvāṇa for his own sake, does not stay in Samsaric life as the lineage of no Nirvāṇa (*aparinirvāṇagotra*) does. Owing to Great compassion, however, he never abandons those suffering people, and having activity in the Samsaric world for the sake of others, he does not abide in Nirvāṇa as do those who seek only for Quiescence (*śamaikāyanagotra*).

Thus standing on intellect and mercy, both being the means for enlightenment,
The saint approaches neither the covered nor the uncovered.[29]

Here the term "the covered" (*saṁvṛti*) means Saṁsāra, while "the uncovered" (*nirvṛti*) means Nirvāṇa. This verse, though counted by the editor as an original verse in its own right, seems to be a quotation from an unknown text. The Chinese translation of the *RGV*, the *Pao sing lun* 寶性論, omits this verse, and instead has another which is again not yet identified.[30] It runs as follows:

A man of indiscriminate (wisdom) discriminates neither the world (Saṁsāra) nor Nirvāṇa; (He perceives) the equality of Nirvāṇa and existence (in Saṁsāra).

無分別之人 不分別世間 不分別涅槃 涅槃有平等

In the *RGV* passage quoted above, we met a quite important phrase which looks like it might be the original of our Chinese phrase *shêng szŭ tsi nieh p'an* (生死即涅槃), namely *saṁsāra eva nirvāṇam*. This is what we have been seeking from the beginning of this paper. Perhaps the reason why this important phrase escaped our notice so far is that neither of the two Chinese translations, the *Fo sing lun* and *Pao sing lun*, translate the phrase idiomatically. Their translations are, respectively, 即是涅槃 即是生死 and 即世間法 名爲涅槃.

The *RGV* might not be the first text to have used this phrase. The words *ity uktam* seem to show the existence of its idiomatic use at the time of the composition of the *RGV*. However, we should be satisfied now by the discovery of this Sanskrit phrase, *saṁsāra eva nirvāṇam*, and might end our present investigation here.[31]

---

29. *RGV* 35.13–16.

30. 究竟一乘寶性論 trans. by Ratnamati (寶性論). *Taishō* no. 1611, vol. 31, p. 831a.

31. I had no chance in the main body of this paper to discuss the term *saṁsāraśāntyekarasa*, quoted from the *Mahāyānasūtrālaṁkāra* above (see n. 7). The said term is found in II.3 (Lévi's ed. p. 9), which runs as follows:

sarvān satvāṁs tārayituṁ yaḥ pratipanno
yāne jñāne sarvagate kauśalyayuktaḥ |
yo nirvāṇe saṁsṛtiśāntyekaraso 'sau
jñeyo dhīmān eṣa hi sarvatraga evaṁ ||
One who is ready to save all living beings,
Is endowed with skill in the vehicle and all-pervading knowledge,
And has one taste of Saṁsāra and Quiescence in Nirvāṇa,
This Bodhisattva is indeed to be known thus as all-pervading.

The third *pada* is quoted according to Prof. Nagao's correction on the basis of the ms. reading and the Tib. trans. The Sanskrit original of Vasubandhu's commentary

Addendum

After sending my manuscript to the editor, I located the source of the erroneously attributed verse, referred to above, cited in Oda's *Bukkyōjiten* as coming from the *Mahāsaṁnipāta-sūtra*, fascicle 90. The passage is rather from fascicle 90 of the *Mahāratnakūṭa-sūtra* translated by Bodhiruci. This is the *Upāli-parṣat*, the twenty-fourth sūtra of the collection, and there the following verse containing the phrase *shêng szŭ tsi nieh p'an* is found.[32] It reads:

了知諸法如實相　常行生死即涅槃　於諸法中實無染　調伏衆生言離欲

Those who realize the real feature of phenomena
Always practise (the idea that) Saṁsāra is Nirvāṇa.
Though (living) in the phenomenal world, they, without pollution,
Guide living beings (to Nirvāṇa) — they are called desireless.

There is another version of this *Upāli-paripṛcchā* in the Chinese Tripiṭaka, called the *Vinayaviniścaya-sūtra* (決定毘尼經; *Taishō* no. 325), and there the equivalent verse runs as follows:[33]

觀世寂靜名勇猛　知法實相亦復然　受五欲利常修行　不生染着度衆生

Those who perceive the world as Quiescence are called the brave,
And who know the real feature of phenomena as well.
They, though perceiving five objects of desire, practise constantly,
And having produced no attachment, guide sentient beings (to Nirvāṇa).

This version is said to be a translation of a certain Bodhisattva of Tun-huang (敦煌菩薩), date unknown, and is nearer the Tibetan version of the *Vinayaviniścaya*, whose equivalent verse (Lhasa Kanjur, *dkon brtsegs*, *ca*, 244a7-b1) runs as follows:

| *gaṅ dag raṅ bshin med chos ḥdi śes pa* |
| *dpaḥ bo de dag ḥjig rten mya ṅan ḥdas* |
| *ḥdod paḥi yon tan spyod kyaṅ chags med ciṅ* |
| *chags pa rnams spaṅs sems can ḥdul bar byed* |

Again, thanks to information I received from the editor, Dr. Jonathan Silk, I came to know that the same verse is quoted twice in the *Prasannapadā* (in chapters XIV and XIII, La Vallée Poussin's ed.,

---

to this verse is missing, while the equivalents to it in Tib. and Chinese run respectively as follows: *mya ṅan las ḥdas pa kun tu ḥgro baḥi don ni ḥkhor ba daṅ shi ba ro gcig paḥi phyir te| de dag gis ñes pa daṅ yon tan la rnam par mi rtog paḥi phyir| de la ḥkhor ba daṅ mya ṅan las ḥdas pa la bye brtag med do||* (D *Phi* (*Sems tsam* 1), 133b5–7), 四者。寂滅一切遍。生死涅槃體是一味。過惡功徳不分別故 (*Taishō* vol. 31, p. 593a).

32. *Taishō* vol. 11, p. 519a.

33. *Taishō* vol. 12, p. 42a.

257.1–4, and 474.7–10, respectively). Both quotations differ from each other in minor points, and Prof. J. W. de Jong offers, in his "Textcritical notes on the *Prasannapadā*" (*Indo-Iranian Journal* 20 [1978]: 25–57), variant readings from a manuscript kept in the IsMEO in Rome ("R"). In light of a comparison of these variant readings and with the help of the Tibetan translation, we can arrive at the following as the presumed original form of the verse:

ye parinirvṛta loki ta śūrā yehi 'sabhavata ñāt'imi dharmā |
kāmaguṇai hi caranti asaṅgā saṅgu vivarjiya satva vinenti || (metre *dodhaka*)

We might render this into Sanskrit as follows:

ye parinirvṛtā loke te śūrāḥ yebhiś [*cā*]*svabhāvato jñātā ime dharmāḥ* |
kāmaguṇair hi caranty asaṅgāḥ saṅgaṁ vivarjiya sattvaṁ vinayanti ||

Those who have completely entered *nirvāṇa* (abiding) in the world, and by whom these phenomena have been known as of no own nature—they are the brave. Though following after sensual objects, they have indeed no attachment, and having gotten rid of attachment, they convert sentient beings.

Turning back to the Chinese translation of this verse, the phrase *shêng szŭ tsi nieh p'an* has been known to be a free rendition of the idea to enter *nirvāṇa* abiding and acting in the world. This idea is nothing but the later developed concept of *apratiṣṭhitanirvāṇa*. With this concept in mind, the translator Bodhiruci must have used the phrase renowned in China in those days.

As for the *Upāli-paripṛcchā*, a critical Tibetan edition with a French translation was published by Pierre Python (Paris, 1973), who actually identified the verse quoted in the *Prasannapadā* for the first time. On the verse in question, see also Jacques May, *Candrakīrti: Prasannapadā Madhyamakvṛtti* (Paris, 1959): 205 and 417.*

---

* A Japanese version of the present paper, with slight differences, has appeared in *Tōhōgaku Ronshū: Eastern Studies Fiftieth Anniversary Volume* (Tokyo: Tōhō Gakkai, 1997): 753–770.

On *Samāropa*

Probing the Relationship of the Buddha's Silence and His Teaching

Teruyoshi Tanji

1.

The word *samāropa*[1] is used together with *apavāda*, the pair forming a dual category, for the first time in the Vijñānavāda school. In the *Mahāyāna-sūtrālaṁkāra*,[2] one of the most basic treatises of this school, these two concepts are defined as a pair which we translate:

1. We do not commit *samāropa* if we realize the non-existence of what is not existent. (*abhāvasya hy abhāvatvaṁ viditvā samāropaṁ na karoti*)
2. We do not commit *apavāda* if we realize the existence of what is existent. (*bhāvasya bhāvatvaṁ viditvāpavādaṁ na karoti*) (MSA 60.20–22)

From these two expressions it follows that *samāropa* is to regard what does not really exist to be existent, while *apavāda* is to hold what in reality exists to be non-existent. Judging from the viewpoint of emptiness, realism stands on the *samāropa* of substance, since it is to assert that what does not actually exist is existent, and nihilism stands on the *apavāda* of experience, since it is to repudiate what does actually exist. Therefore, the concepts of *samāropa* and *apavāda* are used in order to reveal that both realism and nihilism are illusory.

It is to confirm the assertion of presentation-only (*vijñaptimātra*), the pivotal tenet of the school, that these two notions are arranged in an antithesis. The typical application is seen in Sthiramati's commentary on the *Triṁśikā*.[3] The seventeenth verse of the treatise treats of presentation-only:[4]

---

1. Or *adhyāropa*; the latter seems to have been adopted later than the former as its synonym.

2. Sylvain Lévi, ed., *Mahāyāna-Sūtrālaṁkāra: Exposé de la Doctrine du Grand Véhicule, Selon le Systéme Yogācāra.* Tome I: Texte. Bibliothèque de l'École des Hautes Études: Sciences Historiques et Philologiques 159 (Paris: Librairie Honoré Champion, 1907). The page and line reference is given after the quotation.

3. Sylvain Lévi, ed., *Vijñaptimātratāsiddhi, deux traités de Vasubandhu, Viṁśatikā accompagnée d'une explication en prose, et Triṁśikā: avec le commentaire de Sthiramati* (Paris: Librairie Honoré Champion, 1925).

4. *vijñānapariṇāmo 'yaṁ vikalpo yad vikalpyate* | *tena tan nāsti tenedaṁ sarvaṁ vijñaptimātrakam* | | .

> The transformation of consciousness (*vijñānapariṇāma*) is conceptualization (*vikalpa*). All that is conceptualized by that (conceptualization) does not in reality exist. Therefore all things consist of presentation-only.

Sthiramati comments on the verse as follows: "All that is conceptualized by that (conceptualization) does not in reality exist" is said in order to remove the dogmatic extreme of *samāropa*, and "all things consist of presentation-only" is said in order to remove the dogmatic extreme of *apavāda*. "Being conceptualized" (*vikalpyate*) means being cognized as an object. As the object conceptualized on the presentation of consciousness is not existent, all things are nothing but presentations of consciousness. However, presentations themselves are not entirely inexistent. Therefore presentation-only is "the middle way" free from *samāropa* and *apavāda*, realism and nihilism.

In this manner Sthiramati utilizes this pair of categories to expound the middle way in his school. However, the philosophical structure of presentation-only is framed on the basis of the theory of the threefold nature (*trisvabhāva*), as is explained in the above-cited verse of the *Triṁśikā*. Therefore the pair of categories of *samāropa* and *apavāda* does not occupy the position of the central theory in the Vijñānavāda school.

Although *samāropa* in the Vijñānavāda school seems not to mean superimposition or imputation so far as the above definition is concerned, it actually means the superimposition of the object on presentation, or the imputation of objectivity to the presentation of consciousness. In this connection, it may be noted that the Advaita-Vedānta school interprets the same fact as the superimposition (*adhyāsa*) of ignorance and its transformations, *ahaṁkāra* and so on, on Brahman, and thus develops the epistemological theory of error.[5] The structure of error is explained to be the existence or manifestation of a thing on another thing which is not that (former thing: *atasmin tad-*). The stock example is the optical illusion, mistaking a shell to be a piece of silver. The similarity of the two things and a desire for wealth in the perceiver are said to be the causes of this error. This structure of superimposition holds good in the relation of a presentation and its object in the Vijñānavāda school. A presentation "the blue" and an object "the blue" have a similarity of blueness. It is, together with the attachment to the existence of the blue, the cause of illusory manifestation of an object "the blue." Although I am not familiar with the Buddhist epistemological tradition's development

---

5. See the *Vedāntasāra* (VS) [34]: *vastunyavastvāropo 'dhyāropaḥ*|.

of *samāropa* as error, *samāropa* in the Vijñānavāda school seems to mean superimposition. It seems not to be an epistemological concept, but rather an ontological one. This indicates that the word *samāropa* as it had already been used before the Buddhist epistemological tradition prevailed in India was adopted by the Vijñānavāda school and so the philosophy of this school is originally not an epistemological system but rather an ontology of consciousness.

In the Vijñānavāda school, the existence of the presentation of consciousness furnishes an indispensable foundation for the school's philosophical system of yoga-practice, even if consciousness is converted in its final stage. This is the reason why *apavāda* assumes a role relative to *samāropa* in this school. However, the Mādhyamika school and its precursors, historically preceding the Vijñānavāda school, do not accept even the existence of the presentation of consciousness, since the Madhyamakas assert the emptiness of all things unconditionally. Therefore the Vijñānavāda school has to reject emptiness, that is, the non-existence of the presentation of consciousness, as *apavāda* so as to establish its *vijñaptimātra* doctrine. It is unnecessary to add that there is no room for admitting an *apavāda* of this kind in the Mādhyamic system of emptiness.

In the *Laṅkāvatāra* sūtra (LA) too,[6] *samāropa* and *apavāda* are treated as twin categories and are both to be rejected in the system of "mind-only" (*cittamātra*), as is clearly shown in the expression that "neither *samāropa* nor *apavāda* exist in (the state of) mind-only." But the meanings of these terms here are entirely different from those in the Vijñānavāda school. The LA enumerates four kinds of *samāropa*:

1. The *samāropa* of an inexistent characteristic (*asallakṣaṇa*).
2. That of an inexistent view (*asaddṛṣṭi*).
3. That of an inexistent cause (*asaddhetu*).
4. That of an inexistent entity (*asadbhāva*).

The first is commented on as "the attachment to the particular characteristic (*svalakṣaṇa*), that is, own-being (*svabhāva*), and the universal (*sāmānyalakṣaṇa*) such as impermanence of the five aggregates (*pañcaskandha*)." This means that the first *samāropa* is the erroneous view or conviction that permanent and individual *dharma*s are existent, although they really are not. The second has a close relation with the first *samāropa*. As is explained in the commentary, the second *samāropa* of view is the conviction that *ātman* or *sattva* exists in the five aggregates. The third appears to refer to the tenet of eighteen

6. Bunyiu Nanjio, ed., *The Laṅkāvatāra Sūtra* (Kyoto, 1923).

elements (*dhātu*), referring to ideas such as that visual perception (*cakṣurvijñāna*) arises due to its causes such as the eye, form, light, and recollection (*smṛti*). These causes, however, are not in reality existent. Therefore they are mere *samāropa*s of what is not existent. This being the case, this *samāropa* is substantially the same as the assertion that, out of three kinds of elements (sense, object, and consciousness), only consciousness exists. The fourth type is "the attachment to the existence of the unconditioned dharmas: space, *nirodha*, *nirvāṇa* and *akṛtaka*." While the former three deal with conditioned *dharma*s, the fourth is concerned with the unconditioned *dharma*s (LA 70–72).

Apavāda in this sūtra differs from that of the Vijñānavāda school, "because clear insight into non-apprehension is missing in (the above mentioned four kinds of) *samāropa* which are erroneous cognition" (*kudṛṣṭisamāropasyānupaladhipravicayābhāvāt*) (LA 71.6–7). Non-apprehension here, being equivalent to emptiness, is not the lack of cognition or the cognition of nothing in the epistemological sense. And clear insight into it is concerned with emptiness which cannot be an object of cognition at all. Therefore it is suggested that the cognition of the superimposed is devoid of clear insight into reality which is not concerned with objects. Where there is *samāropa*, there is no realization of reality. Accordingly, the word *apavāda* refers to the negative side of *samāropa* and has in itself no particular pregnant import.

Unlike that in the Vijñānavāda school, mind in this sūtra is innately pure mind, called pure *dharmadhātu* or suchness (*tathatā*), which is more substantially existent than the presentation of consciousness in the Vijñānavāda school. The above stated view of *apavāda* accords precisely with this view of mind. Things superimposed on mind are adventitious dirt (*āgantukamala*) to mind. The disappearance of such an adventitious *samāropa* is the manifestation of the innate purity of mind and this is called *apavāda* in the LA. The five aggregates and *ātman* in the first and second *samāropa* are surely adventitious. Once the *samāropa*s of the six senses and the six objects in the third *samāropa*, being the causes of the six perceptions, disappear, the six perceptions also will disappear and innate purity of mind will be manifested. The non-existence of the fourth *samāropa* of the unconditioned *dharma*s is taught to be the realization of ultimate reality, which will be investigated later.

These four kinds of *samāropa* are probably the classification of *samāropa*s which have already been mentioned in Mahāyāna literature.

Among them the first and second types of *samāropa* are found in the *Vimalakīrtinirdeśa* (VKN).[7]

1. The *samāropa* of self is defilement, the absence of self is own-being. (195b6)
2. Enlightenment is the absence of the *samāropa* of all objects. (198b7)
3. "I" and "mine" are two. If there is no *samāropa* of self, there will be no things belonging to self. Thus the absence of *samāropa* is non-duality. (226a4)

It is difficult to elucidate the exact meanings of these fragmentary statements. But we may at least safely say that these maintain that reality (non-self, Enlightenment, and non-duality) is the absence of the *samāropa* of things within and without. The own-being in the first statement seems to be closer to "innately pure mind" than to "innate purity" (*prakṛtiviśuddhi*) or emptiness in the Prajñāpāramitā sūtras. In the Advaita Vedānta school, *apavāda* is said to be neither the non-existence of what really exists nor the non-existence of clear insight into reality, but rather the realization of Brahman through the disappearance of superimposed things.[8] Thus *apavāda* in the Advaita Vedānta school is none other than the VKN's "absence of *samāropa*." It is clear from the above cited usages that *samāropa* is not treated as an antithesis to *apavāda*. These are possibly the original usages of the first and second *samāropa*s in the LA.

Kumārajīva translates these statements of the VKN into Chinese as follows:[9]

1. Grasping self is defilement. Not grasping self is purity. (541b24–25)
2. Enlightenment is not to cognize things as objects, because it is free from objects. (542b–24)
3. Self and belonging to self are two. Belonging to self exists only due to the existence of self. If there is no self, there is no belonging to self. This is the door to enter non-duality. (550c5–6)

Kumārajīva excludes the thought of *samāropa* not only from these statements,[10] but also from his Chinese version of the *Madhyamaka-*

---

7. Peking 843, *'Phags pa dri ma med par grags pas bstan pa shes bya ba theg pa chen po'i mdo.*

8. See VS [161]. To be exact, *apavāda*, according to VS, is that "the *prapañca* which consists of ignorance and so on, and which is not substance but the illusory manifestation of substantial entity, is in nature substance only" (*vastuvivartasyāvastuno 'jñānādeḥ prapañcasya vastumātratvam*).

9. T. 475 (XIV), *Wei mo ch'i so shuo ching*, 維摩詰所説經.

10. Kumārajīva uses the stock Chinese equivalent to *samāropa*, 増益, as the equivalent of the derivation of the root √*vṛdh* (542c16).

śāstra (MMK) which I hold to be a translation of the commentary to the MMK, the *Akutobhayā*.[11] In the MMK, the first three types of *samāropa* in the LA are not found. I am not sure whether the subject matter of the MMK just happens to have no concern with the problem of *samāropa*. If Nāgārjuna consciously avoided using it, he may have been afraid lest the theory of *samāropa* should invite a fatal misunderstanding of emptiness. If enlightenment, the realization of emptiness, were to awaken to the non-existence of what does not exist, i.e., the absence of *samāropa*, it would follow from this that there is neither self nor *dharmas* in enlightenment, because of the non-existence of the superimposed. Emptiness of self and *dharmas* is not in reality their non-existence but the manifestation of empty self and empty *dharmas*. Therefore, *samāropa*, "(the attachment to) the existence of what does not exist," cannot be allowed in the philosophical system of emptiness.

Candrakīrti, who is regarded as the substantial founder of the Prāsaṅgika-Mādhyamika school, uses the notion of *samāropa* and *apavāda* in the *Prasannapadā* (Pr.),[12] his commentary on the MMK, and asserts that these two do not contradict the emptiness of all things.

He uses, it is true, the term *samāropa* in the ordinary sense of the imputation of an inexistent characteristic to a thing in the simile of *samāropa*. For example, in the first chapter Candrakīrti introduces a simile: "A person in erroneous conceptual inversion feels afflicted, imputing an agreeable characteristic to a disagreeable body" (Pr. 57.11–12). In the twenty-third chapter Candrakīrti makes a comment on the perverted cognition: "These six entities (*vastu*), color and so on, are the objects of passion (*kleśa*). Then one feels desire for an object of sight by the imputation to it of an agreeable characteristic. In the same manner, one feels hate (*dveṣa*) by the imputation of a disagreeable characteristic and delusion (*moha*) by the imputation of eternity and *ātman*, etc." (Pr. 457.6–8). These explanations suggest that the absence or extinction of *samāropa* realized through the extinction of passion is the mere manifestation of the disagreeable body and the six objects as such. This means that *samāropa* in these examples

---

11. See my "Mui to Shōmokuchū" 無畏と青目註, *Indogaku Bukkyōgaku Kenkyū* 31/1 (1982): 83–88.

12. Louis de La Vallée Poussin, ed., *Mūlamadhyamakakārikās (Mādhyamikasūtras) de Nāgārjuna avec la Prasannapadā Commentaire de Candrakīrti*. Bibliotheca Buddhica 4 (St. Petersburg: Imperial Academy, 1903–1913).

has the ordinary structure of the imputation of inexistent characteristics to the six objects.

The idea of *samāropa* in Candrakīrti's system of philosophy is different from this ordinarily admitted "imputation of characteristics." According to the fundamental ontological structure of the Mādhyamika school, which is taught in the fifth verse of the eighteenth chapter in the MMK, passion (*kleśa*) ceases only on the cessation of conceptualization (*vikalpa*). The six objects which are the substrata of the imputation of characteristics which are inexistent there also are the effects of conceptualization. So the *samāropa* of characteristics will be extinct only when the six objects are extinct. This is quite clear from Candrakīrti's observation that "the false thing as the *samāropa* of self and the five aggregates appears as really existent (*satyataḥ*) for a person in transmigration following the erroneous inversion of ignorance, but it does not appear for (the sage) who is near to the insight of the reality of things" (Pr. 347.1–3). So far Candrakīrti may be said to accept that *dharma*s as well as self are (the effects of) *samāropa* just as in the LA and the VKN.

However, Candrakīrti asserts that, strictly speaking, the effect of *samāropa* is not a thing but the own-being of a thing, as he observes that "the statement 'things do not arise at all' points out clearly that the first chapter of the MMK is written in order to remedy (*pratipakṣa*) the *samāropa* of perverted (*viparīta*) own-being of things, and then the other chapters are written with the purpose of removing the own-being peculiar to a particular thing in each category" (Pr. 58.10–11). This observation, being the summary of the subjects of the chapters in the MMK, expresses aptly the core of Candrakīrti's philosophy of emptiness. It is so important and cardinal that the meaning of all the other statements in his commentary ought to be estimated by way of meeting the view of this observation. Accordingly, the expression "the *samāropa* of self and *dharma*s" in the *Prasannapadā* should be taken as the meaning of the *samāropa* of the own-being of self and *dharma*s. All the followers of fourteen views in the "fourteen unanswered questions" (*avyākṛtamūla*) are included in those who make the *samāropa* of the own-being of self and *dharma*s, because Candrakīrti states that "the followers of these fourteen views, making the *samāropa* of the own-being of things, consider self or *dharma*s as identical with own-being, or different from it, and conceive and attach to those fourteen views" (Pr. 537.7–8). In this manner, as the effect of *samāropa* is not a thing but its own-being, emptiness devoid of own-being is not the *apavāda* of a thing, that is, is not nihilism. Therefore Candrakīrti asserts that "for you who assert that things have own-being, due to the separation of things from their own-being, the *apavāda* of all things will occur. We, on the other hand, assert that everything, as it arises dependently, has in itself[13] no own-being. Then, of what would we make the *apavāda*?" (Pr. 188.10–12). Although the terms *svabhāvavādin* (those who assert that own-being exists) or *sasvabhāvavādin* (one who asserts that own-being is possessed) are often used by Candrakīrti, they should, strictly speaking, be *sasvabhāvabhāvavādin* (those who assert that things have own-being) as found in this passage.

Candrakīrti also uses the term *apavāda* and admits it as an error the nihilist alone commits. *Apavāda*, being the disappearance of things, occurs, he insists, only for those who assert that things have own-being, because the disappearance of things will occur merely when the extinction of own-being occurs. As he explains: "One who previously accepts that the own-being of all things really exists and who cognizes its extinction afterwards entertains the wrong view of non-existence of things by means of making the *apavāda* of the own-being previously perceived" (Pr. 273.13–14). The cognition of non-existence of all things does not occur without the experience of extinction of really existent own-being. On other occasions, Candrakīrti refers to the nihilist as "one who asserts that everything does not exist and makes the *apavāda* of all things" (Pr. 238.11), or "one who makes the *apavāda* of heaven and deliverance" (*svargāpavarga*) (Pr. 184.11), or "a thorough nihilist who makes the *apavāda* of karma and its result" (Pr. 329.12) or "one who makes the *apavāda* of self and the other world, by means of making the *apavāda* of the past and the future" (Pr. 356.5–6). It goes without saying that nihilism is the false view that all things should be denied. As opposed to the realist who asserts that a thing has an own-being, the nihilist stands at the other of the two extremes and denies this own-being, and denies all things. On the other hand, for one who asserts that everything is empty, the negation of own-being is not the negation of all things because everything arises dependently without an own-being, but to make known that things are in reality empty, i.e., devoid of their own-being. Therefore emptiness is not the *apavāda* of things.

Such being the *apavāda*, we need not be surprised that Candrakīrti regards non-existence as *samāropa* instead of *apavāda* in the observation that "the opponent blames us (who hold that everything is empty), making *adhyāropa* that the meaning of emptiness is the meaning of non-existence" (Pr. 491.16–17, and cf. 499). The opponent confutes

---

13. Read *eva* instead of *evam*, according to the Tibetan version (*ñid*).

the Mādhyamika school in the first verse of the twenty-fourth chapter saying that if everything is empty, then everything comes not to exist. The opponent here does not assert that emptiness does not exist but misunderstands emptiness in the clause "if everything is empty" to be nothing, i.e., the counterpart of the term non-existence (*abhāva*). Non-existence here is an existence called non-existence. The opponent, imputing such an existence to emptiness, blames the Mādhyamika school. And, once he makes the *samāropa* of non-existence on emptiness, understanding the clause "if everything is empty" to mean "if everything does not exist," he comes to commit the *apavāda* of all things in the world. Therefore "if (one who mistakes emptiness for non-existence) does not wish to commit the *apavāda* of all (things), then it is inevitable for him to reject emptiness" (Pr. 496.3–4). In this manner, *samāropa* and *apavāda* directed toward emptiness are faults solely of the opponent who asserts the existence of own-being. There is no room for committing the *apavāda* of things in the philosophy of emptiness.

In the MMK, Nāgārjuna only once uses the term *samāropa* with regard to *nirvāṇa*, which corresponds surely to the fourth *samāropa* of unconditioned *dharma*s in the LA.

> Where there is neither the *samāropa* of nirvāṇa nor the annihilation of saṁsāra, how is there the conceptual dichotomization of saṁsāra and nirvāṇa? (16.10)

Commentators interpret this verse as an exposition of the ultimate reality (*paramārtha*). Kumārajīva holds *paramārtha* to be the real state (*dharmatā*) of things. *Samāropa* is here used as an antithesis of *apakarṣaṇa* (annihilation). While Bhāvaviveka takes it as a mere synonym of *apavāda*, Candrakīrti seems not to accept it as its synonym and adduces the term *parikṣaya* (destruction) as an equivalent (Pr. 299.5). According to his view of *apavāda*, not to make the *apavāda* of *saṁsāra* is to admit *saṁsāra* as a substantial entity.

Ordinarily *saṁsāra* and *nirvāṇa* are treated as twin categories such as conditioned and unconditioned and so on. Therefore *nirvāṇa* is understood to be something that is not *saṁsāra*, or is beyond *saṁsāra*. This view of *nirvāṇa*, however, fatally misunderstands *nirvāṇa* in the perspective of emptiness. The concept of *nirvāṇa* understood as such is no more than a mere product of *samāropa* which is utterly devoid of *nirvāṇa* as reality. *Saṁsāra* also, as long as it is regarded as a mere antithesis of *nirvāṇa*, is definitely no less a product of *samāropa* than *nirvāṇa*. Although *saṁsāra* manufactured by the Abhidharma theory of transmigration of *dharma*s is, to be sure, not real existence but a pure fabrication, *saṁsāra* itself is not illusion, as it is the very world in which we live, or rather the life that we actually live. In this sense, *saṁsāra* is not a relative conception of *nirvāṇa* and is not denied as non-existence. The emptiness of all things mentioned above is the real state (*dharmatā*) of *saṁsāra* understood as such, that is, of the world or life that we live in. At the same time, it is precisely *paramārtha* because *saṁsāra* is not annihilated there and *nirvāṇa* is not *samāropa*. And again, it is the real *nirvāṇa* because the real *nirvāṇa* is the emptiness of *saṁsāra*.

Although Kumārajīva translates this verse rather freely, neglecting the idea of *samāropa*,[14] his version appears to me to be by far more appropriate to what Nāgārjuna means than his own original expression in the verse.

> There is no nirvāṇa independent of saṁsāra. Such is the real state (*dharmatā*) (of all things). How is there dichotomizing conceptualization (of saṁsāra and nirvāṇa)?
>
> It is not taught that there is an independent nirvāṇa, outside of saṁsāra, in the ultimate reality, the real state of all things, just as it is taught in a sūtra "Nirvāṇa is saṁsāra. Saṁsāra is nirvāṇa." In this manner, how is it said in the real state of all things that this is saṁsāra and that is nirvāṇa? (21b15–19)

This idea in the verse is not unique to Nāgārjuna. The same idea in the same expression is taken up in the *Ratnagotravibhāga* (RGV)[15] with respect to real eternity (*nityapāramitā*) as the fourth property (*guṇa*) of the Buddha's *dharmakāya*.

Real eternity should be comprehended according to the following two grounds: (1) It is not reduced to the extreme limit of eradication (*uccheda*), because impermanent *saṁsāra* is not annihilated. (2) It is not reduced to the extreme limit of permanence (*śāśvata*), because permanent *nirvāṇa* is not illusorily constructed (*samāropita*). Then it is taught that *saṁsāra* is *nirvāṇa* in ultimate reality, based on the direct insight of *apratiṣṭhitanirvāṇa* which is not conceptualized into dichotomy, through the door to enter the *dharmadhātu* (RGV 34–35).

This exposition in the RGV makes clear the following two points:

1. It is not Kumārajīva's mere casual idea which leads him to interpret Nāgārjuna's verse as the explanation of the sūtra passage "Nirvāṇa is saṁsāra, saṁsāra is nirvāṇa."

---

14. T. 1564 (XXX) *Chung lun* 中論.

15. E. H. Johnston, ed., *The Ratnagotravibhāga Mahāyānottaratantraśāstra* (Patna: Bihar Research Society, 1950).

2. That *nirvāṇa* is permanent, *saṁsāra* is impermanent, and the characteristic (*guṇa*) of the *dharmakāya*, an equivalent to *paramārtha* and *dharmatā* in the commentaries of the MMK, is the perfection of eternity is the reason why *nirvāṇa* is not imputed and *saṁsāra* is not annihilated in the *dharmakāya*. For the (bad) permanence of *nirvāṇa* should not be imputed to the really eternal *dharmakāya* and the impermanent *saṁsāra* should not be annihilated because the perfection of eternity is realized only in it. Furthermore, this treatise explains the process of realizing the perfection of eternity by means of the tenet of eight erroneous conceptual inversions (*viparyāsa*) (RGV 30ff.). The perfection of eternity is not such (bad abstract) permanence as erroneously conceived in impermanent things by conceptualization. Then it is so called because it is free even from the attachment to the notion of impermanence that is the mere relative conception of the conceptually inverted abstract permanence. The RGV gives the concrete explanation of the perfection of eternity in some detail as follows:

> The pratyekabuddhas, as they are indifferent to the profits of all living beings, are fond of life in solitude. As a remedy (*pratipakṣa*) for such a selfish bias of pratyekabuddhas, bodhisattvas cherish (in their practices of great *karuṇā*) altruistic and impartial attachment to the profit of all living beings as long as saṁsāra continues unceasingly. Therefore it should be comprehended that only as the bodhisattva's actual practice of great *karuṇā* in saṁsāra is the perfection of eternity realized. (RGV 32.2–5)

In this passage, permanent *nirvāṇa* is put out of consideration. It is perhaps needless to say because the perfection of eternity or really living eternity is completely different from abstract, dead permanence as the characteristic of ordinarily understood *nirvāṇa* as a substance which means simply to remain perpetually self-identical at all times. The perfection of eternity is realized only in the flow of life in impermanent *saṁsāra*. *Saṁsāra* here is not a mere spatial world as is ordinarily understood, but the actually lived life itself of all living beings. As long as even one living being is suffering alive, the bodhisattva keeps on unceasingly practising the bodhisattva's practice through his great *karuṇā*. The perfection of eternity is eternity realized as the unceasingness of the bodhisattva's practice. Great *karuṇā* also is nothing other than the bodhisattva's pure and disinterested attachment to the profit of all living beings. While attachment is usually considered to be the cause of defilement, this selfless attachment is, on the contrary, the cause of purification, or purity itself. In sum, real eternity is the bodhisattva's incessant practice in impermanent *saṁsāra*. Therefore in *paramārtha saṁsāra* is not annihilated.

In the RGV also the term "annihilation" is used with regard to *saṁsāra.* The word "annihilation" may be a mere synonym of *apavāda*, or its archaic technical equivalent. However, *paramārtha*, that is, *dharmakāya*, is said to be the field of direct insight of *apratiṣṭhitanirvāṇa* in the commentary to the RGV. This thought seems to me to suggest that the denial of the annihilation of *saṁsāra* implies much more affirming *saṁsāra* positively than the mere absence of the *apavāda* of *saṁsāra*, because the *apavāda* of *saṁsāra* presupposes that *saṁsāra* is the effect of *samāropa*.

Setting aside the *samāropa* of self, both the *samāropa* of conditioned *dharmas*, that is, what is possessed of self, and that of unconditioned *dharmas*, *nirvāṇa* and so on, implies a criticism of the realistic theory of *dharmas* in Abhidharma. Therefore these two kinds of *samāropa* would have been formed about the same period in Mahāyāna Buddhism. On the other hand, as regards *apavāda*, its formal definition, "non-existence of what exists," is commonly accepted in all the Mahāyāna schools. But the meaning and application which *apavāda* has in each system of philosophy differ completely with each system.

2.

The idea of *samāropa* plays a positive role especially in the philosophical system of those who advocate the emptiness of all things. They think that "keeping the Buddha in mind" and "teaching the Dharma (*dharmadeśaṇā*)" are possible only by means of the *samāropa* of the Buddha and that of word. The former case is found in the first chapter, on Meghaśrī, of the *Gaṇḍavyūha*.[16]

Meghaśrī, one of the good friends (*kalyānamitra*) whom Sudhana meets first, becomes a good friend because he has attained "the door of keeping the Buddha in mind" (*buddhānusmṛtimukha*) which is called "the illumination of all the doors that causes the spheres of all the Buddhas to be revealed and all the Buddhas gathered" (49.15–16). This door is open for us to see face to face all the Buddhas equipped with their own Buddha-fields and Buddha-activities. Meghaśrī confesses that though he has already attained this door, he is far behind the great bodhisattvas who have obtained the infinite and pure *maṇḍala* of wisdom, and accordingly he cannot know their activities or talk about their merits. He adduces the reason, saying that these great bodhisattvas have attained as many as twenty-one doors to keep the

16. P. L. Vaidya, ed., *Gaṇḍavyūhasūtra*, Buddhist Sanskrit Texts 5 (Darbhanga: Mithila Institute of Post-Graduate Studies and Research in Sanskrit Learning, 1960).

Buddha in mind, almost all of which are methods to keep in mind the Buddha superimposed on something.

The things on which the Buddha is superimposed are: People (2), the ten powers (3), the Dharma (4), *kalpa* (7), time (*kāla*) (8), the Buddha-field (9), the three times (*tryadhva*) (10), *viṣaya* (11), quiescence (*śānta*) (12), destruction (*vigama*) (13), the wide (*vipula*) (14), the minute (*sūkṣma*) (15), and manifestation (*vyūha*) (16). It is almost impossible to extract any common characteristic from these things. As examples, the full exposition of "people" (2) and "the ten powers" (3) in the sūtra are given here.

(2) (The above mentioned great bodhisattvas) have attained the door of keeping in mind the Buddha superimposed on all the people in order to manifest the Buddha-fields and Tathāgatas in accordance with diverse desires of all the people and to purify them.

(3) They have attained the door of keeping in mind the Buddha superimposed on ten powers in order to be controlled by them willingly. (49.19–20)

In contrast with superimposition as an epistemological error, the Buddha in this superimposition is rather regarded as more real than things on which the Buddha is superimposed. Therefore we may say that the Buddhas seen by means of them are not illusions but realizations of the substrata.

If it is so, these doors may be practical methods to see the Buddha in everything and to know everything to be the Buddha and at least they, being higher in rank than the door attained by Meghaśrī, will be ranked as the second step in order to enter the *dharmadhātu*.

The *samāropa* to make teaching the Dharma possible also appears in some Mahāyāna texts, the subject matter of which is emptiness. Emptiness in them means mainly that the objective counterpart of words does not exist and reality is essentially inexpressible. Therefore the authors of those texts seem to consider that in order to teach the Dharma, it is indispensable to superimpose on the Dharma words which are themselves not the Dharma. In this case also, the structure of *samāropa* is the same as that of the epistemological error, but the meaning and purpose are completely different. This *samāropa* is mentioned in a verse of an unknown sūtra which Candrakīrti cites:

> What is the listening to the Dharma devoid of sounds (*anakṣara*) and what is the teaching of it? The Dharma devoid of sounds is both listened to and taught by means of the *samāropa* (of sounds on the Dharma). (Pr. 264.6–7)

Among important Mahāyāna texts, the *Vimalakīrtinirdeśa* (VKN) develops this *samāropa*. As is well known, the VKN dramatically demonstrates the proposition "reality, once it is subjectively realized, is silence," in the chapter on "The door of entering the non-dual." The author of this sūtra might have felt the necessity of the *samāropa* of words, and thus not silence, in order to teach the Dharma.

> How could we teach such a Dharma? ... Teaching the Dharma is to utter the words superimposed (on the Dharma). And those who listen to it listen to the superimposed (words). ... Where there are no superimposed words there is no teaching the Dharma, no listening to it and no understanding it. It is as if an illusory person were to teach the Dharma to illusory people. (Peking 191a2–4)

This passage is cited from the section where Vimalakīrti criticizes Maudgalyāyana's teaching of the Dharma. Although no concrete exposition of the Dharma which Maudgalyāyana teaches is given here, Vimalakīrti first advises to him to teach the Dharma as it is and then repeatedly puts emphasis on the point that the Dharma is not *ātman* or *sattva* and is beyond words. This means that Vimalakīrti criticizes not Maudgalyāyana's method of teaching but the Dharma itself taught by him, that is, the Hīnayānistic theory of all factors of existence (*dharma*).

In the aforementioned passage that comes just after the criticism of Maudgalyāyana's teaching, Vimalakīrti expounds for the first time how to teach the Dharma. The meaning of the citation is quite clear: The Dharma itself cannot be taught with words. The teaching in fact consists merely of uttering words superimposed on the Dharma. Only when one teaches the Dharma, realizing these facts, can he teach the Dharma without fail.[17] In sum, Vimalakīrti asserts that "the Dharma as the teaching" (*deśanādharma*) is essentially different from "the Dharma as enlightenment" (*adhigamadharma*), and therefore one should teach the Dharma with a precise discrimination of the two Dharmas.

Bhāvaviveka, an advocate of the Svātantrika Mādhyamika, fully accepts the idea of the *samāropa* of this kind which is clearly mentioned in his own introductory verse of the *Prajñāpradīpa*,[18] a commentary on the MMK.

---

17. The present writer actually does not think this theory is successful in teaching the Dharma.

18. Peking 5253, *Dbu ma rtsa ba'i 'grel pa shes rab sgron ma*, Dbu ma, *tsha*, 46b8: *gang gis chos kyi de nyid rnam rtog legs bral ba | | spros pa kun shi blo ngan rab rib kun 'joms can | | tshig gi yul ma yin yang de nyid sgro btags nas | | sa kun 'byor phyir bstan pa de la phyag 'tshal lo | |*.

I salute the Buddha who has taught, through the *samāropa* (of words), the reality of all factors of existence (*dharma*) which is free from thought construction, extinguishes all discursive words (*prapañca*) and is not the object of words.

Avalokitavrata paraphrases in detail the expression "through the *samāropa* (of words)" in his commentary on the *Prajñāpradīpa*:[19]

The expression "through the *samāropa* (of words)" means that (the Buddha) has taught correctly and non-pervertedly (*aviparītam*), through the *samāropa* of (even) the expression (*adhivacana*) "the reality of dharmas" and of the expressions "no destruction, no origination and so on." (Dbu ma, *wa*, 4b7–8)

Avalokitavrata certainly bears in mind Nāgārjuna's introductory verse of the MMK, as the expression "no destruction, no origination and so on" tells us. I think this comment of Avalokitavrata faithfully signifies Bhāvaviveka's real intention in writing the above-quoted verse. Namely, it is Bhāvaviveka's opinion that Nāgārjuna admits that it is by means of the *samāropa* of words on the reality of *dharma* that the Buddha teaches dependent arising free from eight qualities. Nāgārjuna's own view on this problem will be given in some detail below. The *samāropa* of words is for Bhāvaviveka an indispensable foundation of his own philosophy of logic and meets consistently with his theory of *paramārtha*, or ultimate reality. He advocates a twofold *paramārtha*: the *paramārtha* appearing in the range of verbal expression (*sāṁketika-paramārtha*) as well as the inexpressible *paramārtha*, the original one. The former is ordinarily called *paryāyaparamārtha* and the latter *aparyāyaparamārtha*. Due to this distinction of two *paramārthas*, the inexpressibility of the original *paramārtha* becomes a mere antithesis of the expressibility of *paryāyaparamārtha*. Thus the crucial fissure is made between the two *paramārthas*, that is, between reality and its teaching.

As Bhāvaviveka as well as the author of the VKN do not explain the concrete structure of this *samāropa*, we should refrain from applying to this *samāropa* the structure of epistemological error. But at least there must be something between the two *paramārtha* which makes the *samāropa* of words possible, something which corresponds to the similarity between silver and a shell or the characteristic "blueness" common to both what is presented and the object.

Among the Buddha's teachings, Bhāvaviveka asserts, the teaching of "no destruction and so on" alone is *paryāyaparamārtha*, because it

---

19. Peking 5259, *Shes rab sgron ma'i rgya cher 'grel pa.*

is not perverted (*aviprīta*) from the inexpressible *aparyāyaparamārtha*. This understanding of *paryāyaparamārtha* corresponds to the etymological analysis of the compound *paramārtha* as a *bahuvrīhi* to be analyzed as "what has an excellent (*parama*) aim (*artha*)." The teaching of "no destruction and so on" which is not perverted from the *aparyāyaparamārtha* is effective in realizing it. In this respect this *samāropa* alone may be the superimposition of words on the inexpressible reality, unlike the Buddha's other teaching of "destruction, origination and so on."

Candrakīrti also uses the expression "*samāropa*" in a positive sense. As is well known, Nāgārjuna mentions the characteristic of reality in the ninth verse of chapter 18 of the MMK. In his introductory comment to the verse, Candrakīrti states first his own view on the characteristic, quoting Nāgārjuna:

> The characteristic of reality is nothing but that the object of designation ceases and the sphere of thought ceases. (18.7ab; Pr. 372.7–9)

Then he introduces the opponent's claim as follows:

> When this is so, there is no room for further question. Even if so, nevertheless the characteristic of reality also must be mentioned through *samāropa*, just as you allow everyday statements (of judgement that everything is) real (or that it is non-real), and so on as it suits the mundane truth (which you yourself state in the eighth verse of the same chapter). (Pr. 372.10–11)

According to this comment, Nāgārjuna has stated the ninth verse ("Not to be dependent on other, quiescent, not to be expressed by discursive word, free from thought construction and non-plural, this is the characteristic of reality") in order to reply to the opponent's claim. It follows that he asserts positively the characteristic of reality as something which is not to be dependent on other, and so on, while he simply points out the inexpressibility and inconceivability of reality in the seventh verse. Therefore, this comment gives us the impression that the ninth verse alone is offered with the help of the *samāropa* of words. But actually this is not the case.

In the fifteenth chapter of the *Prasannapadā*, Candrakīrti expounds own-being (*svabhāva*) by means of the *samāropa* of words:

> The innate nature (*nijam rūpam*) of fire which is invariable throughout the three times and something that is not dependent on a cause and a condition ... that is what is called "real nature" (*svarūpa*).... Is there such a real nature in fire? That (real nature) is neither existent nor inexistent as a substance (*svarūpataḥ*). Even if it is so, nonetheless with the purpose of dispelling the fears of the audience, we say "[real nature] exists" by means of *samāropa* as a convention (*saṁvṛti*). (Pr. 263.5–264.4)

> If you say "it exists" by means of *adhyāropa*, what is it like? The real nature is the *dharmatā* of dharmas. What is *dharmatā* of dharmas? The own-being of dharmas.... What is the own-being of *śūnyatā*? The absence of own-being. (Pr. 264.11–13)

Samāropa (or its equivalent *adhyāropa*) here is the superimposition of the existence of real nature on "neither being nor non-being," strictly speaking. But it is in fact that of the expressions, real nature, *dharmatā*, etc. The expression "neither being nor non-being" here does not mean the fourth alternative of the tetralemma, or the inexpressibility of the ultimate substance like Brahman which cannot be determined either as being or as non-being. It means the inexpressibility of reality, emptiness. This is why Candrakīrti cites the verse of an unknown sūtra quoted above as an *āgama* (testimony) of this *samāropa*.

Candrakīrti quotes the eleventh verse of the twenty-second chapter of the MMK as another *āgama* of this *samāropa*. The verse reads:

> It should not be said that (the Buddha is) empty, or that he is non-empty, or that he is both (empty and non-empty), or that he is not both. However, in order to make known by words (*prajñapti*), we speak (adopting one of the four alternatives).

In this verse a contradiction between the Buddha and verbal explanation concerning the Buddha is clearly shown. The reason why Candrakīrti introduces the idea of *samāropa* here is to solve this contradiction, as is known from his commentary on this verse in chapter 22:

> We cannot teach [by giving any of] the four alternatives. But without it being spoken in words, the audience can not comprehend the own-being (of the Buddha) as it really is. Therefore we stand on the conventional truth by means of the *samāropa* (of words) in order to use ordinary language and say that (the Buddha is) empty, or that he is non-empty, or that he is both empty and non-empty, or that he is neither empty, nor non-empty, as it suits each one who is to be guided. (Pr. 444.3–6)

The expression "his standing on the conventional truth" seems to be a paraphrase of the *samāropa* (of words). It appears to be substantially the same as "as the convention" in chapter 15 and "following the conventional truth" in chapter 18. It is, I think, simply with the intention of avoiding repetition that Candrakīrti uses the expression *sthitvā* (standing on) in place of *anurodha* (following), because he uses the word *anurodha* in *vineyasattvānurodhena* (as it suits each one who is to be guided), which comes just after this clause in the original Sanskrit text.

However, the expression "his standing on the conventional truth" adequately represents Candrakīrti's view on this cardinal problem of philosophy. In contrast with this, Bhāvaviveka's view may be said to be "standing on *paryāyaparamārtha*" (reality in verbalized form). While Candrakīrti does not allow *paramārtha* in verbalized form, he asserts that the Dharma is taught only by standing on the conventional truth which is radically different from *paramārtha*. Therefore, even if he uses the term *samāropa* it does not mean the superimposition of words on *paramārtha*. In his theory of the two truths, the non-perverted relation between *paramārtha* and the verbal expression, on the basis of which *samāropa* is possible, cannot be established. According to him, *paramārtha* and *saṁvṛti* are completely severed, as is known from the following passage.

> Just as one who does not suffer from an eye disease (*timira*) does not see (illusory) hair in front of his eyes, so when the unreal is not illusorily constructed (*adhyāropyate*), thanks to non-inversion (*aviparyāsāt*), how could one cognize the slightest vestige of what does not exist, by the cognition of which *saṁvṛti* comes into existence? (Pr. 30.4–5)

The theory of the *samāropa* of words on the inexpressible *paramārtha* necessarily results in a dilemma. The necessity of *samāropa* presupposes the position that words do not correspond to reality. If they were to correspond to it, the *samāropa* of words would not be necessary. Even if words were superimposed on reality, the relation of the two would remain merely extrinsic. Therefore Bhāvaviveka had to make it emphatic that *prayāyaparamārtha* is "not perverted" from *aparyāyaparamārtha*. However strongly he may emphasize it, however, he cannot supply grounds for it. It is impossible to find the non-perverted relation between the two, which are intrinsically different.

We ordinarily understand that the Buddha's teachings are about his experience of enlightenment, or the verbalization of reality. In this case, it is very difficult to elucidate the reason why the Buddha's teaching is true, even if the Buddha's enlightenment is the true realization of reality. This is why the Buddha's authority has recently become a question at issue among scholars of Buddhist logic.[20] In the Vijñānavāda school and the Tathāgatagarbha school, it is explained somewhat more technically: the Buddha's teachings are the homogenous outflows (*niṣyanda*) of the *dharmadhātu*, that is, the Buddha's *dharmakāya*, into the range of verbal convention. However, the es-

---

20. See Ernst Steinkellner, "The Spiritual Place of the Epistemological Tradition in Buddhism," *Nanto Bukkyō* 49 (1982): 1–15

sential relation between the Buddha's enlightenment and his teaching is, according to this theory, not any relation, but the identity inherent in *dharma*. Enlightenment is the *dharma* as realization (*adhigamadharma*) and the teaching is the *dharma* as instruction (*deśanādharma*). Therefore there is no room for the matter of non-pervertedness between reality and its teaching.

Although Candrakīrti uses the idea of the *samāropa* of words, I believe he is essentially convinced that inexpressible reality and the Buddha's teaching are one and the same fact, as is clearly mentioned in his comment on the eleventh verse of the twenty-fourth chapter of the MMK.

> The yogin who is awakened to the fact that the conventionally real thing (*saṁvṛtisatya*), the mere (illusory) product of ignorance, is empty of own-being (*niḥsvabhāva*), (not substance), and who contemplates that the *paramārtha* (of conventionally real things) is (not their own-being but) the very emptiness (of all things) falls into neither of the two extremes. (Pr. 495.3–4)

The two extreme (false) views here are: (1) the case in which one denies everyday things (*lokasaṁvṛti*), even in the form of reflection (*pratibimba*) and (2) the case in which one erroneously imagines that *paramārtha* is the own-being of all things (Pr. 495.5–7). A yogin who stands on the middle way free from these two views is one who, "making a correct distinction between *paramārtha* and *saṁvṛti* as taught in the Buddha's teaching, knows the profound reality (*tattva*) in the Buddha's teaching" (MMK 24.9; Pr. 494.4–5). Conventionally real things are things expressed by words and so are by nature inseparably intertwined with words. Therefore it is the yogin's realizing the emptiness of words that he realizes the emptiness of things that are expressed by words in the form of reflection. This view of Candrakīrti's stems from Nāgārjuna's Mādhyamika philosophy which again can be traced back even to the thought of the Prajñāpāramitā sūtras. In the passage of the VKN cited earlier, the teaching by an illusory teacher to an illusory listener is quoted to exemplify the teaching by means of the *samāropa* of words. The notion of an illusory person, as it first appears in the first chapter of the *Aṣṭasāhasrikā*,[21] even in its oldest Chinese version,[22] is considered as an original form of the thought of emptiness in the sūtra, or as a special method of

21. P. L. Vaidya, ed., *Aṣṭasāhasrikā Prajñāpāramitā*, Buddhist Sanskrit Texts 4 (Darbhanga: Mithila Institute of Post-Graduate Studies and Research in Sanskrit Learning, 1960): 8.

22. T. 224 (VIII), *Tao-hsing pan-jo ching* 道行般若經, 427a.

explaining emptiness. Most probably the VKN, taking this idea from the Prajñāpāramitā sūtras, has adopted it as a simile of teaching by means of the *samāropa* of words. We, however, cannot find any passage in the *Aṣṭasāhasrikā* in which an illusory person plays the role of a teacher or of a listener.

This illusory person is illustrative of an empty person, a person who does not exist as an own-being, a substance. Although the activities of the illusory person guide immeasurable and innumerable sattvas to *nirvāṇa*, there is no person who is guided to *nirvāṇa*, or no person who guides to *nirvāṇa* (and no activity, for instance, no teaching the Dharma, which guides persons to *nirvāṇa*). The *Aṣṭasāhasrikā* calls this way activities really are "the real state of things" (*dharmatā*) of illusion (*māyā*) (Aṣṭa 10.28–29). The real state of things here is the pure state of three factors in an activity (*trimaṇḍalapariśuddha*) in which there is no guide, or act of guiding, or persons who are guided. Therefore the real intention of the VKN in adopting the illusory person as a simile for the teaching of the Dharma is to insist that where teaching the Dharma is actually conducted, there is in reality not only no teacher and no person to be taught as a substantial being but even no teaching of the Dharma. Teaching that is actually conducted is not in reality conducted. However, there is no person in the world who is not illusory. Actually living persons are all empty. Likewise there is no teaching that is not empty and empty teaching is conducted only by empty words and by such teaching nothing is taught.

Kumārajīva's version excludes the idea of *samāropa* here too. Thus he comes to translate freely, standing substantially on the above-mentioned thought of the *Aṣṭasāhasrikā*.

> Such is the *dharmatā*. How is it possible to teach? The teacher does not teach or indicate. The listener neither listens nor comprehends. It is just as if an illusory person were to teach the Dharma to an illusory person. (540a17–19)

The *dharmatā* here in the VKN means the absence of self and surpassing verbal expression. Then Kumārajīva asserts that, seen from the *dharmatā* of teaching the Dharma, the teacher who is actually teaching does not in reality teach and the listener who is actually listening does not in reality listen. Therefore teaching the Dharma is in reality non-teaching.

Nāgārjuna develops this aspect of the idea of emptiness with more philosophical accuracy and elaboration. We may even say that it is in order only to elucidate this idea that he has written the MMK, his masterpiece. As his own introductory verses of the MMK shows,

Nāgārjuna takes up the Buddha's teaching as the main topic of the whole śāstra.

> I offer the salutation to the best of the teachers, the Buddha, who has taught that "dependent arising," which is no destruction, no origination, without finitude and without eternity, of no one entity, of no various entities, of no coming, of no going, and which is the cessation of the attachment to verbal expressions as truth and is quiescent. (Pr. 11.13–16)

Although Nāgārjuna propounds here that the Buddha's teaching is "dependent arising" free from eight qualities such as destruction, origination, and so on, there is no specified teaching with such a title in all the Buddha's teachings. It is said that the Buddha has given eighty-four thousand teachings to diverse living beings at various times and places. Nāgārjuna appears to say that it is only "dependent arising" that the Buddha has taught. In other words, he seems to assert that the Buddha's eighty-four thousand teachings, though they seem to contradict one another, are all true, because the real purport hidden in them is to teach one and the same thing, "dependent arising " free from eight qualities. Thus Nāgārjuna endeavors to demonstrate by denying these eight qualities logically that this "dependent arising" is true and at the same time to elucidate the real state of "dependent arising," by pursuing the significance of "the cessation of the attachment to verbal expressions as truth and quiescence" with regard to the *ātman* or the real state of things (*dharmatā*) and the *tathāgata* and so on. Finally, in the last verse of the twenty-fifth chapter, Nāgārjuna seems to indicate, as the conclusion of the above-mentioned investigation, the real aspect of the Buddha's teaching of the Dharma which runs as follows :

> All objectification ceases. The attachment to verbal expressions as truth ceases and it is quiescent. The Buddha does not teach any Dharma to any person anywhere. (25, 24)

If we compare the expressions in this verse with those in the introductory verse, "the cessation of the attachment to verbal expressions as truth" and "quiescence" are commonly used. So "dependent arising free from eight qualities" in the introductory verse appears to correspond to "the cessation of all objectification (*sarvopalambhopaśama*) in this verse. Since the eight qualities may be considered to represent all objectification (*sarvopalambha*), we may safely assert that dependent arising free from these eight qualities will be realized only when all objectification ceases. While the Buddha teaches dependent arising in the introductory verse, the Buddha teaches no Dharma in the twenty-fourth verse. We may say from this contrast that the Buddha's actual teaching of "dependent arising" free from eight qualities is in reality the Buddha's not teaching the Dharma, that is, the Buddha's silence. The real significance of the Buddha's silence is neither to shut his mouth nor to utter words, but not to teach any Dharma anywhere anytime. This is the real aspect (*dharmatā*) of the Buddha's actual teaching of "dependent arising." Therefore, it is said that the Buddha, although teaching eighty-four thousand teachings, does not pronounce even a single word. Nāgārjuna's real intention or purpose in writing the MMK is surely to elucidate that the Buddha's silence is not apart from the real state, *dharmatā*, of the Buddha's teaching, "dependent arising." Therefore, it is entirely needless to use the theory of the *samāropa* of words in order to make the teaching of inexpressible reality possible in Nāgārjuna's philosophy of emptiness.

In this connection, it is not utterly useless to add that, if the structure of the MMK is such as is suggested above, the opinion that the last two chapters (26 and 27) of the MMK were written by Nāgārjuna sometime before or after its first twenty-five chapters is quite plausible.[23]

---

23. See Tillman Vetter, "On the Authenticity of the *Ratnāvalī*," *Asiatische Studien* 45/1 (1992).

Buddhist Liberation and Birth in the Heavens

The Significance of the Earliest Buddhist Icons Found among Grave Objects in China's Yangtze River Region*

Meiji Yamada

Translated by James C. Dobbins

1.

How early did Buddhism in India become linked to funerary rites? Concerning this question, the following passages from various versions of the *Parinirvāṇa Sūtra* are frequently cited. They indicate that, although Buddhism was associated with funerary rites from its earliest period, monks were not permitted to perform them.

1. What are we to do, lord, with the remains [*śarīra*] of the Tathāgata?

   Hinder not yourselves, Ānanda, by honoring the remains of the Tathāgata. Be zealous, I beseech you, Ānanda, in your own behalf! Devote yourselves to your own good! Be earnest, be zealous, be intent on your own good! There are wise men, Ānanda, among the nobles, among the brahmins, among the heads of houses, who are firm believers in the Tathāgata; and they will do due honor to the remains of the Tathāgata....

   And as they treat the remains of a king of kings [Cakravartin], so, Ānanda, should they treat the remains of the Tathāgata. At the four crossroads a cairn [stūpa] should be erected to the Tathāgata. And whosoever shall there place garlands and perfumes and paint, or make salutation there, or become in its presence calm in heart—that shall long be to them for a profit and a joy....

   At the thought, Ānanda: "This is the cairn [stūpa] of the Exalted One awakened for himself alone," the hearts of many shall be made calm and happy; and since they there had calmed and satisfied their hearts they will be reborn after death, when the body has dissolved, in the happy realms of heaven.[1]

2. Ānanda, you should remain silent and think of what should be accomplished yourself. There are undefiled laymen who themselves desire to carry this out.... After they have finished cremating, they will gather

---

* This article is an expanded version of one originally published in Japanese under the title "Gedatsu to Shōten—Kōnan meiki no shoki Butsuzō ni tsuite" 解脱と生天—江南明器の初期仏像について, *Nihon Bukkyō gakkai nenpō* 日本仏教学会年報 59 (1994): 65–78.

1. *Mahā-parinibbāna-suttanta*, PTS, DN ii.141–43. Translation excerpted from T. W. and C. A. F. Rhys-Davids, trans., *Dialogues of the Buddha*. 3 vols. (1910; reprint, London: Luzac & Co. Ltd., 1966), 2: 154–157.

up the relics. They will raise and build a stūpa shrine [for them] at a place where four roads converge, and on the surface of this monument hang silken banners. They will cause all people who pass by to see the stūpa of the Buddha; to reflect on the conversion to the Way [propounded] by the Tathāgata, the Dharma King; and to receive happiness and benefits in this life and to attain birth in the heavens at death.[2]

3. You should remain silent and not concern yourselves. There should be laymen who together will concern themselves with my body.... After they have finished cremating, they will assemble the relics. They will raise and build a stūpa monument [for them] at a place where four roads converge....[3]

4. You should remain silent. There are brahmin laymen who themselves desire to carry this out.... [*The rest of the passage is almost identical to* 2 *above.*][4]

5. You should not concern yourselves with these things beforehand. You yourselves should simply think of upholding the true Dharma after my death. And you should aspire to teach people what you have heard from the past. What is the reason? Heavenly beings themselves will venerate my body. In addition, there are brahmins and warriors, and heads of houses, who themselves will venerate my body.... After they have finished cremating, they will gather up the relics and place them within a gold vessel. Thereupon, they will build stūpas in their own areas.... If at my stūpa sentient beings hang silken banners and canopies, burn incense and scatter flowers, light lamps, worship, and sing praises, these people will continually receive great happiness and benefits, and not long in the future other people will likewise build great stūpas and venerate their bodies....[5]

In all these passages, Śākyamuni responds to Ānanda's question regarding the funerary procedures to be used after the Tathāgata's death. He indicates that the same procedures followed for a Cakravartin king should be adopted. The points made in these passages can be summarized in the following way:

1. Monks should concentrate on efforts and practices leading to Nirvanic liberation, not on matters relating to the funeral of the Tathāgata.
2. Lay people belonging to the *brāhmaṇa*, *kṣatriya*, and *vaiśya* castes will take charge of rituals and events related to the funeral of the Tathāgata.
3. The body of the Tathāgata should be cremated according to the funerary procedures used for a Cakravartin king.

---

2. *Youxing-jing* 遊行經, in *Changahan-jing* 長阿含經, *Taishō shinshū daizōkyō*, Takakusu Junjirō and Watanabe Kaikyoku, eds. (Tokyo: Taishō Shinshū Daizōkyō Kankōkai, 1924–1932), 1: 20a-b. Hereafter, *Taishō shinshū daizōkyō* is cited as *TD*.

3. *Fobanniyuan-jing* 佛般泥洹經, *TD* 1: 169b.

4. *Banniyuan-jing* 般泥洹經, *TD* 1: 186c.

5. *Dabanniepan-jing* 大般涅槃經, *TD* 1: 199c–200a.

4. Detailed instructions are given for the funeral of a Cakravartin, especially the disposition of his body.
5. A stūpa should be erected for the Tathāgata's relics at a crossroads.
6. Those who worship at the stūpa and venerate his relics are assured of great benefits and happiness, and at death will be reborn in the heavens.

With regard to this last point, there is some variation in the expressions found in the various texts. It is important to note, however, that Text 1 and Text 2 both say explicitly that those venerating the Tathāgata's relics at the stūpa will be born in the heavens after death. From the standpoint of Buddhist doctrine, birth in the heavens was considered simply one possible stage in the cycle of Saṁsāra. Hence, from that perspective the fact that the Tathāgata's relics and stūpa perpetuate people's rebirth in Saṁsāra is seen as an anomaly.

What is unclear here is whether Ānanda and other monks are forbidden from venerating the relics of the Tathāgata, or whether they are simply prohibited from participating in funerary ritual.[6] The context seems to indicate that, whether in relic veneration or in funerary ritual, monks should not expect lay rewards such as happiness and benefits within the realm of worldly desires, or birth in the heavens after death. Rather, they should earnestly devote themselves to and strive for the liberation of an enlightened sage.

Nonetheless, it is fair to say that the passages cited above forbidding Ānanda and other monks from participating in funerary ritual implicitly demonstrate, to the contrary, the extraordinary interest people had in it, not to mention in the afterlife. Even though Ānanda, a monk, is admonished not to concern himself with relic veneration, he still displays considerable interest in the funerary procedures of a Cakravartin king. Śākyamuni also goes out of his way in answering Ānanda's question, and expounds on these things in great detail, right down to the virtues of venerating relics. It is clear that sometime after Śākyamuni's death—at the latest, by the time of the *Parinirvāṇa Sūtra*'s earliest redaction—interest in relic veneration and stūpa worship was widespread among monks.

6. Gregory Schopen discusses this subject. See his "Monks and the Relic Cult in the *Mahāparinibbānasutta*: An old misunderstanding in regard to monastic Buddhism," in Koichi Shinohara and Gregory Schopen, eds., *From Benares to Beijing: Essays on Buddhism and Chinese Religion in Honour of Prof. Jan Yün-hua* (Oakville/ New York/ London: Mosaic Press, 1991): 187–201.

2.

The Buddhist order included lay adherents grounded in folk beliefs and practices, who longed for benefits and happiness in both this world and the next, and whose primary activities were almsgiving, worship, and prayer. No matter how vociferously Buddhist doctrine repudiated worldly desires, it could not eradicate the longings of lay adherents for benefits and happiness, not only in the present life but also after death.

Certainly, Buddhism constituted an ethically, conceptually, and existentially sophisticated religion which advocated a path of liberation from this unsatisfactory world by means of three forms of cultivation: the strict observance of religious precepts, the practice of meditation, and the realization of the true aspects of human existence. But to ordinary adherents it was not limited to that. There were many who also revered Śākyamuni, the wondrous "awakened one" of this world, as a sacred figure possessing extraordinary powers. In relying on his miraculous power, they sought to escape the misfortunes of the present life and the dangers of the next one, which were even more disturbing because they were unknown.

Among Buddhist legends, the famous "Division of the Buddha's Relics into Eight Portions" survives in nine different versions preserved in Sanskrit, Pāli, Tibetan, and Chinese sources.[7] Except for the version found in the Pāli *Mahā-parinibbāna-suttanta*, they all describe the fierce standoff and explosive circumstances surrounding the division of the relics among contenders coming from diverse regions seeking a portion.[8] As the story goes, seven tribes assembled from different areas along the Ganges River and surrounded Kuśinagara because

---

7. The nine versions are:
   1. *Mahā-parinibbāna-suttanta*, PTS, DN ii.164–68.
   2. *Youxing-jing* 遊行經, in *Changahan-jing* 長阿含經, *TD* 1: 29b–30a.
   3. *Fobanniyuan-jing* 佛般泥洹經, *TD* 1: 175a-c.
   4. *Banniyuan-jing* 般泥洹經, *TD* 1: 190a-c.
   5. *Dabanniepan-jing* 大般涅槃經, *TD* 1: 200a-c.
   6. *Shisong-lü* 十誦律, *TD* 23: 446b–447a.
   7. *Mahāparinirvāṇa-sūtra*, in pt. 3 of E. Waldschmidt, *Das Mahāparinirvāṇa-sūtra* (Berlin: Akademie Verlag, 1951): 432–450.
   8. *Genben shuoyiqie youbu pinaye cashi* 根本説一切有部毘奈耶雜事, *TD* 24: 401c–402a.
   9. *'Dul ba phran tshegs kyi gzhi*, in the Tibetan Buddhist canon, Peking edition, no. 1035 (reprint vol. 44, p. 235; *Ne* 280a8–285a5); and in Waldschmidt, *Das Mahāparinirvāṇasūtra*, 3.433–454.

8. Yamada Meiji 山田明爾, "Indo oyobi shūhen no shari yōki" インドおよび周辺の舎利容器, *Bukkyō geijutsu* 佛教藝術 (*Ars Buddhica*) 188 (1990): 12–13.

the Malla tribe refused to share Śākyamuni's relics. They all sought the relics, "even at the expense of their own lives."[9] In Kuśinagara preparation for battle extended even to women who took up bows and arrows.[10]

According to the accounts in sources mentioned above, the reasons given by the seven tribes for seeking the Buddha's relics included: "We are *kṣatriya* [warriors]," "We are brahmins," "The Buddha was our benevolent father," "The Buddha was loved and revered as our teacher," etc. But love and reverence for Śākyamuni, no matter how great, are not sufficient explanations for the fierceness of the struggle over his relics—the determination to wage war in order to have exclusive possession of them, or to pursue them "even at the expense of their lives"—if only to build a funeral mound to Śākyamuni.

Their determination to acquire relics, however, becomes understandable once the passage from the *Parinirvāṇa Sūtra* is taken into consideration, specifically, the explanation that venerating the Buddha's stūpa is a source of great reward, i.e., happiness and benefits in this life and birth in the heavens after death. If people in lay life had no access to relics, they would be forced to live without any hope of allaying the misfortunes that beset their lives right up to death. But a reliquary stūpa built in their own territory was taken to be an assurance of happiness and benefits and of birth in the heavens. For that very reason, the *Parinirvāṇa Sūtra* advises that the stūpa for the Tathāgata's relics be built at a crossroads where people come and go frequently. Ordinarily, such a location would not be appropriate for a funeral mound. But in this case setting up a shrine at such a place must be understood in the context of the ancient practice of venerating a sage's relics, of establishing a special site where their influence would be greatest.

It would be wrong to think that the religious phenomenon of venerating a sage's relics, or relic worship, sprang into existence just at the point of Śākyamuni's death. Underlying this practice was an indigenous tradition antedating Buddhism wherein the relics of any sage, not just Śākyamuni, were considered imbued with mysterious power.

This practice is reflected in archaeological evidence found at the great Buddhist site of Sāñcī in India. According to inscriptions on

---

9. *Fobanniyuan-jing* 佛般泥洹經, *TD* 1: 175a.

10. *Genben shuoyiqie youbu pinaye cashi* 根本説一切有部毘奈耶雜事, *TD* 24: 401c–402a.

reliquaries and stone caskets unearthed there, Stūpa no. 3 at Sāñcī was dedicated to the relics of the Buddha's illustrious disciples Śāriputra and Mahāmaudgalyāyana,[11] and Stūpa no. 2 contained the relics of ten sages, (*sapurisa* = Skt. *satpuruṣa*).[12] Also, Stūpa no. 2 at Satdhāra in the region of Vidishā (also known as Bhilsa) near Sāñcī was, according to inscriptions on two reliquaries found there, likewise a stūpa for Śāriputra's and Mahāmaudgalyāyana's relics.[13] In addition, inscriptions on five reliquaries found at Sonari's no. 2 stūpa indicate that they also contained the relics of sages.[14] It is likewise clear from numerous reliquary inscriptions of the second century B.C.E. and earlier from excavations of stūpas located at Bhojpur and Andher[15] that, with the exception of Stūpa no. 1 at Sāñcī, no stūpas in this region contained relics of the Tathāgata. Rather, they all held relics of venerable monks and sages.

It is noteworthy also that in the fifth-century travelogue of India by the Chinese monk Faxian (fl. 399–414), as well as the seventh-century one by Xuanzang (602–664), there are accounts of the confrontation between the kingdoms of Magadha and Vaiśālī over the relics of Ānanda, the disciple who was always at Śākyamuni's side and supposedly heard his teachings more than any other. Faxian's version reads:

> Ānanda departed Magadha and headed for Vaiśālī intending to pass into Nirvāṇa there. The deities reported this fact to King Ajātaśatru who personally led his army in pursuit of Ānanda as far as the Ganges River. On the other side, the Licchavī tribesmen of Vaiśālī heard that Ānanda was coming, and they all went out to the Ganges to meet him. Ānanda was concerned that if he proceeded further he would provoke the enmity of Ajātaśatru and if he turned back he would do the same of the Licchavī. Thus, without going forward or back he entered into the "fire *samādhi*" in the middle of the river, burned up his body, and passed into Nirvāṇa. His remains were thereupon divided into two parts, and one given to each party on the two shores. Thereupon, both armies, having acquired relics of half of his body, returned to their kingdoms and built stūpas.[16]

---

11. H. Lüders, *List of Brahmi Inscriptions*, in *Appendix to Epigraphia Indica*, vol. X (Calcutta: Superintendent Government Printing, India, 1912), inscription nos. 665–668.

12. Lüders, inscription nos. 654–664.

13. Lüders, inscription nos. 152, 153.

14. Lüders, inscription nos. 157–160.

15. Lüders, inscription nos. 678, 681–683.

16. *Gaoseng Faxian-zhuan* 高僧法顯傳, *TD* 51: 862.

Approximately two hundred years after Faxian, Xuanzang also visited the region, and his travelogue relates exactly the same story except in greater detail.[17] It is apparent that the story was widely known in Magadha. From this episode, one can also surmise how extraordinary an attraction relics had, even those of the Buddha's disciples.

The strong interest in relics and stūpas shown in these materials bespeaks the profound concern people had over death and the afterlife. In this context, the hope that such objects would assure birth in the heavens after death was extended to the relics of venerable monks also. If this was the case for relics of monks and sages, then it is fully understandable how much more attachment people felt towards those of the Tathāgata as objects of reverence.

In the conflict over the Buddha's relics, all the parties involved—the seven tribes vying for them, the Malla tribe defending them, and the brahmin acting as intermediary—were lay adherents. Also, King Aśoka of the third century B.C.E., who supposedly built eighty-four thousand stūpas, was likewise a lay believer. Hence, it would seem that relic worship rather centered on Buddhism's lay following. In fact, reliquary stūpas seemed to be at the forefront of the propagation of Buddhism outside India. After the emergence of images of the Buddha, these figures also functioned as an advance guard for its dissemination. Buddhist icons, like stūpas, were considered potent objects connected with happiness in the present life, as well as after death.[18]

Such objects stand out conspicuously at each stage in the spread of Buddhism, e.g., from Gandhāra in northern India to Afghanistan and Chinese Turkestan around the Taklamakan Desert, or from western India to the Deccan and Sri Lanka. When Buddhism was first carried to China also, it was apparently Buddhist icons that led the way, as suggested by the famous dream of a "gold man" that appeared to Emperor Mingdi (r. 57–75 C.E.) of the Later Han dynasty (25–220 C.E.) The same can be surmised from early images of the Buddha excavated from grave sites in the Yangtze (or Changjiang)

---

17. *Datang xiyuji* 大唐西域記, *TD* 51: 909.

18. For a more extensive discussion of this two-dimensional character of Buddhism, see Yamada Meiji 山田明爾, "Bāmiyān no Bukkyō" バーミヤーンの仏教, in *Bāmiyan—Afuganisutan ni okeru Bukkyō Sekkutsu-jiin no Bijutsu Kōkoteki Chōsa 1970–78* バーミヤーン—アフガニスタンにおける仏教石窟寺院の美術考古的調査 1970–78 / *Bāmiyān, Art and Archaeological Researches on the Buddhist Cave Temples in Afghanistan, 1970–78*, vol. 3, ed. Higuchi Takayasu 樋口隆康 (Kyoto: Dōbōsha 同朋社, 1983): 218–238.

River region. Though a number of these icons have been known for some time, they have never been analyzed in the context of Buddhism's historical development. Significant questions can be raised in regard to them, for they were apparently at the leading edge of Buddhism's transmission to China and were intimately connected to funerary rites.

3.

The Yangtze River region extends from Sichuan in the west to Jiangsu and Zhejiang in the east along China's coast. Grave sites in this region dating from the second to the early fifth century have yielded wall carvings and funerary objects displaying unusual and distinctive images of the Buddha. Some of these artifacts were known previously,[19] but up till now have not been examined as Buddhist icons per se, in the context of Buddhist history. Nonetheless, if the evidence from these images is tallied against the conventional assumptions about Buddhism's early history in China, a number of curious problems come to the surface.

The prevailing thesis about Buddhism's entry into China is that it was transmitted via the Silk Road through the oasis towns skirting the Taklamakan Desert around the beginning of the common era, and first put down roots in the so-called Central Plain of China, located in the central region of the Yellow River. From there Buddhism was carried south around the third century to Nanjing, the capital of the Wu dynasty (229–280) during the Three Kingdoms period (220–280). That transmission is thought to be the first appearance of Buddhism in the Yangtze River region. What makes this thesis problematic is that, although Buddhism supposedly spread south of the Yangtze River only in the third century, Buddhist images can be found in graves of this region, and even in Sichuan at the distant headwaters of the Yangtze, dating from around the same time or even earlier.

The oldest surviving Buddhist icons of the Yellow River region include only a few dating from the fourth century—small seated images of the Buddha made of bronze—with the rest dating from the fifth century on.[20] Needless to say, Buddhist images existed in

---

19. For example, see Wu Hung, "Buddhist Elements in Early Chinese Art," *Artibus Asiae* XLVII.3–4 (1986): 263–352.

20. Matsumoto Saburō 松本三郎, *Zōtei Chūgoku Bukkyō chōkokushi kenkyū* 増訂中国佛教彫刻史研究 (Tokyo: Yoshikawa Kōbunkan 吉川弘文館, 1966): 2–4.

the Central Plain prior to this time, but most have been lost in warfare or persecutions of Buddhism. The earliest icons south of the Yangtze and in Sichuan show striking differences in both sculptural form and Buddhist representation from those of the Central Plain. One can only conclude that the two styles represent distinct strains of Buddhist iconography transmitted separately to these two regions.

The specific icons found at sites in the Yangtze region which have greatest relevance to this issue are the following:

1. Images on "Coin-bearing Trees"

Among the funerary objects found in Later and Shu Han 後漢, 蜀漢 period graves (ca. second–third centuries) in Sichuan 四川, Yunnan 雲南, Guizhou 貴州, and southern Shanxi 陝西 are bronze models of trees containing branches which bear copper coins, as if they were fruit, and which have small depictions of the Taoist immortality figure Xiwangmu 西王母 ("Queen Mother of the West") nested in them (plate 1).[21] Appearing on the trunk of these trees, or on ceramic pedestals used to hold them up, are figures of the Buddha. These images are approximately six to eight centimeters in height, and bear certain standard marks of Buddhist iconography: the halo of light, protuberance (*uṣṇīṣa*) on the top of the head, vertical lines delineating hair, and mustache. His right hand is held up in the "Have-no-fear" or *abhaya mudrā*, and his left is holding the edge of his robe at chest level (plate 2). These objects probably express the hope for worldly wealth and possessions even in the next life, symbolized by the copper coins.

2. Images in Cliffside Graves

In the Luoshan 楽山 region of Sichuan 四川 there are many graves located in stone caves dating back to the Later and Shu Han periods. According to some estimates, there are more than five thousand. Among them, the cliffside graves at Mahao 麻浩 and Shiziwan 柿子湾 contain Buddhist images in bas-relief (plate 3).[22] They are located on the rock face above the entrance of the corridor leading to the inner mortuary chamber, and in size they are about thirty-eight centimeters tall. In iconographic features they resemble the Buddhas found on the "coin-bearing trees": the halo of light, *uṣṇīṣa*, folds in the robe, right hand in the *abhaya mudrā*, and left hand holding up the edge of the robe.

3. Images on Spirit Vessels

Excavations of Wu 呉 and Western Jin 西晋 graves (ca. third–fourth centuries) at the lower reaches of the Yangtze River 揚子江 have yielded ceramic funerary vessels known variously as "clay-layered pots" (*duisuguan*

---

21. See also He Yunao 賀雲翱, Yuan Rongchun 阮栄春, Liu Junwen 劉俊文, Yamada Meiji 山田明爾, Kida Tomoo 木田知生, and Irisawa Takashi 入澤崇, *Fojiao chuchuan nanfang zhi lu* 佛教初傳南方之路 / *Bukkyō shoden nanpō rūto* 佛教初傳南方ルート (Beijing: Wenwu Chubanshe 文物出版社, 1993), plates 8–15, 32.

22. See also He Yunao et al., plates 1–2.

堆塑缶), "deity-residing jars" (*shentinghu* 神亭壷), "grain containers" (*gucang* 穀倉), and "five-mouth jars with decoration" (*zhuangshifu wulianguan* 装飾付五連缶). The original term for them is unknown. Concerning their use, one might be tempted to think that things, such as ashes and bones, were deposited in them, but there have been no archaeological reports of such uses. At present, there are several hypotheses, but no prevailing thesis about their use. In height, they stand about fifty centimeters, and on the lower half of the vessel appear figures of animals and humans that are pressed on with molds or are handmade. The upper half has a large central mouth with four miniature openings surrounding it, the whole of which is decorated in the style of a multi-storied palace with figures of humans, animals, and flying birds displayed around the perimeter.

Among these jars there are some which have, at the edge of the upper palace section, a miniature inscription resting on the back of a turtle. There are at least four instances in which the inscription reads as follows: "[This jar] was made in Shining County in Huiji District [present-day Shangyu County in Zhejiang Province]. Use this [jar] in funerals, and it will be beneficial to your descendants. They can become government officials and advance to high rank. The number [that will do so] is without limit" (plate 4).[23] 會稽。出始寧。用此喪葬、宜子孫作吏、高遷、衆無極.

Also, there is one jar on which the inscription reads: "Third year of Yongan (260 C.E.) [This jar] abounds with good fortune, and is beneficial for becoming a government official of high rank. Among your descendants, there will be many to live long, and there will be no end [to your descendants] for millions of years."[24] 永安三年時。富且洋(祥)、宜公綁(卿)、多子孫、寿命長千意(億)萬歳、未見英. Based on these inscriptions, it is clear that such vessels played an important role in funerary ritual. Their efficacy, however, lay primarily in benefiting one's descendants and causing them to flourish, rather than in calming the spirit of the deceased.

On the trunk of the jar or in the upper palace section there also frequently appear images of bearded foreigners wearing pointed hats, characteristic of the horse-riding tribes of Central Asia, some performing music, dance, or acrobatics and others kneeling and holding their hands together in a reverential pose. Interspersed among them are images of the Buddha, pressed on the surface or modeled separately and attached (plates 5–6).[25] Standard Buddhist features found in these images include a halo of light,

---

23. This jar, discovered in Shaoxing County 紹興県 in Zhejiang Province 浙江省, is currently held by the Shaoxing County Office for the Supervision of Artifacts (Shaoxing Xian Wenwu Guanlisuo 紹興県文物管理所). The other three jars are held by: (1) Wuxian Office for the Supervision of Artifacts (Wuxian Wenwu Guanlisuo 呉県文物管理所), originally discovered at Grave Site no. 4, Shizishan 獅子山, Wuxian 呉県, Jiangsu Province 江蘇省; (2) Shanghai Museum (Shanghai Bowuguan 上海博物館); and (3) Shangyu Office for the Supervision of Artifacts (Shangyu Wenwu Guanlisuo 上虞文物管理), originally discovered in Shangyu Country, Zhejiang Province.

24. This jar is currently held at the Beijing Imperial Palace Museum (Beijing Gugong Bowuyuan 北京故宮博物院). Its origins are unknown.

25. See also He Yunao et al., plates 59–106.

the *uṣṇīṣa*, the lotus sitting position, and hands in the meditation *mudrā*. Underneath them is a series of inverted triangles creating a lotus flower pedestal, and flanking them are figures of lions facing outward. Other distinct features not found in other images are the depiction of hair using horizontal lines and of the folds in their robe using a series of curved, parallel lines. These images are about six to eight centimeters in height.

In addition, there are other types of funerary objects, e.g., blue-glazed jars and wide-mouth bowls, which bear the same kind of images of the Buddha. These objects are virtually identical to the spirit vessels described above in dating, geographical origin, material composition, and Buddhist iconographic features. They differ only in their design as vessels.

At present, over two hundred ceramic grave objects of this type, including spirit vessels, have come to light. Among them, over forty bear Buddhist images.

4. Images on Bronze Mirrors

Bronze mirrors found in third- and fourth-century graves also display images of the Buddha, as well as of the Taoist immortality figures Xiwangmu and Dongwangfu 東王父 ("King Father of the East"). These objects are referred to as *foshoujing* 佛獣鏡, "Buddha and Creature Mirrors." Among them, there are several different styles: those with a single-legged phoenix design (*kuifeng* 夔鳳鏡; plate 7),[26] those with a triangular edge (*sanjiaoyuan* 三角縁), and those with concentric patterns (*huawendai* 画文帯). Numerous examples of the phoenix type have been discovered in the Yangtze region, principally in Hubei 湖北 Province. But six out of eight examples of the concentric-patterns type and all seven of the triangular-edge type were in fact excavated from ancient burial mounds (*kofun* 古墳) in Japan. These objects raise formidable questions about the traditional view that Buddhism was first transmitted to Japan in the sixth century.

The Buddhist images appearing on these mirrors are sometimes in a meditative posture with a halo of light, or in other sitting positions. It is difficult to generalize about them at present because there appears to be no set form for these images, and they seem to have developed independently of each other.

5. Other images

There are numerous other examples of Buddhist images, but they have differing iconographic forms, and it is difficult to discern what connection they have to one another. Among them are the following:

a. A standing figure on a bronze censer.[27]
b. A figure in the meditative posture on a bronze censer.[28]
c. A figure in the meditative posture on a celadon censer.[29]

---

26. See also *ibid.*, plates 17–30.
27. *ibid.*, plate 7.
28. *ibid.*, plate 31.
29. *ibid.*, plate 37.

d. A figure on a lidded celadon jar (plate 8).[30] This figure is a Buddha in the meditative posture made from a mold. It is attached to the trunk of the jar, which also has depictions of winged men sketched on it. This figure closely resembles the Buddhist images on spirit vessels.

e. Human figures with halos of light appearing on bricks.[31]

4.

These early Buddhist icons were disseminated across the southern region, from Sichuan in the west to the lower reaches of the Yangtze River in the east. It is possible to identify a number of distinctive characteristics common to them. These characteristics are quite different from those of Buddhist images in China's Central Plain to the north. Their characteristics include:

1. All these images are found on funerary objects excavated from graves, and hence were closely linked to mortuary customs. Among Buddhist images of the Central Plain, there are no known artifacts linked to mortuary customs prior to the fifth century, not even in literary references.[32]
2. All of them are small in size, and were used as accessories or adornments to objects; hence, they did not function as icons of worship.
3. They emerged in the context of China's cult of immortality, as one figure in its pantheon of immortals, and hence were considered influential in the realm of the afterlife.
4. They had no apparent connection to Buddhist temples or priests. Hence, they were not tied to formal doctrine, but belonged to the folk Buddhism of lay adherents.
5. Examples of them cannot be found after the early fifth century at the latest. Apparently, they disappeared in the south after the transplantation of "orthodox" Buddhism from the Central Plain in the north.

---

30. See also *ibid.*, plate 38.

31. *ibid.*, plates 4–6.

32. One source that raises issues concerning this point is the *Luoyang qielanji* 洛陽伽藍記, *TD* 51: 1014a-c, written in 547 by Yang Jiezhi 楊衒之, which indicates that from the time of the death of Emperor Mingdi 明帝 (r. 57–75 C.E.) there developed the practice of building a so-called *futu* 浮圖 on top of the grave. There has been some speculation that this *futu* might refer to an image of or a shrine to the Buddha. For an important recent article on this issue, see Irisawa Takashi 入澤崇, "Butsu to rei—Kōnan shutsudo Busshoku konpei kō" 佛と霊—江南出土仏飾魂瓶考, *Ryūkoku Daigaku Ronshū* 龍谷大学論集 444 (1994): 233–271.

The oldest surviving Buddhist images of the Central Plain date only from the fourth or fifth century, but it is fair to assume that antecedents to them in fact existed in the Yellow River region prior to that time. It is difficult to believe that the earlier images bore any of the features described here of those in the south. The existing fourth- and fifth-century images of the Central Plain apparently developed from these lost prototypes rather than from southern-style images, since no association with mortuary customs can be detected in them. Hence, it would seem that the Buddhist images of the Central Plain were produced from the beginning as objects of worship, not as funerary talismans. One has to assume, by the same token, that these northern prototypes were not the forerunners of early southern iconography. The reason is that it is hard to imagine that Buddhist images from the Central Plain, when transplanted to the Yangtze region, would lose completely their original function as icons of worship and would submerge totally in funerary concerns, with which they had no original connection.

The Buddhist images of the Central Plain and those of the Yangtze region are thus distinct from each other both in iconographic peculiarities and in their character as Buddhist icons. It is in fact difficult to find any common link between them. Consequently, the two should be regarded as separate lineages of Buddhist iconography, not as the transmission of Buddhist images from the Yellow River region to the Yangtze, or vice versa. Ultimately, it is impossible to explain the existence of the earliest Buddhist images in the Yangtze region if one does not assume that southern Buddhism and its iconography were independent of the "orthodox" Buddhism that moved south from the Central Plain in the Three Kingdoms period (ca. 220–280).

Although it is true that Buddhist images of the Yangtze region share the features described above, it is nonetheless possible to divide them into three sub-lineages based on their iconographic characteristics:

1. Sichuan strain (Coin-bearing Trees and Cliffside Graves)

   The prevailing features of images in this strain are the right hand held up in the *abhaya mudrā*, the U-shaped fold of the robe between the two arms, the left hand holding the edge of the robe at chest level, etc.

2. Lower Yangtze strain (Ceramic Grave Objects, especially Spirit Vessels)

   Features found in images of this strain (and this strain only) include hands in the meditation *mudrā*, lotus flower pedestals made up of a series of inverted triangles, and flanking lions facing outward. Not only are these features missing in other strains, but also there are no examples of lower Yangtze images that lack them. Even the two features of the *mudrā* and the pedestal are sufficient evidence for differentiating between the lower Yangtze and the Sichuan strain.

3. Middle Yangtze strain (Bronze Mirrors, etc.)

   If the mirrors found in ancient Japanese burial mounds are included, it would seem that there is no set pattern to the Buddhist images appearing on bronze mirrors. Nonetheless, they clearly differ from the images of both the Sichuan and the lower Yangtze strain. In addition, the figures on censers, lidded jars, and bricks described above (3.5.a-e) also seem to be independent of each other. It is not possible at present to propose a classification for any of them.

Even though one may speak of a southern transmission of Buddhism, it is not plausible to lump these three strains together as a single lineage. The southern transmission is clearly distinguishable as a group from the Yellow River transmission, especially considering the five features identified earlier, i.e., associations with mortuary customs, no apparent connection to priests, etc. But even if the problematic bronze mirror group is set aside for the time being, what significance underlies the indisputable differences between the Sichuan strain and that of the lower Yangtze? It may be that they reflect separate routes of transmission into China. If so, the possible routes they took would include the following:

1. Western Route

   A separate type of folk Buddhism widespread among lay believers in India may have entered China via the so-called Silk Road, skirting the Taklamakan Desert, the path long considered Buddhism's primary route of transmission. Once in China, it could have spread into the Yangtze River region.

2. Assam–Burma–Yunnan Route

   The *Shiji* 史記 of the second century B.C.E. contains a report attributed to Zhang Qian 張騫 (d. 113 B.C.E.) that bamboo canes and linen from Sichuan were being transported via India as far as Afghanistan.[33] It is possible that a folk form of lay Buddhism was transmitted to Sichuan via this trade route, which recently has attracted scholars' attention as a "Southwest Silk Road."[34]

---

33. "Dawan liechuan" 大宛列傳, in *Shiji* 史記, Zhonghua Shuju Bianjibu 中華書局編集部, ed. 10 vols. (Beijing: Zhonghua Shuju, 1959): 10:3166.

34. See Luo Erhu 羅二虎 (Kida Tomoo 木田知生, trans.), "Kanshin jiki no Chūgoku 'Seinan shiruku rōdo'" 漢晋時期の中国「西南シルクロード」, *Ryūkoku Daigaku Bukkyō Bunka Kenkyūjo Kiyō* 龍谷大学佛教文化研究所紀要 33 (1994): 215–254.

3. Sea Route

There are archaeological reports of imported objects discovered in the tomb of a ruler of the Southern Yue kingdom 南越國 in the second century B.C.E., located in Guangzhou 広州 in Guangdong 広東 Province, and also in a Han dynasty tomb located near Hepu 合甫 in Guangxi 広西 Province.[35] In addition, discoveries at the site of a first–fifth century port city known as Oc-èo on the Mekong delta in southern Vietnam have included Roman coins from the second century and standing wooden images of the Buddha over two meters tall, which have not yet been dated.[36] All these objects are testimony to a thriving sea trade with points west, i.e., Persia and India, that existed prior to the common era. With this sea trade as a vehicle, a folk Buddhism may have spread to the southern coastal region of China.

The transmission of the southern strains of Buddhism may also have occurred in some combination or variation of these three possibilities, though verification will have to await further study. What should be noted here is that this form of Buddhism could have traveled via the second and third routes, which up to now have not been examined sufficiently.

These latter two routes apparently flourished as major thoroughfares for east-west commerce from prior to the common era. It is not unreasonable to think that merchants engaging in this trade introduced into this region Buddhist images and a folk form of Buddhism strongly tied to funerary practices, one in which they longed for happiness and benefits in this world through almsgiving and veneration, and aspired to birth in the heavens in the next life. Certainly, the *Jātaka* literature contains frequent references to merchants and traders who are deeply devoted to the doctrine of *karma* and its rewards.

Figurines or effigies of foreigners, both in group sets and in individual models, have been found in tombs of the Han Dynasty and later in the Yangtze River region, including Sichuan, and even in Yunnan (Plates 9–11).[37] These figurines resemble the foreigners that appear

---

35. Guangzhoushi Wenwu Guanli Weiyuanhui 広州市文物管理委員会 (The CPAM of Guangzhou), Zhongguo Shehui Kexueyuan Kaoguxue Yanjiusuo 中国社会科学院考古学研究所 (The Institute of Archaeology, CASS), and Guangdongsheng Bowuguan 広東省博物館 (The Museum of Guangdong Province), eds., *Xihan Nanyue wang mu* 西漢南越王墓 (The Tomb of King Nanyue of the Western Han), 2 vols. (Beijing, Wenwu Chubanshe 文物出版社, 1991), especially 1.209–210, and 2, plate 23.

36. Louis Malleret, *L'archéologie du Delta du Mékong*, vol. 3, "La culture du Fou-nan" (Paris: École Française d'Extrême-Orient, 1962): 115–116, plate XL.

37. See also He Yunao et al., plates 107, 114, 115, 117, 118, 125, 126.

on spirit vessels alongside images of the Buddha. They have the appearance of Central Asian or horse-riding tribesmen. Emerging evidence suggests that from around the common era these foreigners not only embraced the indigenous folk Buddhism of India but also participated in the east-west trade. The key to understanding Buddhism's early influx into China's Yangtze region may lie in future studies of these obscure foreign merchants.

Plates

1: Xiwangmu 西王母 ("Queen Mother of the West"), coins and animals nested in a bronze tree, from the end of the Later Han 後漢 dynasty (ca. second–third cent.). From Pengshan 彭山 City in Sichuan 四川 Province, Chengdu 成都. Sichuan Provincial Museum 四川省博物館.

2: A seated Buddha on the trunk of a bronze tree, from the end of the Later Han. From Mianyang 綿陽 City in Sichuan Province. Mianyang Municipal Museum.

3: A seated Buddha in bas relief, from the end of the Later Han. From cliffside grave no. 1 at Mahao 麻浩, Sichuan Province.

4: A miniature inscription on the back of a turtle on a spirit vessel, from the Wu 呉 to Western Jin 西晉 periods (third–fourth cent.). From Shaoxing County 紹興県 in Zhejiang Province 浙江省. Shaoxing County Office for the Supervision of Artifacts (Shaoxing Xian Wenwu Guanlisuo 紹興県文物管理所).

5: A seated Buddha in meditation *mudrā* on a spirit vessel, from the Western Jin period (third–fourth cent.). From Linhai 臨海 city in Zhejiang Province 浙江省. Linhai Municipal Museum.

6: A seated Buddha in meditation *mudrā* on a spirit vessel, from the Western Jin period (third–fourth cent.). From Wuxian 呉県, Jiangsu Province 江蘇省. Beijing Chinese History Museum 中国歴史博物館.

7: Four seated Buddha images on a bronze mirror with a single-legged phoenix design, from the Wu period (third century). From Ezhou 鄂州 City in Hubei 湖北 Province. Beijing Chinese History Museum 中国歴史博物館.

8: A seated Buddha made from a mold attached to the lid of a lidded celadon jar, from the Wu period (third century). From Nanjing 南京 City, Jiangsu Province. Nanjing Municipal Museum.

9: Bearded foreigners wearing pointed hats on a spirit vessel, with a bird-holding image on the upper portion and a dancing image on the lower. From Shaoxing County in Zhejian Province. Shaoxing County Office for the Supervision of Artifacts.

10: An independent clay image of a bearded foreigner, from a cliffside grave at Mahao, Sichuan Province. Museum of cliffside grave no. 1 at Mahao.

11: Ceramic figures of foreigners with pointed hats playing musical instruments, from the Xiping 熹平 period of the Later Han (172–178) dynasty. From the outskirts of Xiaguan 下関 (Dali 大理) City in Yunnan 雲南 Province. Xiaguan Municipal Museum.

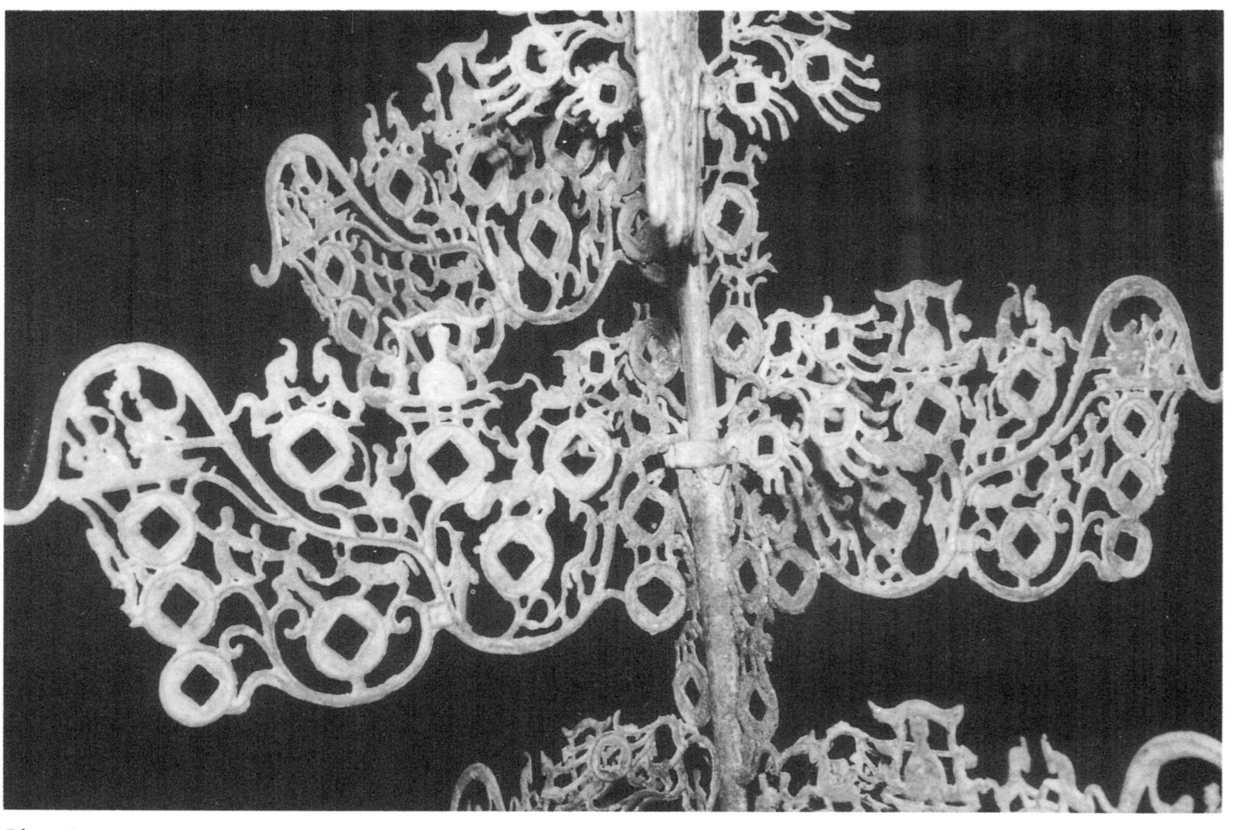

Plate 1

Plate 2

Plate 3

Plate 4

Plate 5

Plate 6

Plate 7

Plate 9

Plate 8

Plate 11

Plate 10

Toward a New Edition of the *Fan-yü Tsa-ming* of Li-yen*

Akira Yuyama

0. Prefatory Remarks

0.0. Traditional Sanskrit studies in Japan, or in the East Asian area as a whole, have upon various occasions captured my interest in the past decades. I feel much indebted to Professor Gadjin Nagao for his enlightening works in related fields of study.[1] In the present paper I intend to offer some preliminary remarks on one particular text, with special reference to research materials I plan to use to study this text with the goal of bringing out a new edition.

0.1. Since the *Fan-yü Tsa-ming* (梵語雜名) of Li-yen (利言) was studied carefully by Prabodh Chandra Bagchi some sixty years ago,[2] it has been somewhat neglected or overlooked, as if no problems remained. In the meantime, however, there has been much progress in the fields of Buddhist studies and Chinese historical phonology, among others.

0.2. This development has stimulated us to make a critical edition of the text, in the first place, from the lexical and lexicographical points of view. Such an edition will certainly shed light on the history of Buddhism from India to China via Central Asia. But this in itself is not the final goal. In order to carry out such a study, needless to say, there must be a mutual awareness of the phonological histories of Indic, Chinese, and Japanese, as well as of other relevant languages in the vast area of Asia. In turn, the results of such work will no doubt also contribute to these varied fields of study. Interdisciplinary cooperation will thus be badly needed. This is not an easy task.[3]

---

* This is a revised version of the paper "Remarks on the *Fan-yü tsa-ming*," which was read in Hong Kong on 27 August 1993 at the 34th International Congress of Asian and North African Studies.

1. See, for example, Gadjin M. Nagao, "Siddham and Its Study in Japan," *Acta Asiatica* 21 (1971): 1–12.

2. Prabodha Chandra Bagchi, *Deux lexiques sanskrit-chinois. Fan yu tsa ming de Li yen et Fan yu ts'ien tseu wen de Yi-tsing*. 2 vols. (*Sino-Indica: Publications de l'Université de Calcutta*, II-III) (Paris: Librairie Orientaliste Paul Geuthner, 1929–1937), (iii), 336; (v), ii, 337–541.

3. See A. Yuyama, "An Appraisal of the History of Buddhist Sanskrit Studies in

I. The Dates of Li-yen's Birth and Death

1.0. In the section of the "Miscellaneous Collection (事彙部)," part 2, of the *Taishō Shinshū Daizōkyō* (大正新脩大藏經) is found the text of the *Fan-yü Tsa-ming* of Li-yen (禮言): Taishō 2135 (LIV) 1223a21–1241b4: *Fan-yü Tsa-ming*, compiled by Śramaṇa Li-yen, from Kučā (歸茲), "Grand Savant in Translating the Canon" and "Imperial Academician" at the Temple Kuang-ting-ssŭ (光定寺) and collated by Śramaṇa Shingen at Eizan (i.e., Mount Hiei): Taishō (LIV) 1223a23–25:

翻經大德兼翰林待詔光定寺

歸茲國沙門　　　　禮言集

叡山沙門　　　　眞源較

This text has so far not been included in any other Buddhist canon (大藏經) in China, Korea, or Japan. The text in the Taishō Edition is based on a 1732 blockprint version (see §3.0–4 below) and an incomplete manuscript dated 1052, indicated by the Taishō editors as Text Kō (甲本: see §4.1 below).

1.1. Li-yen was also called Chên-yüeh (眞月), which suggests his Indic name as Satyacandra, transliterated in Chinese as Ti-ch'an-nieh-lo (地戦涅羅). The first member of this compound (viz., 地) may be made out of its Central Asian (possibly Kuchean) sound. Another name for him is said to be Pu-na-hsien (布那羨: *Pūnasena, Bhvr.-cpd., "purified army"?).[4] Li-yen's correct Chinese characters must be 利言, as proposed in a short notice by Seigai Kimura.[5] Takakusu begins to think that the author of the *Fan-yü Tsa-ming* must be Li-yen (利言, and not 禮言) of the Temple Kuan-chê-ssŭ (光宅寺), a pupil of

---

East Asia," *Studies on Buddhism in Honour of Professor A. K. Warder*, edited by N. K. Wagle and F. Watanabe (*South Asian Studies Paper* V) (Toronto: Centre for South Asian Studies, University of Toronto, 1993): 194–203.

4. Cf. *Répertoire du canon bouddhique sino-japonais. Edition de Taishō* (*Taishō Shinshū Daizōkyō*), compilé par Paul Demiéville, Hubert Durt, (et) Anna Seidel: *Fascicule annexe du Hōbōgirin: Dictionnaire encyclopédique du bouddhisme d'après les sources chinoises et japonaises.* Deuxième édition revisée et augmentée. Publiée par l'Académie des Inscriptions et Belles-Lettres, Institut de France (Paris: Adrien-Maisonneuve / Tokyo: Maison Franco-Japonaise, 1978): 272a, Rigon (Li yen), s.v.

5. 木村西崖 (alias Mukian Shujin 無記庵主人), "Bongo Zōmyō-no Senja" 梵語雑名の撰者 [The Composer of the *Fan-yü Tsa-ming*], *Bussho Kenkyū* 佛書研究 22 (1916, reprinted 1981): 4c–6b. This article has been reproduced in the *Takakusu Junjirō Kyūzō—Nippon Bongogaku Shiryō Shūsei*, edited by Taijun Inokuchi, 井ノ口泰淳編, 高楠順次郎旧蔵・日本梵語学資料集成 (東京・名著普及会, 1988): 872f.

Amoghavajra (不空), and that the text was composed around 750 C.E. (Takakusu, *op. cit.*, p. 497). I have no idea who gave him the name Li-yen, but it seems to me very suggestive of his talent in languages as is seen in the case of Chinese polyglot translators from Central Asian oasis cities. A good example of his predecessors is Kumārajīva from Kučā itself. Li-yen, 利言, "sharp in language(s)," may well have motivated in later ages a word with a similar sound, Li-yen (禮言), "following (i.e., honoring) linguistic rules."

1.2. His lifetime was indeed a period full of eminent scholars. I have appended a chronological table of some important events in connection with Li-yen's *Fan-yü Tsa-ming*. It seems certain that Li-yen was active with Dharmacandra (法月, 653–743) in the capital of Ch'ang-an (長安) between 732 and 741. He returned to Wu-wei (武威) in 755, when he worked with Amoghavajra (705–770/774). He again came back to Ch'ang-an in 788 to work with Prājña (般若: 741–810?)[6] from Greater Kashmir.[7]

1.3. Regarding Kimura's hypothesis about the date of Li-yen's *Fan-yü Tsa-ming* it is worth noting the description given in the *Chêng-yüan Hsin-t'ing Shih-chao Mu-lu* in 30 fasc. (貞元新定釋教目録), a catalogue of the Buddhist canon compiled in 800 by Yüan-chao (圓照):[8] "On the nineteenth day of the fourth month of the fourth year of the Chêng-yüan era (788) … Prājña expounded Sanskrit texts … and Śramaṇa Li-yen of Kuan-chê-ssŭ translated the Sanskrit (into Chinese) … and Śramaṇa Yüan-chao of Hsi-ming-ssŭ recorded his dictation" (貞元四年四月十九日 … 般若宣釋梵本 … 光宅寺沙門利言譯梵語 … 西明寺沙門圓照筆受 …) (Taishō 2157 [LV] 892a21–24). Yüan-chao also notices that Prājña has neither learned Central Asian languages (胡語) nor has he yet understood the language of China (唐言) (*ibid.*, 892a8). It is to be noted that "Li-yen and others were granted an

---

6. For Prājña in connection with Li-yen, see Prabodh Chandra Bagchi, *Le canon bouddhique en Chine. Les traducteurs et les traductions.* 2 vols. (*Sino-Indica*: *Publications de l'Université de Calcutta*, I et IV) (Paris: Paul Geuthner, 1927–1938), vol. II, p. 583 (T'ang period, no. 42).

7. On the regional name *Chi-pin* (Jap. *Keihin*) I wish to refer to an article by Fumio Enomoto: 榎本文雄, "罽賓— インド仏教の一中心地の所在—, 塚本啓祥教授還暦記念論文集・知の邂逅—仏教と科学 (Tokyo: Kōsei Shuppansha, 1993): 259–269. See now the revised English version, "A Note on Kashmir as Referred to in Chinese Literature: Ji-bin," in *A Study of the Nīlamata: Aspects of Hinduism in Ancient Kashmir*, edited by Yasuke Ikari (Kyoto: Institute for Research in Humanities, Kyoto University, 1994): 357–365.

8. *Shōwa Hōbō Sō-Mokuroku*: 昭和法寶總目録 3, Taishō (C) 653b16-c30.

audience (by the emperor) at the Temple Hsi-ming-ssŭ" (*ibid.*, 892b15).

1.4. Incidentally, there was a group of ten translation specialists, including Yüan-chao, the author of this catalogue, and Li-yen, the author of the *Fan-yü Tsa-ming*.[9] It may be noted here that in this group was another Yüan-chao (圓照), but of the Temple Chuang-yen-ssŭ (莊嚴寺). In the tenth year of the Chêng-yüan Era (794) Yüan-chao of Hsi-ming-ssŭ compiled a revised version of the famous *K'ai-yüan-lu*, i.e., *Ta-t'ang Chêng-yüan Hsü K'ai-yüan Shih-chiao-lu* (大唐貞元續開元釋教録) (Taishō 2156).

1.5. In spite of his famed name, Li-yen's *Fan-yü Tsa-ming* must not have entered the Imperial Household Library, i.e., Ta-ts'ang-ching (大藏經). Whether or not a text is incorporated into the Ta-ts'ang-ching is very important for the transmission of the text, and thus in the history of Buddhism in East Asia. In the first place we cannot expect to see Yüan-chao mention Li-yen's lexicographical work even in passing in his catalogue composed around a decade later, although the former must certainly have known the existence of the glossarial work and furthermore even used it in his translation work. Li-yen's dictionary is not really systematic, but must have been more usable than any other lexical work, for example the *Fan-yü Ch'ien-tzŭ-wên* (梵語千字文) of I-ching (義淨, 635–713) (Taishō 2133).[10] Nevertheless, in this way, the *Fan-yü Tsa-ming* came to be forgotten and eventually lost in the land where it was composed.

1.6. The dates of Li-yen's birth and death are not exactly known, but can be placed around 706 and 789, respectively.

II. Transmission of Li-yen's Sino-Indic Glossary—*Fan-yü Tsa-ming*

2.0. Ennin (圓仁, 794–864) who, during his stay in T'ang China from 837 to 847, made an untiring effort to search for important

9. According to the *Fo-tsu-t'ung-chi* (佛祖統記), a chronicle written by Chih-p'an (志盤) in 1258–1269, such a translation group usually consisted of at least nine specialists (Taishō 2035 [XLIX] 398b8–19). Cf. also A. Yuyama, "Classifying Indic Loanwords in Japanese," in *Sauhṛdyamaṅgalam: Studies in Honour of Siegfried Lienhard on his 70th Birthday*, edited by Mirjya Juntunen, William L. Smith, (and) Carl Suneson (Stockholm: The Association of Oriental Studies, 1995): 383f. (§1.1).

10. Incidentally, the Tibetans might have learned of this idea of compiling dictionaries of technical terms. And they were so systematic as to compile the *Vyutpatti*-works, as early as the beginning of the ninth century, or possibly at the end of the eighth.

Buddhist texts, compiled a catalogue in 1 fascicle in the fourteenth year of the Shōwa era (承和十四年, 847):[11] *Nittō Shingu Shōgyō Mokuroku* (入唐新求聖教目録) (Taishō 2167). In it is found the *Fan-yü Tsa-ming* in one fascicle, most probably of Li-yen.[12] It is quite apparent that Ennin began to search for Buddhist works upon his arrival in China in 838: *Nipponkoku Shōwa Go-nen Nittō Guhō Mokuroku* (日本國承和五年入唐求法目録) in 1 fascicle (Taishō 2165). As a matter of fact, more exactly speaking, he compiled this work in the following year (839).[13] In it is found the *Fan-yü Tsa-ming* (one fascicle).[14] This glossarial work is not found in a catalogue sent from China by Ennin (Jikaku Daishi) in 840: *Jikaku Daishi Zaitō Sōshinroku* (慈覺大師在唐送進録), one fascicle.[15]

2.1. In transmitting this important text Shingen (1705–1732) of Mount Hiei, who therefore belonged to the Tendai Sect of Japan, has played a great role. Nevertheless, it seems that he has not enjoyed his fame (§1.0 with footnote 3).[16] Another Shingen (1689/1690–1758) of the Shingon sect seems to be better known.[17] It is rather confusing to see two Shingens whose names are written with the same characters and of almost the same period. One may easily expect Siddham studies of

11. Taishō (C) 654c1–7.

12. Taishō (LV) 1086c10. This is to be found also in the *Dainippon Bukkyō Zensho* (大日本佛教全書) 862 (XCV) (reprint: Suzuki Research Foundation, Tokyo, 1972): 250a8 [cf. "Bibliographical notes," by Ryōshū Misaki: *ibid.* (XCIX) 284c–285b]; and another reprint edition (Tokyo: Meicho Fukyūkai, 1980), II = *Bukkyō Shoseki Mokuroku* (佛教書籍目録), II (1980): 76b2 [orig.ed., 1914: 19b2].

13. Taishō (C) 654b19–26.

14. Taishō (LV) 1075b18. Also in *Dainippon Bukkyō Zensho* 860 (XCV) (1980): 237b8.

15. As for the *Fan-yü Tsa-ming*, one may refer to the following reference works in Japanese:

龍谷大學 (編), 佛教大辭彙 6 (Tokyo: Fuzanbō, 1974; orig. ed., 1922): 4207c–4208a, *Bongo Zōmyō*, s.v.

望月信亨, 佛教大辭典 5 (Tokyo: Sekai Seiten Kankōkai, 1974; orig. ed., 1933, rev. 1958): 4687c–4688a, *Bongo Zōmyō*, s.v.

16. 鷲尾順敬, 増訂・日本佛家人名辞書 (Tokyo: Tōkyō Bijutsu, 1974; orig. ed., 1903, rev. 1911): 457b–458a, *Shingen* (眞源) [of Tendai] (1705–1732), s.v.

17. 種智院大学 (編), 密教大辭典 (増訂版) 3 (Kyoto: Hōzōkan, 1969; orig. ed., 1931), p. 1257b (with a portrait), *Shingen* (眞源) [of Shingon] (1689–1758), s.v.

佐和隆研 (編), 密教辞典 (Kyoto: Hōzōkan, 1975): 406a, *Shingen* (眞源) [of Shingon] (1689/1690–1758), s.v.

斎藤昭俊・成瀬良徳 (編著), 日本仏教人名辞典 (Tokyo: Shin Jinbutsu Ōraisha, 1986): 238c, *Shingen* (眞源) [of Shingon] (1689–1758), s.v.

this type to have been the work of Shingon priest-scholars, but interestingly this is not the case. This may be explained by the fact that the text had been transmitted in the Tendai system of Siddham studies, as it was brought to Japan by Ennin, who was the second head (i.e., Zasu 座主) of the Tendai sect and the first in the lineage of Siddham studies of the Tendai sect of Japan.

2.2. Unfortunately, Shingen died prematurely. Otherwise, he might have left us more works. He compiled a catalogue of Siddham works in 1 fascicle: *Shittan Mokuroku* (悉曇目録), which seems to have been published around 1800.[18] In this catalogue is quoted the *Fan-yü Tsa-ming*, 1 fascicle, compiled by Li-yen (禮言, not 利言!) of Kuan-ting-ssŭ (not Kuang-chê-ssŭ!) and brought to Japan by Jikaku.[19] Regrettably, this description has been followed until today. At the end of this catalogue are shown nine of his works, possibly added by a later publisher. In an anonymously compiled, but rather well-known, catalogue of Siddham works (ca. 1880) the *Fan-yü Tsa-ming* (1 fascicle) is cited in the same manner. But Jikaku Daishi's name is not given here: *Dainippon Bukkyō Zensho* 851 (XCV) (1972): 171a8.[20]

2.3. In 1918 Junjirō Takakusu made an extensive tour to investigate the extant Sanskrit works preserved in Japan. He published its fruit as: "Shittan Senjo Mokuroku (悉曇撰書目録)": *Dainippon Bukkyō Zensho* (XXX) (Tokyo, 1922): 230–257, reprinted with an independent pagination by the Meicho Fukyūkai (Tokyo, 1980): 1–27.[21] It has been further reprinted in Takakusu's collected works.[22]

2.4. From this study we learn that Shingen made the text available immediately before his death. It is to be regretted that Shingen's knowledge of Sanskrit proves to be rather poor. We must not forget,

---

18. "Bibliographical notes," by Shōkō Kanayama, *Dainippon Bukkyō Zensho* (XCIX) (1972): 273a-b.

19. *Dainippon Bukkyō Zensho* 850 (XCV) (1972): 169a15.
Takakusu cites eleven works of Shingen in his *Nippon Bongakushi*: 井ノ口泰淳編, 高楠順次郎遺稿・「日本梵語学史」集成 (Tokyo: Meicho Fukyūkai, 1988): 213f.

20. Shōkō Kanayama, "Bibliographical notes," *Dainippon Bukkyō Zensho* (XCIX) (1972): 273c–274b.

21. *Ibid.*, 274c–275a.

22. 高楠順次郎全集 9 (Tokyo: Kyōiku Shinchōsha, 1978): 395–422; and his *Nippon Bongogaku Shiryō Shūsei* (see n. 6 above): 815–841.

however, that the text is most probably extant today due to his painstaking endeavour.

2.5. It is clear now that Ennin has made a great contribution to the history of Siddham studies in Japan.[23] A catalogue of the books preserved in the Zentōin, the library of Ennin's Vihāra on Mount Hiei, was made known to us by Tetsuei Satō,[24] in which we learn with much interest that the renowned scholar Shūen, or Shinna Shōnin (宗淵 / 眞阿上人, 1786–1859)[25] and Jitsurei (實靈, ?–?) made the catalogue 前唐院見在書目録 in 1819 and 1783 respectively. According to Satō (*op. cit.*, p. 122 [26]), there exists a work copied by Ennin with the title *Hon Bongo Zōmyō* (翻梵語雑名) in one fascicle. Whether it is our *Fan-yü Tsa-ming* or not is unknown.

2.6. As already mentioned above (§2.1 end), Ennin is the successor to Saichō (Dengyō Daishi: 最澄 / 傳教大師, 766–822), the founder of the Japanese T'ien-tai or Tendai sect (天台宗) at Mount Hiei (比叡山).[26] Saichō does not seem to have shown a keen interest in Sanskrit studies, in odd and marked contrast to his contemporary Kūkai (空海, 774–835), or Kōbō Daishi (弘法大師) in his posthumous title, the founder of the Japanese tantric sect Shingon-shū (眞言宗), the headquarters of which is on Kōyasan (高野山).[27] As a matter of fact, both Saichō and Kūkai went together to T'ang China in 804 on board the same governmental fleet consisting of four ships. They went on different ships, both of which arrived safely in the Chinese port, although the other two vessels were wrecked on the way.

---

23. Herewith I wish to quote a single work on Japanese historical phonology, in which the author considers the importance of Siddham studies: 馬淵和夫, 増訂・日本韻学史の研究. 3 vols. (Kyoto: Rinsen Shoten, 1984; orig. ed., Tokyo: Japan Society for the Promotion of Sciences, 1965), [I] 2, 2, 4, 12, 701 pp.; [II] 4, 191, 5, 182, 2, 81 pp., [III] 4, 2, 742, 5 pp. (incl. 1 folded table between 70–71: "Paramparā of Japanese Tāntric Siddham Studies").

24. 佐藤哲英, "前唐院見在書目録 — 慈覺大師將來佛典は如何に傳持されたか —," 慈覺大師研究 (福井康順編) (Tokyo: Tendai Gakkai, 1964): 97–139, with a separate pagination of 1–43.

25. For Shūen, see Yuyama, "An Appraisal of the History of Buddhist Sanskrit Studies in East Asia," 197f.; and "Remarks on the Kōkiji Fragment of the Lokaprajñapti," *India and the Ancient World: History, Trade and Culture before A.D. 650*, ed. Gilbert Pollet (*Professor P. H. L. Eggermont Jubilee Volume Presented on the Occasion of his 70th Birthday*), (*Orientalia Lovaniensia, Analecta*, XXV) (Leuven: Departement Oriëntalistiek, 1987): 216f.

26. See Yuyama, "An Appraisal," 195f.

27. See Yuyama, "An Appraisal," 194f.

2.7. It is strange that Saichō was not interested in Sanskrit, which was more or less a compulsory subject for any serious student of Buddhism in his time in China. This may be explained by the fact that he returned home soon in the year following his arrival there. Or his disinterest in such subjects may have made him return sooner. Anyway, on the contrary, Kūkai enjoyed a name even in the literary circles in the then capital of Ch'ang-an for his Chinese poetry.

2.8. With regard to Sanskrit, Ennin is thus considered to be the first in the lineage of so-called Siddham studies within the Tendai sect. In singular contrast to Saichō again, Ennin studied tantric Buddhism during his stay in China after 838.[28] In this lineage stands a famous scholar in Siddham studies, Annen (安然, 841– ?)[29] (see also §5.1.2–4 below), and much later our Shingen.[30]

III. The *Fan-yü Tsa-ming* in Print

3.0. Shingen died on 14 April 1732, which means that he published his edition a month before his death. The text of the *Fan-yü Tsa-ming* in this edition gives the Chinese terminological words with their Sanskrit equivalents in Chinese transcription of the pronunciations in the then capital of Ch'ang-an, accompanied by Japanese pronunciation in *katakana* (片仮名) as well, and further followed by the Sanskrit originals in Siddham (悉曇) script printed vertically.

3.1. In the first place, the *Fan-yü Tsa-ming*, in 57 × 2 pages, edited by Shingen, appeared in Kyoto from a bookseller named Hasegawa Shōemon (長谷川正右衛門) in the third month of the seventeenth year of the Kyōho era (享保), i.e., 1732.[31] Unfortunately, I do not know who the publisher was. It seems clear, however, that Hasegawa

---

28. For Ennin's travels there one may refer to Edwin O. Reischauer's *Ennin's Diary* as well as *Ennin's Travels in T'ang China* (both New York: Ronald Press, 1955).

29. On Annen one cannot now ignore, among others, Fumihiko Sueki's recent voluminous work: 末木文美士, 平安初期仏教思想の研究 — 安然の思想形成を中心として (Tokyo: Shunjūsha, 1995), (i), vii, 829 pp.; 1, 8 pp.; on Annen's works see also 末木文美士, 安然・源信 (= 大乗仏典, 中国・日本編, XIX) (Tokyo: Chūō Kōronsha, 1991), esp. 245–308.

30. This is briefly mentioned by Tsūshō Kojima: 小島通正, "安然の悉曇學とその展開," 叡山学院(編), 安然和尚の研究 (Kyoto: Dōhōsha, 1979): 61.

31. Cf. Bunyiu Nanjio, *A Catalogue of Japanese and Chinese Books and Manuscripts lately added to the Bodleian Library* (Oxford at the Clarendon Press, 1881), col. 10 [class II: Chinese-Sanskrit-Japanese Vocabularies, Serial no. 7]. Cf. also Mabuchi, *op.cit.*, I, p. 123f.; III, p. 234 (1391).

was the first holder of the printing woodblocks. The name is carved by exactly the same hands as in the following editions. In his edition Hasegawa declares clearly that he has had it printed and published: 書林 長谷川正右衛門 板行 (fol. 57b6). I call this print Ka.

3.2. The very same blockprint text was later handled by another bookseller named Kanbē Murakami (村上勘兵衛) of Heirakuji (平樂寺) in Kyoto. The Heirakuji edition is exactly the same as the previous one with the exception of the last line, i.e., fol. 57b6: 京都東洞院三條上町 書林 平楽寺村上勘兵衛. It has deleted the name of the bookseller Hasegawa Shōemon (cf. §3.1 above). Incidentally, the Heirakuji Bookshop still exists as a publisher of Buddhist works on the same spot. I call this print Kb.

3.3. As far as I know, an edition appeared also from a third bookseller named Sōhachi Shiya (蓍屋宗八) of Kyoto. From an advertisement of 147 items of books produced in blockprint, we learn on folios 58a–59a that Shiya was a Buddhist bookseller for the Tendai, Vinaya, and other sects along the famous street of temples, viz., Teramachi-dōri (寺町通り), where several well-known booksellers and stationery shops have survived until today. After having erased the previous colophons on folio 57, it states on the next folio: 台宗 律宗 諸宗 經師 御書物所 京都寺町通三條下ル町 蓍屋宗八版. But I am not able to identify Shiya with any existing bookshop or publisher in this area of Kyoto. I call this print Kc.

3.4. This last mentioned print, Kc, is the one (and the only one) which Prabodh Chandra Bagchi used for his meticulous work in *Deux lexiques sanskrit-chinois* in two volumes (see n. 2 above).[32] Bagchi reproduced it in facsimile. With the scholarly achievements made during the past decades some further reexamination is now needed, which will lead accordingly to certain revisions.

IV. The *Fan-yü Tsa-ming* in Manuscript

4.0. Thanks to the enormous endeavour of Takakusu (see §2.3 cum nn. 22–23 and 6), we learn that there are manuscripts copied much earlier than 1732 (cf. also §2.5 above). Furthermore, there may be still more copies or manuscripts of this text in some monastic libraries in Japan. It is therefore hoped that investigations into the scriptural

32. Vol. I, pp. 1–117 = photomechanical reproduction of *Kc* (i.e., Hishiya edition); pp. 251–312 = annotated text in Roman script; Vol. II, pp. 337–414 = detailed studies.

libraries of old temples in Japan will be continued. At present, it seems, such searches are being done by Japanese Japanologists, in particular those engaged in Japanese linguistics. To my great regret, with very few exceptions scholars in the field of Indian and Buddhist studies have not shown serious interest in this kind of work, or in traditional Sanskrit studies from a purely scholarly point of view.

4.1.0. The oldest dated manuscript goes back to the eleventh day of the tenth month of the seventh year of the Eishō era (永承七年十月十一日), i.e., 1052. This is about two hundred years after Ennin had obtained the text in China. This incomplete manuscript was used in the Taishō edition as the basic text for collation, noted as Kō (see §1.0 end). It is fortunate that during his investigations Takakusu had this manuscript photographed on dry-plates and later published.[33] Mabuchi thinks that about eight folios are missing at the beginning (see Mabuchi, *op. cit.*, III [1984]: 638 (1796)a: no. 6–6).

4.1.1. It consists of thirty-one folios (62 pages), giving, however, no pagination. Each page contains six lines in three columns, so that there are eighteen key words per page. It seems to me that the missing portion must be the cover of the manuscript in book form and the first five folios. The text begins with the word "fallen" (= Taishō [LIV] 1227a18): 落 / 跛 底 哆 / पतित. As shown here the Chinese words are followed by Indic in Chinese characters (no *katakana*) (cf. §3.0 above). Incidentally, many peculiar characters were invented in order to transcribe the Indic. There may well be an esoteric purpose for this as well. Further investigation in this regard is needed.

4.1.2. The name of the scribe seems to be Tōbō (唐房), as is shown in the colophon. The manuscript was originally kept at the Temple Nisshutsuzan Shinshō-ji (日出山神照寺). The seal of this temple is stamped on the first page of the manuscript. This fact may well suggest that the original from which Tōbō copied must already have been missing the cover(s) and the first five folios. It was copied in the middle Heian period (897–1068). The colophon reads as follows:

此是翻經大德兼翰林待詔光定寺歸茲國沙門禮言集

梵語雜名 一巻

33. *Takakusu Junjirō Kyūzō—Nippon Bongogaku Shiryō Shūsei* (see n. 6 above): 644–659, which corresponds to Taishō 2135 (LIV) 1227a18–1241b3. Cf. "Bibliographical notes," by T. Inokuchi and Junji Uno, *ibid.*, pp. 795b–796a.

本云

永承七年十月十一日賜唐房御本寫畢

4.2. At the Temple Jōrakuin (常樂院) in southern Kyoto (山城宇多野鳴瀧山) is kept a second manuscript copied by Ekō (慧晃), also known as Śramaṇa Shōzan (照山, 1656–1737).[34]

4.3. Takakusu reports a manuscript, copied in the Heian period (781–1183) and bearing a slightly different title, "A Collection of the Miscellaneous Names in Sanskrit (梵語雜名集)," which was then in the possession of Kanbē Tanaka (田中勘兵衛). According to Takakusu, on the cover is written "Konren-in (金蓮院)."[35] This may well be the name of a temple as its former owner. It is a pity that the manuscript does not record any date. Mabuchi thinks that it may well be a copy made in the Kamakura period (1183–1331). The present whereabouts seem to be unknown.[36] This must certainly be the *Fan-yü Tsa-ming* as is proved by another manuscript (see §5.1 below).

4.4. Bearing the same title as that mentioned above (§4.3), another manuscript is said to be kept at the Temple Kongōin (金剛院) within the Compound of the Kyōōgokoku-ji (教王護國寺), better known by its short name Tō-ji (東寺), in Kyoto. This is a monastery founded by Kūkai. This manuscript is also said to have been copied in the Kamakura period. It is noteworthy that the compiler's name is shown as "Rigon (利言)," and not "Raigon (禮言)."[37]

V. The *Fan-yü Tsa-ming* in Fragmentary Manuscript

5.0. The following fragment of the *Fan-yü Tsa-ming* offers some interesting materials and is therefore treated here separately.

5.1.0. There exists a fragment bearing the title *Fan-yü Tsa-ming-chi* (梵語雜名集). It consists of the back cover and the first and last pages, viz., three pages in all. On each page are seemingly seven lines in four columns, i.e., twenty-eight key words per page. It is again fortunate that Takakusu has had a photocopy made on dry-plates and published in facsimile.[38] The present whereabouts of this fragment are unknown.

---

34. Cf. Takakusu, *Nippon Bongogakushi* (n. 19 above): 218.

35. Cf. Takakusu, "Shittan Senjo Mokuroku," *Dainippon Bukkyō Zensho* (XCV) (1972),: 184b: no. 93. Also Mabuchi, *op.cit.*, III (1984): 233 (1391): no. 6–2.

36. Cf. Mabuchi, *op.cit.*, III (1972): 638 (1796)a.

37. Cf. Mabuchi, *op.cit.*, III (1984): 233 (1391): no. 6–1; also I (1984): 124.

38. *Takakusu Junjirō Kyūzō—Nippon Bongogaku Shiryō Shūsei* (see n. 6 above): 660–661

5.1.1. This has not been used in the Taishō edition for its collation. Chinese words are followed by the corresponding Indic in Chinese characters. Neither Siddham script or *katakana* is given.

5.1.2. The colophon read on the last page and the description given on the back cover page offer an interesting fact. The colophon reads: "This very (text) is compiled by Śramaṇa Li-yen, from Kučā (歸茲國), 'Grand Savant in Translating the Canon' and 'Imperial Academician' at Kuang-ssŭ":

此是翻經大德兼翰林待詔光寺歸

茲國沙門礼言集[39]

The back cover page reads: "The author is the Śramaṇa Li-yen from Kučā (龜茲國), i.e., in the *Hakke Sōroku* it is called *Fan-yü Tsa-ming* in one fascicle. (Brought to Japan by En-)nin":

作者龜茲國沙門礼言

八家

惣録云梵語雜名一巻[仁]

5.1.3. This last description is rather important, as it quotes a work entitled *Hakke Sōroku*, which is also known briefly as the *Hakke Hiroku* (八家秘録). Its full title is *Sho-Ajari Shingon Mikkyōburui Sōroku*, "A classified comprehensive catalogue of the tantric-esoteric texts brought by various ācāryas," 諸阿闍梨眞言密教部類總録. This has been transmitted often with a title ending with Sōroku (惣録), instead of 總録. It is said to be the work composed by Annen (§2.6 end) in the ninth year of the Gankei or Gangyō era (元慶九年), i.e., 885.[40]

5.1.4. Nin (仁) here is no doubt for Ennin (see §2.6). As a matter of fact, "Nin" is found in the Sōroku exactly in the same manner. The *Fan-yü Tsa-ming* is attested by Annen under the heading of Bon-Tō Taiyaku, IV (梵唐對譯・四), "Indo-Sinic Translations, IV": 梵語雜名仁.[41]

(3 plates), which corresponds to Taishō 2135 (LIV) 1223a27-b22, and 1241a15-b3 (some being in disorder or missing). Cf. "Bibliographical notes," by T. Inokuchi and Junji Uno, *ibid.*, p. 796a-b.

39. Kuang-ssŭ (光寺) here must be a mistake either for Kuang-chê-ssŭ (光宅寺), or for a false name Kuang-ting-ssŭ (光定寺).

40. Shūyū Kanaoka, "Bibliographical notes," *Dainippon Bukkyō Zensho* (XCIX) (1983): 269c–270c.

41. Taishō 2176 (LV) 1131a 18 / *Dainippon Bukkyō Zensho* 846 (XCV) 156 (*Bukkyō Shoseki Mokuroku*, II), p. 149[41]b1.

VI. Commentarial Works on the *Fan-yü Tsa-ming* (Preserved in Manuscript?)

6.0. The contents of the following texts are not fully known, but seem worth citing here for their rarity.

6.1. A quotation from the *Fan-yü Tsa-ming* is found in a Sanskrit vocabulary compiled anonymously in the Heian period and preserved at the Temple Kongō-Zanmai-in (金剛三昧院) of Kōyasan: *Bongo-shū* (梵語集).[42] Takakusu reports that the said text is cited once (*op. cit.*, p. 184b2). Further, Takakusu thinks that this work was written by Shingaku (心覺, ?–1181).[43] It is also important to learn that Saichō some five years after his return from China (cf. §2.6–8 above) left a work of the same title in one fascicle (ten folios) composed in 810.[44] Whether it is his authentic writing or not needs still further investigation.

6.2. It is reported that there exists a text written by Zuihō (瑞鳳) by name in the year 1775: *Bongo Zōmyō Sōtaishō* (梵語雜名雙對章).[45] The title conveys a hint that it may well be a commentarial work on the *Fan-yü Tsa-ming*.

VII. Two Brief Notes

7.1. It is a great pity that this text has not survived in the western or northwestern areas of China, e.g., in Tun-huang. If a copy of this text were discovered in these regions, it might certainly shed light on such problems as the elements of Northwestern dialects, at least of the T'ang period.

7.2. Some scholars seem to believe that Li-yen has shown the so-called "Prakritism," or "Middle Indicism" (see, e.g., Bagchi, *op. cit.*, II: 364–368). In my opinion, however, such "Middle Indic"–like forms are often seen through the wrong transmission of the text. As we have seen above, Li-yen, being most probably a polyglot, had a great role in translating Indic texts into Chinese. His knowledge of Sanskrit should not be underestimated. In the text compiled by Shingen, whose knowledge of Sanskrit seems rather limited, the original Chinese transliteration was transferred into *katakana* Japanese, and

---

42. See Takakusu, "Shittan Senjo Mokuroku," *Dainippon Bukkyō Zensho* (XCV) (1972): 184b-c: no. 99.

43. See Takakusu, *Nippon Bongogakushi*, p. 508 (also p. 63).

44. See Takakusu, *ibid.*, p. 9 and 557.

45. See Takakusu, *ibid.*, p. 253.

then rewritten back into Siddham script without observing phonetic changes. For example, the technical terms showing consonant clusters are frequently neglected. This has created results which make it appear as if there were epenthetic vowels as seen in Middle Indic or Buddhist Sanskrit. Thus, it seems necessary to make a new edition of the text accompanied by careful and critical apparatuses and translation, as I have already briefly discussed in my prefatory remarks at the beginning of this paper.

Chronological Table
of some important events concerning Li-yen's *Fan-yü Tsa-ming*

653	Dharmacandra (達摩戦涅羅 / 法月) born in Eastern India
664	†Hsüan-tsang (玄奘) born ca. 600
681	Vajrabodhi (金剛智) born in southern India
705	Amoghavajra (不空) born on Laṅkā Island
706(?)	Li-yen (利言 / Satyacandra 眞月) born in Kučā
713	†I-ching (義浄) born 635
715	Amoghavajra arrives in China
720	Amoghavajra starts studying with Vajrabodhi
720	Dharmacandra visits Kučā on his way to China
732	Dharmacandra arrives in Ch'ang-an with Li-yen, staying until 741
735	†Śubhaṁkarasiṁha (善無畏) born 637 in Magadha
741	Dharmacandra and Li-yen visit Kashgar and Khotan (until 743)
741	Amoghavajra revisits Laṅkā and southern India (until 746)
743	†Dharmacandra at Khotan (aged 91)
744	Prājña (般若) born in India, later studies in eastern India
745	Hui-kuo (惠果 / 慧果) born; Kūkai's teacher in China
746	†Vajrabodhi
746	Amoghavajra starts working at Ching-ying-ssŭ (浄影寺) in Ch'ang-an (until 749)
750(?)	Li-yen compiles the *Fan-yü Tsa-ming* (梵語雑名)
753	Amoghavajra stays at Wu-wei (武威) until 754, working with Li-yen (aged 49)
754	Amoghavajra and Li-yen return to Ch'ang-an
766	Saichō (最澄) [Dengyō Daishi 傳教大師] born
774	†Amoghavajra (or possibly 770)
774	Kūkai (空海) [Kōbō Daishi 弘法大師] born

781	Prājña arrives in China by sea, working in Ch'ang-an (785–790 / 792–810)
788	Prājña's translation work with Li-yen, Yüan-chao (圓照), et al.
789	†Li-yen at Kuang-chê-ssŭ (光宅寺) (aged 81 or 82)
790	Prājña visits Central Asia (until 792)
794	Yüan-chao's *Ta-t'ang Chêng-yüan hsü K'ai-yüan Shih-chiao-lu* (大唐貞元續開元釋教録)
794	Ennin (圓仁) [Jikaku Daishi 慈覺大師] born
804	Yüan-chao's *Chêng-yüan Hsin-t'ing Shih-chiao Mu-lu* (貞元新定釋教目録)
804	Saichō and Kūkai arrive in China, Saichō staying until 805 and Kūkai until 806
805	†Hui-kuo
805	Saichō returns home
806	Kūkai returns home
806	†Chih-kuang (智廣), author of the *Hsi-t'an tzŭ-chi* (悉曇字記)
810(?)	†Prājña
814	Enchin (圓珍) [Chishō Daishi 智證大師] born (†894)
822	†Saichō
835	†Kūkai
838	Ennin studies in China until 847, collecting texts at Wu-t'ai-shan (五臺山) and Ch'ang-an
839	Ennin's *Nipponkoku Shōwa Gonen Nittō Guhō Mokuroku* (日本國承和五年入唐求法目録)
840	Ennin sends his catalogue *Jikaku Daishi Zaitō Sōshinroku* (慈覺大師在唐送進録)
841	Annen (安然) born (†915?)
847	Ennin probably brings back a copy of *Fan-yü Tsa-ming* (among others) to Japan
864	†Ennin
885	Annen's *Sho-Ajari Shingon Mikkyōburui Sōroku* (諸阿闍梨眞言密教部類總録) [= 惣録]
…	
1052	Oldest dated manuscript of *Fan-yü Tsa-ming* by Tōbō (唐房) [永承七年十月十一日]
…	
1705	Shingen (眞源) born (†14.IV.1732)
1732	Shingen publishes his edition of *Fan-yü Tsa-ming* in Kyoto [享保十七年三月]

Index

Contributors

Gadjin M. Nagao, professor emeritus, Kyoto University, and member of the Japan Academy.

Noritoshi Aramaki, professor, Otani University.

Mark L. Blum, assistant professor, State University of New York at Albany.

Luis O. Gómez, professor, University of Michigan.

Masaaki Hottori, professor emeritus, Kyoto University.

Masamichi Ichigō, professor, Otani University.

†*J.W. de Jong,* professor emeritus, Australian National University.

Yuichi Kajiyama, professor emeritus, Kyoto University, and professor and head, International Research Institute for Advanced Buddhology, Soka University.

Shōryu Katsura, professor, Hiroshima University.

Leslie Kawamura, professor, University of Calgary.

Katsumi Mimaki, professor, Kyoto University.

Lambert Schmithausen, professor, University of Hamburg.

Jonathan A. Silk, assistant professor, Yale University.

Ernst Steinkellner, professor, University of Vienna.

Jikidō Takasaki, professor emeritus, Tokyo University, and president, Tsurumi University.

Teruyoshi Tanji, professor, Kansai University.

Meiji Yamada, professor, Ryukoku University.

Akira Yuyama, professor, International Research Institute for Advanced Buddhology, Soka University.